2○
6 Oct

13 Oct   Ch 7

20 Oct

27 Oct.   Ch 8

3 Nov   Ch 6

10 Nov

17 Nov   No Class

24 Nov

1 Dec   Ch 10

PUBLIC ADMINISTRATION
An Action Orientation

Sixth Edition

ROBERT B. DENHARDT

Arizona State University

JANET V. DENHARDT

Arizona State University

WADSWORTH
CENGAGE Learning

Australia • Brazil • Japan • Korea • Mexico • Singapore • Spain • United Kingdom • United States

Public Administration: An Action Orientation, Sixth Edition

Robert B.Denhardt, Janet V.Denhardt

Publisher: Michael Rosenberg

Managing Development Editor: Karen Judd

Assistant Editor: Christine Halsey

Senior Editorial Assistant: Megan Garvey

Technology Project Manager: Yevgeny Ioffe

Marketing Manager: Trent Whatcott

Marketing Assistant: Aimee Lewis

Senior Content Project Manager: Josh Allen

Marketing Communications Manager:
Heather Baxley

Art Director: Linda Helcher

Manufacturing Manager: Barbara Britton

Permissions Editor: Mardell Glinksi-Schultz

Production Service/Compositor: Pre-
PressPMG

Cover Designer: Grannan Graphic Design Ltd.

Cover Image: Stockbyte/©Getty Images

For product information and technology assistance, contact us at
Cengage Learning Customer & Sales Support, 1-800-354-9706

For permission to use material from this text or product,
submit all requests online at **www.cengage.com/permissions**
Further permissions questions can be emailed to
permissionrequest@cengage.com

Library of Congress Control Number: 2005923061

ISBN-13: 978-0-495-50516-7

ISBN-10: 0-495-50516-1

Wadsworth
25 Thomson Place
Boston, MA 02210
USA

Cengage Learning is a leading provider of customized learning solutions with office locations around the globe, including Singapore, the United Kingdom, Australia, Mexico, Brazil, and Japan. Locate your local office at **international.cengage.com/region**

Cengage Learning products are represented in Canada by
Nelson Education, Ltd.

For your course and learning solutions, visit **academic.cengage.com**

Purchase any of our products at your local college store or at our preferred online store **www.ichapters.com**

Printed in the United States of America
2 3 4 5 6 7 11 10 09 08

For Michael, Cari, Ben, and Mary

About the Authors

Robert B. Denhardt is Regents Professor, Lincoln Professor of Leadership and Ethics, and Director of the School of Public Affairs at Arizona State University and Visiting Professor at the University of Delaware. A fellow of the National Academy of Public Administration, Dr. Denhardt is a past president of the American Society for Public Administration, the leading national association promoting excellence in public service.

Dr. Denhardt is the author of 19 books, including *The New Public Service, Managing Human Behavior in Public and Nonprofit Organizations, The Pursuit of Significance, In the Shadow of Organization, and Theories of Public Organization*. He is the editor of several others, including *Executive Leadership in the Public Service, The Revitalization of the Public Service, Public Administration in Action,* and *Pollution and Public Policy.* He has published more than a hundred articles in professional journals, primarily in the areas of public sector management, strategic planning and public productivity, and organization behavior. His latest book is *The Dance of Leadership.*

Prior to joining the faculty at Arizona State University and the University of Delaware, Dr. Denhardt taught at the universities of Colorado, Missouri, Kansas, New Orleans, and Central Florida. He has held several major administrative positions in these universities, serving as vice provost at the University of Missouri–Columbia.

Janet V. Denhardt is Professor of Public Administration at Arizona State University. Dr. Denhardt has authored three books: *The New Public Service, Managing Human Behavior in Public and Nonprofit Organizations*, and *Street-Level Leadership*. She has also published more than two dozen monographs, chapters, and articles in journals, including *Public Administration Review, Administration & Society*, and *American Review of Public Administration*. Her latest book is *The Dance of Leadership.*

Prior to joining the faculty at Arizona State University, Dr. Denhardt held faculty and administrative appointments at Eastern Washington University, including associate dean of the College of Liberal Arts and Social Sciences. She has also served in a number of administrative positions at the federal and state levels of government, including senior management analyst in the Department of Health and Human Services in Washington, D.C., and management consultant in the Washington State Office of Financial Management. She received her doctorate in public administration from the University of Southern California.

CONTENTS

CHAPTER 8   THE MANAGEMENT OF HUMAN RESOURCES   285

PREFACE

The sixth edition of *Public Administration: An Action Orientation* updates the text, taking it into the middle of President George W. Bush's second term. But it also adds new material that should be helpful to those becoming acquainted with the field of public service. Most notably, the book has been revised to reflect changes such as developments in e-government, the creation of the Department of Homeland Security, and the intergovernmental and fiscal challenges of coping with the threat of terrorism. In addition, we have included important new material dealing with leadership, organizational theory, and bureaucracy; an expanded discussion of special purpose governments, including school districts; and a closer look at the increasingly important connection between public administration and civic action or citizenship. This book also provides the latest approaches to management in the public sector and continues to pay special attention to the skills needed for administrators at all levels of government and in nonprofit organizations. We have reordered the chapters to create a more logical progression of material given the large number of revisions since the organization of the first edition. Finally, to enliven the text, we have developed and included in an appendix a series of longer and more detailed case studies that challenge students to examine real-world problems in public administration and public policy. Short vignettes asking "What Would You Do?" have been inserted into the chapters to give students the opportunity to think about and discuss their responses to specific and realistic challenges in public service.

Like previous editions, the sixth edition contains subtle but telling differences from other books in the field. We assume that students in an introductory course in public administration don't want to learn about the profession only in the abstract, but are interested in influencing the operations of public agencies, as managers from the inside or as citizens from the outside. They want to acquire the skills necessary for changing things for the better.

For this reason, it is important that the text not only introduce students to the scholarly literature of public administration, but also that it help them develop the insights and abilities that will make them more effective and responsible actors. This book contains a good deal of material that is basic to working in or with public organizations. At the same time, the discussion attends to the complex and often confounding values that distinguish work in the public sector. Most significant, however, is the focus on the technical expertise and interpersonal skills that are crucial to effecting change in public organizations.

Another feature of the book is its balanced attention to the work of managers at all levels of government and in nonprofit organizations. Although the federal government is a powerful model for the study of public administration, managers of state and local agencies are important actors in the governmental process, and their work is acknowledged and examined as well. Similarly, we show how managers of associations, nonprofit and "third-sector" organizations, and even traditionally private organizations are now confronting the same issues faced by administrators in the public sector. In fact, we frequently use the term *public organizations* to describe all such groups involved in the management of public programs.

This edition also gives proper attention to the global dimensions of public administration today. No longer are administrators confined in their work to their own organizations or even to their own jurisdictions. The complexity of modern life means, among other things, that administrators must be attentive to developments around the world as well as to those at home. Decisions made in a foreign capital may affect the work of a public administrator even more significantly than those made only miles away. Today, knowledge of international affairs and comparative issues is important not only to those who work in other countries but to all who work in public administration.

Public Administration: An Action Orientation remains distinctive in its treatment of the ethics of public service. Not only is the topic of ethics thoroughly covered in a separate chapter, but references to ethical concerns appear throughout the text. Ethical issues cannot be separated from action. Indeed, every act of every public servant, at whatever level of government or in any related organization, has an important ethical dimension. For this reason, we have made a strong effort to be attentive to the ethical considerations that are a part of all administrative activities.

Finally, *Public Administration: An Action Orientation* was the first text on this subject to be fully integrated with the Internet resources that are available to assist public administrators and those studying public administration. In each chapter, we highlight "networking" resources available to students, including websites that contain material that supplements the text, provides examples and case studies, and links the student to other materials available online.

In this text we talk about action, but we also invite students to act. At the end of each chapter are self-diagnostic materials and exercises (cases, simulations, discussion points, and so on) designed to supplement students' cognitive learning with behavioral practice. These activities impart a sense of not only what public administration looks like to the impartial observer, but also what it feels like to the manager or private individual engaged in public action. Students have opportunities to test, practice, and improve their skills. Each chapter also contains a list of key terms and definitions (which reappear in the glossary) and recommendations for further reading.

There are very exciting possibilities in public administration today. Working to solve important public problems, sensing the human drama involved in such work, and gaining the satisfaction of doing something really worthwhile make being involved in public organizations quite fascinating. The perspective adopted here—focusing on the experiences of people acting in the real world of public organizations and on the skills needed for managerial success—permits a lively and interesting presentation of the field. We particularly hope to convey, in a personal and direct manner, the challenges and rewards of public service.

Acknowledgments

Many people contributed to this book. From our work with members of the American Society for Public Administration, we have gained special appreciation of the complexity of public management and of the dedication and hard work required for public service.

We hope we have conveyed the commitment and concern that guide the work of the best public managers; they deserve great credit and respect.

In the first edition of the text, Bob's colleagues in the Department of Public Administration at the University of Missouri–Columbia were a great source of help and support. In subsequent editions, good colleagues and friends at the University of Colorado, the University of Central Florida, the University of Delaware, Arizona State University, and Wichita State University have made important contributions.

We wish to thank the reviewers who provided invaluable feedback on the fifth edition for our use in creating this new edition. They are Elizabeth Theiss Smith, University of South Dakota; Robert Blair, University of Nebraska, Omaha; and Carol J. Edlund, San Francisco State University. We also appreciate the help provided by Christine Halsey and the staff of Cengage Learning.

Most importantly, we want to thank our superb graduate assistant, Ljubinka Andonoska, who has been invaluable in constructing the newest edition of this text. Her hard work and careful research made a significant substantive contribution to this edition. She has our deepest gratitude!

Finally, this book is dedicated to Bob and Janet's children, Michael and Cari, Ben and Mary, who have been a constant source of joy, wonderment, and pride. Thanks to all.

Robert B. Denhardt and Janet V. Denhardt

CHAPTER 1

PERSONAL ACTION IN
PUBLIC ORGANIZATIONS

Public administration is concerned with the management of public programs. Public administrators work at all levels of government, both at home and abroad, and they manage nonprofit organizations, associations, and interest groups of all kinds. The substantive fields within which public managers work range across the varied interests of government and public affairs, from defense and national security to social welfare and environmental quality, from the design and construction of roads and bridges to the exploration of space, and from taxation and financial administration to human resources management. Though public administration varies tremendously in its scope and substance, those who work in public organizations share certain commitments. Among these, none is more important than a commitment to *public service*.

In this book, we examine the work of public administrators in many different kinds of organizations and define the political and historical context within which public and nonprofit organizations operate. We examine the commitments that underlie the notion of public service and the opportunities and constraints they place on public action. We examine the many technical fields, such as planning, budgeting, personnel, and evaluation, with which public administrators must be familiar and consider the personal and interpersonal talents needed by successful public managers. Most importantly, we emphasize the knowledge, skills, and values that *you* will need to be both effective and responsible as you act in the public interest.

Although we introduce many different areas of public administration, we do so from a particular point of view that provides a unifying theme in our examination of administrative work in public and nonprofit organizations. This point of view holds that there is something very special about public administration: Your work in the public service is distinguished by its pursuit of democratic values, and this concern affects nearly everything you do as a public manager. As a public administrator, you are obligated not only to achieve efficiency and effectiveness, but to be responsive to the many bodies that help define the public interest: elected officials, members of the legislature, client or constituent groups, and citizens generally. This special obligation requires that you be ever mindful of managerial concerns, political concerns, and ethical concerns, and that you develop structures and processes that take into account all three. The result is a particularly complicated approach to getting things done, but one that has special rewards. From service to the public, you may gain a very special sense of accomplishment and personal satisfaction, one that comes from helping others and from pursuing the public interest.

■ What is Public Administration?

We have already described public administration as the management of public programs. But to elaborate on this definition, it helps to know a little history. Happily, there is only a little history to learn because public administration, at least in this country, is a relatively young field of study. Of course, people have been engaged in the management of public programs for thousands of years. (For example, imagine the administrative headaches involved in building the Egyptian pyramids!) However, the self-conscious study of public administration is a fairly recent development, often dated to the work of French and German scholars in the late nineteenth century. Public administration as we know it today in the United States began as the study of government administration, and that study began as part of late-nineteenth-century efforts to reform governmental operations. Most scholars and practitioners date the beginnings of the self-conscious study of public administration in this country to an 1887 essay written by Woodrow Wilson (then scholar, later president). Although some have recently questioned the influence Wilson had on the field, there is no question that his essay marks the symbolic beginning of American public administration.

Wilson's essay was basically reformist in nature, and highly practical. It was designed to address the inefficiency and open corruption that had become a part of government during the late 1880s and to suggest certain remedies within the administration of government. Wilson argued that although scholars and practitioners had focused on political institutions (such as Congress or the presidency), too little attention had been paid to administrative questions—the questions of how the government actually operates. The result, according to Wilson, was that it was becoming "harder to run a constitution than to frame one" (Wilson, 1887, p. 200). Wilson first wanted the work of government agencies to be accomplished more effectively. He felt that such organizations would operate best if they pursued the private sector's commitment to efficient or "businesslike" operations. Wilson, of course, wrote in a period during which business, industry, and technology were developing in rapid and surprising new ways. Like others, he admired the managerial philosophies that business seemed to be developing. Among these notions, Wilson particularly favored the idea of concentrating power in a single authority atop a highly integrated and centralized administrative structure. His recommendation of a strong chief executive has been echoed by writers (and chief executives!) even to the present.

The men and women who followed Wilson in discussions of what came to be called public administration were very practical people, concerned with reforming governmental structures and making them more efficient. But they were also quite careful to place these concerns within the context of democratic government. How might the principles of democracy, including such lofty ideals as liberty and justice, be extended throughout government and throughout society? Indeed, Leonard D. White, one of the most thoughtful of the early writers, commented that "the study of public administration . . . needs to be related to the broad generalizations of political theory concerned with such matters as justice, liberty, obedience, and the role of the state in human affairs" (White, 1948, p. 10). As we will see, a continued concern for operating efficiently while at the same time operating in a way consistent with democratic values marks the field of public administration even today.

Values of Democracy

Because their commitment to democratic values so clearly affects the work of those in public and nonprofit organizations in this country, it may be helpful to briefly review some of the key commitments we associate with democratic governance. The term *democracy* well reflects its roots: the Greek words *demos,* meaning "people," and *kratis,* meaning "authority." Generally speaking, democracy refers to a political system in which the interests of the people at large prevail. However, it is clear that within these broad parameters there are many different conceptions of democracy. For example, at the end of World War II, representatives of the United States, Great Britain, France, and Russia met to consider the "democratization" of Germany. Yet, it soon became apparent that the Russian idea of democracy was quite different from the Western view. While Westerners associated democracy with such ideas as free elections, freedom of the press, freedom of movement, and the freedom to criticize the government, the Russians had quite a different conception. For them, democracy did not necessarily mean government by or of the people, but rather whether government policy is carried out *in the interest* of the people.

Even today, the term *democratic* is used in many different ways by many different people. Yet in the American experience, there is general agreement that democracy refers to a political system—a way of ordering power and authority in which decision-making power is widely shared among members of the society. Or to put it in terms of control, democracy is a system in which many ordinary citizens exercise a high degree of control over their leaders. (In either case, the opposite would be an *oligarchy*, government by the few, or an *autocracy*, government by one.)

But democracy is defined not only in terms of processes or procedures (for example, rule by many), but also by several important cultural values that are typically pursued in a democratic society. Among these, three—individualism, equality, and liberty—have been of special importance to those who have helped shape the American idea of democracy. The first is *individualism*, the idea that the dignity and integrity of the individual is of supreme importance. Individualism suggests that achieving the fullest potential of each individual is the best measure of the success of our political system. It is the idea of individualism that is reflected in the familiar phrasing of the Declaration of Independence—that all persons are endowed by their Creator with certain inalienable rights and that it is the purpose of government to secure those rights.

Second is the idea of *equality*, which does not mean that all persons are equal in their talents or possessions, but that each individual has an equal claim to life, liberty, and the pursuit of happiness. In this view, each person should be seen as an end, not as a means; no one should be a mere tool of another. Moreover, equality in the field of government would suggest that differences in wealth or position are not sufficient reasons for giving one group preference over another. In a democracy, each one has an equal claim to the attention of the system and should be able to expect just outcomes.

A third central value of a democratic society is *liberty*, or freedom. This idea suggests that the individual citizen of a democracy should have a high degree of self-determination. You should have the maximum opportunity to select your own purposes in life and to choose the means to accomplish them. Liberty is more than just the absence of constraints; it suggests the freedom to act positively in pursuit of one's own ends. Only by allowing individuals the freedom to choose, it is argued, will social progress occur.

The influence of these themes on the development of public administration is undeniable. Though, as we will see, people differ over the degree to which they influence the day-to-day operations of public agencies. Similarly, the way in which democracy has been operationalized in the American political tradition has had important influences on the operation of public organizations. For example, take the traditional separation of legislative, executive, and judicial functions. Although, the primary task of the legislative branch is to make policy through the enactment of legislation, the primary task of the executive branch is the faithful execution or implementation of policy, and the primary task of the judicial branch is the interpretation of the law, especially as it relates to constitutional guarantees.

David Rosenbloom of American University has argued that these three functions of government are related to three views of the role of public administrators in American society (Rosenbloom, 1993, p. 15).

1. The *managerial approach* to public administration, which Rosenbloom connects to the executive function, emphasizes the management and organization of public organizations. As with Wilson, this view sometimes suggests that management in the public sector is very much like that in the private sector; that is, it is primarily concerned with efficiency.

2. The *political approach* to public administration, related to the legislative function in government, is more concerned about ensuring constitutional safeguards, such as those already mentioned. Efficiency becomes less a concern than effectiveness or responsiveness.

3. Finally, the *legal approach* to public administration, related to the judicial function, emphasizes the administrator's role in applying and enforcing the law in specific situations. It is also concerned with the adjudicatory role of public organizations.

While we will examine these various approaches in more detail as we move through the book, it is important to understand at the outset that all actions of public administrators take place within an important political context: a commitment to democratic ideals and practices. Yet, today, that ideal is somewhat tarnished. Americans' trust in government has been steadily declining over the last several decades. Questions are being raised not only about the quality and productivity of government, but about the responsiveness of government to the people (see Box 1.1). This tension will be a persistent theme as we examine contemporary approaches to the study and practice of public administration. Borrowing a phrase from earlier times, the task of public administrators today is still to "make democracy suitable for modern conditions." Doing so in a time of confusion and mistrust will be a special challenge to those in public administration as we move through the twenty-first century. Keep this in mind as we examine the various approaches and techniques that are appropriate to public administration today.

Contrasting Business and Public Administration

One issue, however, deserves further comment up front. Even though work in public and nonprofit organizations is guided by commitments to democratic ideals, it is also involved with management, and, for that reason, public administration is often confused with business management. Indeed, such confusion has occasionally been prominent in the

BOX 1.1

THE DEMOCRATIC DREAM

The predominant American political belief—attained, pretended, or otherwise—from before the establishment of the Republic and throughout the nation's history has been the democratic dream, nominally based on some version of popular representation and governance. Virtually every political structure and reform has been predicated on some mode of the democratic, egalitarian ethos, even as they oscillated back and forth between its Jeffersonian and Hamiltonian poles. Indeed, to imagine a widespread domestic political movement (and probably foreign policy initiative) that does not in some very visible manner drape itself in the sacred vestment of democracy is inconceivable.

It is this ambience that American political philosophies, politics themselves, and even certain professions (e.g., public administration) were created and nurtured.

Not surprisingly, public service and public administration in the United States have shared a similar democratic coloration. From the early days of the professional public administrator—when Woodrow Wilson temporarily partitioned "politics" and "administration" into separate entities—we find a solid stream of democratic theory underpinning and underlining contemporary public administration.

But the Constitution cannot serve as a singular political poultice for whatever ails the body politic. Within the country at large, there is a tangible sense that as often appeals are made to the nation's democratic benchmarks, these are more calls to a fading faith than references to reality. Americans are apparently disenchanted with their politics, both in terms of substance and process. Our public life is rife with discontent. Americans do not believe they have much to say about how they are governed and do not trust government to do the right thing.

SOURCE: Reprinted by permission from *Democracy and the Policy Sciences* by Peter deLeon, State University of New York Press, © 1997, State University of New York. All rights reserved.

field of public administration. (As we have already seen, early writers in the field often suggested that government should become more like business, a sentiment heard even today.) Certainly, there are some similarities between business and public administration. Managers across all sectors—public, private, and nonprofit—are involved in questions of organizational design, the allocation of scarce resources, and the management of people. But most observers would agree that the primary distinction between business and public service is that business is primarily concerned with making a profit, while public service is concerned with delivering services or regulating individual or group behavior in the public interest. All would agree that the context of public and nonprofit management significantly alters the work itself. Three differences are most apparent.

Ambiguity One difference between government and business lies in the purposes to be served. In most businesses, even those with service objectives, the bottom-line profit is the basic measure of evaluating how good a job the organization is doing. In turn, the performance of individual managers can, in many cases, be directly measured in terms of their unit's contribution to the overall profit of the company. This is not true of public or nonprofit agencies, where the objectives of the organization may be more ambiguous and where making or losing money is not the main criterion for success or failure.

Often the objectives of public and nonprofit organizations are stated in terms of service; for example, an agency's mission may be to protect the quality of the environment or to provide an adequate level of rehabilitative services to the disabled. Yet, such service objectives are much harder to specify and to measure. What does "quality" mean with respect to the environment? What level of service to the disabled is "adequate"? The difficulty of specifying objectives such as these makes it harder to assess the performance of government agencies and, in turn, their managers. Moreover, most businesses wouldn't tolerate a money-losing operation in a depressed area, but a public or nonprofit organization, though equally attentive to the money being spent, might well consider meeting human needs more important than the financial "bottom line."

Pluralistic Decision Making   A second difference between work in the public service and in business is that the public service, at least in a democratic society, requires that many groups and individuals have access to the decision process. As a result, decisions that might be made rapidly by one individual or a small group in a business might, in a public or nonprofit organization, require input from many diverse groups and organizations. Consequently, it is difficult to speak of specific decision centers in government. W. Michael Blumenthal, a business executive who became secretary of the treasury in the Carter administration, described the situation this way:

> If the President said to me, you develop [an economic policy toward Japan], Mike, the moment that becomes known there are innumerable interest groups that begin to play a role. The House Ways and Means Committee, the Senate Finance Committee, and every member on them and every staff member has an opinion and seeks to exert influence. Also, the Foreign Relations Committee, the oversight committees, and then the interest groups, business, the unions, the State Department, the Commerce Department, OMB, Council of Economic Advisers, and not only the top people, but all their staff people, not to speak of the President's staff and the entire press. (Blumenthal, 1983, p. 30)

The pluralistic nature of public decision making has led many business executives who have worked in the public or nonprofit sectors to comment that this feature makes public and nonprofit management much more difficult than management in the private sector. But, as Blumenthal points out, "the diversity of interests seeking to affect policy is the nature and essence of democratic government" (Blumenthal, 1983, pp. 30–31). Many have also found that this aspect of public service is particularly challenging and rewarding.

Visibility   Finally, managers in public and nonprofit organizations seem to operate with much greater visibility than their counterparts in industry. The public service in a democratic society is subject to constant scrutiny by both the press and the public. The media seems to cover everything you do, and this may be a mixed blessing. On the one hand, media coverage enables the leaders of the organization to communicate rapidly to external and internal audiences. On the other hand, the media's constant scrutiny of policy positions and their labeling of inconsistencies as weaknesses can be limiting to free discussion of issues in their formulation stage. And, of course, the occasional intrusions of the press into even the most mundane personal matters can be excessive; one local newspaper even reported a problem a new city manager was having with his refrigerator! Yet, executives in government realize that it is essential to a democratic society that their work be visible to the public and subject to the interest and control of the citizenry.

What Would You Do?

You have just been appointed city manager of a city of 30,000 in the upper Midwest. While the economy of the area is generally stable, there is talk of one of the area's major industrial firms moving out. On the other hand, that firm has been a persistent contributor to pollution in the area. The city council seems evenly divided on whether to make an effort to keep the firm and its jobs or simply let it go. In your first six months on the job, what would you do?

why leaving?
where is land?
kind of pollution?
open to change?
opportunity costs?

Thinking about Public Administration Today

With this background, we can now think more carefully about how the field of public administration has traditionally been described and how we might develop an action orientation toward the study of public administration. In terms of definition, many early writers spoke of administration as a function of government, something that occurred in many shapes and forms throughout government. There were obviously administrative activities performed in the executive branch, but there were also administrative functions performed in the legislative and judicial branches. Some even noted that from time to time any single official might engage in both legislative and administrative functions.

Somewhat later, public administration was viewed as merely concerned with the activities of the executive agencies of government. In the words of an early text, public administration is concerned with the "operations of the administrative branch only" (Willoughby, 1927, p. 1). By the 1950s, such a perspective was so firmly entrenched that the leading text of that period stated, "By public administration is meant, in common usage, the activities of the executive branches of national, state, and local governments; independent boards and commissions set up by Congress and state legislatures; government corporations; and certain other agencies of a specialized character" (Simon et al., 1950, p. 7). Modern definitions of public administration have returned to the traditional view, including attention to administrative officials in all branches of government and even focusing on those in nonprofit organizations.

For our purposes, a formal definition of the field may be less important than trying to discover how public administration is experienced by those in the "real world." Our commitment to an action orientation suggests that we try to determine the kinds of activities engaged in by public administrators and the environmental factors that help to shape their work. We have already seen how the ambiguity of service objectives, the pluralistic nature of governmental decision making, and the visibility of management in the public and nonprofit

NETWORKING

The leading national organization for those in the field of public administration is the American Society for Public Administration. See www.aspanet.org. Other related organizations with helpful websites include the National Academy of Public Administration at www.napawash.org; Association for Public Policy Analysis and Management at www.appam.org; Council for Excellence in Government at http://www.excelgov.org; the American Political Science Association at www.apsanet.org; the Alliance for Nonprofit Management at www.allianceonline.org; the Independent Sector at www.independentsector.org; and the Academy of Management, Public and Nonprofit Division at www.aom.pace.edu/pn/index.htm.

sectors create a context in which managerial work is significantly different from that in other settings. From the standpoint of the real-world administrator, the things that really make the difference in the way you operate are not whether you are employed by a government agency, but whether you work under circumstances that feature an ambiguity of objectives, a multiplicity of decision centers, and high public visibility.

Publicness These features in turn all derive from the simple fact that the public or nonprofit manager is pursuing public purposes. In terms of the actions and experiences of the public administrator, therefore, we may say that it is the "publicness" of the work of the public or nonprofit manager that distinguishes public administration from other similar activities. This view of the administrator's role suggests that, as a public or nonprofit manager, you must operate with one eye toward managerial effectiveness and the other toward the desires and demands of the public. It recognizes that you are likely to experience an inevitable tension between efficiency and responsiveness as you work in governmental or nongovernmental organizations, a tension that will be absolutely central to your work.

Let us highlight some of the implications of this orientation. Many commentators point out that the distinction between public and private management is no longer simply a distinction between business and government or between profit and service. In fact, more and more frequently, we encounter situations in which traditionally public organizations are pursuing enhanced revenues (profits?), and traditionally private organizations are concerned with the provision of services. What is important is not merely what is being sought, but rather whose interest is being served. On this basis, a private enterprise is one in which private interests privately arrived at are paramount. A public organization, on the other hand, is one in which public interests publicly arrived at are paramount.

There is a trend in our society for greater openness and responsiveness on the part of many organizations. Most associations and nonprofit organizations would fit this mold, and managers in those organizations must certainly be attentive to both efficiency and responsiveness. But many corporations as well are finding it important to open their decision-making processes to public scrutiny and involvement. The range of organizations engaged in the public service (and the applicability of public and nonprofit management) seems ever-increasing.

On the other hand, our understanding of the manager's role would suggest that there could be managers in governmental or nongovernmental agencies who would be pursuing interests other than those of the public. Certainly, those operating agencies in totalitarian countries could hardly be considered to be pursuing publicly defined values. They would more likely be pursuing the privately defined interests of a political elite. Similarly, we might question from time to time whether all managers in our democratic society have a proper concern for the public interest. Certainly, in cases where managers pursue their own personal agendas, as in cases of empire-building, we would question the "publicness" of their actions.

We now have a notion of the complexity of work in the public and nonprofit sectors—the complexity inherent in the technical work of governmental and nongovernmental agencies, but, even more important, the complexity of the political and ethical context in which managers operate. Indeed, as noted before, this complexity will provide a theme that ties together many aspects of your work as an administrator. The way you set objectives, the way you develop budgets and hire personnel, the way you interact with other organizations and with your own clientele, the way you evaluate the success or failure of your programs—all of these aspects of your work as an administrator, and many more, are directly affected by the fact that you will be managing in the public interest.

■ Why Study Public Administration?

Students come to introductory courses in public administration for many different reasons. Many students recognize the vast array of positions in government (and elsewhere) that require training in public administration and hope that the course will provide basic information and skills that will move them toward careers as public or nonprofit managers. These students seek to understand the field of public administration, but also to sharpen their own skills as potential administrators.

Other students, whose interests lie in technical fields as wide ranging as engineering, teaching, natural resources, social work, and the fine arts, recognize that at some point in their careers their jobs may involve management in the public sector. The engineer may become director of a public works department; the teacher may become school principal; the natural resources expert may be asked to run an environmental quality program; the social worker may administer a welfare program; or the fine arts major may direct a publicly supported gallery or museum. In these cases, and others like them, the individual's technical expertise may need to be complemented by managerial training.

NETWORKING

The National Association of Schools of Public Affairs and Administration is the accrediting body for programs in public administration and pursues other educational matters. See its home page at www.naspaa.org and download a list of NASPAA-accredited MPA programs at www.naspaa.org/accreditation/public/rosterofaccreditedschools2003-04.pdf.

Other students may have no expectations whatsoever of working in a public agency, but they recognize that as corporate executives, as businesspeople, or merely as citizens, they are likely to be called upon to interact with those in public organizations. Someone who owns a small business might wish to sell products or services to a city, a county, or some other governmental body; partners in an accounting firm might seek auditing contracts with a local or state government; or a construction firm might bid on the design and construction of a new public building. In each case, knowledge of the operations of public agencies would not only be helpful, it would be essential.

A final group of students, a group overlapping any of the previous three, might simply recognize the importance of public agencies in the governmental process and the impact of public organizations on their daily lives. They might wish to acquire the knowledge and skills that would enable them to more effectively analyze and influence public policy. Some will find the world of public administration a fascinating field of study in its own right and pursue academic careers in public affairs. Because understanding the motives for studying public administration will also give us a more complete view of the variety and importance of managerial work in the public sector, we will examine each in greater detail.

Preparing for Administrative Positions

You may be among those who wish to use the introductory public administration course as a stepping-stone to a career in the public service. If so, you will find that these careers take many forms. We sometimes make distinctions among program managers, *staff managers*, and *policy analysts*. *Program managers* range from the executive level to the supervisory level and are in charge of particular governmental or nongovernmental programs, such as those in environmental quality or transportation safety. Their job is to allocate and monitor human, material, and financial resources to meet the service objectives of their agency. Staff managers, on the other hand, support the work of program managers through budgeting and financial management, personnel and labor relations, and purchasing and procurement. Meanwhile, policy analysts provide important information about existing programs through their research into the operations and impacts of the programs; moreover, analysts help bring together information about new programs, assess the possible effects of different courses of action, and suggest new directions for public policy. Managers and analysts may work with the chief executive, with the legislature, with officials at other levels of government, and with the public in framing and reframing public programs.

As we will see, the work of public and nonprofit organizations also encompasses a wide variety of substantive areas. Think for a moment of the range of activities the federal government engages in. The federal government touches upon nearly every aspect of American life, from aeronautics, air transportation, and atmospheric sciences; to helping the homeless, juvenile delinquents, and migrant workers; to working with waste management, wages standards, and water quality. In each area, skilled managers are called upon to develop, implement, and evaluate government programs. But the work of managers at the federal level represents only a part of the work of those trained in public administration.

At the state and local levels of government, and in the nonprofit sector, even more opportunities exist. As we will see in Chapter 2, although there is only one federal government in this country, there are almost 88,000 state and local governments (these include cities, counties, and special districts) and more than 1.3 million nonprofit organizations. State and local government employment in this country amounts to over 15 million persons (compared to under 3 million civilians employed at the federal level), and nearly 12 million people work for nonprofit organizations.

Obviously, the work of government at the state and local levels is different from that at the federal level. State and local governments, for example, do not directly provide for the national defense; however, most have police forces, which the federal government does not have. There are also other positions at the state and local levels that do not have exact counterparts at the federal level. For example, consider the president or chancellor of your state university a public administrator with significant and unusual responsibilities, or consider the city manager in a local community a professional administrator appointed by a city council to manage the various functions of local government.

And the public service is not limited to work in government. Beyond employment in federal, state, or local government, those trained in public administration will find many other opportunities. Directors of nonprofit organizations at the state and local levels, as well as those in similar associations at the national level, often find that the skills required for their jobs—skills that combine managerial training with an understanding of the political system—are the skills developed in public administration courses. Again, to demonstrate the breadth of these activities, we might note that there are large numbers of nonprofit associations at the national level alone, ranging from well-known groups such as the American Medical Association or the American Bar Association, to trade groups such as the American Frozen Food Institute and the National Association of Bedding Manufacturers, to professional associations such as the American Society for Public Administration and those representing a particular field of interest, such as the Metropolitan Opera Guild. There is even an association of association executives: the American Society of Association Executives. Beyond these groups at the national level, there are numerous nonprofit groups operating at state and local levels—for example, local United Way organizations, local food banks, art leagues, or historic preservation groups.

Finally, those with training in public administration may work in a private corporation's public affairs division. Because of the increasing interaction across private, public, and nongovernmental sectors, corporations and nonprofit organizations often need special assistance in tracking legislation, developing and monitoring government contracts, and influencing the legislative or regulatory process. Thus, the combination of managerial and political skills possessed by someone with training in public administration can be highly valuable. The career possibilities in the field of public administration are seemingly endless.

Combining Technical and Managerial Training

Many students seek positions in the public service as a primary career objective, whereas many others see the possibility of work in public administration as secondary, but nonetheless important, to their main field of interest. As noted, the work of government spans many areas; consequently, the people who work for government (one out of every six people in this country) come from a wide variety of professional backgrounds. There are engineers who work in the Defense Department and for NASA at the federal level, in state highway departments, and in local public works departments. People interested in natural resources may work for the U.S. Forest Service and the Environmental Protection Agency, in state conservation departments, and local parks departments. Medical personnel may work for the Veterans Administration or the National Institute for Mental Health, for state health departments, and for local hospitals and health offices.

Governments at all levels hire social workers, planners, personnel specialists, accountants, lawyers, biologists, law enforcement officers, educators, researchers, recreation specialists, and agricultural specialists, just to mention a few. To illustrate the magnitude of government employment, over 778,000 people work in the postal service, 390,000 are employed in health care, and 110,000 financial administrators work in the federal government alone. (U.S. Census, ftp2.census.gov/govs/apes/05fedfun.pdf)

People who have worked for some time within a technical field in a public organization are often promoted to managerial positions. A surgeon may become chief of surgery, a water pollution specialist may be asked to direct a pollution control project, or a teacher may become a school principal. Despite having started out in a technical field, these individuals find themselves in a managerial position; they are public administrators. Some people may desire promotion to a managerial position; others may not. (There are some jurisdictions in which continued advancement practically requires moving into an administrative position.) But whatever one's motivation, the new administrator soon discovers a completely new world of work. Now the most pressing questions are not the technical ones, but rather those having to do with management, with program planning and design, with supervision and motivation, and with balancing scarce resources. Often the situation is quite bewildering; it's almost as if one has been asked to change professions in midcareer from technical expert to public manager.

So many people from technical fields find themselves in managerial positions in the public sector that many of them seek training in public administration. For this reason, it is no longer unusual for students majoring in technical fields to take courses in public administration or for students to combine undergraduate training in a technical field with graduate training in public administration (even at midcareer). This, then, is a second reason for studying public administration: to prepare for the eventuality that work in a technical field of interest might lead you to a managerial position in the public sector.

Interaction of Business and Government

Even for students who never work for a public agency of any type, understanding the processes of policy formulation and implementation can be enormously helpful. One of the most important trends in American society is the increasing interaction of business and government. Clearly, the decisions of government affect the environment in which business operates, but government also specifically regulates many businesses and, of course, serves as the biggest single customer of business.

Those in business recognize that governmental decisions affect the economic climate. Most obvious are the effects of governmental decisions at the federal level. Consider, for example, the impact of government economic pronouncements on the stock market.

State and local governments, however, also affect the business climate. The governors of many states have begun major campaigns to attract industry to their states, providing not only information and advice, but specific incentives for plants and industries that might relocate. Similar activities are being undertaken in more and more local communities, as cities recognize that they are in competition for economic development. At a minimum, business recognizes that the political climate of any locality directly affects the area's economic climate.

But the influence of government on business is more specific. At the federal level, major regulatory agencies, such as the Federal Communications Commission and the Federal Trade Commission, provide specific guidelines in which certain businesses must operate. Moreover, requirements of agencies such as the Environmental Protection Agency and the Occupational Safety and Health Administration restrict the operations of business so as to ensure the quality of air and water and the safety of working conditions. Similarly, at the state level, some agencies directly regulate specific businesses, while others act more generally to prevent unfair or unsafe practices. Even at the local level, through licensing and zoning practices, public organizations directly regulate business practice.

Government is also important as a consumer of business products and services. At the federal level, over $330 billion is spent each year on goods and services; in the Defense Department alone, the figure is over $200 billion per year. Similarly, at the state and local levels, these expenditures amount to almost $270 billion a year (www.census.gov/prod/ 2005pubs/cffr-04.pdf and www.census.gov/govs/estimate/0400ussl_1.html). Business is attentive to its customers, so it is not surprising that business is attentive to government!

For all these reasons, people in business are becoming increasingly aware of the need to understand in detail the work of government—how policies are made, how they are implemented, and how they may be influenced. Not only are more and more businesses developing public affairs offices to specialize in governmental operations, track policy developments, and attempt to influence policy, but they are placing a greater premium upon having executives at all levels who understand how government agencies operate. Even if you plan a career in business, understanding the work of public organizations is an essential part of your training.

Influencing Public Organizations

Any of the motives for studying public administration we have discussed so far may bring you to an introductory course. There is, however, another more general reason you may wish to study public administration: to understand one important aspect of the governmental process so you can deal effectively with public issues that directly affect your life. We are all affected by the work of governmental and nongovernmental organizations, so it is helpful, and sometimes even essential, to understand the operations of these organizations.

We have become so accustomed to the pervasiveness of the public service and the range of its influence that we sometimes forget just how often our lives are touched by public and nonprofit organizations. Imagine a typical day: We wake up in the morning to the sounds of a commercially regulated radio station or National Public Radio coming over a patented and FCC-registered clock radio operating on power supplied by either a government-regulated power company or a public utility. We brush our teeth with toothpaste produced under a government patent and trust that it has been judged safe (if not effective) by a federal agency. We use municipally operated water and sewer systems without thinking of the complexity of their operation. We dress in clothes produced under governmental restrictions and eat food prepared in accordance with government regulations and inspected by the government. We drive on a public highway, following government enforced traffic laws, to a university substantially funded by federal, state, and sometimes local dollars to study from books copyrighted and catalogued by the Library of Congress. Though the day has hardly begun, our lives already have been touched by public organizations in a multitude of ways.

The importance of public administration in daily life is tremendous; consequently, the decisions made by governmental and nongovernmental officials (and not just elected officials) can affect us directly. Imagine, for example, that one day you discover that the loan program that is helping to finance your college education is being reviewed and will likely be revised in such a way that you will no longer be eligible for funding. In this case, you might well want to take some action to maintain your eligibility. Obviously, knowing something about the operations of government agencies, especially some of the ways administrative decisions can be influenced, would be of great help.

As citizens affected by the public service, understanding the operations of public and nonprofit organizations is helpful; it is even more important if one becomes personally involved in some aspect of the governmental process. For those reading this book, such involvement is actually rather likely. Indeed, if you are a college graduate, regardless of your major or field of interest, chances are quite good that at some point in your life you will engage in some kind of formal governmental activity. You may be elected to local, state, or national office; you may be asked to serve on a board or commission; or your advice concerning government operations in your area may be sought in other ways. You may also become involved in the work of nonprofit organizations or charities in your local community. In any of these cases, a thorough knowledge of the structure and processes of public organizations, both government and nonprofit organizations, will be of great importance.

Finally, those who are interested in understanding the work of public or nonprofit organizations may indeed find the field of public administration interesting from a more academic standpoint: studying and commenting on the operations of government and nonprofit organizations contribute to our understanding of the process of policy development and support the work of those in public organizations. The opportunities for academic careers in public administration, positions involving teaching and research, are many, and you may find yourself drawn to those opportunities. Even here, however, one begins with a concern for action.

What Would You Do?

You have served three years as head of your state's human services agency. In general, your relationship with the governor has been quite good, and your relationship with the legislature (which is dominated by the governor's party) has been congenial as well. Recently, however, there has been a move in the legislature to reduce funding for a child care program you think is essential to finding and maintaining employment for women on welfare. What would you do?

Making Things Happen

Of the many reasons to learn about public and nonprofit organizations, one theme seems to tie together the various interests: an interest in making things happen. Whether you are preparing for a career in the public sector covering the possibility that you might some-day manage a public agency, or simply preparing to affect the course of public policy and its implementation as it directly affects you or your business, your interest is in taking action and influencing what goes on in public and nonprofit organizations. It's one thing to gain knowledge of the field in the abstract, but most students want to learn those things that will make them more effective *actors* in the governmental process. Some of the more prominent actors are discussed in Box 1.2.

BOX 1.2

PUBLIC SERVICE: A DISTINGUISHED PROFESSION

For my part, when I think of government service, in uniform and out, I think of individual men and women of genuine distinction who have served this country over the years and also of the amazing diversity of a service that can range from defending our borders to delivering our mail, curing disease to exploring outer space. I was looking at a civil service publication the other day containing an alphabetical list of well-known employees through the years "and found it began with a career civil servant named Neil Armstrong who went on TDY (temporary duty) to the moon" and concluded several pages later with Walt Whitman, the poet, who worked in the Department of the Interior and the U.S. Attorney [General's office]. How's that for diversity? Incidentally, the group also included four Nobel Prize winners and several important inventors, including Alexander Graham Bell, who among his other associations worked for the Census Bureau. There also were some other familiar names of people who shared your proud profession: Clara Barton, Washington Irving, Abraham Lincoln, Charles Lindbergh, Knute Rockne, Harry Truman, and James Whistler, to name but a few.

In my own experience, as one who served the federal government for some years, I look back on those periods as among the most exciting, challenging, and thoroughly demanding in life. I have often said, and still say, that I never worked harder than I did in my years as a public servant. I worked alongside some of the finest, most competent, thoroughly committed people I have ever known. I realize this does not comport with everything that you read in the papers or see on television, but I never miss a chance to point it out. My own experience in government left me with an abiding respect for the men and women who serve this nation as public employees.

SOURCE: Norman R. Augustine, Chairman and Chief Executive Officer of Martin Marietta Corporation, Address to the Federal Executive Board, Denver, Colorado, April 26, 1989. Text provided by The Council for Excellence in Government, Washington, D.C.

This book is geared toward action, toward how to make things happen in the public service. Our perspective will be that of the actor, not the scholar, although an understanding of the world of administrative action is the basis for good scholarship as well. Action first requires a base of knowledge; there are certain things that you simply need to know about government and the administrative process to be effective. There are also value questions that must be settled in the course of making and carrying out public decisions. And, finally, there are both technical and interpersonal skills you must acquire to be effective in working with others in your chosen field. Selecting an action orientation, therefore, commits you to emphasizing all three areas: the knowledge, values, and skills that will help you to become more effective and responsible in your work with "real life" public organizations.

■ Issues in Public Administration Theory and Practice

Throughout the chapters to come, our primary emphasis will be on action—those things that real-world actors do in order to be successful in public and nonprofit organizations. But action never stands alone. Without some degree of reflection, action is sterile and unguided. For this reason, we will outline two themes that have traditionally characterized work in public organizations and that continue to be of great importance today. As such, these themes—politics and administration, and bureaucracy and democracy—provide a part of the intellectual and practical context of public administration. Although our purpose is to simply introduce these two themes, we suggest that they are most often manifest in contemporary public administration as a tension between efficiency and responsiveness. This tension is one that is absolutely central to the work of public administrators today and one to which we will return frequently within the context of specific discussions of administrative action.

Politics and Administration

Even though the supposed dichotomy between politics and administration is one of the oldest issues in public administration, it continues to hold great relevance for administrators today. You will recall that an early essay by Woodrow Wilson framed the initial study of public administration in this country. In addition to his emphasis on business-like practices, Wilson was concerned with isolating the processes of administration from the potentially corrupting influences of politics. Wilson wrote, "Administration lies outside the proper sphere of politics. Administrative questions are not political questions. Although politics sets the tasks for administration, it should not be suffered to manipulate its offices" (Wilson, 1887, p. 210). In other words, although policies were to be debated and decided by politicians, they were to be carried out by a politically neutral, professional bureaucracy. In this way, the everyday conduct of government would be isolated from the potentially corrupting influence of politics.

Other early writers joined Wilson in talking, at least analytically, about the distinction between politics (or policy) and administration. More practical reformers went further, creating governmental forms, such as the council-manager plan for local government, that were based on a separation of policy and administration. As we will see later in this form of government, the council presumably makes the policy and the city manager carries it out. The council is engaged in politics (or policy) and the manager in administration.

Over the first few decades of this century, however, the distinction between policy and administration was increasingly broken down, even in council-manager governments. Managers found that they had expertise that was needed by policy makers and began to be drawn into the policy process. By about the middle of the century, Paul Appleby of Syracuse University would write simply, "Public administration is policy-making" (Appleby, 1949, p. 170).

The increasing involvement of administrators in the policy process was in part attributable to the fact that the operations of government, and in contemporary society of nonprofit organizations, were becoming more complex, and the technical and professional skills needed to operate public agencies were dramatically increasing. As people with such skills and expertise became a part of public organizations, they were inevitably called upon to present their views. At the same time, the legislative branches of government (at all levels) found it difficult to be knowledgeable about every detail of government and, consequently, were forced to rely more and more on the expertise of those in public agencies. Additionally, the complexity of government meant that legislative bodies often found it necessary to state laws in general terms, leaving those within government agencies considerable discretion to interpret those laws as they saw fit and, therefore, make policy daily.

Ensuring Accountability The acknowledgment of the interaction of politics and administration does not make the question of their relationship any easier. If public administrators make policy, how can we be sure that the policies they make are responsible to the people (as we would expect in a democratic society)? Presumably, legislators must be at least somewhat responsive, or, come the next election, they will no longer be legislators. But what of administrators?

What Would You Do?

You are the executive director of the Parents Anonymous organization in your area. Your organization is devoted to preventing child abuse and strengthening families. Recently one of your traditional sources of funding was terminated. You are faced with the prospect of reducing staff (and services) or coming up with new revenues. What would you do?

Traditionally, the answer was that the administrators were accountable to the legislators, who, in turn, were accountable to the people. But even that argument is somewhat tricky today. Those in public and nonprofit agencies do indeed both work with and report to legislatures, but they also shape public opinion through the information they provide. They mobilize for support inside and outside government and bargain with a variety of public and private groups. To a certain extent, they act as independent agents.

For this reason, more contemporary discussions of accountability (which we will elaborate on in Chapter 4) place an emphasis on measures that would supplement accountability to the legislature by either seeking a strong subjective sense of responsibility on the part of administrators or by providing structural controls to ensure responsibility. As we will see, some people have tried to assert professional standards in public and nonprofit organizations, while others have developed codes of ethics and standards of professional practice. Others have sought greater legislative involvement in the administrative process or more substantial legislative review. Still others have described mechanisms such as public participation in the administrative process or surveys of public opinion that would bring the administrator in closer alignment with the sentiments of the citizenry.

The relationship between politics (or policy) and administration will be a theme that recurs throughout the remainder of this book. Although the classic dichotomy between politics and administration has fallen, as the role of public administrators in the policy process has become more apparent, the question of the relationship between politics and administration remains central, simply because it goes to the heart of what public administration is all about. If public organizations differ from other organizations in our society, that difference must surely rest in the way public organizations participate in and respond to the public interest. But that issue merely leads us to another: the relationship between bureaucracy and democracy.

Bureaucracy and Democracy

A second theme that grew from early discussions of public administration had to do with the potential for conflict between democracy and bureaucracy. Let's start once again with democracy. One writer has defined the moral commitments of a democracy in terms of three standards. First, democratic principles assume that the individual is the primary measure of human value and that the development of the individual is the primary goal of a democratic political system. Second, democratic morality suggests that all persons are created equal—that differences in wealth, status, or position should not give one person or group an advantage over another. Third, democratic morality emphasizes widespread participation among the citizens in the making of major decisions (Redford, 1969, p. 8).

Set against these tenets of democracy are the ideals of bureaucratic management. The early scholars and practitioners in public administration were, of course, writing at a time when businesses were growing rapidly and beginning to use more complicated technologies and new ways of organizing appropriate to those technologies. To some extent the public sector looked to the field of business for models of organization. They found that the growth of large-scale business had led to the development of large and complex bureaucratic organizations, organizations that were built around values quite different from those of democracy. (Although the term *bureaucracy* is often used in a pejorative sense, as in "bureaucratic red tape," we will use it here in its more neutral and scientific sense: as a way of organizing work.) Consequently, the bureaucratic model of organizing was brought into the public sector.

The values of bureaucracy included first the need to bring together the work of many individuals in order to achieve purposes far beyond the capabilities of any single individual. Second, bureaucratic systems were to be structured hierarchically, with those at the top having far greater power and discretion than those at the bottom. Third, bureaucratic organization generally assumes that power and authority flow from the top of the organization to the bottom rather than the other way around. (We will examine the concept of bureaucracy in greater detail in Chapter 5.)

In contrast to the democratic value of individuality, there stood the bureaucratic value of the group or organization; in contrast to the democratic values of equality, there stood the bureaucratic hierarchy; and in contrast to the democratic values of participation and involvement, there stood the bureaucratic value of top-down decision making and authority.

How these values were to be reconciled became a difficult issue for early scholars and practitioners in the field of public administration, as it continues to be today. A variety of questions are raised. For example, is it proper for a democratic government to carry out its work through basically authoritarian organizations? The key issue turns out to be an emphasis on efficiency as the sole measure of agency success.

Efficiency versus Responsiveness

Those in public administration have long wrestled with the issues of politics and administration, and democracy and bureaucracy, public (and increasingly nonprofit) managers have begun to experience these tensions more frequently in the day-to-day problems they face in terms of efficiency versus responsiveness. Indeed, in a sense, the two earlier issues seem to have dissolved into the single issue of efficiency versus responsiveness. On the one hand, there is the hope that public and nonprofit organizations will operate in the most efficient way possible, getting things done quickly and at the least cost to taxpayers and donors. On the other hand, public managers must be constantly attentive to the demands of the citizenry, whether those demands are expressed through the chief executive, through the legislature, or directly.

A practical and contemporary expression of this difficulty is presented in case study number 5 at the end of the chapter. (You might want to read it now. See number 5 under "Cases and Exercises.") The case relates a dispute that arose in the course of developing a new housing loan program. Although the case presents several different issues, most students reviewing the case focus their attention on the different interpretations that John and Carol have of their work. At first glance, John appears to be solely interested in doing things efficiently, while Carol appears to be much more concerned with responding to the needs of the client group. The case appears to be a classic illustration of the tension between efficiency and responsiveness, and indeed it is. But at a deeper level, the case also illustrates how complex the issues really are. You might say, for example, that John was trying to be efficient in response to the demands of those clients who had been waiting for their loans to be processed. You might also say that Carol, through her educational efforts, was helping to ensure a more efficient, long-term operation.

The main point, of course, is that in public organizations, you may frequently encounter difficulties in reconciling efficiency and responsiveness. A key to resolving the ethical questions raised in situations such as that faced by John and Carol is first understanding the various moral values represented on each side of the equation and second, engaging in ethical deliberation (and perhaps dialogue) to arrive at a proper approach to the problem. Interestingly enough, in this particular case, the real-life characters represented by John and Carol got together and talked through the differences in their respective approaches. The result was a course of action they both agreed on, one they felt met their obligations to be both efficient and responsive. In the real world, dialogue sometimes works!

To summarize this point, the themes of politics and administration, and bureaucracy and democracy have marked much of the history of the field of public administration. Today these themes seem often to manifest in the tension between efficiency and responsiveness. Are public agencies to concentrate only on creating the desired outcomes in the most efficient manner possible? Or should such agencies be responsive to the public interest and the public will, even though the public interest and public will may not have been explicitly articulated by elected officials, especially those in the legislature? Time after time, you'll find evidence of this tension in discussions on public policy, human resources management, budgeting and financial management, and so on. The tension between efficiency and responsiveness remains an "unsolved mystery" of public administration. But perhaps for that reason, it is a tension that helps make public administration such a fascinating and dynamic field.

■ What Do Public Administrators Do?

An action orientation to public administration requires that we focus on what public and nonprofit managers actually do—how they act in real-world situations. How do they spend their time? What skills do they require to do their work well? What are the rewards and frustrations of public service? From the perspective of the administrator, we can ask, What characterizes the most effective and responsible public or nonprofit management? What are the demands on administrators? What are the satisfactions that public managers draw from their work?

We will approach these issues by concentrating on the skills managers need to accomplish their work. In a classic article in the *Harvard Business Review*, Robert Katz provided the first major descriptions of the general skills all managers need: conceptual, technical, and human (Katz, 1974).

1. Conceptual skills include the ability to think abstractly, especially in regard to the manager's concept of the organization. This category also involves the ability to see the organization as a whole, how all the parts or functions work and fit together, and how making a change in one part will affect other parts. Conceptual skills also include the ability to see how the organization, or parts of it, relate to the organization's environment.
2. Technical skills refer to an understanding of, and proficiency in, the methods, processes, and techniques for accomplishing tasks. These are, for example, the skills of an accountant who can conduct an audit or develop an income statement or the skills of a mechanic who can repair an engine.
3. Human skills involve the capacity to work effectively as a member of a group or the ability to get others to work together effectively. ("Others" may include subordinates, superiors, managers at the same level, or virtually anyone with whom one might work on a given project or assignment.)

All these skills are important to managers, but are not equally important to all managers. Katz makes a strong argument that technical skills are most important to managers at the supervisory level who manage day-to-day operations but become less and less important as the level of management increases. On the other hand, conceptual skills are most important to top-level managers who must deal with the organization as a whole rather than with just one or a few parts of it. Conceptual skills are less important at the middle-management level and least important at the supervisory level.

Human skills, however, maintain a constant, high level of importance; they are critical regardless of one's level. How managers' human skills are employed may vary from level to level (for example, top managers lead more meetings than supervisory managers), but as a category, human skills remain the one constant for managerial success. In this book, we will consider the knowledge and values associated with public management (conceptual skills), the techniques public managers require in such areas as budgeting and personnel (technical skills), and the personal and interpersonal qualities that help managers work effectively with others (human skills).

An Inventory of Public Management Skills

One way to elaborate on an action approach is to create an inventory of the skills and competencies required for successful public and nonprofit management. There are many ways such an inventory can be constructed. One of the best ways is to talk with public and nonprofit managers about their work, as we suggest in exercise 1 at the end of the chapter. Several research studies have sought to answer this question by identifying the skills that are critical to managerial success. Of these studies, an early study by the federal government's Office of Personnel Management (OPM) is particularly helpful (Flanders & Utterback, 1985). The OPM study was based on information gathered from a large number of highly effective federal managers and produced a description of the broad elements of managerial performance at the supervisory, managerial, and executive levels.

NETWORKING

Websites dealing with management issues at the federal level include the Office of Personnel management at www.opm.gov and those services listed at www.usa.gov. In addition to the journals listed in the back of the book, you might be interested in the websites of the following: *Governing* magazine at www.governing.com; the *Chronicle of Philanthropy* at www.philanthropy.com; *Government Executive* magazine at www. govexec.com; *Government Technology* magazine at www.govtech.com; and *The Public Manager* at www.thepublicmanager.org.

According to the OPM study, the competencies of managers include being sensitive to agency policies and national concerns; representing the organization and acting as a liaison to those outside the organization; establishing organizational goals and the processes to carry them out; obtaining and allocating necessary resources to achieve the agency's purposes; effectively utilizing human resources; and monitoring, evaluating, and redirecting the work of the organization. But the OPM researchers recognized that managerial excellence requires not only doing the job, but doing it well. For this reason, they developed a set of skills, attitudes, and perspectives that seemed to distinguish the work of highly successful managers.

But different skills are required at different levels. As managers move up the organizational ladder, they must accumulate increasingly broader sets of skills. The researchers suggest, for example, that first-line supervisors must apply communication skills, interpersonal sensitivity, and technical competence to ensure effective performance on their own part and within the work unit. In addition, their actions must begin to reflect those characteristics in the next ring: leadership, flexibility, an action orientation, and a focus on results.

Middle managers, on the other hand, must demonstrate all these characteristics of effectiveness and begin to acquire the skills listed in the outer ring: a broad perspective, a strategic view, and environmental sensitivity. Executives at the highest levels of the public service who are responsible for the accomplishment of broad agency objectives must demonstrate the full complement of effectiveness characteristics to be most successful. Clearly, a wide diversity of skills, regardless of how the job is constructed or of the style in which it is executed, will be essential to your success as a manager.

A more recent study by the OPM detailed the core qualifications expected of the highest-level government executives, those comprising the Senior Executive Service. This study first presented five executive core qualifications: leading change, leading people, results driven, business acumen, and building coalitions. These were complemented by six "competencies": interpersonal skills, oral communication, integrity/honesty, written communication, continual learning, and public service motivation. (OPM, 2006)

Voices of Public Administrators

Studies such as that of the OPM are helpful in understanding what you need to know and what you must be able to do to be successful in public administration. But how does it actually "feel" to work in a public or nonprofit organization? The best way to answer this question is to let some public servants speak for themselves (see Box 1.3). Recently, we spoke to three outstanding professionals in the field of public administration about their views of the field and their feelings about their work. The following accounts are based on those interviews. Jan C. Perkins served for many years as city manager of Fremont, California. When asked about her motivations for entering the field of public administration, this was her reply.

> I was interested in improving the quality of life for all people and increasing the access of women and minorities. I believed that I could have the most impact by being involved in local government at a management level.
>
> The most rewarding aspects of my work have been being able to articulate the mission of the city and focus my resources and efforts in effectively meeting that mission, solving the problems of residents, and seeing employees grow and develop.

Those considering public service careers should understand that managing in the public arena is different from that in a private corporation. It requires a commitment to values such as providing quality services for all and dealing with all people on an equal level. It is very important that people who enter the public service do so with a high standard of ethical behavior and an ability to deal honestly and directly with all people.

BOX 1.3
REFLECTIONS OF A PUBLIC SERVICE JUNKIE

In reviewing my own motivations for staying in public service, I found several, rather than one single answer.

First, there is a joy in the use of skills learned through a long apprenticeship. After twenty years in public service, I realize my skills and abilities were not easily or painlessly acquired. My education in public service has been costly, and I feel an obligation to repay the resources, energy, and interest others have invested in teaching me.

A second factor is the conviction that the work is important. There is an underlying assumption in public service that we are all part of an effort that leads to a better life for individuals in our society. Public service is ultimately based on the view that the human condition can be improved, an optimism which perhaps forms the core of the motivation for staying in public service. In order to remain in government, you have to believe that your actions can have some small impact on the public good.

Only in public service can you find the sense of completion that comes from working on a successful program to reduce infant mortality, for example, and then realizing that thirty-five more children are alive this year as a result of that effort. Only in public service can you participate in a process that helps move individuals from mental hospitals back into the community. The opportunity to help solve a community problem and then to witness the changes that occur is the cement that binds us to public service.

A final motivation for public service is the importance of constantly reaffirming the legitimacy and credibility of government services in the public's mind. One vital way to reaffirm our ability to govern ourselves, to control our own fate, is to have government, at all levels, that delivers the services expected of it. This presupposes a cadre of individuals who can understand and manage public institutions. If there is no response when the public demands action, then it confirms our sense of alienation and powerlessness, and we lose our ability to cooperate. If, as public servants, we are rusty, run-down, obsolete tools of government, then there will only be further reaction against the institution of government. The challenge is to be there whether or not we are wanted, to be committed to the public's business whether or not we are noticed, to carry the public trust whether or not we are asked, and to pick up the garbage.

In the end, regardless of the personal reasons to stay in public service, the process of government demands dedicated professionals to make it work. The ability to continue day-to-day government operations in the face of all difficulties is what public service is about. That ability is what creates a legitimate government, what creates the public trust. If that is too abstract, then let us say that public service is about babies living, fires being extinguished, garbage collected, crimes solved, people moved. That is all there is, ever.

SOURCE: Thomas Downs, "Reflections of a Public Service Junkie." Reprinted with permission from the March 1988 issue of *Public Management (PM)* magazine, published by the International City/County Management Association, Washington, D.C. (Tom Downs has served several communities as city manager and also served as the president of Amtrak.)

Michael Stahl works for the federal government in the Environmental Protection Agency. He reflected on his motivations for public service.

I entered public service because I viewed (and still do) government as an instrument to solve social problems. Democratic government can be a tremendous positive force in society, and in spite of recent political rhetoric and prevailing political ideology, I am convinced that the institutions and programs of government are of vital importance to the nation and that public service is a noble calling.

There is great satisfaction in knowing that your work has made an impact on persons who could only have been helped through the intervention of the government. In my own experience, for example, schoolchildren across the country have been helped by elimination of exposure to asbestos in their schools that were unable to remove asbestos materials without federal financial assistance from a program I helped implement. Government service provides opportunities to help people through means that are beyond the capabilities of the private sector.

If you are considering a career in the public service, take the time to reflect on your motivation for entering the public service, because there are right reasons and wrong reasons. You are entering for the right reasons if you want to make a contribution to the solution of social problems, promote democratic values and ethical standards on using the powers of government, and if the concept of serving the public good is a passion. You are entering for the wrong reasons if you are looking for public adulation and recognition for your accomplishments, seeking material or financial rewards as compensation for your hard work, or expecting to acquire levels of power and change the world according to your own plan. Those entering for the wrong reasons will be bitterly disappointed. Yet, for those whose passion is to contribute to the public good, government service can represent the single most satisfying way of translating your passion into ideas and events for improving the quality of life for scores of people. Very few professions offer this kind of opportunity, and that is why public service will always be an exciting, challenging, and satisfying endeavor.

Obviously, these professionals, as well as Tom Downs, the "public service junkie" (see Box 1.3), take very seriously their commitment to serving others. In making such a commitment, these administrators participate in a long and proud tradition. Indeed, the public service has historically been considered one of the highest callings in our society and has been even more highly regarded in other countries, such as France and Japan.

Without question, the idea of serving others has enormous appeal, in part because of the great joy and satisfaction it brings. Those working in public organizations experience almost daily the rewards of public service.

■ Summary and Action Implications

As noted, our focus in this book is on the individual administrator or the individual citizen seeking to influence public policy through the agencies of government or through other public and nongovernmental organizations. We consider in some detail the institutions, processes, and techniques required for work in the public and nonprofit sectors. But, most importantly, we examine the "real world" of public administration, the world as experienced by the administrator.

That world, as we have seen, is one for which you will need to develop certain capabilities to operate effectively and responsibly. Among these we include an understanding of the institutions and processes of government; an appreciation of the values underlying public service; technical skills in such areas as program design, budgeting, and personnel; interpersonal skills in communications, leadership, and decision making; and a capacity to "put it all together" to integrate knowledge, skills, and values appropriately.

Ideally, in studying the issues discussed in this book, you will develop a good sense of the political context of public administration; a sound understanding of your role in both policy development and policy implementation; a sensitivity to the moral and ethical questions inherent in the notion of public service; technical competence in areas such as planning and program development, budgeting, personnel, and productivity; facility with interpersonal relationships (including leadership, decision making, and communications), and the self-confidence and self-awareness to act effectively and responsibly in real-life situations. Though public administration in the abstract sometimes appears lifeless and remote, the real world of the practicing public administrator is a quite lively and interesting place, filled with challenging problems and unique opportunities.

TERMS AND DEFINITIONS

Autocracy: Government by one.

Democracy: A political system in which decision-making power is widely shared among members of the society.

Equality: The idea that all persons have an equal claim to life, liberty, and the pursuit of happiness.

Individualism: The idea that the dignity and integrity of the individual is of supreme importance.

Liberty: The idea that individual citizens of a democracy should have a high degree of self-determination.

Oligarchy: Government by the few.

Policy analysts: Persons who provide important information about public programs through research into the operations and impacts of the programs.

Program managers: Persons ranging from the executive level to the supervisory level who are in charge of particular governmental programs.

Public administration: The management of public programs.

Staff managers: Persons who support the work of program managers through budgeting and financial management, personnel and labor relations, and purchasing and procurement.

STUDY QUESTIONS

1. Discuss some of the career opportunities available to those trained in public administration.

2. "One of the most important trends in American society is the increasing interaction of business and government." This quotation signals the need for better recognition and understanding of the interactions between business and government. Discuss the importance of this interaction and why a clear understanding of the relationship between the public and private sector is necessary.

3. The differences between public administration and business management are profound. Explain how the two fields differ and why the two terms are not interchangeable.

4. How did early scholars, such as Woodrow Wilson, view the role of public administration in a democracy?

5. The term *democracy* can be interpreted in a variety of ways. What significant concepts helped form the democratic society within which American government operates?

6. What is the role of "publicness" in defining the work of public and nonprofit managers?

CASES AND EXERCISES

1. Interview a public administrator. Locate one or more people who work as managers or analysts in a public or nonprofit organization and interview them. The interviewees might work for a public university, local government, state or federal agency, or nonprofit organization. They might be a university administrator, a city manager or department director (public works or parks and recreation), a county official (such as a county clerk), a manager in state government (perhaps someone in a welfare office or a highway department), a federal government manager (in a local office of a department such as Social Security, Agriculture, or the FAA), or someone such as an association executive. They might be a program manager, a staff manager, or a policy analyst.

    Ask the people you interview to describe their jobs, including the range of responsibilities they have and the knowledge, values, and skills that are important to them in their work. The following are some examples of questions you might want to ask.
    - Describe the work you do and how you came to this position. What is your educational and work background?
    - What impact does the work you do have on the community/state/nation/and so on?

- What do you find different or unusual about working in a public organization? How do you think your job compares to other jobs at a comparable level in business or industry?
- What knowledge, values, and skills are important to your work? For instance, if you were hiring someone to take your place, what would you look for?

2. Consider the following case. As an administrative assistant in the Department of Finance of a midsize suburban community, you are asked by the director to contract with an accounting firm to audit the books of the 10 major city departments. You develop a request for bids, advertise in the local newspaper, and send written notices to all the local accounting firms. In response, you receive five proposals, four from local firms and one from a Big Eight accounting firm based in a nearby city. The proposals are essentially the same with respect to cost and expected quality of work. However, one firm, Jones and Denham, appears to have considerably more experience, having done similar audits locally in the past. Having gathered all the information you feel you need to make a decision, you make an appointment to report to the director early Tuesday morning. At lunch on Monday, however, a friend who knows you are working on the auditing contract casually mentions that a certain Mr. Howard of the Firm T. P. Howard and Co. is the brother-in-law of the mayor. T. P. Howard and Co. is one of the five firms that has submitted bids for the auditing contract. Later that afternoon, you receive a call from the mayor, asking for a report on the auditing contract. What do you say to the mayor? What do you recommend be done about the contract? What does this case say about the relationship between business and government?

3. Consider the following case. There wasn't much that David Wood couldn't do. He was an excellent teacher, a dedicated scholar, and a good department chair. He had been called to the chancellor's office to comment on a new curriculum proposal, one his faculty and he had discussed, and one they firmly opposed. The chancellor began the meeting by commenting on the excellent administrative work that David had been doing and on the possibility that he might be considered for a deanship that was opening up soon. David had always wanted to be a dean. He voiced very mild objection to the curriculum proposal and then promised to try to convince his faculty to support it.

   Moving from an academic position into an administrative position or from any technical position into an administrative position puts you in a different world, one with greater complexity and different pressures. What are some of the factors that affect those holding managerial jobs as opposed to technical jobs?

4. Recently fraternities and sororities at a major midwestern university were informed that the property tax classification for their houses was being changed from "residential" to "commercial," a change that would increase the assessed values of the properties from 19 percent to 32 percent and would cost the Greek houses thousands of dollars in new taxes. The Greeks felt the change was inappropriate because, as one

member stated, "There's not a fraternity or sorority on campus that makes a profit." On the other hand, a county official pointed out that the houses contain more than "four dwelling units," as the law describes it. Moreover, fraternities and sororities are probably not residential enterprises and are definitely not agricultural ones (as specified in the law), so they are relegated to the third "catch-all" category, "commercial and all others."

If you were advising the Greek organization as to how they might seek relief, what would you recommend? What kind of action should they take? Where should an appeal originate? How might it proceed?

5. Consider the following case study (see the discussion under "Efficiency versus Responsiveness" earlier in this chapter).

> John Taylor and Carol Langley worked for a local, nonprofit community development agency. Following a rather massive reorganization of the agency in which a number of new programs were taken on, John was asked to supervise a new housing loan program and Carol was asked to assist him. The program was designed to provide low-interest loans to people in rehabilitating housing in certain parts of the city. Although John and Carol had experience in related areas, neither was familiar with this particular program. To make matters worse, seminars to provide help in establishing such programs had been held some months earlier. John and Carol were simply given a manual and told to begin.
>
> The program involved a number of new activities and took considerable time to set up. For example, it was necessary to train new housing inspectors to coordinate their inspection activities with those provided by the city government, and relationships had to be established with the other public and nonprofit agencies that would provide information about the applicants being processed.
>
> John soon began receiving considerable pressure to complete the processing of the first group of applications within a brief period of time. For one thing, the first group of applicants consisted of some forty people who had originally applied for other programs but had been turned down. Because their applications had been on file in the agency for as long as one year, they were quite anxious to have their applications processed quickly. Initial visits and phone calls from several of the applicants made John quite aware of their feelings. In addition, however, John knew that this particular loan program would have a significant impact on the community and that, consequently, his doing an efficient job under these difficult circumstances would be important both to the agency and to his own future in public service.
>
> Carol recognized the necessity to do the work as quickly as possible, but she also felt a special obligation to the applicants themselves. She took seriously the agency director's comment that the agency could use this opportunity to help "educate" the applicants about the procedures involved in such projects. She felt it was very important to check periodically on the inspections, cost estimates, loan amounts, financial information, and terms and conditions of the loans. Unlike John, who spent most of his time in the office, she talked frequently with the applicants, many of whom she knew personally from her previous position in the agency.

For each applicant, John and Carol were to accumulate a complete file of information about the financial status and rehabilitation project the applicant had in mind. This file was to be received and signed by the applicant, then forwarded to the federal regional office of HUD for further action.

John felt the process could be completed more quickly if Carol would simply get the applicants to sign a blank set of forms that could be kept at the office.

When information was received regarding a loan, the appropriate items could be entered on the signed forms, bypassing the time involved reviewing each form with the applicant. Also, this procedure would eliminate the often lengthy process of coordinating several office visits to discuss the material.

When John asked Carol to obtain the signed forms, she refused. Not only was she concerned that the applicants see and understand the materials before signing, she was afraid that getting people to sign blank forms might be illegal. When she talked with John's supervisor about the request, she was told that the procedure was not illegal and had been used before by people in the regional office.

FOR ADDITIONAL READING

Ban, Carolyn. *How Do Public Managers Manage?* San Francisco: Jossey-Bass, 1995.

Cohen, Steven, and William Eimicke. *The New Effective Public Manager.* San Francisco: Jossey-Bass, 1995.

Cayer, Joseph N., and Louis F. Weschler. *Public Administration: Social Change & Adaptive Management.* 2nd ed. San Diego, CA: Birkdale Publishers, 2003.

Doig, Jameson W., and Erwin C. Hargrove. *Leadership and Innovation.* Baltimore, MD: Johns Hopkins University Press, 1987.

Frederickson, H. George. *The Spirit of Public Administration.* San Francisco: Jossey-Bass, 1997.

Ingraham, Patricia, and Donald F. Kettl, eds. *Agenda for Excellence.* Chatham, NJ: Chatham House, 1992.

Hal, Rainey G. *Understanding and Managing Public Organizations.* 3rd ed. San Francisco: Jossey-Bass, 2003.

Kettl, Donald F., and Brinton Milward, eds. *The State of Public Management.* Baltimore, MD: Johns Hopkins University Press, 1996.

King, Cheryl Simrell, and Camilla Stivers. *Government Is Us: Public Administration in an Anti-Government Era.* Thousand Oaks, CA: Sage Publications, 1998.

King, Cheryl Simrell, and Lisa A. Zanetti. *Transformational Public Service: Portraits of Theory in Practice.* Armonk, NY: M. E. Sharpe, 2005.

Lynn, Naomi B., and Aaron Wildavsky, eds. *Public Administration: The State of the Discipline.* Chatham, NJ: Chatham House, 1990.

Meier, Kenneth J., and Laurence J. O'Toole, Jr. *Bureaucracy in a Democratic State: A Governance Perspective.* Baltimore, MD: Johns Hopkins University Press, 2006.

Perry, James. *Handbook of Public Administration.* 2nd ed. San Francisco: Jossey-Bass, 1996.

Peters, Guy B., and Jon Pierre, eds. *Handbook of Public Administration.* Thousand Oaks, CA: Sage Publications, 2003.

Pollitt, Christopher. *The Essential Public Manager.* Maidenhead, England: Open University, 2003.

Rosenbloom, David H., and Howard E. McCurdy, eds. *Revisiting Waldo's Administrative State: Constancy and Change in Public Administration.* Washington, DC: Georgetown University Press, 2006.

Rutgers, Mark R., ed. *Retracing Public Administration.* 1st ed. Amsterdam: Elsevier, 2003.

Stivers, Camilla. *Democracy, Bureaucracy and the Study of Public Administration.* Boulder, CO: Westview Press, 2000.

APPENDIX

OPM List of Core Executive Qualifications

■ Leading Change

Competency	Description
Vision	Takes a long-term view and acts as a catalyst for organizational change; builds a shared vision with others. Influences others to translate vision into action.
External Awareness	Identifies and keeps up to date on key international policies and economic, political, and social trends that affect the organization. Understands near-term and long-range plans and determines how to best be positioned to achieve a competitive business advantage in a global economy.
Creativity and Innovation	Develops new insights into situations and applies innovative solutions to make organizational improvements; creates a work environment that encourages creative thinking and innovation; designs and implements new or cutting-edge programs/processes.
Strategic Thinking	Formulates effective strategies consistent with the business and competitive strategy of the organization in a global economy. Examines policy issues and strategic planning with a long-term perspective. Determines objectives and sets priorities; anticipates potential threats or opportunities.
Continual Learning	Grasps the essence of new information; masters new technical and business knowledge; recognizes own strengths and weaknesses; pursues self-development; seeks feedback from others and opportunities to master new knowledge.
Resilience	Deals effectively with pressure; maintains focus and intensity and remains optimistic and persistent, even under adversity. Recovers quickly from setbacks. Effectively balances personal life and work.

Flexibility	Is open to change and new information; adapts behavior and work methods in response to new information, changing conditions, or unexpected obstacles. Adjusts rapidly to new situations warranting attention and resolution.
Service Motivation	Creates and sustains an organizational culture which permits others to provide the quality of service essential to high performance. Enables others to acquire the tools and support they need to perform well. Shows a commitment to public service. Influences others toward a spirit of service and meaningful contributions.

■ Leading People

Competency	Description
Conflict Management	Identifies and takes steps to prevent potential situations that could result in unpleasant confrontations. Manages and resolves conflicts, and disagreements in a positive and constructive manner to minimize negative impact.
Leveraging Diversity	Recruits, develops, and retains a diverse high quality workforce in an equitable manner. Leads and manages an inclusive workplace that maximizes the talents of each person to achieve sound business results. Respects, understands, values, and seeks out individual differences to achieve the vision and mission of the organization. Develops and uses measures and rewards to hold self and others accountable for achieving results that embody the principles of diversity.
Team Building	Inspires, motivates, and guides others toward goal accomplishments. Consistently develops and sustains cooperative working relationships. Encourages and facilitates cooperation within the organization and with customer groups; fosters commitment, team spirit, pride, trust. Develops leadership in others through coaching, mentoring, rewarding and guiding employees.
Integrity/Honesty	Instills mutual trust and confidence; creates a culture that fosters high standards of ethics; behaves in a fair and ethical manner toward others, and demonstrates a sense of corporate responsibility and commitment to public service.

■ Building Coalitions/Communication

Competency	Description
Oral Communication	Makes clear and convincing oral presentations to individuals or groups; listens effectively and clarifies information as needed; facilitates an open exchange of ideas and fosters atmosphere of open communication.
Written Communication	Expresses facts and ideas in writing in a clear, convincing and organized manner.
Influencing/Negotiating	Persuades others; builds consensus through give and take; gains cooperation from others to obtain information and accomplish goals; facilitates "win-win" situations.
Partnering	Develops networks and builds alliances, engages in cross-functional activities; collaborates across boundaries, and finds common ground with a widening range of stakeholders. Utilizes contacts to build and strengthen internal support bases.
Political Savvy	Identifies the internal and external politics that impact the work of the organization. Approaches each problem situation with a clear perception of organizational and political reality, recognizes the impact of alternative courses of action.
Interpersonal Skills	Considers and responds appropriately to the needs, feelings, and capabilities of different people in different situations; is tactful, compassionate and sensitive, and treats others with respect.

■ Results Driven

Competency	Description
Accountability	Assures that effective controls are developed and maintained to ensure the integrity of the organization. Holds self and others accountable for rules and responsibilities. Can be relied upon to ensure that projects within areas of specific responsibility are completed in a timely manner and within budget. Monitors and evaluates plans, focuses on results and measuring attainment of outcomes.
Problem Solving	Identifies and analyzes problems; distinguishes between relevant and irrelevant information to make logical decisions; provides solutions to individual and organizational problems.

Decisiveness	Exercises good judgment by making sound and well-informed decisions; perceives the impact and implications of decisions; makes effective and timely decisions, even when data are limited or solutions produce unpleasant consequences; is proactive and achievement oriented.
Customer Service	Balancing interests of a variety of clients; readily readjusts priorities to respond to pressing and changing client demands. Anticipates and meets the need of clients; achieves quality end-products; is committed to continuous improvement of services.
Entrepreneurship	Identifies opportunities to develop and market new products and services within or outside of the organization. Is willing to take risks; initiates actions that involve a deliberate risk to achieve a recognized benefit or advantage.
Technical Credibility	Understands and appropriately applies procedures, requirements, regulations, and policies related to specialized expertise. Is able to make sound hiring and capital resource decisions and to address training and development needs. Understands linkages between administrative competencies and mission needs.

■ Business Acumen

Competency	Description
Financial Management	Demonstrates broad understanding of principles of financial management and marketing expertise necessary to ensure appropriate funding levels. Prepares, justifies, and/or administers the budget for the program area; uses cost-benefit thinking to set priorities; monitors expenditures in support of programs and policies. Identifies cost-effective approaches. Manages procurement and contracting.
Human Resources Management	Assesses current and future staffing needs based on organizational goals and budget realities. Using merit principles, ensures staff is appropriately selected, developed, utilized, appraised and rewarded; takes corrective action.
Technology Management	Uses efficient and cost-effective approaches to integrate technology into the workplace and improve program effectiveness. Develop strategies using new technology to enhance decision making. Understands the impact of technological change on the organization.

SOURCE: https://www.opm.gov/deu/Handbook_2003/DEOH-MOSAIC-5.asp

CHAPTER 2

THE POLITICAL CONTEXT OF PUBLIC ADMINISTRATION

Your involvement in public organizations, whether in your career or as a private citizen, will inevitably center on the development, implementation, and evaluation of public policies. You may work for an agency charged with devising new approaches to familiar problems, you may want to see that a particular policy or proposal is framed in a way that is consistent with your beliefs, or you may simply want to better understand the implications of a particular direction in national policy. In any case, it will be helpful for you to know how public policies are designed and put into practice.

Talk of public policy is, of course, quite familiar. From one day to another, we hear criticisms of the U.S. policy in the Middle East, calls for a more effective drug enforcement policy, challenges to a school district's approach to violence in the schools, ideas for changing a city's policy toward the homeless, or proposals for altering an organization's hiring practices. Uses of the term *policy* are varied and the process by which policies are developed is even more complex.

We may think of a policy as a statement of goals and intentions with respect to a particular problem or set of problems, a statement often accompanied by a more detailed set of plans, programs, or instructions for pursuing those goals. Public policies are authoritative statements made by legitimate governmental actors (the chief executive, the legislature, public agencies) or nongovernmental actors (nonprofit organizations, foundations, quasi-governmental organizations, private corporations) about important, and sometimes not so important, public problems. We expect decision makers at all levels to spend considerable time and energy dealing with such topics as foreign affairs, health, education, employment, the economy, civil rights, the environment, energy, transportation, housing, agriculture, law enforcement, and myriad other issues. But in each of these areas, *public policy* is simply what an agency or an entire network of public, private, and nonprofit organizations decides to do or not do.

Organizations in all sectors are deeply involved in carrying out public policy—executing or "implementing." But these organizations are also involved in developing policy. Governmental and nongovernmental organizations play an important role in shaping public policy. Proposals are written and submitted by agency personnel; testimony and other expert advice are presented; and representatives of various agencies, especially political appointees who head agencies, often seek to build public support for particular ideas. Those in government agencies, and increasingly in nonprofit organizations, are often asked to elaborate on or clarify legislative intentions, and, in doing so, they continue the process of policy development.

Moreover, public, private, and nonprofit organizations not only develop policies that guide their own activities, but they also seek to influence the course of public policy on behalf of their members or other constituencies. Many such groups limit their activities to providing public information and seeking to affect indirectly the formation of policies in their area of interest. But others are far more direct, employing lobbyists and others whose specific job is to influence the policy process.

To understand the conduct of specific groups, namely public and nonprofit organizations, in the policy process, you must have some understanding of the context in which these organizations operate. That context is not merely physical; it includes the beliefs and values that shape our expectations of the organizations as well as the structures we have developed to try to maintain those values. In large part, the complexity of the policy process in this country is the result of the Founding Fathers' fear of concentrated power, a fear they sought to allay by organizing the federal government into three branches—executive, legislative, and judicial—so that no one branch could exert itself above the others. As we will see, our political system has evolved in such a way that the relations between and among the various branches, and between governmental and nongovernmental institutions, remain a central issue in conducting public programs. This chapter focuses on the process of public policy and especially the relations between public administrators and the executive, the legislature, and the judiciary as they work together to seek important policy goals.

■ Administrative Organizations and Executive Leadership

As we saw in Chapter 1, public administrators work in the federal, state, and local governments and in nonprofit organizations and associations. But, understandably, the federal government, simply by virtue of its size and the range of its activities, has become the model against which others are often judged. For that reason, we begin our discussion of the political context of American public administration by examining the development of the national administrative system and the role of the chief executive in that system.

Again it is helpful to begin with a brief historical review, primarily because some of the arguments that characterized discussions of administration in the early days of our nation are quite similar to those that continue to confront us. Take, for example, the difference between the Federalist view, expressed most forcefully by Alexander Hamilton, and that of the Jeffersonians, led by (you guessed it!) Thomas Jefferson. Hamilton and his Federalist colleagues argued for a strong centralized government, staffed and managed by men of wealth, class, and education. "The Federalist preference for the executive branch was a faithful reflection of their distrust of the people. An intelligent perception of sound public policy, in their view, could come only from well-educated men of affairs, men with trained minds and broad experience—in short from the upper classes" (White, 1948, p. 410).

The Jeffersonians, on the other hand, saw the administration of government as intimately connected to the problem of extending democracy throughout the nation. They thus preferred a more decentralized approach to the executive function and sought formal legal controls on the executive so that executive power would not be abused (Caldwell, 1964). These democratic views reached their pinnacle in the administration of Andrew

Jackson, known for its openness to the "common man." But the Jacksonian era was also notable for extension and formalization of the administrative apparatus of government; the administration of government began to form "a link between the nation's political authorities and its citizens" (Crenson, 1975, p. 10; see also Nelson, 1982).

Despite these developments, the president's role as chief executive officer, the head of the federal bureaucracy, was not clearly established until well into the twentieth century, when Franklin Roosevelt was able to assert his administrative management of the executive branch and to set a model for all the presidents who have followed him. Some changes were inevitable: The growing size and scope of governmental activity simply required greater attention to management and organization. Other changes reflected a greater understanding of the administrative process, how the work of government might be accomplished more effectively.

In 1936, President Roosevelt appointed a committee on administrative management, chaired by Louis Brownlow, which included a number of respected scholars and practitioners in the emerging field of public administration. The Brownlow committee concluded that "the president needs help" and recommended a series of possible steps to improve the president's management of the executive branch (Karl, 1963). Though initially sidetracked in the wake of the president's attempt to "pack" the Supreme Court, the major recommendations of the Brownlow committee were finally approved in the Reorganization Act of 1939. This act authorized the president to take the initiative in reshaping and reorganizing the executive branch, subject only to congressional veto. The Reorganization Act also allowed President Roosevelt to create the Executive Office of the President, composed of six assistants, to give the president the help he needed. (The Executive Office of the President continues today, but now it employs nearly 2,000 people.)

All presidents since Roosevelt have continued to assert their executive power in various ways. President Nixon, for example, sought to further centralize managerial power in the White House; President Carter sought greater managerial responsiveness through the Civil Service Reform Act. President Reagan and the first President Bush pursued the same ends, by extending political control further into the bureaucracy while also developing programs to reduce costs and increase productivity. President Clinton carried through on many of his promises to streamline government and improve quality and productivity through implementing the National Performance Review (NPR).

Although President Clinton's National Performance Review officially ended in January 2001, the larger "Reinventing Government" movement has become a central current in the "tides" of public and nonprofit reform (Light, 1995, 2000). Reinvention and NPR will be discussed in more detail in later chapters, but it is important that you understand generally what that effort is and why it was undertaken. Basically, NPR was a Clinton administration initiative headed by Vice President Gore and aimed at increasing the trust of the American people in their government through a broad range of improvements in the quality and productivity of government (as well as through reductions in the size of government). The National Performance Review, first presented to President Clinton in September 1993 and implemented over the next several years, made hundreds of recommendations aimed at cutting unnecessary red tape and burdensome regulations, empowering federal employees to make decisions while holding them accountable for the results, and emphasizing service to "customers."

cut the fat + made it better for 'customers'

President George W. Bush introduced substantial changes in management practices, many of which we will discuss later. However, his reforms did not stop with the management practices. Referring to Bush's decisions on national intelligence, including the establishment of the new Department of Homeland Security and his initiatives in international affairs (primarily the Iraq and Afghanistan interventions), Pfiffner (2007) describes Bush as the President who "undertook the most far-reaching reorganization of the executive branch since the National Security Act of 1947" (p. 14–15). According to Pfiffner, Bush has had huge success in extending presidential powers: "Although presidents of both parties have sought to enhance and protect executive prerogatives, President Bush's grasp has exceeded that of most of his predecessors in scope and degree, if not in kind" (Pfiffner, 2007, p. 17).

Returning to the subject of executive powers, one important tool that presidents have employed is the *executive order*, a presidential mandate directed to and governing, with the effect of law, the actions of government officials and government agencies. Over time, the executive order has become a chief instrument of presidential power. President Bush, for example, used one of his first executive orders (no. 13199, January 29, 2001) to create the Office of Faith-based and Community Initiatives, which will serve as the center-point for his administration's effort to extend federal funding to faith-based organizations. In this case and many others like it, the president is essentially making law by decree, occasionally in direct opposition to the wishes of Congress and constituent groups.

The president, as the chief executive officer of the federal government, exercises power over an enormous and wide-ranging set of public organizations. In 2006, there were some 2.7 million civilians employed by the federal government and another 1.4 million uniformed military personnel (http://www.whitehouse.gov/omb/budget/fy2008/pdf/hist.pdf). In addition, the federal government supports and pays for the work of a wide variety of activities in which the actual work is performed by someone other than a federal civil servant. The Defense Department, for example, supervises almost 2 million persons in private industry involved, directly or indirectly, in defense-related work.

Administrative Organizations

You are probably already familiar with many of the agencies of government at the federal level; however, several types are particularly important: (1) the Executive Office of the President; (2) the cabinet-level executive departments; (3) a variety of independent agencies, regulatory commissions, and public corporations; and (4) administrative agencies that support the work of the legislature and the judiciary.

The Executive Office of the President

The various administrative bodies located in the Executive Office of the President both advise the president and assist in formulating and implementing national policy. Several offices have come to play especially important policy roles. The *Office of Management and Budget,* for example, assists the president in preparing the budget, submitting it to

Congress, and administering it. OMB is also involved in reviewing the management of various agencies, suggesting changes in structures and procedures, and searching out capable executives for service in government. The *National Security Council* is charged with integrating domestic, military, and foreign policy; it is made up of the president, vice president, and secretaries of state and defense and is directed by the national security adviser. Finally, the *Council of Economic Advisers* consists of three economists who develop proposals to "maintain employment, production, and purchasing power." The council also develops a variety of economic reports.

Obviously, each of these groups, and others in the Executive Office of the President, are used in different ways by different presidents according to the personality of the president and the particular issues that are most pressing at that time. Some presidents, such as Eisenhower and Reagan, have relied very heavily on their staffs, whereas others, such as Carter, have been much more personally involved in management and policy development.

NETWORKING

To locate information about the executive branch of the federal government, check out the following websites: http://www.whitehouse.gov and http://www.usa.gov/Agencies/Federal/Executive.shtml. For access to executive orders, go to http://www.archives.gov/federalregister/index.html.

Cabinet-Level Executive Departments These agencies are among the most visible, if not always the largest, of the federal executive agencies. There are currently fifteen cabinet-level departments. They are the Departments of Defense, Health and Human Services, Treasury, Agriculture, Interior, Transportation, Justice, Commerce, State, Labor, Energy, Housing and Urban Development, Education, Veterans Affairs, and—the newest—Homeland Security, established by the Homeland Security Act of 2002. Several departments, such as Treasury and State, date back to the nation's founding; others were created by Congress as needed.

Each cabinet-level department is headed by a secretary, who, along with a group of top-level staff people, is appointed by the president with the approval of the Senate. Each cabinet-level department is organized into smaller units, such as offices, services, administrations, branches, and sections. The Department of Health and Human Services, for example, includes the Public Health Service, which in turn includes the Food and Drug Administration, the National Institutes of Health, and the Center for Disease Control and Prevention. Though each department is headquartered in Washington, D.C., their offices are, of course, spread across the country. Indeed, just over 10 percent of the federal workforce lives in or around the District of Columbia.

The cabinet-level secretaries, along with a few others, such as the director of the Office of Management and Budget and the ambassador to the United Nations, constitute the president's cabinet, a group that some presidents have used sparingly and primarily for formal matters and others have employed extensively for help and advice. Inevitably, a

only 10% of Federal work is done in D.C.

president will come to rely informally on certain advisors, cabinet members, or others outside the formal inner circle for advice and consultation. Historically, for example, President Kennedy relied heavily on the advice of his brother, Robert, during the Cuban Missile Crisis, even though as attorney general his brother held no formal position that would involve him in foreign affairs.

What Would You Do?

You are in charge of the federal government's effort to assess the scientific, technical, and socioeconomic impact of greenhouse gas emissions and to understand the potential for climate change caused by these emissions. Your agency has recently been accused of "sugarcoating" the data to protect the administration from potential political damage. What would you do?

Independent Agencies, Regulatory Commissions, and Public Corporations A variety of *independent agencies* have been created intentionally outside the normal cabinet organization. Some are engaged in staff functions in support of other agencies. The Office of Personnel Management, for example, oversees the federal personnel function, and the General Services Administration oversees the government's property. Other agencies have simply not been viewed as appropriate to include in cabinet-level departments; among these are the Environmental Protection Agency and the Small Business Administration. With rare exceptions, these independent agencies are directed by persons appointed by the president with the confirmation of the Senate.

Regulatory commissions, which are formed to regulate a particular area of the economy, are structured quite differently. Typically, they are headed by a group of individuals (variously called directors, commissioners, or governors) appointed by the president and confirmed by the Senate. These persons are protected in various ways from removal by the president; in some cases, their terms of appointment overlap presidential terms. Presumably, the regulatory commissions are to perform their tasks independently and objectively, free from undue influence either by the political incumbent or by the affected clientele. As we will see later, however, the nature of regulatory work makes this task exceedingly difficult. (Note that not all regulatory bodies are located outside the cabinet departments; for instance, the Food and Drug Administration is part of the Department of Health and Human Services.)

Public corporations are employed where the objective of the agency is essentially commercial, where the work of the agency requires greater latitude than would be typical, and where the agency will acquire at least a portion of its funding in the marketplace (Moe, 2001; Walsh, 1978). The Tennessee Valley Authority, which has provided power in the Tennessee Valley for over fifty years, is a classic example of a public corporation. Somewhat more recent additions to the growing list of government corporations include the U.S. Postal Service and the National Rail Passenger Corporation (AMTRAK), both established in 1970. (Periodically, there are questions raised about the status of these two operations, indicating that the structure of public organizations is constantly subject to question.)

Agencies Supporting the Legislature and the Judiciary Whereas both the legislative and judicial branches require considerable direct administrative support for their members (legislative staff, committee staff, and court administrators), there are also several specific agencies attached to the legislative branch that are of special significance. You are probably already familiar with the Government Printing Office and the Library of Congress. But, although less is known about the Government Accountability Office (formerly the General Accounting Office), its duties have become increasingly important. Established in 1921, and headed by the Comptroller General, the GAO is responsible for auditing funds to see that they are properly spent. In recent years, however, the agency's mission has broadened to include formal program evaluations within various agencies. The GAO studies the way federal money is spent and advises Congress and executive agencies on ways to improve the efficiency and responsiveness of government. Finally, Congress is supported by the Congressional Budget Office, an agency that supports the budget process and whose operations we will examine more carefully in Chapter 7.

The State Level

The organization of state governments varies considerably, according to each state's policy interests and political development; however, there is little question that state government in this country is "big business." In fact, if you compare the expenditures of state governments with those of the largest private companies in America, the results are striking. California would rank third between Exxon Mobil and General Motors, and New York would be seventh, just above ConocoPhillips. Even Delaware, a small state would rank in the top 500 (rank 327) near such well-known corporates as Dynegy and Federal-Mogul (http://money.cnn.com/magazines/fortune/fortune500_archive/full/2005/). Recent efforts to decrease federal involvement in domestic policy have combined with a general growth in the range of activities undertaken at the state level to support a vast increase in state activity. Between 1980 and 2006, state government employment rose from 3.7 million to 5.1 million, with an even more dramatic rise in state expenditures (from 391 billion in 1985 to 1,187 billion in 2006). From time to time, states in fact play an important role in the redistribution of governmental power. For example, in 1996, states were central to the federal government's move to reform the nation's welfare system, a reform agenda that has led to the devolution of many public assistance programs and a further expansion in the role of state government.

The organization and structure of state government in many ways mirrors that of the national government, but there are some distinctive features. You should note, for example, the large number of elected administrative officials in most state governments. In most states, the people elect not only the governor and lieutenant governor, but also the attorney general, the secretary of state, and the state treasurer. Many states still elect the head of the Department of Agriculture by popular vote, and it is not uncommon to have members of various boards and commissions (for instance, the Public Service Commission) elected by the public. Obviously, these latter offices are filled at the federal level by presidential appointment. (The large number of elected officers at the state and local level is a carryover from a period in which democratic tendencies in this country were especially strong and it was felt that nearly all major officials of government should be elected directly by the people.)

In addition, many state departments do not report directly to the governor, but rather to boards or commissions isolated from executive control in the same way as regulatory commissions at the federal level. For example, a Department of Conservation may report to a commission appointed by the governor for periods exceeding those of the governor and, indeed, may have dedicated sources of revenue essentially outside the governor's budgetary control. Obviously, under such circumstances, the governor's power as chief executive is severely limited.

NETWORKING

For information about state governments, start with the Council of State Governments at http://www.csg.org/csg/default. Then see the state and local gateway at http://www.gov.com/statelocal and these two library-based sites: http://www.loc.gov/rr/news/stategov/stategov.html and http://www.law.indiana.edu/v-lib.

Despite structural limitations on gubernatorial powers, contemporary governors exercise a broad range of political and executive influence that enable them to play a major, even central role in the operations of state government. In recent years, these powers have even had an impact on national policy making, particularly in the welfare reform agenda mentioned previously. For example, Governors Thompson of Wisconsin and Engler of Michigan were instrumental in the framing of the 1996 federal welfare reform legislation, which built upon innovations at the state level (Katz, 2001). Most important, governors play a key symbolic role, helping to set the political agenda and to focus the attention of other political and administrative actors on a limited number of special topics. Many governors have accumulated special powers with respect to the budget process through which they are able to dramatically affect the allocation of state resources and to mediate policy disputes among executive agencies (Bowman & Kearney, 1986, p. 54).

Beyond these somewhat informal powers, the strength of the governor's formal executive powers is often gauged by three measures: the presence or absence of the item veto, the ability of the governor to reorganize state agencies, and the number of other elected officials. All state governors have the power to veto legislation. Most states also give the governor the power of an item veto (also called "line-item veto"), the capacity to veto specific items within an appropriations bill (as opposed to accepting all or nothing), which is a helpful tool in shaping legislation according to the governor's preferences. (During his final term, President Clinton, himself a former governor, supported passage of the line-item veto at the federal level. The federal provision, however, was ultimately invalidated by the Supreme Court in *Clinton v. City of New York* [1998].) The gubernatorial power to reorganize is more

Power + # of these officials

limited. Roughly half the states require either statutory or even constitutional action to reorganize. Finally, as we have seen, nearly all states have a variety of statewide elected officials in addition to the governor and lieutenant governor. Indeed, most states have between four and eight agencies that are controlled by individuals elected statewide rather than appointed.

The growing importance of state government suggests that governors will likely continue to assert their executive leadership role and will seek greater control by reorganizing the executive branch. So far, however, relatively few structural moves have been made. However, some procedural changes have occurred; for example, many states have moved in the direction of more clearly establishing the governor's leading role in the budgetary process and establishing centralized management improvement programs.

Although the organization of government varies considerably from state to state, most states have a variety of substantive agencies concerned with state and local needs (Natural Resources, Highways and Transportation, and so on), as well as several agencies, such as the Department of Social Services, that largely administer programs funded by the federal government. These agencies are likely to be assisted by a central management support unit, called an Office of Administration or some similar title, that provides budget, personnel, and other general services. As mentioned, if there is one trend in the reorganization of state agencies, that trend would seem to be the creation of a greater number of state departments devoted to economic development. In some cases, these departments seek to coordinate many economic development activities; in others, there is a more specific focus on small business or on providing incentives for industrial location or relocation.

The Local Level

According to the most recent data available, there are almost 88,000 local governments (see Table 2.1). Many of these are municipalities, cities, and towns of varying sizes offering a full range of services; others are counties, typically more limited in their role but still embracing a variety of governmental functions. But most are special districts, created to serve one particular function, such as education, fire protection, or parks and recreation. (Only special districts have substantially increased in numbers over the past several years.)

Cities   American cities are organized in three ways. The mayor-council form is used by about 49 percent of all municipalities, about 56 percent of those having a population over 250,000, and three-fourths of those with a population over 1 million. In all cases, both the council and mayor are elected, the latter either by direct popular vote or a council election. One variation of the mayor council form features a *strong mayor*, with almost total administrative authority, including preparation and administration of the budget. Policy making in this form is a joint endeavor of the mayor and council. The *weak mayor* type places primary administrative control, including most appointments and development of the budget, in the hands of the council.

The power of the mayor as chief executive is obviously greater in the strong mayor system, and, consequently, that system is used in most large, industrial cities. At least in a

TABLE 2.1

Number of Governmental Units, by Type of Government

Federal	1
State	50
Local	87,849
County	3,034
Municipal	19,431
Township and town	16,506
School district	13,522
Special district	35,356
Total	87,900

SOURCE: U.S. Bureau of the Census, *Statistical Abstract of the United States,*
2002 (http://ftp2.census.gov/govs/cog/2002COGprelim_report.pdf).

formal sense, however, several large cities, including Chicago, still maintain a weak mayor
system, although even under such circumstances, a particular mayor may assert considerable strength. The legendary Mayor Richard Daley of Chicago, for example, was able to
utilize a well-oiled political machine to assert substantial administrative power. Though he
operated in a weak mayor system, Daley was unquestionably a strong mayor.

A recent variation on the mayor-council form is the use of a professionally trained chief
administrative officer (sometimes called a "deputy mayor") to oversee the administrative
operations of city government (such as Los Angeles, New Orleans, Washington, D.C.).
We find this administrative arrangement in many big cities, where mayors are often more
interested in campaigning and in working with external constituencies and like to have
someone else oversee the internal management of the city. But city administrators are also
being hired in an increasing number of smaller mayor council communities as well, mostly
in an effort to bring professional expertise to local government.

The council-manager form of local government is of special interest. It represents a
structural effort to solve the classic question of the relationship between politics (or policy)
and administration. In this form, the city council, usually five to seven people, has responsibility for making policy, including passing appropriations and supervising in a general
way the administration of city government. The primary executive responsibility, however,
lies with a full-time professionally trained city manager; the mayor has no involvement in
the administration of the city and performs primarily ceremonial duties and legislation. In
its classic formulation, therefore, the council-manager form is designed so that the council
makes policy and the city manager carries it out.

The council-manager plan was first tried in Staunton, Virginia, in 1908, and a few years
later it was adopted in Dayton, Ohio, with great success. Several reform organizations,
such as the National Municipal League, felt the council-manager plan would be a good
way to insulate the management of city government from the vagaries of local politics and
consequently added their endorsement.

NETWORKING

For information about local government, see the National Civic League at http://www.ncl.org and the National League of Cities at http://www.nlc.org. See also the Local Government Institute at http://www.lgi.org; the Local Government Network at http://www.lgcnet.com; and the U.S. Conference of Mayors home page at http://www.usmayors.org.

The number of council-manager governments has grown steadily throughout this century and continues to increase. Today, some 42 percent of American communities employ the plan. Whereas the mayor-council system is associated with larger, industrialized, and heterogeneous cities, the council-manager plan is most frequently found in medium-sized cities. Over 60 percent of American cities with populations between 25,000 and 250,000 operate with the plan, and 32 percent of the cities with a population below 5,000 have adopted it. Although a number of large cities, such as Phoenix, San Antonio, and Kansas City, use the plan, it is rare among cities over 1 million in population. The council-manager form continues to grow, however, with the number of council-manager adoptions outrunning those of the mayor-council form by three to one over the past twenty years. Those favoring the council-manager plan usually argue that it emphasizes professional expertise and administrative accountability; those favoring the mayor-council plan emphasize its adaptability and its responsiveness to community needs. As a result, more than 89 million Americans now live in communities with council-manager governments (*American City and County*, 2006).

A small number of American cities use the commission form of government. Under this form, the people elect a set of commissioners. Each acts as a council member, but also as director of a particular city department; for example, one commissioner might head the Parks Department and another the Public Works Department. The commission form is fading; we find it today primarily in smaller rural communities, although it is still found in a few cities such as Portland, Oregon.

Counties Counties (or variations, such as *parishes* in Louisiana) are found in nearly every state and range in population from very small to huge. Once considered an unexplored area of local government, counties are emerging as important actors in the modern governmental system. Counties have traditionally provided a range of services in behalf of state government, a role that has expanded considerably in the past few years. In addition, counties have recently assumed a wide range of new services (such as mass transit, mental health, waste disposal, and police services) that, for one reason or another, cannot be offered by individual municipalities (Dodge, 1988, pp. 2–3).

The traditional form of county government has been a combination of a county commission and a series of elected administrative officials, such as sheriff, auditor, treasurer, and so on. An emerging trend in county government, however, is the use of appointed county administrators, similar in many ways to the city manager at the municipal level. Still another type of county government, also increasing in use, involves the combination of a city council and an elected executive. In this system, a chief executive is elected by the people and holds powers similar to that of a governor in a state system. For example, the elected executive often has veto power over council actions (Henry, 1980, pp. 158–164). Trends toward a greater range of activities, especially in the social services, combined with the increasing professionalism of county government make this often overlooked area one of the most interesting arenas for public service today.

Native American Tribes

Native American tribes have a special relationship with the U.S. government. This relationship was first articulated by Supreme Court Justice Marshall in three decision between 1827 and 1832 known as the Marshall Trilogy. In these decisions, Marshall acknowledged that American Indians had inherent rights to possess and use their land and that they had sovereignty to run their own affairs. But even though they were seen as nations, the tribes were not foreign nations. They could not sell their land without the consent of the federal government. And the federal government had responsibilities to protect Indian land from incursions from the states and others. Marshall described this relationship as similar to guardianship.

In the last 150 years, this relationship has evolved. Influenced greatly by European settlers' desire to move westward, Congress made treaties, fought wars, and otherwise moved Indians out of the way of western expansion. Despite efforts to assimilate Indians into the dominant culture, many Indians have clung to their heritage and maintained their tribal governance systems. Today, the Department of the Interior recognizes more than 500 tribes who have sovereignty over their internal affairs and tribal management is emerging as a growing and significant field in public administration. Not only do those engaged in tribal administration need to understand the special circumstances surrounding tribal governance, but also public administrators who work near or with tribes need to be aware of the legal history that has led to Native American rights that are unique in America.

Special Purpose Governments   Finally, we should note again the large number of special purpose governments that operate in the United States. One type are special districts that exist at the local level: limited-purpose districts, which may operate in the areas of natural resources, fire protection, libraries, schools, housing and community development, and so forth, are typically governed by an appointed part-time governing board and a full-time general manager or executive director, who plays the most significant role in the operation of the district. Critics claim the proliferation of special districts causes fragmentation and lack of coordination, but others argue that such districts remain important because they are "close to the people."

The largest group of special districts are school districts. There are roughly 14,000 local school districts in the United States, serving over 72 million students—55 million kindergarten, elementary, and secondary, and 17 million post secondary (http://nces. ed.gov/programs/digest/d05/tables/dt05_002.asp). School districts employ over 8 million teachers, administrators, and other staff to provide elementary and secondary education to the nation's school children, making educators the largest single category of public employees in the nation.

School districts vary in their size, organizational structure, governance, and mix of federal, state, and local funding sources. Approximately 44 percent of U.S. school districts serve fewer than 5,000 children. Only a little over 10 percent of school districts serve 40,000 students or more, but together these large districts serve over 62 percent of the school-age population.

One significant trend, however, is the takeover of local school systems by local governments. About a dozen of the largest school districts in the country are now under the control of local governments. Boston's mayor was given control of the schools in 1992, Chicago's in 1995, and New York's in 2002. Washington, D.C.'s mayor is currently moving to take over the school system, as is the mayor of Los Angeles. The Los Angeles mayor, however, suffered a setback in his efforts to control the schools, when a California court declared a law giving the mayor substantial control over schools unconstitutional.

Other major types of special purpose governments include public nonprofit corporations such as economic development corporations and housing finance corporations at the local and state level. For example, the City of Baltimore Development Corporation is a nonprofit corporation chartered by the city to promote economic development by attracting new business and assisting new and growing companies. Housing finance corporations may, for example, issue housing bonds, offer tax-exempt financing, or other assistance to facilitate the development of low-income housing and address other housing needs.

Nonprofit Organizations and Associations An increasingly significant set of institutions in the American system of public policy falls between what we think of as the "public sector" and the "private sector." These institutions may be described as belonging to an independent or third sector of our economy. For the most part, independent-sector organizations do not have the distribution of profits to shareholders as one of their major objectives. They exist instead to meet the needs of the public at large, a particular portion of the public, or the needs and interests of their own members (Boris, 1999; Salamon, 1999). Technically, *nonprofit organizations* are defined as those prohibited by law from distributing surplus revenues (profits) to individuals (typically, members). Such organizations may in fact make a profit; however, the profit must be used for the purposes of the organization.

Nonprofit organizations may include churches, educational institutions, civic organizations, schools and colleges, charitable organizations, social and recreational groups, health and human service organizations, membership organizations (including labor unions and fraternal organizations), conservation and environmental groups, mutual organizations (including farmers' cooperatives), trade associations, community chests, youth activities (such as Boy Scouts), community betterment organizations, advocacy groups of all kinds, and many others. Their numbers range into the millions, depending on how they are counted and, as noted earlier, include some 22,000 national nonprofits and more than a million organizations of varying sizes across the country (see Table 2.2).

While private nonprofit organizations account for between 6 percent and 10 percent of employment in the United States (depending again on how you count), the voluntary effort that is expended in support of these groups makes their impact far greater. Nearly 100 million American adults devote volunteer time to such organizations, an investment of time that has been estimated as the equivalent of over $200 billion a year. Over the last twenty-five years, the third sector has been the fastest-growing segment of our economy.

During the past decade, nonprofit organizations have taken a leading role in the delivery of public services. As mentioned previously, change in the federal welfare system has led to the devolution of services to the state and local level (a trend we will explore later), where

TABLE 2.2

National Nonprofit Organizations by Specialty, 2004

Category	Number
Trade, Business, and Commercial Organizations	3,795
Health and Medical Organizations	2,800
Social Welfare Organizations	1,931
Public Affairs Organizations	1,821
Cultural Organizations	1,746
Hobby and Avocational Organizations	1,433
Engineering, Technical, and Natural and Social Sciences Organizations	1,325
Educational Organizations	1,294
Religious Organizations	1,151
Environmental and Agricultural Organizations	1,133
Legal, Government, Public Administration, and Military Organizations	830
Veterans, Hereditary, and Patriotic Organizations	808
Athletic and Sports Organizations	759
Fraternal, Nationality, and Ethnic Organizations	552
Fan Clubs	344
Greek and Non-Greek Letter Societies, Associations, and Organizations	309
Labor Unions, Associations, and Federation Organizations	211
Chambers of Commerce, Trade and Tourism Organizations	138
Total	22,380

SOURCE: *Encyclopedia of Associations*, 29th ed., Vol. 1, No. 2 by Gale Group © 2004. Reprinted by permission of The Gale Group.

networks of agencies, many of which are nonprofits, manage the implementation of public programs (Light, 2000). The current system has been characterized as "an extended chain of implementation," in which recipients of public support in some cases will "not even encounter a government employee—federal state or local" (Kettl, 2000, pp. 492–493). Moreover, nonprofits have become active in other areas of service delivery, including hospitals, museums, colleges and universities, the performing arts, religion, advocacy, and research (Boris, 1999).

Nonprofit organizations can be categorized in many ways, but perhaps most easily according to their purposes and sources of financial support. Some nonprofits are *charitable* or *public benefit organizations*, which provide services to the public at large or to some segment of the public. These organizations, such as social service organizations or art museums, may receive some funding from government and some from private contribution; they are generally tax-exempt under federal statutes. Other nonprofits are *advocacy organizations*, groups that espouse a particular cause and seek to lobby for that cause, or *mutual benefit organizations*, which produce benefits primarily for their members. The former would include groups like Common Cause and the Sierra Club; the latter would include trade associations, professional organizations, labor unions, and others that directly promote the interests of their own members. Obviously, however, from these examples, the line between the two is not completely clear. Finally, *churches* are obviously charitable organizations, but are difficult to classify in the categories mentioned.

Indeed, the entire "independent sector" is sometimes confusing to categorize. For one thing, the distinctions among the three sectors are not clear, even to the point that a particular individual might find the same service provided by one or more sectors. For example, you can play golf at a municipal course (public sector), a private driving range (private sector), or a country club (independent sector). Furthermore, the sources of funding are often intermixed. For example, both governments (public sector) and private corporations (private sector) often contribute financial support to local chambers of commerce.

The fact that nonprofit organizations are required to pursue a public interest is reflected in their legal structure (and tax-exempt status). Typically, so government can feel that a public purpose is being carried out, there are requirements that the organization be governed by a board of trustees (or directors or commissioners), the purpose of which, at least in legal terms, is to promote and protect the public interest (Boris, 1999; Salamon, 1999). Such persons will also likely establish the mission and operating policies, hire an executive director, and generally oversee fiscal and programmatic operations. The executive director is responsible for day-to-day operations and often becomes the organization's chief spokesperson. Most nonprofit associations are highly dependent on their executive director's leadership. More and more, such persons (and other major staff persons in nonprofit organizations) are coming from a background in public administration.

■ Relationships with the Legislative Body

In examining the political context of public organizations, we have thus far emphasized the importance of executive leadership. For example, we noted the emergence of the president as the chief executive officer of our national government and the pivotal role of the chief executive in state and local governments and in nonprofit organizations and associations. But although we tend to associate public agencies with the executive branch of government, there are numerous administrative bodies associated with the legislative and judicial branches. More importantly, wherever agencies are located, their role in the policy process will be especially clear in their relationship with the legislature. In discussing the relationship between public agencies and legislative bodies, we will focus much more directly on the policy process.

The Policy Process

Before we examine the role of public and nonprofit organizations in developing public policy, we should review the process by which public policies are developed. We may think of the policy process as involving five stages: agenda setting, policy formulation, policy legitimation, policy implementation, and policy evaluation and change (see Box 2.1). Whereas public and nonprofit organizations are the primary actors in implementing public policy (indeed, most of this book focuses on ways to effectively carry out public policy), they are also significant players in the first two phases.

BOX 2.1

STAGES IN THE POLICY PROCESS

1. Agenda Setting
2. Policy Formulation
3. Policy Legitimation
4. Policy Implementation
5. Policy Evaluation and Change

SOURCE: Kraft, Michael E., and Scott R. Furlong. (2007). *Public Policy: Politics, Analysis, and Alternatives.* 2nd ed. Washington, DC: CQ Press, pp. 80–85.

Agenda Setting Obviously, before policies are acted upon, they must get the attention of major decision makers. From among all the many and competing claims on their time and interests, decision makers must select issues that will be given priority and those that will be filtered out. Through the *agenda-setting* phase, certain problems come to be viewed as needing action, whereas others are postponed. Naturally, there is a great deal of ebb and flow in what is considered most important. In the 1970s and 1980s, U.S. foreign policy was dominated by concerns for Soviet movement into such areas as the Middle East; in the 1990s attention shifted to a variety of "flash points" such as Somalia and Bosnia. More recently, foreign policy has focused on Afghanistan and Iraq, Iran and North Korea. Similarly, any particular issue area can gain or decline in prominence over time, as has the attention to energy policy over the past twenty years.

Many people contribute to setting the public policy agenda. The president, for example, has a special claim on the attention of the American people and their elected representatives; a presidential speech or press conference can significantly affect what decision makers see as important. But there are many others whose actions can give certain topics greater or less visibility. Members of Congress, executive branch officials, political parties, interest groups, the media, and the general public can all significantly shape the question of what will be considered important. Think, for example, how concern for teen pregnancy has been recently brought to public awareness. Who have been the leaders in shaping public opinion on this issue?

The agenda-setting process may be viewed as the confluence of three streams of events: policy recognition, policy generation, and political action (Kingdon, 1995). The first, *policy recognition*, has to do with the way certain topics emerge as significant issues that demand action. As you can well imagine, decision makers are subject to many influences in choosing what items are significant. They may respond to particular indicators that come to public view, such as an increase in air traffic problems or a rise in unemployment. Or they may get feedback on current programs that indicates some need to reassess the status of a particular issue. Finally, some items are brought to the policy agenda by events that simply demand attention, such as AIDS in Africa or the damage brought about by hurricanes, tsunamis, or other natural disasters.

NETWORKING

See the home pages of various "think tanks" such as the Brookings Institution at http://www.brookings.org and the American Enterprise Institute at http://www.aei.org. Especially interesting is the site for the Urban Institute at http://www.urban.org.

There are many ways people try to affect the degree of attention given to particular items. Sometimes called *policy entrepreneurs*, those who are willing to invest personal time, energy, and often money in pursuit of particular policy changes can use a variety of personal tactics, such as publicity campaigns, direct contacts with decision makers (letters, phone calls), petition drives, and many others. Or they can involve themselves in major institutions, such as the media, political parties, or interest groups, that provide access to decision makers. Election campaigns, for example, often help clarify or focus the policy agenda.

A second phase of the agenda-setting process may occur almost simultaneously. At the same time that attention is focusing on a particular issue, it is likely that many will be involved in trying to *generate solutions* to the problem. Ideas may come from decision makers themselves, members of their staffs, experts in the bureaucracy, members of the scientific community, policy think tanks (such as the Brookings Institution or the American Enterprise Institute), or from the public generally. Typically, proposed solutions swirl around through speeches and articles, papers, and conversations until a few ideas begin to gain special currency. Most often these will be the ideas that not only seem to correctly address the problem, but also seem to be politically acceptable.

A third stream of events affecting the policy agenda is concerned with *political action*. For a proposal to reach the top of the policy agenda, it must be consistent with emerging political realities. Items that are consistent with the prevailing political climate, those that are favored by the incumbent administration and legislative majority, and those that have interest group support (or at least lack organized opposition) are more likely to reach the top of the agenda. These political realities, the proposed ideas or solutions, and the recognition of particular topics represent streams that must come together at just the right moment for action to occur. The windows of opportunity for policy action are narrow, and it takes great skill in managing the various streams so that one's interests are best served.

Policy Formulation Formulation of public policy involves development of formal policy statements (legislation, executive orders, administrative rules, and so on) that are viewed as legitimate. Again, we will focus here on policy making by the legislature and on the role of public administrators in the legislative process. The basics of how a bill becomes law are well known. At the federal level and in most state governments, a bill is introduced and referred to a committee (and perhaps a subcommittee), hearings are held, the committee reports to the larger body, a vote is taken in both houses, a conference committee works out any differences in the two versions, and the bill is sent to the chief executive for signature. In most other jurisdictions, a similar, though often simplified, approach is used. In any case, the complexity of the legislative process, and the fact that many different decision points must be passed before anything is final, means there are many occasions when those seeking to shape legislative outcomes can seek to exert their influence.

The president, of course, has both formal and informal means of influencing legislation, most notably through program initiatives and budget proposals. Others in the government, including many agency personnel, interact with Congress on a regular basis and may also affect policy outcomes. At the same time, those outside the government—from individual citizens to well-organized interest groups—also seek access and influence. Agency personnel become involved in the legislative process in several ways. In many cases, agencies actually send program proposals to the legislature for its consideration. Such proposals are usually submitted to the legislative leadership, then passed on in turn to the appropriate committee chairs. Though a member of Congress will actually be the one to introduce the proposed legislation, that person may depend on those in the agency for background information and other support. Whether or not legislation has been submitted by an agency, agency personnel will often be called upon to provide testimony regarding particular proposals. As you might imagine, those who staff major public agencies constitute an important source of expertise concerning public issues. For example, it's hard to imagine a group of people better able to understand the tax laws of a particular state than those who work in the state revenue department.

Over time, the relationship between agency personnel and representatives of Congress (either members or staff) can become quite strong. After all, the two groups share common interests and concerns, along with representatives of certain interest groups. A subcommittee on aging, a senior citizen's lobbying organization, and the Social Security Administration, for example, are likely to agree on the need for more Social Security benefits. When the relationship among such interest groups, agency personnel, and members of Congress becomes especially frequent and intense, the resulting alliances are sometimes called *subgovernments* or *iron triangles*. These coalitions can often exert great, possibly even unwarranted, influence.

You should be aware of some of the special considerations facing public administrators at the local level and in nonprofit organizations as they are called upon for advice and help during the process of policy development. As noted, the council-manager form of government was actually founded on a separation of policy and administration—the council made policy and the city manager carried it out. Over time, however, many city managers have become valued by their councils for their expertise in local government and frequently find themselves commenting on or even proposing particular policies. While this situation is quite at odds with the theory underlying council-manager government, it is the reality in most council-manager cities. The same is true of executives in nonprofit organizations and associations. Such situations are not without risk, however, for a delicate balance must be maintained between the executive and legislative functions. Council or board members who feel that their policy-making territory has been intruded upon may exercise another of their council prerogatives: firing the manager or executive!

Policy Legitimation

Kraft and Furlong (2007) define policy legitimation as "giving legal force to decisions or justifying policy action" (p. 86). Legitimation, as the authors point out may be seen as simple and complex. When the legitimation is analyzed in terms of a policy being approved by a recognized authority (such as passing a bill), then we may talk about a simple process of legitimation. But, the authors suggest that legitimation is more about acceptance of a new policy from the broader public. The process of policy acceptance should, therefore, be considered from the legal aspect, political culture and values, and from the level of popular support. Many times, the authors suggest, politicians bring in actors or other celebrities to testify in front of congressional committees. Frequent public meetings and public hearings as well as participation of citizen advisory bodies are other ways to legitimize policies.

The authors give the Nuclear Waste Policy Act from 1992 as an example of adopting a law that was not embraced by the public or interest groups. Since lawmakers were 'rushing' to adopt the new law, they misjudged public unwillingness to accept the new piece of legislation. The act was revised when "Congress voted to study only one possible site in the nation, at Yucca Mountain in Nevada" (p. 87). The process again was not embraced by the public or interest groups, and as a result fifteen years later the controversy over these decisions continued as Nevada fought the federal government's actions.

The whole process of legitimation, according to the Kraft and Furlong (pp. 87–88) is mostly political. They suggest that lawmakers ask questions before they decide to adopt a policy. Referring to public opinion poll data, considering the views of the interest groups, initiating a broad political debate, and developing an ethical analysis of the issue are only few of the many ways for achieving policy legitimation.

Policy Implementation

Members of public and nonprofit organizations play important roles in building the policy agenda and shaping legislative policy, but they are also involved in policy making as part of the implementation process. By its very nature, legislation is general and lacking in detail. Legislators cannot foresee all the individual questions that might come up in implementing a program. Moreover, legislators don't want to tie the hands of program managers by being too restrictive. Consequently, legislation typically leaves a great deal of discretion to public managers in working out the details of a particular program. The Federal Trade Commission, for example, is instructed to prevent deceptive advertising, but has to decide what is deceptive; the Occupational Safety and Health Administration is asked to define and set safety standards for the workplace, but must define more clearly what that means (Meier, 1987, p. 52). In these and many other cases, managers develop administrative rules or policies to give detail to the legislation or to fill in the gaps, and, in effect, they make policy.

Policy implementation is the "set of activities directed toward putting a program into effect" (Jones, cited in Kraft & Furlong, 2007: pp. 82–83). According to Kraft and Furlong, policy implementation includes organization, interpretation, and application. Organization refers to the use of resources and methods to administer a particular program. Interpretation involves translating the language of regulation (or law) into language understandable to the affected parties. Application is the "routine provision of services, payments, or other agreed upon program objectives or instruments" (pp. 82–83). Policy implementation is the stage of policy process in which the public sees concrete governmental actions/interventions. Implementation involves following the rules imposed in the law (or the regulation), developing program details, and then putting them into effect.

An early case involving the Environmental Protection Agency illustrates the latitude administrators are often given by Congress (and other legislative bodies) and the difficulties they can cause (Reich, 1985). The EPA is required by law to develop national standards limiting the emission of hazardous air pollutants so as to provide an "ample margin of safety" to protect the public health. But there is no definition in the legislation of ample. This question was especially problematic in the case of a copper smelter in Tacoma, Washington. The EPA determined that, in the absence of any controls on emissions of arsenic from the plant, four new cases of cancer each year could be expected. Even with the very best control equipment, there would still be one new case each year. On the other hand, requiring actions to eliminate the threat would cost the company so much money that it could not afford to continue operations, and its annual $23 million payroll would be lost to the Tacoma community. Obviously, then EPA administrator William Ruckelshaus faced a difficult exercise of discretion. (We'll see in Chapter 4 what he did.)

There have been several recent debates concerning the amount of discretion given to administrative agencies. Some analysts argue that broad grants of discretion amount to an abdication of legislative power; others point to the advantages of expertise and flexibility residing in the agencies or with the executive. Currently, the trend appears to be in the direction of greater detail in federal legislation, though occasionally less so at other levels.

In any case, there inevitably remain many opportunities for the exercise of administrative discretion.

Policy Evaluation and Change

Policy evaluation "is an assessment of whether policies are working well" (Kraft & Furlong, 2007, p. 84). Policy evaluation asks whether the policy that is implemented has met the goals and the objectives of the legislation. Cost benefit analysis is one of the most frequently used methods for evaluating policies. But, certainly this is only one of many evaluation methods. Evaluation methods, in this regard, should not only be considered as technical, but many times, these may involve "political judgments about a program's worth, decisions that are likely to be of great interest to all policy actors involved. In this sense, programs are continually, if often informally, evaluated by members of Congress, interest groups, think tanks, and others" (p. 85).

The purpose of policy evaluation is to determine whether a certain program is effective, that is, whether it produces the intended results. After the evaluation stage, changes in the policy may be introduced. These changes can expand, reduce, or eliminate the program. But most programs undergo continuous incremental changes in an effort to make the policy more effective and more responsive. In this sense, the policy process actually never ends.

Types of Policy

The government develops and carries out several different types of policies, and the involvement of public and nonprofit organizations in the policy process varies somewhat according to type. We will examine four types: regulatory, distributive, redistributive, and constituent policy (Meier, 1987). These classifications are not precise, however, and indeed, many agencies work in several different areas at the same time.

Regulatory Policy Regulatory policy is designed to limit the actions of persons or groups so as to protect the general public or a substantial portion of the public. For example, people are prohibited from selling certain drugs, polluting the air and water, and engaging in monopolistic business practices. One form of regulation simply focuses on illegal criminal activity; it is a crime to do certain things. State and local governments have special responsibilities in this area, and certain federal agencies, such as the Drug Enforcement Administration, are active here as well. Another form of regulation focuses on American business and seeks to ensure fair and competitive practices. Indeed, the first major regulatory effort in this country came in 1887, when the federal government created the Interstate Commerce Commission to regulate the railroads. Similar regulatory agencies today monitor securities (Securities and Exchange Commission), commodity exchanges (Commodity Futures Trading Association), and labor relations (National Labor Relations Board), among others.

A modern regulatory area is concerned with limiting access to certain goods available to the public generally, such as the airwaves (regulated by the Federal Communications Commission) or clean air and water (regulated by the Environmental Protection Agency). Other regulatory bodies focus on protecting health and safety in such areas as consumer protection (Consumer Product Safety Commission), air travel (Federal Aviation Administration), food (Food and Drug Administration), and workplace safety (the Occupational Safety and Health Administration).

Although federal regulation of economic activities has seen several waves of growth through the past century (Ripley & Franklin, 1987), the last two decades have seen somewhat of a movement in the opposite direction. Late in the Carter administration and extending through the Reagan administration, there were several efforts to deregulate certain industries. The Civil Aviation Board was disbanded in 1984, and over the following decade significant areas of transportation, telecommunications, and banking were deregulated. Moreover, regulations were eliminated or enforcement slowed down in areas such as the workplace, auto, and consumer products safety.

During the 1990s, however, even as other federal agencies relaxed their regulatory grip, the Food and Drug Administration attempted to expand its jurisdiction to include one of the largest industries in the country—and certainly the industry with the most profound impact on public health: tobacco. Under Commissioner David Kessler, the FDA tried to establish nicotine as a drug, a move that would have given federal regulators the power to control cigarettes and other tobacco products. Tobacco companies quickly challenged, and in *FDA v. Brown & Williamson Tobacco Corporation et al.* (2000) the Supreme Court ruled against the federal government. Justice O'Connor, in her summary of the majority opinion, wrote that although smoking should be considered "one of the most troubling public health problems facing our nation today . . . the FDA's assertion of jurisdiction is impermissible" (cited in Kessler, 2001, p. 384). Regulatory activities during Clinton's administration culminated in the last three months of his term. As Dudley (Winter 2004/2005) puts it, "Using numbers of *Federal Register* as a proxy, President Clinton's regulatory activity in the post-election quarter (November, December, and January) represented 52.5 percent increase over the volume of regulation issued during the same three months of his previous seven years (1993–1999)" (p. 4).

However, the new Bush administration withdrew those regulations that were not yet published and postponed the recently issued regulation for 60 days. The Bush administration established two sets of guidelines: scientific peer review "developed with President's Office of Science and Technology" and "guidelines for conducting regulatory analysis," which was developed in coordination with the Council of Economic Advisors (Dudley, p. 6). With these guidelines, the administration imposed additional obligations for the regulatory agencies, but at the same time "reinvigorated the regulatory review process, exhibiting a willingness to return regulations that do not meet analytical requirements" (p. 9).

Distributive Policy   *Distributive policy,* perhaps the most common form of government policy, uses general tax revenues to provide benefits to individuals or groups, often by means of grants or subsidies. If the country faces a large agricultural surplus, for example, the federal government may provide incentive payments to farmers to not produce crops that would add to the surplus. Similarly, the federal government provides direct grants to state and local governments for a variety of purposes. Finally, governments often create "public goods" that all citizens can enjoy. In some cases, such as national defense, the good is provided for all; in others, such as city, state, or national parks, it is anticipated that some citizens will use the benefit and others will not. (In Chapter 3, we will examine the growing trend toward employing user fees for certain of these traditionally public goods.)

Unlike regulatory agencies that are often at odds with a clientele group they are seeking to regulate, agencies that carry out distributive policies often develop close relationships with their constituencies and, in turn, with interested members of Congress. The growth of veterans' benefits over the past several decades is an almost classic example of the operation of such a subgovernment. The Veterans Administration is now one of the largest federal agencies and provides a broad range of health benefits, educational assistance, pensions, and insurance for veterans. Such a development would not have been possible without the VA's close relationship with veterans' groups (such as the American Legion and the Veterans of Foreign Wars) and with the veterans' committees in Congress.

Redistributive Policy *Redistributive policies* take taxes from certain groups and give them to another group. On rare occasions, redistribution is from the less-well-off to the better-off; many charge that capital gains proposals are of this type. Redistribution is, however, generally thought of as benefiting less-advantaged groups at the perceived expense of the advantaged. Among major redistributive policies are those that deal with (1) income stabilization, helping to support those who are unemployed or retired; (2) social welfare, providing either direct payments to individuals or supporting state and local efforts for the indigent; and (3) health care programs, such as Medicaid and Medicare. Most federal agencies active in the redistributive area, such as the Social Security Administration or the Office of Human Development, are located in the Department of Health and Human Services.

Since redistributive policies are often (though sometimes incorrectly) viewed in win-lose terms—that is, if one group benefits, another will surely lose—they generate perhaps more intense discussion than any other area of public policy. Despite this controversy, every American president since Roosevelt and prior to Reagan has supported some major redistributive effort. Presidents Reagan and George H. W. Bush, however, took the opposite position, seeking to limit and even reduce redistributive programs. The reform agenda also influenced President Clinton, whose pledge to "end welfare as we know it" resulted in legislation placing a five-year cap on public assistance and tying welfare benefits to a work requirement. And within the first six months of his term, President George W. Bush showed his administration's commitment to continuing this trend by advancing a $1.3 trillion tax cut and encouraging Congress to trim federal spending. In addition, as we noted earlier, President Bush used executive orders to implement a faith-based initiative designed to employ private and nonprofit organizations in the delivery of social services. During these Bush years, federal, state, and local governments have sought to recruit, train, and assist religious groups to provide a broad array of social services.

Constituent Policy *Constituent policies* (Lowi, 1972, p. 300) are intended to benefit the public generally or to serve the government. Foreign and defense policies are good examples of the first set of constituent policies, as well as good examples of the operations of a significant subgovernment. The Air Force had lobbied since the 1960s to build the B-1 bomber as a mainstay of our air defense. In 1978, President Carter was able to "kill" the B-1; however, only three years later, a combination of Defense Department officials, representatives from the defense industry (especially contractors), and congressional supporters of increased military capabilities helped President Reagan resurrect the B-1. Incidentally, even though more than a hundred B-1 bombers were built and were in service at one time, the B-1 remains controversial, and in 2004 several B-1s were retired and cannibalized for spare parts to keep the remaining bombers flying.

The other set of constituent policies are those directed toward the agencies of government itself. Legislation affecting the structure and function of government agencies, as well as policies governing their operations, falls in this area. President Carter was especially interested in policies impacting government agencies and was instrumental in such changes as a reorganization of the federal personnel system and a re-emphasis on affirmative action in hiring practices. Presidents Reagan and George H. W. Bush were more interested in matters of technical efficiency and problems of waste in government. President Clinton, early in his term, expressed an interest in managerial issues, pledging to implement some version of Total Quality Management in the federal government, as he had done in Arkansas.

As mentioned previously, President Clinton, later in his tenure and assisted in significant measure by Vice President Gore, developed the National Performance Review to make government work better and cost less (and a topic we will examine in detail later). More recently, President George W. Bush has rejuvenated the Reagan-Bush drive for technical efficiency. In an article titled "Trying to Run a Country Like a Corporation," the *New York Times* characterized President Bush, the first president with an MBA, as "the chairman of the board of the world's biggest conglomerate . . . They said his administration would apply business discipline to a bloated government. And cabinet sessions do look a lot like the Business Roundtable" (Sanger, 2001, p. 1). Led by a cabinet of former CEOs, the Bush administration has placed an emphasis on developing more efficient, businesslike practices of government.

Sources of Bureaucratic Power

There are several reasons governmental agencies have become so influential in the policy process. First, those who staff the agencies constitute an enormous source of expertise with respect to their areas of interest. No president, governor, mayor, or legislator could ever be expected to gain comparable expertise in all areas. Consequently, to make informed decisions, elected officials must often rely on those in the various agencies. It is often said that information is power; the information that is stored in government agencies is a distinct source of power.

What Would You Do?

You are testifying before a congressional committee in behalf of an increase in your agency's budget so that you can better investigate intellectual property claims involving software development. It is clear that one member of the committee, who is very supportive of the increase, really doesn't understand what's going on, and if he did, he might not support the budget increase. What would you do?

Second, as noted earlier, legislation is often both inevitably and intentionally vague, leaving considerable discretion to the administrator. In some cases, legislators simply wish to defer to the expertise of those in the agencies to provide detailed rules and interpretations. In others, they are recognizing the necessity of some flexibility in administering public programs. In still others, they are responding to the pressures of the legislative process itself, where specificity leads to disputes, and vagueness can often promote agreement.

Administrative discretion is also necessary because changing conditions necessitate changing policies, and it is not always possible to wait for new laws to be passed. In the 1960s, for example, the Department of Agriculture sought to maintain farm income by lowering the supply of agricultural products. Following shortages in the 1970s, the department sought increased production. In the 1980s, the policy once again became one of limiting production.

Flexibility is also needed as new information is discovered. For example, a few years ago, the surgeon general sent a brochure to all households in the country outlining the latest information about AIDS, an action not mandated by Congress but, in the judgment of the surgeon general, required by emerging events.

Through their expertise and discretionary power, those in public agencies help shape public policy. But there are more active and more political ways in which certain agencies become involved in the policy process. Whereas all agencies participate in making policy at some level, some agencies clearly are more politically adept than others. The Defense Department and the Veterans Administration, for example, both wield considerable power, whereas the Government Printing Office has little.

The power, influence, and, in turn, the resources an agency is able to generate depend on several factors, some external to the agency, some internal. Obviously, shifts in public opinion concerning the agency's tasks are likely to affect the support the agency receives. The National Aeronautics and Space Administration has experienced wide variations in public support over the years, riding a crest of popularity with the first lunar landing, but later coming under special scrutiny in the wake of the *Challenger* disaster. More recently, the agency has been fighting desperately to maintain projects such as the space station in light of proposed budget cuts. Not surprisingly, there seems to be a close correlation between favorable public opinion concerning an agency's area of interest and the support it receives from Congress.

More specific support comes from clientele groups, members of the legislature, and others in the executive branch. We have already noted the support certain agencies receive from clientele groups who benefit from the agencies' actions. Obviously, the larger and more powerful the supporters of the agency, the more powerful the agency is likely to be. But agencies also develop opposition, which can be damaging to the agencies' programs. The Environmental Protection Agency, for example, interacts with many different groups, including businesses, state environmental agencies, members of the scientific community, and groups like the Sierra Club or the National Wildlife Federation; the EPA is likely to receive support from some groups and opposition from others.

Special support can also come from individual members of the legislature who decide, for whatever reason, to champion an agency's cause. But, as we have seen, the combination of congressional and clientele support can lead to the development of "subgovernments" within particular policy areas. These subgovernments come about, in part, because each group has something to give and something to gain from the relationship. The agency can provide quick and favorable responses to congressional requests for help as well as rulings favorable to clientele groups. In return, the agency might receive support for expansion of its budget and programs.

Support may also come from other members of the executive branch. Presidential support is obviously important, whether it is diffuse support of an agency's general work or more specific, such as in a president's support for AIDS research, increased drug enforcement, or a particular new weapons system. But agencies are also attentive to their relationships with other agencies. The development of a new state park may raise environmental issues, economic development issues, and health issues. The parks department will clearly fare better if all the relevant groups and agencies are "on board."

For nonprofit organizations, the capacity to influence public policy tends to be limited as much by informal as formal mandates. Although federal law does set guidelines for the use of public and charitable resources for lobbying purposes, some nonprofit leaders assume that these limitations prevent them from representing their constituents' interests in policy decision making. Or they refrain from taking a stand on issues so as not to isolate themselves from opposing parties. Philanthropy groups, such as the Independent Sector with its Charity Lobbying in the Public Interest initiative, have launched campaigns to encourage nonprofit leaders to be more proactive in their lobbying and to expand the advocacy role of nonprofits in the public policy process. The Internal Revenue Service has assisted in this effort by making available a simplified set of guidelines from the federal tax code, which nonprofits can use to map their lobbying strategies.

In addition to the external sources of bureaucratic power, there are several internal sources of power. We have already noted the importance of the *information* and expertise of agency personnel. Especially in highly technical areas, such as medicine or agricultural economics, those in the agencies are likely to be far more knowledgeable than many others involved in setting policies and priorities. If they can employ their expertise credibly, demonstrating effective performance over time, the agency will surely benefit.

NETWORKING

For information on the advocacy role of nonprofit organizations, see Center for Lobbying in the Public Interest at http://www.clpi.org. A copy of the *Nonprofit Lobbying Guide* can be downloaded at http://www.clpi.org/CLPI_Publications.aspx.

Agencies are also likely to benefit by their *cohesion*—the degree to which members are uniformly committed to the organization and its goals. An agency that is seen as divided over major issues will suffer a loss of credibility. Conversely, a sense of unity within an agency is likely to make the agency more effective, both internally and externally.

Finally, agencies benefit from strong and effective *leadership*. For example, James Baker became known as a highly effective leader (as well as an effective politician) in his several roles during the Bush administration. As secretary of state, Baker played a strong leadership role in U.S. policy in the Middle East and elsewhere. Similarly, in the Clinton administration, Madeline Albright quickly emerged as a strong secretary of state and enjoyed a good relationship with Congress, especially in her early days in office. On the other hand, the impact of effective versus ineffective leadership is illustrated by the change in the EPA under the highly effective William Ruckelshaus and the ineffective Anne Burford.

The power of particular agencies, therefore, is the result of interaction between the agency and its environment, a process to which the agency brings certain strengths, but it must also exercise considerable skill to reach its goals. The external support an agency can generate and the internal combination of its knowledge, cohesion, and leadership affect the amount of power and influence it can command. Whatever an agency's degree of power and influence, however, that power and influence must be exercised judiciously. The agency is a creation of the legislature, and its programs are always subject to the legislature's review, alteration, and even termination.

Legislative Supervision: Structural Controls

Obviously, most governmental programs (and the agencies that administer them) first take shape in the legislative process. In response to public demands, and perhaps also executive leadership, Congress or a state legislature or a city council or a board of directors passes legislation or policies to correct a particular problem. The problems vary widely, from federal environmental policy to state education requirements to local trash collection practices to the establishment of local health centers, but in most cases legislation authorizes the program. Typically, especially in larger jurisdictions, money to operate the program is authorized separately through an appropriations process. With a program authorized and money appropriated, the building (or expansion) of a public organization can commence.

NETWORKING

For information on Congress, see the following: http://www.loc.gov/index.html for the Library of Congress; http://www.house.gov for the House; and http://www.senate.gov for the Senate.

Legislation is, however, somewhat limited as a device for controlling the day-to-day activities of public organizations, especially at the federal and state levels. (Remember that legislation is usually intentionally vague at some points.) But legislation can be used as a control device. After a program is under way, legislation may be passed to prevent members of the executive branch from taking certain actions (Meier, 1987, pp. 140–141). For example, the Boland Amendment sought to prevent covert action in support of the Contras in Nicaragua in the mid-1980s. Whereas legislation authorizing programs must inevitably be somewhat general, legislative prohibitions on administrative actions can be quite specific. However, as in the Iran-Contra scandal, members of an administration may go to great lengths to reinterpret legislation to avoid even those specific prohibitions.

Legislative Veto

One specific device legislatures employ to control public agencies is the *legislative veto*, a statutory provision that essentially says that any action proposed by the executive (or administrative agency) under provisions of a particular piece of legislation is subject to the approval or disapproval of Congress (or some portion of Congress), usually within thirty to ninety days. For example, legislation might authorize a new highway program, but require legislative consent to undertake specific projects. The legislative veto was first used in the 1930s to permit the president to reorganize, subject to review by Congress. In the 1970s and early 1980s, however, the legislative veto began to be used in many other areas, most notably in the War Powers Resolution of 1973, which required the president to notify Congress of military action and to cease such action within sixty days unless Congress acts to continue it.

The effect of a legislative veto provision on a public agency is illustrated in the experience of the Federal Trade Commission in the late 1970s and early 1980s. An aggressive consumer protection effort by the FTC in the late 1970s was countered by business groups in Congress, which successfully passed legislation to the effect that Congress could disapprove any FTC rules it didn't like. Congress used that provision in 1982 to disapprove an FTC rule that had been developed over a 10-year period which required used-car dealers to disclose any defects in cars they sold (Ripley & Franklin, 1987, pp. 141–142). In a similar case that found its way to the Supreme Court as *Immigration and Naturalization Services v. Chadha* (1983), the Court ruled the legislative veto unconstitutional. The Court argued that the constitutional process for passing legislation requires the involvement of the president, and actions under a legislative veto provision violate the separation of powers by failing to involve the executive.

Despite the unconstitutionality of the legislative veto, the interest of Congress in controlling the work of administrative agencies has not diminished. Indeed, Congress has found a variety of ways to get around the *Chadha* ruling, either informally, by adding detailed rules to legislative authorizations, or by simply continuing to include veto provisions in legislation despite the court's ruling. More recently, Congress in 1996 approved a legislative review process that, although providing a veto alternative, would not be open to the types of legal challenges that limited previous procedures (Cooper, 2000, p. 172).

It should be noted that the question of legislative control over administrative agencies is not limited to the federal government. At the state level, the use of the legislative veto has been growing rapidly, and many states have adopted the veto either in the form of legislation or as part of state administrative procedures. Moreover, while state courts have reinforced the principles of *Chadha* (the *Chadha* ruling in a federal case does not itself limit the use of the legislative veto at the state level), state lawmakers continue to employ vetolike actions in their processes of legislative review (Cooper, 2000, p. 172).

Sunset Laws

Another control device that legislatures employ, to assess the performance of agencies and to eliminate those that are not successful, is the *sunset law*. Sunset laws are based on the assumption that certain governmental programs should periodically terminate, to continue only after an evaluation of the program's effectiveness and a specific vote by the legislature. A classic case on the problem of program continuation is the military commissary system, which was created to provide foodstuffs to the cavalry on the Western Plains in the 1800s. The program continues today, although nearly all military commissaries are within ten miles of two or more supermarkets!

Sunset laws became popular in the late 1970s and early 1980s, after the state of Colorado, at the urging of Common Cause, passed a set of laws requiring that certain regulatory agencies be terminated at a given point unless given new life by the legislature. Soon dozens of other states and many municipalities passed general sunset laws, applying termination dates to a set of programs, or included sunset provisions in legislation creating new programs. Proposals containing sunset provisions were also presented at the federal level.

The purpose of specifying a particular life span for a program is to force careful evaluation of the program at some future point. Critics of automatic terminations point out several problems, not the least of which is the cost of evaluations and the burden to the legislature and legislative staff if all programs were periodically evaluated in great detail. Questions also arise about whether sunset legislation actually changes our assumptions about continuing most programs; for example, no one would seriously anticipate that a police or fire department would be eliminated. Finally, critics point out that most programs are reviewed periodically anyway and that highly ineffective programs are often eliminated even without "sunset" provisions.

The debate over sunset provisions was fueled once again in 2001, as Congress acted to phase in key elements of the Bush administration's $1.3 trillion tax cut over a ten-year period, but then established a sunset deadline for the end of the 10th year. Critics of the legislation viewed this as a political remedy, one that would carry serious economic implications if the then-sitting Congress failed to reinstate the tax measures. In other words, if the 2010 Congress (or one before) failed to make the tax cuts permanent, as President Bush desires, the cuts would expire and go back to the levels in place at the time the legislation was first passed in 2001.

A final mechanism through which legislative bodies formally exert control over administrative agencies is passage of broad legislation to govern agency conduct. Such legislation, applicable to all agencies, might affect administrative procedures, contracting or purchasing arrangements, human resources management, or other areas. A good example is the continuing congressional interest in access to governmental information. Following World War II, governmental agencies, probably in keeping with the military mentality of the war years, could legally classify as "confidential" all records for which there was "good cause" to hold secret. As you can imagine, it was not difficult to come up with all kinds of "good causes" or reasons to withhold records. The practice of keeping secrets became so widespread that one congressional investigating group found that the Pentagon had classified as secret the construction of the bow and arrow and the fact that water runs downhill! Similarly, the General Services Administration had decided photographs could not be taken in federal buildings without permission of the janitor (Archibald, 1979, p. 314).

What Would You Do?

You are the superintendent of schools in an urban school district. The mayor has approached you about using two of your high school gyms to house a nighttime recreational basketball league for inner-city youth. You are concerned that there could be serious damage to the gyms themselves and that the school buildings nearby would become a target for graffiti. What would you do?

As a result of findings such as these, and in the belief that the public has the right to information gathered by the government, Congress passed the Freedom of Information Act (FOIA) in 1966. The law was based on the assumption that the public has the right to know, except in clearly defined and exceptional cases; in other words, it limited those in the executive branch from classifying documents for ill-defined purposes. Implementation of the new law was hindered by confusion about certain parts and by some agency officials who still tried to maintain as much secrecy as possible. These problems were addressed in a series of amendments in 1974, 1986, and 1996. The amendments required agencies to respond to inquiries quickly and even sought to penalize government officials who hid government records from the public. Although problems with the Act have persisted, nearly all federal agencies have now implemented the Freedom of Information provisions. In fact, processing and responding to FOIA requests has become a substantial activity in federal agencies. The Department of Justice alone, for example, received over 235,000 requests in the year 2000 (Piotrowski and Rosenbloom, 2002).

Sunshine Laws These examples of constraints on the operation of government agencies are closely related to *sunshine laws* that require various agencies, especially regulatory agencies, to conduct business in public view (except under specific conditions). For example, early in 1993, based on a Freedom of Information request from a New York artist, NASA released forty-five photographs of wreckage of the space shuttle *Challenger*, which had exploded some seven years earlier.

Florida's Government-in-the-Sunshine Law provides the public the right of access to governmental proceedings at the state, county, and municipal levels, as well as other political subdivisions, such as authorities and special districts. This law requires that any gathering of two or more members of any board or commission be subject to the requirements of the Sunshine Law if they discuss any matter that will, in the foreseeable future, come before that board for action. The three basic requirements of the law are (1) meetings must be open to the public, (2) reasonable notice of such meetings must be given, and (3) minutes of the meetings must be taken. In effect, the law prohibits members of any board or commission from having informal or casual discussions of board business outside an open public meeting for which reasonable notice was given.

All fifty states now have "sunshine" provisions for their own legislative bodies, administrative agencies, and local governments. In all these cases, the legislative body, in expressing its concern for the public's right to be informed about the public's business, has exercised control over a broad range of administrative agencies.

Legislative Supervision: Oversight

In addition to the "structural" mechanisms for legislative control, the legislature also exercises continuing supervision of administrative agencies through what is called the oversight function. Each house of Congress has a government operations committee charged with overseeing the activities of all government agencies, including their relationships with other levels of government. In addition, each of the other congressional committees exercises oversight responsibility with respect to its particular area of interest and expertise (such as defense, welfare, the post office). Oversight is especially connected to the legislative and appropriations processes (see Box 2.2), but may occur at any time. For this reason, it is not unusual to see a cabinet secretary, complete with charts and documents, testifying before a congressional committee that is interested in his or her programs.

BOX 2.2

TESTIFYING BEFORE THE APPROPRIATIONS COMMITTEE

> The most important thing in a committee hearing is creating an atmosphere of confidence—so that you have confidence in the committee and they have confidence in you. I tell my people to be perfectly honest and to have a full, free, and frank discussion with the committee, even if it hurts you a little bit. That will mean more than anything else in getting your money. Nobody likes to admit things and cast reflections on his own shop, but don't try to fool the congressmen. You can't. They have a sixth sense when someone is not talking freely and frankly. If you have a perfectly open discussion, they'll have more confidence in you, and your appropriations troubles will be minimized.

SOURCE: An agency budget officer quoted in Richard F. Fenno, Jr., *The Power of the Purse* (Boston: Little, Brown, 1966), 298.

Holding hearings is probably the most visible oversight activity of Congress, at times assuming a circuslike atmosphere. The Iran-Contra hearings, for example, were essentially an investigation of the activities of the National Security Council, an executive agency, but they became the arena for considerable political infighting concerning the Reagan administration's conduct of foreign policy. (They were also noteworthy for their revelations of intentional efforts by Lt. Colonel Oliver North and Undersecretary of State Elliot Abrams to deceive Congress in the course of normal oversight activities.)

The exposure that hearings provide members of Congress is obvious. Politicians from Harry Truman to Sam Ervin to Daniel Inouye to Fred Thompson have built national reputations through their involvement in congressional hearings. But hearings can also provide excellent opportunities for administrative officials at the federal, state, and local levels, and in nonprofit organizations, to tell their side of the story, to help educate members of the legislature and the public generally, and to build support for their programs. Consequently, most agencies devote considerable time and attention to legislative relations, often—at the federal level—working through a legislative liaison office or—at the state and local levels—on a more individual basis.

Perhaps the most extraordinary example of legislative oversight in recent years occurred in 1998–1999, when Congress impeached, and then acquitted, President Clinton on charges stemming from an adulterous affair with a White House intern. The House of Representatives approved two articles of impeachment against the president, claiming that he perjured himself in his testimony before a federal grand jury and that he obstructed justice by interfering with the investigation of the Independent Council, Ken Starr. However, the Senate voted to acquit the President on both articles of impeachment, a decision that in many ways brought to a close eight years of allegations, investigations, and scandal that had plagued the Clinton presidency.

Nationally, Congress can also exercise oversight through its staff agencies, most of which were significantly enhanced by legislation in the early 1970s that created the Congressional Budget Office. The CBO was charged with furnishing certain program information to Congress. At about the same time, Congress shifted the focus of the General Accounting Office from its traditional financial auditing to program evaluations. Now, in addition to holding hearings, Congress can exercise oversight responsibility through staff evaluations of agency operations by requesting information from the Congressional Budget Office or by initiating audits or program evaluations by the General Accounting Office. Although legislative staff capabilities at the state and local levels are considerably less, and often more focused on policy development than oversight, all levels of government have witnessed a general increase in legislative staff over the past twenty years.

Finally, there are myriad informal relationships between legislators and those in executive agencies. In fact, such nonstatutory controls may be the most common form of congressional oversight.

Despite the array of oversight activities available to members of Congress and despite devoting increased staff resources to oversight, questions remain concerning the effectiveness of legislative oversight of executive branch operations. Part of the problem is simply that many legislators have relatively little interest in oversight activities. Instead, they tend to focus on policy issues, recognizing that they are much more likely to build their reputations in the policy arena than in oversight. Moreover, interest in oversight activities is likely to vary from time to time, increasing in times of crisis or public outcry, when new and different program requests are forthcoming from an agency or when a member feels a particular agency has not been responsive to constituent groups. Generally, when a member has high confidence in a set of leaders and tends to agree with policies, the motivation for oversight decreases; conversely, when trust is low or when the member's favored programs are being ignored, the incentive for oversight is greater.

Legislative Supervision: Casework

Legislators also interact with those in public agencies on an individual basis, usually on behalf of their constituents. Obviously, legislators who wish to be re-elected must be attentive to requests for information or influence from those in their districts. On the other side of the coin, individual citizens have come to expect that they can and should receive help from their senator or representative in dealings with government. Thus, members of the legislature receive a multitude of requests for assistance, from someone who needs help to collect Social Security benefits to someone who hopes to influence the award of a particular governmental contract. Intervention on behalf of individuals or groups that need assistance with or access to government agencies is called legislative casework.

At the federal level, providing services for constituents has become one of the most time-consuming and important activities for Congress members. Requests for assistance are typically handled by congressional staff members who specialize in casework. If the request requires an inquiry into an agency activity, the staffer will likely approach the agency's congressional liaison office or perhaps go directly to the agency head or a regional office. In most instances, inquiries are responded to promptly, and information about the case and any necessary explanations of the agency's action are returned quickly to the member of Congress.

Federal officials, in both the legislature and the agencies, feel the process is useful not only in providing a mechanism for review, but in clarifying agency policies and procedures and assessing agency performance (Johannes, 1984). Occasionally, however, pressure to "bend the rules" or to play political favoritism occurs. Several years ago, for example, Congressman Daniel Flood of Pennsylvania was charged with conspiracy, bribery, and perjury in connection with his efforts to obtain certain federal grants and loans for a hospital in his district.

Casework activities seem less routine and institutionalized at the state and local levels. Here there appear to be both benefits and costs. On the one hand, casework activities serve to "humanize" the bureaucracy; on the other, there are disadvantages in the disruption of administrative processes and in the possibility of political influence. Certainly in the more highly professionalized governmental agencies, agency heads view legislators' involvement positively.

In many European countries, and in some American states and localities, the legislature's casework function has been paralleled or even turned over to the office of the *ombudsman*, a permanent office that receives complaints and acts on behalf of citizens in securing information, requesting services, or pursuing grievances. Many other jurisdictions have created similar, though less formal, structures, such as public advocates, citizens' assistance offices, and so on (Hill, 1982).

■ Relationships with the Judiciary

The relationship between administrative agencies and the judiciary derives, as you might expect, from the legal foundations of administrative actions, some of which are quasi-legislative and others of which are quasi-judicial. Those that are *quasi-legislative* elaborate the details of legislation. As we have noted, most legislation is necessarily and intentionally general, leaving considerable room for interpretation or discretion on the part of the administrator. For example, an agency might be required by law to set safety standards for nuclear-powered electric utilities but receive little guidance about which specific standards should be employed. The agency would seek to determine appropriate standards, then develop rules to govern implementation of the legislation. *Rule making* is concerned with establishing general guidelines that would apply to a class of people or a class of actions in the future.

At the federal level, rule making by administrative agencies, as well as many other aspects of administrative law, is governed by the Administrative Procedures Act (APA). (Similar statutes exist in each state to provide the legal framework for administrative actions.) The Act seeks to ensure that rules are based on proper legal authority; that there are both adequate notice of the rule making and an opportunity for citizens to be heard; that the rule is clear and unambiguous; and that people are given sufficient advance warning that the new rule will take effect (*Federal Administrative Procedures Source Book*, 1992, p. 416).

In 1996, the APA celebrated its 50th anniversary, an anniversary that had some questioning whether the act still provided an adequate framework to resolve the increasingly complex legal questions in contemporary society. Recent challenges to the APA have centered on issues of regulatory reform, including efforts by Congress to curb powers of administrative agencies. The discourse on Capitol Hill, however, has tended to be divided along partisan lines, with only a trace of common ground to advance the reform agenda, and, in fact, most of the recent criticism from Congress had little to do with "poor administrative practices." The courts, on the other hand, remain favorable to the APA and during the past three years have sustained the act's administrative framework. So while the legislative debate goes on, the APA continues to be the primary guide for the practice of administration.

NETWORKING

For legal research on issues of administrative law, go to http://www.findlaw.com, or explore specific Supreme Court decisions at http://www.findlaw.com/casecode/supreme.html. Information relating to the Administrative Procedures Act can be found at http://www.fda.gov/opacom/laws/adminpro.htm.

In most cases, rule making is fairly straightforward, involving notice, comment, and steps to ensure an adequate record; in others, legislation requires greater detail and great formality in the rule-making process. Food and Drug Administration regulations and others that involve high risks require a formal rule-making process. Formal rule-making procedures require that the agency issue its rule only after trial-type hearing procedures are completed.

Several important provisions were added to the APA during the 1970s and 1990s. These included measures that reduced regulatory demands in some circumstances involving smaller for-profit, nonprofit, and public-sector organizations. The first of these changes, which appeared in the APA as part of the Regulatory Flexibility Act (RFA), gained approval during the Carter administration. Under the RFA, administrative agencies not only must take into account the impact of new regulations on smaller agencies, but also must ensure a requisite level of flexibility in the rules to accommodate agency compliance and reporting without adding to administrative costs. In 1996, Congress expanded the RFA, as part of the debt limit extension bill, by adding three statutes and approving a legislative review process for proposed regulations. With the review process, lawmakers would now have a window of opportunity to adopt a "resolution of disapproval" prior to final decision making (Cooper, 2000, p. 139).

The Negotiated Rule Making Act of 1990 continued a trend toward the use of alternative means of dispute resolution—that is, mechanisms for resolving disputes that would not require formal legal processes. As with other alternative means of dispute resolutions, "negotiated rule making provides a means of using consensual techniques to produce better, more acceptable results, reducing the likelihood of protracted legislation." Essentially, negotiated rule making brings together various parties involved in a particular issue to discuss potential rules and to try to arrive at a consensus in advance of the structure and content of those rules.

Like other forms of dispute resolution, such as mediation or arbitration, no agency is forced to use these techniques; however, many public agencies are finding it very helpful to do so (*Federal Alternative Procedures Source Book*, 1992).

Other administrative actions are quasi-judicial in that they produce orders relating to individual cases. For example, following the issuance of safety standards for nuclear power plants, an administrator might have to decide if a particular plant has met those standards. Similarly, an administrator might have to decide if a specific individual is eligible for workers' compensation. In such cases, the administrator is making decisions that determine one's status under the law. The substantive decisions are obviously important, but so are the procedures under which they are resolved. For example, a woman denied welfare support might request a hearing to argue her case before a final decision is made. The administrator's decision to grant or refuse the hearing represents another kind of quasi-judicial administrative action.

In quasi-judicial administrative actions, often called *adjudication*, procedural issues such as those just mentioned are of special importance. There is a desire that citizens be treated fairly and not subjected to arbitrary decisions. Consequently, where standards of due process are applied, notice of the proposed action must be given, there must be a chance for the affected party to respond, and there must be an independent decision maker and an opportunity for appeal.

The courts may review administrative actions (in rule making, adjudication, or other areas) through *judicial review*. Such review typically occurs when a party "suffering legal wrong because of agency action, or adversely affected or aggrieved by agency action" seeks judicial remedy (5 U.S.C., Section 702). The court reviews the case in light of constitutional, statutory, and executive provisions and determines the appropriateness of the administrative action. Generally speaking, courts may find unlawful and set aside agency actions that are unconstitutional, that extend beyond the limits of statutory authority, that are "arbitrary, capricious, or an abuse of discretion," that are procedurally unfair or without substantive justification (5 U.S.C., Section 706). However, following the Supreme Court's finding in *Chevron v. National Resources Defense Council* (1984), if a statute is silent or ambiguous with respect to the issue at hand, the agency's interpretation of the statute must be upheld if its interpretation is a reasonable one.

The deference to administrators underlying *Chevron*—a position referred to as contemporaneous administrative construction—stems from the court's belief that an administrative agency responsible for implementing a piece of legislation has the most knowledge of the policy and of existing legislation concerning the issue. The courts may ultimately disagree with the agency interpretation, but they start with a heavy presumption that the agency was correct. Although some suggest that *Chevron* is being called into question, recent Supreme Court decisions have reinforced the doctrine of judicial deference to administrative agencies.

For example, in *Rust v. Sullivan* (1991), the high court considered a challenge to the Bush administration's abortion "gag rule," which prevented family planning clinics that receive federal funding from offering counseling or referrals for abortion services, but allowed information concerning childbirth and related services. The gag rule resulted from a fundamental reinterpretation of the existing statute by the Secretary of Health and Human Services. Despite the fact that the Secretary's position went against the long-standing interpretation, a divided court ruled that the agency's policy should stand because Congress had given responsibility to HHS for implementing the statute. (The *Rust* decision also carries important implications for nonprofit organizations in that it holds employees of nonprofit organizations that receive government funding responsible for the same requirements as public officials. For instance, *Rust* was applied recently in a case challenging the ability of nonprofit organizations to lobby for their constituents. The Supreme Court in *Legal Services Corp. v. Velazquez* [2001] ruled that employees of nonprofit organizations that receive government funding must adhere to the same standards and limitations as government workers with regard to advocating on issues of public policy.)

In more recent cases, including *Smiley v. Citibank* (1996), *Auer v. Robbins* (1997), and *Regions Hospital v. Shalala* (1998), the Supreme Court has continued to reinforce the *Chevron* standard, based on the principle that unless legislators give clear direction to the administering agency, the administrator's interpretation must be upheld as long as it is permissible under the statute.

On the other hand, the courts have established parameters for *Chevron*, limiting the standard to regulatory measures and to circumstances in which the administering agency clearly acts within the confines of the statute. The courts have maintained that petitions regarding administrative issues, but whose primary concerns relate to legal matters such as contracts, should be viewed as "a question of law clearly within the competence of the courts" (Cooper, 2000 p. 254). Despite these limitations, the consistency with which the court has reinforced *Chevron*, and in light of lower court decisions during the same period, it can be presumed that the judiciary will maintain the capacity and scope of administrative agencies into the "post-*Chevron*" era. The list of cases in Box 2.3 provides a summary of the principles established during the past two decades.

That is not to say that the court always rules in favor of the administrative agency. Of particular interest are those cases in which the court determines that the agency has misinterpreted (or gone beyond) the intent of the legislation. As an example, the statute creating the Occupational Safety and Health Administration (OSHA) in the Department of Labor charged the agency with developing a standard for toxic substances in the workplace "which assures, to the extent feasible that no employee will suffer material impairment even if such employee has regular exposure to the hazard for the period of his working life" (Cooper, 1983, p. 192). After extensive studies, OSHA determined that exposure to the toxic substance benzene created a risk of cancer and other health hazards and set a standard accordingly.

The American Petroleum Institute sought judicial review that led the courts to a discussion of two rather interesting issues. One aspect of the case had to do with legislative intent. The Fifth Circuit Court focused on this issue, finding that the phrase "to the extent feasible" in the legislation meant that a standard had to be both technologically and economically feasible. For this reason, the court set aside the OSHA standard. The Supreme Court concentrated more on the health aspects of the case, with the majority concluding that existing standards were not dangerous and the new standard was not necessary. The justices who dissented argued that the Court should not substitute its own judgment on the technical merits of the case for that of experts within the agency. The case illustrates several of the most important difficulties that face the courts in reviewing administrative actions (Cooper, 2000).

BOX 2.3

LEGAL PRINCIPLES RELATING TO JUDICIAL REVIEW AND DEFERENCE TO AGENCY INTERPRETATION

The standard for judicial review requires the court to address two questions: First, has the legislature provided clear direction to the administering agency with regard to the implementation of the statute? If so, then the court and the agency must follow the direction established by the legislative body. Second, if the legislature has left the implementation of the statute relatively vague, and thus granted an implicit level of authority to the agency, is the agency's interpretation a permissible one under the statute?

Interpretation	Relevant Cases
The premise that a long-standing agency interpretation of a statute should be given considerable notice, although having legal precedence, does not override an administrator's prerogative to reinterpret a statute, even if the reinterpretation represents a substantive change in policy direction. Administrators must be given the opportunity to keep pace with changing conditions, and their decisions merely have to be permissible under the statute. In other words, the administrator's interpretation does not have to be the best or brightest choice, only a permissible one.	Chevron U.S.A. v. Natural Resources Defense Council (1984)
The power of judicial review in cases of administrative interpretation must be limited because it is not up to the courts to negotiate among alternate interpretations of a statute or to determine which interpretation would be better from a regulatory standpoint. In such cases, the agency's interpretation must be followed—that is, as long as the interpretation adheres to the language and principles of the statute.	Motor Vehicle Manufacturers Association v. State Farm Mutual Ins. Co. (1983) INS v. Cardozo-Fonzeca (1987) Rust v. Sullivan (1991) NationsBank v. Variable Annuity (1995) Smiley v. Citibank (1996) Auer v. Robbins (1997) Regions Hospital v. Shalala (1998) Martin v. Occupational Safety and Health Review Commission (1991) Thomas Jefferson University v. Shalala (1994) United States v. O'Hagan (1997)

SOURCE: Reproduced by permission of the publisher, F. E. Peacock Publishers Inc., Itasca, IL. From P. Cooper, *Public Law and Public Administration*, 3rd ed. © 2000. pp. 250–264, 269–270.

The courts lately have more frequently acted not only to review agency actions, but to compel agency action "unlawfully withheld or unreasonably delayed" (5 U.S.C., Section 706). A few years ago, the Food and Drug Administration received a petition from a group of death row inmates to determine whether the materials used for lethal injections were safe and painless or whether they might leave the prisoner conscious but paralyzed, a witness to his or her own slow death. The FDA responded that it did not have jurisdiction to review the practices of state corrections systems in cases such as this; however, on review, the circuit court concluded that the FDA did indeed have jurisdiction. The court wrote, "In this case FDA is clearly refusing to exercise enforcement discretion because it does not wish to become embroiled in an issue so morally and emotionally troubling as the death penalty. As a result of the FDA's inaction, appellants face the risk of cruel execution" (Cooper, 1985, p. 649).

Closely related to the FDA's failure to undertake an investigation are cases in which the agency refuses to make rules or delays the issuance of rules required by statute. But there have also been several recent cases in which agencies have been found to have exceeded their authority in rescinding previously established rules.

Concerns for Due Process

At the heart of our system of jurisprudence is the assurance that people will be treated fairly, that they have a right to present arguments and evidence in their own behalf, and that those who make the decisions will be unbiased and impartial. As with issues of due process in administrative adjudication—whether a hearing is required, at what point, and the format of the hearing—some patterns have emerged in the Supreme Court's evaluation of administrative matters. During the 1950s, 1960s, and early 1970s, the Court sought to protect the rights of citizens from arbitrary action on the part of administrative agencies by requiring that a person be allowed an opportunity to challenge a proposed action before being made to suffer serious harm. The Court would not allow cost or inconvenience to the agency as an excuse for causing harm to an individual.

Through the 1970s and 1980s, however, the Supreme Court, under the leadership of Chief Justice Warren Burger, began to alter its approach to administrative due process, treating administrative hearings not as a means of protection, but as devices for fact-finding. Most frequently, the Court has employed a "balancing test," weighing the interests of the individual (rather narrowly defined), the value of additional safeguards, and the government's interest (including the fiscal and administrative burdens that additional procedural safeguards might impose). The material in Box 2.4 illustrates the application of this balancing test. As a result, it has become much more difficult for someone who feels that adequate protections have not been provided to prevail in the courts (Cooper, 2000).

The flexibility in administrative law for due process has contributed to a variety of alternative dispute resolution (ADR) strategies, namely mediation and arbitration. In fact, the adoption of the Alternative Dispute Resolution Act of 1990 helped remove many of the barriers administrators face to such alternative approaches. For the most part, ADR strategies are easier to employ in less complex cases. Yet ADR should not be used to obtain settlements that fail to protect the public interest. The spirit and letter of the agreement must be clear or else face considerable challenge, and potential failure, during the implementation stage.

BOX 2.4

THE SPOTTED OWL AND AGENCY INTERPRETATION OF THE LAW

When a court reviews an agency's construction of the statute it administers, it is confronted with two questions.

First, always, is the question of whether Congress has directly spoken to the precise question at issue. If the intent of Congress is clear, that is the end of the matter; for the court, as well as the agency, must give effect to the unambiguously expressed intent of Congress.

If, however, the court determines Congress has not directly addressed the precise question at issue, the court does not simply impose its own construction of the statute, as would be necessary in the absence of an administrative interpretation. Rather, if the statute is silent or ambiguous with respect to the specific issue, the question for the court is whether the agency's answer is based on a permissible construction of the statute.

Given the ubiquity of ambiguity in regulatory statutes, *Chevron* looked like a recipe for judicial acquiescence to agency interpretations. It hasn't worked out that way.

Sometimes, to be sure, the Court gives full scope to the doctrine announced in *Chevron*. Other times, however, the Court virtually ignores the *Chevron* test. Most importantly, only three years after *Chevron*, the Court recognized a major escape hatch from the doctrine of deference to agency interpretation.

Babbitt v. Sweet Home Chapter of Communities for a Great Oregon—the celebrated Spotted Owl case—illustrates the indeterminacy of the *Chevron* doctrine. At issue was the meaning of the term *harm* in the Endangered Species Act. The act prohibits the "taking" of endangered animals and defines "take" to mean "to harass, harm, pursue, hunt, shoot, wound, kill, trap, capture, or collect." According to Secretary of the Interior Bruce Babbitt, "harm" includes destruction of habitat that has the effect—although not the purpose—of harming endangered wildlife. Oregon business interests challenged this interpretation as contrary to the statute.

The fundamental problem in administrative law is that a congressional majority typically favors some federal response to a problem, but no congressional majority favors any particular response. Rather than do nothing, Congress adopts general language and leaves it to the agencies—and the courts—to make the controversial choices. The Endangered Species Act is a good illustration of this. Congress knew quite well that habitat destruction poses the biggest threat to endangered species. Congress also knew, however, that regulating habitat destruction would conflict with economic development. So Congress waffled.

The only clear intention Congress had regarding habitat destruction is a clear intention to have no clear intention. The problem calls less for lawyerly interpretations of authoritative language than for a policy decision made by an institution that is familiar with the problem and is held politically accountable. The agency has the advantage (over) the courts on both counts.

SOURCE: Donald A. Dripps, *Trial* 32, no. 2 (February 1996): 70–71. Reprinted with permission of the author.

The Courts and Agency Administration

Over the past twenty years, one of the most dramatic developments in the relationship between administrative agencies and the judiciary is the direct involvement of federal district courts (and some state courts) in agency administration, including decisions on spending, personnel, organization, and management. This involvement has come about through court rulings in *administrative equity* cases, wherein individual rights, such as the prohibition against cruel and unusual punishment, have been violated by state and local administrative organizations.

Two landmark cases in the early 1970s set precedents for such rulings. In the first, prisoners in the Arkansas penitentiary system alleged a large number of abuses, including dangerous and unhealthy conditions in the prisons. The court ruled that confinement in the Arkansas system amounted to cruel and unusual punishment and ordered corrections officials to devise a plan to remedy the problems. Similarly, in Alabama a federal district court judge found "intolerable and deplorable" conditions in that state's largest mental health facility and ordered corrective actions. The court also established a constitutional right to treatment, detailing actions required to meet that constitutional standard (Gilmour, 1982, pp. 26–29).

The involvement of courts in the management of public agencies is especially well illustrated in a federal judge's order demanding reform of the New Orleans Parish Prison. In addition to ordering adequate medical services, improved security, and development of recreational facilities, the judge directed that "the management and operation of the prison be improved immediately," that a professional penologist be hired to manage the prison, and that personnel practices (filling vacancies, raising wages, etc.) be improved in specific ways. Although court actions such as this have obviously corrected constitutional inequities, there are questions as to whether the courts are well suited for involvement in the details of administration. Moreover, many states and localities argue that court-ordered expenditures of funds on projects such as desegregation or prison reform take money away from other needed services, such as education, social welfare, or mental health. Indeed, for these various reasons, the Supreme Court has recently taken steps to limit the involvement of courts in the work of administrative agencies, requiring carefully tailored plans of limited duration based on specific constitutional violations.

■ Summary and Action Implications

This chapter has explored the political context of public administration, including things you will simply need to know to operate effectively in or with public or nonprofit organizations. The material in this chapter (and in Chapter 3) constitutes a knowledge base on which to build your action skills. Understanding the political context of work in the public sector will enhance the effectiveness of your actions.

Public managers, and their counterparts in nonprofit organizations, work in many different institutional settings, but those institutions all reflect important political values that lie at the heart of a democratic system. Whether at the federal, state, or local level, in the governmental or nongovernmental sector, a democracy's values, especially a concern for operating in the public interest, affect the structure of public and nonprofit organizations.

For example, the division of powers at the federal level expresses a fear of concentrated power; similarly, the council-manager plan expresses one way to view the relationship between politics and administration. Finally, the structure of nonprofit organizations reflects their operation in the public interest. Knowing something about how democratic values are reflected in the structure of the various organizations and knowing something about the role of executive leadership in administrative organizations will enable you to act with greater confidence and authority.

As a manager, you may have important interactions with a legislative body, either the national Congress, a state legislature, a local city council, or a nonprofit organization's board of directors. Those serving in the public interest participate in one way or another in nearly all policy areas—a situation that our political system encourages. The distinction Woodrow Wilson suggested between politics (or policy) and administration no longer accurately describes the relationship between the legislative and the executive branches. Today, the legislature and the various agencies of government share in the policy process, either working together in developing policy or making separate decisions in different realms.

As a manager, you will also deal with the legislature in many other ways. Most importantly, the legislature will establish the tasks your agency or association will undertake and provide human and financial resources to carry them out. Moreover, the legislative body will exercise continuing, although sometimes intermittent, supervision over your work. Thus, you may spend a great deal of time developing effective working relationships with those in the legislature.

The involvement of the courts in the work of administration is both intense and inevitable. For this reason, your understanding of the legal system and your ability to interact with legal and judicial officers will improve your effectiveness as a public manager. Whether you are dealing with the legislative body or the courts, your relationship with either need not be adversarial. Indeed, in many cases, the legislature and the courts can help to substantially improve administrative practices.

By now you should be coming to realize that your behavior as a public or nonprofit manager is bounded by a vast and complicated network of relationships in which you are but one of many players. Within this network, you must be attentive to questions of executive leadership, legislative intent and oversight, and judicial interpretation. The world of the public administrator is indeed complex!

TERMS AND DEFINITIONS

Agenda setting: Phase in public policy process when certain problems come to be viewed as needing attention.

Cohesion: Degree to which members of a group are uniformly committed to the group and its goals.

Constituent policy: Policy designed to benefit the public generally or to serve the government.

Distributive policy: Policy involving use of general tax funds to provide assistance and benefits to individuals or groups.

Executive order: A presidential mandate directed to and governing, with the effect of law, the actions of government officials and agencies.

Independent agencies: Agencies intentionally created outside the normal cabinet organization.

Iron triangle: Term given to a coalition of interest groups, agency personnel, and members of Congress created to exert influence on a particular policy issue.

Legislative veto: Statutory provision that gives Congress the authority to approve or disapprove certain executive actions.

Nonprofit organizations: Organizations prohibited by law from distributing surplus revenues to individuals.

Ombudsman: Permanent office that receives complaints and acts on behalf of citizens to secure information, request services, or pursue grievances.

Policy: Statement of goals and intentions with respect to a particular problem or set of problems.

Policy entrepreneur: A person willing to invest personal time, energy, and money in pursuit of particular policy changes.

Public corporation: An essentially commercial agency where work requires greater latitude and acquires at least a portion of its funding in the marketplace (such as the Tennessee Valley Authority).

Public policy: Authoritative statements made by legitimate governmental actors about public problems.

Redistributive policy: Policy designed to take taxes from certain groups and give them to another group.

Regulatory commission: Group formed to regulate a particular area of the economy, usually headed by a group of individuals appointed by the president and confirmed by the Senate.

Regulatory policy: Policy designed to limit actions of persons or groups to protect all or parts of the general public.

Rule making: Administrative establishment of general guidelines for application to a class of people or a class of actions at some future time.

Sunset law: Provision that sets a specific termination date for a program.

Sunshine law: Provision that requires agencies to conduct business in public view.

STUDY QUESTIONS

1. What do we mean by the term *public policies?*

2. Describe how the president's role in the administration of government has changed since the framing of the Constitution.

3. Describe the administrative system at the federal level.

4. State and local governments have been designed to operate similarly to the national level; however, both have distinct structures for administering government initiatives.

5. Explain each level's structure and the different approaches to operating the government bureaucracy.

6. Describe the policy process and actors who play significant roles in shaping administrative issues.

7. What are the four types of policy? Define and give examples.

8. How do agencies maintain a power base within the government?

9. Describe some of the structural controls on bureaucratic power and how government, as a whole, benefits from these controls.

10. Discuss several ways the legislative and judicial branches interact with the bureaucracy. Explain why these interventions are necessary and useful.

CASES AND EXERCISES

1. We have discussed the various powers, both formal and informal, that affect the governor's ability to exercise executive power in the administration of state government. Among the informal powers that governors exercise are political powers (including agenda setting), budgetary powers, and executive leadership.
   Among the formal powers are the presence or absence of an item veto and the ability of the governor to reorganize state agencies. Another indicator of gubernatorial power is the number of other elected statewide officials. Analyze the power of the governor in your state, giving special attention to the governor's power to exercise executive leadership over the agencies of state government. How do your governor's executive powers

compare to those of the president of the United States? How do they compare to those of your local mayor?

2. The *United States Government Manual* is the handbook or encyclopedia of federal government programs and activities. (See, as an alternative, www.usa.gov.) It contains descriptions of the many programs the federal government operates, as well as information about how the government is organized to conduct those programs. Obtain a copy of the *Manual* (or check the Web site) and analyze the organization and structure of one cabinet-level department, such as Transportation or Health and Human Services. Then, using local sources, try to develop similar information about how your state and your local government are organized to deal with the same subject matter. What are the similarities and what are the differences? How do you explain them?

3. Attend a meeting of a congressional or state legislative committee, your local city council, or the board of directors of a local nonprofit organization. Watch the pattern of interaction between elected members of the legislative body and full-time administrators. (The latter may be agency staff called to testify, legislative support staff, a city manager or executive director, or many others.) What strengths does each side bring to the exchange? What is the level of cooperation or competition? If possible, try to follow up with the administrator to see how he or she felt about the interchange. To what extent did the legislative body set a clear direction for the administrator's ensuing actions? What discretion did the administrator have (or claim to have) following the meeting?

4. Consider the following case: Billie Jackson was the leader of a nonprofit, economic development corporation in a small community in Colorado. For six years, Billie had been trying to interest members of the city council in purchasing an abandoned downtown hotel for conversion to a city-owned long-term care facility. Billie felt strongly that the community needed such a facility and that the city had a golden opportunity to meet that need through purchase of the hotel. The problem was that several extremely conservative members of the council felt differently. In their view, the city shouldn't get into providing social services, especially where the need might be met by a private firm at some point in the future. Moreover, they felt the cost of the purchase and renovations would be more than the community could bear.

The hotel issue was once again on the council agenda, and Billie was determined to make the strongest appeal possible. With the help of a nearby university, she had prepared a lengthy report documenting the need for the facility and the desirability of purchasing the hotel. Just as she was beginning her presentation, one of the conservative council members said, "Mrs. Jackson, we have heard more on this topic than we care to. I just don't want to go through all this again. I move to table the issue indefinitely." The motion to table carried by a quick and somewhat confused voice vote.

Assume the role of Billie Jackson. What is your immediate response? What would you do in the days and weeks that followed? Would you continue to pursue the issue? Why or why not?

FOR ADDITIONAL READING

Anderson, James E. *Public Policymaking: An Introduction.* 2nd ed. Boston, MA: Houghton Mifflin, 1994.

Barry, Donald D., and Howard R. Whitcomb. *The Legal Foundations of Public Administration.* Lanham, MD: Rowman & Littlefield Publishers, 2005.

Beckett, Julia, and Heidi O. Koenig, eds. *Public Administration and Law.* Armonk, NY: M. E. Sharpe, 2005.

Boris, Elizabeth T., and C. Eugene Steuerle, eds. *Nonprofits and Government: Collaboration and Conflict.* Washington, DC: Urban Institute, 1999.

deLeon, Peter. *Democracy and the Policy Sciences.* Albany, NY: State University of New York Press, 1997.

Goodsell, Charles T. *The Case for Bureaucracy.* 3rd ed. Chatham, NJ: Chatham House, 1994.

Holden, Matthew. *Continuity and Disruption.* Pittsburgh: University of Pittsburgh Press, 1996.

Kraft, Michael E., and Scott R. Furlong. Public Policy: *Politics, Analysis, and Alternatives.* 2nd ed. Washington, DC: CQ Press, 2007.

Light, Paul C. *Making Nonprofits Work: A Report on the Tides of Nonprofit Management Reform.* Washington, DC: Brookings Institution, 2000.

Meier, Kenneth J. *Politics and the Bureaucracy.* 2nd ed. Pacific Grove, CA: Brooks/Cole, 1987.

Mier, Robert. *Social Justice and Local Development Policy.* Newbury Park, CA: Sage Publishers, 1993.

Nalbandian, John. *Professionalism in Local Government: Transformation in Roles, Responsibilities and Values of City Managers.* San Francisco: Jossey-Bass, 1991.

Peters, B. Guy. *American Public Policy: Promise and Performance.* 3rd ed. Chatham, NJ: Chatham Books, 1993.

Pfiffner, James P., ed. *The Managerial Presidency.* Pacific Grove, CA: Brooks/Cole, 1991.

Piotrowski, Suzanne J., and David Rosenbloom. "Nonmission-Based Values in Results-Oriented Public Management: The Case of Freedom of Information." *Public Administration Review* 62(6), 643–657, 2002.

Reich, Robert. *Locked in the Cabinet.* New York: Alfred A. Knopf, 1997.

Roberts, Nancy C., and Paula J. King. *Transforming Public Policy.* San Francisco: Jossey-Bass, 1996.

Salamon, Lester M. *America's Nonprofit Sector: A Primer.* 2nd ed. New York: Foundation Center, 1999.

Svara, James H. *Official Leadership in the City: Patterns of Conflict and Cooperation.* New York: Oxford University Press, 1990.

Rosenau, Pauline Vaillancourt. *Public-Private Policy Partnerships.* Cambridge, MA: MIT Press. 2000.

Rosenbloom, David H. *Administrative Law for Public Managers.* Boulder, CO: Westview Press, 2003.

CHAPTER 3

THE INTERORGANIZATIONAL CONTEXT OF PUBLIC ADMINISTRATION

As a manager, you will interact not only with many others at your level of government or the independent sector, but also with those throughout our system of governance at the federal, state, and local levels. More and more, public administrators recognize that managing an agency requires paying attention to what happens in other organizations and that relations with those outside the agency are just as important as relations with those inside. This chapter examines the interorganizational context in which public administrators operate.

The traditional focus in public administration has been the agency, and that is the focus we have largely taken so far. However, given the "transformation of governance" that has occurred during the past decade, it may be more helpful to focus not on the individual agency, but on the *relationships* among many different groups: public, private, and nonprofit (Kettl 2000). Indeed, today more than ever, the effectiveness of public programs depends on the ability of various agencies to cooperate in processes of service delivery.

Government resources, from federal grants for public assistance to local funding for health and human services, go to a variety of actors, and although the funding usually contains guidelines and performance objectives, the implementing agencies often have a certain amount of leeway for running the program or for forging relationships with other groups to deliver the services.

For example, Temporary Assistance for Needy Families (TANF), the federal program that replaced Aid to Families with Dependent Children (AFDC) under the Personal Responsibility and Work Opportunity Reconciliation Act of 1996, the federal welfare reform legislation, provides funding to the states for public assistance and welfare-to-work initiatives. The states rely on a variety of local government, for-profit, and nonprofit organizations for service delivery. These organizations, in turn, may provide the services themselves, or they may contract with other organizations (again, public, private, or nonprofit) for carrying out the programs. In many cases, it's possible for an individual or family to receive an array of public assistance without ever coming into contact with a government employee (Kettl 2000).

Another example of intergovernmental and interorganizational cooperation is in the area of emergency management and disaster relief. Hurricane Katrina was the single most destructive and costly natural catastrophe in U.S. history. In August 2005, the hurricane struck the Gulf Coast, affecting four states: Alabama, Florida, Mississippi, and Louisiana. Immediately after the disaster, 42 states and the District of Columbia received Presidential emergency declarations to shelter the evacuees. The Federal Emergency Management Agency (FEMA, which became part of the Department of Homeland Security in March 2003), in coordination with the American Red Cross, state and local governments, nongovernmental organizations, local communities, and businesses worked (and still work) on relief and recovery of the regions hit by the hurricane. FEMA provided $6 billion to the direct victims for housing and other assistance. An additional $4.8 billion in federal funds was reimbursed to the states for "mission assignments." According to FEMA, "The U.S. Small Business Administration has approved more than $10.4 billion in disaster loans to homeowners, renters and businesses as a result of damages caused by the hurricane. More than $15.3 billion has been paid out to National Flood Insurance Program policyholders" (www.fema.gov/news/newsrelease.fema?id=29109). What was most striking, however, was the failure of various public and private agencies to effectively coordinate services to the victims of the hurricane. Katrina made policy makers reevaluate the emergency management programs on national and state level, but also provides a significant example of the importance of interorganizational cooperation and coordination.

These examples illustrate the complexity of the interactions triggered by federal policies and natural disasters. But equally complex relationships can develop as a result of a local initiative. A local community that wants to attract new industry might develop a coalition of government, business, labor, and education groups to promote the city's image and to work with groups at other levels of government. These groups might include a state department of economic development to help contact prospective employers wishing to relocate. Or the city might request that the state or federal government designate a particular area in the city as an *enterprise zone*, thus permitting special tax incentives and other benefits for businesses willing to locate there. Again, a variety of government and nongovernment entities are involved in the task of economic development.

One can easily understand why the effectiveness of many public programs depends on the quality of the relationships among various organizations. Some analysts for this reason emphasize the importance of the *interorganizational networks* that develop in various policy areas (see Box 3.1). Obviously, the various groups and organizations involved in any policy arena do not report to a single director, nor are they structured in a typically hierarchical fashion. Rather, they are loosely joined systems that often have overlapping areas of interest, duplication of effort, and lack of coordination. Hult and Walcott wrote, "Governance networks link structures both within and across organizational boundaries. Like governance structures, networks may be permanent or temporary, formal or informal. They may be consciously designed, emerge unplanned from the decisions of several actors, or simply evolve. A given governance structure may be part of one or several networks" (Hult & Walcott 1990, p. 97).

Whether the growing dependence on such systems is a helpful development is a matter of some debate. Many experts have suggested that the use of intermediaries in the delivery of services is a major reason for the difficulties many programs encounter. On the other hand, many such networks have proven enormously stable over time, and others have capitalized on the inherent flexibility and adaptability of such systems. In any case, because interorganizational networks are such an important part of the management of public programs, they deserve our attention.

BOX 3.1

NETWORKS AND NETWORK MANAGEMENT

The first type is a *service implementation network* that governments fund to deliver services to clients. Collaboration is critical because these networks are based on joint production of services, often for vulnerable citizens like the elderly, families on welfare, or the mentally ill. Integration of services is critical so clients will not fall through the cracks. The second type of network is an *information diffusion network*, whose central purpose is to share information across governmental boundaries to anticipate and prepare for problems that involve a great deal of uncertainty, such as earthquakes, wildfires, and hurricanes.

The third type of network (which often grows out of an information diffusion network) is a *problem solving network*. The purpose of this network is to solve a proximate problem like the response to the attack on the World Trade Center and the Pentagon on 9/11. The problem that the managers confront demands immediate attention and shapes the nature of the response and the set of interorganizational relations that emerge. Past cooperative relationships prove useful in managing a problem solving network.

The fourth type of network is a *community capacity building network*, whose purpose is to build social capital in a community so that it is better able to deal with a variety of ongoing and future problems, such as substance abuse among youth. An effective community capacity building network allows a town or city to be more resilient and responsive when new problems emerge, as when methamphetamine emerged from drug labs to ravage certain communities.

Managing networks that do not have a hierarchical chain of command but which rely on trust and reciprocity as the levers of collaboration makes the tasks of managers much different from those in organizations. These tasks must be performed by network managers, like Coast Guard vice Admiral Thad Allen, who led the recovery of New Orleans and the Gulf Coast in the wake of the devastation of Hurricane Katrina. But the tasks must also be performed by the managers of organizations who are part of a network, for example, the local police chief with a DARE (Drug Abuse Resistance Education) program in district schools that is part of a substance abuse prevention network but also manages a police department.

There are five different tasks that lead to effective network management. The first task is the *management of accountability*. With no chain of command, this is a critical issue that both network managers and managers of organizations in a network must successfully negotiate. Key issues are determining who is responsible for what and how to respond to free riders who don't contribute their fair share but continually demand more resources.

The second task is the *management of legitimacy*, which is more critical for networks than organizations. A public organization is created by law to serve a particular purpose. A network is usually a cooperative venture that must continually negotiate its legitimacy, particularly if, as is often the case, its boundaries cross the public, private, and nonprofit sectors. Managers of organizations in networks must continually work to convince their stakeholders that their work with other organizations in the larger network continues to be valuable and worthwhile.

(Continued)

(Continued)

> *Management of conflict* is the third task of network managers. Conflict can develop from differing goals among the organizations in the network, and the result cannot be resolved by commands issued from on high. It is important that network managers listen to the voices of their members and provide mechanisms for conflict resolution. These devices help to create dispute resolution mechanisms for conflicts that arise between managers of network organizations and network managers.

SOURCE: H. Brinton Milward and Keith G. Provan, "A Manager's Guide to Choosing and Using Collaborative Networks," Washington, DC: *IBM Endowment for the Business of Government, 2006* (www.businessofgovernment.org/pdfs/ProvanReport.pdf).

■ The Development of Intergovernmental Relations

In terms of your ability to operate public programs effectively and responsibly, you must understand the relationships among levels of government. There are various ways to define the relationship between a larger comprehensive unit of government and its constituent parts. A *confederation,* for example, is a system in which the constituent units grant powers to the central government, but do not allow it to act independently. A unitary system is one in which all powers reside with the central government, and various units derive their powers from that unit. France and Sweden, for instance, are characterized by unitary systems, as is the relationship between states and localities in the United States; localities hold only those powers specified or permitted by the state.

The relationship between our national government and the states, however, is *federal.* It involves a division of powers between the two levels of government, federal and state. (Local governments exist under the legal framework of the states.) As you know, some powers are granted specifically to the central government (to conduct foreign relations, to regulate interstate commerce, and so on); some are reserved by the states (to conduct elections, to establish local governments, and so on); and some are held by both levels (to tax, to borrow money, to make laws, and so on). (This system of governance is also referred to as federalism.) A federal structure has many advantages. It allows for diversity and experimentation, but can lead to the development of a highly complex intergovernmental system, a fact of life with important implications for the management of public programs.

The term *intergovernmental relations* is often used to encompass all the complex and interdependent relationships among those at various levels of government, as they seek to develop and implement public programs. The importance of intergovernmental relations has been recognized in several structural developments. At the federal level, a permanent Advisory Commission of Intergovernmental Relations was established in 1959 and continued to operate until the mid-1990s. All states and nearly all major cities have a coordinator for intergovernmental relations (though the specific titles vary). Finally, many scholars and practitioners have begun to emphasize the managerial processes involved in intergovernmental relations by employing the term *intergovernmental management.*

A key to understanding intergovernmental relations in this country involves understanding the changing patterns used to fund public programs. Although intergovernmental relations consist of much more than money, financial questions are inevitably at the core of the process. Thus, definitions of various types of *grants or* transfers of money (and property) from one government to another, are a helpful starting place.

Some grants give more discretion to the recipient than do others. *Categorical grants* or *project grants* are spent for only a limited purpose, such as building a new sewage treatment plant. Categorical grants have historically been the predominant form of grants in this country; however, in recent years, many categorical grants have been consolidated into *block grants*, which are used for nearly any purpose within a specific functional field, such as housing, community development, education, or law enforcement. For example, the recipient government might spend a law enforcement grant on police training, new equipment, or crime prevention programs. Finally, *revenue sharing* makes funds available for use by the recipient government in any way its leaders choose (within the law).

Grants may also be classified in terms of how they are made available. A *formula grant* employs a specific decision rule indicating how much money any given jurisdiction will receive. Typically, the decision rule is related to the purpose of the grant (for example, money for housing might be distributed to qualified governments based on the age and density of residential housing). A *project grant*, on the other hand, makes funds available on a competitive basis. Those seeking aid must submit an application for assistance for review and approval by the granting agency.

Grants may also be categorized as to the purposes they serve. *Entitlement grants* provide assistance to persons meeting certain criteria, such as age or income—for example, TANF or Medicaid. *Operating grants* are used in the development and operation of specific programs, such as those in education or employment and job training. *Capital grants* are used in construction or renovation, as in the development of the interstate highway system.

NETWORKING

Some basic information on federal-state-local interactions can be found at www.usa.gov. For coverage of the changing roles of state and local government, go to *Governing* magazine at www.governing.com.

Finally, grants may vary according to whether they require matching funds from the recipient agency. Some federal grants require the state or locality to put up a certain percentage of the money for the project; in the case of the interstate highway system, states contribute one dollar for every nine dollars of federal money. Other grants require different matching amounts, and some require no matching at all. Different types may be combined in different ways to create quite a variety of grant possibilities. A specific grant might be made available on a competitive basis strictly for use in programs for job training and may require local matching funds.

What Would You Do?

You are a member of a task force that has been asked to consider ways your local parks and recreation service could be delivered at less cost to the city. You have been considering alternatives such as special charges, citizen involvement in service delivery, and limitations on services. But you strongly feel that parks and recreation are essential functions of local government and should be protected from cuts. What would you do?

Dual Federalism

Historically, the various grant types have been employed in different ways and in different times. The earliest period in our country's intergovernmental history, a period that lasted well into the twentieth century, was characterized by what has been called *dual federalism.* Both federal and state governments sought to carve out their own spheres of power and influence during which there was relatively little intergovernmental cooperation—indeed, there was substantial conflict.

However, some programs cut across the strict divisions of federal, state, and local responsibility associated with dual federalism. A notable example is the Morrill Act of 1862, which granted land to universities to establish agricultural programs and was the basis for the eventual development of "land-grant" colleges. It was important in the development of higher education, but was also precedent-setting in terms of the structure of its grants (Nathan et al. 1987). No longer were grants made in a fairly open-ended fashion; specific instructions were attached, requiring that they be used for "agriculture and the mechanical arts." In addition, new reporting and accounting requirements were added as a condition of receiving the grants.

The adoption of grant programs such as the Morrill Act was accompanied by considerable anguish, because some saw such programs as a drastic departure from the dual federalism they preferred. The Morrill Act itself, signed by President Lincoln, had previously been vetoed by President Buchanan, who commented "Should the time arrive when the State governments shall look to the Federal Treasury for the means of supporting themselves and maintaining their systems of education and internal policy, the character of both Governments will be greatly deteriorated" (Nathan et al. 1987, p. 25).

In any case, the period of dual federalism was marked by considerable conflict among the various levels of government. The federal government sought to deal effectively with the increasingly broad issues being raised in a more complex, urbanized society by developing new grant programs in such areas as highway construction and vocational education. The states, though they appreciated federal money, were cautious of federal interference in their spheres of responsibility. The localities, though creatures of the state and dependent on state grants of authority or money, sought to build their own political base. The resulting pattern of federalism resembled a layer cake, with three levels of government working parallel to one another but rarely together (see Figure 3.1).

FIGURE 3.1

Images of American Federalism

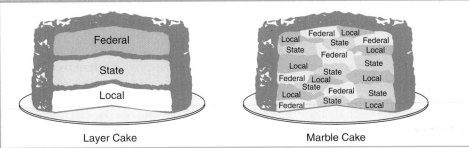

Layer Cake   Marble Cake

Cooperative Federalism

If the layer cake was the prevailing image associated with dual federalism, the marble cake was the image for the period that followed, notable for its increasing complexity and interdependence. As opposed to the conflict and division of the earlier period, the emerging era of *cooperative federalism* was characterized by greater sharing of responsibilities. The marble cake image implied a system in which roles and responsibilities were intermixed in a variety of patterns vertical, horizontal, and even diagonal (see Figure 3.1).

The great impetus for the development of cooperative federalism was the Roosevelt program for economic recovery following the Great Depression. Although the majority of President Roosevelt's programs were national in scope and could have been national in execution, a political choice was made to operate many of the programs through the states and their localities. The pattern of intergovernmental relations that emerged revealed a dramatically increased federal role, accompanied almost paradoxically by greater federal/state/local sharing of responsibilities. In addition, there was greater attention to vertical relationships within functional areas such as social welfare or transportation.

The pattern of federal/state/local relations that emerged from the New Deal is illustrated by several key programs. The first was the Federal Emergency Relief Administration, which provided grants to states for both direct and work relief. It also revitalized many weak state relief agencies. A variety of public works and employment security programs also supplemented relief efforts. The best known was the Works Progress Administration (WPA), a program that used federal money to hire state-certified workers for locally initiated construction projects. Finally, the Social Security Act of 1935 brought the federal government into direct relief for the poor, disabled, and unemployed, an area that had previously been reserved for states and cities.

Through the middle part of the twentieth century, the structure of the various grant programs initiated at the federal level featured:

1) A federal definition of the problem
2) A transfer of funds, primarily to the states (rather than localities)

3) A requirement that plans for use of funds be submitted to the federal government

4. A requirement for state matching funds

5. A requirement for federal review and audit of the programs (Nathan et al. 1987)

For the most part, these grant programs were categorical—that is, directed to a particular category of activity, such as public works. Indeed, the use of categorical grants as the primary mechanisms for federal/state transfers continued until the 1970s. Throughout this period, various groups appointed to review the state of intergovernmental relations returned the same verdict: The federal government and the states should begin "cooperating with or complementing each other in meeting the growing demands on both" (cited in Nathan et al. 1987, p. 33). Today, the principle of cooperative federalism is well established.

Picket-Fence Federalism

Through the 1960s, 1970s, and 1980s, there were dramatic shifts in the pattern of intergovernmental relations. Nowhere were these shifts more striking than in the contrast between the activism of the Kennedy and Johnson years and the cutbacks of the Reagan and Bush years. President Johnson used the phrase "creative federalism" to describe his approach to intergovernmental relations, which included a huge increase in the number and amount of federal grants available to states, localities, and other groups. Over three years, the number of available grants from the federal government grew from about 50 to nearly 400. Federal aid to states and localities rose from $7 billion in 1960 to $24 billion in 1970 (Wright 1987, p. 236). Interestingly, state aid to local governments also nearly tripled during this period.

The new federal programs focused mainly on urban problems and problems of the disadvantaged. Medicaid, for example, the largest of the new grant programs, provided funds to states to assist in medical care for low-income people. (Medicaid is largely administered by the states [eligibility requirements vary from state to state], but it also requires state matching funds, which became a fiscal problem for many states.) But there were also new programs in education aimed directly at school districts, new programs in employment and training run by cities and other independent providers, and new programs in housing and urban development in major metropolitan areas.

Probably the most publicized domestic program of the Johnson years was the "War on Poverty," launched with the passage of the Economic Opportunity Act of 1964. The War on Poverty and other Johnson programs were significant for both their size and shape. Substantially more aid was aimed directly at local governments, school districts, and various nonprofit groups, as opposed to the previous pattern of aid primarily to states. In addition, there were requirements for detailed planning and for streamlined budgeting systems, as well as demands for public participation in management of the programs. Finally, and most importantly, the majority of new programs involved project grants, requiring grant applications for specific purposes. States and localities began to spend enormous amounts of time playing the federal grant game trying to obtain grants, searching for matching funds, and trying to meet planning and reporting requirements. As a result, intergovernmental relations took on an increasingly competitive tone (Wright 1988, pp. 81–90).

Through this period, the intergovernmental system was becoming increasingly dominated by the relationships among professionals within various substantive areas at various levels of government. For example, the relationship among mayor, governor, and president might be less important than that involving a local health department official, someone from a state department of health, and the manager of a federal program in health care. A new image emerged, replacing the "cakes" of earlier periods—that of *picket-fence federalism.* The horizontal bars of the fence represented the levels of government, and the vertical slats represented various substantive fields, such as health, welfare, education, employment, and training (see Figure 3.2).

President Nixon's administration brought about a reaction against many of the developments we have just described. Claiming that programs of the Great Society were too detailed to administer effectively at the local level and that subgovernments were coming to dominate the intergovernmental system, Nixon proposed what he termed a *"New Federalism"* that would reestablish greater local autonomy in the use of federal funds. Although a part of his program involved administrative changes, lessening certain requirements, the most notable changes President Nixon proposed involved changes in the structure of grant programs.

FIGURE 3.2

Picket-Fence Federalism

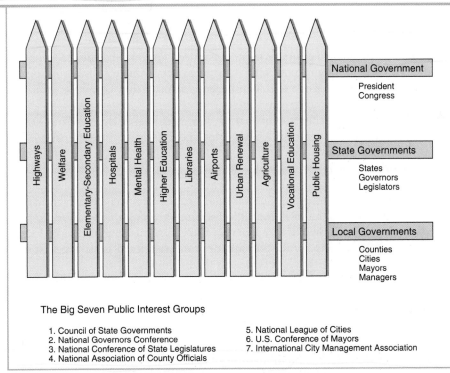

The Big Seven Public Interest Groups

1. Council of State Governments
2. National Governors Conference
3. National Conference of State Legislatures
4. National Association of County Officials
5. National League of Cities
6. U.S. Conference of Mayors
7. International City Management Association

SOURCE: From *Understanding Intergovernmental Relations,* 4th edition, by D. Wright © 2003. Reprinted with permission of Wadsworth, an imprint of the Wadsworth Group, a division of Thomson Learning.

One way to return power to state and local leaders—especially elected leaders as opposed to program professionals—was through general revenue sharing. The Nixon plan for general revenue sharing involved transfers of money from the federal government to states and localities to use for any purpose they wished. The funds were distributed based on a complex formula, but once in the hands of the state or local political leadership, they could be used for tax reduction, transportation, community development, law enforcement, or any other area. First passed in 1972, the Nixon revenue-sharing program provided approximately $6 billion a year for five years and was continued through the Nixon, Ford, Carter, and early Reagan years before being eliminated in 1986.

The Nixon administration also sought to consolidate large numbers of categorical grants into block grants, two of which were passed. The Comprehensive Employment and Training Act (CETA) provided funds to local "prime sponsors," usually a local government or group of governments, for manpower training. Which specific programs would be developed was up to the prime sponsor at the local level. Similarly, two weeks after President Nixon resigned, President Ford signed the Community Development Block Grant program (CDBG) consolidating several categorical grant programs, including urban renewal and the model cities program. Despite these successes in altering the pattern of federal grants, the Nixon and Ford years actually increased the total amount of aid available to states and localities.

The dependency of state and especially local governments on federal aid became more apparent during the administration of President Carter. The Carter years saw few dramatic departures in intergovernmental relations, continuing the general revenue sharing and block grants of the Nixon administration, though there was a greater tendency to target funds through categorical grants. Among the more important initiatives were expansion of public service employment under CETA, so local government jobs would be filled by the unemployed, and passage of the Urban Development Action Grant program to stimulate economic development in distressed cities.

As a former governor, President Carter was attentive to the needs of state and local governments to more effectively operate intergovernmental programs, so he proposed a series of administrative steps for improving intergovernmental management. In this effort, he worked closely with a group of seven major public interest groups, known as the PIGs, that were active in the intergovernmental system. These included such groups as the Council of State Governments, the National League of Cities, the National Governor's Association, and others. Later in the Carter years, however, a new mood of fiscal restraint combined with Carter's own fiscal conservatism, was something states and localities found difficult to handle. From the standpoint of state and local governments, however, the reductions of the late Carter years were just the beginning.

The Reagan and Bush Years

The Reagan and Bush administrations brought major structural changes in the pattern of fiscal federalism, including elimination of general revenue sharing and a reworking of the block grant system. However, these years were more significant (in intergovernmental terms) because of the administration's efforts to reduce the size of the federal government through a variety of tax and spending cuts and to return responsibility for major areas, especially social welfare, to the states.

A strong ideological commitment undergirded President Reagan's efforts to eliminate federal funding and federal regulation of state and local activity wherever possible. In his inaugural speech, the president stated, "It is my intention to curb the size and influence of the federal establishment and to demand recognition of the distinction between the powers granted the federal government, those reserved to the states or to the people" (Reagan 1981). One way he proposed to do this was by turning back responsibility for a variety of federal programs, and the resources to pay for them, to the states. (President Bush employed the same ideology, emphasizing the term *turnovers* rather than *turnbacks,* in promoting his programs.) Proposals along these lines, however, quickly became intertwined with the president's 1981 efforts to reduce taxes and spending under the banner of *supply-side economics,* an approach that holds that decreased taxes and spending will stimulate capital investment and in turn economic growth (Stone & Sawhill 1984). The defense budget was protected by the Reagan administration, so the majority of cuts were sought in federal grant programs and general government operations. Indeed, during 1981, the Reagan administration achieved the first absolute decline in federal expenditures in decades. As part of these reductions, federal grants were lowered from about $95 billion in fiscal year 1981 to about $88 billion in fiscal year 1982, with a major portion of the cuts coming in employment and training programs (Beam 1984, p. 420).

Meanwhile, state and local officials decried the depth of the cuts and the administration's failure to make available any revenue sources to pick up the slack, especially as the tax cuts failed to produce the expected economic growth. Moreover, concerns were increasingly voiced that efforts to balance the budget had been especially damaging to the poor—for example, by reducing eligibility for Aid to Families with Dependent Children (AFDC) payments (Nathan et al. 1987, pp. 52–57). The public was concerned about excessive spending, yet it became clear that neither Congress nor the public considered spending for social welfare, environmental protection, and infrastructure maintenance excessive.

Thus, by the middle of the second Reagan term, eligibility requirements in AFDC were restored; the environmental Superfund, designed to clean up toxic wastes and repair leaking underground tanks, was funded by Congress at a significantly higher level than the president requested. Additionally, the Highway Trust Fund for highway improvement, including urban mass transit, was passed despite Reagan's veto.

On the other hand, reductions continued in specific areas, most notably in general revenue sharing. Recall that the Nixon general revenue-sharing program had been continued through the Carter administration; however, early in the Reagan years, revenue sharing for states was eliminated. Finally, in 1986, revenue sharing for local governments was also ended. Many saw general revenue sharing as a way to equalize the disparity between rich and poor communities and allow greater flexibility at the local level; others saw revenue sharing as providing too much money and discretion, especially to wealthy communities.

President Bush continued the Reagan approach to federalism, making important, but largely stylistic, gestures to the states and localities. In part, he could do little else. The budget deficit continued unabated and led to the Budget Enforcement Act (BEA) of 1990. Under the new law, as we will see later, any legislation that exceeds the budget ceiling in its category will trigger an across-the-board cut in that category. In this way, the BEA effectively pits each domestic program against all others. When this legislation was combined with the savings and loan bailout, there was little enthusiasm left for expanding domestic spending, including state and local aid.

As mentioned earlier, President Bush continued the Reagan strategy of turning over various programs to the states, but just as in Reagan's case, there was great skepticism about whether the proposed turnovers were based on a commitment to states' rights and responsibilities or whether they were just a strategy to place the funding of various programs in state hands. For example, the administration's highway plan proposed to turn over four-fifths of the federal highway system to the states with funding to be on a 60–40 basis, federal to state. According to Transportation Secretary Skinner, the proposal was designed not only to permit greater local flexibility, but also to turn over more financial responsibility to the states, shifting the burden to the states.

The Clinton Presidency

During the Clinton presidency, the philosophical foundation of New Federalism remained in place. The primary themes were regulatory reform and shifting decision-making authority to state and local governments. However, the character and scope of this devolution of power was interpreted in vastly different ways by the president, the Republican House, and the more moderate leadership in the Senate. In latter stages of the Clinton administration, state and local governments offered their own ideas on federalism and the overall system of intergovernmental relations. Such diverse viewpoints generated a number of questions concerning not only the state of federalism but also the implications for government practice.

Early on, President Clinton left little doubt as to his administration's position on intergovernmental relations, a position characterized by a sensitivity to state and local governments. The president quickly showed his gubernatorial roots, for example, by choosing four of his cabinet members from the subnational level. And within months of taking office, the administration identified the removal of burdensome federal regulations as a primary objective. In September 1993, President Clinton issued Executive Order 12866, which along with a subsequent order prevented federal agencies from imposing mandates without financial support. Although administrative agencies would gain regulatory powers under the order, central review was to continue to ensure that new regulations conformed with the president's priorities. President Clinton reinforced his stance soon after by issuing Executive Order 12875, establishing a system of state and local review of intergovernmental regulations.

The Clinton administration's New Federalist philosophy also carried over into programmatic areas. In championing the drive to "end welfare as we know it," for example, the administration transformed the nation's system of public assistance by turning to mainly market forces for public well-being and placing service-delivery into the hands of nongovernmental actors. Key provisions in the 1996 welfare reform legislation included setting time limits on benefits, tying welfare to work requirements, handing over authority for welfare programs to state government, and limiting (in some cases eliminating) access to public assistance for legal immigrants and the disabled.

President Clinton's New Federalism could also be seen in his administration's main community and economic development initiative, the Empowerment Zone/Enterprise Community Program, and its key education initiative, the Goals 2000: Educate America Act. In both programs, "the administration persuaded Congress to expand state and/or local discretion" (Walker 1996, p. 274), reinforcing the belief that by reducing federal regulations and handing decision-making power to the state and local levels, those closest to the issue would be in a better position to effect innovation and change in the given policy area.

Vice President Al Gore further advanced the administration's position on intergovernmental relations. In his National Performance Review (NPR) and related efforts, the vice president highlighted a variety of alternative strategies for managing public programs. These strategies, which echoed Osborne and Gaebler's (1992) *Reinventing Government,* injected a new spirit of entrepreneurialism into the federal government. Gore's NPR called for "a new customer service contract with the American people, a new guarantee of effective, efficient, and responsive government." Although the vice president focused mainly on the national level, the philosophy driving his reinvention agenda fostered a greater appreciation for innovation by local and state administrators. NPR also featured several practical measures that affected intergovernmental relations, such as collapsing categorical grants into more flexible funding streams and removing unfunded federal mandates.

On this latter issue, the adoption of New Federalist ideals extended beyond the Clinton administration. Regulatory reform and the removal of unfunded mandates became key issues for the 104th Congress. As cited in the Republican Contract with America, conservatives argued that federal agencies placed too great a burden on state and local administrations by imposing regulations without adequate financial resources for their implementation. Republican lawmakers thus returned to two measures from the preceding Congress (H.R. 4771 and S. 993) and, with assistance from the Clinton administration, revised the bills into the Unfunded Mandate Reform Act (1995). Under the resulting act, the cost of any future mandate would need to be spelled out by the Congressional Budget Office. The act also raised the President's Executive Orders (cited preceding) to a statutory level, binding agencies by law to find less expensive, more flexible ways of instituting regulations.

During President Clinton's second term, however, ties with the Republican Congress degenerated into political gridlock, and the administration devoted as much time to avoiding scandal as it did setting public policy. Though the two camps did come together on measures to eliminate the federal deficit and reform the nation's welfare system, the prevailing story from Washington during the last years of the twentieth century was one of partisan extremism, culminating in President Clinton's becoming the first elected president to be impeached, then acquitted, by Congress. Moreover, even the hallmarks of the period failed to gain support among many state and local governments. Governors and mayors across the country, though recognizing the need for fiscal constraint and welfare reform, remained concerned that the cost of the measures would, over time, fall primarily on the subnational levels administration.

The impact of NPR and "reinventing government" at the federal level also remained in question. While a variety of federal agencies implemented reform initiatives during President Clinton's consecutive terms, many were fraught with political and administrative challenges.

An example of this can be seen in the president's national service initiative. In championing the National and Community Service Trust Act (1993), which created the Corporation for National Service (CNS), President Clinton set out to construct a model of reform based on the principles of reinvention and performance-driven government. But reform under CNS proved to be a difficult path. From the beginning, the agency was a target of controversy, with questions about whether CNS was simply a way to supplement funding of federal programs, questions about accountability, and concerns about how much competition was desirable in the public service.

CNS during its early years does not give a full picture of the reinvention movement. Examples can be found at all levels of government, and in the nonprofit sector, as reformers strive to create a more responsive, entrepreneurial, and results-based system of governance. Indeed, reinvention, compared to many political reform movements, has had a fairly long lifespan. On the other hand, a growing number of scholars and practitioners have taken issue with the assumptions underlying the reform agenda. Although few would dispute the values of making federal agencies more responsive, or ensuring effectiveness in delivering public services, many have come to recognize that productivity and performance should not be the only measures of success.

The Bush Administration

President George W. Bush continues the New Federalism of his predecessors, as evident in his agenda to streamline the federal government, increase the role of nongovernmental organizations (nonprofit, for-profit, and faith-based) in the policy process, and shift to more market-based models of service delivery (see Box 3.2). For instance, the Bush administration's first legislative victory came with a $1.3 trillion tax cut, which supporters said would force the federal government to tighten its belt on spending and stimulate economic growth by returning money to taxpayers. (Many compared the measure to the major tax cuts early in the Reagan administration.) Since then, Bush has succeeded in pushing through three more major tax cuts that are expected to reduce revenue by $1.9 trillion over a 10-year period.

The Bush administration has also emphasized program decentralization. As mentioned in Chapter 2, the president used one of his first executive orders to create the Office of Faith-Based and Community Initiatives (see www.whitehouse.gov/government/fbci/index.html). The goal of this program is to strengthen the role of faith-based and community organizations in addressing social problems by removing barriers to their participation in federally funded programs and increasing funding targeted specifically at these groups. Since the inception of the faith-based initiative, nearly $200 million of federal funding has been awarded to support the work of organizations in social services, mentoring, and addiction recovery programs. Although many nonprofit leaders support the program, which expands the amount in social service spending for which faith-based organizations could compete, others (including many religious leaders) are concerned that without a substantial increase in the level of funding, the Bush initiative has the effect of pitting religious groups against each other for a share of the pie. Others argue that although federal funding helps enhance the role of faith-based nonprofits as service providers, most of the smaller religious organizations simply lack the expertise needed to administer federal grants.

BOX 3.2

TRANSFORMATION OF GOVERNANCE: GLOBALIZATION, DEVOLUTION, AND THE ROLE OF GOVERNMENT

Over the last generation, American government has undergone a steady, but often unnoticed, transformation. Its traditional practices and institutions have become more marginal to the fundamental debates. Meanwhile, new processes and institutions—often nongovernmental ones—have become more central to public policy. In doing the people's work to a large and growing degree, American governments share responsibility with other levels of government, with private companies, and with nonprofit organizations.

This transformation has two effects. First, it has strained the traditional roles of all the players. For decades, we have debated privatizing and shrinking government. While the debate raged, however, we incrementally made important policy decisions. Those decisions have rendered much of the debate moot. Government has come to rely heavily on for-profit and nonprofit organizations for delivering goods and services ranging from antimissile systems to welfare reform. It is not that these changes have obliterated the roles of Congress, the president, and the courts. State and local governments have become even livelier. Rather, these changes have layered new challenges on top of the traditional institutions and their processes.

Second, the new challenges have strained the capacity of governments—and their nongovernmental partners—to deliver high-quality public services. The basic structure of American government comes from the New Deal days. It is a government driven by functional specialization and process control. However, new place-based problems have emerged: How can government's functions be coordinated in a single place? Can environmental regulations flowing down separate channels (air, water, and soil) merge to form a coherent environmental policy? New process-based problems have emerged as well: How can hierarchical bureaucracies, created with the presumption that they directly deliver services, cope with services increasingly delivered through multiple (often nongovernmental) partners? Budgetary control processes that work well for traditional bureaucracies often prove less effective in gathering information from nongovernmental partners or in shaping their incentives. Personnel systems designed to insulate government from political interference have proven less adaptive to these new challenges, especially in creating a cohort of executives skilled in managing indirect government.

Consequently, government at all levels has found itself with new responsibilities but without the capacity to manage them effectively. The same is true of its nongovernmental partners. Moreover, despite these transformations, the *expectations* on government—by citizens and often by government officials—remain rooted in a past that no longer exists. Citizens expect their problems will be solved and tend not to care who solves them. Elected officials take a similar view: They create programs and appropriate money. They expect government agencies to deliver the goods and services. When problems emerge, their first instinct is to reorganize agencies or impose new procedures—when the problem often has to

(Continued)

(Continued)

> do with organizational structures and processes that no longer fit reality. The performance of American government—its effectiveness, efficiency, responsiveness, and accountability—depends on cracking these problems.

SOURCE: Donald F. Kettl, "Transformation of Governance: Globalization, Devolution and the Role of Government." *Public Administration Review* 60, no. 6 (November/December 2000): 488–497. Reprinted by permission.

Another example of President Bush's New Federalism can be seen in his administration's reliance on the market for delivering public services. In July 2001, the president outlined a plan to reduce the cost of prescription drugs for the elderly. The Bush plan offered seniors the opportunity to join buying clubs, which would be administered by for-profit firms, and use discount cards to save 15 to 25 percent on their pharmaceutical purchases. Several such buying clubs already existed, including a cooperative venture between Merck-Medco, a pharmaceutical firm, and the Readers' Digest Association. Some health-care companies and other Bush supporters viewed the plan as a way to improve access to health care for the elderly, but doing so without increasing federal spending. Critics said the proposal would not produce the types of changes needed in the Medicare system. They argued that under the Bush plan pharmaceutical companies would still be able to set their own prices, and, rather than relying purely on the market, the federal government should require discount clubs to negotiate with drug manufacturers and pharmacists should be asked to set prices prospectively. President Bush agreed that the proposal was simply the first step in a major overhaul of the thirty-six-year-old federal program, adding that the government should explore additional market approaches like expanding the role of health maintenance organizations and other private health plans (Pear 2001, p. A1). In 2003, Congress passed Bush's Medicare Prescription Drug Improvement and Modernization Act, which provides discount cards until 2006, when seniors will be able to buy into a federally supported prescription drug insurance program.

His commitment to partnering with the private sector and to nongovernmental strategies continues. In 2004, Bush first proposed allowing younger workers to privately invest some of their Social Security contributions instead of paying into the Social Security system. This continues as one of his major domestic initiatives. Supporters claim that doing so will help workers to realize greater gains and thus build a bigger nest egg toward retirement. Assuming workers will receive a higher rate of return in these private accounts, the pressures on the Social Security system will lessen. Critics argue that doing so will cause a reduction in benefits and, rather than saving the system, will ultimately cause greater financial problems.

Judicial Influence

One final point relates to the role of the judiciary in shaping intergovernmental relations. Through the 1990s, students of federalism became increasingly aware of the role of the judiciary, especially the Supreme Court, in defining the relationship between the federal government and the states. Although the recent judicial activism has produced varied results, with the scope of federal authority limited in some cases and reaffirmed in others, an important outcome emerged. The Court once again established itself as "a conscious arbiter of the respective powers of the national government and the states" (Wise 2001, p. 343).

At issue has been Congress's constitutional authority to regulate activities at the state level. For much of the twentieth century, the Commerce Clause, which gives Congress the power to regulate trade between the states, has been the center point of federal legislation. However, regulations also have been imposed under the Fourteenth Amendment, which grants Congress the power to enforce by appropriate legislation the rights provided in the amendment. Regardless of its legal basis, federal regulatory authority has been allowed to expand virtually unchecked by the Court since the 1940s. In fact, some scholars of federalism began to wonder whether any boundaries would be established to limit the scope of the federal government relative to the states (see Wise 1998, 2001). The tides began to change, however, during the 1990s.

Among the first key decisions setting parameters on Congress's regulatory power was *Gregory v. Ashcroft* (1991). In this case, the Court ruled that the Missouri constitution's rule that state judges must retire at age seventy does not violate the federal Age Discrimination Act, as the Equal Employment Opportunity Commission had ruled. "The significance of this [the *Gregory* ruling] is that it bars individuals and groups who wish to use federal statutes of general applicability adopted under the Commerce Clause to attack state regulation in federal court from doing so, unless Congress makes it clear that the statute applies to the states" (Wise 2001, p. 344). Justice O'Connor, in her opinion, emphasized the constitutional principle of dual sovereignty and the importance of maintaining a certain degree of state authority.

Congress's regulatory power under Commerce came into question again in *United States v. Lopez* (1995) and *United States v. Morrison* (2000). In *Lopez,* the Court considered a challenge to federal restrictions placed on handgun possession in a school zone. The *Morrison* case focused on provisions in the Violence Against Women Act, which allow victims of violent crimes motivated by gender to seek federal civil action. The Supreme Court ruled in both cases that Congress had overstepped its regulatory jurisdiction because the statutes were not consistent with the authority afforded under the Commerce Clause. At the heart of the Court's decisions was the premise that clear lines must be established between national and state powers and that, under Commerce, these lines must be limited to matters of interstate trade.

Of course, the *Lopez* and *Morrison* decisions focused primarily on restoring a balance of regulatory power between the national government and state governments. The recent judicial activism, however, also can be seen on issues of administration, such as in *New York v. United States* (1992) and *Printz v. United States* (1997), where the Court placed restrictions on Congress's ability to compel state and local actors to implement federal statutes.

The *New York* case involved a challenge from local governments against the Low-Level Radioactive Waste Policy Act, which required state and regional authorities in certain circumstances to assume ownership of radioactive waste and commanded them to implement provisions of the federal legislation. The Court ruled unconstitutional both alternatives, stating that Congress must not view state/local governments as "mere political subdivisions . . . [or] regional offices" (Wise 1998, p. 95) of the national government and must afford the level of state sovereignty guaranteed under the Tenth Amendment.

In *Printz,* the Court reviewed a challenge to provisions of the Brady Handgun Violence Prevention Act, which mandated background checks on prospective buyers and required local law enforcement officers to serve as entities of the national government in executing the regulation. The federal government, in an interesting twist, argued that unlike *New York,* the Brady Act did not place responsibility on the states for policy making and that, given the rewards, the cost to the states would be minimal. The Court disagreed. In its rejection of the federal claim, the Court stated that *New York* established, in very clear terms, that Congress cannot command state officials to execute or administer federal regulations, nor can the national government bypass the *New York* limitations by directly enlisting state actors.

However, the decisions cited here should not be taken as a complete shift toward state sovereignty. Several recent rulings, including *Davis v. Monroe County Board of Education* (1999), *Saenz v. Roe* (1999), and *Sabri v. United States* (2004), have reinforced the national government's capacity to monitor state activities.

In *Davis,* for example, the Court reaffirmed Congress's authority to establish state liability for certain actions as part of the states' agreement to receive federal funding. The majority of the justices ruled that, under the Spending Clause, Congress could use its control over appropriations to enforce constitutional rights—in this case, the guarantee against third-party discrimination in public schools—as long as the language in the funding program remained clear enough so that states would have adequate notice of the federal requirements.

The main issue in *Saenz* was the state of California's revision to its welfare laws to set a twelve-month residency requirement for certain levels of public assistance. Although the Court had previously invalidated residency requirements for eligibility (in *Shapiro v. Thompson* [1969]), Secretary Saenz, of California's Department of Social Services, claimed that the new welfare reform provisions did not exclude new arrivals from welfare benefits but simply maintained their assistance levels to those of the states where they resided previously. The Court disagreed, ruling that the Fourteenth Amendment does not assign levels of citizenship according to length of residence but instead links citizenship with residence generally. Although the Court appreciated California's desire to reduce the cost of welfare benefits, a majority determined that fiscal efficiency could not be allowed to outweigh citizen guarantees against discrimination.

In the *Sabri* case, Sabri was accused of offering bribes to a Minneapolis councilman to facilitate city construction projects. The constitutional question before the Court was whether Congress could criminalize such bribes under its Spending Power. Even though it was not possible to establish a direct link between the bribes and a particular federal project, the Court held that the federal government could act to safeguard the integrity of local government administration involved in federally funded projects.

When taken as a whole, the decisions cited here present a mixed image of federalism (see Box 3.3). On one hand, the Court clearly has reconsidered its deference to Congress on issues of intergovernmental relations, a practice it had followed throughout

BOX 3.3

BALANCE OF POWER? THE CHANGING FACE OF JUDICIAL FEDERALISM

The authority of states protected under the Constitution, based on a balance of power between the national government and the states and the principle of *dual sovereignty.* Limitations placed on Congress's regulatory authority under the Commerce Clause of the Constitution.	Gregory v. Ashcroft (1991) Gregory v. Ashcroft (1991) Gregory v. Ashcroft (1991) *United States v. Morrison* (2000)
State sovereignty reaffirmed, in that state and local actors cannot be compelled by Congress to implement federal regulatory statutes.	New York v. United States (1992) *Printz v. United States* (1997)
The authority of Congress to regulate activities in the states, based on powers granted under the Spending Clause of the Constitution. State and local actors may be required to accept certain standards as a condition of receiving federal funds.	*Davis v. Monroe Co. Board of Education* (1999) *Saenz v. Roe* (1999)

SOURCE: Charles R. Wise, "Judicial Federalism: The Resurgence of the Supreme Court," *Public Administration Review* 61, no. 3 (2001): 343–358. Reprinted by permission.

— Courts reconsidered deference to Congress on intergovernmental issues

the twentieth century, setting restraints on the scope of federal power. On the other hand, federal regulatory authority in other areas has been reaffirmed, particularly under the Spending Clause and the Fourteenth Amendment. Despite the significance of these decisions in themselves, the implications go even further. Indeed, the most significant outcome is that the Court appears to have reassumed its responsibility for judicial review on questions of federal-state authority, which it had all but abandoned in *Garcia v. San Antonio Metropolitan Transit Authority* (1985). (The *Garcia* case will be discussed in more detail in the next section.) Given not only the nature of the decisions but the mere fact that the judiciary has been willing to intervene, we can be assured that the Supreme Court once again has become the "arbiter-in-chief" in our federal system (Wise 1998, p. 98).

The State and Local Perspective

We have described the system of intergovernmental relations primarily from the federal perspective, but states and localities are also major actors in the intergovernmental system, both as they participate in federal programs and as they interact state to state, state to locality, and locality to locality. Here, also, intergovernmental relations have seen great changes. Although budgetary shifts have created serious problems for state and local governments, the governments have proven remarkably well equipped to deal with these dilemmas, both financially and administratively.

Funding Patterns

Although federal aid to state and local governments declined in the early 1980s, this trend soon reversed. Federal grant funding grew from $91.4 billion in 1980 to $225 billion in 1995 and $434.1 billion in 2006 (Table 3.1). This roller-coaster ride adversely affected both state and local governments, and federal aid has still not returned to the levels of 30 years ago. Throughout the 1980s and 1990s, the impact on state and local governments, as well as other service delivery organizations, was severe. As Table 3.1 shows, in 1980 total federal grants made up about 27.4 percent of state and local government expenditures. The figure dropped to about 22.8 percent by 1995 but increased (slightly) to 23.3 percent in 2006.

TABLE 3.1

Federal Grants: Federal Aid to State and Local Governments 1980–2006 (in billions of dollars)

Fiscal Year	Composition of Federal Grants				State/Local Expenditures (%)
	Payments for Individuals	Physical Capital	Other Grants	Total Grants	
1980	32.6	22.6	36.2	91.4	27.4
1985	50.1	24.9	30.9	105.9	22.0
1990	77.3	27.2	30.9	135.4	18.9
1995	144.4	39.6	41.0	225.0	22.8
2000	182.6	48.7	54.6	285.9	22.2
2006	272.6	64.1	97.4	434.1	23.3

SOURCE: U.S. Office of Management and Budget, Crosscutting Programs, Budget of the United States Government, FY2008, Table 8.3 Trends in Federal Grants to State and Local Government [Electronic version], p. 91, Retrieved March 25, 2007, from www.whitehouse.gov/omb/budget/fy2008/pdf/apers/crosscutting.pdf.

All of these changes occurred at a time during which state governments were experiencing significant fiscal stress related to other factors such as the recession; inelastic tax systems; growing expenditures in health, poverty, and immigration; and so on. For example, states spent approximately $40.1 billion on health care in 1996, and by 1999, that number had almost quadrupled to $157 billion (U.S. Census Bureau 2002). Medicaid accounted for 13 percent of state spending in 1990; today it accounts for almost a quarter of state expenditures (*PA Times* August 2004). Consequently, state and localities found it necessary to curtail or even terminate many programs, while at the same time trying to develop new sources of revenue. According to researchers at Harvard University, states continue to face serious budgetary strains, which can be expected to last through the decade. Part of the reason for this is that spending has surpassed the ability of states to collect revenues.

Although median state spending per capita increased threefold between 1982 and 2002, revenues have grown much more slowly. In 2001 alone, state revenues decreased over 7 percent (*PA Times* August 2004).

Without question, the last several decades have presented a variety of fiscal challenges to state and local governments. One surprising development, however, is that the states have proven capable of managing their new responsibilities far better than many predicted. Indeed, although the federal government has a huge deficit, many states have continued to operate with balanced budgets over the past decade.

An important boost to state governments came in 1998, as attorneys general across the country reached a landmark settlement with tobacco companies to recoup expenditures from health costs associated with smoking and other forms of tobacco use. The settlement, which amounts to $246 billion nationally over the next twenty-five years, has given states much-needed resources for antismoking campaigns, health care, and a variety of other needs. In fact, since the settlement set few limitations on how the proceeds could be used, the approximately $8 billion per year has been used for a wide variety of purposes.

Once considered a weak link in the federal system, over the past thirty years, states have dramatically increased their capacities. Although there are still considerable variations in states' powers, most states have undertaken important institutional reforms (such as developing legislative audits), expanded the scope and professionalism of their operations (to include new services in areas such as energy planning and conservation or new programs in areas such as productivity improvement), and demonstrated remarkable fiscal restraint. Indeed, the states are operating balanced budgets, and some are even making investments for the future.

The states also are moving into areas of responsibility once thought to rest at the federal level. International trade is one area where shifting roles already seem to be taking place. Whereas the federal government has traditionally played the leading (if not the exclusive) role in foreign affairs, economic forces are precipitating much greater state and local activity in the international arena. For example, all states have offices of economic development involved in some way with international economic development. Through such units, the states provide local businesses with seminars and conferences on how to market themselves overseas. Over 40 states also maintain permanent offices overseas, with some of the larger states having offices in several countries.

Preemptions and Mandates

Preemptions   As discussed previously, although our federal system of government establishes certain federal powers, reserves certain powers to the states, and permits certain actions at both levels, there has long been controversy about the exact definitions of these categories. Intense controversy surrounds the issue of the right of the federal government to preempt the traditional powers of states and localities or to coerce states and localities into doing (or not doing) certain things.

As a case in point, the Fair Labor Standards Act (FLSA) of 1938 set the minimum wage and the maximum hours that could be worked before overtime pay was required. The act originally applied only to the private sector, but 1974 amendments applied it to all state

NETWORKING

For data relating to federal funding to state and local governments, go to the Statistical Abstract of the United States at www.census.gov/prod/www/statistical-abstract-1995_2000. html or to the Office of Management and Budget at www.whitehouse.gov/omb/budget/fy2005. Analyses of the changing character of intergovernmental relations under the "New Federalism" can be found at http://www.urban.org/center/anf/index.cfm.

and local governments. Many state and local officials argued against the amendments, citing the difficulties in applying the standards to government—for example, how do you measure the hours a firefighter works in off-and-on shifts of several days' duration? Soon the amendments were challenged in court, and, in the case of *National League of Cities v. Usery* (1976), the Supreme Court decided that the functions of "general government" were part of the powers "reserved" to the states by the Tenth Amendment and therefore could not be regulated by the federal government. Consequently, the FLSA did not apply.

The Court's ruling in many ways raised as many questions as it answered, especially around the issue of what could be included under the notion of "general government." The confusion persisted until, nearly ten years later, the Court reviewed a case that sought to determine whether the San Antonio transit authority was performing "general government" functions and was therefore exempt from the Fair Labor Standards Act.

In *Garcia v. San Antonio Metropolitan Transit Authority* (1985), however, the Court went beyond the narrow question of whether transit is a general government function and decided that, under its responsibilities to regulate commerce, Congress did in fact have the power to intervene in the affairs of state and local governments.

The effect of *Garcia*, a direct reversal of the Court's earlier position in the *Usery* case, was to remove questions about the scope of the federal government's powers from the realm of judicial inquiry. The Court essentially held that states have sufficient input into the national legislative process, through the election of members of Congress and the influence of their governors and mayors, to protect themselves politically from burdensome legislation. That being the case, the question of whether the federal government could act in areas previously believed reserved to the states should be decided through legislation rather than judicial action. The rights of the states were, therefore, viewed as raising political rather than judicial questions.

A similar argument was developed by the Court in *South Carolina v. Baker* (1988), a case viewed by many at the time as putting a nail in the coffin of the Tenth Amendment rights of the states. *South Carolina* asked whether the federal government had the right to dictate the form of bonds issued by the states. The Court not only answered "yes," but it also indicated that the federal government had the right to tax income earned on tax-exempt bonds. Obviously, if the federal government had this right, then the states would have to compete directly with private firms issuing bonds. Although political leaders tried to assure the bond market that the federal government would not try to balance its budget by intruding on the states' abilities to issue tax-exempt bonds, several such proposals were introduced in Congress. As you can imagine, states and localities were incensed at this intrusion into a critical area of state financing, but, again, the states were precluded from a judicial remedy and asked to rely on their political power to see that Congress did not act to tax state and local bonds.

The *Garcia* and *South Carolina* cases open the door for the federal government to move into areas once thought to be the purview of state and local governments. Certainly, state and local officials, who have seen the federal government act in areas from rat control to minimum drinking ages, have been skeptical of the self-restraint of Congress. At a minimum, *Garcia* and *South Carolina* set a precedent for expanded federal action directed at state and local governments.

We should not, however, rush to judgment, because many of the Supreme Court rulings handed down in the past decade have been decided by 5–4 votes, and in several key cases, the majority has clearly reaffirmed the sovereignty of state governments (for example, *New York v. United States* [1992], *Seminole Tribe of Florida v. Florida* [1996], *Printz v. United States* [1997], and *Alden v. Maine* [1999]). In fact, a recent commentary on emerging judicial federalism noted that majority opinion maintained the theme "that state sovereignty may not be invaded, not only because it is rooted in the nation's constitutional structure, but also because such invasion undermines the very operation of American democracy" (Wise 2001, p. 354).

These cases deal with the powers of the federal government over states and localities, but somewhat less complex issues have been raised with respect to the powers of the states over local governments. As noted, our intergovernmental system does not allocate separate spheres of power to state and local governments, but rather treats local governments merely as "creatures of the state," having only those powers granted by the state. In what has come to be known as *Dillon's Rule*, Judge John Dillon declared in 1868 that municipalities had only those powers granted in their charters, those fairly implied by the expressed powers, and those essential to the purposes of their being granted a charter. In other words, Dillon's Rule allowed for state control over all but a narrow range of local activities. Dillon's Rule has been somewhat relaxed, especially in states that permit cities greater autonomy through *home-rule* provisions, but the powers of local government continue to derive directly from the actions of the state.

There are various mechanisms involved in the relationship between the federal government and the states and between the states and localities. *Preemptions* involve the federal government preempting state action traditionally associated with the lower level of government. For example, the federal Nutrition Labeling and Education Act of 1990 preempted many state and local laws regarding food labeling. Such assumptions of power have been particularly significant in the last few years. For example, federal preemptions of state and local authority more than doubled after 1970. More than 50 percent of the preemption statutes enacted in the entire history of our country were enacted in the last twenty years. Not even Ronald Reagan, despite his rhetoric promising a return of more power to the states, was exempt from this trend, endorsing federal limits on the regulation of business, as well as restraints in health and the environment (Kincaid 1990, p. 149).

Mandates The *New York* and *Printz* cases deal with what are called *direct orders*, requirements or restrictions enforced by one government upon another (the federal government on states and localities, the states on the cities). Direct orders might include a federal requirement that cities meet certain clean water standards or a state requirement that a city pay part of the costs of certain welfare programs. Another way control can be exercised over another government is through *conditions* tied to grants-in-aid. These conditions are typically of the type parents use with children: "You can go outside to play after you have cleaned your room." Conditions of aid might require land-use planning or an assurance of making facilities accessible to the handicapped prior to a capital construction project.

Because cities derive their powers from the states, most state requirements are direct orders. But most federal requirements are conditions-of-aid tied to a particular grant program. "Conditions-of-aid" are of two varieties. *Cross-cutting requirements* are rules that apply to most, if not all, grant programs. For instance, the federal government requires environmental impact statements before undertaking capital projects, certain personnel provisions in agencies receiving grant funds, and compliance with civil rights legislation. Other conditions-of-aid are program-specific, applicable only to the particular program. They may include rules about program planning, implementation, and evaluation. For example, a particular program might prescribe certain maximum salaries for individuals employed under the grant or some form of citizen participation in program design (most federal programs have this latter requirement).

What Would You Do?

You are in charge of a coalition combating domestic violence. The various nonprofit organizations that are the primary service delivery groups in this area have complained to you that a new state initiative to stop human trafficking will have the effect of reducing their capacity to help current victims of domestic violence and abuse. What would you do?

Congress imposes such conditions-of-aid requirements under the Spending Clause of the Constitution. For the terms to be valid, though, federal lawmakers must clearly state the conditions in the legislation, making certain that state and local governments are aware of the requirements. The legality of Congress using funding conditions as a way of advancing regulatory and administrative objectives has been reaffirmed in several Supreme Court decisions, notably *Cedar Rapids Community School District v. Garret* (1999) and *Davis v. Monroe County Board of Education* (1999) (see Box 3.3).

The term *mandate* has been used to embrace both conditions-of-aid and direct orders, in either case an order requiring a government to do something it might not otherwise do. And mandates often require states or localities to spend money they would not otherwise spend. Today it is estimated that federal mandates cost state and local governments an estimated $100 billion a year. State spending mandated by the recent immigration bills alone is estimated to be over $1 billion. Moreover, states and cities claim that mandates unduly impinge upon the autonomy of their level of government. Consequently, mandates have become a source of considerable frustration for those on the receiving end. The argument continues today by mayors and governors across the country—the mayors concerned with both federal and state mandates, and the governors concerned primarily with federal mandates.

For nonprofits, mandates tend to be a part of daily life. The key difference is that where a local government may have mandates from a relatively narrow number of sources, such as the federal and state levels, a nonprofit agency often will face direct orders or conditions-of-aid requirements from each of its funding sources, and the larger the funder (and funding amount), the greater the burden. Those in the nonprofit sector sometimes speak of mandates as the "golden handcuffs"—the funding is great, but grant maker demands usually place an excessive administrative strain on the organization. As Paul Light concluded, the situation has been exacerbated in recent years by trends in nonprofit management reform: "Unfortunately, the nonprofit sector is caught in the middle of an unrelenting contest between competing philosophies and advocates of reform, all of which produce significant motion back and forth across different reform ideologies" (Light 2000, p. 45). The varying philosophical positions can become manifested in an array of reporting standards and administrative procedures imposed by grant-makers.

The United Way of America, for example, plays a leading role in establishing guidelines for performance (or "outcome") management by nonprofit organizations, and an increasing number of local United Ways have set reporting standards for agencies receiving grants. Similarly, many foundations (large and small) have made interagency partnerships an eligibility requirement for grant programs. If a nonprofit service provider wants to apply for a grant, the leadership must show how the agency will "collaborate" with other nonprofits, government, and even for-profit firms.

At the federal level, every president since Nixon has pledged to reduce the burden of mandates on states and local governments. In his 1992 State of the Union address, President Bush said, "We must put an end to unfinanced Federal Government mandates... If Congress passes a mandate, it should be forced to pay for it and to balance the cost with savings elsewhere. After all, a mandate just increases someone else's burden, and that means higher taxes at the state and local level" (Bowman & Pagano 1992, p. 4). However, shortly after the president made his remarks, he signed a budget agreement that contained twenty new mandates expected to cost state and local governments about $17 billion over the next five years.

An important step forward was taken in March 1995, when President Clinton signed the Unfunded Mandate Reform Act (UMRA) of 1995, presumably an effort to limit the effects of federally imposed mandates. Although this legislation does not provide federal funding for all mandated activities, it does require that Congress recognize the implications of mandates for state and local activities and, in some cases, authorize funding for such mandates. According to Gullo (2004) UMRA increased the amount of information that federal agencies are required to provide Congress when proposing a bill that will impose costs for the state, local, and tribal governments. UMRA also gives Congress the authority to defeat or alter a bill that would impose costs for the state, local, and tribal governments above the 1996 threshold of $50 million (Gullo 2004).

However, there seem to be a variety of "loopholes" through which Congress might avoid funding. Although most state and local government associations (such as the Big Seven Public Interest Groups) actively supported the act, most also realize that it provides limited relief from federally imposed mandates. Also, the act does nothing about mandates imposed on local governments by state governments.

And, according to many, unfounded mandates continue. For example, the Bush administration has received criticism from educational groups as well as state and local officials for the presumedly unfounded mandates required by the No Child Left Behind Act. According to the National Education Association (NEA), "Since the law's enactment in 2002, there has been a $27 billion funding shortfall in what Congress was supposed to provide schools to meet the law's regulations and what has been funded. Cost studies in Ohio and Texas estimate that the price of the regulations to state taxpayers could run as high as $1.5 and $1.2 billion, respectively" (www.nea.org/lawsuit/nr050420.html). For this reason, the NEA and others filed a national lawsuit seeking remedy from this unfunded mandate.

Subnational Relationships

Even focusing on state and local activities, we find the federal government involved in some way—at a minimum, in providing funds for states and localities. But important intergovernmental activity also occurs at the subnational level: state to state, state to local, and local to local.

State to State Relationships between and among states are mentioned several times in the U.S. Constitution, most notably in the requirement that states recognize the rights and privileges of citizens of other states and give "full faith and credit" to the public acts and legal proceedings of other states. Some of the most important intergovernmental relationships involving various state governments are not based in constitutional doctrine, however, but are rather the result of political practices over the years.

Relationships among states are not without conflict. States may differ over census counts (important in determining the number of representatives in Congress), shifting state boundaries (as when a river changes course), and a variety of substantive policy issues (such as the rights to underground water or the degree to which dumping pollutants into a river affects water quality in states downstream). In addition, states must increasingly compete with one another for economic development; for example, when General Motors announced plans to build a plant to produce the Saturn, many states entered an intense bidding war, each hoping GM would locate the plant within its boundaries.

States also cooperate. There are many opportunities for officials in one state to seek the advice of those in other states with respect to policy alternatives or new administrative arrangements. Many organizations, including the Council of State Governments, the National Governor's Association, the National Council of State Legislators, and groups that bring together state officials in personnel, budgeting, purchasing, social welfare, health, and so forth, have been created to help officials share information and expertise. These groups, along with the Washington offices of various states, constitute an important lobbying group in Washington.

One way the states come together to resolve potential disputes or work together on common problems is through *interstate compacts*. These agreements have historically been bilateral, involving only two states; however, increasingly, they involve a number of states within a region or even all 50 states. Originally used to resolve boundary disputes, interstate compacts today cover a wide variety of topics, most arising from the fact that today's policy problems do not confine themselves neatly to the borders of one state. Imagine, for example, the common interests of people in several states sharing the same underground water supply. Think also of the problems that are of interest to all who live in metropolitan areas, such as Cincinnati or Kansas City, that cross the boundaries of two or even more states. It is not uncommon in such areas to find interstate compacts covering air and water pollution, transportation, law enforcement, and so on.

States may also use interstate compacts to symbolize their agreement to cooperate in especially important policy areas. For example, Arizona, California, and Nevada have a definite interest in ensuring access to water from the Colorado River. The states' governments follow compacts dating back to 1922, which lay out strict guidelines on access rights and water usage. In cases such as this, an interstate compact provides a way for states to formalize resolution of a dispute or to work together without involving the federal government.

State to Local   We have seen that the relationship between states and localities is unitary—that is, local governments have only those powers granted by the state. However, the nature of the powers may vary considerably. Most cities operate under some form of *charter*, the local government equivalent of a constitution. But a state may grant charters in several ways. Some states develop *special charters* for each individual local government; others take exactly the opposite approach and grant a *general charter* for local government. The *classified charter* approach seeks to avoid the restrictive nature of the special charter and the rigidity of the general charter by granting charters to various classes of cities. For example, all cities over 1 million in population might be designated Class A and have one set of charter provisions, whereas cities from 250,000 to 1 million might be Class B and have a different set of provisions. A final means of chartering cities, called home rule, permits cities to write their own charters, within very broad state guidelines and generally subject to voter approval.

Home rule obviously provides the greatest flexibility for local governments in terms of basic structure; however, even under home rule, there is substantial state involvement in local government affairs. For one thing, the states are an important source of funding for local activities. Indeed, at a time when federal aid has leveled somewhat, state aid to local governments has increased dramatically. Between 1980 and 2004, for example, state aid to local governments increased from about $83 billion to over $379 billion in 2004, with most of that targeted for education and lesser amounts for welfare, highways, and other purposes (US Census, www.census.gov/govs/www/estimate.html).

But states do not only provide money; they also regulate local government activities. State governments tell local governments what taxes they can levy, what services they can provide, and what types of management systems they must employ. In doing so, states pro-

What Would You Do?

You are city manager for a medium-sized community in the Northwest. The state legislature is considering a bill intended to prevent underage drinking. It would require local police departments in the state to perform additional spot inspections of bars and restaurants serving alcohol after midnight. Although you think the cause is an important one, you simply don't have the resources in your police department to do this. The state is not willing to provide more money. What would you do?

vide needed uniformity, as in the case of highway signs, and ensure minimum standards of performance, as in education or welfare programs. Because states have virtually unlimited power over local governments, there is an obvious temptation to compel local governments to assume new responsibilities. In most states, there are twenty to thirty statutes that impose substantial financial burdens on local governments. The total number of mandates or regulations may number in the thousands (Berman 1992, p. 53).

Just as states complain about federal mandates, many local officials view state mandates as unnecessary intrusions on local prerogatives. The mandates may require local expenditures that might not otherwise be made. Recently, localities have complained especially about *sneaky mandates*, actions that are required of local governments by the inaction of state governments. For example, Georgia failed to pick up prisoners housed "temporarily" in county jails, resulting in overcrowding in the prison system, to say nothing of the additional financial burden on the counties. There is, however, new sympathy for localities in terms of mandates, and about one-third of the states now have requirements for at least partial reimbursements of expenses created by mandates (MacManus 1992).

Localities are not powerless in their relationship with the states, especially as they constitute an important base of political support for those in the legislatures. Local representatives and senators can and often do voice the local message loudly and clearly in the state legislature. Moreover, various patterns of state/local cooperation have emerged in the past several years. Many states, for example, have developed state-level equivalents of the federal Advisory Commission on Intergovernmental Relations. These state commissions bring together state and local officials to discuss problems in the intergovernmental system and devise ways to work together more effectively. Among the recommendations that have emerged are suggestions for greater local discretionary authority and for reductions in the number of state mandates.

Local to Local In discussions of intergovernmental relations, there is an understandable tendency to focus on national patterns, but for those who work at the local level, relationships with other local governments are extremely important. One reason is that many citizens live in one jurisdiction, work in another, shop in another, and pay taxes to several. They naturally expect services, such as quality streets or law enforcement, to remain fairly constant as they move from one place to another.

From a political standpoint, the fragmentation of government, especially in urban areas, often means that problems are separated from the resources that might be employed to solve them. Wealthier cities have the money; poorer cities have the problems. But even where resources are evenly distributed, it is difficult to get several local governments together to resolve common problems. In such cases, citizens often turn to higher-level governments for help, thus taking the problem (and its solution) out of the hands of local authorities (Nice 1987, p. 191).

But many inter-local problems are resolved at the local level. Natural, though informal, patterns of cooperation develop, especially in the relationships among local professionals. The police chief in one community talks with other police chiefs, the health officer talks with other health officers, and so on. More formally, one government may actually purchase services from another, contracting for police or fire protection, wastewater treatment, or trash collection. Los Angeles County, for example, provides a variety of services to local governments through contract arrangements. Additionally, *Councils of Government* (COGs), oversight bodies representing various localities, may be created to help coordinate local affairs.

In recent years, partnerships between local governments have entered the information age as many cities and counties started to share technological innovations across jurisdictions. In the city of Sunnyvale, California, for example, the local government worked with other municipalities and the Microsoft Corporation to develop online permitting software. The Silicon Valley Smart Permit initiative proved to be so successful, Sunnyvale has created a public-private partnership with a management firm and its e-government affiliate to market the application to other local authorities that are interested in enhancing their efficiency and responsiveness (Hernandez 2001; Mariani 2001).

Finally, *special districts* may be created to solve problems that cross governmental boundaries. As mentioned, special districts are local governments created for a specific purpose within a specific area (not necessarily coinciding with the boundaries of a city or county). Although special districts may promote coordination of health, education, or other services, they also add to the number of governments within a particular area. Thus, one city block may be governed by the city, a county, and several special districts. A resident may have difficulty figuring out which government can help with a particular problem. The difficulties in coordinating efforts are substantial, as are the problems of holding the various governments accountable.

■ Working with Nongovernmental Organizations

It is impossible to speak of intergovernmental relations without discussing the role of nongovernmental organizations (NGOs) in the policy process. Nonprofit, for-profit, and faith-based organizations have taken a leading role in the delivery of public services. NGOs can be found at all levels of governance and in a variety of policy areas. However, NGOs must be considered not only for their part in implementing public programs, but also their growing influence in raising issues to the public agenda, lobbying for particular policy alternatives, and guiding political and administrative decision making. In many respects, even the term "intergovernmental relations" seems a bit outdated; perhaps we should opt for the more inclusive term *interorganizational relations*.

The use of NGOs in the delivery of public services has grown markedly in the last several years. Figure 3.3 compares, at the federal level, civilian employment and overall governmental expenditures. Between 1970 and 2004, government spending increased by over 400 percent, even holding inflation constant, but government employment grew only about 25 percent, with practically no significant growth in the last twenty-five years. This substantial growth in federal programs, occurring without comparable growth in federal employment, is explained by the fact that parties other than the federal government are actually conducting the programs and delivering the services. Federal money, for example, goes to private firms, such as defense contractors or banks that administer school loan programs, and to nonprofit organizations, especially those that provide human services such as care for the homeless or disabled.

FIGURE 3.3

Federal Spending and Payroll, 1970–2000 (in Billions of Dollars)

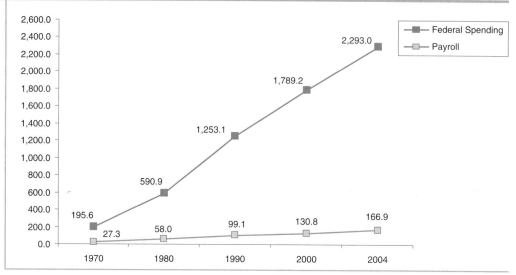

SOURCE (numbers): http://www.whitehouse.gov/omb/budget/fy2008/pdf/hist.pdf https://www.opm.gov/feddata/factbook/2005/factbook2005.pdf, (p.62)and https://www.opm.gov/feddata/factbook/2005/factbook2005.pdf, (p.62).

Much of the attention on NGOs tends to focus on the nonprofit sector, which we will discuss later in this chapter, but for-profits also deserve attention. Traditionally, business was seen as the antithesis to government, with clear boundaries between the public and private sectors. Today, we have experienced a significant blurring between sector lines, with only vague distinctions between for-profit firms and government agencies. Such involvement of private-sector firms in public programs, of course, isn't completely new. Defense and aerospace companies have contracted with government for decades, and for-profit prisons were actually the norm in the nineteenth century. In fact, many of our technological innovations stem from public-private partnerships. Increasingly, though, these partnerships can be found in areas once viewed as purely public in nature, including health and human services, trash collection, education, environmental protection, and parks and recreation (Rosenau 2000; Sagawa & Segal 2000).

Governments have entered into public-private partnerships to conserve revenues, to reduce crime in blighted areas, and to promote economic growth. We mentioned previously the partnership between Sunnyvale, California, and other municipalities with the Microsoft Corporation to create online permitting software. Other examples include an alliance between the city of Daytona Beach, Florida, and a private development firm to renovate a dilapidated boardwalk and build a beachfront hotel; a partnership between the state of Michigan and other states for correctional services; and relationships across the country between school districts and private computer firms to bring public school classrooms into the information age. In each case, the interorganizational relationships that arise are important to the success or failure of public programs.

Privatization and Contracting

The movement toward greater involvement of NGOs in the delivery of public services is partly ideological. Some people simply feel that services should be provided by those outside government wherever possible. But the movement has also been stimulated by recent restrictions on government spending and a resulting effort to find more efficient ways to conduct the public's business. Both motives have been discussed under the heading *privatization*—the use of NGOs to provide goods or services previously provided by government. It is important to be clear about its various meanings because the term is used several different ways (Kolderie 1986).

In its broader sense, privatization refers to efforts to remove government from any involvement in either the design or conduct of a particular service. In Great Britain, for example, major industries such as steel or coal, once nationalized, are returning to private control, typically through direct sales to individuals, firms, or other groups. In the United States, most such major industries, including most utilities, are already in private hands, so there are relatively few examples of such magnitude (the sale of Conrail and certain petroleum reserves are exceptions). There are many more limited examples of privatization, however; a city might, for example, sell a golf course to a country club development, thus ending the government's involvement in golf.

The rationale for removing government from a particular area varies. In some cases, people may feel that clients will receive more personal attention from a nongovernmental or private group, such as one that operates a drug abuse program or a day-care center. Others suggest that privatization enhances competition among service providers, thus ensuring that the new means of delivering services will provide higher quality at a lower cost to the client. Programs also can be turned over to the private sector because the programs seem inappropriate to government or because the private firm operates more efficiently.

NETWORKING

To trace some innovative practices in government, check out the Alliance for Innovation at http://transformgov.org and the Ash Institute for Democratic Governance and Innovation at Harvard University's Kennedy School of Government program at www.ashinstitute.harvard.edu/Ash/index.htm. For innovations in nonprofit organizations, see the Leader to Leader Institute at www.pfdf.org.

Privatization is used in a more narrow sense (and more frequently) to refer to various devices through which a government retains a policy role regarding a particular service but engages someone else to actually deliver the service. A federal agency might decide to contract with a private firm rather than handle computer programming itself; a state might contract with a nonprofit organization to deliver services to welfare recipients; or a local government might lease a public hospital to a private firm. In each case, the services would be spelled out in detail by the government and some, if not all, funding might be provided, but day-to-day operation of the program would be the responsibility of the for-profit or nonprofit agency.

During the past decade, government at all levels has explored a variety of mechanisms for privatizing public services, the most popular being the use of *contracting* (see Box 3.4). Supporters view fee-for-service and similar arrangements with NGOs as a more efficient method of service delivery, given the greater flexibility, different labor costs, and economies of scale offered by for-profit and nonprofit organizations. Some of the most publicized examples of contracting in recent years have been in human services, because the federal government shifted to state and local authorities (and in turn to NGOs) a larger role in the nation's welfare system under the Personal Responsibility and Work Opportunity Reconciliation Act of 1996.

In the city of West Palm Beach, Florida, the local Work and Gain Economic Self-sufficiency (WAGES) board, the public-private partnership that oversees implementation of welfare reform in regions statewide, invested $6.2 million on welfare-to-work programs in fiscal year 1998–1999. The WAGES Board contracted with Lockheed Martin IMS, a subsidiary of the aviation-aerospace giant, to run the programs, and in a short period reduced the number of welfare cases by 45 percent. Advocates say the for-profit firm was able to be more innovative than government agencies in its hiring and development of service systems, and in the future the WAGES Board intends to examine ways to use privatization to streamline even the determination of program eligibility (Walters 2000, pp. 34–35).

The state of Kansas used contracts to hand over most of its child welfare services to the private sector. Several years ago, government officials recognized that the state's foster care, adoption, and related programs simply had to change. "We had a failed child welfare system in this state," said State Rep. Melvin Neufeld, who played a key part in drafting the reform legislation. Excessive costs and declining effectiveness on the part of government agencies,

BOX 3.4
TAKING CONTRACTING SERIOUSLY

A government that took contract management seriously would
- Regard resources required to manage contracts as part of the cost of contracting, funded from cost savings and performance improvements they are likely to produce.
- Train contracting people, especially those developing contract requirements and doing contract management, in selection and use of performance measures for contracts.
- Take evaluation of contractor past performance seriously, as a method for incentivizing good performance, particularly for complex "relational" contracts where there is a danger the contractor will exploit the government post-award.
- Look for ways to hire relatively young "doers" (such as software programmers, bench engineers) from industry to do stints as contract managers, to give government the technical expertise to manage technical contracts in situations where the government has few "doers" itself.
- Reconceptualize—in terms of training and self-image—contract management as a high-level management job.

SOURCE: Steven Kelman, "Reflections on 21st Century Government Management," *IBM Center for The Business of Government* (2008 Presidential Transition Series), "What Might the Next Decade's Trends Be" (If We Get to Focus on Performance)?, p. 45, www.businessofgovernment.org/pdfs/KettlKelmanReport.pdf.

coupled with newly elected conservative state leadership, prompted state officials to shift virtually the entire system of service delivery over to NGOs, mostly for-profit firms. Under the new system, state government contracts with lead agencies at a regional level, which in turn subcontract with NGOs to handle actual service delivery. State officials act mainly to administer the contracts and ensure standards for service quality (Gurwitt 2000, p. 40).

As these cases may suggest, privatization has transformed public welfare into a major growth industry. Maximus, Lockheed Martin IMS, and other for-profit corporations have capitalized on the new arrangements to expand their business operations. The Lockheed Martin IMS story is particularly interesting because it also reflects changing priorities in public policy in the aftermath of the cold war. As the number of defense contracts dwindled during the 1980s and 1990s, Lockheed Martin IMS picked up the slack in its parent company's defense-related operations by contracting for delivery and administration of welfare services. The strategy has proven to be quite a success. Lockheed Martin IMS has experienced a significant jump in the number of government clients, from 0 to 25, since the passage of welfare reform in 1996.

But privatization of human services has its challenges. Even as supporters point to Kansas and Florida as success stories, a closer look reveals major problems relating to sustainability. Next door to its thriving effort in West Palm Beach, Lockheed Martin IMS struggled in Miami-Dade County. The company's costs exceeded $38 million in the same fiscal year, but failed to make a significant impact on caseloads. In fact, the county government has since handed the contract for welfare-to-work services over to a local community college (Walters 2000, p. 35).

In Kansas, the state's transformation of child and family services has come under attack not only from liberal critics, who argue that public welfare should not be left up to firms whose primary motive is profit, but also from the businesses themselves. *Governing* magazine reported that "Kansas's story isn't really about *privatization*: It's about a rushed, no-holds-barred effort to build a public-private social services system using managed-care principles, as well as its struggle to recover from the fallout" (Gurwitt 2000, p. 40). What was the fallout? State officials have been forced to pick up the pieces from what can only be considered a managed-care revolution. Unlike other states, Kansas bypassed smaller scale, experimental initiatives, choosing instead sweeping reforms. The change inside the state resulted in confusion, as state officials struggled to learn new roles as contract managers rather than caregivers. For private firms, the reforms opened a floodgate on newly created service networks, swamping many businesses that simply did not have the expertise or capacity to deal with the demands of public welfare programs.

Contracts used to provide public services certainly have promise; however, as the Kansas example has shown, building effective alliances with NGOs must not be taken for granted. Nor should contracts be seen as the only mechanism. There are a variety of options for partnering with NGOs. A *franchise* can be awarded to a private firm to perform a certain service within a state or locality. The firm charges citizens directly for the services it provides. Typically, rates and performance standards are established by the government, and there is often some continuing regulation of the firm. Examples include electric power, taxi services, cable television, and emergency ambulance services. Similarly, governments may provide *grants* or *subsidies* to private or nonprofit organizations that are performing needed public services. The government provides full or partial support for activities that will benefit the community but that the local government, for financial or other reasons, does not wish to operate on its own. Examples include local government support for the arts, child care, or shelter for the homeless.

All levels of government have experimented with the use of *vouchers*, which are coupons citizens redeem for goods or services. The federal food stamp program, for example, provides recipients with vouchers to purchase food, but it permits the individual to choose both the supplier and the items to be purchased (within stated limits).

At the local level, many jurisdictions have explored the use of vouchers for education. But although proponents suggest it would lead to more effective, efficient options than the public schools, the issue has become one of the most controversial topics in current education policy.

Increased privatization means that public officials need to be attentive to the process of contracting for services. In the words of Ruben Berrios (2006), "The government purchases the expertise of private firms to provide services. The goal is to create a more effective and efficient delivery through a system that fosters and creates competition, provides better management, and helps reduce the size of the government" (p.119). Although government contracts are not new, they create the new relations between government organizations and private or nonprofit organizations. Cooper (2003) describes a shift from the traditional authority-based relations (vertical model) as in regulatory enforcement to negotiation relations (horizontal model) in today's public contract relationships.

The vertical model is about authority relationships: the way that decisions get from the democratically appointed executives and down through agencies to the contracting officer who is ultimately authorized to negotiate for the needs of the community and then to commit its resources in a legally binding relationship. . . . The second model comes into play once the decision to contract for goods or services has been made and operates in tandem with the vertical model. . . contractual relationships are horizontal in character and operate from the base of mutual commitment in which, theoretically at least, the parties are equal. (Cooper 2003, p. 48).

Recent trends with government contracting refer to so-called public/private partnerships, where the term "partnership" indicates more than cooperation. These partnerships may include long-term agreements for activities that are inherently considered governmental, such as commercial operation of prisons, or including contractors in rule-making policy procedures (Cooper 2003, p. 57). Public/private partnerships and alliances operate between government agencies and for-profit companies and between government agencies and nonprofit organizations. Nonprofit organizations are a convenient choice for governments for at least two reasons: they are often fervently committed to providing assistance for people in need, and they have close relations with the communities. In addition, volunteers in these organizations often deliver public services for lower costs than if these services were provided by government agencies. However, government grants to nonprofit organizations impose additional administrative requirements for these organizations, frequently requiring more resources and paid personnel.

While public/private partnerships and alliances may provide better services for lower costs, they present a huge challenge for government officials. When entering a partnership with a for-profit company, public managers should be aware that these companies operate for making profit. "Whatever else is promised, the most common way in which for-profit firms seek to make money on government contracts for the same amount of money government is spending now to do the job itself, is to reduce personnel costs" (Cooper 2003, p. 63). There are also moral issues related to government contracting. Berrios (2006) talks about some flaws that complement the contracting process: favoritism for companies that already have contracts with the government, preferences for large firms over small firms, and corrupt behavior of the government officials that in some instances grant contracts to private companies without following legal requirements. Finally, where government programs are run directly by government, responsibility for their success lies squarely with the government agency. But where such programs are actually delivered by those in the private or nonprofit sector, traditional mechanisms for control and account-ability may not work. Maintaining a proper concern for democratic values such as equity and responsiveness may, in the long run, prove more difficult than the managerial chal-lenges of creating appropriate interorganizational policy networks.

■ The Management of Nonprofit Organizations

As we have seen, nongovernmental organizations have become important players in public policy and administration. Unfortunately, many public administrators fail to appreciate the distinct challenges faced by these organizations, especially in the nonprofit sector. In order to develop more effective interorganizational, cross-sector relations, it may be help-ful to identify some of the key elements of organizational capacity within nonprofits.

Operational Leadership

Nonprofit management begins with effective leadership. By leadership, we mean an organi-zation's internal systems for establishing a mission and vision to guide organizational action, for engaging in strategy-making and planning as a way of setting goals and objectives, and for developing an operational structure to facilitate the translation of strategy into action.

Creating effective leadership systems in nonprofits starts with forging a sound mission and vision. The mission represents the purpose the organization will serve in its commu-nity. This vision is the guiding image of what members want the organization to become in the future (Bryson 1995; Smith, Bucklin & Associates 2000). Although these factors are critical in virtually all organizations, they are especially important in nonprofits. Indepen-dent sector groups depend on a lot more than paid staff to carry out organizational objec-tives, including volunteers, donors, board members, and other resources. Without a strong sense of purpose, or a clear vision for the future, nonprofit leaders will find it extremely difficult to build the "critical mass" necessary for success.

Of course, setting a mission and vision must be combined with sound planning—in par-ticular, establishing clear, measurable goals and objectives. A recent survey of nonprofits found that the "level of support and commitment to planning by the leadership of the orga-nization is . . . a crucial element in an assessment of organizational capacity. If management neither plans nor possesses the support systems needed to enable planning (such as budget-ing systems, planning models, information about past organizational experiences), then the issue of capacity is largely moot. Organizational survival generally requires planning and the development of a shared vision and goals" (Fredericksen & London 2000, pp. 234–235).

NETWORKING

To explore some of the aspects of nonprofit management, go to the Aspen Institute at www.aspeninstitute.org; the Hauser Center for Nonprofit Organizations at Harvard University at www.ksghauser.harvard.edu; and the Institute for Not-for-Profit Management at Columbia University at www.gsb.columbia.edu/execed/inm/index.cfm. See Chapter 2 for a list of sites relating to the advocacy role of nonprofit organizations.

Leadership also involves building a solid organizational foundation that allows nonprofits to transform their strategy into action. For those working in the charitable sector, this often proves to be the most difficult task. Most nonprofits begin with an idea, which translates very well into mission and vision. Things get much tougher, though, in trying to turn the idea into an organizational reality.

In fact, one of the biggest challenges confronting today's nonprofits involves creating effective, high-capacity systems of operation. Much of this stems from an unwillingness on the part of government and foundation grant-makers to provide funding for administrative costs. Nonprofit agencies could gain access to resources for programming and service delivery, but they struggled to find support for the basics of management: staff, equipment, technology, and related expenses. Fortunately, foundations have begun to realize that although restricting funding to program-related needs sounds good, it's impossible to deliver quality services without a well-developed administrative structure (Greene 2001).

Resource Development

Speaking of financial support, resource development represents another key element of nonprofit management. Agencies in the independent sector receive their funding from a variety of sources, including fees and charges, government grants-in-aid, and private giving. According to the National Center for Charitable Statistics, of some 1.4 million nonprofit organizations registered with IRS, nearly half have collected more than $25,000 in gross receipts. They reported more than $299 billion in revenues in charitable contributions during 2004, with 83 percent from individual contributions, 11 percent from private foundations, and 5 percent from corporations (*The Nonprofit Sector in Brief—Facts and Figures from the Nonprofit Almanac 2007*. . . Center on Nonprofits and Philanthropy at the Urban Institute, p.5, www.urban.org/UploadedPDF/311373_nonprofit_sector.pdf).

These figures don't include funding from fees and government grants, which make up an additional $400 billion. With such a diverse revenue base, it might seem strange that a primary weakness of nonprofits (especially the smaller organizations) is to rely on a single source of support, and not look beyond the next grant cycle for their funding. Successful nonprofits, on the other hand, diversify their revenue streams, balancing between grants, fees-for-service, and other sources.

Nonprofit organizations that are classified as either a public charity or private foundation under IRC 501(c)(3) benefit from their tax-exempt status, which allows taxpayers to deduct contributions as charitable donations. Some nonprofits also may receive discounts on postal rates, special provisions for financing, as well as various exemptions from state and local taxes.

To assure sustainability, many nonprofits and their associations have developed innovative strategies for maintaining a sound financial base for the next generation. For example, the National Committee on Planned Giving has initiated the Leave a Legacy program, a nationwide effort to encourage people of all socioeconomic groups to include charitable contributions as part of their estates. The program in large part aims at attracting charitable contributions from the "baby-boomer" generation, which over the next few decades will retire with unprecedented wealth. An important element of Leave a Legacy is its community-based focus—that is, a single organization cannot adopt the program, but instead the program brings together nonprofits from around a given community. Prospective donors are asked to work directly with the planned giving officers of the foundations or with estate planners to decide upon a charitable beneficiary.

As any nonprofit manager will tell you, resource development goes well beyond grants and other types of financial contributions. Although most people recognize the challenge nonprofits face in competing for donors, few appreciate the level of competition for other vital resources, such as in-kind support and volunteerism. Although charitable giving certainly remains central to a nonprofit organization's balance sheet, more and more nonprofits depend on in-kind contributions and the time, energy, and expertise of volunteers to meet their objectives. A study conducted by the Independent Sector found that while charitable giving by individuals had declined in recent years, more Americans were volunteering than ever before. In 2004, about 65 million volunteered in charitable organizations (http://www.urban.org/UploadedPDF/311373_nonprofit_sector.pdf).

Keys for successful resource development include being able to articulate a case for your organization, exploring a diverse array of support, identifying an appropriate development strategy and action plan, and ensuring effective implementation of the action plan. Most importantly, at the heart of the resource development strategy must be a commitment to building and maintaining relationships with funders, donors, and volunteers (Smith, Bucklin & Associates 2000).

Financial Management

Running a nonprofit also depends on sound financial management. The benefits of being a charitable organization were discussed previously, but with these benefits come important requirements for accounting and public disclosure of financial transactions. For example, all 501(c)(3) organizations must maintain open records and prepare financial reports for their stakeholders on a periodic basis. Many foundations and other grant makers ask grant recipients to undergo periodic audits, sometimes as an eligibility requirement. And charitable organizations with annual gross receipts of $25,000 or more must submit to the IRS each year a Form 990 (Return of Organizations Exempt from Income Tax), as well as file disclosure statements with state and local tax authorities.

To satisfy these requirements, nonprofits must maintain detailed financial records. At the very least, this includes following basic accounting standards and procedures. But financial management includes much more than reporting. It should be at the heart of a nonprofit's strategic planning and management. Without the ability to generate clear, meaningful financial information, and incorporate this information into organizational decision making, a nonprofit agency limits its overall capacity. Unfortunately, many nonprofits fail to follow established procedures, and some do not have in place even the simplest mechanisms for accounting. Small- to medium-sized nonprofits have the greatest need in this area.

The basics of financial management include monitoring the assets, liabilities, and net assets of the organization, as well as the revenues and expenses for established reporting periods. Moreover, nonprofit managers should make sure that the budget and financial management process is undertaken in coordination with the governing board. In many cases, such coordination is mandated in the articles of incorporation, but it also makes sense to have those responsible for setting the strategic direction informed on the organization's financial condition.

Board Governance

Most of the principles of nonprofit management discussed here have focused on the operational side of the organization. However, independent-sector agencies also must have an effective governance system. Nonprofit boards are, in some respects, even more vital to the organization than to the staff, because some smaller agencies rely on board members for performing day-to-day tasks. Regardless of an agency's size, its board represents the final decision-making body of the organization. By law, board members are bound (in the articles of incorporation) to ensure the fiscal and legal health of the agency.

The board is responsible for several important roles. These include setting the strategic direction for the organization, serving as champions in the external community, and overseeing organizational planning and implementation (Carver 1996). First, with regard to strategic direction, board members act as the primary source of vision, mission, and values for the agency. They ensure that these strategic factors become reflected in organizational action. An excellent example of this can be seen in Porter Hills Retirement Communities and Services, a nonprofit health-care provider in Grand Rapids, Michigan. The Executive Leadership Team at Porter Hills actually brings the outline of the Porter Hills mission, vision, and values into its strategy sessions and considers these principles prior to moving ahead on decisions. If a new venture, partnership, or internal change does not reflect the core principles of the organization, or doesn't coincide with where the board wants to be in the future, then the issue is either dropped or taken back to the board for direction.

Second, board members also must be the organization's champions in the community. They are the principal spokespeople, representing the organization on key issues, but also the role models for donations and volunteerism. In this capacity, the board should set the policies and procedures for the operational staff and leadership on strategies for external communication. Board members, consequently, must always be kept "in the loop" on factors affecting the organization.

A vital point here is that the board must speak with one voice, or it shouldn't speak at all. This means that board members should support decisions of the governance body once a consensus has been achieved. Too often, and particularly with smaller, community-based organizations, members of nonprofit boards go into the community and speak against other members or against the organization. This does nothing but send a signal to those listening that the disgruntled board member has failed to appreciate the core values of governance.

Third, the board must support the organization's leadership on issues of planning and implementation. The board should make sure that the organization has an effective and ongoing planning process and work with staff to establish priorities and goals. This doesn't mean that board members should try to manage day-to-day activities on the part of the staff. It does mean, though, that those on the operational side of the organization should coordinate and seek direction from the board on issues that are truly strategic in nature.

Nonprofit boards vary in size with some organizations having fewer than ten, and others having more than fifty members (which is toward the extreme!). The composition of the board will reflect the history and mission of the organization, but most nonprofits strive to ensure that the governance system will reflect the diversity and values of the constituent community. Here are a few of the considerations relating to board size.

- What functions are required of the board?
- How many individuals, and in what roles, are needed to accomplish those functions?
- How many board committees are needed to accomplish the organization's goals?
- Are there sufficient individuals on the board to participate on board committees? (Smith, Bucklin & Associates 2000, p. 29)

A primary source of failure for nonprofit boards relates to the leadership's inability to manage the board's time wisely. Most often the greatest inefficiency happens at board meetings. How many hour-and-a-half meetings have turned into three-hour marathons? Agenda setting is a valuable beginning point, but also the presiding officer must set clear time constraints for each of the agenda items, making sure that everyone has the opportunity to participate when necessary but limiting comment to only the key points.

Boards are perhaps one of the most important attributes for effective nonprofit management. A high-impact board with an effective board chairperson can have an extraordinary influence on the organization's success. Unfortunately, the opposite is also true. Many a good nonprofit has been severely limited, and in some cases completely destroyed, due to an ineffective, divisive board.

Board-Staff Relations

Among the greatest challenges faced by nonprofits is the need to strike a balance in board staff relations. As the previous discussion suggested, board members have a central role to play in the organization's strategy making and in representing the organization in the external community. However, once the parameters for action have been established, board members must step back and allow staff adequate room to achieve the goals and objectives. Frequently, boards (especially those consisting of inexperienced members) tend to micromanage the operational staff. But this does little more than foster distrust and frustration, and, in many cases, it contributes to high staff turnover.

There are several keys to effective relationships. First, the board must set clear expectations for leadership and staff. At least once a year, board members should sit down with the executive director and lay out the goals and objectives for the coming term. Second, the expectations must be reinforced by lines of communication between board and staff. Communication channels should be maintained by the executive director, and in some rare events directly between the board and staff. Third, the board must reinforce success. As part of its oversight function, the governing board should be ready to celebrate the good work being done, not just sanction the shortcomings.

In many respects, the primary buffer between the board and staff is the executive director (ED). Although some EDs position themselves in ways that cut off the governance and operational sides of the agency, with very little direct involvement between board members and staff, this takes things a bit too far. The most effective relationships feature EDs as the main conduits or brokers. Staff should be present, when appropriate, at board meetings, mainly to offer expertise and inform the board on key decisions; similarly, the board must provide oversight and guidance to the staff on key issues of agency strategy. How far to go on either side will depend on the organization, but it's up to the executive director and members of the leadership team to determine the appropriate balance.

Advocacy   The advocacy role of independent-sector organizations is perhaps the most overlooked and misunderstood aspect of nonprofit management. This stems from the fact that the federal tax code limits lobbying activities by charitable organizations and, depending on the party affiliation or political position, some legislators and policy makers have frowned upon nonprofit activism. But nonprofit organizations may, even under federal tax law, engage in advocacy as a way of amplifying the voice of their constituents in the policy process.

In 1976, Congress granted nonprofits the right to lobby in the public interest without having to worry about losing their status as tax-exempt organizations (Pub. L. No. 94–455, 1307 [1976]). While the IRS deliberated on the issue for more than a decade, in 1990 the federal tax code was revised to expand the advocacy rights of nonprofits. Under the 1976 tax law, nonprofits that choose to come under its jurisdiction must comply with the definition of lobbying as "the expenditure of money by the organization for the purpose of attempting to influence legislation. Where there is no expenditure by the organization for lobbying, there is no lobbying by the organization" (Smucker 1999, p. 51).

The tax law establishes two types of lobbying: *direct* and *grassroots*. In direct lobbying the organization communicates with legislators or other public officials on matters concerning legislation in which they have a role to play or with the nonprofit organization's own membership. In grassroots lobbying, the organization influences the legislative process by attempting to sway public opinion on policy issues.

The tax law also establishes ceilings for expenditures that may be allocated to lobbying, based on the total level of tax-exempt expenditures for the organization. A nonprofit with annual expenses of up to $500,000, for example, may allocate 20 percent of these expenses for lobbying activities, whereas an organization with tax-exempt expenditures of over $17 million may spend a total of $1 million for lobbying (Smucker 1999, p. 55).

We should point out that many activities by nonprofits, and even a wide array of expenditures that may be connected with the legislative or public policy process, are not considered "lobbying" under the 1976 law. For instance, using contacts with officials in the executive branch to influence proposed legislation; communicating to members of the organization—as long as they are not encouraged to lobby—even if the organization itself takes a certain position; and advocating legislators on issues that affect the existence, tax-exempt status, or other aspects of operations (the so-called "self-defense" activity) would not be viewed as lobbying on the part of the nonprofit.

The right of nonprofits to lobby in the public interest was reinforced by the Supreme Court in *Legal Services Corp. v. Velazquez* (2001). At issue in the case were provisions in the 1996 welfare reform law, which attempted to prohibit legal challenges to the reform legislation from local organizations funded by the Legal Services Corporation. The Court struck down these provisions, stating that because Congress allowed Legal Services Corporation lawyers to advocate for the poor on some matters, federal lawmakers could not deprive a Legal Services client of his or her rights to a full and complete legal defense, which might well happen if a lawyer couldn't challenge the legitimacy of the welfare law (Lenkowsky 2001, p. 40). The ruling has been viewed by many in the nonprofit community as a potential expansion in the capability of independent-sector organizations, even those that receive federal funding, to advocate for their constituents on legislative issues.

For others, however, the ruling may have the opposite effect. In its analysis of the decision, the *Chronicle of Philanthropy* characterized *Velazquez* as a Pyrrhic victory, stating that although the ruling may have some positive impact on the advocacy role of nonprofits, it also reaffirmed the Court's decision in *Rust v. Sullivan* (1991), in which employees of NGOs that receive federal funding were held to be agents of the government. They forfeit their First Amendment rights to free speech by agreeing to accept the federal grants and contracts (Lenkowsky 2000, p. 40).

As future nonprofit managers, you should take caution to explore the legal constraints before engaging in lobbying activities, but by no means should you shy away from attempting to influence policy decision making on behalf of your constituents. The law is on your side, and you certainly will have greater protection than you may have originally thought for lobbying without fear of threatening your organization's tax-exempt status.

■ Summary and Action Implications

Given the complexity of modern society, your work as a public administrator will likely involve a complex set of relationships with all kinds of external groups. Many of these groups will be agencies at other levels of government. Our federal system has evolved from a pattern in which the various levels of government were relatively distinct to a pattern in which funding and programmatic relationships are extremely intense.

The fact that public programs today operate through vast and complex webs of people and organizations—public, private, and nonprofit—means that new skills are required of the public manager. Any particular program may involve various levels of government, organizations from all sectors of society, and clients or citizens with many different interests and concerns. As a public manager, you must be able to identify the network that is or should be involved in a particular situation and assess the effectiveness of that network.

To make that judgment, you will need to consider several factors. The first is *communications*, the type of information that goes from one organization to another and how it is transmitted. Second, you might focus on *exchanges* of goods and services, money, and personnel among the organizations involved. Third, you might examine the normative aspect of the relationship—that is, what each organization expects of the other and what each is willing to contribute to the alliance. Examining these same categories may also suggest ways to improve the effectiveness of interorganizational relationships.

The interorganizational nature of modern public administration also has interesting implications for the interpersonal skills you must bring to the job. Increasingly, the government official responsible for a given program must be skilled in negotiating relationships with those outside the agency to ensure that the program proceeds effectively and responsibly. More and more, the public administrator works in a world in which older images of organizational hierarchy and control are quickly giving way to newer images of "managing in ambiguity" and "negotiating organizational boundaries." The interorganizational nature of public administration today has a direct effect on what skills managers need.

TERMS AND DEFINITIONS

Block grants: Grants in which the money can be used for nearly any purpose within a specific functional field.

Capital grants: Grants for use in construction or renovation.

Categorical or project grants: Grants requiring that the money may be spent for only a limited purpose; typically available on a competitive basis.

Charter: Local government's equivalent of a constitution.

Cooperative federalism: Greater sharing of responsibilities between federal and state governments.

Coproduction: Using volunteer activity to supplement or supplant the work of government officials.

Councils of government: Oversight bodies representing various localities to help coordinate local affairs.

Cross-cutting requirements: Rules that apply to most grant programs.

Dillon's Rule: Municipalities have only those powers granted in their charters; cities are creatures of the state.

Direct orders: Requirements or restrictions that are enforced by one government over another.

Dual federalism: Pattern in which federal and state governments are struggling for power and influence with little intergovernmental cooperation.

Entitlement grants: Grants that provide assistance to persons who meet certain criteria.

Formula grants: Grants that employ a specific division rule to indicate how much money any given jurisdiction will receive.

Grants: Transfers of money (and/or property) from one government to another.

Home rule: Provision allowing cities greater autonomy over local activities.

Intergovernmental relations: A term encompassing all the complex and interdependent relations among those at various levels of government.

Interorganizational networks: Pattern of relationships within and among various groups and organizations working in a single policy area.

Mandate: Order requiring a government to do something.

Negotiated investment strategy: Bringing together representatives of all affected groups to set priorities for funding.

Operating grants: Grants for use in development and operation of specific programs.

Picket-fence federalism: Pattern of intergovernmental relations in which the horizontal bars represent levels of government and the vertical slats represent various substantive fields.

Preemption: Federal government efforts to preempt an area traditionally associated with state government.

Privatization: Use of nongovernmental agencies to provide goods and services previously provided by government.

Revenue sharing: Grant pattern in which the money can be used any way the recipient government chooses.

Special districts: Local governments created for a specific purpose within a specific area.

Supply-side economics: Argument that decreased taxes and spending will stimulate capital investment and economic growth.

STUDY QUESTIONS

1. Although intergovernmental relations involve more than financial matters, funding programs have a significant role in the process. Define and give examples of the various kinds of grants and funding programs.

2. Compare and contrast "dual federalism," "cooperative federalism," and "coercive federalism." Describe the approach to federalism used during the Clinton presidency.

3. In the last decade, states and localities have faced significant changes in funding from the federal government. Discuss the reasons for the changes and how they affect relations among the various levels.

4. How do governmental mandates and regulations affect operations at the state and local levels?

5. Government has been moving to "privatization" of some goods and services. How will this trend affect intergovernmental relations?

6. Explain the importance and use of contracting for services and goods.

CASES AND EXERCISES

1. Analyze the relationship between state and local governments in your state. What legal requirements govern state-local relationships? What, if any, bodies exist to help in intergovernmental cooperation? What kinds of mandates has the state imposed on local governments? What has been the reaction to these? How do you think state-local relations could be improved?

2. Divide the class into several groups of six to eight students each. Have one group assume the role of a granting agency charged, by legislation, with providing funds to local communities to help in projects that improve the economic potential of the community and assist low-income and disadvantaged groups in the community. Assume that the agency has $50 million to distribute, but that the legislation has given the granting agency the authority to determine all other details of the grant program.

   The agency group must first define as clearly as possible the intent of the legislation and then prepare guidelines outlining the types of projects that will be funded under the program. A written Request for Proposals (RFP) should then be prepared and distributed to a set of potential applicant communities, each represented by one of the other groups in the class. The RFP should contain, at a minimum, a description of the program, criteria by which proposals will be evaluated, examples of projects that might be funded, and instructions for submitting proposals for funding (including a deadline for applications).

Each community group will then prepare a grant application to support a project or projects it wants for its community. Members of each community group may communicate with one representative of the agency designated as liaison to that community, but should not talk with other agency members. Community groups can communicate with one another if they wish. By the deadline contained in the RFP, all proposals should be submitted to the agency. The agency will then determine which, if any, projects will be funded and at what levels. The results should be communicated to all the communities.

Following the exercise, the class as a whole should discuss the entire process. You might want to focus on issues such as these.

- What is the role of the agency in defining the kinds of projects that will be funded?
- What types of instructions are necessary to enable communities to compete fairly and effectively?
- What was most attractive about the proposals that were funded?
- For what reasons were other proposals not funded?
- What effect on the final decisions did communications between the community and the liaison from the agency have?
- Did "politics" play any role?

FOR ADDITIONAL READING

Bernstein, Susan R. *Managing Contracted Services in the Nonprofit Economy*. Philadelphia: Temple University Press, 1991.

Boris, Elizabeth T., and C. Eugene Steuerle. *Nonprofits and Government: Collaboration and Conflict*. Washington, DC: Urban Institute, 1999.

Cook, Brian J. *Bureaucracy and Self-Government*. Baltimore: Johns Hopkins University Press, 1996.

Cooper, Phillip J. *Governing by Contract*. Washington, DC: CQ Press, 2003.

Cooper, Phillip J., and Chester A. Newland. *Handbook of Public Law and Administration*. San Francisco: Jossey-Bass, 1997.

Cooper, Phillip J., et al. *Public Administration for the Twenty-First Century*. Fort Worth, TX: Harcourt Brace College Publishers, 1997.

Gage, Robert W., and Myrna P. Mandell, eds. *Strategies for Managing Intergovernmental Policies and Networks*. Westport, CT: Greenwood Press, 1990.

Goldsmith, Stephen, and William D. Eggers. *Governing by Network: The New Shape of the Public Sector*. Washington, DC: Brookings Institution Press, 2004.

Hill, Kim Quaile, and Kenneth R. Mladenka. *Democratic Governance in American States and Cities*. Pacific Grove, CA: Brooks/Cole, 1992.

Hill, Larry B., ed. *The State of Public Bureaucracy*. Armonk, NY: M. E. Sharpe, Inc., 1992.

Judd, Dennis R., and Todd Swanstrom. *City Politics: Private Power and Public Policy*. New York: HarperCollins College Publishers, 1994.

Katz, Michael B. *The Price of Citizenship: Redefining the American Welfare State*. New York: Metropolitan Books, 2001.

Kemp, Roger L., ed. *Privatization: The Provision of Public Services by the Private Sector*. Jefferson, NC: McFarland & Company, 1991.

Kettl, Donald F. *Government by Proxy.* Washington, DC: Congressional Quarterly Press, 1988.

Kettl, Donald F. *Sharing Power: Public Governance and Private Markets.* Washington DC: Brookings Institution Press, 1993.

Levin, Martin, and Mary Sanger. *Making Government Work.* San Francisco: Jossey-Bass, 1994.

Light, Paul C. *Sustaining Innovation: Creating Nonprofit and Government Organizations that Innovate Naturally.* San Francisco: Jossey-Bass, 1998.

Light, Paul C. *Making Nonprofits Work: A Report on the Tides of Nonprofit Management Reform.* Washington, DC: Brookings Institution Press, 2000.

McLaughlin, Curtis. *The Management of Nonprofit Organizations.* New York: Wiley, 1986.

National Academy of Public Administration. *Privatization: The Challenge to Public Management.* Washington, DC: National Academy, 1989.

Nice, David C. *Federalism: The Politics of Intergovernmental Relations.* New York: St. Martin's Press, 1987.

Peirce, Neal R., Curtis Johnson, and John Stuart Hall. *Citistates: How Urban America Can Prosper in a Competitive World.* Washington, DC: Seven Locks Press, 1993.

Peterson, Paul. *The Price of Federalism.* Washington, DC: Brookings Institution Press, 1995.

Rivlin, Alice M. *Reviving the American Dream: The Economy, the States, and the Federal Government.* Washington, DC: Brookings Institution Press, 1992.

Rosenbloom, David H. *Building a Legislative-Centered Public Administration: Congress and the Administrative State, 1946–1999.* Tuscaloosa, AL: University of Alabama Press, 2000.

Rusk, David. *Cities without Suburbs.* Baltimore: Johns Hopkins University Press, 1993.

Salamon, Lester M., ed. *Beyond Privatization.* Washington, DC: Urban Institute Press, 1989.

Salamon, Lester M. *Partners in Public Service: Government-Nonprofit Relations in the Modern Welfare State.* Baltimore: Johns Hopkins University Press, 1995.

Smith, Steven Ragbeth, and Michael Lipsky. *Nonprofits for Hire: The Welfare State in the Age of Contracting.* Cambridge, MA: Harvard University Press, 1993.

Vincent-Jones, Peter. *The New Public Contracting: Regulation, Responsiveness, Relationality.* New York: Oxford University Press, 2006.

CHAPTER 4

THE ETHICS OF PUBLIC SERVICE

So far we have focused on the context of public administration—the values, structures, and relationships you need to act effectively and responsibly in public organizations. Now we begin a transition to more skill-based issues by exploring the ethical issues raised in public service. An ethical posture toward work in public organizations requires not only knowing the right answers, but also being willing and able to do what is right. You must be prepared to act.

As a public manager, you will often face difficult ethical choices. These choices may present themselves in several ways. "It is certainly true that in many administrative ethics dilemmas, multiple rationales for action can be considered. It is also true there is no science or set of fixed rules for resolving the dilemmas. Without question, ethical tensions are inevitable" (Goodsell, 2006, p. 136). Understanding the moral implications of your actions and resolving the dilemmas they pose is one of the most difficult problems you will face working in the public sector. Consequently, your ability to understand the context in which public problems arise and to work them out in a careful, reasoned, and ethical fashion will be essential to your success (and your own sense of personal well-being).

In this chapter, we examine a variety of ethical issues faced by public managers. Some involve concerns that might arise in any organization—cases of lying, cheating, or stealing, or questions about what to do when you feel compelled to refuse an order from your boss. Others are more directly connected to the special values that underlie public service, involving the relationship between political leaders and career civil servants or between competing demands for efficiency and responsiveness.

■ Approaches to Ethical Deliberation

Recall that ethics is a branch of philosophy concerned with the study of moral principles and action. To properly define *ethics*, therefore, we must first understand the meaning of morality. *Morality* is concerned with those practices and activities that are considered right or wrong; it is also concerned with the values those practices reflect and the rules through which they are carried out. The morality of a society, a political system, or a public organization concerns what is considered to be right or wrong within that group. Morality expresses certain values that members of the group hold to be important and is reflected in laws, rules, and regulations, or in policies and procedures. Moral action, in turn, is action that is consistent with the group's morality—that which expresses the group's most basic commitments about what is right and what is wrong.

Ethics, on the other hand, can be defined as "a systematic attempt through the use of reason to make sense of our individual and social moral experience in such a way as to determine the rules which ought to govern human conduct" (DeGeorge, 1982, p. 12). Ethics is concerned with the process by which we clarify what is right and wrong and by which we act on what we take to be right; ethics involves the use of reason in determining a proper course of action. Ethics is the search for moral standards.

Though we have defined ethics as the study of morality, the two terms are often used interchangeably. For example, we often call an action that is morally correct an ethical action. Similarly, we speak of codes of moral conduct as codes of ethics. Despite the overlapping uses of the terms, the distinction between morality and ethics is important not only for philosophical reasons, but because focusing on ethics emphasizes the individual's active involvement in searching out morally correct positions. Ethics calls us into action; it requires us to reason, to analyze, and to seek guidance as to the proper course of action.

This deliberative aspect of ethics is important because the issues you will face in public organizations are rarely black or white. Should you lie to a legislator so as to carry out a policy you think is correct? Should you bend the rules to benefit a client in need? Should you follow orders from an organizational superior even if you know you are being asked to do something wrong? These questions and the thousands of others you may encounter in public organizations don't have easy answers. To act properly, you must be able to sort through the many and often competing values that underlie your work, and you must be able to come to a reasoned conclusion that will form the basis for action.

It's not enough to simply say, "It depends," and then go about your business, though such a position has gained widespread currency in our society. *Ethical (or moral) relativism* is the belief that actions that are immoral in some places or circumstances are moral in others and that one can make moral judgments only by taking into account the context in which an action occurs. According to this view, there are no universal rules of conduct that apply in all situations. A defense of the relativist position is that different cultures have different rules of conduct. One culture may consider it proper to leave elderly people to die in solitude, whereas another may give them considerable care and attention.

Such arguments, however, often fail to take into account larger and more unifying moral principles, such as respect for the elderly. Furthermore, the relativist position seems at odds with our moral experience. When we make the judgment that murder is immoral, we don't mean that it is immoral for some individuals and not others. We don't even mean that murder is immoral in some countries and not in others. We claim that murder is immoral for all people at all times—and we can defend our statement on both rational and emotional grounds. This position suggests that there is only one right answer to moral questions, (even though that answer may be hard to find!). Nevertheless, by understanding the context in which an action occurs, working through the various arguments in behalf of one position or another, and arriving at a set of guidelines for action, one can at least act with greater clarity and confidence.

What are the steps in ethical deliberation? First, you should attempt to *clarify the facts*. Although most ethical issues involve both facts and values, and the facts alone are not likely to resolve the issue, it is important to establish the facts as clearly as possible. A pollution control policy may require precise measurements of pollutants released into the air; knowing the exact measurements, rather than speculating about them, may resolve the issue. In other cases, merely clarifying the facts will help resolve certain ethical problems.

Second, it is easier to resolve ethical issues if those involved come to *some agreement about basic principles*. These may be broad moral standards (such as freedom or justice), laws or rules accepted by society, or standards of behavior appropriate to a particular group or organization. These ideas are, of course, deeply held by members of any society or organization, so disagreements may be marked. For example, two detectives may have dramatically different views about how to treat criminals, but if they clarify their agreement on the basic goal of fighting crime, they may be able to reconcile their differences. Generally speaking, any progress you can make in establishing a common ground or in bringing about agreement on basic principles will help resolve the issue.

Third, one of the central aspects of ethical deliberation is the *analysis of arguments* presented in behalf of various viewpoints. The arguments may be articulated by different individuals or different groups, or they may simply be arguments and counterarguments you think through yourself. In either case, you will need to consider the evidence presented, the justifications for various viewpoints, and possible fallacies of the justifications. Throughout the process of argumentation, dialogue is extremely helpful in clarifying one's position. (If the problem is one you are considering alone, finding someone to talk through the issues with you is a good idea.) Ultimately, however, you will need to make a decision and act on it. Ethical deliberation will lead you to a decision, but acting in a way that is consistent with that decision is also important, though often difficult.

Reasoning, Development, and Action

You will be better prepared to deliberate if you become familiar with some basic approaches to ethical reasoning: moral philosophy, moral psychology, and moral action. In each case, we will present only a brief overview. You should be aware that there are varying and sometimes conflicting interpretations of these issues, and you may find others (perhaps including your teacher) who disagree with the formulation presented here. Consider this material merely an invitation for further learning!

Moral Philosophy   Regarding *moral philosophy*, we can ask: given a particular set of circumstances, how do we determine what is right and what is wrong? In other words, how do we go about figuring out the proper course of action? One approach is to consider who will benefit and who will suffer from various alternative actions, then ask which course of action provides the greatest benefit at the least cost. Another approach is to search for a moral principle or rule against which to measure aspects of the particular case. In the first approach, one focuses on the consequences of the action; in the second, one looks for universal rules of conduct.

One of the most common forms of ethical deliberation, which focuses on the consequences of actions, is *utilitarianism*. Utilitarianism holds that an action is right, compared to other courses of action, if it results in the greatest good (or at least the minimum harm) for the greatest number of people. Proponents of this view contend that there are no universal principles guiding action, but rather the likely benefits and costs associated with any action must be calculated to judge the action either moral or immoral.

Obviously, this view leans toward relativism; according to a utilitarian, telling the truth cannot be judged a priori either right or wrong. Rather, the rightness or wrongness of telling the truth depends on a calculation of who is helped and who is harmed. Only then can a moral judgment be rendered. In the utilitarian view, "Actions themselves have no intrinsic values. They are simply means to attain things which do have value" (DeGeorge, 1982, p. 40).

An administrator employing a utilitarian approach to moral reasoning in a specific situation would ask what the likely outcomes of one course of action or another might be. If building a new highway through a particular neighborhood would inconvenience a few people but benefit many others, then building that highway in that location would be considered a proper course of action. The administrator would not follow any predetermined moral principle (such as that citizens should not be arbitrarily displaced), but would calculate costs and benefits relative to the specific case. Moreover, the administrator would not generalize beyond the specific case; each act would be judged on its own merits.

A contrasting approach to moral reasoning based on the search for general rules or principles of conduct is often called deontological. Deontology holds that broad principles of rightness and wrongness can be established and that these principles are not dependent on the consequences of a particular action. Those who hold this view tend to focus on duties or responsibilities (*deontology* derives from the Greek word for "duty"). Quite simply, one's duty is to do what is morally correct and avoid doing that which is morally wrong, regardless of the consequences. Deontologists thus tend to focus on broad principles of right and wrong, such as those embodied in concepts like "rights" or "justice."

Using the deontological approach, an administrator would act in accord with generally accepted moral precepts, such as honesty or benevolence. Administrators are expected, for example, to tell the truth, keep their promises, and respect the dignity of the individual. Doing so does not derive from laws or codes of ethics, but from generally accepted moral principles. In particular situations, these actions might even be harmful to the overall interests of the organization or the society, but because the actions could be justified as consistent with a shared sense of moral order, the administrator should feel strongly compelled to act in that way.

Philosopher John Rawls presents one contemporary deontological theory that has received considerable attention. His approach emphasizes fairness or equity in policy decisions (Rawls, 1971). Rawls's theory suggests that if decisions were made under conditions in which the decision maker had no knowledge of whether they would personally accrue harm or benefit by choosing one way or another, then fairness would likely prevail. Imagine a city council committee deciding where to spend $1 million on street improvements. If all members of the committee acted in their own interest, they might spend the money in their own neighborhoods (and those would likely be the more affluent neighborhoods). On the other hand, if all members of the committee acted under a "veil of ignorance," not knowing where they lived or whether or not they were affluent, they would most likely spend the money to bring the poorer streets up to some standard level (and in doing so, they would likely spend more in less affluent neighborhoods). If all public decisions were rendered by acting out of concern for fairness rather than self-interest, Rawls argues, a far different moral order would prevail—one that was much more consistent with the basic principles of liberty and justice.

Moral Psychology   Psychologist Lawrence Kohlberg devised a scheme outlining three levels of moral development through which people pass: the preconventional, conventional, and postconventional stages (Kohlberg, 1971). According to Kohlberg, most people operate on one of the first two levels of moral development, and no one operates exclusively on the third level.

At the *preconventional level,* children begin to develop certain ideas about right and wrong. They interpret these ideas in terms of the consequences of their actions or the physical power of those around them. At an early stage, the ideas are associated with punishments; for example, if the child writes on the wall with a crayon, the child will be scolded. To avoid the negative consequences associated with writing on the wall, the child avoids that behavior. Later on, the child begins to behave in certain ways to receive rewards, such as parental praise.

Whether to avoid negative consequences or to receive praise, the child begins to behave in ways that we characterize as right rather than wrong. Of course, from the child's point of view, there is no moral code; the child is merely doing things to avoid punishments or to seek rewards. At this level of moral development, therefore, the consequences of our actions—the rewards or punishments we receive—determine whether we consider our actions right or wrong. The preconventional orientation is, of course, one that we all carry into adulthood.

At the *conventional level* of moral development, people behave morally in terms of conformity to various standards or conventions of the family, group, or nation. The individual seeks to conform to given moral standards and, indeed, to actively support and maintain those standards. This level involves two stages. Kohlberg calls the first the "Good Boy/Nice Girl" stage, at which we conform to expectations of parents, teachers, or peers and to the norms we learn at home, church, or school. We develop moral rules or codes, standards of right and wrong; though what we think of as good behavior is really just that which meets the expectations of others.

A second stage in the conventional level of moral development is the "Law and Order" orientation. At this stage, we develop an orientation toward authority and the social order. We learn what it means to be a "good citizen" and accept the importance of living by the conventional rules of society. Notions of duty and honor tend to dominate one's moral perspective at this level. We recognize that certain behaviors are wrong—lying, cheating, stealing—but if asked why, we can only answer, "Because everyone knows they are wrong" (DeGeorge, 1982, p. 25). Most adults continue to operate, at least in part, at this level of moral development.

Few adults reach the final level, the *postconventional,* but some do. At this level, people accept moral principles and behave according to those principles, not merely because someone says they should, but because they know themselves what makes these principles right. The individual seeks to define moral principles and to understand how those values operate independently of any group or society. A first postconventional stage is called the "social-contract" or "legalistic" stage, which has a strong utilitarian bias. The individual recognizes the rights of other individuals, including the right to one's own beliefs and values, and how societies are constituted to support those rights. The result is a legalistic viewpoint, though it recognizes the possibility of changing the legal order (rather than freezing it, as in the previous level). Changes of this sort are often supported based on the greatest good for the greatest number.

The second stage of the postconventional level represents the highest stage of moral development. At this stage, the individual freely chooses to live by a particular set of

What Would You Do?

You were recently appointed city manager in a small community in Tennessee. Yesterday, the mayor gave you an envelope filled with receipts from a recent trip he took to an economic development conference. Included were receipts from a four-day vacation that the mayor and his wife took at a resort near the conference city. It was clear the mayor wanted the city to reimburse him for everything that was included in the envelope. What would you do?

abstract moral principles, such as justice, equality, and respect for individual dignity. One chooses to follow these precepts not for reward or punishment and not to meet others' expectations, but because one understands why the principle should be supported and chooses to live by that standard. The actual standards may be the same in both the conventional and postconventional levels, but there is an important difference in the *reason* one holds an action to be right or wrong.

Although we have focused on Kohlberg's work here, we should point out that there are several alternatives to his interpretation that have been voiced recently. One important alternative, for example, is that suggested by Carol Gilligan. Gilligan argues that, in contrast to the rational and impartial perspective of Rawls and Kohlberg, one may interpret moral theory in terms of care and relationships. According to Gilligan, a final and mature morality involves an interaction between the concerns of impartiality and those of personal relationship and care (Blum, 1988, pp. 472–491).

As you work in and with public organizations, you will come to recognize that many of the ethical decisions you make are based in a level of moral development. We do certain things because they will lead to rewards or punishments, and we do other things because we must adhere to laws or organizational standards of conduct. For example, you may obey an order from a superior so that you won't be fired, or you may purchase a new piece of equipment through a bidding process rather than from a friend because that's the law. But you will also encounter cases that will require you to think more carefully and personally about the standards you are willing to live by. For example, purchasing a piece of equipment might be complicated by the fact that your supervisor *ordered* you to purchase the equipment from a friend without other bids. In cases such as these, postconventional or "principled" reasoning may be essential. Certainly if you recognize that not all answers come from the power or expectations of others and that careful deliberation concerning moral principles is often quite appropriate, you will be better positioned to make the correct ethical decisions, time after time.

Moral Action   Knowing the proper and correct course of action is not enough. You must act in a way that is consistent with what you consider to be right. (After all, we describe people as having "integrity" not merely on the basis of what they believe, but on the basis of how they act.) This concern is especially significant for a public manager (or, for that matter, any other professional) who wishes to act ethically. Questions of ethics in the public service are not abstract; they are real. And they have immediate and sometimes serious human consequences. It is thus important to consider how we can ensure moral actions in public organizations.

A long-standing philosophical tradition holds that putting principles (whether utilitarian, deontological, or otherwise) into action requires the development of "character" on the part of the individual. In other words, it is necessary to apply a complex set of general principles to specific cases—something that requires more than abstract knowledge. Aristotle spoke of the importance of gaining "practical wisdom" so as to make morally correct judgments in specific situations. This practical wisdom or "virtue" requires that the individual not simply know how to apply given principles, but rather why to do so. That is, to bring moral knowledge to bear in the "real world," the individual needs a strong sense of what is ideal in human conduct. Terry Cooper, for example, argues that virtues are character traits acquired through reflection and conduct. They involve an integration of both thought and feeling where potentially conflicting tendencies are brought under control (Cooper & Wright, 1992, p. 6).

This "ethics of virtue," then, is not merely another philosophical approach but a way of developing the skills one brings to the problem of ethical decision making. Aristotle speaks of developing the skills of virtue in the same way we develop other skills—that is, by practice: "The virtues we get first by exercising them . . . For the things we have to learn before we can do them, we learn by doing them . . . We become just by doing just acts, temperate by doing temperate acts, brave by doing brave acts" (McKeon, 1941, p. 952).

But what are the virtues that we must practice? Obviously, this question has challenged philosophers over the centuries. Answers range from honesty, courage, and trustworthiness to kindness, fairness, and dependability, but most seem to center around concerns for *benevolence* and *justice*. If this is the case, then all persons should practice these virtues, whereas members of specific professions (such as public administrators) should practice applications of these virtues in their specific situations (Tong, 1986, pp. 91–92).

How then, does one sort out the various philosophical and psychological approaches one might employ to make ethical choices in the "real world"? First, if you set about solving difficult moral problems through the application of broad moral principles in specific situations, you need to understand the principles and moral reasoning that underlie them. Second, you must engage in careful and consistent ethical deliberation, through self-reflection and dialogue with others. Third, you must understand how virtues such as benevolence or justice are played out in public organizations; that is, you must recognize the political and ethical context that conditions the moral priorities of the public service.

James Svara has suggested an approach to ethics that takes various considerations into account. The first is the duty-based approach which emphasizes the responsibilities of public administrators, accentuating to the public service (Svara, 2007, p. 28):

1. Put the public interest over personal interest.
2. Display a service orientation and commitment to serve.
3. Have a commitment to procedural fairness.
4. Exercise fiduciary responsibility.
5. Be bound by and uphold the law.
6. Support the democratic process.
7. Be responsive to the policy goals of political superiors while fairly examining all policy options and exercising leadership appropriate to position.

The duty-based approach is a useful tool for public administrators, but if used alone, it may impose unanticipated problems. It also may be used as a loose guide for administrators who often face complicated situations which cannot be easily resolved if virtue, principle, and consequences are not taken into account.

The virtue-based approach concentrates on what 'a good person would do' and is highly intuitive. It reflects the values and norms widely accepted in society. But when used alone, this approach could put the administrator in a dilemma because what is good for one person is not always considered good for others.

The principle-based approach guides the administrator in what is right to do (unlike duty, which says what is obligatory). While this approach may be useful for the public administrator because it relies on a broader perception of what is good and what is bad (external source), it still should not be used alone for many reasons. Some principles are contradictory, such as the principle of doing no harm and the principle of honesty.

Consequential approach is the least accentuated approach in public administration. Utilitarian approach that calls for 'the greatest good for the greatest number' seems right, but also is difficult to implement. What if the greatest good for greatest number harms minorities in an unethical way? Can we justify that? Are the means used for the ends ethical?

The questions that come from any approach used alone indicate that public administrators should use a comprehensive approach that would put duty in the center but also would take into account virtues, principles, and consequences. For this reason, Svara proposes an ethical triangle model, which according to the author "conveys the idea that administrators should act on their duty to promote public interest by seeking a balance of virtue, principle, and good consequences" (Svara, p. 67). The use of an ethical triangle prevents under- and overutilization of any approach taken alone, but also "helps to prevent the shortcomings of using any of the approaches alone" (Svara, p. 68). It allows utilization of the advantages of the separate approaches. Their combination avoids the emphasis of the disadvantages of the 'pure' approaches. For example, if we have the intent to achieve the greatest good for the greatest number, the ethical triangle helps us to look in our duties (serve the public interest), principles (no harm for anyone), and virtues (being fair and just) and to measure the 'good' consequences in terms of every approach.

As you approach similar questions, it may be helpful to consider first the utilitarian position: What are the costs and benefits, and which alternative will bring the greatest benefits? Next, you might ask whether the alternative you chose will infringe upon the rights of others and, if so, whether there are overwhelming factors that justify such an outcome. Then, you might ask whether the chosen alternative violates principles of equity and fairness and, if so, whether again there are overwhelming factors that would justify the outcome. Finally, you might ask whether the alternative is consistent with your ideals with respect to human conduct (especially the conduct of public affairs) and whether by choosing this alternative you will be acting in a way you consider virtuous. At any point, you may find that the alternative comes up short, and you must search for another. Remember that your ultimate goal is the development of virtue and the application of sound ethical reasoning to public problems.

■ Issues of Administrative Responsibility

People who work in or with public organizations face literally dozens of ethical dilemmas. Some—like lying, cheating, or stealing—are the same problems that many others face. But some, like the public manager's commitment to democratic standards or feelings about the political involvement of public employees, are peculiar to public organizations.

One of the most troublesome "broad-range" issues in the field of public administration is that of administrative responsibility. (In the section that follows, we focus much more specifically on issues where personal values, such as honesty, equity, and justice, become deeply intermingled with the broader values of public service.) As a public manager, you may often confront the potentially conflicting demands of operating as efficiently as possible while, at the same time, being fully responsive to administrative superiors, to the legislature, to the citizenry, and to the principles of democratic governance generally. This tension between *efficiency* and *responsiveness* characterizes many of the problems public managers face.

As we have seen, the tension between efficiency and responsiveness grows from two other issues that are deeply rooted in the history of public administration: those of politics and administration, and bureaucracy versus democracy. Early writers in the field sought a clear distinction between *politics* and *administration*, arguing that, wherever possible, administrative activities should be insulated from the potentially corrupting influence of politics. Obviously, this idea was based on the assumption that policy making could be distinguished from policy implementing. Making such an assumption allows easy resolution of questions of democratic responsibility: The legislature, charged with making policy, should be responsive to the people; the administrative agencies, charged with implementing policy, should be responsive to the legislature. The requirements of democracy will be met by a neutral and competent public bureaucracy that follows the mandates of the legislative body. This is called the doctrine of *neutral competence.* Most writers and practitioners clearly preferred this somewhat narrow view of administrative responsibility. Indeed, the doctrine of neutral competence, and the politics-administration dichotomy on which it is based, continues to influence the field. But there were and are many who recognize the difficulty of maintaining a neutral public bureaucracy. Some even argue that the role administrative agencies play in the policy process is not only inevitable, but proper.

NETWORKING

For general discussions of ethics in government, see the following: Center for Public Integrity at www.publicintegrity.org; Institute for Philosophy and Public Policy at www.puaf.umd.edu/IPPP; and the Josephson Institute of Ethics at www.josephsoninstitute.org. Organizations that seek to promote citizen action include the Center for Civic Networking at www.civicnet.org and the Center for Democracy and Technology at www.cdt.org.

The Limits of Administrative Discretion

We have noted that administrators take their primary cues from the actions of legislatures that initiate programs and from executives who are charged with carrying out the programs. If you are hired to manage a new agency, one of your first priorities will be to familiarize yourself with the legislation that created the agency and with any executive orders or directives outlining the agency's responsibilities. But if your situation is typical, you will find that neither the legislation nor the directions you receive from the executive are sufficiently detailed to answer all the questions your work raises. There will be a need to develop policies regarding these issues—policies that are, in effect, merely more detailed pieces of "legislation." In addition, as you get into the work, you may find it necessary to ask the legislature or the chief executive to make certain changes in the rules and regulations under which you operate.

The problem, of course, is to make sure that your policies or recommendations for change are consistent with the wishes of the citizenry (see Box 4.1). In most jurisdictions, of course, the legislature and the chief executive are popularly elected, and their reelection depends on their response to the public's perceived needs and interests. For them, the electoral process assures responsiveness, at least in theory. As long as you are acting in a way that is clearly consistent with legislative intent, you are likely to be considered appropriately responsive. But because most situations aren't that clear, the question becomes "How can we assure that the administrator is exercising discretion in a way consistent with the will of the people, whether expressed in the Constitution, the laws of the land, or the preferences of citizens?" Historically, two answers to this question have been offered. In an important debate in the pages of the *Public Administration Review* and other journals some 40 years ago, Herman Finer argued that, to maintain responsiveness to the public, managers in public organizations should be subjected to strict and rigid controls by the legislature. His question was straightforward (though perhaps overdrawn): "Are the servants of the public to decide their own course, or is their course of action to be decided by a body outside themselves?" (Finer, 1972, p. 8). His answer was equally direct: Only through specific and detailed legislation carefully limiting the work of public managers could responsiveness to the legislature be maintained. This interpretation of how to assure responsiveness is often called *objective responsibility*, depending as it does on objective external controls.

Carl Friedrich, on the other hand, argued that the increasing complexity of modern society made such detailed legislation difficult, if not impossible. Consequently, Friedrich felt that the administrator's own concern for the public interest was often the only real assurance that his or her actions would be responsive to the electorate. Fortunately, wrote Friedrich, the growing number of professionals in government increases the likelihood that a sense of democratic responsibility will be part of the administrator's makeup (Friedrich, 1972).

Others, following Friedrich's lead, noted the growing number of governmental officials in schools of public affairs and public administration. These schools take quite seriously the need to expose students to the ethical issues they may encounter in public organizations and to ways these issues might be resolved. This way of assuring responsiveness is often called *subjective responsibility*, depending as it does on the subjective nature of the individual.

Recently, Terry Cooper has argued that citizenship involves both rights and responsibilities and that the citizen must assume a positive role in the betterment of society as a whole. In doing so, he or she acts in pursuit of the common good and in accord with values such as political participation, political equality, and justice. When a citizen becomes a public administrator, he or she assumes the role of "citizen-administrator, both a citizen and someone working for the citizenry." In this case, the administrator's ultimate obligation is to

[margin note:] objective responsibility —
specific + detailed legislation to limit the work of managers

BOX 4.1

TODAY'S LEADERSHIP CHALLENGE—ENGAGING CITIZENS

Citizen engagement is part of a family of democratic reform ideas—an aspect of our political culture—that includes public participation, public involvement, participatory democracy, deliberative democracy, and collaborative governance. These terms make distinctions about the purpose, scope, and techniques of participation, but they all recognize and build upon a belief that citizens have the right to participate in decisions that affect their lives. Citizen participation policies and programs thus reflect a basic commitment to this principle and invite citizens to engage in policy development and decision-making activities.

Citizen participation activities revolve around six general aims:

- Inform and educate the public on important policy issues.
- Improve government decisions by supplying better information upward from citizens to decision makers.
- Create opportunities for citizens to shape and, in some cases, determine public policy.
- Legitimate government decisions by ensuring that the voices of those impacted by government policy have been heard, considered, and addressed.
- Involve citizens in monitoring the outcomes of policy for evaluation.
- Improve the quality of public life by restoring trust and engagement of citizens in public life.

Since the modern era of citizen participation in federal policy decision making was entered . . . government is being asked to adopt a more active stance toward involving citizens in service-delivery; democratic activists are saying this is not enough.

As a result of these influences, citizen participation is being recast as an instrument to improve the quality and legitimacy of government action. "One of the powerful things about citizen engagement," a senior manager told us, "is that it takes government out of the middle role—as a broker for all information in techniques where people don't get to hear each other's point of view." We see this shift as the establishment of a new role for government in the twenty-first century: convener of the public. To fulfill and sustain this role, public agencies need to adapt existing policy and administrative processes and support the development of new national mechanisms to share knowledge, promote practice, and evaluate results of citizen engagement in ways that improve outcomes over time. Another participant in our June conference observed, "The public voice should not be echoing alone in one out of several silos of variables in a project; it should be the overarching sound that integrates all the silos." As convener, government's role is to help create that "overarching sound."

SOURCE: Carolyn J. Lukensmeyer, Lars Hasselblad Torres. (Fall 2006) Today's Leadership Challenge—Engaging Citizens. *Public Manager*. Potomac: (35), 3: 26–31.

deliver public goods and services "in ways that enhance the common good of community life through which character and civic virtue are formed" (Cooper, 1991, p. 161).

One approach to ensuring responsiveness that cuts across the objective/subjective distinction is *representative bureaucracy*—the idea that public agencies whose employees reflect certain demographic characteristics of the population as a whole are likely to operate more in line with the policy preferences of the general citizenry. According to this view, an agency with a substantial number of women or minority employees is more likely to take into account the views of women and minorities in the population than would an agency of white males. Experience with representative bureaucracy has produced mixed results. Whereas we might indeed expect greater responsiveness with respect to race and gender, there is no reason to think that such an agency would be more or less representative on other types of issues. Moreover, there is no real assurance that a person from one particular group would necessarily or always reflect that group's policy preferences. Those preferences might well be displaced by the professional or bureaucratic norms that person adopts.

Avenues for Public Participation

Another way to assure that public managers and employees act in a way consistent with the desires of the public is to involve citizens directly in the decision-making process through membership on advisory boards, open hearings, or direct polling. Such techniques, which have now become widespread, took their initial impetus from passage of the Economic Opportunity Act of 1964, legislation that required the "maximum feasible participation" of the poor in the design and conduct of antipoverty programs. In this case, the question of involvement itself became quite an issue, especially as the representatives of the poor came into direct confrontation with those holding established positions of power. The movement toward widespread citizen participation was soon well established, however, and spread quickly to local school boards, universities, and other government agencies. Today, for example, the practice of holding hearings prior to administrative decisions is commonplace at all levels of government.

There are questions, of course, as to whether real power is transferred to the citizens or whether citizen involvement is merely a device for defusing protests. Some use the term *cooptation* to describe situations in which citizens are given the feeling of involvement but little real power. On balance, it is probably accurate to say that there are some cases in which citizens have been coopted through involvement in advisory boards or even public hearings, but in most cases, administrators are truly interested in receiving input from the public that will help them make difficult decisions.

The complexities of public involvement in administrative decision making are illustrated in the following "classic" case, actually a continuation of one we encountered in Chapter 2. The Clean Air Act required the EPA to set national emissions standards for hazardous air pollutants to protect the public health. But no definition was given as to what would be considered "an ample margin of safety."

> The issue received national attention in 1983 when EPA was trying to decide what, if anything, should be done about inorganic arsenic, a cancer-causing pollutant produced when arsenic-content ore is smelted into copper. The problem was particularly serious in the area around Tacoma, Washington, where the American Smelting and Refining Company (ASARCO) operated a copper smelter. The EPA had concluded that, in the absence of any controls on ASARCO's arsenic emissions, approximately four new cases of lung cancer would be contracted each year in the Tacoma area.

Even after installation of the "best available" pollution-control equipment, there would still be one new case of cancer per year. But there was an important consideration on the other side of the issue as well. If the EPA were to impose any more onerous conditions on ASARCO—for example, that it use ore containing less arsenic or install a new and far more expensive electric smelter—the company could not afford to continue to operate the plant. ASARCO employed 570 workers, with an annual payroll of approximately $23 million; the company bought an additional $12 million worth of goods from local suppliers. Closing the plant therefore would pose serious economic problems for the local economy.

William Ruckelshaus, then administrator of the EPA, decided that the citizens of the Tacoma area ought to wrest with the problem. Accordingly, Ruckelshaus flew to Tacoma to announce a series of three public workshops to be held during the summer of 1983. The purpose was to acquaint residents with the details of the pollution problem, help them prepare for subsequent formal hearings, and enable them to deliberate about what should be done.

Some questions concerned technical matters, like the reliability of the proposed control equipment and the risk figures and epidemiological studies on which the EPA had based its estimates. Other questions revealed the inadequacy of the EPA's explanation of the relative health risk posed by the smelter: One resident asked whether that risk was greater than the risk posed by auto emissions.

Residents were not solely concerned, however, with the factual basis for the agency's claims. Several residents wanted to discuss the effects of the arsenic emissions on their gardens, their animals, and on the overall quality of life. Several residents expressed hostility toward the EPA for involving them in this difficult decision making in the first place. These issues are very complex, and the public is not sophisticated enough to make these decisions. This is not to say that the EPA doesn't have an obligation to inform the public, but information is one thing—defaulting its legal mandate is another.

These numerous workshops, together with the national attention that Ruckelshaus had deliberately drawn by traveling to Tacoma, created considerable and often unfavorable press coverage. In an editorial on July 16, 1983, entitled "Mr. Ruckelshaus a Caesar," the *New York Times* argued that "Mr. Ruckelshaus has it all upside down . . . . What is inexcusable is for him to impose such an impossible choice on Tacomans." An article in the *Los Angeles Times* pointed out the difficulties "in taking a community's pulse . . . [Should one] poll the community . . . [or] count the pros and cons at the massive hearing?" Ruckelshaus was not surprised by the controversy. He said, "Listen, I know people don't like these kinds of decisions . . . Welcome to the world of regulation. People have demanded to be involved and now I have involved them, and they say, 'Don't ask that question.' What's the alternative? Don't involve them? Then you are accused of doing something nefarious" (Reich, 1985).

SOURCE: Reprinted by permission of the Yale Law Journal Company and William S. Hein Company. From *The Yale Law Journal*, Vol. 94, pp. 1617–1641.

The outcome of the case is anticlimactic: Before the EPA promulgated its regulations, declining copper prices led to the closing of the ASARCO smelter anyway. The case does, however, point out some of the difficulties in designing adequate programs for public participation. Certainly there is every reason to think that Ruckelshaus really wanted to test the pulse of the citizens before making regulations. But his attempt was met not only with ambivalence, as is often the case, but with outright hostility. Moreover, despite his efforts, there were few clear signals to the agency about what to do. The ethical issues posed by the requirements of administrative responsibility are indeed complex.

The Ethics of Privatization

We noted in Chapter 3 the increasing involvement of for-profit and nonprofit organizations in the delivery of public programs. Especially as governments have contracted for or otherwise sought to "privatize" services, private and nonprofit organizations have become major providers of public services. But, as we also saw, transfer of responsibility may raise significant ethical questions regarding equity and accountability. The government might find it necessary or expedient to contract out for garbage collection, for example, but neither necessity nor cost savings would justify allowing contractors to engage in discrimination or other unethical practices.

The issue is particularly critical for private-sector providers, who could have a tendency to maximize profits even at the sacrifice of some other public value. A private organization might be tempted to provide either more services than necessary for clients (to increase payments and therefore revenues) or fewer services than necessary (to cut costs). Actions such as these, clearly motivated by concern for profit, are less likely to occur in service delivery by nonprofit organizations, simply by virtue of their service "ethos," but even they require mechanisms to ensure equity and accountability (Rubin, 1990).

In any privatization arrangement, the government's responsibility is not only to ensure quality and cost consistent with stewardship of public resources, but also to promote democratic ideals and ensure constitutional protections. There are at least two different types of delegation to consider: those that involve no transfer of discretionary authority and those that do. Obviously, many contracts involve no transfer of authority. Public works contracts, for example, can usually be standardized and highly specified so as to grant virtually no discretionary public authority to contractors (though there are exceptions). The government retains responsibility for exercising public authority (such as determining eligibility for and frequency of garbage collection or street repair) and for holding contractors accountable for quality, quantity, and cost of work.

Other arrangements may involve transfer of discretionary authority—for example, the authority to determine details of eligibility requirements for student loans or the authority to decide what services to provide to inmates of a privately operated prison. In situations such as these, appropriate accountability structures must be in place to assure responsiveness to the government agency that administers the contract as well as to the public generally. Developing contractual arrangements that fully incorporate appropriate concerns for the public interest presents one of the most significant challenges in privatizing public services.

■ Ethical Problems for the Individual

Even the most straightforward ethical problems may be problematic, especially in the context of work in public organizations. Think for a moment about telling the truth. At first glance, nothing could seem more obvious than to tell "the truth, the whole truth, and nothing but the truth." But is that really the proper ethical position (outside a courtroom)? Should you be prepared to lie to protect matters vital to the national defense? Should you tell the whole truth in response to questions from the press about confidential matters affecting your clients? Is it proper to "stretch" research findings so they better support a policy position you feel is in the public interest? These are just a few of the most pressing and difficult questions you may face that will test not only your principles but also your willingness to act in accord with those principles.

Interacting with Elected Officials

The relationship between public managers and elected officials, either chief executives (such as mayors or governors) or members of a legislative body, presents a unique but nearly pervasive set of issues for the public manager. Whether as a department head working with a legislative committee, a city manager working with a city council, or an executive director working with the board of a nonprofit organization, the relationship between manager and the legislative body presents special problems.

We have examined some of the implications of this relationship for the development of public policy, but we should also be aware of possible ethical implications. On the one hand, an administrator should be accountable to the legislative body, but on the other hand, responding blindly to legislative decree may not always be in the public interest.

The latter situation might arise in several ways. Certainly, differing strongly with members of the legislature on policy questions presents great difficulties. As an administrator, to what extent should you seek to persuade the legislature to your position? Is it proper for a manager to try to build a power base in the legislature to enable special consideration of legislation favorable to the agency? If the legislature acts contrary to your strong beliefs, should you continue in your position or should you resign? If you continue, is it proper to try later to shape implementation of the legislation to fall more closely in line with your beliefs?

Similarly, difficult questions might arise if the manager is asked to do something improper. For instance, what would you do if a legislator asked you to do something illegal, such as permitting health care payments to an ineligible client? How would your decision change if the legislator only asked you to "bend the rules" a little bit? How would your decision change if the legislator chaired the committee that passed on your agency's appropriation?

These issues may arise in any public organization; however, they are especially well illustrated at the local level with the council-manager form of government, which is built around the distinction between policy and administration. Theoretically, the council is responsible for determining policy and the manager is responsible for carrying it out. In practice, however, the line between policy and administration is never so clear; inevitably, the manager becomes involved in policy matters and the council in administrative matters.

Because of this overlap, the Code of Ethics of the International City Management Association contains several statements that influence the council-manager relationship. The code's first item emphasizes the manager's dedication to "effective and democratic local government by *responsible elected officials*" and recognizes the contribution professional management can make in this regard. More specifically, on the manager's policy role, the code suggests that the manager "submit policy proposals to elected officials; provide them with facts and advice on matters of policy as a basis for making decisions and setting community goals, and uphold and implement municipal policies adopted by elected officials." Similarly, the manager is advised to "recognize that elected representatives of the people are entitled to the credit for the establishment of municipal policies; (while) responsibility for public execution rests with the members."

Despite these helpful guidelines, city managers often face difficulties in relationships with city councils. One city manager disagreed strongly with a council move to limit widening a particular city street, an improvement the manager felt was essential to local economic development, another felt that a council member was acting irresponsibly in proposing legislation that would help his contracting business, and still another was asked to process travel vouchers that included payment for personal vacation expenses. Simply figuring out how to respond effectively to these situations is hard enough, but the problem is even greater when you remember that the city manager who forces an issue of policy or ethics may be seen as "attacking" the boss—and may, at any time, be summarily fired. It's no wonder that the average tenure of city managers in this country is four to five years!

Following Orders

Another problem has to do with limits to organizational authority. What would you do if your boss asked you to do something you felt was morally wrong? Suppose you are asked to "bury" a report on toxic wastes you consider potentially dangerous to the public or that, under pressures of time, you are asked to give quick approval to a piece of equipment that might be unsafe. Imagine that you are asked to approve an expense reimbursement for your boss, when you know the amount has been "padded."

In such cases, you face difficult choices—choices made even more difficult by the very logic that causes us to employ bureaucratic means of organizing. Bureaucratic organizations are attractive because they enable people to accomplish large-scale tasks they would not otherwise be able to undertake, but bureaucracy as a social form also demands a certain amount of obedience to authority. Presumably, if orders are not obeyed, the whole system falls apart—so there are strong pressures for individuals to follow orders rather than their consciences.

The most dramatic example of unquestioning obedience to authority comes from Hitler's attempt to exterminate the European Jews during World War II. Although the killings were ordered by political leaders, they were carried out through German bureaucracy. The problem faced not only those at the top of the organization but those throughout. Raul Hilberg, author of a classic study of the Holocaust, writes the following.

Most bureaucrats composed memoranda, drew up blueprints, signed correspondence, talked on the telephone, and participated in conferences . . . However, these men were not stupid; they realized the connection between their paperwork and the heaps of corpses in the East. And they realized, also, the shortcomings of those rationalizations which placed all evil on the Jew and all good on the German. That was why they were compelled to justify their individual activities. The first rationalization was the oldest, the simplest, and therefore the most effective: the doctrine of superior orders. First and foremost there was duty. No matter what objections there might be, orders were given to be obeyed. A clear order was like an absolution; armed with such an order, a perpetrator felt that he could pass his responsibility and his conscience upward (Hilberg, 1961, p. 649).

This manner of justifying one's actions became central to the defense of those accused at the Nuremberg trials. Many defendants argued, as did General Alfred Jodl, that it is "not the task of a soldier to act as a judge over his superior commander" (Arendt, 1963, p. 133). But despite the rationale of "superior orders" for the German bureaucrats and their more contemporary counterparts, the moral dilemma posed by such orders remains.

One might argue, of course, that the German example is overdrawn—that such a thing could never happen in a democratic society such as ours. But perhaps it could. Indeed, a remarkable series of studies conducted by Yale psychologist Stanley Milgram many years ago suggests that Americans are often quite willing to obey, even where doing so causes them extreme moral discomfort.

In an elaborate series of experiments, Milgram asked subjects to administer shocks to a person supposedly involved in a memory experiment. Even though the person receiving the shocks writhed in pain (he was actually an actor and an accomplice), the subjects continued to follow Milgram's orders to administer the painful shocks—simply because they were told to do so! Milgram concluded that "a substantial proportion of people do what they are told,

What Would You Do?

The dean at the university where you are a department chair forwards an e-mail to you that is clearly an advertisement for a consulting firm's seminar on grant writing and asks you to send the note on to your faculty. You are concerned about using the university's e-mail for commercial purposes. What would you do?

irrespective of the content of the act and without limitations of conscience as long as they perceive that the command comes from a legitimate authority" (Milgram, 1974, p. 189).

Contemporary examples of problems with orders from above are perhaps less dramatic than the German illustration, but they present equally difficult choices for the individual. You may, of course, protest the action, either directly to your superiors or more indirectly, although in doing so, you may place yourself in jeopardy. Or you may leave the organization, resigning in protest, even though the available alternatives—such as unemployment—may not be attractive. Or you may simply keep quiet and do what you are told. The latter alternative is certainly the easiest in most cases. By obeying orders, you feel you have someone else (your superior) to blame if something goes wrong. In any case, many feel that if people in large organizations fail to follow orders, things won't get done. Unfortunately, rationalizations such as these don't allow you to escape the moral consequences of your actions.

Conflicts of Interest

Another area of potential ethical difficulties for public officials involves conflicts of interest. Finding ways to avoid conflicts of interest, especially financial, has been central to federal, state, and local ethics legislation for the past twenty-five to thirty years. At the federal level, legislation proscribing the ethical behavior of public officials has deep historical roots; however, the tone of modern ethics legislation was set by Executive Order 11222 issued by President Johnson in 1965. In part, the policy reads as follows.

> Where government is based on the consent of the governed, every citizen is entitled to have complete confidence in the integrity of his government. Each individual officer, employee, or advisor of government must help to earn and must honor that trust by his own integrity and conduct in all official actions.

The executive order then provides a set of "standards of conduct" that covers such topics as accepting gifts, financial conflicts of interest, misuse of federal property, and limitations on outside employment. The policy also bars use of public office for personal gain or for the gain of those with whom the individual has family, business, or financial ties.

The Johnson policy also initiated public disclosure of financial statements, something that was given greater prominence in the Ethics and Government Act of 1978. This act codified many of the previously established standards and created the Office of Government Ethics to establish more detailed regulations to monitor the behavior of public servants and provide ethics training for managers and other officials.

Under existing legislation, officers of the executive branch of the federal government are required to refrain from participating "personally and financially" in deciding, approving, recommending, or advising with respect to matters in which they, family members, or close associates have a financial interest. An official facing a possible conflict of interest has a number of avenues available. First, the official can simply withdraw from participating in the particular case. Second, the official may seek a waiver, especially when his or her interest is not considered substantial or the relationship is too remote to affect the integrity of the action. Third, the employee may choose to place his or her assets in a "blind trust." Finally, the official can sell, give away, or otherwise divest himself or herself of the financial interest in question.

Other parts of the federal ethics legislation restrict outside income and the acceptance of gifts or favors. For example, as a federal employee, you are prohibited from accepting any

What Would You Do?

Your wife's brother has applied for a job in the state-level department that you head. What would you do?

salary or contribution from any source other than the federal government. The law also limits the acceptance of meals, entertainment, and gifts. For example, meals can usually be accepted if offered during the course of a working meeting, but there are prohibitions on "one-on-one" meals in which you are being treated.

There are also prohibitions on what a federal employee can do after leaving a government position. Sections of the Ethics and Government Act prohibit former officials from representing outside parties before the federal government with respect to matters in which they had some personal involvement or official responsibility for a period of two years. There is also a one-year "cooling-off period," during which you cannot represent parties before your agency even on matters that were not your responsibility while working for the government. The Bush commission recommended strengthening provisions dealing with activities of former federal officials by requiring a prohibition not only against personally representing outside interests before government agencies but also "aiding or advising any other person." The proposal would eliminate not only direct representation, but "behind the scenes" advice and counsel as well.

Legislation such as this is obviously intended to prevent "influence peddling" by those who have recently left government and to limit the "revolving door" phenomenon, wherein people move in and out of government to acquire knowledge and information valuable to external groups. This issue became particularly prominent during the Reagan administration, when several officials, including Michael Deaver and Lynn Nofziger, were accused of using their previous contacts to unduly influence the governmental decision process.

Finally, the potential for conflicts of interest is decreased by requirements for financial disclosure on the part of executive officials. A commission created by the first President Bush, for example, wrote "financial disclosure has been variously described as the linchpin of the ethical enforcement system, as the disinfectant sunlight which makes possible the cleaning up of abusive practices" (President's Commission, 1989, p. 5). Though financial reporting requirements have sometimes been criticized as excessively detailed and intrusive, they have been, in the view of most ethics experts, highly valuable in maintaining public confidence in the integrity of government. If nothing else, the reports have meant that individuals are forced to carefully review potential conflicts of interests that they may bring to government, and thus be more aware of those interests should conflicts arise.

The recommendations of the Bush commission led, in February 1993, to new standards creating greater uniformity across all agencies of the federal government. The rules cover seven areas: (1) gifts from outside sources, (2) gifts between federal employees, (3) conflicts of financial interests, (4) impartiality in performing official duties, (5) other employment, (6) misuse of position, and (7) outside activities. In many respects, these standards reflected the new president's pledge for a return to values-based leadership. As a candidate, President Clinton had voiced sharp criticism against the ethical shortcomings of preceding administrations. Then, on Inauguration Day, he used his first executive order to require new ethics commitments of executive branch appointees, restricting an appointee's lobbying or trying to influence an agency where he or she worked.

However, despite the efforts of the Clinton administration to set a high moral tone, it is unlikely that the Clinton presidency will be remembered for its stance on ethics (more likely for its unethical behavior!). As mentioned in Chapter 2, President Clinton was impeached by Congress for lying under oath to a federal grand jury, and even though the Senate later acquitted the president, the fact that President Clinton lied to the grand jury (and to the public) to protect his political career was never disputed. President George W. Bush's administration has not been immune from ethical conflicts. His actions against terrorism, while supported in general, opened the administration to harsh criticism. Specific actions, such as the U.S. Patriot Act (adopted 2001) that gives permission for "warrantless searches of phone and Internet records," raise concerns for protecting the basic civil liberties. Questions have also been raised about the honesty of the president's justifications for the war in Iraq and the political motivations for firing federal attorneys. Ethics is an ever present issue, and political leaders, including presidents, sometimes fail to meet the highest standards.

Many of the same provisions for preventing conflict of interest in federal ethics legislation have been paralleled at the state level. Many states have passed detailed ethics legislation, often using financial disclosure as a chief mechanism for preventing abuse. Indeed, almost all have some form of financial disclosure provision for some state employees. In addition, more states have adopted ethics codes and ethics commissions. For example, in 1991 the state of Texas established an ethics commission to review the conduct of lobbyists, candidates, and elected officials. Similarly, given the influence of money

NETWORKING

The primary federal agency dealing with ethics issues is the Office of Government Ethics at www.usoge.gov.

in politics, other states have sought to establish controls on political money. Florida, for example, reduced the limits on campaign contributions and created a fully funded public campaign finance system. Many states have adopted similar versions of the federal conflict of interest legislation passed during the Bush administration.

Whistle-Blowing

There has been a marked increase over the last 20 years in employee disclosure of problems in public organizations. Public employees have exposed defense contract overruns; spoken out against corruption in local police departments; and revealed abuses of the merit system, improper enforcement of toxic waste legislation, and other matters. Alan Campbell, director of the Office of Personnel Management during the Carter administration, described these public disclosures, or "whistle-blowing," in this way: "Quite simply, I view whistle-blowing as a popular short-hand label for any disclosure of a legal violation, mismanagement, a gross waste of funds, an abuse of authority, or a danger to public health or safety, whether the disclosure is made within or outside the chain of command" (Bowman, 1983, p. 91). In other words, the *whistle-blower* reveals information about fraud, waste, or abuse in government, including actions that might endanger the safety or liberty of other government employees or citizens at large.

Generally, employees who decide to blow the whistle move through several stages. First, the employees become aware of an organizational practice that is unethical or dangerous. Second, they express concern to their immediate supervisor or those further up in the hierarchy; and third, unsatisfied that anyone in the organization will take appropriate action, they take the issue outside, either through "leaks" to the press or to external public interest groups. (The press, of course, may independently play an important role in revealing instances of wrongdoing.)

Unfortunately, whistle-blowers in both government and industry have often been subjected to abuse and retaliation by superiors. One study of whistle-blowers shows a large number who were fired or forced to resign or retire, as well as others who were refused promotions or given less desirable work assignments. Others felt excluded from communication within the organization and were avoided by both supervisors and coworkers (Truelson, 1986, p. 9). Studies show that, as a result, many public employees who have knowledge of corruption don't bother to report it, and many who do report abuses suffer reprisals (Bowman, 1983a, p. 91).

If you discover improper actions on the part of persons in your organization, you have a strong obligation to report those actions; however, you should be careful that your allegations are based on fact and are properly reported. Norman Bowie suggests that an act of whistle-blowing can be justified if the following conditions are met.

1. If it is done with an appropriate moral motive
2. If all internal channels of dissent have been exhausted
3. If it is based on evidence that would persuade a reasonable person
4. If analysis has been made of the seriousness, immediacy, and specificity of the problem
5. If it is commensurate with one's responsibility
6. If it has some chance of success (Bowman, 1983a, p. 91)

At the federal level, codes of conduct have encouraged public servants to expose corruption wherever it is discovered, and protection for whistle-blowers has been provided through the Civil Service Reform Act. Moreover, some agencies have established formal *dissent channels,* confidential patterns of communications outside the normal chain of command, that allow a potential whistle-blower or someone who merely disagrees with a proposed policy to express a dissenting opinion without fear of reprisal. Consequently, whistle-blowing has become somewhat more common at the federal level. But wherever you work, if you decide to blow the whistle, you should be fully aware not only of potential dangers, but also of the protection available to you based on rights of free speech and of prohibitions against discriminatory actions. Encouraging greater communication by providing freer and more open channels of dissent is one way to ensure more ethical behavior in public organizations (see Box 4.2).

Prohibitions on Political Activities

Political neutrality has traditionally been considered important to effective democratic governance. President Jefferson, for example, issued an order against federal government employee partisanship, an order whose essence was repeated by Presidents Grant and Hayes. Legisla-

BOX 4.2

TEN TIPS FOR POTENTIAL WHISTLE-BLOWERS

1. Consult your loved ones. Blowing the whistle is a family decision. Before taking any irreversible steps, talk to your spouse, your family, or close friends—the support group you will need to depend upon in the coming days—about your decision to blow the whistle. If they are not with you, you may want to rethink your path.

2. Check for skeletons in your closet. Any personal vulnerability or peccadillo you possess can, and most likely will, be used by the agency against you. One practical step is to make a copy of the complete contents of your personnel file as insurance that new but backdated "dirt" cannot be later slipped in.

3. Document, document, document. Keep copious records and a daily diary of relevant information, memorialize conversations with letters to the file, and maintain a separate set of documents outside of work in a safe place. Your chances of success will likely depend on how powerful a paper trail you produce. After you blow the whistle, your access to agency records may be immediately cut off.

4. Do not use government resources. Do not engage in whistle-blowing activity on agency time, even to defend yourself in a retaliation case unless you have specific approval, such as through a union collective bargaining agreement.

5. Check to see who, if anyone, will support your account. Gauge the level of concern among your coworkers for the concerns you might raise. If you can't count on others to later testify as supporting witnesses, you may be well advised to wait before challenging misconduct. Try to stay on good terms with administrative staff members who may be in a position to know of impending agency actions.

6. Consult an attorney early. Do not wait until you are in the "career emergency room" before seeking professional help.

7. Choose your battles. Pick favorable terrain for highlighting your issue. Don't sweat the small stuff. In any personnel action, the advantage is with the employer, not the lone employee.

8. Identify allies. There is strength in numbers. Do not wait to be isolated by the agency. If possible, line up the assistance of sympathetic interest groups, elected officials, or journalists. The strength of your support coalition may determine the outcome of the battle ahead.

9. Have a well thought-out plan. Be clearheaded about precisely what you expect to accomplish and how. Try to prepare for agency countermoves by anticipating agency responses to your charges and mapping out the counter to those charges.

10. Get yourself a little career counseling. Map out where your actions will leave you a year from now, two years from now, five years, and so on. Plan out the route you want to take and how you reasonably expect your professional path to proceed. There is no doubt that you are about to embark upon a professional journey (Svara, 2007, p. 127).

SOURCE: POGO/GAP/PEER 2002, 4–7, in Svara, James. (2007). *The Ethics Primer for Public Administrators in Government and Nonprofit Organizations.* Sudbury, MA: Jones and Bartlett Publishers.

tive action occurred with the adoption of the Pendleton Act in 1883, which "prohibited political assessment, solicitations, subscriptions, or contributions from or by any employee of the United States." The most sweeping ban on political activity, however, occurred during Theodore Roosevelt's administration. He declared that classified civil service employees "shall take no active part in political management or in political campaigns" (Masters & Bierman, 1985, p. 519). Later, Congress passed the Hatch Political Activities Act in 1939, stating that "no officer or employee of the executive branch of the federal government, or any agency or department thereof, shall take any active part in political management or in political campaigns." (A set of amendments passed in 1940 extended the ban on political management and campaigning to state and local employees whose programs were financed fully or in part by federal funds.)

Under the Hatch Act, public employees can register to vote, contribute money to campaigns, assist in voter registration drives, and express opinions about candidates and issues; however, the following activities are prohibited.

1. Endorsing partisan candidates
2. Listing or raising money for political action committees
3. Participating in partisan voter registration and get-out-the-vote drives
4. Distributing campaign material on behalf of candidates
5. Serving as a delegate to a political convention
6. Making campaign speeches
7. Seeking public office in partisan elections (Masters & Bierman, 1985, pp. 519–520)

Although the Hatch Act seeks both to protect public employees from political harassment and the political process from special influence, it has been subject to various interpretations and has proven confusing in its application. Moreover, many have claimed that it unduly restricts public employees' political freedoms by disenfranchising them from important political activities during the time they were employed by the government. Others have pointed out that the Hatch Act places more stringent restrictions on United States government employees than on those of Great Britain, Canada, and Australia. For this reason, there have been recent efforts in Congress to change the Hatch Act, to permit a greater range of political activities by those in government. Many support the proposed legislation, especially those in public employee unions, who feel that public employees should be able to run for office and solicit campaign funds on their own time. Others, however, have argued that the Hatch Act is still necessary to prevent coercion of political officials. Reform of the Hatch Act has been considered for a number of years, with Congress passing major reform legislation in 1991 (though it was vetoed by President Bush).

In 1993, Congress changed the Hatch Act, generally strengthening those sections dealing with activities while on duty and expanding the off-duty activities of federal employees. Basically, with the exception of running for office, which is still prohibited, the new act permits federal workers to participate in a full range of political activities on their own time, not while on the job (*Congressional Quarterly Weekly*, 1993, p. 511).

■ Managing Ethics

How does a manager promote more ethical practices in an organization? First, of course, there are a variety of formal controls, including legal, on the behavior of those in public organizations—the courts may direct public officials to undertake specific actions or to "cease and desist" from certain courses of action. They may also be required, on behalf of their agencies, to provide individuals with damages or other compensation. And, of course, any public employee may be prosecuted for breaking the law. But what if you are sued as an individual for actions you have undertaken in the course of your official duties?

Actually, this question has been the subject of considerable legal debate throughout our country's history. Early interpretations of the law generally protected public officials against suits, claiming they violated an individual's rights in the course of one's duties. Recent interpretations have severely limited the immunity granted to public officials. Speaking broadly, there are two types of immunity: absolute immunity and qualified (or "good faith") immunity. Absolute immunity, which means that an official is not liable for damages under any circumstances, has been granted to certain legislative and judicial officers and, in limited cases, to members of the executive branch. (The president has been granted absolute immunity, but state governors have not.)

Most other officials have only qualified immunity; they may be sued, but they can defend themselves by showing they were acting in good faith. They must show that they were unaware of impropriety at the time and that any reasonable person might have acted similarly. Although the current legal position allows most officials to be sued, relatively few suits have been successful; most public managers have been found to have acted in good faith. In any case, knowing something about public officials' liability for their actions will better enable you and those in your organization to avoid problems in the first place or to respond to them when they arise.

Besides legal proceedings, other formal devices are available to protect against waste or fraud by public officials or the private individuals or groups with which they interact. For example, most major federal agencies have an Office of the Inspector General to investigate cases of fraud, waste, and abuse in government. The inspectors general are charged with looking into situations in which federal employees or funds are used improperly. Targets of investigations may be either public employees or private individuals, such as contractors, who might attempt to defraud the government.

Through their internal investigations of federal agencies, the inspectors general have occasionally revealed major problems. For example, the Office of the Inspector General of the Department of Health and Human Services initiated several studies related to excessive billings for Medicaid payments. Selling samples, billing Medicaid at higher prices than charged the public, and billing for brand-name drugs while dispensing generic drugs are among the suspected abuses. Similarly, the inspector general's office in the Defense Department recently announced plans to probe the military fastener industry—makers of bolts, screws, and other hardware—to see if substandard parts contributed to military accidents. In a related case, two Maryland defense contractors pleaded guilty to a decade-long scheme to sell cheap, low-grade fasteners for military equipment. The contractors admitted to substituting commercial-grade bolts, screws, and other fasteners for more expensive military-grade hardware ordered by defense contractors for radar and sonar systems, satellites, Trident submarines, and armored earthmovers like those used in the Persian Gulf War (*Washington Post*, 1992).

Establishing an Ethical Climate

In addition to formal controls, you can help promote ethical behavior by providing strong ethical leadership, creating a climate in which ethical behavior is valued, and encouraging free and open communications throughout the organization. "Managing ethics involves more than making public statements espousing a particular set of values and more than selecting employees with good moral character. Managing ethics also involves careful analysis of the organizational culture, working to develop a cultural environment that places high value on ethical integrity and developing policies and procedures and systems that enable organization members to act with ethical integrity" (Denhardt, 1989, p. 1). Unfortunately, most organizations, including most public organizations, have not undertaken active programs to promote ethics (see Box 4.3).

BOX 4.3

INTERVENTION TECHNIQUES FOR INTEGRATING ETHICS INTO AGENCY OPERATIONS

- Do both compliance and integrity training and counseling.
- Give briefings on common ethical problems on the job for new hires.
- Give termination briefings on potential postemployment problems.
- Designate senior manager(s) for integrity issues, separate from compliance/ investigative unit.
- Require annual sign-off on prospective commitment and compliance.
- Consider ethical values and character in recruitment.
- Integrate ethical performance into promotional exams and annual reviews; link ethical behavior to incentives.
- Publicize positive, noteworthy role models.
- Raise ethical concerns at meetings and through regular communication channels.
- Train middle managers to recognize and commend subordinates' statements about ethical concerns.
- Review management practices and administrative routines at every level and in every type of unit in the organization.
- Get the whole team—all employees, all levels, all units to participate; ethics is not a spectator sport.
- Give earnest attention to ethical treatment of subordinates, clients, and others.

SOURCE: Carol W. Lewis, *The Ethics Challenge in Public Service.* © 1991 by Jossey-Bass. This material is used by permission of John Wiley & Sons, Inc.

Many organizational members feel that, in the absence of an ethics program, the requirements of large bureaucracies tend to promote unethical, dishonest, and inhumane behavior. "Managers perceive that the bureaucratic environment is less ethical than their own values and beliefs, that they are under pressure to compromise personal standards to achieve organizational goals, and that their supervisors are interested only in results, not how they were obtained" (Bowman, 1983a, p. 74).

A first step in promoting more ethical practices in your organization is to analyze the basic ideas, beliefs, and attitudes that guide the behavior of the organization's members.

One device for assessing the prevailing beliefs of your organization is an *ethics audit*, an assessment of the value premises that guide action in the organization. The audit provides a methodical review of the organization's activities and the implicit values that underlie the activities. Importantly, these values may not turn out to be those contained in public pronouncements. One student of organizational behavior concluded that "the key to learning the ethics of individuals or organizations is simple: *Do not listen to what they say about ethics; observe what they do*" (Pastin, 1988, p. 92). By clearly establishing the values that guide behavior in the organization, you and other members can more consciously and clearly begin to alter those values that seem inappropriate.

As an example, after numerous incidents of defense contract violations, the General Dynamics Corporation brought in an outside consultant to help establish an ethics program. The consultant conducted an ethics audit, which helped members of the organization recognize that they shared a basic, though unstated, assumption that the government was their adversary and that taking advantage of an adversary was quite acceptable. Once this assumption was understood, it could be addressed openly and replaced with more appropriate assumptions about the relationships between government and its contractors. An example of an ethics audit conducted by a public agency is contained in Carol Lewis's book, *The Ethics Challenge in Public Service* (1991, pp. 199–202).

Following an ethics audit, your organization may wish to develop a clearer statement of values to guide individual behavior. The statement should include general moral guidelines, but also articulate a vision of the organization's mission—what it stands for, what it seeks to achieve, and how it plans to go about its business. Developing such a statement should involve many members of the organization and have the full support of top management. (We will examine statements of values in more detail later.)

Besides developing a statement of management philosophy for your organization, you may also wish to employ more general codes of ethics developed by other organizations. The federal government, for example, has promulgated a Code of Ethics for Federal Service, and many state and local government organizations have developed similar codes. Professional organizations such as the International City Management Association (ICMA) also have codes of ethics related to members of their profession. Perhaps the most comprehensive code of ethics for public-sector managers is that of the American Society for Public Administration (ASPA). The ASPA Code of Ethics and accompanying guidelines illustrate the variety of ethical concerns public managers face and provide guidance for resolving ethical issues (see Appendix at the end of this chapter).

After assessing values and adopting statements to express the desired values, you might wish to develop training programs or other devices for communicating these ideals within the organization. The Office of Government Ethics, for example, conducts frequent seminars for federal managers on ethics in the public service. Similarly, organizations such as ASPA and ICMA have developed training programs that are available nationally or can be adapted to local circumstances. Training programs are also available for executives in nonprofit organizations.

As a manager, however, you should not neglect the fact that your own actions will be taken as a "model" of appropriate behavior. The example you set will be one of the most important "training" devices to members of your organization. If you wish them to take the moral "high road," you must demonstrate by example that ethics is a substantial concern and that unethical conduct will not be tolerated.

■ Summary and Action Implications

As we move from the context of public administration to the ethics of public service, we also move from areas where abstract knowledge is helpful to areas where the ability to act is important. In dealing with the many ethical dilemmas that confront public officials, you must know not only what the correct action is, but be able to act in a way consistent with that judgment. Understanding how ethical choices are made is helpful, as is recognizing the importance of deliberation in making ethical decisions. But what will ultimately make the difference will be your willingness to act on the basis of moral principles.

The particular ethical issues you may face range from matters of individual integrity to those that derive from the special value commitments associated with working in the public interest. Most of the latter are associated with the tension between efficiency and responsiveness that seems to pervade public organizations. That tension, as well as issues of accountability and responsiveness to public demands, are especially intense in the relationship between administrators and the legislative branch.

Many of the concerns you may encounter as a public manager are similar to those other managers face, but some are especially conditioned by the fact that you are operating "in the public interest." In either case, you must exhibit the virtues of benevolence and justice (including honesty, trustworthiness, and fairness) in your behavior. In any case, as you face some of the difficulties that arise, careful self-reflection and dialogue with others about ethical concerns will be especially helpful.

It is within your power as an administrator to undertake programs to encourage and facilitate a more ethical climate within your organization. Conducting an ethics audit, developing a statement of organizational philosophy or a code of ethics, and establishing training programs to deal with ethical issues will help improve your organization's ethics.

As a manager, however, perhaps the most important message you can send is that communicated by your own actions. If you seem to attach great importance to ethical concerns, others in the organization will attach similar importance. The model you provide can make an important difference in the ethics of your organization.

TERMS AND DEFINITIONS

Cooptation: Situations in which citizens are given the feeling of involvement while exercising little real power.

Deontology: Belief that broad principles of rightness and wrongness can be established and are not dependent on particular circumstances.

Ethical (or moral) relativism: Belief that moral judgment can be made only by taking into account the context in which action occurs.

Ethics: Process by which we clarify right and wrong and act on what we take to be right.

Ethics audit: Evaluation of the value premises that guide action within an organization.

Morality: Practices and activities considered right or wrong and the value those practices reflect.

Neutral competence: The belief that a neutral public bureaucracy following the mandates of a legislative body will meet the requirements of democracy.

Objective responsibility: Assurance of responsiveness through external controls.

Subjective responsibility: Assurance of responsiveness based on an individual's character.

Utilitarianism: Philosophy of the greatest good for the greatest number of people.

STUDY QUESTIONS

1. Although ethics and morality are similar, what is the distinction between the terms?

2. Discuss the steps in ethical deliberation.

3. Compare the two approaches commonly used in moral philosophy.

4. Discuss the three levels of moral development devised by psychologist Lawrence Kohlberg.

5. What is meant by an "ethics of virtue"?

6. Discuss the conflict between efficiency and responsiveness.

7. Explain the limitations on administrators' discretion with regard to responsiveness and efficiency.

8. Discuss some of the ethical problems individuals who work in public organizations encounter and how they can deal with them properly.

9. The Hatch Act defines prohibited activities of public employees. Explain the significance of these prohibitions with regard to an individual's political actions.

10. Explain ways to improve the ethical behavior of those in a public organization and provide examples of managing ethics.

CASES AND EXERCISES

1. To illustrate various aspects of ethical deliberation, read and discuss the following case.

There is a raging river that can be crossed only by boat. The only boat is owned and operated by a person we shall call A (in order to protect the innocent as well as the guilty). On the tame side of the river, X is deeply and sincerely in love with a person, C, on the other side of the river. X goes to A and asks to be taken across the river, offering to pay for the service. A declines any money, but agrees to take X across the river if X will sleep with A. Person X refuses, of course (!), but argues and then pleads with A to name some other price. A, however, remains firm.

Person X leaves, but returns a second day to seek a way across the river. A remains as adamant as before. In frustration, X seeks out a third person, B, who hears the situation sympathetically, agreeing that A is certainly a rogue. But B says, "I have other matters to deal with just now and cannot help you."

In desperation, X goes to A a third time, only to be met with the same deal for the trip across the river. X finally agrees to the price and sleeps with A, who then delivers X across the river as promised.

X and C are joyously reunited, until C asks how X got across the river. X truthfully replies, "I had to sleep with A to earn the trip across the river." C replies indignantly, "Out of my life! I will have nothing to do with one who holds honor and principle so lightly!"

X, of course, is frustrated and desperate again, and appeals to another person, D, who replies, "I understand and am deeply sympathetic. I'd do anything I can to help you." (The curtain falls.) (ASPA, n.d.)

Following your discussion of the case itself, consider to what extent the discussion reflected moral relativism, utilitarianism, or deontology. Then, reconsider the case, following the steps of ethical deliberation presented in this chapter. Clarify the facts, find basic principles, and analyze the arguments. How could you establish a moral action?

2. A random check of long-distance telephone calls at the Department of Housing and Urban Development, conducted by the agency's inspector general, indicated that some 30 percent were personal calls (though charged to the government). The cost of the calls was estimated at $73,000 for the sample and, by extrapolation, $290,000 for the agency as a whole. Many calls were placed to the homes of employees or their relatives; others were calls to prerecorded messages, such as time and temperature, horoscopes, and financial information. Penalties for unauthorized use of federal telephone lines include fines, suspension, and dismissal.

Why do you think employees at HUD, and presumably elsewhere, misuse official telephone lines? What, if anything, should be done to limit such excesses? How do you respond to employees who argue that using agency telephone lines for personal business is necessary from time to time? What about those who argue that telephone use is an essential benefit the organization should provide? If you crack down on unauthorized calls, what will happen to morale in the agency?

To put the case in a more intense, real-world setting, imagine that you are secretary of Housing and Urban Development. You have just finished testifying at a congressional hearing. On your way out the door, a senator corners you and waves a copy of the inspector general's report in your face, saying, "This is an outrage! These people are stealing from the public, and you've been letting it happen! I want some action on this right away!" Next, a reporter, who has seen the report and heard the exchange with the senator, shoves a microphone in your face and asks, "Well, what are you going to do?" What is your response, both immediately and over the next several days?

3. Consider the following cases. Sidney Franklin knew that one of his most valued employees, Anderson Hayes, was stealing from the organization—not much, and in a way that no one but Sidney would ever know—but he *was* stealing. Sidney also knew that without Anderson, his unit could never complete a newly assigned task on time. He decided to do nothing about the stealing incident and secretly hoped that success in the new assignment would bring about a long-desired promotion and get him out of this awkward situation.

Analyze and discuss this case in terms of the moral position that the individual involved should have taken. Then consider the nature of your own ethical reasoning. What types of moral philosophy, moral psychology, or moral action have you been using?

4. As a class, conduct an ethics audit (or survey) of your college or university and recommend ways the institution might begin to develop higher standards of ethical conduct.

Begin by considering in detail what might be expected from such an audit (or survey) in any organization and what is practical and ethical to expect from such a project conducted by students within the institution. Recognize your available resources, but also the limitations on your work. (You might even want to discuss your project with several university officers before proceeding.)

As a practical matter, consider basing your work primarily on interviews with important decision makers throughout the institution, including administrators, deans and department chairs, members of the faculty (especially members of the faculty council or faculty senate), representatives of the school's athletic programs, and staff support in areas such as budget and accounting and personnel or human resources. Also consider interviews with members of the school's governing board. You might also want to collect material based on public record: newspaper reports, magazine articles, editorials, and so forth. *The Chronicle of Higher Education* and other materials dealing with higher education show what kinds of efforts other schools have undertaken.

Throughout your interviews and other research, you should first seek to determine the major ethical concerns facing institutions of higher education. Topics you will likely encounter are plagiarism and other forms of academic dishonesty (on the part of both faculty and students), the integrity of the research process, matters of institutional governance, questions of equal opportunity and affirmative action, institutional policies toward drugs and alcohol, the school's position on certain political issues, and athletic recruiting policies—just to name a few. You may find that your institution has taken strong moral positions in some areas (perhaps many areas). You may even find parts of the institution that have undertaken serious and detailed appraisals of their ethical positions. You may also find, however, that many of these issues simply haven't been considered, at least in terms of ethical implications.

If you can simply develop an inventory of ethical issues that should receive greater attention from members of the institution, you will have done a great service. But you may also identify cases where actual behavior seems to imply an ethical position different from the position espoused by those with whom you talk. If you discover such cases, be prepared not only to document your findings, but also to present your report in such a way that will be helpful and constructive. Remember that you are seeking to provide a service to the institution, not an exposé.

Based on your research and analysis, prepare a written report for the school's president or chancellor and offer to have a delegation meet with him or her (or a representative) to discuss your findings. Again, your approach should be to provide preliminary findings that will be helpful in terms of institutional ethics. It may be helpful to think of yourself as a member of the president's or chancellor's staff, developing a report upon which constructive action can be taken. As in any such situation, you should be prepared to suggest specific action steps that will enable the school to give serious and sustained attention to its ethical posture.

After you finish spend some time considering as a class what you have learned from this exercise—about institutional ethics and the administrative process, and what will make you a more effective and responsible administrator in the future. Try to develop specific action-oriented statements to guide your actions in the future. Finally, consider whether there were any ethical questions you faced in the course of this project. How did you resolve them? Or did you?

FOR ADDITIONAL READING

Adams, Guy B., and Danny L. Balfour. *Unmasking Administrative Evil*. Rev. ed. with a new foreword by Charles Perrow. Armonk, NY: M. E. Sharpe, 2004.

Bowman, James S., ed. *Ethical Frontiers in Public Management: Seeking New Strategies for Resolving Ethical Dilemmas*. San Francisco: Jossey-Bass, 1991.

Bowman, James, ed. *Public Integrity Annual*. Lexington, KY: Council of State Governments, 1997.

Bruce, Willa. *Classics of Administrative Ethics*. Boulder, CO: Westview Press, 2001.

Burke, John P. *Bureaucratic Responsibility*. Baltimore: Johns Hopkins University Press, 2000.

Cooper, Terry L. *The Responsible Administrator: An Approach to Ethics for the Administrative Role*. 3rd ed. San Francisco: Jossey-Bass, 1990.

Cooper, Terry L. *An Ethic of Citizenship for Public Administration*. Englewood Cliffs, NJ: Prentice-Hall, 1991.

Cooper, Terry L. *Exemplary Public Administrators: Character and Leadership in Government*. San Francisco: Jossey-Bass, 1992.

Cooper, Terry, ed. *Handbook of Administrative Ethics*. New York: Marcel Dekker, 1994.

Denhardt, Robert B. *Theories of Public Organization*. 5th ed. Belmont, CA: Thomson/Wadsworth, 2007.

Frederickson, George H., and Richard K. Ghere, eds. *Ethics in Public Management*. Armonk, NY: M. E. Sharpe, 2005.

Harmon, Michael M. *Public Administration's Final Exam: A Pragmatist Restructuring of the Profession and the Discipline*. Tuscaloosa, AL: University of Alabama Press, 2006.

Harmon, Michael. *Responsibility as Paradox*. Thousand Oaks, CA: Sage Publications, 1995.

Hodgkinson, Christopher. *Administrative Philosophy*. Oxford: Pergamon Press, 1996.

Jun, Jong S. *The Social Construction of Public Administration: Interpretive and Critical Perspectives*. Albany: State University of New York Press, 2006.

Kellar, Elizabeth, ed. *Ethical Insight/Ethical Action.* Washington, DC: ICMA, 1988.

Pasquerella, Lynn, Alfred G. Killilea, and Michael Vocino. *Ethical Dilemmas in Public Administration.* Westport, CT: Praeger, 1996.

Richardson, William D. *Ethics and Character: The Pursuit of Democratic Virtues.* Durham, NC: Carolina Academic Press, 1999.

Rohr, John. *Ethics for Bureaucrats.* New York: Marcel Dekker, 1978.

Rohr, John. *To Run a Constitution.* Lawrence, KS: University Press of Kansas, 1986.

Rohr, John. *Ethics and Public Administration.* Armonk, NY: M. E. Sharpe, 1993.

Svara, James. *The Ethics Primer for Public Administrators in Government and Nonprofit Organizations.* Sudbury, MA: Jones and Bartlett Publishers, 2007.

Tong, Rosemarie. *Ethics in Policy Analysis.* Englewood Cliffs, NJ: Prentice-Hall, 1986.

Washington, Sally. *Ethics in the Public Service.* Paris: OECD, 1996.

APPENDIX

Code of Ethics of the American Society for Public Administration (ASPA)

I. Serve the Public Interest

Serve the public, beyond serving oneself. ASPA members are committed to

1. Exercise discretionary authority to promote the public interest.

2. Oppose all forms of discrimination and harassment, and promote affirmative action.

3. Recognize and support the public's right to know the public's business.

4. Involve citizens in policy decision-making.

5. Exercise compassion, benevolence, fairness, and optimism.

6. Respond to the public in ways that are complete, clear, and easy to understand.

7. Assist citizens in their dealings with government.

8. Be prepared to make decisions that may not be popular.

II. Respect the Constitution and the Law

Respect, support, and study government constitutions and laws that define responsibilities of public agencies, employees, and all citizens. ASPA members are committed to

1. Understand and apply legislation and regulations relevant to their professional role.

2. Work to improve and change laws and policies that are counterproductive or obsolete.

3. Eliminate unlawful discrimination.

4. Prevent all forms of mismanagement of public funds by establishing and maintaining strong fiscal and management controls, and by supporting audits and investigative activities.

5. Respect and protect privileged information.

6. Encourage and facilitate legitimate dissent activities in government and protect the whistle-blowing rights of public employees.

7. Promote constitutional principles of equality, fairness, representativeness, responsiveness, and due process in protecting citizens' rights.

III. Demonstrate Personal Integrity

Demonstrate the highest standards in all activities to inspire public confidence and trust in public service. ASPA members are committed to

1. Maintain truthfulness and honesty and to not compromise them for advancement, honor, or personal gain.

2. Ensure that others receive credit for their work and contributions.

3. Zealously guard against conflict of interest or its appearance: e.g., nepotism, improper outside employment, misuse of public resources, or the acceptance of gifts.

4. Respect superiors, subordinates, colleagues, and the public.

5. Take responsibility for their own errors.

6. Conduct official acts without partisanship.

IV. Promote Ethical Organizations

Strengthen organizational capabilities to apply ethics, efficiency, and effectiveness in serving the public. ASPA members are committed to

1. Enhance organizational capacity for open communication, creativity, and dedication.

2. Subordinate institutional loyalties to the public good.

3. Establish procedures that promote ethical behavior and hold individuals and organizations accountable for their conduct.

4. Provide organization members with an administrative means for dissent, assurance of due process, and safeguards against reprisal.

5. Promote merit principles that protect against arbitrary and capricious actions.

6. Promote organizational accountability through appropriate controls and procedures.

7. Encourage organizations to adopt, distribute, and periodically review a code of ethics as a living document.

V. Strive for Professional Excellence

Strengthen individual capabilities and encourage the professional development of others. ASPA members are committed to

1. Provide support and encouragement to upgrade competence.

2. Accept as a personal duty the responsibility to keep up to date on emerging issues and potential problems.

3. Encourage others, throughout their careers, to participate in professional activities and associations.

4. Allocate time to meet with students and provide a bridge between classroom studies and the realities of public service.

SOURCE: WWW.ASPANET.ORG

CHAPTER 5

DESIGNING AND MANAGING ORGANIZATIONS

A public administrator needs a good understanding of the values and principles underlying work in the public and nonprofit sectors, knowledge of how public policy is developed and executed, and familiarity with a number of administrative techniques peculiar to public and nonprofit organizations. But the real key to managerial success is not what you know, but what you can do. How effectively and how responsibly can you deal with the seemingly endless series of problems and opportunities that confront you in an organizational setting? A legislator or foundation program officer calls to ask for an immediate report on a matter you know will require a week to examine properly; a subordinate confesses that he has grown dependent on drugs and needs your help; someone in a meeting becomes outraged over what you perceive as a minor matter and threatens to have you fired; your boss asks your assistance in designing a completely new program and asks if you would be interested in running it. These situations and many more like them constitute the real challenges of public administration.

Your response to each event, of course, is spontaneous; yet, your actions will soon add up to a pattern that reflects your knowledge, values, and most of all, skills in dealing with other people. Organizations create the environment or context for these actions and set the stage for how your choices and behaviors will be seen and reacted to by others. An understanding of organizations—how they are structured, how they influence behavior, how they both limit the range of possibilities and facilitate new opportunities at the same time—is crucial to success in public administration. If, time after time, you act effectively and responsibly in situations that arise unexpectedly and require immediate answers with little time to think through the "theoretical" possibilities, you will be considered a highly successful manager.

Fortunately, the skills required for managerial effectiveness can be developed over time. In this and the following chapters, we examine how your knowledge and values can be brought to bear in real-world situations. We focus on the nature and structure of organizations, the specific personal and interpersonal skills a manager requires, and some ways you might further develop those skills. In this chapter, we look at several broad approaches to understanding the structure and design of public and nonprofit organizations, as well as people's behavior within those organizational settings.

■ The Organizational Context

To gain the ability to function well within organizations, it is useful to begin by asking some basic questions about how and why we create organizations in the first place. What are the reasons for and advantages of formal organizations? What do we gain and lose by creating organizations? Is there a best way to organize or reorganize public and nonprofit programs? We all have certain ideas and assumptions about how to organize and structure work. For instance, you may have preferences about how you would organize a group project for a school assignment or how you would organize tasks if you and several of your friends decided to throw a party. Where do these ideas about organizing come from, and what have we learned about how these structures work?

Organizations are as necessary as they are unavoidable in the modern world. When you think about all the organizations that you are connected to and rely on, the list can seem endless: your school, the businesses you buy goods and services from, the power company, the government organizations that you depend on for services and programs ranging from streets and fire protection to national defense and education. Yet, because we sometimes get frustrated with these organizations, we forget why people create them in the first place. Because they are so much a part of our lives, almost all of us can relay personal "horror stories" about dealing with organizations and how an organization was slow, rigid, or unresponsive. So why don't we just get rid of them?

The simple answer is that organizations exist because we need them. Think of what school would be like without an organization with job descriptions, multiple offices, schedules, rules, procedures, regulations, and all the features that can make organizations such as universities seem very frustrating at times. How would you know when classes are offered? Would each professor get to decide who gets to take his or her class and when and where it would be held? Imagine if the number of classes you were required to take in order to graduate depended on whom you asked? What if there wasn't any particular department or procedure for applying for financial aid? What if the library was open only when the library staff felt like it and people could just take books without checking them out and keep them as long as they wanted?

Obviously, there are advantages to organizing formal structures for getting things done. At the most basic level, we can often accomplish more by working together with other people than we can alone. But there are other advantages as well. By organizing, we can achieve cooperation between people and coordination between tasks. Organizational structures, and the rules and procedures that go with them, create predictability and regularity for the people who work in those organizations and those that interact with them. When you create schedules and processes, then people are not dependent on the whim of any particular individual. When rules are formally established, then we can increase consistency and fairness. Organizational structure allows people to know what to expect and what is expected of them. Organizations also provide the framework for dividing work so people can develop skills in a particular area—not everyone in the organization has to be an expert in everything the organization does.

[handwritten margin note: argument for organization]

At the same time, there are disadvantages to formal organizations. Putting limits on individual choice is unavoidable if you are to gain the advantages of formal organization structure. The same procedures that ensure fairness and consistency in the treatment of individuals in organizations often keep individuals from getting what they want when they want it. Although in our interactions with organizations, we would like to bypass the rules on occasion, if there were no rules, each of us would be forced to act alone and beg, bribe, or convince individuals to help us. As individual employees of organizations, we may feel limited in our freedom to decide when we will go to work and the tasks we will (or will not) accomplish. If we were completely free to do so, however, it would be very difficult to accomplish shared tasks, much less be fair to the needs of the people we are supposed to be serving. When we create, design, and manage organizations, we want to gain the advantages of predictability and fairness while being mindful of the disadvantages and limits we are placing on individuals. Given this challenge, what are some ways to evaluate the alternative ways of managing and designing organizations?

■ Images of Organizing in the Public and Nonprofit Sectors

All managers carry around in their heads ideas or images of how public and nonprofit organizations should operate and how individual managers should act. These images, built up through experience, reading, discussion, and reflection, include notions about the most effective structures for public agencies, the best way to manage employees, and the proper relationship between elected and appointed officials. Depending on your particular view, you will tend to look for and emphasize certain things and ignore others. The images you carry in your head will lead you to emphasize certain aspects of organizational life and to de-emphasize others.

Some of these images derive from our experiences in our families, others come from school experiences, and still others are a result of work in other organizations. Some are general lessons we learned about topics, such as power and authority, communications and cooperation, and so forth. Others are more specific to the world of work or the public service. Some are fairly conscious; others lie far beneath the surface.

Whatever their form, these images direct our actions in specific ways. They make us see the world in a particular way and, correspondingly, act in a particular way. So it is important to carefully consider how individuals think about public and nonprofit organizations. What images do we have, and how do they direct us to act? Which images allow us to be most successful, and which hold us back or get in the way?

As you begin to think more carefully about the images that shape your work, and especially as you begin to accumulate experiences, you will begin to identify areas where your insight (and consequently your actions) might be improved. One way to sharpen your images of public and nonprofit organizations is to consider what scholars and practitioners in the field of general management, particularly public and nonprofit management, have said and written. Fortunately, there is a considerable and growing body of material to draw upon that offers many categories and approaches you might use in thinking about your involvement.

For the most part, this literature has developed out of the experiences of practicing managers. (Because the literature on nonprofit management is still in its early stages, much of the following discussion relates to public-sector management.) Reflective practitioners and thoughtful academics have asked over and over how public and nonprofit managers can be helped to select those features of organizational life that will be most helpful to them. Many students and practitioners of public administration have contributed to our understanding of the management of public agencies. They have developed "word pictures" (often simply called theories) to suggest what will be most helpful when you approach similar problems.

Each theoretical approach directs attention toward certain topics or ideas and away from others. It is up to you to select the most relevant and most helpful approaches to your particular situation. In this chapter, we review some of the most influential ways of thinking about organizations and management in the public sector. Some early approaches focused on fairly obvious points, but more recent approaches are more complex and sophisticated.

■ The Functions of Management

In the twentieth century, French management theorist and practitioner Henri Fayol (1949) identified five general functions managers should perform: planning, organizing, commanding, coordinating, and controlling. Several years later, Luther Gulick compiled a similar list. Gulick, an advisor on federal government reorganization, described the functions of public management in terms of an acronym, POSDCORB: planning, organizing, staffing, directing, coordinating, reporting, and budgeting (Gulick, 1937a). To Fayol and Gulick, these activities were the essence of management and identified functions that had to be performed if organizations were to be managed effectively. They constituted advice to managers about what they should be doing.

Planning involves preparing yourself and your organization to move effectively into the future. All managers engage in planning at least to some extent, and for some managers, such as those on strategic planning staffs, planning is almost a full-time activity. Some managers make plans for the entire organization, while others make plans for the units they directly supervise, but all managers plan for their own activities. Unfortunately, as we noted earlier, planning is one managerial function that is often easy to overlook. Managers get caught up in the hectic pace of conversations, meetings, and deadlines and often neglect planning. Yet, the most effective managers are aware that time taken out for planning, whether for the organization or for oneself, pays rich dividends.

Planning is closely related to decision making, an aspect of managerial work that cuts across many of the other areas. The ability to make thoughtful decisions seems to distinguish the more successful managers. Because decision making is so fundamental to managerial work, it has been studied intensively for many years. In most organizations, decision making is a central activity. (We will discuss decision making in more detail later.)

Organizing refers to many different activities, including division of the organization into different departments, creating levels in the organization's hierarchy, and deciding who reports to whom. In a specific department or division, organizing also includes the task of defining specific positions and jobs. Note that organizing includes job design, but the assignment of individuals to specific jobs involves the staffing rather than the organizing function.

Staffing is the process of acquiring, training, and developing the personnel to conduct the organization's activities. It is generally described as "personnel management" or sometimes "human resources management." As we will see in Chapter 6, specific tasks such as hiring, training, firing, and so forth are examples of the staffing or personnel function. Obviously, dealing with people involves important skills in communication and motivation, as well as the ability to make sound decisions about whom to hire.

Directing is often the most dynamic and most visible management function. It includes three critical management activities: leading, motivating, and changing things when necessary. Providing direction to an organization is a subtle and complex task that involves the full range of personal and interpersonal skills.

Coordinating the work of many different people in many different places is also a central managerial function. The complexity and diversity of most modern organizations means that a great deal of time must be spent making sure that all the "pieces" fall into

What Would You Do?

You have been given the assignment of managing a brand new federal program designed to assure an adequate supply of flu vaccine each year. Your first task will be to explore whether provision of vaccine should become a public function or remain in private hands (or something in between). You are then to prepare a plan for organizing the transition to whatever new system you recommend. What would you do?

place at the right time. Coordinating involves special skills in problem solving—how to make things work—but it also involves skills in communicating and negotiating.

Reporting provides the basis for accountability. It involves analyzing and keeping records of organizational activities and performance, and then providing meaningful and useful information to elected officials, citizens, and others to whom the manager is accountable. Reporting and record keeping is also important so that the manager and others can keep track of tasks and activities, analyze performance and progress toward goal attainment, identify problems in a timely fashion, and find opportunities for improvement.

Budgeting involves managing the organization's resources, especially financial. It also involves securing, planning for, and managing the organization's funds. As we will see in Chapter 7, budgeting is a technical field, but it also involves human skills, especially those of developing funding for one's programs and allocating scarce resources among competing programs and people.

In addition to these standard management functions, there are also a number of miscellaneous tasks that are usually considered managerial work. One of the most important is dealing with people from outside the organization. Skills in presenting your organization and point of view to others are becoming increasingly important as the relationships among organizations at different levels become more intense. Representing your organization before outside groups and organizations has come to be known in the literature on management as *boundary spanning*.

The Early Writers: A Concern for Structure

The question of how to best organize and manage work has occupied theorists and practitioners for many years. When you think about setting up an organization, you might think, for example, about establishing who will be "in charge" of what, making assignments and delegating tasks, and maybe even setting up some rules and timetables. Although this may feel like the "natural" or obvious way to organize, many of these ideas can be traced to the work of a German sociologist named Max Weber, who observed the emergence of large-scale organizations in the late-nineteenth and early-twentieth centuries. He was the first to use the term *bureaucracy* and to write comprehensively about the structure of these large-scale organizations. According to Weber, bureaucracy meant any large organization, public or private, characterized by a clearly defined hierarchy of impersonal offices and employment of qualified people who are subject to strict discipline and control (Weber in Gerth and Mills, 1946, p. 328). More specifically, Weber said that bureaucracies could be characterized as follows.

1. There is a fixed and stable structure for dividing tasks and responsibilities established and operated according to rules and regulations.
2. The authority to give orders related to these duties is set forth in official rules.
3. Only people who are qualified to do the work are employed in order to provide consistent and ongoing accomplishment of organizational tasks.
4. There is a system of graded authority or hierarchy in which each level of the organization, from bottom to top, is supervised by the next higher level.
5. Management is based on written records and documents to keep track of correspondence, decisions, financial matters, and other items of importance.
6. Office management is based on thorough and expert training.
7. Working in a bureaucracy is a vocation or profession. It is generally a full-time activity, not a secondary activity.

Though we now often use *bureaucracy* pejoratively, Weber's more technical use of the term carries no negative connotation. In fact, Weber argued that bureaucracy is the most efficient way to organize: "Experience tends to universally show that the purely bureaucratic type of administration [is] capable of attaining the highest degree of efficiency and is in the sense formally the most rational known means of carrying out imperative control over human beings" (Weber in Gerth and Mills, 1946, p. 337). On the other hand, Weber was also concerned about some of the drawbacks of the bureaucratic form. First, he cautioned that fully developed bureaucratic power and expertise could come to "overtower" or surpass democratic controls. Second, he was concerned about the effects of bureaucracy on individual freedoms.

Despite these concerns, the bureaucratic form of organization has long served as the foundation for many of our ideas about organizational design and structure. Early writers on public administration thought of management in highly mechanical terms and considered questions of organizational structure and design of paramount importance. Recall that the birth of public administration as a separate field of study occurred during a time of impressive gains in science and industry. New ideas and new products were changing society almost overnight, as were the industrial and organizational processes that made them possible. It was a time of rigid control by "captains of industry"; it was also a time of fostering the birth of the assembly line.

In such an era, the machine became the leading image for how to organize technical and human processes. Just as the machine was precise, mechanical, and efficient, so should be the organizations that built the machines. The result was a highly mechanical approach to organization that valued the idea of developing proper structures and operating them with great efficiency.

This orientation was epitomized in the influential work of Frederick W. Taylor, who developed what he termed *"scientific management,"* an approach based on carefully defined "laws, rules, and principles" (1923, p. 7). Taylor focused first on the individual worker, designing detailed measurements of time and motion to discover how the worker might become more efficient. For example, one might measure the distance from where a particular piece of equipment was stored to where it was used and then try to reduce the distance, time, and motion required to use the equipment. (In one example, Taylor sought to develop a "science of shoveling" based on the premise that the size of each individual shovel load would affect the daily output of "first-class shovelers." After careful and detailed experiments, it was determined that the greatest tonnage per day would be achieved with an average shovel load of about twenty-one pounds!)

Taylor's approach could be applied to a wide variety of work-process problems, from the design of assembly lines to the arrangement of items on one's desk. But beyond these efforts to turn workers into highly tuned machines, Taylor's work provided guidance for managers throughout the organization. The manager's role became that of making the organization more efficient through the application of detailed "scientific" information. The smooth-running organization was to be highly mechanical, with the human elements strictly controlled to contribute to overall efficiency. The manager's job was to ensure the efficient operation of the system.

Just as Taylor and others emphasized the efficient operation of industrial systems, others soon applied this emphasis in public administration. Leonard White wrote, "The objective of public administration is the most efficient utilization of the resources at the disposal of officials and employees" (1926, p. 2). "In the science of administration, whether public or private, the basic 'good' is efficiency," Luther Gulick concurred (1937b, p. 192). Though several writers objected, pointing out that other values such as responsiveness come into play and that mechanical efficiency is "coldly calculating and inhuman" (Dimock, 1936, p. 120), efficiency was clearly the primary interest of most early public administrationists.

Early writers in public administration transferred other lessons from the field of business to the design and structure of organizations, specifically the importance of establishing single centers of power controlling basically top-down structures. At the top of the organization there was to be one single authority to whom all subordinate personnel ultimately reported. Though the organization would be characterized by many managers, and perhaps many organizational units, the ultimate responsibility and authority lay at the top.

NETWORKING

The Academy of Management Online at www.aomonline.org, the Society for Industrial and Organizational Psychology at www.siop.org, and the Institute for Operations Research and the Management Sciences at www.informs.org offer research and information sources concerning the general principles of organization theory and behavior. For an alternative, visit the Electronic Journal of Radical Organisation Theory at www.mngt.waikato.ac.nz/ejrot. This site is published by the University of Waikato School of Management Studies in Hamilton, New Zealand.

To reconcile this view with the democratic requirement that public organizations be responsive to the popular will, early writers suggested that the organization's head, the single source of power and authority, should simply be accountable to the legislative body in much the same way a corporate chief executive officer is accountable to a board of directors. (Recall this idea as "the doctrine of neutral competence.") In describing the role of an agency chief executive, early writers advised to vest all administrative authority in a single executive who would be given power to carry out the work and the responsibility for seeing that the work was done. According to W. F. Willoughby, this was the first step in making the executive branch a "single, integrated piece of administrative machinery" (1927, p. 37). (This advice was at odds with the standard political practice of that period: the election of many administrative officers and the use of many large executive boards. As we saw earlier, even today, most states elect officers such as secretary of state or treasurer rather than having such officers report to a single chief executive—in this case, the governor.)

The early writers who put forth the administrative management viewpoint were practical people who drew on their experience in managing public agencies. Consequently, when they described their work, they tended to emphasize how organizational structures might be built. Luther Gulick, for example, wrote extensively about the formation of agencies. After the agency was created and an executive chosen, Gulick saw the next task as one of dividing the necessary work, and then establishing proper means of coordination and control. The new organization would move through four phases in which the legislature or chief executive would (1) define the job, (2) select a director, who would (3) determine the nature and number of required units, and (4) establish a structure of authority through which he or she would coordinate and control activities of the units (1937a, p. 7).

The division of labor, which amounted to creation of an organizational structure, was a critical element. The logic was compelling: Because people differ in knowledge and skills, and because the amount of time any one person can contribute to the solution of large-scale problems is limited, it is necessary to divide the work of the organization into manageable portions. As we saw earlier, division of labor could be accomplished in a limited number of ways. Recall that Gulick suggested organizing on the basis of (1) the major purpose served (such as education or welfare), (2) the process (engineering or medicine), (3) the persons or things being dealt with by the unit (veterans or convicts), or (4) the place or geographic location where the work is done (1937a, pp. 21–29).

Having established a division of labor, the next problem facing the new director or manager was to create a structure of authority to coordinate and control the various parts of the organization. Gulick's answer to this question, like others during this period, was again drawn from orthodox practice in business: The organization should feature unity of command exercised through a hierarchical structure of authority. By the early 1900s, hierarchical organizations, like those symbolized in the standard organization chart (see Figure 5.1), had become models for industry (as they had previously been in the military and the Catholic church). Gulick and many other early scholars and practitioners in public administration suggested a similar approach in the public sector.

Guidance for creating such structures was given by two former General Motors executives, James Mooney and Alan Reiley (1939). Mooney and Reiley described four main principles for structuring large organizations. The first, *coordination through unity of command,* emphasized the importance of strong executive leadership exercised through a specific and formal chain of

1) Coordinated Command
   - know who gives *your* orders
2) Scalar (Vertical) Principle

3) functional principle (horizontal)
   - infantry + Air force
4) line + Staff
   - line; info goes up
   - Staff; info to chief.

FIGURE 5.1 General v. Private

Typical Organization Chart Showing Line and Staff

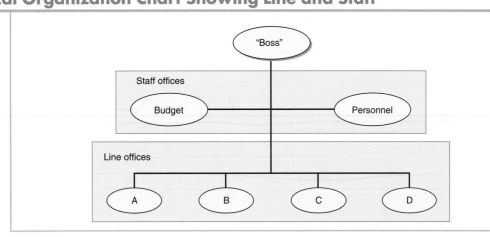

command. In this structure, each person would have only one boss, and each boss would have a limited span of control—that is, a limited number of people reporting to him or her. Mooney and Reiley argued that there should be no question about whose orders to obey.

The second principle was the *scalar principle*, which described the vertical division of labor among various organizational levels. (In military terms, the difference between a general and a private reflects the scalar principle.) Third was the *functional principle*, describing a horizontal division of labor. (Again, in military terms, the difference between Infantry and Air Force would be a functional difference.) Finally, Mooney and Reiley discussed the relationship between *line and staff*, with line offices representing the direct flow of authority, and staff offices (such as personnel or finance) available to advise the chief executive, but not exercising direct authority over line offices.

The language of hierarchical structures became somewhat standard. Just as distinctions were often drawn between line and staff, managers were (and are today) often classified as top, middle, or supervisory. Supervisory managers are at the bottom of the hierarchy, top managers at the peak, and middle managers in between. A supervisory manager directly manages the people involved in producing the organization's output. The supervisory level is the first level of management, so supervisors are sometimes called first-line managers. Normally, no managers are below the supervisory level. An example of a supervisory manager is the person to whom your mail carrier reports at the post office.

Supervisors report to middle managers, usually defined as "managers who manage other managers." If the organization is small, there may be only one level of middle managers; large organizations usually have more than one middle-management level. The highest level of management, the top level, usually has the fewest managers. Top managers, often called "executives," are responsible for entire organizations, whereas middle- and supervisory-level managers focus on increasingly smaller sections of the organization. Top managers are usually the most involved in relationships with other groups and agencies.

It is easy to distinguish supervisory-level from middle-level managers, but often ambiguous where middle management stops and top management begins. Titles often confuse things more than they help. The title of vice president, for example, indicates a top manager in some organizations; in others, the vice president is only a middle manager. Banks are particularly well known for having many vice presidents, most of whom are obviously not part of top management. Similarly, titles in public organizations, such as division director, branch chief, and department head, are used in different ways and are usually only meaningful if you understand the conventions of the organization.

In any case, early writers on public administration generally sought to apply what they saw as the correct "principles" of administrative management to the conduct of public organizations. They implied that the problems and solutions facing government were much the same as those in industry: centralization of authority and the development of hierarchical structures. But this assumption sidestepped several important issues essential to the operations of public agencies. Is the criterion of efficiency the only criterion by which the work of public organizations should be evaluated? Is it incompatible to create highly authoritarian structures to carry out the work of a democracy?

There were also questions about whether approaches to organization based on structural analysis alone were even the most efficient. In both the public and private sectors, for example, managers and researchers began to ask whether the rigid structures described in the principles of administrative management could effectively adapt to change. And, perhaps most important, where does the individual enter into the equation, other than as a potential machine? The structural lens through which many early scholars and practitioners viewed the world proved to be somewhat limiting; something else was needed.

■ Recognizing Human Behavior

In the mid-1920s, an impetus to further investigation of informal or human factors in organizational life came from studies conducted by Harvard researchers at the Hawthorne Works of the Western Electric Company. The studies, which began in a way largely consistent with the scientific management tradition, were designed to measure the relationship between working conditions (such as lighting, temperature, and humidity) and worker productivity (such as monotony and fatigue). In the experiment, certain groups were isolated from their coworkers and placed in carefully controlled environments where conditions could be varied systematically. But as the experiment developed, regardless of the changes in environmental conditions—lighter or darker, hotter or colder, more or less humid—the productivity of the experimental group tended to increase. Can you guess why?

Researchers discovered that the experimental group was responding not to the conditions around them, but to the fact that they had been singled out for special attention. As a result, the researchers developed a new interest in the human aspects of organizational life. Those in the Hawthorne study began to see organizations as not only meeting the stated goals of producing goods or services, but also as being concerned, even if implicitly, with the distribution of "satisfactions"—some monetary, others social and psychological—to members of the organization. The informal organization (in other words, the human interactions that paralleled those prescribed by the organizational structure) was viewed as important or even more important than the formal organization. If this were the case, then it made sense that the manager's role involved attention to both the formal structure of the work process and the pattern of informal relationships among the workers. Either one could affect efficiency and effectiveness.

There was abundant advice on how to manage the formal structure, but only speculation on how to manage the informal or human side of organizations. Consequently, a number of studies were undertaken that dealt with the critical human relationship between manager and worker. Many of the studies suggested that changes in one's approach to managing, or management style, could lead to important differences in productivity. By treating workers differently, you could affect the work they did.

An example of this orientation was Douglas MacGregor's discussion of Theory X and Theory Y. After reviewing other work on management, MacGregor suggested that a better theory of human behavior (not structure) might make it possible to more effectively control workers in organizations. MacGregor contrasted a set of assumptions about human behavior that appeared to form the basis for traditional management techniques (Theory X) with a set of assumptions he felt would underlie a new, more enlightened approach (Theory Y). Traditionally, MacGregor argued, managers assume that human beings are lazy and dislike work, that they must therefore be coerced to produce, and that most in fact want such direction. MacGregor suggested in contrast that work is quite natural, people do not need to be coerced, they will devote energy to objectives to which they are committed, and they will make commitments to objectives that, when completed, will lead to rewards. As a consequence, MacGregor suggested that most workers were not being utilized to their full potential. The lesson was straightforward: Managers must take care to determine the needs and desires of their employees, then help orient the individual's objectives so that they are met by work toward the organization's objectives.

Two Classic Works

Two writers on organizational behavior, both stimulated by the new attention to human factors in organizational life, wrote "classics" on the subject during the 1940s and 1950s. One author, Herbert Simon, came from the field of public administration; the other, Chris Argyris, began his work in industrial psychology. Both have influenced all fields of management even to the present.

Simon suggested that the reason we have large organizations in the first place is that human beings are limited or "bounded" in their rationality or capacity to solve the complex problems of the modern world. "The capacity of the human mind for formulating and solving complex problems is very small in comparison with the size of the problems whose solution is required for objectively rational behavior in the real world or even for a reasonable approximation to such objective rationality" (1957, p. 198). Organizations are seen as devices for molding our sometimes erratic behavior to rational patterns of obtaining our objectives.

In the abstract, it's not difficult to design a rational system for reaching organizational objectives. The difficulty comes when human beings, with all their emotions and interests, are inserted into the system. Because they are human, they often appear "irrational" in terms of the system, even though what they are doing, from their point of view, may be perfectly rational. The chief problem for Simon, therefore, became how to understand and direct human behavior in such a way that it aids in pursuit of the organization's objectives in a rational (that is, efficient) way.

Simon described the organization as a decision-making system involving two primary sets of decisions on the part of the individual: the decision to be a part of an organization and the decision to contribute desired behaviors to the organization. Simon approaches each problem through a rational calculation of costs and benefits. For example, a person may be expected to remain a member of an organization as long as the benefits exceed those that might be obtained elsewhere.

The same approach is used with respect to the individual's contributions to the organization, an issue closely tied to the question of authority. Simon argued that each individual establishes "an *area of acceptance* within which the subordinate is willing to accept the decisions made for him by his superior" (Simon, 1957, pp. 74–75). But because it is in the interest of the organization to have the "zone" or area of acceptance as wide as possible, the organization, through its managers, offers certain "inducements" designed to increase the individual's "contributions." Inducements include money and status, but they also involve creating a state of mind in which individuals tend to obey rather than disobey.

Simon argues that you cannot expect people to make perfectly rational decisions. Indeed, most human beings act with *bounded rationality*; they seek the best possible solution, though not necessarily the most rational from a purely economic standpoint. Members can be made to fall in line with the organization's expectations by means of inducements that are just good enough to elicit the desired contributions. In this way, what Simon terms "administrative man" (in contrast to "economic man") becomes a part of a rationally behaving system.

Rather than focusing on rational systems, Chris Argyris focused on the interaction of the individual and the organization. He suggested, like MacGregor, that formal organizational structures and traditional management practices were inconsistent with a natural human striving for growth and development. Individuals in our society, Argyris concluded, develop from infancy through adulthood along several important dimensions: from passivity to activity, dependence to independence, a limited to greater range of behaviors, shallow to deeper interests, shorter to longer time perspectives, positions of subordination to those of equality or superordination, and lack of awareness to greater awareness. Movement along each dimension contributes to what we know as the healthy adult personality.

Yet, argued Argyris, these goals are exactly those that traditional management practices prevent. For example, standard patterns of management give the individual little control over his or her work. Workers are expected to be passive, submissive, and limited in the range of their responses. They are expected to behave like children. Moreover, if individuals express frustration at such a situation, managers often see their behavior as hostile and dysfunctional. The typical managerial response is to crack down, to assert even more severe methods of control.

A healthier approach, suggests Argyris, would be to understand the basic tendencies of the human personality for growth and development, then to "fuse" these tendencies with the objectives of the organization. Achieving this congruence or fusion is the task of the manager. This requires that the manager develop "skill in self-awareness, in effective diagnosing, in helping individuals grow and become more creative, in coping with dependent-oriented . . . employees, and in surviving in a competitive world of management" (1962, p. 213).

Both Simon and Argyris shift from concerns with structure to concerns with human behavior. Each offers a new way of looking at organizations and the people in them. The manager, according to this new view, needs to take structure into account (for that will affect human behavior), but the "bottom line" is how people behave. And, of course, the behavior of human beings is affected by more than the structures in which they reside. The attention of the manager is redirected from structure to behavior, in Simon's and Argyris's works. In this new view, the job of the manager is to mold human behavior toward the purposes of the organization.

■ The Organization and Its Environment

The early emphasis on structure and the later emphasis on human behavior proved helpful in focusing attention on important aspects of life in complex organizations. But neither viewpoint considered the relationship between the organization and its environment. This missing element began to appear, however, as writers in the field of public administration returned to issues of structure, though they viewed structure in a quite different way. The new concern for structure was stimulated by two emerging approaches to public organizations: systems theory and the political economy approach. The *systems approach* suggested that public (or other) organizations could be viewed in the same way as biological or physical systems as whole "organisms," independent of their parts and pursuing specific purposes within a complex environment. The *political economy approach* focused on politics and economics as categories for analyzing organizational behavior.

Systems Theory

The systems model suggests that the organization receives from its environment the human and material resources it requires to function, as well as requests and directives about how it should operate. These resources, requests, and directives are processed through the organization and transformed by it. The resulting outputs (products, services, and so on) are transmitted back into the environment. In turn, these outputs are taken into account as new inputs are developed, and, over time, a balancing point is reached that makes possible the survival of the organization.

A classic study of the relationship between an agency and its environment was Selznick's analysis of the Tennessee Valley Authority (TVA) in the 1940s. Selznick argued that, in contrast to the closed, mechanical systems implied in many approaches to public organization, organizations are in fact open systems. That is, they exist within an institutional framework, which includes political parties, pressure groups, and special interests. Though the groups' demands may appear "irrational" from the perspective of the organization, they simply cannot be ignored.

The TVA sought to involve already existing local agencies in planning power distribution systems and other programs, in order to anticipate potential demands and be prepared

What Would You Do?

You have been taking doctoral-level classes at a local university while continuing to work as a mid-level manager in state government. Some of your fellow workers have been teasing you lately about your "theoretical" approach to management, which, they say, just doesn't work in the "real world." You are beginning to wonder yourself whether theoretical ideas really make a difference in practice. What would you do?

to respond. Additionally, the TVA wanted to get local groups committed to the TVA program by making them feel part of the organization. By bringing outside groups into the structure of the organization (by placing persons on advisory groups or negotiating service contracts with them), TVA sought support for its own programs. You will recall this idea as cooptation, a term Selznick defined as "the process of absorbing new elements into the leadership or policy-determining structure of the organization as a means of averting threats to its stability or existence" (Selznick, 1949, p. 13).

Another study examining the influence of environmental factors on the operations of public agencies was Herbert Kaufman's analysis of the U.S. Forest Service (Kaufman, 1960). The Forest Service faced the problem of how to secure compliance and consistency from forest rangers scattered across the country and who were subjected to pressure from their local communities. Rangers often served, of course, in isolated locations. Although they sought to carry out the policies of the Forest Service, they also developed loyalties to their local communities. They often had to carry out regulations that would adversely affect their friends and neighbors and, in such cases, might be tempted to deviate from central office directives. The agency's response was to devise a series of training programs, procedural devices, inspections, and sanctions as efforts to reduce the influence of the local environment and to ensure that central office orders were actually carried out.

Looking at how environmental factors influence public organizations led other writers to characterize public agencies as interdependent systems operating in a complex environment. No longer could one agency's work be viewed in isolation from other public and private agencies. One would simply not be able to understand how an agency operated without understanding the myriad external influences on the agency. Imagine, for example, the difficulty of implementing a new set of standards for water quality in a city located on a state boundary, such as Cincinnati. Think of all the agencies, public and private, that would have to be notified and would wish to express their views. Think of the various political jurisdictions—states, cities, counties, and special districts. Think of the various bodies within each jurisdiction that might want input: the mayor, legislature, and administrative agencies.

The complexity of administrative activities has led some scholars to suggest that it is no longer meaningful to focus on a specific agency's contribution to implementing policy, but to think in terms of programs. Recall that many federal programs operate through a pattern of funding in which money, rules, and guidelines are established for programs that are delivered at the state and local levels through both public and private agencies. For example, in the delivery of social services, such as drug prevention efforts, state and local governments use federal money to fund private or nonprofit providers of the services. In many cases, the money goes to fund programs, not specific agencies, so that these programs operate through rather diffuse networks of loosely joined groups rather than through traditional hierarchical structures. In such ill-structured "structures," older notions of organizational control give way to new emphasis on bargaining and negotiation, in which the systems perspective has much to offer.

From Political Economy to Organization Development

Interest in interorganizational policy networks was further stimulated by the emergence of the political economy approach to understanding public organizations. Wamsley and Zald (1976) suggest that public organizations can best be understood in terms of the conjunction of political and economic factors influencing their operation. These factors affect the organization both internally and externally, leading to four categories through which we might view organizations. First, the external political environment involves the interplay of various interest groups and other organizations that affect the organization's political climate. Second, the external economic environment consists of market exchanges that influence the available supply of resources. Third, the internal political category focuses on the distribution of power and authority. Fourth, the internal economy concerns the allocation of resources and how they are used.

The Wamsley-Zald approach is related to a more sophisticated, complex approach most often associated with Vincent Ostrom. Ostrom's public choice approach begins with examining how individuals might make choices if they were free to act rationally and in their own self-interest. Under some circumstances, people might be expected to engage in collective action, especially where "public goods" are involved or where situations are neither purely public nor purely private. (Public goods are distinguished from private goods—those that can be measured, marketed, and maintained—by the fact that they are highly indivisible; a public good such as the national defense is available to all once it is provided for one.)

Following this logic, Ostrom sees public organizations as "a means for allocating decision-making capabilities in order to provide public goods and services responsive to the preferences of individuals in different social contexts" (Ostrom & Ostrom, 1971, p. 207). Ostrom argues that the best structures for satisfying individual preferences are not centralized bureaucratic agencies, but rather more fragmented, multiorganizational arrangements.

Although earlier behavioral studies like Simon's and Argyris's were important in countering the field's dependence on a structural interpretation of organizational life, they were limited in certain ways. First, most of the behavioral literature failed to question the top-down pattern of organizational authority; many people thought it merely provided more sophisticated mechanisms for managerial control. Second, there seemed little interest in organization change processes, at a time that rapid social change was becoming a dominant feature of the landscape. Third, as open systems theorists pointed out, the perspective failed to comprehend the complexity of interorganizational bargaining and negotiation. Similarly, the political economy approach seemed to unnecessarily limit creativity and communication and seemed, at least to some, to place values in a secondary position.

Among major critics of earlier approaches were a group of scholars in the early 1970s whose collective work came to be known as "the New Public Administration." In contrast to older approaches that emphasized efficiency and control, the New Public Administration heralded openness and change, equity and involvement. In a rapidly changing society populated by diverse groups, the New Public Administrationists felt the key element in the survival of organizations—indeed, of society—was the capacity to adapt to rapid social change. Organizations would have to find ways to deal with an increasingly "turbulent" environment.

Doing so would require stimulating the creativity of everyone involved in any public program, both within the agency and in the environment. Involving the organization's members and its clients in the decision-making process would, the New Public Administrationists felt, foster creativity. Moreover, such an approach seemed far more consistent with democratic norms and practices than operating through top-down structures of control. The key words in the New Public Administration were *equity* and *involvement*.

Many of those associated with the New Public Administration became students of organizational change processes and sought ways to help organizations implement needed changes. One of the most important approaches they employed was *organization development*, a process-oriented approach to planned change. Organization development suggests many techniques for change that we will examine later, but it also offers another approach to view the work of organizations.

Robert Golembiewski, a leader in the application of organization development strategies and techniques to the public sector, points out that organization development represents a particular philosophy of management that is considerably at odds with traditional top-down tendencies and values the following.

1. Mutual accessibility and open communications
2. A willingness to experiment with new behaviors and to choose those that seem most effective
3. A collaborative concept of authority that emphasizes cooperation and willingness to examine conflicts openly
4. Helping relationships involving a sense of community and acceptance of responsibility for others
5. Authenticity in interpersonal relationships (Golembiewski, 1972, pp. 60–66)

Decision Making in Organizations

As suggested in our discussion of the public policy process, decision making represents one of the most critical functions of public and nonprofit organizations. Although the scope and nature of decision making varies from issue to issue, the process itself is a daily activity. Some have even suggested that organizations can be viewed as living histories of their decision-making processes. To better appreciate this important function, it may be helpful to examine some of the core concepts of organizational decision making and to understand how leaders use these concepts in their management practice (Hatch, 1997, pp. 270–281).

Scholars of organizations traditionally followed an economic view of decision making, which assumed that decisions were the result of rational, well-informed selection procedures. (Much of our discussion to this point reflects this traditional viewpoint.) In the rational model, management recognizes the problem, identifies alternatives, selects and implements the most efficient alternative, and monitors the results.

However, a series of works, beginning with March and Simon (1958), and Cyert and March (1963), challenged this rational viewpoint, arguing that decision making can be viewed as rational only in certain circumstances. Most often, organizations lack the information and capacity needed for making rational decisions. Simon, who received a Nobel Prize for his work in artificial intelligence, referred to this phenomenon as a "bounded rationality." He identified five of the most common constraints.

1. Imperfect and incomplete information
2. The complexity of the problem
3. Human information-processing capacity
4. The time available for decision-making processes
5. The conflicting preferences decision makers have for organizational goals (Hatch, 1997, p. 274)

Despite attempts on the part of managers to use more rational processes, these factors pose insurmountable barriers to rational decision making. The implications are two-fold. First, managers will never have enough data to adequately inform decision-making processes. Second, even if they did, they would face conflicting goals from stakeholders, to the point that they would be unable to make a truly rational selection of the most efficient alternatives. For Simon, the best that managers can do involves what he called, "satisficing"—that is, making do with the most information possible at the time and attempting to balance between competing demands.

But what happens when the goals of a particular decision-point are relatively clear and the only true variable lies in the uncertainty of the policy direction or outcome? Henry Mintzberg and his colleagues (1976) referred to this as the "trial-and-error" model of decision-making. Managers take an incremental approach to implementing policy alternatives, assess the impact, and then move to the next decision-point. Over time, the belief is that a comprehensive solution to the issue will be attained, but the process will allow decision makers to proceed with caution.

Often the opposite may also be true. Decision makers may (and will!) face a variety of competing demands from stakeholders, which they must balance before even moving to the decision stage. Handling the complexity of these situations requires what organization theorists refer to as the "coalition model" of decision making. The coalition model involves a search for "interest-accommodating alternatives" as opposed to the "problem-solving information" in the rational model. Policy leaders recognize that what may be the most efficient alternative will not be acceptable to different interest groups. The best option is the one they can "sell" to their key constituencies. Although some believe that the coalition model implies some sort of breakdown in "normal" decision making, in today's dynamic, multicultural world (particularly in the public and nonprofit sectors) it tends to be the rule more than the exception.

Of course, both the trial-and-error and coalition models of decision making assume that either the certainty of approach or the goals of the process has been determined. All that's left is "filling in the blank" of the other variable. Anyone who has served in a public or nonprofit organization will tell you that many times both sets of questions need to be answered. In these situations, which are characterized by a continuous ebb and flow of leadership, ongoing change in the policy environment, and shifting sets of coalitions among stakeholders, leaders find themselves using the "garbage can model" of decision making. (Does this sound familiar? If not, it will very soon!) Randomness replaces rationality. Indeed, Cohen, March, and Olsen (1972) used the term "organized anarchies" to describe organizations that practice the garbage can model as normal policy.

The approaches to organizational decision making described here should not be taken as mutually exclusive. Leaders in public and nonprofit organizations should explore a variety of methods, depending on the changing conditions in the policy environment. In fact, the most effective managers will be able to "read" the shifting conditions and balance their desire for rationality with a sensitivity to their "political barometers."

■ Organizational Culture, Organizational Learning, and Strategic Management

During the past generation, many discussions of management and organizations, especially in the private sector, have emphasized the importance of understanding the "culture" of the organization. Most writers refer to *organizational culture* as the basic pattern of attitudes, beliefs, and values that underlie the organization's operations. An organization's culture consists of shared assumptions that members of the organization hold. Edgar H. Schein (1997, pp. 8–10) notes that culture can be manifested in many ways, including the following.

1. *Observed behavioral regularities when people interact.* The language they use, the customs and traditions that evolve, and the rituals they employ in a wide variety of situations.
2. *Group norms.* The implicit standards and values that evolve in working groups, such as the particular norm of a "fair day's work for a fair day's pay" that evolved among workers in the Hawthorne studies.
3. *Espoused values.* The articulated, publicly announced principles and values that the group claims to be trying to achieve.
4. *Formal philosophy.* The broad policies and ideological principles that guide a group's actions toward stockholders, employees, customers, and other stakeholders.
5. *Rules of the game.* Implicit rules for getting along in the organizations and "the ropes" that a newcomer must learn to be an accepted member—"the way we do things around here."
6. *Climate.* The feeling that is conveyed in a group by the physical layout and the way in which members of the organization interact with each other, customers, or outsiders.
7. *Embedded skills.* The special competencies group members display in accomplishing certain tasks, the ability to make certain things that gets passed on from generation to generation without necessarily being articulated in writing.
8. *Habits of thinking, mental models, and/or linguistic paradigms.* The shared cognitive frames that guide the perceptions, thought, and language used by the members of a group and are taught to new members in the early socialization process.

9. *Shared meanings.* The emergent understandings that are created by group members as they interact with each other.
10. *"Root metaphors" or integrating symbols.* The ideas, feelings, and images groups develop to characterize themselves that may or may not be appreciated consciously, but that become embodied in buildings, office layout, and other material artifacts of the group.

As these manifestations suggest, some of the most important aspects of an organization lie outside of the explicit characteristics shared in normal group interaction. The unique ways in which an organization communicates internally and externally, its system of reward and punishment, and the way group members perceive themselves and the outside world all stem from the deeper, mostly undiscussed system of values and beliefs that define the group as a whole (Schein, 1997).

What Would You Do?

As a newly hired city manager, you want to shift the culture of your organization to reflect a greater commitment to citizen service. What would you do?

These layers of culture represent key concerns in their own right. They yield insight in very different ways about the nature of the group. However, organizational culture becomes even more critical as it relates to planned organizational change. Organizations face dynamic conditions in their internal and external environments—a variety of social, economic, and political factors impact group performance. The successful organization remains flexible to meet these changing conditions. Yet, given the multiple levels of organizational culture, change within the group cannot simply occur on the surface. The organization's underlying system of beliefs and values must be transformed if change is to be sustainable (Schein, 1997; Senge, 1990).

In this context, the notion of organizational culture becomes closely related to another important management concept: *organizational learning.* Learning organizations recognize that the primary contributors to error, or the disparity between what the group intends to happen and what actually occurs (Argyris, 1993) and thus barriers to change, are embedded deep within the organization's collective consciousness. They are not talked about, or even immediately acknowledged by group members. Therefore, groups that succeed in becoming learning organizations, those that are able to correct error and overcome their barriers, can successfully bring about change both in surface behavior and in the underlying levels of culture in the organization.

For example, say an organization's performance has started to suffer because of a decline in employee satisfaction and infighting among staff members. An immediate response may be to alter the group's behavior to reduce the infighting and improve the quality of work life. This type of surface-level change would be a form of single-loop learning. However, such behavioral change more than likely would not resolve the deeper problem that produced the infighting in the first place. To resolve this more tacit concern, double-loop learning, or a change in the underlying system of beliefs, would need to occur. Both the actions and values of the group would need to be affected.

Peter Senge, writing in *The Fifth Discipline*, suggests five elements that contribute to building a learning organization.

1. *Personal Mastery.* A discipline that connects individual learning, personal skills, and spiritual growth with organizational learning. It involves one's inherent capacity to continuously focus on what's most important, while ensuring that the view of reality remains clear and truthful (Senge, 1990, p. 141).

2. *Mental Models.* A discipline that links the way in which we view the world—our assumptions about "how things work"—with innovation and learning. Our mental models may pose substantial barriers to new ideas, those that conflict with our current understanding of reality, or they may become a source of new knowledge and creative learning (Senge, 1990, pp. 174–178).

3. *Shared Vision.* A discipline in which an image or idea becomes transformed into a powerful force that is shared throughout the organization or group. The organization that has a shared vision is "connected, bound together by a common aspiration" (Senge, 1990, p. 206).

4. *Team Learning.* A discipline that reflects the capacity of a group of individuals to coalesce, to engage their respective energies into an integrated team. The team remains connected through its shared vision, thus ensuring that the individual learning that occurs becomes translated into a group—indeed, a shared—experience (Senge, 1990, pp. 234–235).

5. *Systems Thinking.* A discipline that shows how human action—whether in business, government, or other pursuits—represents a systemic, interrelated set of events. Thus, we may understand and effect change by recognizing the interconnectedness of our actions and their consequences in the broader system. Those who are able to achieve this type of systems thinking—what Senge calls "the fifth discipline"—have embodied the concept of individual and organizational learning (Senge, 1990, p. 7).

NETWORKING

For a less formal introduction to organizational culture, begin with a website developed by graduate students at the University of Toronto at www.oise.utoronto.ca/~vsvede/culture.htm. Next, visit MIT's Society for Organizational Learning at www.solonline.org. This site discusses research about organizational culture and change.

The convergence of the concepts of organizational culture and organizational learning provides an important foundation for understanding organizational change. Yet these concepts also relate to an older concept, one that remains crucial in contemporary society: *strategic management.* Peters and Waterman's *In Search of Excellence* (1982) introduced this concept in its analysis of implicit philosophies that guide most successful American companies. Much of the work remains just as valuable today as it was nearly three decades ago. In particular, Peters and Waterman state the importance of establishing a core set of values that comprise the organization's mission and shape decisions throughout the structure. They suggest the importance of constant interchange between managers and workers, the organization and its clients. Though terms like "MBWA," or Management by Walking Around, may seem dated, the supporting principle of leadership maintaining close contact with members of the organization has even grown in significance.

These criteria for excellence can be translated into a public-sector context without great difficulty. For example, the International City Management Association and the Center for Excellence in Local Government adapted Peters and Waterman's criteria to define "excellence in local government."

1. *Action orientation.* Excellent local governments identify problems and deal with them quickly, fighting through structural, political, legal, and environmental constraints that make action more difficult than in the private sector.

2. *Closeness to citizens.* This criterion includes establishing and maintaining a variety of close links with citizens who are served by the local government, including those who are regulated against their will. Excellent local governments listen and are sensitive and responsive to public input.

3. *Autonomy and entrepreneurship.* Excellent local governments have developed climates conducive to conceiving ideas and doing new things to solve problems. They have track records for implementing creative solutions, even in the face of declining resources.

4. *Employee orientation.* This criterion demands more than lip service to employees and their needs. Excellent local governments insist on intensive, pervasive treatment of employees as human beings and adults.

5. *Values.* Excellent local governments have a defined set of values. Their overall focus is on being the best by providing superior quality service to the public. Their values are communicated clearly and demonstrated regularly to employees. Those values also provide the source of enthusiasm and pride among employees.

6. *Mission, goals, and competence.* Mission is the underlying premise of the organization. Excellent local governments have evaluated their missions based on changing resource levels and citizen demands, and they have used mission statements as the foundation for establishing community and organizational goals. Within their defined mission, excellent local governments provide consistent, uniform service levels.

7. *Structure.* In excellent local governments, the potential negative effects of antiquated, bureaucratic structures have been minimized. These organizations have fewer management levels and fewer centralized support staffs. They provide firm central direction while giving maximum autonomy to employees.

8. *Political relationships.* Political relationships refer to more than how the elected governing body and management staff work together. In excellent local governments, managers and policy makers are tuned in to the political environment; have established positive, open, and respectful relationships with each other; and have established political stability (Barbour et al., 1984).

More recently, Robert B. Denhardt (1993) elaborated several approaches to public management based on interviews with highly successful public managers in Australia, Canada, Great Britain, and the United States. Denhardt's research shows that these managers, highly regarded by their peers for improvements in quality and productivity, have a distinctive style from the traditional rule-driven bureaucratic mode of operations, but still have much in common. Among the approaches used by these "revolutionary" public managers are the following.

1. *A commitment to values.* The manager seeks organizational change less by attention to structure than by developing a pervasive commitment to the mission and values of the organization, especially the values of professionalism and integrity, service and quality. Values are clearly articulated by the chief executive and shared throughout the organization.

2. *Serving the public.* The manager gives priority to service to both clients and citizens. That priority is supported by high standards of performance and accountability and by a constant emphasis on quality. Most important, the manager recognizes that technical efforts alone will fail unless equal or even greater attention is given to the human side, especially to building a sense of community within the organization and a sense of cooperation outside.

3. *Empowerment and shared leadership.* The manager encourages a high level of participation and involvement by all members of the organization in efforts to improve the quality and productivity of the organization (see Box 5.1). Leadership from the top is complemented by empowering individuals throughout the organization to assume leadership within their own realms.

4. *Pragmatic incrementalism.* Change occurs through a free-flowing process in which the manager pursues a wide variety of often unexpected opportunities to move the organization in the desired direction. The manager views change as a natural and appropriate feature of organizational life and employs a creative and humane approach to change, taking into account the personal concerns and interests of members, clients, and others.

5. *A dedication to public service.* Individuals throughout the organization understand and appreciate the special character of public service, especially the role of public organizations in the process of democratic governments. The manager insists that members maintain high levels of standards and encourages them to make the organization a model of integrity for similarly situated groups.

Denhardt argues that these approaches to public management are not merely techniques to be used in pursuit of the organization's interest, but are ideas consistent with the history and tradition of public service. For many public managers and employees the driving motive behind their best efforts is not the pursuit of self-interest, but rather the pursuit of the sense of meaning or significance in their work. As managers become more aware of this factor and take it into account, public organizations can become more flexible, more creative, and more responsive to both clients and citizens.

Even more recently, Jim Collins, an author well known in the field of business management, built a concept for reaching "great" levels of achievement in the public service. His book *Good to Great: Why Some Companies Make the Leap . . . and Others Don't* (2001) and the subsequent *Good to Great and the Social Sectors: A Monograph to Accompany Good to Great* (2005), make it clear that public organizations should not blindly follow business practices for a simple reason: public organizations' achievement cannot be measured though earned profit. While for the "great" private companies, it is perfectly legitimate to measure the input and output in monetary terms, for the "great" public organizations, money is the measure for the input, but delivering "superior performance" and "a distinctive impact over a long period of time" are legitimate measures for successful output (Collins, 2005, p. 5).

BOX 5.1
TOP 10 TIPS TO REDISCOVER YOUR STAFF

1. Dump contingency management practices. Read up on the subject and identify how contingency manifests itself in tangible ways in organizations; set about changing habits and processes.

2. Embrace complexity. Complexity management practices are the antithesis of contingency management. Complexity is a nonlinear management model. It is not just a theory. Learn what it means in practice and develop staff to work in new ways.

3. Make plans and stick to them. All the unpredictability and uncertainty around contingency management in practice is unsettling for staff. It gives the impression of a lack of direction, lack of conviction, and inconsistency. Learn to have plans that can absorb and accommodate challenges rather than plans that keep attuned to outside demands. Plan for the unexpected and expect the unpredictable.

4. Reassess your approach and attitudes toward organizational culture. Know that organizational culture can be influenced but not controlled by senior managers. Do not mistake quiet compliance for cultural change. It is a staff survival mechanism; fury may be bubbling beneath!

5. Find ways to involve all staff in culture renewal, evaluation, and development initiatives. Remember that your staff creates the culture, so getting them positive and excited leads to a positive and exciting culture.

6. Look carefully at your cultural messages and symbols, and ask whether you and your top team are really delivering on them. Would I, as an outsider coming to your place for the first time, see that you mean what you preach or is it just more empty rhetoric? Take the time to make your values mean something.

7. Think about how you can stop talking about empowering work practices and begin enshrining them so that people believe you mean it. A charter is one good idea.

8. Remember that delegation is not empowerment. Review your approach and make sure managers do not pass on work to others as a "development opportunity." Staff always sees this for what it really is, and it does only damage.

9. Invite staff to take the initiative. Real empowerment is about creating the space for people to empower themselves. Support and encourage this but do not dictate it.

10. Retain your awareness that the changes managerialism dictates might make the organization meaner and leaner but that the effects on people policies must be carefully managed.

SOURCE: Davis, Paul. (January/February 2007). Too Busy Managing to Lead? A View from "Down Under," *Public Management* 89 (1): 28–32.

Collins (2005) offers five essential elements for building "great" public organizations.

1. *Defining "Great"—Calibrating success without business metrics* (p. 4). Public organizations should strive for excellence in delivering services. According to the author, "what matters is not finding the perfect indicator, but settling upon a *consistent and intelligent* method of assessing your output results, and then tracking your trajectory with rigor" (Collins, 2005, p. 8). His advice to public organizations is to actually be concentrated on great outputs.

2. *Level 5 Leadership—Getting things done within a diffuse power structure* (p. 9). Level 5 leader is the leader who can "build enduring greatness through a paradoxical blend of personal humility and professional will" (Collins, 2005, p.12, "Level 5 leadership/ level 5 hierarchy"). True leaders, as the author implies, are those who empower people. These leaders are followed by the people when people have the freedom not to follow them (Collins, 2005, p. 13).

3. *First who—getting the right people on the bus, within social sector constraints* (p. 13). True leaders also know who should be "on the bus" and how to attract the right people to "get on the bus"; that is, they know how to overcome social sector constraints and recruit motivated and competent "great" (not good or average) people.

4. *The hedgehog concept—rethinking the economic engine without a profit motive* (p. 17). In order to be effective with all the constraints in the social sector, social sector managers should concentrate on three elements: "passion," "best at," and "resource engine" (Collins, 2005, p. 19). "Passion" refers to the organization's values and core mission; "best at" refers to the activities that are unique to the organization; "resource engine" refers to the appropriate combination of time, money, and brand.

5. *Turning the flywheel—building momentum by building the brand* (p. 23). Organizations in the social sector should build brand, by which they are recognized in a positive manner. The brand helps these organizations achieve superior performance. But organizations will be able to build the brand only if they recognize that they should make a change within the organization. In other words, while the sector itself may face huge challenges, social sector organizations should recognize what is their (own) advantage and work on building and advancing their "pocket of greatness" (Collins, 2005, pp. 28–31).

Guidelines for Public Management

What lessons can you draw from these various perspectives that might guide your actions as a public manager? One way to begin to answer that question is to summarize some of the thinking about management in terms of guidelines for practice. The recent literature on strategic management seems to suggest the following guidelines.

1. *Maintain clarity about organizational priorities, goals, and objectives.* Although some ambiguity is often unavoidable in stating organization priorities, goals, and objectives, most organizations are far too confused on these issues. This confusion leaves people throughout the organization, including people who are required to make frequent decisions about organizational direction, without an appropriate basis for making such decisions. The direction of the organization should be stated as clearly as possible and widely communicated to all members.

2. *Make decisions today in terms of the most likely future circumstances.* Strategic management implies making all organizational decisions in terms of "futurity"—that is, how they will meet expected changes in the environment. It suggests taking every action in light of anticipated conditions, thus putting the organization in the best position to take advantage of future opportunities.

3. *Be attentive to the context in which you operate, especially relationships with other actors in the governmental system.* There is a natural but unfortunate tendency toward

"tunnel vision" in most organizations. Actions are viewed in immediate terms, without duly considering who will be affected by the action. Acknowledging the importance of the environment is essential to strategic thinking.

4. *Understand clearly the organization's capacities and limitations.* New programs and policies can be effectively implemented only if they fall within the existing capacity of the organization or provide sufficient opportunity to build capacity. There are dangers in both underutilization of resources and becoming overextended.

5. *Balance program goals with attention to organizational values and processes.* It is important to state programmatic objectives clearly; however, the organization's culture and the prevailing norms, beliefs, and values of its members are equally important. Organizational processes, such as leadership, communications, motivation, group dynamics, and so forth, need constant attention, because they are essential to goal accomplishment.

6. *Create diverse mechanisms, both temporary and permanent, for constantly renegotiating programs and processes.* Both programmatic concerns and organizational processes are constantly changing in ways that affect persons throughout the organization. Thus, clarity with respect to priorities, goals, and objectives must not lead to rigidity. Mechanisms must permit and, in fact, encourage the entire membership of the organization to contribute regularly to refining programs and processes.

7. *Build trust and commitment through open communications and genuine participation.* Guidelines by which we measure the degree of participation the organization encourages include members' access to information and to forums of decision making, their ability to open any issue without fear of retaliation, and their feeling that their ideas will at least be considered by major decision makers (Redford, 1969, p. 8).

Much of the work reviewed here applies equally to management in the public and private sectors. But it is interesting to note that some of the most recent general trends in management have been anticipated in public-sector management. Public organizations' dependence on pluralistic decision processes—that is, processes through which different people and groups are likely to be involved—makes the process of managing change in the public sector quite complicated. It also means that a high degree of ambiguity and uncertainty is likely to surround most efforts to implement or alter programs. Managers must be especially skillful in negotiating across organizational boundaries rather than expecting to control circumstances "from the top." In addition, public organizations must have a service orientation—specifically, an understanding of and an attempt to act in accord with the public interest. We noted that organizations seeking public purposes must operate openly, be cognizant of client interests, and understand the political context within which they operate.

Under these circumstances, it is not at all surprising that the values and perspectives that now seem so much a part of "modern management," such as those associated with strategic management or Total Quality Management, have always been central (if not dominant) in public administration theory. Thus, for example, Marshall Dimock's (1936, p. 120) comment that "successful administration is warm and vibrant. It is human." sounds very much like a quotation from Peters and Waterman. One might thus argue that, in contrast to Woodrow Wilson's admonition that public agencies should operate like businesses, it seems that public organizations and the values and interests they represent today should be and are becoming models for organizations of all types.

However, in this age of reinvention and managerialist government, there are reasons to be concerned that business values have overshadowed the ethic of citizenship that accompanies our theory of democracy. Public administration sometimes seems to be more concerned with promoting the entrepreneurial spirit than fostering meaningful engagement and sustaining citizen participation in civil society. There is a danger of devoting ourselves to satisfying the customer while neglecting to ensure equity, justice, and equality for citizens.

We will note later, in discussing recent critiques of the reinvention movement, that citizens are more than mere customers of government, they are its owners. Placing this relationship in economic terms reduces the role (and responsibility) of the citizen in the governance process. This critique carries important implications for our notions of public management. Specifically, in the current framework, public administrators can afford to view citizens in instrumental terms, and thus believe that by achieving an efficient, market-oriented system of service delivery that citizen trust and participation will be maintained. Citizen engagement, in this context, may be limited to a source of legitimation for public decisions that have already been made in more rational forms (for different perspectives, see Bryson & Crosby, 1992; Chrislip & Larson, 1994; Thomas, 1995).

Such a limited concept of engagement not only weakens our systems of public management and administration—it removes decision-making processes from the public realm—but it also threatens to destroy the remaining level of citizen trust we as public servants enjoy. Citizens have expressed that their confidence is less contingent on managerial pursuits, such as efficiency and performance, and more on the values of responsiveness and equity. Yet, sometimes it is tempting to forget this important message and to continue to strive simply for greater productivity.

The question we encounter once again is "How can we balance efficiency and responsiveness in the operation of public programs?" The field of public administration has generally leaned toward the efficiency side of the equation. Now, however, there is growing evidence that emphasizing responsiveness is not only consistent with democratic principles, but, in the long run, may also be the most effective way of operating. Whereas a structural view of organizations tends to emphasize internal efficiency, it is apparent that greater attention to external relationships and the ability to negotiate across organizational boundaries will become more and more necessary in our increasingly complex society, as will an organizational environment that fosters creativity.

Developing a "democratic" approach to management has often been attractive to public administration theorists because it seems only proper that government institutions in a democracy should operate democratically. What we are finding more and more is that such an approach is not only appealing but necessary for organizations of all types—not only those in the public sector—to survive.

■ Postmodern Narratives on Management

In recent years, the images of organizations just discussed have come under criticism from a variety of standpoints. Some challenge the notion of a single, unifying concept of management and organizations. Others bring into question the overly functionalistic nature of management theory. And still others attempt to counter the political context of traditional theory, particularly the use of power by elites to marginalize the powerless. We will now discuss these contrary perspectives on organizations under the heading of *postmodernism*. But as we will see even this term is problematic, because postmodernism defies our tendency for categorizing diverse viewpoints into a single, definitive theory.

Postmodernism

The philosophical roots of what we call postmodernism can be traced to the late 1960s and a school of French philosophy known as *poststructuralism*. Poststructuralists took issue with many of the core assumptions underlying modernist philosophy. For example, highlighting modernity's debt to the Enlightenment, the poststructuralists opposed modernity's primacy of rationality, objectivity, and the application of scientific principles in the development of a universal explanation of the social world. They argued for more diverse "readings" of society—that is, for new ways of knowing, based on semiotics and linguistics, to help explore the symbolic content of social phenomena. Such influences helped to bring about what has been called the "linguistic turn" in social theory.

In management theory, a key theme underlying the postmodernist critique centers on the multiple sources of knowledge that confront us in our organizational experience— what we may refer to as *fragmentation*. As Hatch explained, "Postmodernists challenge the modernist desire for unifying views with their belief that knowledge is fundamentally fragmented—that is, knowledge is produced in so many different bits and pieces that there can be no reasonable expectation that it will ever add up to an integrated and singular view" (Hatch, 1997, p. 44). Consequently, we are faced with this question: Given the increasingly global, networked nature of public and nonprofit organizations, how can we cling to a belief in a central, complete theory of management?

A second important theme involves a postmodernist challenge to what is called the *progress myth*. This stems from modernity's premise that our scientific knowledge is the result of a cumulative process, with one theory building uniformly on previous theories toward a shared end of advancing the human condition. Rather than some altruistic enterprise, postmodernists argue that the Enlightenment, and its offspring of modernity, proved to be a wholesale abuse of scientific knowledge by the powerful for the purpose of maintaining the status quo. Indeed, even the notion of a common human goal reveals the power-saturated, neocolonial character of modernism. So how can we presume to be in a position to determine what's in the best interest of societies around the world, much less to impose a particular form of knowledge to identify and evaluate policy alternatives?

To counter these tendencies, postmodern theorists employ a narrative device known as *discourse analysis*. It begins by viewing presentations of organizational inquiry—such as oral, textual, or visual narratives—as forms of discourse and then using discourse analysis to deconstruct the narratives to reveal modernist assumptions underlying the content. Discourse analysis exposes (and challenges) any attempt on the part of the "author(s)" to provide some type of *grand narrative*, in the modernist tradition, of organizations or society. Another purpose, however, is more action oriented and involves the use of discourse analysis to reverse the power-saturated state of language in the organizational context.

It opens the door for more diverse "voices" in organizational narratives—that is, the inclusion of traditionally dispossessed participants in social experiences of management.

Issues of Gender and Power

Feminist scholars have used elements of discourse analysis, as well as the liberating experience of postmodernism generally, to launch a sustained critique against traditional organization and management theory. At the heart of their critique is the segmentation of power along gender lines in organizational hierarchies—what the feminist scholar Jane Flax refers to as a "sexual division of labor" in modern management.

In Chapter 8, we will discuss the "glass ceiling" that limits the advancement of women in the workplace. However, Flax points out that the corollary to such structural barriers is that women tend to be employed in occupational areas that consist overwhelmingly of other women, jobs that are paid less and subject women workers to gender-stereotyped roles, like child care (school teachers), housecleaning (secretaries), and other forms of "women's work" (cited in Hatch, 1997, p. 293).

Mary Guy and Meredith Newman (2004) have explored this issue by asking what is it about women's jobs that causes them to pay less? They employ the term "emotional labor" to indicate that some tasks require "the emotive work thought natural for women, such as caring, negotiating, empathizing, smoothing troubled relationships, and working behind the scenes to enable cooperation" (p. 298). This work is largely invisible and not fully compensated. Public service relies heavily on such skills, yet pay and promotion systems fail to acknowledge and compensate this work.

This concern for the powerless provides perhaps the most compelling argument of feminist theories. From a foundation in neo-Marxian critical theory, feminist scholars draw into question the very legitimacy of our ways of organizing in the postindustrial era. To them, studies of organization and management theory have become little more than sources of intellectual justification for an abuse of power by elites whose only purpose is to maintain social, political, and economic order. Even postmodernism itself has come under attack from feminist critics, who see these theories as shifting the concern away from substantive issues of power and inequality in daily work life.

Moreover, contrary to what advocates depict as a democratization of economic and political space in the global marketplace, feminist critics argue globalization and the imposition of new forms of governance by industrialized nations have done nothing but take the northern, western drive for power and economic supremacy to new frontiers. The result has been a further marginalization of women, especially in what the development community refers to as "third world" societies.

■ Summary and Action Implications

As we have seen, your behavior is guided by the images you carry around in your head. Images that have to do with the role of public agencies in a democratic society, that have to do with the most effective and responsible way to run a complex public organization, and others that have to do with the relationships you establish with other actors, both within and outside the governmental system. Over your career, you will develop and refine your images based on experience, careful reflection, and self-critique. You will also benefit from comparing your images (and approaches) to those that other people recommend.

Through the years, students and practitioners of public administration have spent considerable time reflecting on the nature of their work and sorting out the factors that make for successful public management. Each resulting "theory" represents an attempt to suggest where you should cast your attention. Because you can't attend to all things at once, a certain amount of selectivity goes into theory building. Each theory implies evaluating what is most important to be aware of and to do to manage successfully.

Early writers thought that issues of organizational structure were most important, so they spent considerable time detailing concerns for structure. Later theorists (some of them practitioners) felt that structural issues should be balanced, if not outweighed, by a concern for the behavior of individuals in the organization. Still others sought further refinements, moving from behavior to structure and back again. More recent approaches have emphasized the organization's culture or value structure, but others have challenged the very notion of our ways of organizing in contemporary society.

For the time being, however, we should note the special sensitivity that those in public organizations have always shown for value questions. We have seen time and again how the values of public service—the pursuit of the public interest—affect the work of those in public organizations. The concern of contemporary writers in business and related fields of service and human values is something that those in public administration have always had to contend with, especially as they have been challenged to find a form of management compatible with the requirements of a democratic society.

TERMS AND DEFINITIONS

Area of acceptance: Area within which the subordinate is willing to accept the decisions made by the supervisor.

Boundary spanning: An organization's representation to outside groups and organizations.

Bounded rationality: An individual's search for the best possible solution, but not necessarily the most rational from an economic standpoint.

Functional principle: Horizontal division of labor.

Organization development: Process-oriented approach to planned change.

Organizational culture: Basic patterns of attitudes, beliefs, and values that underlie an organization's operation.

Organizational learning: The process of correcting errors by recognizing the disparity between what the group intends to happen and what actually occurs, and then drawing appropriate lessons for the future.

Political economy approach: A focus on politics and economies as categories for analyzing organizational behavior.

Scalar principle: Vertical division of labor among various organizational levels.

Scientific management: Approach to management based on carefully defined laws, rules, and principles.

Strategic management: A systems-based approach to management that seeks clarity with respect to goals and objectives, strategies to achieve those goals and objectives, and processes of evaluation to measure accomplishments.

Systems approach: Suggestion that public (or other) organizations can be viewed in the same general way as biological or physical systems.

STUDY QUESTIONS

1. Discuss the approaches to public management espoused by early writers.

2. Explain Douglas MacGregor's Theory X and Theory Y management concepts.

3. Compare the management approaches of Herbert Simon and Chris Argyris.

4. Two management approaches combine the human element with the structural aspect of the organization. Discuss the differences between the systems approach and the political economy approach.

5. What shared assumptions, as outlined by Edgar H. Schein, seem consistent in organizational cultures? What features do Peters and Waterman contribute to the list?

6. What basic philosophies underlie recent work in organizational culture and strategic management?

CASES AND EXERCISES

1. Divide the class into four small groups (or multiples of four). Have each group analyze your class as an organization, taking into account questions of power and authority, communications, motivation, group dynamics, and so on. One group should employ only a structural perspective, the second group should employ only a behavioral perspective, and the third group should employ only a systems perspective. The fourth group should employ whatever perspective (or combination of perspectives) that its members consider most modern and most complete. Have each group (or a representative of each type of group, depending on the numbers) report their conclusions to the

entire class. Think of each perspective as allowing you to see certain things and preventing you from seeing others. What do you see from the structural perspective? What about the behavioral perspective? The systems perspective? The combination perspective is likely to seem most complete, but consider the possibility that this modern viewpoint overlooks a great deal, and that, though we think it is complete (as those using earlier perspectives considered them complete), there may be much left to understand about organizations, even small ones. What other questions might we encounter in the future?

2. As a class, study the interorganizational relationships of one small organization. The organization might be a unit at the university (either an academic or a staff unit); a unit in city, state, or federal government; or a local nonprofit organization. Pick an organization that is clearly identifiable and, if possible, that appears to have considerable autonomy. Based on interviews with its top administrators and top staff people, develop a chart showing the organization's relationships with others in its environment. (A model resembling a molecular structure might be appropriate.) Indicate the importance of each relationship, the degree to which that relationship is considered positive or negative, and the degree to which it is considered essential. Try to develop some sense for how much time administrators and staff members spend on external relations versus internal organizational work.

3. The following statement is a mission statement from the City of Oakland (California). The City of Oakland is committed to the delivery of effective, courteous, and responsive services. Citizens and employees are treated with fairness, dignity and respect. Civic and employee pride are accomplished through constant pursuit of excellence and a work force that values and reflects the diversity of the Oakland community. First, this statement permeates the organization. For something that is well-established, what elements would you wish to add to the statement? Second, think about the relationship between a city and its citizens. What statements of philosophy dealing with the relationship between city and citizens would be appropriate to add? Third, given the statement and your modifications, what specific steps would you recommend to the elected and appointed officials in the city for putting their commitments (and yours) into practice?

FOR ADDITIONAL READING

Ban, Carolyn. *How Do Public Managers Manage?* San Francisco: Jossey-Bass, 1995.

Baum, Howell S. *The Organization of Hope.* Albany: State University of New York Press, 1997.

Bennis, Warren, Jagdesh Parikh, and Ronnie Lessem. *Beyond Leadership.* Cambridge, MA: Basil Blackwell, 1994.

Block, Peter. *Stewardship.* San Francisco: Berrett Koehler Publishers, 1993.

Boje, David M., Robert P. Gephart, Jr., and Tojo Joseph Thatchenkery, eds. *Postmodern Management and Organization Theory.* Thousand Oaks, CA: Sage Publications, 1996.

Box, Richard C. *Critical Social Theory in Public Administration.* Armonk, NY: M. E. Sharpe, 2005.

Caiden, Gerald. *Administrative Reform Comes of Age*. Berlin: W. de Gruyter, 1991.

Carnavale, David G. *Trustworthy Government*. San Francisco: Jossey-Bass, 1995.

Cohen, Steven, and Ronald Brand. *Total Quality Management in Government*. San Francisco: Jossey-Bass, 1993.

Collins, Jim. *Good to Great and the Social Sectors: A Monograph to Accompany Good to Great*. New York: HarperCollins, 2005.

Crosby, Barbara C., and John M. Bryson. *Leadership for the Common Good: Tackling Public Problems in a Shared-Power World*. 2nd ed. San Francisco: Jossey-Bass, 2005.

Davis, Charles R. *Organization Theories and Public Administration*. Westport, CT: Praeger, 1996.

Denhardt, Robert B. *The Pursuit of Significance*. Belmont, CA: Wadsworth, 1993.

Denhardt, Robert B. *Theories of Public Organization*. 2nd ed. Belmont, CA: Wadsworth, 1993.

Diamond, Michael A. *The Unconscious Life of Organizations: Interpreting Organizational Identity*. Westport, CT: Quorum Books, 1993.

Dunn, Delmer. *Politics and Administration at the Top*. Pittsburgh: University of Pittsburgh Press, 1997.

Farmer, David John. *The Language of Public Administration*. Tuscaloosa, AL: University of Alabama Press, 1995.

Farmer, David John. *To Kill the King: Post-Traditional Governance and Bureaucracy*. Armonk, NY: M. E. Sharpe, 2005.

Fox, Charles, and Hugh Miller. *Postmodern Public Administration*. Thousand Oaks, CA: Sage Publications, 1995.

Fredrickson, H. George. *New Public Administration*. Tuscaloosa, AL: University of Alabama Press, 1980.

Frost, Peter J., Arie Y. Lewin, and Richard L. Daft, eds. *Talking About Organization Science: Debates and Dialogue from* Crossroads. Thousand Oaks, CA: Sage Publication, 2000.

Grubbs, Joseph W. "Cultural Imperialism: A Critical Theory of Interorganizational Change." *Journal of Organizational Change Management* 13, no. 3 (2000): 221–234.

Guy, Mary Ellen, and Meredith A. Newman. "Women's Jobs, Men's Jobs: Sex Segregation and Emotional Labor," *Public Administration Review* 64 (3), 289–298, 2004.

Ingraham, Patricia W., Philip G. Joyce, and Amy Kneedler Donahue. *Government Performance: Why Management Matters*. Baltimore: Johns Hopkins University Press, 2003.

Kass, Henry D., and Bayard L. Catron, eds. *Images and Identities in Public Administration*. Newbury Park, CA: Sage Publications, 1990.

Kettl, Donald, et al. *Cutting Government*. Washington, DC: Brookings Institution, 1995.

Lee, Dalton M. *The Basis of Management in Public Organizations*. New York: R. Long, 1990.

Milakovich, Michael. *Improving Service Quality*. Delray Beach, FL: St. Lucie Press, 1995.

Morgan, Gareth. *Images of Organization*. 2nd ed. Thousand Oaks, CA: Sage Publications, 1997.

Omar, Ray. *Management Analysis in Public Organizations: History, Concepts, and Techniques*. New York: Quorum Books, 1992.

Peters, B. Guy. *The Future of Governing*. Lawrence, KS: University Press of Kansas, 1996.

Peters, B. Guy, and Bert Rockman. *Agenda for Excellence 2*. Chatham, NJ: Chatham House, 1996.

Rainey, Hal G. *Understanding and Managing Public Organizations*. San Francisco: Jossey-Bass, 1997.

Schein, Edgar H. *Organizational Culture and Leadership*. San Francisco: Jossey-Bass 1987.

Senge, Peter M. *The Fifth Discipline*. New York: Currency Doubleday Dell Publishing, 1990.

Senge, Peter M., et al. *The Fifth Discipline Fieldbook*. New York: Currency Doubleday Dell Publishing, 1994.

Shafritz, Jay M. *Classics of Organization Theory*. Pacific Grove, CA: Brooks/Cole, 1992.

Stever, James A. *The End of Public Administration: Problems of the Profession in the Post-Progressive Era*. Dobbs Ferry, NY: Transnational Publishers, 1988.

Stivers, Camilla. *Gender Images in Public Administration: Legitimacy and the Administrative State*. Newbury Park, CA: Sage Publications, 1993.

Terry, Larry D. *Leadership of Public Bureaucracies: The Administrator as Conservator*. 2nd ed. Armonk, NY: M. E. Sharpe, 2003.

Wamsley, Gary, et al. *Refounding Democratic Public Administration*. Thousand Oaks, CA: Sage Publications, 1996.

White, Jay D. *Taking Language Seriously: The Narrative Foundations of Public Administration Research*. Washington, DC: Georgetown University Press, 1999.

CHAPTER 6

PLANNING, IMPLEMENTATION, AND EVALUATION

Developing policies and programs, putting them into operation, and measuring their success or failure constitute an important and recurring cycle for public and nonprofit managers. A new monitoring program is initiated in the Balkans. To support that policy, the U.S. Navy organizes a fleet of vessels to patrol the Adriatic Sea, while political and military leaders assess the operation and decide what to do next. Similarly, a new policy involves sending literature on AIDS to all households in the United States. A group in the surgeon general's office convenes to monitor the operation. Both the efficiency of the mailing and its effectiveness as an educational device are discussed. Meanwhile, a local parks and recreation department joins with nonprofit organizations to develop a program for handicapped athletes. After staff and money are acquired to support the program and it begins operations, the department director asks whether the program is worth the time and energy it seems to be taking from other tasks. Repeatedly, plans are made, policies and programs are implemented, and the work of the organization is evaluated.

Recently these issues have taken on increased importance as managers in the public and nonprofit sectors have been asked to do more with less, while at the same time providing more and better services. This has led many to call for "managing for results"—that is, clearly stating goals and objectives in terms of public outcomes, designing and implementing programs, and then measuring the performance of the government or other agency against established standards. The idea of "managing for results" or "performance management" suggests the importance of bringing together careful planning, implementation, and evaluation.

Although planning, implementation, and evaluation all require knowledge of the political and ethical context of public administration and certain personal and interpersonal skills, various technical aids have been developed during the past decade to assist the manager in these three areas. These technical aids can include Web-based participative planning, strategic planning, or specific quantitative methods for measuring performance. Moreover, these techniques reflect a change in the way public and nonprofit organizations account for their actions. Citizens, lawmakers, and other advocacy groups increasingly hold agencies accountable not only for their efficiency in expending public and charitable resources, but also their effectiveness in achieving public outcomes. Techniques such as *strategic planning, reengineering*, and *performance measurement* link the actions of public and nonprofit organizations with specific, measurable results. Through the use of such techniques, public administrators may account for both their own efforts and the impact those efforts have in each given policy area.

NETWORKING

The Government Accountability Office website at www.gao.gov provides resources relating to managing for results. For additional resources on productivity and performance management, see the American Productivity and Quality Center at www.apqc.org.

■ Planning

On a daily basis, all managers engage in planning. But organizations, and indeed entire governments, engage in more formal planning processes, often involving a wide range of participants and the development of considerable data and other information. Planning typically leads to the development of alternative courses of action, and each must be examined to decide which way to go. Depending on the level of the problem, the process of examining and choosing among alternatives may involve the manager in either "policy analysis" or "program design" or both.

In a planning effort that captured the public's attention like few in recent memory, New York City was faced with the momentous task of deciding how to rebuild the devastated downtown area after the September 11, 2001 terrorist attacks. New York's Regional Planning Association convened the "Civic Alliance" to spearhead a participative planning process (see www.civic-alliance.org). The Civic Alliance is a coalition of approximately 85 different civic groups, businesses, universities, foundations, and community groups that joined together to solicit public comment and involvement and provide recommendations to the Lower Manhattan Development Corporation, a joint city and state organization charged with the rebuilding and revitalization effort. Several different approaches were used to provide citizens with the opportunity to become involved and have their ideas heard in the process. For example, an event called "Listening to the City" employed both face-to-face dialogue and technology in one-day forums. Over 4,500 people participated in small roundtable discussions while a network of people with laptop computers recorded and immediately transmitted the ideas generated to a "theme team." The theme team identified key themes and concepts and reported them back to all of the participants. Participants also had electronic keypads to record their preferences and answers to specific questions. Subsequent to these forums, an additional 800 people exchanged approximately 10,000 messages in small virtual discussion groups and participated in numerous polls in online dialogue over a two-week period to express their views and preferences.

Additional projects included "Imagine New York," which was sponsored by the Municipal Art Society of New York (see www.imagineny.org/aboutimagineny/index2.html). In the first phase of this project, 230 workshops and an interactive website were used to solicit answers to three primary questions: What have we lost? How have we changed? What should be done? Approximately 3,800 people participated either in workshops or online to generate 19,000 ideas. In the subsequent phases, participants were asked to react to proposed designs for rebuilding on the site of the World Trade Center. Although the revitalization project is not completed, the process used in New York City illustrates the potential of using innovative strategies and approaches to garner public participation in large-scale planning projects.

■ Strategic Planning

Planning is not only used when responding to a crisis, but has been increasingly employed in the public and nonprofit sectors. A number of writers have commented on the rapidity of the social and technological changes we are now experiencing and on the turbulence and complexity that such changes generate. In an effort to recognize and respond to such changes, many private corporations began programs in the 1960s and 1970s to systematically plan for future development. The success of these programs is now confirmed by the fact that more than half of publicly traded companies use strategic planning in some form. Strategic planning helps an organization match its objectives and capabilities to the anticipated demands of the environment to produce a plan of action that will ensure achievement of objectives. We can differentiate strategic planning from more familiar long-range planning activities in several ways. Long-range planning primarily concerns establishing goals or performance objectives over a period of time; it is less concerned with specific steps that must be undertaken to achieve those goals. Strategic planning, on the other hand, implies that a series of action steps will be developed as part of the planning process and that these steps will guide the organization's activities in the immediate future. Strategic planning takes the future into account, but in such a way as to improve present decisions.

A second way that strategic planning differs from long-range planning is its special attention to environmental complexity. The organization is not assumed to exist in a vacuum; rather, both the organization's objectives and the steps to achieve them are seen in the context of the resources and constraints presented by the organization's environment.

A final distinction between the two types of planning is that strategic planning, especially in the public sector, is a process that must involve many individuals at many levels. As most managers know quite well, effective changes in organizational practices are most readily accomplished by involving all those who will be affected by the change. This general rule is especially applicable to changes generated through a process of strategic planning.

Public organizations undertake strategic planning efforts for many reasons: (1) to give clarity and direction to the organization, (2) to choose from among competing goals and activities, (3) to cope with expected shifts in the environment, and (4) to bring together the thoughts and ideas of all participants in the work of the organization. Most importantly, planning activities provide an opportunity for the widespread involvement of leaders and citizens in defining the direction of the community or the agency as it moves into the future, thus building trust and commitment.

Planning for Planning

As a manager, you may wonder whether such activities are appropriate for your jurisdiction or agency. Whatever your work—at any level of government or in a nonprofit organization—you will find precedents for planning. Many federal, state, and local agencies have begun strategic planning programs over the past several years, as have voluntary associations, human service organizations, and job training programs. The key seems to be that any organization is a candidate for strategic planning if, by allocation of resources, it can significantly influence either formulation or implementation of public policy.

You may, of course, question whether strategic planning is worth the costs in terms of consultant fees, research and data analysis, and time away from other duties. The best gauges for assessing costs are: (1) Is it likely that careful planning will lead to reduced operating costs or increased productivity over the long run? and (2) What might the organization lose in the absence of a more comprehensive and integrated approach to the future?

The latter question has become increasingly important to those in local governments, who now realize that they must compete with other communities in attracting industry, providing amenities, and maintaining the population base. The issue, however, must be treated differently when an administrative agency such as a state government department is considering planning. Although strategic planning might make the agency more competitive in attracting resources from the executive or legislature, this clearly should not be the purpose of planning. Rather, the agency should use strategic planning to involve key "stakeholders" in assessing the unit's work and the possibilities for improving its services. The process may indeed lead to requests for further funding, but it may also suggest ways to more effectively utilize existing resources or even ways to reduce the scope of activities.

What Would You Do?

You are a member of the management team of a medium-sized Florida oceanfront vacation and retirement community. You have been asked to make recommendations to the city council concerning elements that should be a part of a new vision and an accompanying strategic plan for the city. What would you do?

Because of budgetary uncertainties, you may also question whether time is right for planning activities. Some say that planning can't take place without solid information about funding levels. But the opposite argument is compelling—that planning is most essential in times of uncertainty, for these are exactly the times when you most need to be in control of your own destiny. Times of uncertainty do not mitigate the need for planning; they intensify it.

Managers in the public sector voice a related argument; that periodic changes in political leadership make planning more difficult than in private industry. Again, the opposite argument is compelling: In times of transition, planning can provide continuity. Even when the new leadership wishes to change the directions specified in an earlier planning effort, changes can be made with greater clarity and aimed more readily toward critical concerns if a plan is in place.

Finally, you may wonder whether strategic planning efforts are consistent with your organization's commitment to democratic or participatory processes. Here lies the most significant difference between strategic planning in the public and private sectors. Whereas planning in the private sector may involve many people throughout an organization, it remains centered and directed at the top, because that is where the private interests of the firm are most clearly articulated. In the public sector, however, every effort must be made to significantly involve all those who play an important role in the jurisdiction or the agency. For example, a local government planning effort should involve not only elected leadership and city staff, but also many others with a stake in the outcome: unions, neighborhood associations, chambers of commerce, civic organizations, and so forth. Similarly, a state government agency's planning effort should involve people from all levels of the organization, members of constituent groups, elected officials, people from other agencies and other levels of government, and representatives of the general citizenry.

Strategic planning in the public sector must be a highly participatory process; consequently this participation opens the possibility of building new understanding among various groups. Many communities that have engaged in strategic planning have found that the process brought together various groups in a way not previously possible. Strategic planning may therefore be undertaken to achieve both direction and commitment.

Organizing for Planning

The planning process can proceed in a number of different ways, but the most common approach is to form a central planning group to work closely with an outside consultant to obtain information and make commitments to various new directions. In a local community, the group might include the city's political leadership; representatives of city administration (for example, the city manager); representatives of business, industry, and labor; members of neighborhood associations; and so on. For a federal or state agency, on the other hand, the major planning group might consist of the agency director, managers from the next organizational level below, and selected program directors. The planning group in a nonprofit organization might include the executive director, members of the board, staff members, and representatives of constituent groups.

Steps in Planning

Once it has been brought together, the planning group will want to give its attention to four primary concerns: (1) the organization's mission or objectives, (2) an assessment of the environment in terms of both opportunities and constraints, (3) an examination of the organization's existing strengths and weaknesses, and (4) the values, interests, and aspirations of those important to the organization's future (see Box 6.1). Consideration of these issues will lead to several strategic alternatives—perhaps stated as "scenarios for the future"—and to the choice of a particular direction in which the organization should

BOX 6.1

STEPS IN STRATEGIC PLANNING

1. Statement of mission
2. Environmental analysis
3. Strengths and weaknesses
4. Values of organizational leaders
5. Development of alternative strategies

move. Finally, a set of action steps or implementation items will be developed to indicate what must be done immediately to put the organization in the proper position to face the future most effectively.

Mission or Objectives   Arriving at a concise, yet inclusive, mission statement of the organization is a difficult step in the planning process. Although most organizations have a general sense of their mission, questions often arise that cannot be readily answered in terms of stated objectives. Having a specific mission statement, however, provides an identity for the organization, as well as a guideline for future decisions and a standard against which to measure specific actions.

Because arriving at a mission statement may imply certain strategies, care should be taken to consider alternative approaches to the organization's goals. A mission statement might indicate, for instance, whether a city wishes to seek a broad industrial base or focus on particular types of businesses, such as tourism or high-tech industries. Similarly, a university mission statement might indicate whether the institution seeks a broad range of programs in all areas or a limited number of exceedingly high-quality programs. The mission statement of a state agency might comment on the desired range of clientele, responsiveness to changes in the environment, or quality of service. If there is doubt or debate about items, they should be carried forward as elements of strategy for later consideration.

Environmental Analysis   After developing a mission statement, the planning group should move to an analysis of the environment within which the organization operates. This assessment should include legal and political considerations, social and cultural trends, economic circumstances, technological developments, and, where appropriate, the organization's competitive or "market" position. Each area should be examined in terms of the present environment and how it is likely to change in the future. This assessment leads the group toward identifying possibilities for reducing constraints and extending opportunities.

Strengths and Weaknesses   At this point, the planning group can turn its attention toward assessing the organization's existing capabilities—its strengths and weaknesses. The analysis should be as forthright and inclusive as possible, taking into account financial resources (including changing patterns of funding), human resources (including political and managerial strengths and weaknesses), the operation of both technical and organizational systems, and quality of work. This assessment of capabilities should relate as directly as possible to the stated mission of the organization. For example, an agency involved in facilities design and construction might want to consider the age and condition of facilities, the number and abilities of architects and engineers, the number and frequency of design projects, and the unit's standing among other similar organizations. Examining strengths and weaknesses should be accompanied by some attention to programs that might significantly improve capabilities in one or more areas.

Values of Organizational Leaders   A final step in preparing to develop strategic alternatives is to take into account the values, interests, and aspirations of those who will guide the organization into the future. People will respond to the same environmental and organizational analysis in different ways. In business, for example, some will be perfectly satisfied with the security of a stable market share, whereas others will be willing to take greater risks in the hope of greater payoffs. Leaders vary in terms of creativity, energy, and commitment. Yet, to effectively implement a plan, it must reflect the concerns and interests of those who will play major roles in shaping the future of the organization.

Development of Alternative Strategies   At this point, the planning group can move to formulate alternative strategies. These strategies can take several forms; however, one useful way to proceed is to draw up alternative "scenarios of the future," indicating what the organization might look like five, ten, or twenty years into the future. The scenarios should indicate new directions the organization might take; pessimistic, realistic, and optimistic interpretations of its future; and factors likely to influence these future patterns. It is helpful to develop more than one scenario, then use them as competing viewpoints from which to debate the merits of various alternatives. From a thorough discussion of the scenarios, one or more strategies will emerge. The strategy should be chosen that most effectively moves the organization toward its mission, given environmental opportunities and constraints, organizational strengths and weaknesses, and the values, interests, and aspirations of the leadership. After developing the strategic orientation, the planning group should be pressed to identify specific action steps for implementing the strategy. For example, a local job-training program went through an extensive planning exercise involving thorough analysis of environmental opportunities and constraints as well as organizational strengths and weaknesses. Based on the information developed and future funding patterns, the program's directors chose to deemphasize subsidies for local businesses to employ those without work and to try for longer-term benefits through skills training and job preparation.

The Logic of Policy Analysis

One possible outcome of a formal planning process is that the need for new policies will be identified. (The need for new policies can be generated in other ways as well, many of which we discussed in Chapter 2.) A local group considering economic development issues might recognize the need for new tax incentives for industries interested in locating in the community. A state welfare department planning group might focus on the relationship between providing day care and job training. Or a nonprofit organization might decide there is a need for a new publications program. In each case, a problem is identified and the question arises as to whether a new approach to the problem—a new policy—might help.

Many issues may come up. Exactly what is the nature of the problem? What would we be trying to achieve with the new policy? What might be alternative approaches? What might we expect from each alternative? What criteria would we use to evaluate alternatives? Which alternative would best meet our criteria? Answering questions like these is the basis of analyzing public policies. We can therefore define *policy analysis* as the process of researching or analyzing public problems to give policy makers specific information about the range of available policy options and their advantages and disadvantages.

There are several ways you might become involved in policy analysis. All managers engage almost daily in a sort of informal analysis of public policies; they encounter new problems and consider alternative policies. Often a more formal review of policy options is called for. Sometimes staff members perform the analysis; many public organizations employ policy analysts to work on just such problems. In other cases, another governmental agency may help; for example, the Office of Management and Budget, as well as its counterparts in many states, develops policy reports. Policy analysis might also be performed by legislative staff or legislative research groups. Finally, many analyses are performed by consultants, including university consultants, where the public manager acts as a client, issues the contract, monitors the work, and receives the final report. Even though, as a manager, you may perform the analysis yourself, you must be able to distinguish between high-quality analysis and work of limited usefulness.

Broadly speaking, most policy analyses attempt to follow a "rational" model of decision making, involving five major steps: (1) formulating the problem, (2) establishing criteria for evaluation, (3) developing policy alternatives, (4) considering the expected impact of the various alternatives, and (5) ranking the alternatives according to the established criteria (see Box 6.2). As a simple illustration, think about how you might decide what would be the best route from home to work (Quade, 1989, pp. 33–34). If we assume at the outset that the "best" route is the shortest, then we could simply lay out the alternative routes on a map and select the shortest. (Using a map would in effect create a "model" that would help in our analysis.) As in almost all policy analyses, however, there may be more than one criterion involved. For example, the shortest route might involve more traffic and take longer to drive. The shortest travel time might then constitute a second criterion, but would require a more sophisticated model than a map, taking into account traffic congestion and perhaps other variables. Just thinking through the various complications that might arise in this "simple" example, you can get some sense of the difficulties you might encounter in moving through the five stages of a more comprehensive policy analysis.

BOX 6.2

STEPS IN POLICY ANALYSIS

1. Problem definition
2. Setting objectives and criteria
3. Developing alternatives
4. Analyzing various policies
5. Ranking and choice

Problem Definition

There are obviously many problems facing any public organization and, correspondingly, many opportunities to analyze policy alternatives. Someone, however, must decide about the problem and how the analysis will proceed. This someone—the *sponsor* of the analysis—may be a legislator, an elected chief executive, or an agency manager. But, in any case, the one who will perform the analysis—the *analyst*—should seek as clear a statement of the problem as possible and as much information about the nature of the problem and the range of solutions. Why has the problem surfaced? Who is affected? How does this problem relate to similar problems? What policy options have already been tried? What is the range of policies that would be feasible, both economically and politically? What resources are available to support the analysis?

Obviously, how the question is initially formulated will guide the analyst toward certain possibilities and away from others, so it is important at the outset to be as clear as possible, without unnecessarily cutting off alternatives. The sponsor might ask, for example, "How can we provide adequate shelter for the homeless in our community this winter?" This statement permits exploring alternatives ranging from subsidizing existing shelters to building new shelters. If, however, certain options, such as building new shelters, are clearly out of the question due to time or money, then the analyst should be advised of these limitations.

Sometimes the problem is only vaguely understood at the outset, and part of the analyst's job is to develop a background statement or issue a paper that outlines the problem. In some cases, gathering information at the library will be helpful, especially in laying out the history of the problem, discovering approaches used in other jurisdictions, and in becoming aware of technical developments in the field. The analyst may want to talk with other people, perhaps in other jurisdictions, to see what their experience has taught them. People in other governments, other levels of government, and other agencies at the same level can be helpful. The analyst can also gather information from those involved. In our example, the analyst would probably want to talk with those already involved in providing shelter. A statistical survey might even be possible. Finally, agency records and statistics might be helpful. Throughout these initial information-gathering efforts, the analyst wants to develop an idea of how different people and different groups perceive the problem and possible solutions.

Setting Objectives and Criteria

As we have seen, establishing objectives for a new policy or criteria for judging alternatives is often quite difficult. In some rare agencies, the existing values and preferences are clear enough to guide choices. The manager might be able to say, "It's worth much more to our agency to achieve result A than result B, C, or D. Therefore, whenever the choice presents itself, choose A." But in most policy areas, there are likely to be multiple and often conflicting objectives. To route a highway through an urban area, for example, one must consider factors such as the cost of the project, how many and who might use the highway, the number of houses and other properties that might be displaced, and the impact of noise and pollution on adjacent neighborhoods. How does one begin to rank all the factors?

There are other problems in selecting criteria. For example, criteria may differ among different levels of the organization. A constant problem for decision makers is to be sure that criteria used at one level are consistent with those at another level. A particular course of action might fit the criteria developed at one level, but so distort the use of resources at the next higher level as to make the choice inappropriate. Criteria must also be stated as completely as possible. An analyst might be told to seek a solution that maximizes output at minimum cost, then discover that no single alternative can meet both criteria. Which is more important?

Finally, choosing criteria depends on individual perspective. Most policy areas have many different *stakeholders*—people who are involved in and affected by the policy decision. These may include legislators, agency personnel, client groups, and other interest groups, and each group may feel quite differently about what is most important. In the design of a new highway, for example, a neighborhood association might place highest value on environmental concerns, while someone who lives in the suburbs might be most concerned with finding the shortest, quickest route to work. Different criteria compete for prominence in any policy analysis. And, often, which criteria receive greatest prominence is a political decision of legislators or high-ranking administrators.

Developing Alternatives Developing alternative policies is without question the most creative phase of policy analysis, for it is here that the analyst must move beyond easy solutions and develop innovative approaches to public problems. Different alternatives often derive from different assumptions about the problem. For example, should the welfare system be oriented toward providing support at home for impoverished mothers or should it enable mothers to work by providing day care? Should day care be addressed by building new centers or by providing tax credits or vouchers to subsidize attendance at existing centers? Obviously, answers to questions about alternative approaches to child support depend on interpretation of both the causes of poverty and the motivations of the mothers. To develop a complete range of alternatives, the analyst must assume the perspectives of many different stakeholders.

Another way to develop far-ranging alternatives is to consider the relationship between the particular problem and other similar issues. For example, adequate care for the homeless ties to issues of health care, financial support for housing, welfare policy, and perhaps such areas as mental health and Social Security. Again, alternatives that take the various interrelated concerns into account are likely to be generated if the analyst takes into account the views of many different stakeholders. Rather than saying, "How can my organization solve this problem?" the analyst should ask, "How can this problem be solved?"

Analyzing Various Policies Having generated a number of realistic policy alternatives, the analyst must now assess the likely impact of each alternative. How one analyzes the impact will vary according to the particular type of policy. In some policy areas, including some of major importance, limited information about possible impacts will be available. The analyst can only make intuitive judgments based on his or her experience and the experience of others. In other cases, however, one can gather specific data and analyze it by means of quantitative techniques. In the urban highway example, data could be gathered and analyzed to determine cost per mile, load-bearing capabilities, travel time for users, and a variety of other factors.

Occasionally, actual experiments with several policy options may be possible, sometimes with an experimental design similar to that used in the natural sciences. That is, the behavior of a particular target population may be compared to that of a control group when only one variable (the policy) is changed. Applied to large-scale social problems, such experiments may be quite costly, but they may also save considerable time and money in the long run. Sometimes it is appropriate to spend millions to save billions. (We should also note the ethical problems associated with providing a treatment expected to be beneficial to one group, but intentionally denying it to another "control" group. Is it ethical to deny some people a treatment you think will be beneficial?)

A less formal means of policy experimentation occurs when one state or locality tries a particular policy approach and makes the results available to other communities. Sometimes this form of experimentation is simply the result of different groups trying different programs, but sometimes it is conscious. When state and local groups pressured the Carter administration to move the administration of the small cities' portion of the Community Development Block Grant program to the states, Wisconsin and Kentucky were asked to run the program on an experimental basis. Their success in tailoring programs to local needs led to legislation allowing all other states to assume administration of the program (Jennings et al., 1986).

Ranking and Choice   The final step in the analytic process is to compare the impacts associated with various alternatives and the criteria for evaluation established earlier. Alternatives can then be ranked in terms of their respective impacts. When both the criteria and impact levels are fairly straightforward, a simple comparison of possible effects may readily show which choice should be made; other cases may be more complex. The highway construction example, for instance, might yield three or four alternative proposals and as many as twenty criteria by which to evaluate the alternatives. One way to treat such cases is to simply lay out the expected results of each alternative in terms of the various criteria, leaving the task of comparing the data and ranking the alternatives to the decision maker. Sometimes more sophisticated quantitative techniques are available to the analyst.

Costs and Benefits

One of the most straightforward quantitative techniques is the *cost-effectiveness* approach, which compares policies by quantifying their total costs and effects. Costs are usually measured in monetary terms, but effects may be measured in units of any type.

Typically, the cost-effectiveness approach takes one of two forms. First, the level of *effectiveness* can be fixed, and one can search for the alternative that achieves this level at the least cost. If, for example, we want to increase the number of houses in a community tested for radon by 25 percent, would it be cheaper to hire inspectors or to spend money on advertising so that homeowners would do the inspection themselves? A second approach fixes the budget amount and then asks which alternative will provide the highest level of effectiveness for that amount. If we want to spend no more than $50,000 a year on radon inspections, which two approaches will result in a higher number of inspections?

The cost-effectiveness model is widely used because it is quite flexible and does not demand the same degree of precision as other approaches. Cost-effectiveness is especially useful when the relative merits of competing proposals, such as different childcare delivery mechanisms, are being debated. It is not as useful in comparing questions of absolute merits, however, such as whether to allocate resources to early childhood programs or to radon testing. Moreover, the cost-effectiveness approach may be somewhat limited where criteria and impacts are more complex.

Closely related to cost-effectiveness is *cost-benefit* analysis. Essentially, the cost-benefit approach involves identifying and quantifying both negative impacts (costs) and positive impacts (benefits) of a proposal, then subtracting one from the other to arrive at a measure of net benefit. In contrast to cost-effectiveness analysis, the cost-benefit approach seeks to establish both the total monetary costs and total monetary benefits of a proposal. The logic of cost-benefit analysis is obvious, but applying it to policy proposals that involve large expenditures and produce difficult-to-measure results can be quite complicated.

There are several advantages to cost-benefit analysis. If programs can be evaluated in terms of costs and benefits, the approach can result in rather precise recommendations. But even if it is difficult to calculate costs or benefits, focusing on the two areas may help clarify the manager's thinking about a proposal. Legislation often requires that cost-benefit analysis precede particular policy changes, especially in environmental or regulatory policy.

Several factors make it difficult to assess the costs and benefits of a particular program. First, the analyst will be asked to come up with measures of both costs and benefits and reduce them to a common unit of measure (usually money). But in analyzing a proposed new highway, can we accurately portray the fatality rate for similar highway segments as a measure of safety? And, if so, how can we translate the rate of fatalities into dollars? Second, we should always remember that the final calculated cost-benefit ratio is not the only basis for choosing one alternative over another. Despite the ratio of costs and benefits in our highway example, a particular level of fatalities may simply be considered too high, either politically or ethically.

Typically, costs are thought of as inputs and benefits as outputs. Costs might include one-time items such as research and development, buildings and facilities, land acquisition, equipment purchases, and so on. Costs might also include recurring budgetary items such as personnel, rent, maintenance, administrative overhead, insurance, and so forth. Because these expenditures take place over time, calculations usually take into account the *time value of money*—the fact that people generally are not as willing to pay for something in the future as in the present. Although the particular calculations are beyond the scope of this text, taking time into account enables us to answer questions such as whether Project A with low initial cost but high maintenance is better than Project B with high initial cost but low maintenance.

Benefits, based on outputs, include both positive and negative effects. (The negative effects of a program obviously might be calculated either as increases in cost or decreases in benefits. They are usually the latter.) Positive benefits might include reduction in disease or improved drinking water or increased highway safety. Negative benefits might include increased noise and pollution from constructing a new airport. Again, some effort to translate positive or negative benefits into monetary terms would have to be made.

Obviously, measuring outputs and translating them into dollars are exceedingly difficult tasks. For example, eliminating a disease might increase productivity, which could be measured, but also reduce pain and suffering, which would be more difficult to measure. Omitting these factors because they are hard to measure biases the analysis, but assigning a dollar value to them might do the same. Consequently, the quantitative presentation of costs and benefits is often accompanied by an explanation of additional qualitative considerations.

Other Quantitative Techniques

In addition to cost-effectiveness and cost-benefit analyses, there are many other techniques to aid policy analysis. It is not necessary to examine the mathematical formulas, but it is helpful to understand the logic they depend on. Let us examine the following *payoff matrices* with that goal in mind. Assume a simple example: hiring an office worker who will need proficiency in computer operation and budgeting. After interviewing two applicants, A and B, you feel that A is stronger than B in both areas. Your thoughts might be modeled as shown in Table 6.1.

TABLE 6.1

Value Measures

Possible Actions	Computers	Budgeting
Choose A	1	1
Choose B	2	2

Your choice here is simple, because one candidate is clearly superior in both respects. But what if your decision appears to be structured as shown in Table 6.2.

TABLE 6.2

Value Measures

Possible Actions	Computers	Budgeting
Choose A	1	2
Choose B	2	1

Now there is no clear choice. Even if you thought computer skills were more important than budgeting skills, you couldn't choose, because candidate A might be a little better with computers, but candidate B may be much better in budgeting. To decide, you need either more sophisticated measures of ability or a way to weight the two factors, as we do in the example Table 6.3.

TABLE 6.3

	Computers	Budgeting	Combination
Choose A	.9	.3	.8
Choose B	.5	.8	.6
Weight	.7	.3	

Here we are assuming that we can measure ability in the two areas on a 10-point scale and that we have established that computer skills are more important than budgeting skills. By multiplying the scores by the weights, we obtain a combined value measure for the two candidates, thus enabling us to choose the better candidate. (This classic example is adapted from Latane 1963.)

We could extend the logic of the payoff matrix even further. One way is to combine scores under differing working conditions. Indeed, following the logic of the payoff matrix, we could accommodate large numbers of weighted variables, as might be involved in a large-scale policy analysis; the logic remains much the same. Remember that one can adopt different decision rules and that the choice of criteria is subjective.

Another tool of policy analysis is *decision analysis,* a technique for use where decisions are likely to be made sequentially and with some degree of uncertainty. Decision analysis is applicable to a variety of complex problems, such as choosing airport sites or developing plans for commercial breeder reactors, but the underlying logic is fairly straightforward and often quite helpful. Consider another classic illustration.

> The officer in charge of a U.S. Embassy recreation program has decided to replenish the employees' club funds by arranging a dinner. It rains nine days out of ten at the post, and he must decide whether to hold the dinner indoors or out. An enclosed pavilion is available but uncomfortable, and past experience has shown turnout to be low at indoor functions, resulting in a 60 percent chance of gaining $100 from a dinner held in the pavilion and a 40 percent chance of losing $20. On the other hand, an outdoor dinner could be expected to earn $500 unless it rains, in which case the dinner would lose about $10. (Stokey & Zechauser, 1978, p. 202)

Using decision analysis to structure the officer's dilemma involves first constructing a *decision tree* to show the various possible outcomes, given the risks associated with each (see Figure 6.1).

Obviously, the decision tree lays out the options, probabilities of various occurrences, and anticipated outcomes in much the same way as a payoff matrix. It is easy to imagine how much more complicated the situation could become, however, with the addition of other variables or other decision options. Even in this simple case, matters might be complicated by other variables, such as whether the weather will be hot or cold, whether there are other ways to increase attendance (advertising, and so on), and whether the commanding officer prefers indoors or outdoors. You can imagine the sequences and variables involved in a decision concerning location of a nuclear facility.

And as if this weren't enough, consider what happens when you take into account competition from others. Let's imagine a chess match in which we have decided on some evaluation criterion, such as king safety or center control that we can measure (see Figure 6.2). That is, we have identified a way to place a value on each outcome that might result from a given set of moves. Let's say that White is ready to move and has two options, W1 and W2, leading to the decision tree in Figure 6.2. (If we move W1, then Black can move either B1 or B2; if we

FIGURE 6.1

Decision Tree

	.6	
	Attendance fair	+$100
Indoors	.4	
	Attendance very poor	−$20
	.1	
	No rain; attendance excellent	+$500
Outdoors	.9	
	Rain; attendance poor	−$10

FIGURE 6.2

Chess Match Decision Tree

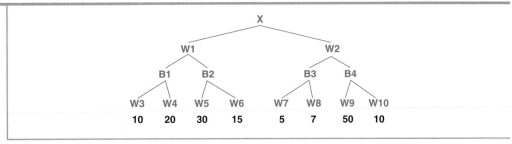

move W2, then Black can move either B3 or B4; and so on. We will take the values across the bottom to be the outcomes.) We would obviously prefer to choose W2, and then have Black choose B4, so we could choose W9, the alternative with the highest value for us. But taking into account what Black is likely to do, we recognize that if we take W2, then Black will take B3, leading us to the two lowest payoffs. Recognizing this probability, we will instead take Wl, expecting that Black will take B1, and we will have a satisfactory outcome.

Although our examples have been quite simple, their logic can support far more sophisticated applications of policy analysis. Moreover, the discipline these techniques impose makes them useful for even relatively simple applications. The models force us to examine our assumptions, structure the problem clearly and logically, and consider the full range of available options. The models also allow us to more effectively communicate our analysis to others.

That brings us to one final point. No matter how sophisticated the analysis and how rational its conclusions, a policy analysis must be effectively communicated to the actual decision makers. Communication is often quite difficult, because decision makers are extremely busy and have a variety of conflicting demands on their time and interests. Sometimes even those who are invited to do a policy analysis find themselves and the analysis swept aside by political or other considerations, and, indeed, that is the prerogative of major decision makers. A rational analysis is helpful in the decision process, but political considerations, in the positive sense, must also be taken into account before any actions are taken.

Bardach (2005) suggests that policy analysis is more art than science and emphasizes the importance of intuition as a complementary part of the methodology used for a policy analysis. He develops eight useful steps in the policy analysis process that can be used as a practical guide when constructing policy proposals.

1. Define the problem. A clear operational definition of the problem to be solved is a crucial step that gives "both a reason for doing all the work necessary to complete the project and a sense of direction for your evidence-gathering activity" (p. 1).

2. Assemble some evidence. Before gathering evidence, it is important for the analyst to think carefully as to what is relevant to the problem. Pertinent literature review, applied best practices, and analogies are some of the sources for supporting the argument for the existing policy problem.

3. Construct the alternatives. When looking for alternatives, use a comprehensive and focused approach. The alternatives should address the problem and should be feasible.

4. Select the criteria. Commonly used evaluative criteria are: efficiency, equality, equity, fairness, and justice. Commonly used practical criteria are legality, political acceptability, robustness, and improbability.

5. Project the outcomes. Policy analysis along with the policy proposal refers to results that will come in the future. Most important for this step is to be realistic (not too optimistic, which is a common pitfall) in the expectations for the future.

6. Confront the trade-offs. "As economics teaches us, trade-offs occur at the margin" (p. 48). In other words, it tells us how much extra money we should pay to receive an extra unit of some service.

7. Decide! With this step, the policy analyst makes a decision on which policy alternative to concentrate his or her attention.

8. Tell your story. This step implies that the intention of the analysis is to suggest a solution for a certain problem. The policy analyst should be aware that clarity of presentation of his or her analysis is very important.

■ Implementation

In the cycle of planning, implementation, and evaluation, implementation is the action phase. Once plans have been made and policies decided on, you must put them into operation. Financial and human resources must be allocated and mobilized, organizational structures and systems must be devised, and internal policies and procedures must be developed. During implementation, you may be involved in issuing and enforcing directives, disbursing funds, awarding grants and contracts, analyzing programmatic and operational problems, taking corrective action, and negotiating with citizens, business, and those in other public and nonprofit organizations.

Recently, a body of literature dealing with the implementation process has emerged. Some of the literature merely uses new terms to talk about the general processes of administration in the public sector. Other parts of the literature focus on the relationship between policy development and program implementation. This literature specifically alerts us to the difficulty of effective program implementation and to how implementation may distort or even subvert the intent of policy makers. Most pointedly, one commentator has written, "It is hard enough to design public policies and programs that look good on paper. It is harder still to formulate them in words and slogans that resonate pleasingly in the ears of political leaders and the constituencies to which they are responsive. And it is excruciatingly hard to implement them in a way that pleases anyone at all, including the supposed beneficiaries or clients" (Bardach, 1977, p. 3).

A classic study of the relationship between policy and implementation was suggestively titled *Implementation: How Great Expectations in Washington Are Dashed in Oakland; or Why It's Amazing That Federal Programs Work at All* (Pressman & Wildavsky, 1973). *Implementation* described a particular economic development program in the Oakland, California, area that was less than successful. Pressman and Wildavsky concluded that "what seemed to be a simple program turned out to be a very complex one, involving many participants, a host of different perspectives, and a long and tortuous path of decision points that had to be cleared" (p. 94). Implementation was characterized by multiple and conflicting interests, each trying to influence the program's direction to suit their many and divergent needs. The major recommendation of the study seemed to be that people involved in designing public policies "pay as much attention to the creation of organizational machinery for executing a program as for launching one" (pp. 144–145).

This lesson has been clearly recognized in the literature of strategic planning. Plans remain sterile without implementation, so there has always been a close connection between planning and execution. As noted, planning is most beneficial where it can help make immediate decisions in light of future impact. Thus, a final step in any planning process is to arrive at a series of specific actions to take in the near future—the next six months, or the next year or two years—who does what, when, and to what effect. These steps, which may detail new policy positions or new organizational processes, will form a new action agenda for the community or the agency.

Organizational Design

Some of the classic approaches to implementation, formerly called "organization and management," focused on the structure and design of new organizations and their work processes or flows. The traditional organization chart expresses both the division of labor within an organization and the structure of command or control.

In the late 1930s, Luther Gulick advised managers developing new organizations that there were several ways they could divide work (Gulick, 1937, pp. 21–29). Among these were (1) purpose, (2) process, (3) people or things, or (4) place. Dividing work according to purpose might result in distinctions such as between providing education or controlling crime, while dividing work according to process might lead to a legal unit, a medical unit, or an engineering unit. One could also divide work according to the people served or the things being dealt with—for example, the Veterans Administration deals with all problems that veterans face, whether legal, medical, and so on. Finally, one may organize according to geographic area, as would a state welfare department that has regional or county offices.

NETWORKING

Online resources and case studies relating to the planning and implementation of productivity initiatives can be found at the U.S. Conference of Mayors site at www.usmayors.org/uscm/best_practices. For information on scenario planning, go to the Global Business Network at www.gbn.org.

Gulick and his contemporaries also talked about the number of levels that would be appropriate to an organization. Obviously, many organizations are fairly "tall"—they have many levels; others are "flat"—they have relatively few levels. The number of levels is guided to a degree by the type of work and by the number of people who report to any one manager. The term *span of control* signifies the number of people that one individual supervises; although there are significant variations, depending on the type of work, it is generally considered difficult to supervise more than six to ten people.

In addition to developing organizational structures, early writers urged charting work processes as an aid to organizational design. *Process charting* or *flowcharting* can provide a graphic demonstration of the various steps in an operation, the people performing each step, and the relationships among these elements. Figure 6.3 shows a simple illustration of process charting, though charts can become far more sophisticated in actual applications. This process chart uses a variety of symbols to indicate different activities. The vertical lines set the basic framework of the chart. The columns show the flow of work from one person to another and vary depending on the complexity of the process and the degree of analysis desired. The column headings indicate the positions under study. In Figure 6.3, the ovals indicate a specific task (sorting, conferring, and so on); the circles indicate transportation of work from one person to another. The triangle indicates storage, a period during which operation is stationary. Finally, the rectangle indicates an inspection, usually to check for quality or quantity. As illustrated here, one can make notations on the chart to indicate the nature of particular steps in the process.

Process charting is most useful where a considerable number of clerical or nonprofessional employees perform the same general classes of work and follow the same general sequence of operating steps. Although process charting is less useful in analyzing the work of professionals, there are possible applications here as well. For example, charting a professional operation may reveal bottlenecks, excessive periods of review, or excessive checkpoints that inhibit the flow of work. As with other techniques, process charting can become quite complex, but

FIGURE 6.3
Process charting

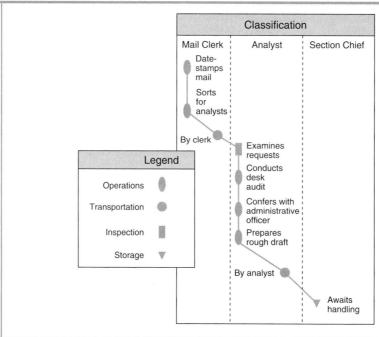

its logic is both simple and compelling. Process charting simplifies analysis because it sharply points out backtracking, excessive detail, unnecessary repetition, poor distribution of functions, and other administrative defects. For this reason, process charting has enjoyed a revival of interest by those implementing total quality management programs.

Systems Analysis

There are many other sophisticated devices that have been developed for analyzing the design and operations of both public and private organizations. Many of the approaches are based in *systems theory*, an effort to identify, in logical fashion, the interactions of various internal and external elements that impinge on an organization's operations. The systems approach has been used in a variety of fields, including physics, biology, economics, sociology, and information science, but the basic concepts are much the same regardless of discipline. Generally speaking, a *system* is a set of regularized interactions configured or bounded in a way that differentiates and separates them from other actions that constitute the systems environment. Thus, we can speak of a biological system, a physical system, an economic system, or a political system. Any such system receives *inputs* from its environment, then translates these through some sort of *conversion process* into *outputs* that are returned to the environment. These outputs in turn affect future inputs to the system through a *feedback loop*. Presumably, if the outputs of a system are valued by the environment, new inputs will be forthcoming and the organization will survive. A basic systems model is illustrated in Figure 6.4.

FIGURE 6.4

A Basic Systems Model

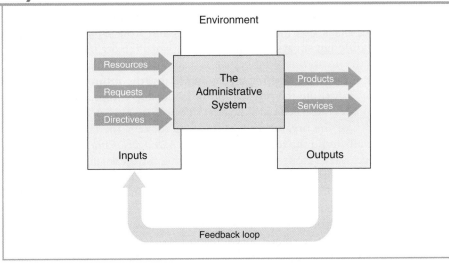

Following this model, consider the operation of a thermostat. The thermostat takes in information about the heat in a room, and then measures the heat against some standard. If the level of heat is below the standard, the thermostat causes more heat to be put out into the room. The additional heat becomes part of the environment and creates new information (feedback), which becomes part of the next input into the system.

The systems concept works similarly in human organizations. A business might receive input from its environment that customers are demanding more red shoes. A decision might be made to produce more red shoes, and those shoes would be part of the organization's output. The new red shoes become part of the environment and affect new inputs into the system, which might range from comments about the quality of the shoes or information that the demand has not yet been met. This new information guides the operation of the system in the future.

Like many of the other models we have discussed in this chapter, the systems approach has been used in highly sophisticated applications ranging from analysis of organizational design and processes to creation and modification of major weapons systems. Indeed, the first major applications of systems analysis occurred in the military during and soon after World War II. For some time thereafter, the Defense Department was the major user of systems analysis, depending on a variety of contractors, most notably the Rand Corporation. Yet, it is possible to apply systems logic to a variety of problems public organizations face, and, as with other techniques, the systematic discipline that the approach brings to problem solving is perhaps its greatest strength.

Systems analysis emphasizes the relationship between the organization and its environment, suggesting that public managers carefully consider factors in the environment that impinge on their operations. These factors include legal and political matters, support and opposition generated by interest groups and client organizations, human and financial resources, and applicable technology. Naturally, the environment also includes a large number of other organizations with which the agency interacts, such as the chief executive's office, the legislature, the budget office, related agencies at the same level of government, parallel agencies at other levels of government, and a variety of private and nonprofit groups and associations.

Many systems analysts tend to ignore what occurs within the system itself, preferring to think of it as a black box into which inputs go and from which outputs come. Others speak of several different subsystems that carry forward the organization's work. In a classic formulation, the *institutional subsystem* is responsible for adapting the organization to its environment and for anticipating and planning for the future. People involved in this activity generally constitute the organization's leadership cadre. The *technical subsystem*, on the other hand, is concerned with the effective performance of the organization's actual work. If the work of the organization is building rockets, the technical subsystem is the people who actually build the rockets. Finally, the *managerial subsystem* is concerned with providing the necessary resources for accomplishing the technical task, as well as mediating between the technical and institutional subsystems (Thompson, 1967, pp. 10–11).

Outputs of public organizations range from goods (such as highways or buildings) to services (such as student loans or employment counseling), but also include regulations, adjudication, and support for other programs. To know the effect of their efforts, managers need some sort of feedback mechanism. Feedback often occurs naturally: Clients write letters of appreciation; legislators inquire about program operations; a program may even become an issue during an election campaign. Sometimes, however, you will want to secure more systematic and accurate feedback, for which you can use devices such as questionnaire surveys, field testing, or spot checks of service provision. Recall that systems analysis helps focus on how an organization interacts with its environment; developing effective feedback mechanisms helps the manager in that process.

PERT/CPM

Other techniques for guiding implementation of public programs are the *Program Evaluation Review Technique (PERT) and the Critical Path Method (CPM)*. (These two techniques were developed separately and have minor differences, but we can treat them as one, using the title PERT.) PERT is a system for organizing and monitoring projects that have a specific beginning point and a specific ending point. NASA used the system extensively in developing the manned spacecraft program; it can accommodate quite substantial projects. We will focus on the basic logic underlying the system.

A *PERT* chart uses a series of circles (which designates events) and arrows (which designates time or costs) to indicate various activities for completing a project and the necessary sequence. One circle might show the beginning of a particular effort and be connected by an arrow to another circle, which might show the end of the first activity and the beginning of a second. Any activity that must be completed before the start of another activity should appear to the left of that activity. Thus, the key elements in a PERT chart might look like this

Put on socks: Put on shoes

Activities that are independent of one another are shown in separate sequences. For example, if you could put on your shirt while you are putting on your shoes, that activity could be parallel to putting on your shoes.

A more complex PERT chart appears in Figure 6.5, showing a variety of activities that might be undertaken to hold a conference. As in all PERT charts, no activity can take place until everything prior to that event occurs. For instance, to print and mail the brochures (I), it is necessary to develop a budget (H), contract for the space (D), and identify the conference speakers (K). Each event is necessarily preceded by others. Time estimates for each activity are entered above each line. (Some PERT charts give a normal, an optimistic, and a pessimistic time projection, but we give one figure—the expected time in days. PERT charts can also be constructed with cost estimates substituted for time estimates.)

Various paths lead from the decision to hold the conference (A) to the opening session (G). If you add the times required to complete all the steps along any particular path, you arrive at an expected time to complete that path—ABCDEFG requires twenty-two days; ABJKIFG requires forty-two days. The path that takes the most time is the *critical path* (in this case, path ABHKIFG) and is usually highlighted in some way. Any delay in the critical path will delay the entire project. Other paths may have built-in slack times, where small delays will not cause that path to exceed the time required for the critical path. The critical path in this example tells us that the conference organizers have forty-three days to complete their project. If for some reason the conference must be held sooner, they must find some way to decrease the time required to complete the critical path.

FIGURE 6.5

Chart for organizing a Conference

Key to Action Steps

(A) Decide to hold conference.
(B) Organize planning group.
(C) Assess possible locations.
(D) Contract for space.
(E) Set up rooms.
(F) Conduct registration.
(G) Hold opening session.

(H) Develop budget.
(I) Print and mail brochures.
(J) Establish conference theme.
(K) Contact and confirm speakers.
(L) Develop conference materials.
(M) Deliver materials to site.

→ Critical path
( ) Expected time in days

In summary, program implementation involves the full range of administrative skills and concepts, but implementation can occasionally be facilitated by using certain techniques. Our examples are simplified to illustrate the logic of the technique. All the techniques, however, can be applied to projects of much greater magnitude and complexity. Regardless of the complexity of the application, the result should be the same: a more disciplined and precise view of the implementation of a program.

Reengineering Recently, some public administrators have adopted a more comprehensive, even radical technique for enhancing organizational performance, called *reengineering*. The core tenet of reengineering centers on redesigning work processes and organizational structures to be in line with agency outcomes. Proponents of the technique view existing bureaucracies as relics from the industrial age and seek to restructure public organizations. Through this technique, they attempt to make public organizations more flexible and capable of responding to the dynamic conditions in contemporary society.

In some respects, reengineering builds upon systems theory, PERT, and other techniques in that it involves the recognition of core processes and the systemic context of staff behavior. However, the outcome of reengineering goes well beyond simply making alterations within the existing bureaucratic structure. Its goal is to overhaul rigid government agencies into what one author calls seamless organizations: "In contrast to the fragmented bureaucracies of the past, seamless organizations provide a smooth, transparent, almost effortless experience for their customers. Staff in seamless organizations perform the full job, in direct contact with their end users" (Linden, 1994, p. xii).

Implementation of a reengineering process begins with an identification of the organization's desired outcomes. These include the short- and long-term impacts the agency wants to achieve. Then, the organization is redesigned around the core and support processes that will produce these outcomes. Given the hierarchical, inflexible nature of many public organizations, though, this is not as simple as it may seem.

Reengineering requires that public administrators change their current assumptions, those equating organization with traditional bureaucracy. Such a reorientation helps to transform work processes and agency structures to those driven by meaningful outcomes—a shift from segmentation to integration, from division of labor to seamless work (Linden, 1994).

Reengineering involves enhancing those activities that may be considered value-added—activities that give customers more of what they are willing to pay for and cutting functions that merely stand in the way. Of course, some functions remain crucial for the organization's success. Central administration activities such as budgeting, accounting, and quality inspections cannot simply be removed from the picture. On the other hand, these functions often hinder the completion of the more value-added activities. The key to successful reengineering is to separate the core processes from the other tasks, enabling the critical activities to be carried out more effectively.

While management plays a central role in any reengineering effort, the technique's success depends on the capacity of key teams engaged in project design and implementation. The first team is responsible for identifying organizational processes in need of change. Next, the second group leads the change initiative. Individuals from throughout the organization, as well as members of the organization's stakeholder groups, are brought in to inform the process and to develop indicators that will help keep the initiative on track. Leaders emerge from each of these teams—individuals who guide the reengineering process by ensuring that it has adequate resources, administrative support, and overall organizational commitment (Hammer & Champy, 1993; Linden, 1994).

Evaluation

The sequence of planning, implementation, and evaluation is completed by asking whether the program goals and objectives have been achieved in a way that was both efficient and effective. Such evaluations may, however, operate at a variety of different levels. Some may respond to the interest of the legislature in knowing whether the intended benefits of legislation were achieved; others may be designed to communicate to the public what is happening in areas of broad citizen interest; still others may be oriented toward improvements either in the design of the policy being implemented or in the way it was conducted. An understanding of contemporary approaches to evaluation requires attention to both the performance measurement movement mentioned earlier and more traditional program evaluation approaches.

Whereas program evaluation offers insight into each policy or program's direction, effectiveness, and sustainability, performance measurement generates information concerning the organization or network as a whole. When combined within the framework of evaluation research, these strategies not only assist in the decision-making process, but they improve the overall accountability of public organizations. In turn, evaluation research enhances legislative oversight and administrative control.

Several legislative groups conduct or "sponsor" evaluation research at the federal level. These include the Government Accountability Office (GAO), the Congressional Budget Office, and various legislative committees, primarily those concerned with the budget and oversight of specific programs. Executive agencies, such as the Office of Management and Budget and the Executive Office of the President, also conduct evaluation research. Much of this research, however, is sponsored by the agencies themselves, as managers seek to determine how they can better manage or generate greater productivity from their organizations.

There is also great interest in performance measurement and program evaluation at the state and local levels, although resources to support such activities have often been limited. State governments have developed analytic capabilities within the executive branch, often through the budget office. In recent years, many states have restructured their budgets to be in line with predetermined performance standards. This has enabled state governments to link fiscal resources to the desired results targeted by each agency. Evaluation research is then used to help state government determine how successful it has been in achieving its performance goals. Consequently, state legislatures and citizens can now see what services and impacts were gained with public resources.

Again, at state and local levels and in most nongovernmental organizations, as at the federal level, a great deal of evaluation research is done as part of the agency or program manager's ongoing responsibility. Particularly in the era of "reinvention" and the National Performance Review, public administrators increasingly must show not only the efficiency of their actions, but also the results of their actions within the broader stakeholder community. Examples of performance measurement and program evaluation range from complex, detailed, one-time studies to the ongoing, integrated monitoring of performance goals. Regardless of the level of sophistication, evaluation research offers important details in support of the organization's overall strategic planning and to assist the organization in determining the direction of individual programs.

Performance Measurement

The most recent addition to the field of evaluation research—*performance measurement*—emerged during the late 1980s, as citizens, legislators, and advocacy groups started to demand more value from public organizations. Government was pressured to show its efficiency in expending public resources and prove that substantive results, or outcomes related to a program's public effectiveness, had been generated by its activities. As the call for "reinventing government" gained strength in the early 1990s, the move toward performance measurement occurred at all levels of government. Federal agencies developed performance standards at the program level and in their management and administrative functions. State and local governments followed suit, both as a means of assessing their activities and of enhancing their reporting under federal programs (Wholey, Hatry, & Newcomer, 1994).

In 1993, performance measurement became law under the Government Performance and Results Act (GPRA). This act mandates that federal agencies undergo a strategic planning process to identify five-year performance outcomes. Organizational activities toward these outcomes, then, would be measurable through annual performance reviews. The performance review plans were required starting in fiscal year 1999. Within these plans, federal agencies identified *performance indicators*—specific, quantifiable goals that the agency strives for in pursuit of its objectives. These indicators reflect each agency's outputs and outcomes.

NETWORKING

The federal government provides updates and related information concerning evaluation strategies under its Government Performance and Results Act (GPRA) at the GPRA Report site at www.ombwatch.org/gpra and the Congressional Institute at www.conginst.org. For information concerning evaluation activities by state and local governments, visit these sites: www.policyworks.gov and www.auditor.leg.state.mn.us/ped/pedintro.htm.

A distinction should be made here between inputs, outputs, and outcomes: Inputs are resources—financial, human, and otherwise—available to the organization; outputs are actual goods or services produced by an organization; and outcomes, as we have mentioned, are long-term objectives that the organization wants to achieve. As an illustration, the Federal Aviation Administration issues regulations, which constitute one type of its outputs. But someone measuring the performance of this organization would be only moderately interested in the number of regulations it issues. More important would be the effect of the regulations on desired goals, such as improved air safety. Improved air safety would be an outcome. (Generally speaking, objectives are likely to be narrow and specific, directly tied to each organization's particular activities; outcomes, on the other hand, are related to the larger purposes to be served by the organization's work.)

"The Bush administration believes that GPRA has to date involved little more than the production of data, with virtually no evidence that this information has been used to guide decisions" (Joyce, 2007, p. 27). Performance measurement, however, is one of the top priorities for the Bush administration, one to be carried out through the Program Assessment Rating Tool (PART) that has become part of the President's Management Agenda (PMA). PART is conceived as a tool for measuring performance and was used for the first time in the FY 2004 budget process. "A PART review helps identify a program's strengths and weaknesses to inform funding and management decisions aimed at making the program more effective. PART therefore looks at all factors that affect and reflect program performance including program purpose and design; performance measurement, evaluations, and strategic planning; program management; and program results. Because PART includes a consistent series of analytical questions, it allows programs to show improvements over time, and allows comparisons between similar programs" (OMB web site: www.whitehouse.gov/omb/part/index.html).

Evidently PART is used as a tool that will evaluate all agencies' programs by contrasting them with consistent criteria. But, as Joyce (2007, p. 29) points out, the major problem when PART was introduced was the fact that many programs could not "demonstrate results, at least according to the PART criteria"; that doesn't necessarily mean, however, that these programs are ineffective. Although the main function of PART is to help decision makers when deciding which programs are to receive more funds, Joyce (p. 29) points out that "for the vast majority of programs, the relationship between funding and performance is not well understood, even where good performance data exist." This comes from the fact that some federal programs cannot be abandoned solely on performance criteria. The long-term impact of PART remains to be seen; while there are critics of PART as a tool that cannot be uniformly used for evaluating all federal programs, agency commitment to following the standards has been evident in ensuing budget proposals.

What Would You Do?

You are part of a state-level task force charged with integrating the work of multiple agencies dealing with children, youth, and their families. You have been asked to come up with a set of broad outcome measures that will enable state decision makers *and the public* to know how well the state is doing in addressing concerns ranging from employment and child health to substance abuse, teen pregnancy, and school dropouts. What would you do?

The long-term impact of GPRA remains to be seen; however, in a recent symposium, representatives from federal agencies and the academic community had a chance to reflect on some of the reactions to federally mandated performance measurement. Kathryn Newcomer, one of the scholarly participants, wrote, "The message given at the conference was certainly mixed. There are benefits in the form of improved dialogue about Federal government performance in this GPRA era, but there is still much progress to be made in improving dialogue across agencies and across congressional committees. And the report cards on performance reporting in the federal government [based on reporting standards for federal agencies] are not out yet. The criteria to be used by Congress in grading performance reports are still big—and significant—unknowns in the performance rating game" (Newcomer, 1999, p. 10). All else aside, GPRA certainly has helped to broaden the dialogue to include issues of government effectiveness and the capacity of federal agencies to achieve public objectives.

Of course, the move toward performance measurement goes well beyond GPRA and its requirements for federal agencies. Public organizations at all levels, as well as organizations in the nonprofit sector, have begun to tie evaluation research to their planning and implementation functions. Most state governments and many local governments, for instance, now use performance measurement as a means of assessing their activities in terms of both outputs and outcomes. Accordingly, these states can associate budget decisions and program directives with specific performance standards set by each agency. And, as a result, the states enjoy a more effective system of accounting for their efficiency and effectiveness to citizens and other stakeholders.

"By 2004, 33 states had maintained, amended, or added legislation that prescribe performance-based application, while 17 states had an administrative requirement or executive mandate for such application" (Melkers & Willoughby, 2007, p. 80). Despite these requirements, in most states there is neither legislative nor administrative requirement for comprehensive performance-based application. Only 11 states have some type of statewide performance-based requirements: Arizona, Delaware, Louisiana, Maryland, Minnesota, Missouri, New Mexico, Oregon, South Dakota, Virginia, and Wyoming (p. 83).

Several years ago, for example, Texas instituted a performance-budgeting system as a means of enhancing agency accountability and productivity. Under the new system, state agencies must determine the resources necessary to accomplish performance goals, and then negotiate the goals and resources with the state legislature. Once the outcomes and allocations have been established, lawmakers grant spending authority based on the performance goals. The move away from program categories and line items, thus, gives administrators in Texas greater flexibility in meeting their performance objectives. And the budget system ensures that evaluation and measurement is based on productivity rather than on agency processes (Carter, 1994). However, as we see in Box 6.3, the task of identifying measures is not always easy.

BOX 6.3
SEEING EYE TO EYE: PERFORMANCE MEASURES THAT MATTER TO CITIZENS

Citizen participation has often been the square peg that public administrators try to squeeze into the round holes of government, whether it is for strategic planning, budgeting, land-use planning, or other key processes. This is especially true when it comes to performance measurement. Most participation is input driven (citizen satisfaction surveys) or output driven (annual performance reports). While both are important components of a performance measurement system, neither impact the design of the system or influence what is actually measured. Barbara J. Cohn Berman's Listening to the Public presents the results of a multi-year research project conducted by the Fund for the City of New York that provides local governments with a rounder peg that has the potential to greatly influence the design of their performance measurement systems.

Taking its cue from private sector market research practices, the Fund's Center on Municipal Government Performance set out to listen to the citizens of New York City through focus groups, surveys, and interviews over a six-year period between 1996 and 2001 to determine how the public perceived local government performance. Overall, researchers found participants to be knowledgeable about public services and realistic in their expectations. Their opinions were shaped by their own personal experiences and most critically influenced by their interactions with government employees and agencies.

The value of Berman's work is her methodology and its potential widespread application and impact. During the focus groups, participants were provided brief descriptions of thirty different city responsibilities so that all had an equal base level of understanding. Participants then ranked how familiar they were with each service, how important they believed each service to be, and how well each service is performed. While not scientific, these ratings provide insight into the public's perception of city services, allowing researchers to draw the conclusions mentioned.

From focus group discussions stimulated by this activity and subsequent phone interviews, Berman extrapolates common themes and presents potentially new performance measures that are important to citizens. For example, one person had this comment: "I called 911 for my grandmother. They came quickly, knew what to do, and got her to the right hospital on time." From this one comment Berman derived three potential performance measures: (1) the

(Continued)

(*Continued*)

initial response time to reach the patient, (2) the elapsed time to transport the patient to the appropriate hospital, and (3) the knowledge, compassion, competence, and responsiveness of personnel. Berman documents comments and potential performance measures for each of the thirty services ranked. Such an exercise could be easily replicated by jurisdictions and used to validate their current measures and/or provide new ones that are more important to citizens.

The Center also identified governmental functions regarded by citizens as very important, but for which there was no performance data. The Center then developed new tools to produce reliable performance information and applied them to New York City. The first tool was concerned with the quality of the roads—roadway maintenance ranked second in the 2001 focus groups for being very important but low performing. Berman describes how the Center adapted a pavement-roughness measurement technology known as profilometry to produce a smoothness score and jolt score for city streets. Volunteers and focus groups were used to calibrate the technology to easy-to-understand performance measures, and maps were produced to spatially depict the results and observe changes over time. Since this technology was first deployed in New York, other cities have begun conducting similar studies.

As noted, Berman discovered that citizens perceive government much differently than does government itself. For citizens, problems do not fit neatly into departmental structures. Consider street-level issues such as garbage, vacant lots, unsafe buildings, and graffiti that together influence citizen perception of government but are not the responsibility of a single department. The Center developed a system called Computerized Neighborhood Environment Tracking (ComNet) to provide a means for citizens to easily communicate these problems to the appropriate local authority without having to know departmental responsibilities. Citizens or government employees use hand-held computer devices while walking pre-determined routes to record observable problems. Detailed summaries are tabulated and the problems are automatically routed to the correct department. This also provides data that can be mapped to determine service level disparities and note changes over time. Numerous cities across the country have now used ComNet for similar systems.

The final tool developed by the Center is an online survey instrument called CitizenGauge, which allows citizens to rate their interactions with government employees based on the qualities the Center found to be most important during its research: accessibility, courtesy, knowledge, timeliness, and responsiveness. While CitizenGauge offers an additional feedback mechanism that should be welcome to agencies concerned about their performance, it also carries the weaknesses inherent in a "suggestion box" system—feedback that is anecdotal and not representative. Local governments might receive more useful data through community surveys and use CitizenGauge to pinpoint interim problems between surveys.

SOURCE: John Ruggini. (2005). Seeing Eye to Eye: Performance Measures that Matter to Citizens, *Government Finance Review*. Chicago: Dec 2005. Vol. 21, Iss. 6; pg. 62–63.

Similarly, the United Way of America has implemented a comprehensive *outcome measurement* program to foster a consistent, effective system of performance management across United Way–funded agencies (Hatry et al., 1996). The United Way approach concentrates on a logical chain—linking program inputs, activities, outputs, and outcomes—with outcomes measured by specific points of information, referred to as indicators. The goal for the United Way is to encourage agencies to move away from traditional, efficiency related measures to more meaningful assessments of program impact, based on the number and percentage of clients, to achieve the program outcomes (Hatry et al., 1996, pp. 1–2).

In identifying performance standards, public and nonprofit organizations may pull from a variety of sources. This is usually done in what is called a process of *benchmarking*. Benchmarking features the targeting of specific goals based on previous performance levels, standards set by similar organizations, objectives created through a strategic planning process, or any combination of these. Public administrators then assess agency performance, using comparisons with these predetermined indicators. Through benchmarking, administrators are able to connect their evaluation research directly with the agency's planning and implementation strategies.

The most effective application of performance measurement integrates evaluation and measurement within the broader context of performance management. A recent report on one successful performance management exercise was developed by Jay Hakes, at the time the administrator of the Energy Information Administration (EIA) of the U.S. Department of Energy. Based on his EIA experience, Hakes suggests that organizations that attempt to pattern assessment strategies, without first sequencing these strategies in the overall process of organizational change, may lose sight of important organizational barriers both to performance measurement and to the change itself. These groups may fall into the trap of monitoring activities without linking them to the targeted goals and outcomes of the organization.

To prevent this, Hakes suggests several action steps that lay a foundation for successful performance measurement.

- Analyzing goals deriving from statutes and historic practices
- Discussing desired outputs and outcomes with major customers in and out of government
- Writing a strategic plan
- Drawing an input/output map of the organization (Hakes, 1997, p. 10)

It is important to note that these steps represent merely the beginning of successful performance management. Commitments from top leadership, organizational members, stakeholders, and those overseeing agency resources must be gained for the change strategy to be effective. The performance measures themselves must be linked with the organization's budget allocations and reward systems. In this regard, creating an effective measurement strategy means transforming the organization into a performance-based organization.

The next steps in the process involve integrating the measures throughout the organization. This can be done, according to Hakes, by involving organizational members in the process and by gaining feedback to enhance the measures. Data sources, complete with baseline indicators, should be established and a benchmarking process initiated to ensure that the goals will be measurable and the activities geared toward predetermined performance standards.

Finally, clear decisions must be reached on how the performance measurement system will be used. Some may opt for a more punitive application of assessment, choosing to use the techniques to play a watchdog role. Hakes encourages public administrators to employ measurement strategies in a more constructive way: "If workers can use measures for self-correction and continuous improvement without risk of punishment or with some prospect for reward, progress on providing value for dollar (maximum outputs and outcomes for minimal inputs) will surpass the expectations of most observers" (1997, p. 17).

As with any successful approach to organizational change, Hakes reveals that the most meaningful attempt at performance management will occur when leadership engages members throughout the organization and, in turn, connects the assessment strategy to the organization's long-term outcomes. More importantly, Hakes suggests that public administrators must become less concerned with strictly the quantitative indicators and more concerned with creating a culture of success within their organizations. (The challenges of applying performance management in practice are discussed in Box 6.4.)

An interesting approach to performance measurement that has begun making its way into the public and nonprofit sectors is Kaplan and Norton's (1996) "Balanced Scorecard." The Balanced Scorecard balances concerns for financial performance and internal business processes with customer service and organizational learning. This enables decision makers to track various dimensions of an organization's performance and communicate more

BOX 6.4

PERFORMANCE MANAGEMENT: THEORY AND PRACTICE

In theory, measures of performance are thought to be answers to questions. In practice, performance measures are often themselves questions, or at least they raise as many questions as they answer. Performance measures are exactly that, quantitative representations of some reality. Because performance measures are represented quantitatively, they have the appearance of fact and convey impressions of objectivity and neutrality. In practice, such measures are quantitative interpretations of reality in exactly the same way words are narrative interpretations of reality. In practice, very little is judged to be neutral and objective; all performance measures may be used as arguments and weapons in policy debates.

Measuring Performance

	In Theory	In Practice
Measures of	answers objective neutral	facts evidence
performance are . . .	questions interpretations arguments	slanted weapons
Results are . . .	aggregated for everyone	for some but not others
Performance is . . .	long term	short term
Policy is moved by . . .	data and analysis	rhetoric
What to measure . . .	the important	the measurable
Program domain . . .	comparable	particular
Causal assertions can be . . .	demonstrated	unclear
"This program . . ."	performs poorly	performs poorly, but things would be worse without it

SOURCE: H. George Frederickson, "Measuring Performance in Theory and Practice." *PA Times* 23, no. 8 (August 2000): 8–10. Reprinted by permission.

effectively with stakeholders. Kaplan and Norton point out, however, that the Balanced Scorecard is not just a technique to control behavior or evaluate past performance. Rather it should be used to communicate, to inform, and to enable learning and growth. Through the use of this technique managers should be able to monitor and adjust the implementation of their strategies and make fundamental changes in the way the organization operates (Kaplan & Norton, 1996, pp. 18–24).

Not only those in the United States, but government agencies around the world have begun to develop strategies to help them evaluate their efforts and assume more client centered approaches to meeting public outcomes. A recent study examined reform efforts in member states of the Organization for Economic Cooperation and Development (OECD) and selected nonmember nations. Nations such as Canada, Spain, and Sweden were targeted for their efforts to develop and implement performance measurement techniques on a nationwide basis. Other countries, like the United States, Germany, Korea, Mexico, and the Netherlands, were cited for implementing performance monitoring in specific policy areas. The areas sampled included health care, police and public safety, and policy advice.

The findings from this research suggested that several requirements influence the success of performance monitoring by public organizations: the need for "strategic leadership from central units," "the establishment of the proper organizational incentives which support and encourage results-based management," and "the use of program evaluation as a complement to ongoing performance measurement systems to address performance issues that performance measurement cannot well deal with so as to make the best use of these two measurement tools" (Mayne, 1997, p. 16).

The research showed that the dynamic environments in which the organizations functioned had a significant impact on each agency's capacity for performance and its measurement. In fact, the study found that the ability of an organization to adapt to changing conditions exceeded raw performance as the primary indicator of organizational success. Mayne (1997) wrote, "Maximizing flexibility may be more important than maximizing short-term utility" (p. 16). The study concluded that organizational survival depended on each group's ability to integrate performance measurement with the organization's overall capacity for problem solving and strategic management.

Of course, such a capacity depends on each agency's ability to monitor both the broader organizational performance as well as the effectiveness of individual programs. We have noted the significance of these evaluation strategies in our discussion of performance measurement. However, additional attention should be given to program evaluation, which generates valuable insight into organizational processes and the programmatic impacts produced by policies and initiatives. If performance measurement connects the organization as a whole to specific results and outcomes, then program evaluation reveals how actions by an organization contribute to the objectives within each policy area.

Program Evaluation

There are a variety of ways to classify the approaches to program evaluation. These are, for example, outcome evaluations and process evaluations. *Outcome evaluations* are closely tied to the type of assessment in performance measurement; they focus on the results of program ty—that is, the extent to which a program meets its objectives in terms of impact on environment (for example, the previous discussion of the United Way). If the work of an organization is to improve adult literacy, then an evaluation might measure the number of individuals who learned to read. That information would likely then be related to program inputs to show, in a cost-benefit ratio (in this case, based on allocative efficiency), the number of individuals learning to read per thousand dollars spent. In general, an outcome evaluation seeks to determine whether X causes Y, where X is the activity of the program and Y is the desired outcome or goal. As you can imagine, outcome evaluations are particularly valuable to legislators, grant makers and others concerned with performance of various programs.

In contrast to outcome evaluations, *process evaluations* focus on ways program implementation might be improved to better meet the program's objectives. The question here is what can be done to X, the program's management, to improve Y, the desired outcome. Whereas an evaluator interested in outcomes might spend a great deal of time developing systematic measures of program results, someone interested in process evaluation would analyze the organization and management of the agency's activities, including distribution of financial and human resources and design of service delivery mechanisms. Process evaluations also determine if legally prescribed processes are being followed and assure that individual rights are not violated.

Relevant measures here would fall more on the input side and might include such items as workload measures or data on resource allocation. In such studies, it may be important to distinguish between *efficiency* and *effectiveness*. Efficiency is concerned with the relationship between inputs and outputs, usually expressed in a ratio per unit of input. For example, a measure of streets paved per thousand dollars spent would be a measure of efficiency. Effectiveness, on the other hand, is concerned with the extent to which a program is achieving or failing to achieve its stated objectives Effectiveness measures are outcome-oriented; they focus on the real changes the program produces, such as a decrease in airline deaths.

Sometimes process evaluations occur after the fact—that is, upon completion of the program; but often they occur during program operation. Indeed, some process evaluations are almost continuous in their ongoing review of program operations. In either case, the information that emerges in the course of a process evaluation is likely to be of greatest interest to the program manager who hopes to improve his or her organization's performance.

Program evaluations may therefore be directed toward many different audiences and serve many different purposes. The specific kinds of information required vary from evaluation to evaluation. Eleanor Chelimsky, former head of the General Accounting Office's Program Evaluation and Methodology Division, lists the following types of information that may be developed retrospectively.

- Information on program implementation (such as the degree to which the program is operational, how similar it is across sites, whether it conforms to the policies and expectations formulated, how much it costs, how stakeholders feel about it, whether there are major problems of service delivery or of error, fraud, and abuse, and so on).
- Ongoing information on the current state of the problem or threat addressed by the program. (Is the problem growing? Is it diminishing? Is it diminishing enough so that the program is no longer needed? Is it changing in terms of its significant characteristics?)
- Information on program outcomes. (What happened as a result of program implementation?)

- Information on the degree to which the program made, or is making, a difference. (That is, what change in the problem or threat occurred that can be directly attributed to the program?)
- Information on the unexpected (as well as expected) effects of the programs. (For instance, was a program of drug education accompanied by an increase in the use of drugs?) (Chelimsky, 1985, pp. 8–9)

Evaluation Designs and Techniques

Approaches to the evaluation of public programs range from historical analysis to sophisticated experimental designs. Indeed, over the years, there has been a recurring debate over the proper approach to evaluation. Some argue that such research should be primarily qualitative, concerned with tracking program development and indicating forces that helped shape the program. Advocates of this approach tend to be most interested in process questions, such as reasons for success or failure and unanticipated consequences of the program; they ask, "What happened?" Others argue that program evaluations should, wherever possible, employ the most rigorous scientific methods appropriate to the subject matter, including the design and execution of formal experiments. These analysts tend to be more interested in program outcomes; they ask, "Does it work?" (Chelimsky, 1985, p. 14).

Whatever the approach, those involved in program evaluation must confront two challenges to the validity of their work. The first question, concerning *internal validity*, asks whether the approach measured what was intended. Was the design consistent with the goals of the program and the needs of the sponsor? Were the methods most appropriate for answering the questions that needed to be asked? Were the results as free from bias as possible? A second question, concerning *external validity*, asks to what extent the findings may be applicable to more general circumstances. What does the study say about similarly situated programs? Can the study be replicated and expected to produce similar results? These and other questions can be directed toward the various techniques employed in evaluation research.

Qualitative Techniques Many program evaluations depend on qualitative information derived from reading about the program, from interviewing important actors (including agency personnel, clients, and others) and sometimes from actually participating in the work of the program. The initial step in a qualitative evaluation project is usually to read everything available about the program and the subject matter, including background material on the subject of the program (flu vaccines, child nutrition, rapid transit systems, and so on), agency documents, operating procedures, internal memoranda, newspaper and magazine articles, articles on similar programs elsewhere, and reports issued by various concerned groups. The researcher would also likely make a few phone calls to identify the significant actors in the program and determine where the most important activities are taking place.

Following an initial reconnaissance, the analyst settles on a limited number of sites (schools, hospitals, highway systems, and so on) as the focus of the investigation. Most qualitative evaluations are largely exploratory, designed to explore a variety of hunches or intuitions about the program's operation. For these cases, the analyst will probably try to select sites that vary

What Would You Do?

You have been asked to assess the effectiveness of a new program aimed at reducing teen pregnancies by providing birth control information through the high schools. You have heard several suggestions about how to design the study—and some comments that it's simply impossible to measure something like this. What would you do?

widely along several crucial dimensions. Some evaluations, however, are *hypothesis-guided*, designed to demonstrate the plausibility of a particular hypothesis, so the analyst might choose a limited number of crucial sites that are especially illustrative of the issue under investigation.

Once the research sites have been chosen, the analyst may choose to gather most of his or her information through *intensive interviews*, detailed information-gathering sessions involving major actors both inside and outside the agency responsible for the program. Interviewing skills include establishing the interviewer's credentials, setting the proper climate, arranging questions effectively, asking reasonable but challenging questions, and keeping a good record of all that is said. Perhaps most important, the interviewer must keep the discussion on the subject, in a way that is neither obvious nor embarrassing to either party. Immediately following the interview, the interviewer should review and expand upon the notes taken during the interview session. These notes will form an important basis for drawing conclusions about the program.

An alternative means of gathering qualitative information is the use of a *participant observer*, someone involved in either the target population or the agency itself, who makes observations and draws conclusions based on firsthand data. For example, an evaluation of an antipoverty program in eastern Kentucky some years ago employed a participant observer who lived in the community, talked daily with others in the community about the program, and reported back to the overall evaluation staff.

Either technique can be questioned with respect to both internal and external validity. Biased information and questions about internal validity can arise if the wrong people are chosen to interview or if those interviewed provide misleading information, intentionally or unintentionally. Participant observers can affect the program's operation through their own presence, leading to outcomes far different from what would otherwise have happened. Questions concerning external validity (or generalizability) might be raised with either technique based on the choice of only a limited number of sites for investigation.

Quantitative Techniques Policy evaluations often endeavor to approximate the scientific methods of the physical sciences, though such efforts are extremely difficult. In its classic formulation, an *experimental design* involves examination of two or more groups under carefully controlled conditions. One group, the *experimental group*, receives a treatment or intervention; in the case of program evaluation, members of the experimental group receive the benefits of the program being evaluated. Another group, the *control group*, consists of individuals who are as similar as possible to those in the experimental group and who act under the same general conditions, yet do not receive the intervention. Members of both groups are tested before and after the experimental intervention (pretest and posttest measures), and the results are compared. If the program has had either a positive or negative effect, the differences should show up in the data.

We can illustrate the difficulties in designing a rigorous experimental design with respect to social programs by imagining that we are interested in analyzing the effectiveness of a new approach to mathematics education in the fourth grade. One classroom might be designated an experimental group and be taught using the new approach; another classroom might be designated the control group and be taught using traditional methods. The mathematical abilities of all students would be measured both before and after the period in which the new program was being taught. If the new technique is indeed more effective in educating children in mathematics, the posttest scores of the children in the experimental group should be higher than those of the children in the control group.

In a very general sense, this is an application of an experimental design to a social program, and you can easily imagine how similar designs might be used to measure other programs, ranging from immunizations to welfare incentives to highway designs. But we can observe difficulties in such designs, some of which relate to questions of internal validity. One might respond to the study by saying that students in the experimental group were smarter to begin with, or that the absence rate was higher among those in the control group. Or you might suggest that one teacher was better than the other, and that made the difference. Or even if the same teacher taught both groups, you might speculate that he or she taught the new material with more enthusiasm. Similar questions might be raised about external validity. For instance, if the results were obtained in a rural school, would they apply as well to an urban setting?

Some, if not all, of these questions could be anticipated by slightly altering the research design. For example, students could be randomly assigned to the two groups, thus eliminating any possibility of bias in the group's composition. But questions such as these show the difficulty of achieving true experimental conditions in measuring social programs. For this reason, most evaluations of social programs are called quasi-experimental.

Quasi-experimental designs retain the requirement for systematic data gathering that should be part of any quantitative approach, but free the researcher from some of the difficulties of developing experimental designs, such as the need for random assignment of subjects to various groups. Here again, different groups may be compared, but an essential task for the researcher is to separate the effects of a treatment from effects of other factors. Only the effects caused by the treatment are of interest.

Quasi-experimental approaches are not only more adaptable to social situations, but they also better fit the situation in which program evaluators often find themselves—assigned to the evaluation long after the program has begun and having little influence on patterns of intervention. In such a case, a historical approach may be of special value. For example, one quasi-experimental design—*time series analysis*—involves making a number of observations about the target population both before and after the program intervention. (These observations may even be made retrospectively by gathering historical data.) In one case, basic information about neighborhood crime was developed for a period of years prior to the introduction of a new patrol pattern, then similar data followed after the new approach was introduced.

■ Summary and Action Implications

As a public manager, you will become quite familiar with the cycle of planning, implementation, and evaluation. In practice, the phases of the cycle will rarely appear as distinct as in our discussion, but you will still find that you must devote a portion of your time to each phase. In middle and upper management, the planning, implementation, and evaluation cycle will become especially complex because you will find yourself engaged in all three phases almost simultaneously. That is, you will be planning for one project at the same time that you are implementing a second and evaluating a third, and so on. Obviously, maintaining a good sense of the timing of the various projects and knowing when and how to shift from one to the next will be extremely important.

As we have seen, techniques have been developed to help you work through the typical problems you will encounter in each phase of the cycle. Although many of the techniques can be elaborated in highly complex ways, the logic on which they are based can be helpful in dealing even with fairly simple and immediate problems.

Throughout the planning, implementation, and evaluation cycle, you should remember that, whereas we have focused on technical aids to your administrative work, each of the three areas will be strongly affected by how you interact with the *people* in your organization (and elsewhere). Planning, implementation, and evaluation are human processes and are thus subject to people's shifting values, attitudes, and behaviors. In planning, implementation, and evaluation, as with budgeting, financial management, and personnel, techniques are successful only when you use them with full regard for democratic values, clear leadership, and humane management.

TERMS AND DEFINITIONS

Benchmarking: Targeting of specific goals based on previous performance levels, standards set by similar organizations, objectives created through a strategic planning process, or any combination of these and other relevant sources.

Cost-benefit: Identifying and quantifying both negative impacts (costs) and positive impacts (benefits) of a proposal, then subtracting one from the other to arrive at a net benefit.

Decision analysis: Technique wherein decisions are likely to be made sequentially and under some degree of uncertainty.

Decision tree: Technique that identifies various possible outcomes, given the risk associated with each.

Effectiveness: Extent to which a program is achieving or failing to achieve its stated objectives.

Efficiency: Relationship between inputs and outputs.

Institutional subsystem: Responsible for adapting the organization to its environment and for anticipating and planning for the future.

Managerial subsystem: Concerned with providing necessary resources for accomplishing a technical task and mediating between the technical and institutional subsystems.

Outcome evaluations: Evaluations that focus on the results of program activity, the extent to which a program meets its objectives in terms of impact on the environment.

Participant observer: Someone in either the target population or the agency who makes observations and draws conclusions based on firsthand experience.

Performance indicators: Specific, quantifiable goals that the agency strives for in pursuit of its more substantive objectives.

Performance measurement: Careful and detailed measurement of the achievement of program objectives and outcomes by a program or agency.

PERT: A way to monitor the time or costs of various activities required to complete a project, showing the sequence in which the activities must be completed.

Policy analysis: Process of researching or analyzing public problems to provide policy makers with specific information about the range of available policy options and advantages and disadvantages of different approaches.

Process charting or *flowcharting:* Graphically demonstrating the various steps in an operation, the people who perform each step, and relationships among those elements.

Process evaluations: Seeking ways to improve program implementation so as to better meet program objectives.

Reengineering: Radically redesigning work processes and organizational structures to be in line with agency outcomes.

Stakeholders: The many different people who are involved in policy decisions and are affected by the results.

Strategic planning: Matching organizational objectives and capabilities to the anticipated demands of the environment to produce a plan of action that will ensure achievement of objectives.

System: Set of regularized interactions configured or "bounded" in a way that differentiates and separates them from other actions that constitute the system's environment.

Systems theory: Effort to identify the interactions of various internal and external elements that impinge on an organization's operations.

Technical subsystem: Concerned with effective performance of an organization's actual work.

Time series analysis: Making a number of observations about the target population both before and after program intervention.

STUDY QUESTIONS

1. Planning is one aspect of the policy process. Discuss the various types of planning and their objectives.

2. In organizing a planning process, what are the primary concerns of the planning group?

3. Discuss the necessary steps for comprehensive policy analysis.

4. Identify some of the quantitative techniques used for policy analysis.

5. The second phase of the policy process is implementation of plans. Discuss some of the techniques available to help in the beginning stages of the implementation process.

6. Compare and contrast the several different subsystems that carry forward an organization's work.

7. What does the phrase "managing for results" mean? How might such a program be implemented?

8. What are the different types of evaluation approaches? Discuss the distinctions among them.

CASES AND EXERCISES

1. As a class or working in small groups, assume the role of a task force that the governor has asked to develop plans for a new university that the legislature has created in a rapidly expanding area in the corner of your state. Your plan should be based on whatever assumptions you wish to make by explicitly stating them in writing; however, all your assumptions should be consistent with the following guidelines.

    a. Assume that you have full legal authority to develop the university, including the power to develop a full range of undergraduate programs and a limited number of graduate programs in areas of special interest to the state. Assume a high degree of political support within the corner of the state where the university will be built, and general support throughout the state, but assume major opposition from the state's leading public university.

    b. Assume that the area where the new university is to be located already houses a community college, which the university will take over, and a couple of small, private liberal arts colleges. Assume that the community college has 2,000 freshmen and sophomores and operates in two large buildings on a large tract of otherwise undeveloped land, which is sufficient to accommodate the new university.

c. Assume that the area in which the university will be built has traditionally had an agricultural and tourist-based economy, but is experiencing rapid growth in high-tech industry, primarily because companies are attracted to the area's natural beauty and comfortable climate.

d. Assume that you can anticipate a budget starting at $12 million for the first year of operations (this is inclusive of the community college budget), but rising at a rate of $7 million a year for the next nine years. Assume also that, in addition, there is adequate financing available for whatever new construction will be required during the first ten years of the university's existence.

e. Assume that you have full control over the curriculum of the university and authority to propose to the Coordinating Board on Higher Education any new program offerings. Assume, however, that the major university in the state will fight hard to protect its engineering and computer science programs from competition.

You should create a plan for development of the new university over the next ten years. You should take into account all aspects of development, including all academic programs, student services, administrative support (including the physical plant, personnel, and financial and accounting systems), capital construction, and intercollegiate athletics. You may wish to establish subcommittees or task forces to work on particular areas; however, all reports should be combined into a single planning document to be submitted to the governor's office.

2. Imagine that your city council is considering a proposed ordinance to require an 8-percent deposit on each beverage container sold in the city. Each beer can, soft drink bottle, or other container would carry a city sticker or imprint. Retailers would collect the deposit on each container sold and would be required to pay 8 cents for each empty container returned to the store. Proponents of the bill argue that it would help clean up the city and provide better recycling of containers. Opponents argue that the bill would be difficult for stores to adhere to and a nightmare for the city to enforce. Develop a research design—that is, a plan for conducting research—that would enable you to report to the city council on the potential costs and benefits of the proposed ordinance.

3. Complete the following exercise: The newly elected governor of a large Middle Atlantic state has asked you to assist in developing a plan to revise the method of patrolling the highways. The problem stems from a report by the federal Department of Transportation, showing that an independent sampling of traffic in the state indicates far too many motorists are exceeding the federally mandated speed limit. The report goes on to threaten a cutoff of all federal highway funds to the state if something is not done. Perhaps of greater urgency, however, is the finding that the number of accidents per 1,000 miles driven is rising dramatically.

The governor's office has provided you with a set of alternative strategies for patrolling the highways and the associated costs and probable reductions in both accidents and speeders. Also included in the materials is a study of the revenue generated by the issuance of citations. You are asked to write a report indicating the various payoffs associated with each strategy. These are the types of patrols.

stationary radar trap patrol
cruising car patrol
airplane/chase car patrol

These are the costs per shift for each patrol type.

stationary = $600 per patrol
cruising = $800 per patrol
airplane = $1,500 per patrol

The cost of servicing each accident that occurs during a patrol is $250. The likelihood of accidents, however, differs, depending on the type of patrol: The stationary patrol results in a .50 probability of two accidents; the cruising patrol results in a .30 probability of two accidents; and the airplane patrol results in a .25 probability of two accidents. Finally, the number of citations issued varies by type of patrol: Stationary patrols issue eight citations on average; cruising patrols issue five citations on average; and airplane patrols issue three citations on average.

A previous study indicated that accident rates of less than an average of one per patrol were typical of states where the Department of Transportation found acceptable levels of speeding.

In a concluding paragraph, the governor indicates that it costs the state $50 to process a citation (which averages a fine of $85), but the governor goes on to say that may not be relevant to the choice of patrol type because the whole idea is to prevent accidents by slowing traffic to the legal speed limit (and preventing a cutoff of federal money).

How would you go about developing the report to the governor?

4. Complete the following exercise: You have been hired by Expert Analysis consulting firm to work on a project for New York City. The city has hired the firm to analyze the advisability of contracting out garbage collection, expanding city garbage collection capacity, or going to a twenty-four hour collection system.

The city currently operates a sanitation department of 2,538 people using 781 garbage trucks of two different sizes. The large trucks carry 35 tons per trip and make two trips per day. The small trucks carry 15 tons and make three trips per day. There are 537 small trucks and 244 large trucks. The cost of one day for a large truck is $720 in wages for three people (eight-hour shift) and $200 for maintenance. The cost of one day for a small truck is $480 for wages for two people (eight-hour shift) and $150 for maintenance. The collective bargaining contract calls for a "shift differential" of 15 percent above the standard $30 per hour for the truck crews, if the crews work other than 6:00 A.M. to 3:00 P.M. The contract has three years to go before it expires. A recent study indicates that the amount of garbage to be collected in the city will increase 14 percent in the next year and 18 percent in the following year. The study also shows that many of the larger firms in the city are contemplating using a private garbage service, We-Haul, Inc., which has recently begun competing with the city. The study concludes that, although the amount of garbage to be collected will increase, the amount the city will be required to collect might decrease slightly or remain steady.

A quick check of the maintenance records indicates that you can expect a 20 percent increase in maintenance costs for the large trucks and a 30 percent increase for the small trucks, if you operate twenty-four hours a day. You call the Tidy-Truck manufacturer and get a quote of $82,000 for a new large truck and $59,000 for a new small truck if you order this year. They expect a 6 percent price increase next year.

Just as you put down the phone, your liaison with the city calls to tell you that We-Haul, Inc. has offered to collect the additional garbage at a "special rate" for the city of $18 per ton for the first year and $20 per ton for the second year.

Making reasonable assumptions about information you may need, develop a recommendation as to whether the city should expand its service by buying more trucks and hiring more people, operate its service twenty-four hours a day, or contract with We-Haul, Inc. to pick up the increase.

SOURCE: This case was adapted from material provided by Barry Hammond of Slippery Rock University, Pennsylvania.

5. The governor of a large Midwestern state has recently introduced a performance management initiative to enhance the activities of state agencies and, more specifically, to reverse downward trends in educational achievement and increases in juvenile crime. The governor, responding to increasing public outcry, has encouraged her cabinet to develop ten outcomes in the area of human and social services, then identify performance indicators that can be used in monitoring the state's progress in achieving these outcomes. As a senior cabinet member, you have been called upon to play a leadership role in this process. What are the primary outcomes that the state would need to accomplish in order to reverse the downward trends? What performance indicators could be used to help keep the statewide initiative on track? How would you ensure that these performance measurement strategies are implemented throughout the state and that the necessary organizational change has occurred to ensure their effectiveness?

FOR ADDITIONAL READING

Adler, Matthew D., and Eric A. Posner. *New Foundations of Cost-Benefit Analysis*. Cambridge, MA: Harvard University Press, 2006.

Allison, Michael, and Jude Kaye. *Strategic Planning for Nonprofit Organizations*. New York: John Wiley & Sons, 1997.

Abramson, Mark A., and Ann M. Kieffaber, eds. *New Ways of Doing Business*. Lanham, MD: Rowman & Littlefield, 2003.

Bardach, Eugene. *A Practical Guide for Policy Analysis*. Washington, DC: CQ Press, 2004.

Bingham, Richard D., and Claire L. Felbinger. *Evaluation in Practice: A Methodological Approach*. 2nd ed. New York: Chatham House, 2001.

Boyne, George A., et al., eds. *Public Service Performance: Perspectives on Measurement and Management*. Cambridge, NY: Cambridge University Press, 2006.

Bryson, John M. *Strategic Planning for Public and Nonprofit Organizations: A Guide to Strengthening and Sustaining Organizational Achievement*. 3rd ed. San Francisco: Jossey-Bass, 2004.

Bryson, John, and Farnum Alston. *Creating and Implementing Your Strategic Plan.* San Francisco: Jossey-Bass, 1995.

Chambers, Donald E. *Social Policy and Social Programs: A Method for Practical Public Policy Analysis.* Boston: Allyn & Bacon, 1999.

Forester, John. *Planning in the Face of Power.* Berkeley, CA: University of California Press, 1989.

Geva-May, Iris. *Thinking Like a Policy Analyst: Policy Analysis as a Clinical Profession.* New York: Palgrave Macmillan, 2005

Greene, Jennifer C., and Valerie J. Caracelli. *Advances in Mixed Method Evaluation.* San Francisco: Jossey-Bass, 1997.

Goggin, Malcolm L., Ann O. Bowman, James P. Lester, and Laurence O'Toole, Jr. *Implementation Theory and Practice: Toward a Third Generation.* New York: HarperCollins, 1990.

Hatry, Harry P., Therese van Houten, Margaret C. Plantz, and Martha Taylor Greenway. *Measuring Program Outcomes: A Practical Approach.* Alexandria, VA: United Way of America, 1996.

Kaufman, Roger. *Strategic Planning Plus: An Organizational Guide.* 2nd ed. Newbury Park, CA: Sage Publications, 1992.

Kearns, Kevin. *Managing for Accountability.* San Francisco: Jossey-Bass, 1996.

Keehley, Patricia, et al. *Benchmarking for Best Practices.* San Francisco: Jossey-Bass, 1996.

Koteen, Jack. *Strategic Management in Public and Nonprofit Organizations.* 2nd ed. Westport, CT: Praeger Publishers, 1997.

Kraft, Michael E., and Scott R. Furlong. *Public Policy: Politics, Analysis, and Alternatives.* Washington, DC: CQ Press, 2004.

Krause, George A., and Kenneth J. Meier, eds. *Politics, Policy, and Organizations: Frontiers in the Scientific Study of Bureaucracy.* Ann Arbor, MI: University of Michigan Press, 2003.

Lejano, Raul P. *Frameworks for Policy Analysis: Merging Text and Context.* New York: Routledge, 2006.

Linden, Russell. *Seamless Government.* San Francisco: Jossey-Bass, 1994.

Meehan, Eugene. *Assessing Governmental Performance.* Westport, CT: Greenwood Press, 1993.

Meier, Kenneth J., and Jeffrey L. Brudney. *Applied Statistics for Public Administration.* 3rd ed. Belmont, CA: Wadsworth, 1993.

Mintrom, Michael. *People Skills for Policy Analysts.* Washington, DC: Georgetown University Press, 2003.

Peters, Guy B. *American Public Policy: Promise and Performance.* New York: Chatham House, 1999.

Poister, Theodore H. *Measuring Performance in Public and Nonprofit Organizations.* San Francisco: Jossey-Bass, 2003.

Quade, E. S. *Analysis for Public Decisions.* 2nd ed. New York: North-Holland, 1989.

Rabin, Jack, W. Bartley Hidreth, and Gerald J. Miller, eds. *Handbook of Strategic Management.* New York: Marcel Dekker, 1989.

Starling, Grover. *Strategies for Policy Making.* Pacific Grove, CA: Brooks/Cole, 1988.

Sylvia, Ronald, et al. *Program Planning and Evaluation for the Public Manager.* 2nd ed. Prospect Heights, IL: Waveland Press, 1997.

Vines, David. *Information Strategy and Public Policy.* Cambridge, MA: B. Blackwell, 1991.

Wholey, Joseph, Harry P. Hatry, and Kathryn Newcomer, eds. *Handbook of Practical Program Evaluation.* San Francisco: Jossey-Bass, 1994.

Wye, Christopher G., and Harry P. Hatry, eds. *Timely Low-Cost Evaluation in the Public Sector.* San Francisco: Jossey-Bass, 1988.

Zey, Mary, ed. *Decision Making: Alternatives to Rational Choice Models.* Newbury Park, CA: Sage Publications, 1992.

CHAPTER 7

BUDGETING AND FINANCIAL MANAGEMENT

Public budgeting and financial management are concerned with allocating limited resources to problems that governments and other public organizations face. Just as you establish a personal budget to track your income and expenses and, just as businesses create budgets to aid in decisions affecting profits and losses, so do public organizations employ budgets to help in planning and management. Public organizations must carefully and responsibly manage large amounts of money and other resources—taking in taxes and other revenues, purchasing goods and services, investing surplus funds, and managing debt wisely.

From the point of view of the manager or citizen trying to influence public policy, the budget is an extremely important tool for planning and control. To manage public programs effectively, you must be able to manage resources, both practically and politically. In this chapter we focus on the budget process from the standpoint of the individual public manager, examining how budget decisions are made and how you can influence budgetary outcomes. Although much of the budget process is highly charged politically, specific technical knowledge about budgeting systems will give you a distinct advantage.

The elaborate systems that public organizations have developed to manage their fiscal affairs are relatively recent. Prior to the turn of the century, revenues were easily sufficient to cover the expenses of government, and financial management was merely record keeping. As the scope of government grew and new demands were placed on its resources, the need for more sophisticated systems of decision making became apparent. Moreover, repeated instances of corruption and waste made more effective control over the public's resources necessary.

In establishing its executive budget process through the Budgeting and Accounting Act of 1921, the federal government followed the lead of several local and state governments that had already taken similar actions. This municipal reform movement emphasized the budget process as a means of bringing order to public spending; consequently, by the 1920s, most big cities had established a formal budget process. Similar developments were also occurring at the state level. In 1910, Ohio became the first state to require an executive budget; within the next decade, similar actions took place in most other states. At the federal level, a special Commission on Economy and Efficiency, known as the Taft Commission, recommended establishing an executive budget in 1912; the recommendation was implemented nearly a decade later.

Since the 1920s, the federal budget has grown in both size and complexity, as have budgets at the state and local levels. This growth means that budgeting and financial management have come to involve far more than keeping a record of income and expenses. Today, how government spends its money affects many other areas of the economy; consequently, the budget is an instrument of fiscal policy. Moreover, the budget is a primary expression of government priorities; it constitutes a record of the decisions that are made concerning various public policies.

NETWORKING

General information on budgeting organizations can be found at www.gasb.org and at www.nasbo.org.

■ The Budget as an Instrument of Fiscal Policy

Budgets express the public policy choices of governments and others. Among these are choices with respect to the impact of the public sector on the economy. *Fiscal policy* is concerned with the impact of government taxation and spending on the economy generally. Before the Great Depression, little attention was paid to how the federal budget affected the economy, which was presumably regulated by the *business cycle*. Periods of economic growth featuring inflation and high employment, were followed by periods of recession or depression featuring deflation and unemployment. Meanwhile, the federal government sought to balance its budget each year—that is, to make revenues and expenditures approximately equal.

Economists soon began to realize, however, that this pattern of government spending was influencing the economy in a negative way. In periods of economic growth, government revenues naturally increased. In an effort to balance the budget, taxes could be lowered to the level of expenditures; in periods of economic decline, the budget was balanced by lowering spending to meet the lower revenues. The unanticipated result was to increase citizens' income during good times and decrease their income in bad times—just the opposite of what would be desirable. Government taxation and spending had the effect of accentuating economic instability (Pechman, 1983, p. 8).

Economists such as the British scholar John Maynard Keynes argued, in contrast, that all else being equal, positive government action could lead to greater economic stability. A key to Keynes's analysis was the relationship between inflation and unemployment. Keynes noted that periods of rapid economic growth are typically accompanied by high inflation, which is harmful to individuals because it lowers their purchasing power, especially if they are on fixed incomes. On the other hand, periods of economic decline are typically accompanied by high unemployment, which not only hurts individuals, but lowers revenues for government. In either case, government action aimed at achieving greater stability might be both possible and desirable.

There are many ways the federal government can influence the economy, but one important way is simply by varying its own spending or, somewhat more indirectly, by raising or lowering taxes. The capacity of government spending patterns to influence the economy so dramatically is not hard to understand if you recognize the enormous role of government in the economy. The Gross Domestic Product (GDP), the rate of inflation, and the rate of unemployment are the key indicators of economic health. *Gross Domestic Product,* a measure of total economic output, is measured by the market value of goods and services. Almost two-thirds of our current GDP is private in nature, but about one-third (31.8 percent in 2006) is based on government spending. Based on revenues, the U.S. federal government is the single largest organization in the world, almost 10 times the size of General Motors, Wal-Mart, or Exxon. Obviously, decisions at the federal level play an important role in the health and stability of the economy generally.

The key relationships are these: (1) If the economy is experiencing rapid growth—with high inflation and low unemployment—the government might seek to "cool off" the economy by taking money out of the economy through lowering spending, raising taxes, or both. This limits private demand and slows economic growth. On the other hand, (2) If the economy is experiencing recession or depression—with falling prices and high unemployment—the government might want to stimulate the economy by putting more money into circulation, through increasing spending, lowering taxes, or both. This stimulates private demand and increases economic growth. Creating a surplus, as might occur in the first case, would help restrain private spending during prosperity; creating a deficit, as might occur in the second case, might stimulate spending during a recession.

Cumulative state and local spending also affects the economy. State and local government expenditures constitute close to 12 percent of the GDP and must be taken into account in discussions of fiscal policy. If the federal government cuts taxes, but also cuts aid to states and localities, those governments may find it necessary to raise taxes themselves, thus offsetting any economic gains caused by lower federal taxes.

Patterns of spending in many states and in major cities do have some effect on the local economy, and consequently, state and local officials are becoming more cognizant of their role in fiscal policy and especially economic development. These governments, however, often don't have the tools or authority to make certain kinds of decisions. For example, nearly all the states have either constitutional or statutory provisions requiring a balanced budget. (Various political leaders have called for a balanced budget amendment at the federal level as a way to eliminate deficit spending. If balanced budgets are achieved in other ways, however, calls for an amendment will be undercut. In any case, such a proposal, though attractive in a symbolic sense, would limit the flexibility of the federal government in seeking to influence the economy.) In any case, it is clear that the budget process has important effects on the economy that must be anticipated when structuring overall patterns of public spending.

■ The Budget as an Instrument of Public Policy

Although the overall pattern of spending represented in a government budget has an important effect on the economy, individual entries in the budget represent important choices with respect to public policies of all types. The budget is, essentially, a measure of support (or lack of support) for specific programs. Those in favor are funded; those out of favor are not. For this reason, discussions of budgetary priorities are of special importance to political leaders, government officials at all levels, and representatives of various interests in society. As a manager, you will need to understand both where the money comes from and where the money goes (see Figure 7.1).

FIGURE 7.1

The Federal Government Receipts: Fiscal Year 2007 Estimate

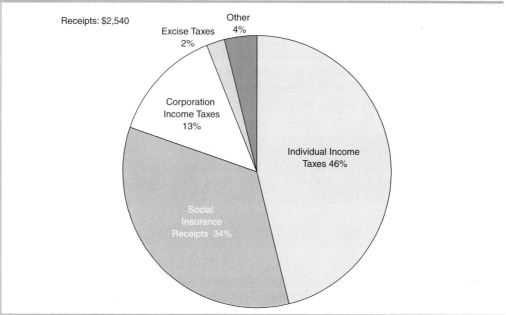

SOURCE: Historical Tables, Budget of the US Government, FY2008 (Table 2.1 Receipts by Source, p. 30), retrieved April 4, 2007, from www.whitehouse.gov/omb/budget/fy2008/pdf/hist.pdf.

Where the Money Comes From

Governments obtain funds either from their own sources or through transfers from other governments to operate programs deemed important. There are a variety of ways governments can raise their own revenues, including levying taxes and charging individuals or groups for specific services. Because all public programs are affected by the way governments raise revenues, and because revenue administration is itself an important part of public administration, you will find it helpful to understand the way taxes are structured.

Developing tax policies requires attention not only to the level of taxes being taken from individuals or groups, but to the fairness, efficiency, and simplicity of the tax system. Everyone agrees that the tax system should be fair and that everyone should pay his or her "fair share." But what exactly does that mean? Some argue that each should pay according to the benefits they receive; others argue that those who have a greater ability to pay should in fact pay more.

One way to approach the issue is to think in terms of the relationship between one's tax rate and one's income (vertical-equity concept). A tax structure is *proportional* (or "flat") if it taxes everyone at the same effective tax rate. If an effective tax rate is applied to $20,000 income (yielding $2,000) and the same rate is applied to a $200,000 income (yielding $20,000), even though the amounts differ, the tax is proportional to the amount of income. A tax is *progressive* if it taxes those with higher income at a higher effective tax rate. Income tax is often cited as progressive. For example, a person with a $20,000 income and tax rate of 10 percent will pay $2,000 in taxes; another individual with a $200,000 income will be taxed at 10 percent for the first $20,000 (yielding $2,000), 20 percent for the next $80,000 (yielding $16,000), and 50 percent for the remaining $100,000 of income (yielding $50,000). Total tax paid on $200,000 will be $68,000, or an effective rate of 34 percent. Finally, a tax is *regressive* (such as sales taxes) if it taxes those with lower incomes at a proportionally higher effective rate than those with higher incomes. For example, if an individual with a $20,000 income buys a car and pays $500 in taxes, then the effective tax rate for this individual relative to his income is 2.5 percent. If another individual with a $200,000 income buys the same car and pays $500 in taxes, then the effective tax rate for that individual relative to his income is 0.25 percent.

Individual Income Tax   All methods of taxation involve application of a *tax rate* to a particular *tax base*; the product of these yields *tax revenue*. The individual income tax is the single most important tax in our country. It calls for individuals to add up all income from taxable sources, reduce that amount by certain deductions or exemptions, and then apply a tax rate to that base to arrive at the individual's income tax. The current federal income tax, for example, applies rates between 15 and 35 percent to six income brackets.

All advanced industrial nations use some form of income tax. In the United States, income tax is the primary source of revenue for the federal government and is used to a lesser extent in many states and some cities. In most cases, a higher rate is applied to higher incomes, making the income tax a progressive tax. For nearly thirty years after its passage in 1913, the federal income tax applied only to a fairly small number of high-income people. With the advent of World War II, deductions were reduced significantly and higher rates applied.

Managing the task of collecting income tax from everyone in the country is obviously difficult. Yet, the Internal Revenue Service (IRS) has developed a relatively efficient mechanism for collection and does so at a cost of about one-half of 1 percent of the revenues produced. Key to the existing system is the requirement that each individual calculate his or her own tax liability. IRS auditors then select a few returns for closer inspection, concentrating on those with unusual features. The extent of compliance with tax regulations in this country, though far from complete, is considered comparatively high.

Corporation Income Tax   The corporation income tax, also a progressive tax, actually predates the individual income tax by several years and, for most of the last century, was a key source of federal revenue. Its proponents justify it as a way of taxing capital accumulation that is not specifically distributed to individuals. Moreover, the corporation income tax is needed to support the individual income tax; without it, individuals could simply keep their income in corporations and avoid paying income taxes. Though most states have corporation income taxes, the tax is far more substantial at the federal level; yet, even here, corporation income tax is declining in contrast to other sources of revenue. Where it once yielded more revenue than the individual income tax, the corporation income tax has declined to only about one-tenth of federal revenues.

Payroll Taxes   Taxes on payrolls support a variety of social security and other social insurance programs, such as unemployment compensation and medical care for the aged. (Do not confuse these specific taxes with the general income taxes that may be deducted from a payroll check.) These programs are primarily financed by taxes paid either by the employer or by the employer and employee in equal amounts. Payroll taxes overall are regressive because there is a flat rate, with no deductions or exemptions, and maximum amounts above which taxes are not required. Payroll taxes at the federal level now constitute the second largest source of federal revenue.

Sales and Excise Taxes   Both sales and excise taxes are applied to goods and services. *Sales taxes* are applied to a broad range of goods and services at either retail or wholesale levels and are a popular source of income at state and local levels. There are significant variations in sales tax rates and in items covered by sales taxes—for example, some jurisdictions exempt food, clothing, and medicine from sales tax. *Excise taxes* are applied to the sale of specific commodities such as gasoline, tobacco, or alcohol, and are the primary form of consumption tax at the federal level. Typically, excise taxes are applied at specific rates (such as two cents per gallon of gasoline), but may be applied to the total sales price. Some excise taxes are, in effect, user charges that help support particular activities. Gasoline taxes, for instance, are typically used to support highway construction and maintenance.

A major issue concerning sales and excise taxes is that of equity. Because the poor consume a greater portion of their income than the rich, the burden of consumption taxes tends to fall more heavily on the poor, so the taxes are regressive. These taxes also tend to penalize certain groups, such as those with large families or those just starting a household. On the other hand, these taxes tend to provide more stable revenues, something that is especially important at state and local levels.

Property Taxes   Taxes on personal property are widely used at the local level and provide about half of local government revenues. Administration of a property tax involves assessment of an individual's property, most often land and buildings, then the application of a tax rate. About half the revenue generated by the property tax derives from residential property and half from businesses. Although the property tax is progressive in its effect (those who spend more on housing pay more), administration is difficult and has often not been highly professional. Moreover, recent tax limitations have severely restricted the capacity of local governments to raise additional revenue through the property tax.

Other Revenue Sources   There are, of course, a variety of other sources of government revenues. Whereas public organizations have often charged fees for the use of specific government services, recent limitations on other tax revenues have made such charges increasingly attractive, especially at the local level. For example, fees for the use of parks and recreational facilities are becoming increasingly important. Another recent development in terms of revenues at the state level is the use of lotteries. Nearly half the states and several local governments now conduct lotteries, which provide a highly visible, but relatively small and unstable, source of funds. Lotteries are also highly regressive in their effect (because poorer citizens tend to play the lotteries more); indeed, they are more regressive than even the sales tax.

Nonprofit organizations, which lack the power to tax, derive revenues from quite different sources and, indeed, engage in a wide variety of efforts to support their programs. Obviously, membership organizations depend in large measure on member dues for revenue, but such organizations, along with many others, have recently sought to diversify revenues. Although grant funding remains an important source of revenue for many nonprofit organizations, recent reductions in federal social service programs have seriously limited grant opportunities for many nonprofits. Additional sources of funds include donations (from individuals, corporations, and foundations), sales of goods and services (from books to coffee cups), and joint enterprises involving commercial firms (such as insurance plans or "affinity" credit cards).

Patterns of Government Revenues As we have seen, different levels of government vary in their dependence on specific revenue sources. Figure 7.1 shows the distribution of receipts at the federal level. The president's budget for fiscal 2007 estimates total revenues of $2.54 trillion, including the following major categories:
Individual income taxes: $1,168.8 billion
Corporation income taxes: $342 billion
Social insurance and retirement receipts: $873.4 billion
Excise taxes: $57.1 billion
Other receipts: $98.8 billion
Estate and gift taxes: $25.3 billion
Customs duties and fees: $26.8 billion
Miscellaneous receipts: $46.7 billion

NETWORKING

For the budget of the United States, and how to get to the budgets of other governments, see the Department of the Treasury at www.ustreas.gov. For details on the current fiscal year federal budget and access to historical budget data, go to www.gpoaccess.gov/usbudget/index.html.

Although the federal government relies heavily on income tax, state governments are much more dependent on sales taxes, and local governments are primarily dependent on property tax. All state and local governments combined generated $1,464 billion in revenues in 2003–2004, with $360.6 billion coming from sales taxes of one kind or another and only $249 billion coming from individual and corporate income taxes. In addition to tax receipts, the combined governments counted as revenues $425.7 billion in intergovernmental (primarily federal) transfers. The property tax accounted for $318 billion in revenues. (U.S. Census Bureau, Table 1 State and Local Government Finance by Level of Government and by State 2003–04, retrieved April 4, 2007, from www.census.gov/govs/estimate/0400ussl_1.html.)

Where the Money Goes

These revenue figures are staggering, but they hardly match up to the demands on governments at all levels. There simply isn't enough money to meet every need or cure every problem, even if money alone were the solution. Instead, difficult choices must be made each year about which programs will be funded and at what levels. The choices made through the public policy process are reflected in the government's budget. The budget, therefore, stands as a record of the government's priorities.

What Would You Do?

You are the director of Motor Vehicle Registration for your state. Your agency, with offices scattered across the state, is responsible for registration and licensing of cars, trucks, and other motor vehicles. About six months into the fiscal year, the governor announces that all state agencies will have to finish the fiscal year with expenditures five percent less than originally budgeted. You have already spent half your yearly budget allocation, so the reduction means you actually have to cut spending by ten percent over the next six months. What would you do?

But government priorities are always shifting. As new conditions arise, new programs are proposed and old programs are expanded or contracted. The emphasis the federal government gives to various areas has reflected the condition of the country and the world at times, as in the large percentage of national resources devoted to national defense during periods of international conflict.

We can also trace budgetary changes over shorter time spans, thus indicating the policy priorities of various presidents, governors, mayors, or other public officials. Restrictions, however, have been built into the federal budget over the years that somewhat limit the choices any president or Congress can make. Over the past thirty years, for example, Congress has passed a variety of *entitlement programs* that provide specified benefits to those who meet certain eligibility requirements. For example, legislation might provide benefits to people above a certain age or below a certain income level. The implication, supported by several judicial rulings, is that individuals are entitled to or have a right to certain benefits (primarily social welfare benefits).

For these programs, Congress essentially agrees to provide whatever money is necessary from year to year to ensure a certain level of benefits to all eligible people. Legislation is typically written so that new action is not required each year to keep the program going. Only a projection of likely beneficiaries is needed to determine the level of expenditures for a given year. Unless Congress takes specific steps to limit benefits or eligibility—something that legislators are reluctant to do—funding of these programs is practically automatic.

These programs vary in size over time. In a recession, for example, unemployment would be high, and spending for unemployment compensation would rise. Similarly, the changing character of the population—for example, a larger number of older Americans—would also change the amount of money required to provide benefits to that group. Moreover, most entitlement programs have now been *indexed* to the cost of living (or related measures) so that benefit levels automatically rise with inflation. (Over the past decade, Congress has passed major expansions of indexing in Social Security and Medicare.) Expenditures for entitlement programs thus increase almost every year.

Such programs constituted just over 50 percent of the fiscal year 2006 federal budget. When they are combined with farm price supports (also indexed), interest on the national debt (which must be paid), and expenditures based on previous commitments, these so-called *uncontrollable expenditures* constitute almost two-thirds of the federal budget.

The remainder of the federal budget might be termed *discretionary spending*; meaning the president and Congress are open to make changes in this relatively small portion of the budget. This includes defense spending (about 20 percent) and domestic discretionary spending (only about 19 percent). These are the areas that generate the most difficult policy choices.

From Deficits to Surplus and Back

A great deal of political debate in the 1980s and early 1990s centered on strategies for controlling the federal deficit. However, by 2000, a booming economy and fiscal measures taken by Congress in the late 1990s changed the debate from how to control the deficit to ways to spend a growing budget surplus! To understand this change in fortune, it may be helpful to examine some of the deficit reduction methods employed by the federal government during the past decade.

Let's begin with the deficit. As noted, traditional economic theory does not necessarily disapprove of public borrowing; indeed, there may be benefits to deficit spending in particular years. But at some point, a growing deficit becomes unmanageable, especially as interest payments become a substantial part of government spending. Large deficits are generally thought to limit both short-term and long-term economic recovery, especially because they limit private investment. Moreover, large deficits contribute to an understandable lack of public confidence concerning their political leaders' ability to deal effectively with the budget.

The budget deficits of the Reagan years were substantial. The administration's accumulated debt exceeded that of all previous administrations combined. By 1984 it became clear that if no further actions were taken to reduce the deficit, by the end of the Reagan years, the accumulated deficit would total over $2.6 trillion. Interest payments alone would require one out of every six federal dollars. Facing this prospect, Congress passed the Gramm-Rudman-Hollings Act of 1985. Under this legislation, deficit targets were set for each of the next five budget years and aimed at reducing the deficit to zero in 1990 (though a later amendment pushed the target to 1992). Unfortunately, the president and Congress were overly optimistic in their economic projections and employed several questionable budget techniques to evade the restraints set by Gramm-Rudman-Hollings.

With the deficit still out of control in 1990, President Bush and Congress faced very difficult budget deliberations. For the 1990 budget, the Gramm-Rudman-Hollings law had targeted an annual deficit of no more than $110 billion. By October, when the fiscal year began, there was still no agreement on the budget. (As we will see, it is not unusual for a federal fiscal year to begin before the year's budget is approved.) Consequently, automatic, across-the-board spending cuts were applied to all federal agencies.

Finally, in late November, a deficit-reduction plan was approved that would bring the projected deficit below the Gramm-Rudman-Hollings target. The plan that was agreed to, however, contained a number of provisions that appeared to be budgetary "smoke and mirrors." For example, part of the plan would save money by having the government lease rather than buy buildings, something that would obviously save up-front costs within 1990, but likely increase costs in the long run. Similarly, certain payments to doctors under Medicaid were shifted to the following fiscal year. The biggest reduction item was to simply maintain for another 130 days the across-the-board cuts that had been imposed in October. Many observers read this as a failure of the administration and Congress to come to grips with the hard choices that deficit reduction requires.

As part of the budget agreement, the Budget Enforcement Act (BEA) was passed to police the deficit even further. The BEA set annual ceilings on several categories of discretionary spending, with violation of the caps requiring across-the-board cuts. BEA also required that legislative actions affecting mandatory spending not increase the deficit in any year. (This is known as the "pay as you go" provision.) Though these provisions seem to have had the desired effect on the budget process, the deficit continued to grow, driven in part by incorrect economic assumptions and in part by increased spending for health care programs and the savings and loan bailout.

NETWORKING

Check out the National Debt Clock at www.brillig.com/debt_clock and the Treasury Department's FAQs about the budget at www.ustreas.gov/topics/accounting-and-budget. Also, for simulations of financial conditions at the federal level, go to www.thirdmil.org.

In 1997, the Clinton administration led a bipartisan effort in Congress to pass yet another landmark piece of legislation aimed at balancing the federal budget. The budget agreement was originally scheduled to eliminate the deficit by 2002, phasing in $121 billion in spending cuts over a five-year period. Much of the savings were planned to come from reductions in Medicare payments to health providers and hospitals. An additional $55 billion was to have been saved each year through mandates imposed on future spending bills. The budget agreement also featured $95 billion in tax cuts over the five years, including credits for higher education, relief for families with children, and reductions in capital gains.

When President Clinton signed the measure into law, few would have imagined that in less than three years the Congressional Budget Office would be projecting a budget surplus. But the federal government turned the tide, thanks to a variety of factors—including old-fashioned good luck! One of the most significant contributors to the government's change in fortune came in the "dot-com" craze of 1999–2000, as thousands of Internet companies went public on the stock market, leading to a dramatic increase in tax revenues and an overall expansion in the American economy. Reductions in military spending in the wake of the cold war also helped, as the government was able to invest its resources in more productive areas (Uchitelle, 2000, p. A1). The net outcome was a projected surplus of $81 billion, scheduled to materialize during the next decade. This is a far cry from the crisis years of the early 1980s!

The Bush Tax Plan

President George W. Bush seized upon the opportunity afforded by this emerging surplus to advance one of the key themes in his election platform: a reduction in federal taxes. Given the estimates early in the year from both the Congressional Budget Office and the president's Office of Management and Budget, few could stand in the way of the new administration's drive for sweeping tax reform.

The administration's original plan called for a $1.6 trillion cut in the federal income tax, but even the president's most ardent supporters on Capitol Hill cautioned that it would be extremely difficult to pass such an enormous reduction plan. Recognizing the importance of a victory on his administration's first key policy initiative, President Bush worked with lawmakers to pare down the original proposal and gain the necessary votes. The final measure, which was signed into law on June 7, 2001, featured a $1.3 trillion tax cut to be phased in over the next decade and a fundamental restructuring of federal income taxes.

Supporters of the plan said that reducing the tax burden on the American public, particularly with the projected federal surplus, was a way to return "an overcharge" to taxpayers and to curb federal spending. For example, House Majority Leader Dick Armey said, "The addicts are going to have to take the cure. We're no longer going to get stoned on the other people's money" (Stevenson, 2001, p. A1). Proponents also argued that the tax rebates, which the IRS began sending out in the summer of 2001, would help to stimulate an economy that had declined sharply in the preceding months.

Some of the central elements of the Bush plan included reducing personal income tax rates, phasing out the estate tax, increasing the child tax credit (and expanding the number of low-income families eligible for this credit), and increasing the contribution limits to 401(k) and individual retirement accounts. For nonprofits, the tax reduction plan that finally passed Congress lacked many of the provisions from the original Bush proposal that would have encouraged increases in charitable giving. As the *Chronicle for Philanthropy* reported, the law lacked provisions that would have achieved the following:

- Allowed people who do not itemize on their federal income tax returns to write off charitable deductions.
- Permitted people to donate to charity directly from their individual retirement accounts, without incurring taxes.
- Increased the annual limit on charitable deductions taken by corporations from 10 percent to 15 percent of a company's taxable income. (Williams, 2001, p. 26)

Critics of the Bush tax plan in the governmental sector predicted that it would prove to be too much, too soon. Senator Tom Daschle, who became majority leader when the Democrats took control of the Senate in June 2001, said, "We think this is good short-term politics. [But] it is disastrous long-term policy" (Stevenson, 2001, p. 26). Daschle and others suggested the plan would not leave enough in reserve to cover the cost of upgrading the military, much less the substantial reforms to Social Security and Medicare that remain on the horizon. And even the president's own economic advisors moved away from their original optimism, saying that the more cautionary estimates of the federal surplus, which were released just weeks after the tax plan became law, may require Congress to revisit some of its main provisions.

Since then, Bush has succeeded in pushing through three more major tax cuts that are expected to reduce revenue by $1.9 trillion over a ten year period. Unfortunately, the surplus did not materialize and spending has far outstripped revenue to produce high levels of debt. Since Bush took office, an economic recession, terrorist attacks, and corporate scandals, coupled with new spending for military action in Iraq and Afghanistan have put the federal government further and further into debt. Instead of the surplus forecasted at the beginning of the Bush administration, the U.S. Office of Budget and Management now projects an extra $5 trillion in debt in this decade. A record-breaking $412.7 billion in debt accumulated in fiscal year 2004 alone. Although the estimated annual deficit for 2007 has dropped to $244 billion, the estimated accumulated debt for the same year is above $9 trillion. As a result, the government currently has to borrow an average of about $1 billion a day to cover its bills and is spending about $159 billion per year for interest payments on its debt (*Washington Post*, Oct. 8, 2004, p. A01).

State and Local Expenditures

Expenditure comparisons at the state and local levels are complicated by our system of intergovernmental transfers. In education, for example, the federal government provides money directly to individuals (in the form of student grants and loans), but it also transfers large sums to state and local governments. States spend money directly (for colleges and universities), but they also transfer money received from the federal government and some raised at the state level to local governments, primarily to support education. Consequently, local governments provide less than 30 percent of the money spent on education in this country and actually are involved in spending 70 percent of that money. If we include intergovernmental transfers spent at the state and local levels in our calculations of state and local spending, the following patterns emerge: States spend the greatest portion of their funds on education, with public welfare next, followed by highways, health, and natural resources. At the local level, the largest amount again is spent on education, with health, public works, and social welfare next (see Figure 7.2). Because of intergovernmental transfers, federal fiscal policies can have a significant impact on state and local governments. Cuts at the federal level directly affect not only federal agencies, but also state and local governments that depend on federal funding. In fact, in a statement by the National Council of State Legislatures, states have an "incalculable stake" in the manner in which the federal government balances its budget (see www.ncsl.org/statefed/fedbud.htm#FederalGrants).

The Budget as a Managerial Tool

As a public manager, you will find that the budget process is critical to your success and that of your agency, quite simply because it establishes the level of funding for your programs. A variety of steps are required to enable an agency to spend money. First, legislation

FIGURE 7.2

The State and Local Dollar, 2003–2004 (In Billions of Dollars)

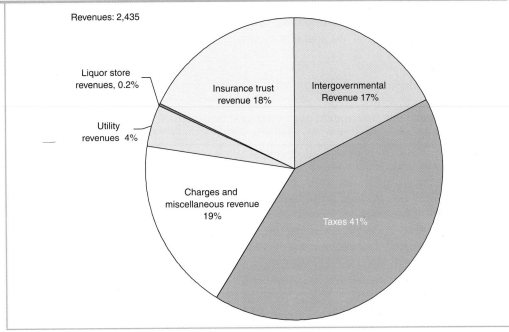

Revenues: 2,435

Liquor store revenues, 0.2%

Insurance trust revenue 18%

Intergovernmental Revenue 17%

Utility revenues 4%

Charges and miscellaneous revenue 19%

Taxes 41%

SOURCE: U.S. Census Bureau, Table 1 State and Local Government Finance by Level of Government and by State 2003–2004, retrieved April 5, 2007, from www.census.gov/govs/estimate/0400ussl_1.html.

must be passed and signed by the chief executive to authorize the program. This *authorizing legislation* permits the establishment or continuation of a particular program or agency. (Authorizing legislation usually covers multiple years or is even open-ended, although some programs, such as the space program, require new authorization each year.) Next come *appropriations*, whereby the legislature sets aside funds and creates budget authority for the funds' expenditure. Only after both steps have been taken can an agency spend money in pursuit of its stated objectives.

In most cases, governments use a *fiscal year* as their basic accounting period. The federal fiscal year begins on October 1 and runs through September 30 of the following year. The fiscal year carries the name of the year in which it ends; thus, fiscal year 2002, or FY 02, begins October 1, 2001, and ends September 30, 2002. States and localities differ widely in terms of fiscal years; some follow the federal pattern, whereas others start July 1 (as did the federal government until 1976). Still others match the fiscal year to the calendar year. Kentucky and a few other states actually have a two-year-long fiscal year because their legislatures meet and pass a budget only every other year.

The fiscal year is the key period in which money is spent, but a variety of steps must be taken before and after the fiscal year that can affect an agency's expenditures. The budget must be developed, typically by the chief executive (president, governor, mayor), and transmitted to the legislature; it must be approved by the legislature prior to the beginning of the fiscal year; it must be executed during the fiscal year; and it must be reviewed and audited following the fiscal year. At any given point in the *budget cycle*, there are actually several budgets being worked on. While one budget is being executed (say, FY 06), another (FY 07) is being formulated and approved, while another, (FY 05) is being audited.

Budget Formulation

In the federal government and in many state and local jurisdictions, the chief executive has primary responsibility for preparation of the budget. The budget cycle (see Figure 7.3) typically begins with a letter from a central budget office to agencies outlining the timetable for preparing the budget, transmitting forms for use in the process, and indicating any policy concerns of special priority for the fiscal year. The agencies then prepare their own budget requests and forward them to the central budget office for review (see Box 7.1). Often a series of meetings (or sometimes hearings) are held to negotiate differences in the views of the central budget office (reflecting the priorities of the chief executive) and the agencies. Finally, the budget document is prepared by the central budget office and transmitted by the chief executive to the legislature for approval.

FIGURE 7.3

The Budget Cycle at The Federal Level

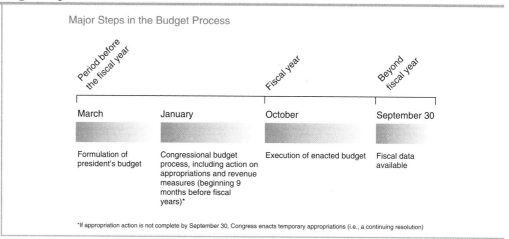

*If appropriation action is not complete by September 30, Congress enacts temporary appropriations (i.e., a continuing resolution)

BOX 7.1

FINANCIAL MANAGEMENT: THE PROGRAM MANAGER'S ROLE

Many in government think financial management is the responsibility of financial offices, accountants, and the like. Most program managers, in particular, feel they do not have to be concerned with financial management.

WRONG. Nothing could be further from the truth. Successful program managers appreciate that, in government, they have the responsibility for financial management. They understand what this entails, and thus have a far better chance of successfully delivering their programs despite reduced budgets.

What is financial management? It is nothing more than obtaining and effectively using funds and other resources to accomplish the goals and objectives of the organization. It typically entails:

- Defining people, materials, and services for achieving a program's goals and objectives.
- Defining the sources of resources that can be used to fund the program's costs.
- Obtaining the resources.
- Managing and minimizing the costs.
- Obtaining results from the expenditure of the resources.
- Preventing waste in the expenditure of the resources.
- Reporting accountability for both the use of resources and delivery of the results.

SOURCE: Harold I. Steinberg, "Improving Financial Management: The Program Manager's Role," *PA Times*, Vol. 20, No. 11 (November 1997): 1. Reprinted by permission of the author.

In some jurisdictions, responsibility for preparing the budget may not lie completely with the chief executive, and the budget cycle may vary accordingly. In many states, for example, responsibility for budget formulation may be shared among the governor, other elected officials, and members of the legislature. Cities with a strong mayor form usually give responsibility to the chief executive, whereas cities that operate under other forms tend to disperse budget authority. The city manager usually prepares the budget in council-manager cities, though typically with substantial input from the mayor and other council members.

The Office of Management and Budget (OMB) is the central budget office at the federal level and has evolved from an office established in 1921. Originally called the Bureau of the Budget, President Nixon renamed the Office of Management and Budget in 1970 to reflect an emphasis on management concerns in addition to budgetary responsibilities. At the outset of the budget process, OMB collects information on projected revenues for the coming fiscal year, as well as information on the outlook for the economy. In addition, OMB develops information on the progress of the current year's budget, as well as the budget being considered by Congress. After a beginning consultation with the agencies to assess their program priorities, OMB works with the president to establish basic policy guidelines for developing the budget.

NETWORKING

Federal organizations involved in budgeting and financial management include the Office of Management and Budget at www.whitehouse.gov/omb, the Congressional Budget Office at www.cbo.gov, and the General Accountability Office at www.gao.gov.

These guidelines are communicated to the agencies, along with detailed forms for budget requests. In turn, managers in the various agencies assess their program priorities and decide the necessary level of funding for accomplishing objectives in the next fiscal year. Starting about September, a period of negotiation occurs with OMB. The central budget office represents the president's policy concerns and usually takes a generalist perspective, in contrast to the more narrow, specialized interests of the agency representatives. About November or December, the president becomes more actively involved in the budget process and makes final decisions with respect to both revenue and fiscal considerations and individual program needs.

The final budget document, which is submitted to Congress early in the new year, represents the culmination of a long process of analysis and interaction among a wide variety of groups. Obviously, given the magnitude and complexity of the federal government, the process of budget formulation at that level is the most complex in this country. But the difficulties of reconciling different and competing interests in the budget process are significant at all levels of government. In addition, chief executives at the state and local levels face constraints not found at the federal level. For example, most governors are required by constitution or statute to submit a balanced budget to the legislature, making it essential that they project anticipated revenues as closely as possible.

Budget Approval

The budget approval phase begins with submission of the budget to the legislature and ends with approval of the budget. The legislature, in most cases, can approve, disapprove, or modify the chief executive's budget proposal; it can add or eliminate programs; and it can alter methods of raising revenues. Remember that first programs must be authorized and then money appropriated for their implementation. In some cases, appropriations are contained in one bill that is debated, amended, and passed by the legislative body. In other cases, appropriations may be divided among several different appropriations bills.

The budget submitted to the legislative body is first sent to the committee or committees responsible for appropriations. These committees review the submitted document and hold hearings involving agency personnel, representatives of interest groups, other legislators, and private citizens. After consideration by the full legislative body, the bill as amended is passed and sent to the chief executive for signature (where approval is required). In the case of bicameral legislatures, the bill is sent to the other legislative body for similar consideration. If there are differences in the bills produced by the two houses of the legislature, the differences are worked out in a conference committee, and the bill is passed again by the two houses and sent to the chief executive.

Again, there are wide variations in the approval process from jurisdiction to jurisdiction. At the federal level, granting budget authority—the authority to obligate funds for immediate or future *outlays* (government spending)—can come about in several ways. Budget authority for most programs must be granted annually through passage of an appropriations bill. Congress has voted permanent budget authority for some programs, so funds become available each year without further congressional action.

In addition, within any given fiscal year, some outlays will be based on obligations made in previous years. Thus, total budget outlays for any fiscal year include previously granted budget authority, authority granted through appropriations for the current year, and money obligated in previous years for spending in the upcoming fiscal year, minus outlays deferred to later years.

Under procedures established by the Congressional Budget Act of 1974, Congress considers budget totals before considering individual appropriations measures. Based on work by the budget committees of both houses, a first *concurrent resolution* (a resolution of both houses not requiring the president's signature) is passed by May 15. It establishes targets for total revenues and total spending authority within various functional areas for the upcoming fiscal year. Although the president is not formally involved in this part of the budget process, consultation frequently occurs so that all parties will be informed of developments in the approval process. In some cases, the various parties even agree on a set of budget totals to be honored by both the president in his budget submission and Congress in its approval process.

Congressional review of appropriations requests begins in the House of Representatives, where the Ways and Means Committee considers revenue estimates and the Appropriations Committee (through various subcommittees) reviews spending recommendations. Appropriations are considered within thirteen different appropriations bills covering groups of departments and agencies within related functional areas. After initial passage by the House, all tax bills and the thirteen appropriations bills are forwarded to the Senate for consideration. Differences in the appropriations measures coming from the two houses are worked out in conference committee and, following approval by both houses, are forwarded to the president for signature. The two budget committees are charged with drawing up a second concurrent resolution—this one binding in nature—setting limits on total spending. Finally, a separate *reconciliation bill* attempts to reconcile individual actions in taxes, authorizations, or appropriations with the totals.

What Would You Do?

The budget of the Parks and Recreation Department that you head is stretched to the limit. The city council seems unwilling to add any resources to support new programs you think would benefit the community. You have called a staff meeting to consider alternative sources of revenue, but now you are wondering if the council will be offended if you try to come up with funds on your own to do something they chose not to support. What would you do?

If action on appropriations for the fiscal year is not completed by the beginning of the fiscal year (October 1), Congress enacts a continuing resolution, which permits the government to keep operating until an appropriations measure is passed. Through the 1970s until 1987, continuing resolutions became more than interim funding measures and instead provided funding through the end of the fiscal year. More recently, continuing resolutions have returned to a more limited scope and duration.

Throughout its consideration of the budget, Congress is aided by the work of budget committee staff members (whose numbers have grown substantially in recent years) and by the Congressional Budget Office. This agency provides basic budget information and its own economic forecasts and indicates to Congress how its conclusions differ from those of the executive branch. Such differences have, in several years, led the Congressional Budget Office to predict a more substantial budget deficit than that anticipated by the administration.

An increase in staff capabilities has been among the most important developments in the legislative approval process in most states and some larger cities. Legislative budget staffs vary in structure and composition—partisan or nonpartisan, centralized or decentralized, joint (both houses) or single house, and so on. Their responsibilities usually include analyzing the governor's budget, forecasting revenues and expenditures, and developing alternatives to the executive budget. In all cases, greater staff capabilities have considerably aided the resurgence of state legislative involvement in the budget process.

One important feature of the approval process at the state level is the existence in most states of the *line-item veto*. (The line-item veto allows the executive to veto specific items in an appropriations bill rather than having to decide between "all or nothing.") Such authority has been sought at the federal level by recent presidents, and President Clinton became the first chief executive granted such capacity when the federal Line-Item Veto Act (P.L. 104–130) took effect in January 1997. The act, though stopping short of extending full constitutional line-item veto power, gave the president authority to strike items from a federal appropriations bill without having to veto the entire piece of legislation. The Clinton administration, like its Republican predecessors, argued that the powers granted under the act would enable the president to make significant cuts in federal spending. Proponents added that a great deal of time and energy would be saved because the executive and legislative branches would not have to renegotiate an entire budget when only specific items are at issue.

Despite the value inherent in such a measure, the Supreme Court invalidated the federal act in *Clinton v. City of New York* (1998), stating that although there may be procedures for amending or repealing federal statutes, the process must be consistent with the constitutional powers afforded each branch of government (see *Immigration and Naturalization Services v. Chadha* [1983]). In the case of the line-item veto, the president simply did not have the constitutional authority to amend or repeal a spending bill passed by Congress. In the absence of any suitable formulation that would meet the constitutional test, it appears that the federal line-item veto will wind up a historical anomaly (Joyce, 1998).

Budget Execution

The budget execution stage, generally coinciding with the fiscal year, is that part of the budget cycle in which the agencies of government carry out agreed-upon programs and policies. The execution stage involves public administrators in all aspects of the management process—planning, analysis, personnel management, communication, and other interpersonal skills.

Basic financial controls are exercised during the budget execution phase through the mechanism of *apportionment*, a process by which funds are allocated to agencies for specific portions of the year. Typically, the central budget office asks for submission of spending plans indicating what money the agencies anticipate spending in each quarter of the year. Because the agencies may not have received all they wanted in the appropriations process, the apportionment mechanism also acts as the basis for required changes in programs and policies. As soon as there is agreement between the central budget office (acting on behalf of the chief executive) and the agencies on the changes embodied in the apportionment plan, agencies begin receiving *allotments* to spend within a given period.

To ensure that funds are expended for the purposes for which they were intended and that there is enough money budgeted to cover a proposed expenditure, a *preaudit* (a review in advance of an actual expenditure) is usually required. Depending on the jurisdiction, the preaudit may be conducted by an agency's own budget office, by an independent agency, or even by an elected state official. Once approval has been given, the treasurer will "write a check" for the expenditure.

Even though budgets are not passed until just before (or even well into) the fiscal year, important changes may occur during the year that require changes in an agency's budgeted expenditures. Some changes may require greater funding—for example, when an unexpected natural disaster, such as a drought, places special burdens on farmers. If the need must be met prior to the next budget cycle, the president and Congress can work together to provide a *supplemental appropriation,* a bill passed during the fiscal year to add new money to an agency's budget for that fiscal year. Such a bill may simply provide more money for existing programs or money for a newly authorized program.

There are also devices, used primarily by chief executives as a matter of administrative discretion, to restrict agencies' spending below budgeted amounts. Presidents throughout the nation's history have sought to limit agency spending by *impoundment*—withholding—funds authorized and appropriated by law, typically in the case of emergencies or where the purpose of the money had been achieved and budgeted funds still remain. At the state level, governors regularly withhold agency funds when revenue projections fall below levels on which the budget was based.

The 1974 Budget Act sought to clarify matters by defining two types of legal impoundments. The first, a *deferral*, is a decision by the president to withhold funds for a brief period. In such circumstances, the president must inform Congress, and either house of Congress may veto the action. The second, a *rescission*, is a presidential decision to withhold funds permanently; a rescission must receive the positive approval of both houses of Congress. Through these devices, Congress has sought to maintain its involvement in budget execution while at the same time allowing some administrative discretion to the president. (Not surprisingly, recent presidents, including President Clinton and President Bush, have argued for expanded rescission authority.)

Because situations change, public managers are often accorded some flexibility in the use of allocated funds. Money originally allocated for salaries and wages, for example, might be shifted (with appropriate approvals) to an equipment and expense category. On a broader scale, some agencies engage in *reprogramming*—that is, taking money appropriated for one program and diverting it to another that emerges as a higher priority. This strategy must be undertaken with great care because of legal and ethical implications, and because efforts to subvert the legislature's intention are likely to incur retribution in the next year's budget process.

Audit Phase   The final phase of the budget process is the postexecution or audit phase. *Postaudits* take place following the end of the fiscal year and are concerned with verifying the correctness and propriety of agency operations. These audits were originally designed to ensure financial control; as such, they focused on accuracy of record keeping; compliance with statutes; and uncovering fraud, waste, and mismanagement. More recently, the concept of auditing has been broadened to include *performance auditing*—analyzing and evaluating the effective performance of agencies in carrying out their objectives. Three purposes are served by postaudits: (1) financial viability, as indicated by efficient use of resources; (2) compliance with statutes and other limitations; and (3) program performance, including the results of program operations.

Agencies themselves can carry out audits; we have already seen how the auditing work of inspectors general has revealed waste and fraud in some agencies. There is a clear trend, toward broader use of independent agencies. Moreover, to maintain detachment in their review of executive agencies, the postaudit function is increasingly being attached to the legislative rather than the executive branch. In 1921, for example, the federal government created the General Accounting Office (GAO) as a support agency of Congress, although President Wilson had previously vetoed such legislation on the grounds that the officers of such an agency should be answerable to the executive rather than the legislature. Recall that the GAO was originally concerned primarily with the financial auditing of selected federal agencies; however, more recently, it has not only changed its name—to become the General Accountability Office—but it has extended its activities to include program evaluations as well.

At the state level, organizational arrangements vary; however, the trend toward having postaudit agencies attached to the legislature is clear. In 1938, there were five states in which the audit function was part of the legislative branch; in 1960, there were 15; today, there are more than 40 (CSG, 1993). A large number of states retain an elected state auditor, whose office often goes beyond detached analysis and becomes embroiled in political controversy. Finally, a number of large cities, including Dallas and Seattle, have developed legislative postaudit functions.

Approaches to Public Budgeting

To be an effective tool in management and decision making, the budget must present information about the purposes of the proposed activity and resources to be expended. There are a variety of different ways to present such information. Some approaches to budgeting, for example, are based on the assumption that budget decisions are (and should be) largely *incremental*—policy makers start with the given situation (last year's budget) as a base and make only marginal adjustments to that base. Following this approach, managers build budgets by asking for limited increases in spending rather than focusing on major programmatic concerns. Similarly, the legislature focuses on individual expenditures rather than the "big picture." According to proponents of *incrementalism*, this approach is an accurate representation of the actual behavior of decision makers and is an appropriate way to maintain balance among different interests represented in the budget. In contrast, other budget theorists argue for a more rational, comprehensive, and programmatic approach.

Budgets can be categorized according to the purposes they serve. Allen Schick (1987), a leading scholar in the field of budgeting, has suggested that budgets can have at least three different purposes, all of which are reflected in any approach to budgeting. These purposes are planning, management, and control. *Planning* involves the determination of organizational objectives and the development of strategies to meet those objectives; *management* involves the design of organizational means by which approved goals can be translated into action, as well as developing the staffing and resources necessary for execution; *control* refers to the process of ensuring that operating officials follow the policies and plans established by their superiors. According to Schick, each attempt at budget reform changes the balance among the three purposes—sometimes inadvertently, sometimes deliberately. Understanding how budgets are put together will help you present an effective case for program changes.

The Line-Item Budget

Those who established the first systematic governmental budgeting schemes were concerned primarily with assuring the public that expenditures were properly made and accounted for. Consequently, the systems they designed emphasized the control function. Because all agencies purchase essentially the same kinds of goods and services, it was argued, account classifications could be designed that would be broadly applicable to various agencies or departments. It would then be possible for auditors to apply uniform criteria to evaluate the expenditures of all.

In what is called a line-item or *objects of expenditure* budget, categories of expenditures are listed with amounts allocated to each. Typically, *line-item budgets* are organized by departments, so that the budget for one agency might look something like this:

Organizational Unit: XXXXX

Expenditure Code	Category/Subcategory	2007	2008
100	Salaries and Wages	2,585,400	2,879,000
200	Other Operating Expenses	887,250	1,102,000
2100	Travel	150,000	200,000
2200	Supplies	250,000	370,000
2300	Utilities	88,000	93,000
2400	Maintenance	78,500	89,000
2500	Other	320,750	350,000
Total		3,472,650	3,981,000

The cost of each object of expenditure is generally based on the agency's past experience and analysis of expected changes during the budget year. Because personnel costs (salaries, wages, and other personal services) typically constitute over half the budget, special attention is given to projected staffing changes, and such changes are often appended to the budget. (Our example projects, among other things, the addition of one clerical person during the upcoming year.)

The line-item budget continues to be widely used, because it is easy to understand and offers political leaders the more palatable option of reducing items (such as travel) rather than eliminating "programs." Moreover, it is well suited to incremental decisions, which make only minor modifications in the previous budget. However, because in the line-item budget, the focus is on expenditures and not on their results, it is of little benefit to planning or management.

The Performance Budget

The 1930s proved a turning point with respect to public budgeting. The federal budget grew tremendously, the Bureau of the Budget became attached to the White House, and, in general, greater attention was paid to the executive management of government agencies. This interest in management was paralleled at the state and local levels, where efforts to relate budget presentations to programmatic activities had been under way for some time. The result was a new approach to budgeting: the performance budget.

The *performance budget* is organized around programs or activities rather than departments. It includes various performance measurements to indicate the relationship between the work actually done and its cost. As the Hoover Commission described it, a performance budget "would analyze the work of government departments and agencies according to their functions, activities, or projects. It would concentrate attention on the work to be done or the service to be rendered, rather than the things to be acquired." By focusing on the relationship between available resources and the work to be done, performance budgeting is well suited to the purposes of management.

To construct a performance budget, the manager must first determine appropriate program categories, such as highway safety, and then break down that program into appropriate subprograms, such as school visitations or advertising programs. It is then necessary to establish detailed work measures for each activity—for example, a highway safety program might anticipate twenty-seven school visitations during the course of the year. These data would then be related to the cost of making such visits. In its most detailed presentation, a performance budget requires identifying the work activity, establishing an output unit, calculating the cost of each unit, and projecting the units required and the associated costs for the coming year.

Although performance measures are obviously helpful in making budgetary decisions, not all organizations can easily develop such information. A license bureau can report the number of licenses issued and fairly easily calculate the cost per license issued, but a research unit or a group promoting civil rights would find its work much more difficult to measure. Performance budgeting also tends to concentrate on quantity of work rather than quality.

Finally, performance budgeting somewhat diffuses organizational responsibility because one program or function may be located in several different units. "Public information," for example, may involve work in the mayor's office, police department, fire department, and elsewhere. To sort out costs by department, one would need to construct a crosswalk or matrix of expenditures. A matrix might place various activities on one dimension and departments on another.

Activities	1	2	3	Total
Division A	$10,000	$20,000	$15,000	$45,000
Division B	12,000	16,000	10,000	38,000
Division C	5,000	12,000	13,000	30,000
Total	27,000	48,000	38,000	

A matrix could also be constructed relating activities to traditional objects of expenditure; such calculations are typical in performance budgets.

Program Budgeting

Another approach to budgeting had its origins in the Defense Department in the early 1960s. Soon after taking office as secretary of defense, Robert McNamara discovered that his ability to manage the department was severely restricted by the lack of coordination between planning and budgeting. Each service (army, navy, air force) prepared its own annual budget, reflecting its own priorities, and then submitted the documents to the secretary. This plan failed to give proper attention to system-wide issues. But, equally important, because the budgeting system was based on a one-year time frame, it bore little relation to the multi-year projections of the department's planning and analysis staff. The development of major weapons systems, for example, involves research and development, assembly, and operations over many years. Yet, this fact was not clearly reflected in the annual budget submissions.

McNamara instituted a new approach, which came to be known as the *planning-programming-budgeting system (PPBS)*, an effort to connect planning, systems analysis, and budgeting in a single exercise. In the Defense Department, PPBS began with the identification of nearly 1,000 program elements, each grouped under one of nine major programs or missions—that is, strategic retaliatory forces, continental air and missile defense forces, civil defense, and so on. Not only was extensive study required to identify the right combination of program elements to support each mission, but, once having established the combinations, units in the department were required to submit detailed analyses of proposed program changes. In addition, the new budget system was designed to cover a nine-year period and to show detailed projections for the first six years. President Johnson was so impressed with the operation of PPBS in the Defense Department that he ordered the new system extended to all federal agencies. Each cabinet-level department was asked to identify a limited number of purposes to be served by the agency, then to organize budget requests around those themes. The Department of Health, Education, and Welfare (HEW), for example, chose topics such as "social and rehabilitation services" that cut across several agencies within HEW. Costs for each program element were projected five years into the future, and extensive documentation justifying each element was required, especially in areas undergoing significant changes. Most agencies were able to develop their budgets using the new approach, but there was considerable confusion in the implementation of PPBS. As a result of this confusion, and for a variety of other political reasons, President Nixon formally terminated PPBS in 1971.

During its relatively short tenure, PPBS attracted great attention, with many cities, states, and other countries embracing the new technique. PPBS not only emphasized the planning aspect of budgeting, but it appeared to bring greater rationality and comprehensiveness to the budget process. These goals, however, were accomplished at great cost. Substantial numbers of new staff members were needed, both in the central budget office and in the various agencies to provide the kind of analysis PPBS required. The process proved extraordinarily time-consuming. Consequently, very few full-blown PPBS systems remain, although many of the principles of PPBS have been incorporated into other approaches, often under the more general label *program budgeting*.

There are important differences between performance budgeting and program budgeting. "As a general rule, performance budgeting is concerned with the *process of work* (what methods should be used), while program budgeting is concerned with the *purpose of work* (what activities should be authorized)" (Schick, 1987, p. 53). Moreover, although both systems urge measurement of work being done, performance budgeting is more likely to employ measures related to the work (for example, the number of tons of garbage collected) and a program budget might concentrate instead on measures related to the purpose of the work (for example, the rate of infectious disease in the community). Performance data are of great interest to individual managers who seek to improve productivity, but legislators and other policy makers are more likely to be interested in the purposes of various activities.

Outcome-Based Budgeting

A recent trend in government budgeting involves increasing the level of accountability for public resources. Citizens, elected officials, and administrators want to be able to determine how much is being spent on each program or agency and the return on the public's investment—that is, the substantive impact of each policy. In practical terms, this requires linking budget information with some type of a performance measurement system. The resulting budget enables administrators to track levels of expenditures and report on the outcomes being achieved.

Unlike performance budgeting mentioned previously, outcome-based budgeting goes beyond looking at mere issues of productivity and unit cost. It assesses the long-term impact of each policy, program, or agency within its targeted area. Though based on quantitative measures, *outcome-based budgeting* determines the qualitative results of government initiatives. Many government agencies have incorporated outcome-based budgeting within their strategic planning processes, making it possible to observe the level of resources needed to reach goals and objectives and then use that information for budget decision making.

In Catawba County, North Carolina, local officials used outcome-based budgeting to enhance their government's system of service delivery. The county in the past few years had experienced limited growth in revenues; yet, during this time the call for human services continued to rise. County leadership responded by handing decision-making authority to agency administrators, challenging them to reduce costs while more effectively meeting citizen demands. Those who achieved 90 percent of their goals would be able to apply their savings to unrestricted needs. Catawba County administrators embarked on a citizen-driven, outcome-based system of budgeting to ensure that resources were targeted to meet specific community goals. Over time, they not only saved money, but enhanced government responsiveness.

We will see later the way performance or outcome measurement has affected the conduct of the public's business at all levels of government. For now, we should simply note that the current federal budgeting system, like most at the state and local levels, is a combination of elements from several of the approaches we have discussed. What is most important is not whether one particular system or another is being used, but rather what political and administrative choices underlie the selection of a particular budget approach. That is, what are decision makers trying to emphasize by using the type of budget they select?

Budgetary Strategies and Political Games

Despite all attempts to rationalize the budget process, public budgeting is an inherently political activity. The changing demands on government and its programs, the shifting interests that are brought to bear in policy decisions, and the many different actors (and personalities) that are part of the budget process mean that budget decisions will always occur in a highly charged political environment. Because agency managers typically (and properly) believe in the programs they operate and would like to see the programs be of even greater benefit to the public, they tend to become advocates of an agency position, often seeking to expand the size and scope of the agency's work.

If you can deal effectively with the political environment in which budgeting occurs, you will likely be more successful in expanding, or at least maintaining, your agency's programs. (There are, of course, many cases in which you will be judged on your capacity to hold the line on expenditures or to manage program reductions.) Whatever your intent, understanding the politics of the budgetary process will be helpful.

In discussions of budgetary strategies, two basic concepts will help orient your thinking. The first is the notion of program base. The *base* refers to those elements of an agency's program that everyone expects will be continued from year to year. Under normal circumstances, the program's base is assumed to remain pretty much the same from one year to the next and is not subject to special scrutiny. Having an activity approved for one year is one thing; having that activity considered a part of your agency's base budget is far more important. A second concept is that of receiving a *fair share* of the overall budget. Managers often measure success in terms of whether their program receives a proportionate amount of any increases or decreases that the government generally supports. Agency personnel often work for years to build a base that they consider a fair share of the overall budget.

As we saw earlier, budget requests typically originate with the agencies. They are then reviewed and often changed by a central budget office (acting in behalf of the chief executive) and submitted to the legislature for approval. In constructing a budget request, you need to take into account several different types of expenditures. Many departments at the federal level have a large budget component that is essentially *uncontrollable*. The Department of Health and Human Services (HHS), for example, which administers many entitlement programs, has a large percentage of its budget that is essentially fixed. A second part of an agency's budget is likely to be devoted to *adjustments for inflation*. The rising cost of utilities, telephones, postage, and other essential services must be taken into account, either absorbed in the base or covered by increased expenditures. Finally, some part of the agency's budget is *discretionary*, subject to increase or decrease according to the agency's priorities. The discretionary portion of the budget allows you to decide which new programs to propose and which existing activities to recommend for more (or less) funding. Understanding these categories will help you argue for changes in a particular budget.

Strategies for Program Development

These choices lead to strategic questions you must answer in building a budget—including the important question of what total amount to request. Although an overall budget is likely to differ only incrementally from that of the previous year, some agencies are clearly more assertive in their requests than others. They are more willing to request large increases rather than small ones. How assertive to be, however, is conditioned by several factors.

Support from the chief executive (the president, governor, mayor, and so on) is highly important, whether the support is specifically advocacy for a particular program or more generally interest in a particular field, such as law enforcement. Legislative support is also highly important. Agency personnel work throughout the year to maintain contact with key legislative leaders and to build the kinds of alliances that will be helpful in supporting programs of mutual interest. Finally, your personality—especially your willingness to take risks and defend risky choices—will play a strong role in deciding how much to request.

Aaron Wildavsky, who wrote a landmark study of the politics of the budgetary process, suggested three other strategic elements that affect the nature of the request and help build political support for it. The first of these is *clientele support*. The support of client groups and other associations interested in the agency's work will be helpful in developing testimony and lobbying in behalf of programs. An agency that is confident of the testimony of "satisfied customers" or able to show support for proposed changes will likely fare much better than others. Obviously, the most effective way to build support is to serve a client group well, but agencies may also try to stimulate supportive clientele to communicate with legislators about the agency's good work.

Wildavsky's second element of political support is the *confidence* of higher executives and legislative officials in your character and ability. The magnitude of government budgets is so great that higher officials or legislators simply cannot know all the details necessary for making a purely rational analysis. At some point, they must simply trust the manager. Managers who enjoy a good reputation are typically more successful, especially in dealings with the legislature (see Box 7.2). One administrator commented, "If you have the confidence of your [appropriations] subcommittee your life is much easier and you can do your department some good; if you don't have confidence you can't accomplish much and you are always in trouble" (Wildavsky, 1988, p. 105). There are many ways to build confidence, but highly successful managers seem to agree that a reputation for integrity (telling the whole truth) and responsiveness (keeping in touch and responding completely to inquiries) are particularly important.

Third, agency officials can take certain tactical positions to attempt to develop or protect their favorite programs. One approach, verging on the unethical but nonetheless common, is *budget padding*—that is, proposing a higher budget than is actually needed.

BOX 7.2

PLAY IT STRAIGHT

> Everyone agrees that the most important requirement for confidence, at least in a negative sense, is to be aboveboard. . . . A lie, an attempt to blatantly cover up some misdeed, a tricky move of any kind, can lead to an irreparable loss of confidence. A typical comment by an administrator states, "It doesn't pay to try to put something over on them [committee members] because if you get caught, you might as well pack your bags and leave Washington." And the chances of getting caught are considerable because interested committeemen and their staffs have much experience and many sources of information.
>
> Administrators believe that punishments for failure to establish confidence are greater than the rewards for achieving it. But at times they do slip up, and then the roof falls in. When Congress limited the amount of funds that could be spent on personnel, a bureau apparently evaded this limitation in 1952 by subcontracting out a plan to private investors. The House Subcommittee was furious:
>
> *Representative Jensen:* It certainly is going to take a house-cleaning . . . of . . . all people who are responsible for this kind of business.
>
> *Official:* We are going to do it, Mr. Chairman.
>
> *Representative Jensen:* I do not mean "maybe." That is the most disgraceful showing that I have seen of any department.
>
> *Official:* I am awfully sorry.

SOURCE: Excerpted from Aaron Wildavsky and Naomi Caiden, *The New Politics of the Budgetary Process*, 3rd ed. (New York: Longman), p. 60. © 1997 by Addison-Wesley Educational Publishers Inc. Reprinted by permission of Pearson Education, Inc.

Agency officials assume that after the central budget office and legislature cut the budget, you will have what you wanted in the first place. Another strategy is one Wildavsky terms the "camel's nose." The manager asks for a small amount to begin a program, then later treats this program as part of the base and argues that it would be unfortunate to lose the money already invested by not finishing the job (Wildavsky, 1988, p. 115).

Over the past couple of decades, many programs at all levels of government have experienced lower revenues and more limited funding. In some cases, such as in the social services, programs have been reduced or eliminated. In other cases, changes such as the termination of revenue sharing at one level of government have resulted in lower revenues at another. In still other cases, popular efforts to limit either revenues or expenditures, such as Proposition 13 in California, have limited government funds. Many public managers have had to turn their attention from developing new programs to maintaining or even reducing existing ones. This has been referred to as managing fiscal stress or, where serious reductions have occurred, cutback management.

As you would expect under retrenchment conditions, many managers have used budgetary tactics of the sort outlined by Wildavsky to lessen the impact of fiscal stress on their agencies (Wildavsky, 1988, p. 113). Any attempt to resist cuts is risky because it can quickly undermine the manager's credibility. Under conditions of long-term fiscal limitations, resistance to cuts is simply not a realistic option for many managers. Other ways of dealing with fiscal stress have been tried with some success.

- Following a *multiyear plan* to preserve the administrative capacity and the capital investment of the jurisdictions.
- *Targeting* cuts in specific programs rather than cutting across the board (all programs cut at the same percentage).
- *Smoothing out* the impact of the cuts (lessening their immediate effect). Smoothing out may occur through improvements in productivity, so the organization can accomplish more with less, or by generating new revenues, such as imposing new user charges for services.

Aspects of Financial Management

Although those in public organizations need to budget their resources, they must also attend to other aspects of managing the public's money. They must be concerned with the long-term financing of buildings, roads and highways, and equipment; they must carefully plan and manage borrowing; they must ensure against future losses; and, in all cases, they must try to get the most for the money they spend (see Chapter 6).

NETWORKING

Professional associations for budgeting and financial management can be found at www.aabpa.org, www.abfm.org, and www.gfoa.org.

Capital Budgeting

In addition to budgeting annual expenditures, public policy makers and managers need to invest in facilities and equipment that will be used over a period of time. For example, government is primarily responsible for developing and maintaining the country's public works *infrastructure*—streets and highways, tunnels and bridges, sewers and water treatment facilities, and so on. Governments invest in a variety of major facilities, including schools and universities, hospitals and mental health centers, public housing, and correctional institutions.

Innumerable equipment purchases (especially military equipment at the federal level) are intended for long-term use. Expenditures on items that will be used over a period of several years are called *capital expenditures.*

Budgeting for capital expenditures is similar to the process of budgeting for annual expenditures, but differs in some ways. In most jurisdictions, except the federal government, capital expenditures are treated in a separate budget called a *capital budget.* Most states have a separate capital budget, and nearly all give special treatment to capital expenditures in budget presentation. Nearly all major cities and most local governments use a capital budget. For many years, the federal government treated capital spending merely as part of the regular budget. Only recently has it begun to provide a special analysis of capital spending. There is still not a separate capital budget at the federal level.

The primary argument in favor of separate consideration of capital items is that the benefits of these items are spread over future generations, so it is not unreasonable to share the burden of repaying the money borrowed. A separate capital budget may also encourage more long-term thinking—the lack of which is often decried in the annual budget process. On the other hand, the capital budget can become a political "pork barrel," in which each legislator seeks to gain his or her share of projects (and their funding). A capital budget can become a device for avoiding fiscal responsibility by pushing expenditures that should be faced immediately into an indefinite future. Whether a separate budget is developed or not, one should keep in mind the relationship between capital and operating expenditures. Building a new swimming pool, for example, implies that annual expenditures will be forthcoming in future years to keep it operating.

What Would You Do?

A friend who is a city manager once commented that he liked to put a "radio" item in each budget—an item that would make a lot of noise and attract attention but could be "unplugged" easily. He said that after the council focused all its attention on that item and it was finally removed, everything else would be approved with little question. You are preparing your budget for presentation to the council. What would you do?

Ideally, a capital budget develops in the context of a fairly comprehensive planning process, undertaken either for the government as a whole or by the various agencies within their functional areas (such as health or criminal justice). Whether or not a planning process is in operation, an important intermediate step (and one followed by nearly all governments considering capital projects) is development of a *capital investment program*— a timetable indicating various projects to be undertaken, schedules for their completion, and methods of financing. A capital investment plan is usually written to cover a three- to five-year period and is moved forward each year. Georgia, for example, has a capital budget that is mainly a gathering of capital outlays by agency and project category, as these have been requested by various agencies' submissions to the budget office. For each category, the financing source is identified (Thomassen, 1990, p. 73).

To undertake such a plan, government decision makers often solicit proposals from agencies and then try to bring order to the resulting submissions. Among the criteria decision makers might use would be the essentiality of the project, especially for health and safety; whether the project fills a gap in existing services; whether it builds effectively on existing services; and whether it meets an unforeseen emergency need. Because financing for capital projects is usually spread over many years, as are the benefits, complete analysis of each project is likely to involve detailed consideration of both costs and benefits over time.

Debt Management

One part of the capital budgeting process is careful consideration of the source of funding. Some jurisdictions try to operate on a "pay-as-you-go" basis, paying in full for all projects during the fiscal year in which they are authorized. (One variation of this idea is the accumulation of money in a *sinking fund*, something like a Christmas Club account, which is then used to pay for the needed improvement.) Other jurisdictions may be willing to borrow money for a project, either because waiting to accumulate funds would simply take too long or the costs as well as the benefits of the project should be spread over a period of years—a "pay-as-you-use" approach.

Borrowing is often used to finance capital improvement projects; but borrowing may be employed to meet a variety of other needs as well. In some cases, anticipated revenues will simply not be available at the time spending is necessary. To solve the resulting "cash flow" problem, governments undertake short-term borrowing. (In more questionable cases, money is borrowed from future years' revenues to pay operating expenses within the current year. Such a practice was partly responsible for the financial crisis in New York City in the mid-1970s.) Borrowing is also used for emergency needs; for example, a natural disaster, such as fire or flood, might require funds far beyond the capacity of the annual budget. Especially when such spending will be used to reconstruct facilities that will have long-term benefits, borrowing may well be justified. Finally, at least at the federal level, borrowing is sometimes justified as a way of stimulating the economy.

Governments may undertake various types of borrowing. The primary mechanism for financing government debt is the issuance of a *bond*—that is, a promise to repay a certain amount (*principal*) at a certain time (*maturity date*) at a particular *rate of interest*. One of the most common bonds is the *general obligation bond*, which pledges the "full faith and credit" of the jurisdiction—in other words, the government provides as security all its revenues and resources. In contrast, *revenue bonds* promise as security the anticipated revenues that a capital project will produce. Revenue bonds might be issued based on the future toll receipts of a new highway or on the gross receipts of a new municipal sports complex.

Both from the standpoint of a jurisdiction, and of potential investors who might purchase the bonds, it is helpful to know something about the jurisdiction's *debt capacity*. For example, you would want to know the value of a city's resources combined with the ability of its government to provide payment. As a service to investors, several firms provide bond ratings for cities and other jurisdictions. The ratings are also important to the jurisdiction because a lower rating means higher costs of borrowing for the government. Standard and Poor's reference guides rate bonds in descending quality from "AAA" to "AA" to "A" to

"BBB" to "BB," and so on. Cities or other government units that carry high ratings will be more successful than others in selling their bonds.

Risk Management

Public organizations are subject to a variety of risks that can prove extremely costly. For example, an individual lost control of his car, bounced off a guardrail, and into a ditch. The driver suffered serious injuries, then sued the city for several million dollars, arguing that the guardrail had been improperly installed. Similarly, a city employee with no previous health problems began to suffer back pain on the job. After several operations, high medical bills, and physical therapy, he was given disability retirement at age 26 (Lynch, 1985, p. 316). Another city was sued by residents who lived near the municipal airport, because the noise of aircraft landing and taking off supposedly lessened the value of their property. Over the years, cases such as these involving civil damages, breach of contract, workers' compensation, and related legal problems have cost cities, states, and other jurisdictions millions of dollars.

Risk management is concerned with how public organizations anticipate and cope with these risks. A first step in risk management is to identify potential areas of loss and then to attempt to reduce the probability of losses occurring. Risk reduction programs might include improved work safety, periodic inspections of physical property owned by the city, and employee health programs. But, whatever the success of risk reduction efforts, losses do occur. The government has a variety of options for meeting losses, including payment from operating funds or financial reserves, levying special taxes to cover the loss, or even floating bonds.

In anticipation of losses, many public organizations purchase insurance often from private firms. In recent years, this option has become more difficult, as insurance rates for governments and other public organizations have risen dramatically and put many traditional forms of insurance beyond reach. (The difficulty of purchasing insurance has also led some jurisdictions to eliminate uninsured services such as recreation programs.) Another possibility, however, is *self-insurance*, the development of an insurance pool by the jurisdiction itself. Many governments are larger than insurance companies, so such an undertaking is not only financially feasible, but provides some administrative control and flexibility that is not present when private firms are used. An increasingly popular means of self-insurance involves pooling risks in a shared program operated by several municipalities (see Box 7.3).

Purchasing

A final aspect of financial management in public organizations is the purchase of goods and services. Because public organizations are typically not equipped to produce all the goods and services they require (and in most cases would not find it financially feasible to do so), they must acquire some goods and services from the private sector. Like individuals and businesses, public organizations want to get the most for their money. But at the

BOX 7.3

RISK AND REACTION—WHERE DO WE GO FROM HERE?

Misperceptions of risk and interdependencies pose enormous challenges for individuals, firms, and the public sector in managing catastrophic risks. By recognizing the nature of people's decision processes and the limitations of the private sector in coping with these risks on its own, creative partnerships between the public and private sectors can be developed. There is the inevitable tension between letting individuals make their own choices and imposing requirements on them. But because individuals ignore a problem because they do not think it will happen to them and believe the public sector will rescue them if it does, there are grounds for imposing requirements in advance of a possible catastrophe. This point was highlighted almost thirty years ago by Finn Kydland and Edward Prescott in their Nobel-prize winning paper arguing for rules rather than discretion. The challenges of managing the risks of global catastrophe are even more significant today than they were then.

The gravity of the challenges of interdependent risks is particularly apparent when considering a potential avian influenza outbreak. Much as we were aware of the possibility of an event like Hurricane Katrina, we are aware of the danger of a possible outbreak as a result of human-to-human transmission of the virus. Each country in the world can undertake its own preparations, but if some do not, the scope and spread of the disease will be much greater than if every country took the same measures to prevent an epidemic from occurring. Countries must be induced through collective agreements to work together to mitigate the potential catastrophic risk of a pending avian influenza outbreak. Unlike the case of Hurricane Katrina, however, there is no global government to come to the rescue.

We need to rethink ways of reducing the likelihood and consequences of catastrophic risks. During the past five years, the United States has been hit by a series of unprecedented major disasters, opening a new era of large-scale catastrophes. Perhaps some decision makers still prefer not to think about the problems caused by these disasters because it means that they can devote time to the short-term issues that demand immediate attention. After the next disaster strikes, the consequences will be much greater than they imagined. More than ever, governments, firms, and individuals must take steps to address these risks before they become the next catastrophes.

SOURCE: Howard Kunreuther. (2006, Fall). Risk and Reaction. *Harvard International Review*. 28 (3): 38–42.

same time, because government purchasing involves such substantial sums of money and is capable of influencing the structure of the market generally, public purchasing must also take into account social and political goals.

Governments have often found that centralizing purchasing in one agency, rather than having each agency buy what it needs, results in considerable savings. For one thing, a central purchasing unit can buy in sufficient volume to get better prices; for another, those in the purchasing unit can develop expertise with respect to pricing, business conditions, and market practices. Finally, experts in purchasing are likely to be more successful in the negotiating process. Although individual agencies occasionally complain that their specific needs are not met by the purchasing unit, most state and local jurisdictions use centralized purchasing operations.

In most cases, a purchasing unit circulates and advertises the government's needs and solicits bids for the required goods and services. The resulting bids are evaluated in terms of cost, and the lowest bid is usually, though not automatically, chosen. Consideration is also given to the quality of the product and to the ability of the firm to actually deliver the goods or services in a timely fashion. In addition, purchasers are often required to give special preference to certain groups, such as minority-owned firms or in-state companies. Several jurisdictions often join together to cooperate in purchasing activities. In some instances, several local governments may form a common purchasing unit; in other cases, prices negotiated by the state purchasing office are available to local governments as well.

Accounting and Computer-Based Information Systems

Keeping track of the revenues and expenditures of government and other public organizations is an enormously complex task. Not only are there billions of dollars to record and report, but the presentation of financial information must serve several purposes at once. Certainly financial data should be developed and reported in such a way that public officials can be held accountable for the use of public funds. At the same time, the accounting and reporting system should provide managers with information they can use to operate their organizations more efficiently and effectively. This dual requirement means that financial information should correlate closely with other managerially relevant material, such as personnel data or productivity measures.

Government Accounting

Accounting, whether in the public or private sector, is simply "the process of identifying, measuring, and communicating economic information to permit informed judgment and decision making by users of the information" (Berne & Schramm, 1986, p. 12). But because the purposes of public organizations differ from those of private organizations, accounting practices also differ. Those in public organizations are generally not concerned with making a profit; rather, they tend to focus on achieving a balance between revenues and expenditures—what comes in and what goes out. There are some exceptions, such as public corporations, hospitals, and water companies that are more like profit-seeking groups; however, in nearly all public organizations, accountability is more important than profit maximization.

Governmental accounting systems reflect these different purposes. The cornerstone of accounting in the public sector is the allocation of resources to various funds, each of which is designed to record transactions within a particular functional area and assure that funds are used in accord with the purposes sought. (Use of such funds is uncommon in the private sector.) The funds typically reflect policy makers' intent in authorizing certain activities and appropriating funds for them. The legislature may decide, for example, that certain gasoline taxes should be used exclusively for highway maintenance—in which case a separate fund might be created to keep track of money produced by the tax and spent for highways. In all cases, a primary concern is that the accounting system show whether the organization's activities have been consistent with the purposes for which it was created. There are several broad types of funds that are used in public organizations.

1. *General government funds* are used to account for most of the ordinary or routine functions of government. Most important among the general government funds is what is called the *general fund*, which handles the "unrestricted" funds of government, those not restricted to specific purposes (and typically allocated to other funds). The general fund is the dominant fund in most jurisdictions and handles most of the government's operational activities. Related general government funds might include those that account for special revenues, like a dedicated gasoline tax, or those that monitor expenditures for capital projects.

2. *Proprietary funds* are used to account for government activities or enterprises that more closely resemble private business in their orientation toward profit. This does not mean that all agencies employing funds are required to make a profit; indeed, they may break even or perhaps require a subsidy. What is implied is that a measure of profit is possible and usually desirable in such operations; examples include a local transit system or a state printing operation.

3. Finally, *fiduciary funds* are used when the government must hold assets for individuals (such as those in a pension fund) or when the government holds resources to be transmitted to another organization (such as property taxes that a county collects for a city).

Within each fund there is an accounting of the resources available and the flow of funds in and out of the account. There are *assets*—what the government owns; and, there are *liabilities*—what the government *owes*. Assets include items such as cash, capital facilities, equipment, and money owed to the government; liabilities include items such as bills that the government has yet to pay. When the organization's liabilities are subtracted from its assets, the remainder is called a *fund balance* (and may be expressed either in positive or negative terms). An organization with $2,525,000 in assets and $2,300,000 in liabilities has a fund balance of $225,000. Note that a fund balance does not mean the amount of "cash on hand," but rather signifies a relationship between all assets (including cash) and all liabilities. Broadly, the fund balance is the key measure of the viability of the operation monitored by the fund and is one of many items contained in financial reports issued by governments and other public organizations.

Both accounting practices and financial reporting are guided by standards referred to as "generally accepted accounting practices." The Governmental Accounting Standards Board (GASB) was established in 1984 to develop standards for accounting and financial reporting at the state and local levels. The GASB has been especially attentive to multiple users of public financial information, including citizens, taxpayers, legislative bodies, upper-level executives, labor and employee groups, interest groups, contractors, and the press. Again, an important characteristic of governmental accounting is that it must serve multiple purposes, including accountability within a democratic system.

Computer-Based Information Systems

The emergence and widespread use of computers in tracking financial data as well as other program-relevant information has led to what one writer has called a "quiet revolution" in the analysis and use of information in public organizations. Not only do computers make easier the accumulation and manipulation of vast amounts of data, they also greatly facilitate analysis of that data in terms that are meaningful to decision makers at all levels. Computers have also increased the probability that information can be provided when it is needed, not weeks later. Consequently, a great deal of attention is being given to the design and implementation of computer-based information systems in the public sector and to the political and organizational implications of such systems. Applications in the area of financial management have led the way in these efforts.

A distinction is often made between management information systems and decision support systems. *Management information systems* collect and summarize routine information as a basis for structuring decision making. Relevant databases might include budgetary information, expenditures for salaries and wages, and personnel data. The system might be asked, for example, to produce a list of employees eligible for salary increases based on length of service in the agency (McGowan & Lombardo, 1986, p. 581).

Decision support systems, on the other hand, are interactive systems that can assist in the solution of unstructured or nonroutine problems. These systems allow the manager to manipulate data within the system to produce a specific analysis for a particular decision, or provide optimization models to use in analyzing a particular policy recommendation. Although most public organizations are developing management information systems of various sorts, the development of decision support systems remains somewhat behind. We can expect increasing attention to this area in the future.

Applications of computer-based information systems are as wide-ranging as the work of public organizations. Most organizations are quickly becoming familiar with the use of spreadsheets and statistical packages for budget analysis, financial management packages for revenue and expenditure forecasting, and accounting packages for fund accounting and analysis. Far more extensive applications of information technology (IT) have been developed in government agencies. A recent survey indicates that federal agencies vary considerably in use of computer-based information systems, but in the area of financial management, some agencies have developed quite sophisticated systems. The Department of State, for example, has developed and implemented a comprehensive system designed to operate in the department's financial management centers around the world. Other federal agencies have yet to develop agency-wide financial management information systems, though all seem to be moving in that direction. All agencies report extensive and varied applications of information technology throughout their organizations.

At the state and local levels, one of the most interesting developments in information technology has been the design and implementation of information systems integrating budgeting, personnel, performance reporting, and auditing. Several states have begun this process of integration, including Michigan, Oregon, Texas, Wyoming, and Washington. Efforts of this nature reflect an overall shift on the part of states toward more sophisticated systems of accounting. State governments over the past decade have used information technology to enhance their capacity to generate more detailed financial and productivity data, thus allowing for extensive analyses at a programmatic level and a link between expenditures and actual performance.

To the extent that budgetary and performance data are made available to the chief executive and other top managers on a timely basis, more effective management decisions may be possible. In addition, freeing budget analysts from the more mundane aspects of budgetary procedures should allow more attention to planning and analysis.

Similar developments have occurred at the local level. Baltimore, Maryland has implemented a comprehensive accounting and performance measurement system, called Citistat, to track (virtually in real time) the productivity and fiscal efficiency of city departments. In a room lined with large projection screens and computer terminals, Baltimore's Mayor Martin O'Malley meets weekly with top aides and department heads to hear the latest reports on the city's service delivery. If a department's numbers lag behind its performance targets, the manager must account to his or her peers for the difference. "If we only looked at performance every year at budget time, I'd be old and gray before anything would change. Citistat brings the sense of urgency we need around here," said O'Malley (cited in Swope, 2001, p. 20). Thus far, the information system has contributed to significant improvements in public safety and public health, as well as opened new doors for collaboration between city departments.

Whether Citistat or similar IT initiatives will have across-the-board improvements for public organizations remains to be seen. Some argue that change of this nature requires far more than increased capacity to handle information. Moreover, the implementation of these types of systems may have negative consequences on the organizational culture and relationships within affected agencies.

■ Summary and Action Implications

Budgeting and financial management in public organizations have a lot in common with those activities elsewhere. But there are also important differences, most of which flow from the necessity for public organizations to be accountable to elected officials and, ultimately, to the people.

The centrality of the budget to any organization can hardly be underestimated; if you want to know what's going on in an organization, look at where the money is going. Establishing budget processes that reflect the organization's priorities, while securing appropriate levels of involvement from those who want to affect the budget, is extremely important. Finding ways to present budgetary information clearly and comprehensibly is a great aid to decision makers and to the public. Finally, developing mechanisms to ensure that the public's money is being spent both efficiently and responsibly is essential. You will find that knowing the technical side of the budget process—being able to follow the budget process and clearly understand preparation, administration, and review—will be extremely helpful as you try to influence the operations of your organization.

If you work in a central budget office, you will find that the period during which the budget is formulated is intense, and your technical expertise will be put to the test. But you will also recognize that you are playing an important role in shaping public policies. Similarly, if you are managing an agency, you will place your imprint on the policies and directions of your organization through the budget process. Your skill in presenting and supporting requests for programs may determine whether or not they are undertaken.

The budget process at the federal level, and in some state and local jurisdictions, is integrated with a process for long-range planning. Federal agencies are asked to provide certain projections for the two-year period following the year for which the budget is being prepared, thus adding an element of long-range planning to the process.

Budgets and financial management systems are important tools for planning, prioritizing, and operating public programs, as well as important mechanisms for accountability and control. Public access to budgets and financial statements allows citizens to see how their interests are reflected in the actual conduct of government. Budgets and other financial documents that clearly show what is happening in an agency are a necessary part of operating in the public interest.

TERMS AND DEFINITIONS

Accounting: The process of identifying, measuring, and communicating economic information to permit informed judgment and decision making.

Allotments: Amounts that agencies are authorized to spend within a given period.

Apportionment: The process by which funds are allocated to agencies for specific portions of the year.

Appropriation: Legislative action to set aside funds and create budget authority for their expenditures.

Authorizing legislation: Legislative action that permits establishment or continuation of a particular program or agency.

Bond: Promise to repay a certain amount (principal) at a certain time (maturity date) at a particular rate of interest.

Budget padding: Proposing a higher budget than is actually needed.

Business cycle: Periods of economic growth featuring inflation and high employment followed by periods of recession or depression and unemployment.

Capital expenditures: Spending for items that will be used over a period of several years.

Continuing resolution: Resolution permitting the government to continue operating until an appropriations measure is passed.

Debt capacity: Value of a city's resources combined with the ability of the government to draw on them to provide payment.

Deferral: Decision by the president to withhold expenditure of funds for a brief period.

Discretionary spending: That portion of the budget still open to changes by the president and Congress.

Entitlement programs: Programs that provide a specified set of benefits to those who meet certain eligibility requirements.

Excise tax: Tax applied to the sale of specific commodities.

Fiduciary funds: Funds used when government must hold assets for individuals or when government holds resources to be transmitted to another organization.

Fiscal policy: Public policy concerned with the impact of government taxation and spending on the economy.

Fiscal year (FY): Government's basic accounting period.

General fund: Fund that handles the "unrestricted" funds of government.

Gross Domestic Product (GDP): A measure of total output of the economy, measured by the market value of goods and services.

Impoundment: Withholding of funds authorized and appropriated by law.

Item veto: Allows the executive to veto specific items in an appropriations bill.

Line-item budget: Budget format for listing categories of expenditures along with amounts allocated to each.

Outcome-based budgeting: Budgeting system that takes into account long-term effects or outcomes.

Performance auditing: Analysis and evaluation of the effective performance of agencies in carrying out their objectives.

Performance budget: Budget format organized around programs or activities, including various performance measurements that indicate the relationship between work actually done and its cost.

Planning-programming-budgeting system (PPBS): Effort to connect planning, systems analysis, and budgeting in a single exercise.

Preaudit: Review in advance of an actual expenditure.

Progressive tax: One that taxes those with higher incomes at a higher rate.

Proportional tax: One that taxes everyone at the same rate.

Proprietary funds: Used to account for government activities that more closely resemble private business.

Reconciliation bill: Legislative action that attempts to reconcile individual actions in taxes, authorizations, or appropriations with the totals.

Regressive tax: One that taxes those with lower incomes at a proportionally higher rate than those with higher incomes.

Rescission: Presidential decision to permanently withhold funds.

Risk management: Ways that public organizations anticipate and cope with risks.

Supplemental appropriation: Bill passed during the fiscal year adding new money to an agency's budget for the same fiscal year.

Zero-base budgeting: Budget format that presents information about the efficiency and effectiveness of existing programs and highlights possibilities for eliminating or reducing programs.

STUDY QUESTIONS

1. Discuss how government uses the budget to affect fiscal policy.

2. Describe some of the ways government obtains funds for operation. Identify the various types of taxes that governments use.

3. How does the government spend the money it collects?

4. The budget cycle consists of four major phases. Discuss government's role in the budget cycle and the components of each phase.

5. Allen Schick suggests three different purposes of the budget. Identify and define these purposes.

6. Compare and contrast the different types of budgeting processes.

7. Explain the two basic concepts of budgetary strategies.

8. Political influence has a major impact on the budgetary process. What are some of the strategies managers use to influence the budget process?

9. Financial management is an important part of fiscal activities. Discuss some of the concerns fiscal managers deal with, including capital budgeting, debt management, risk management, and purchasing.

10. Discuss the broad types of funds that public organizations use.

CASES AND EXERCISES

1. Figure 7.4 contains several pages from the City of Tempe's budget document. Analyze these budget pages from the perspective of: (1) a city council member who will have to make decisions about which city services to fund; (2) the public works department director who wants to improve services to the community; and (3) an average citizen interested in seeing whether the city's tax dollars are being put to good use. For the purposes of each viewpoint, how complete and clear is the information? Does the budget tell you what you want to know in order to act? How might the budget presentation be improved?

2. Consider the following case: You are Mike Smith, chief procurement officer for a major university. Work generated by your staff of twenty procurement specialists includes writing proposals to vendors and evaluating the vendors' bids. To write those bids, the procurement specialist works with someone from the university agency who is knowledgeable about the project. Tom Drake, a procurement specialist, is currently working with Kathy Kline of the Communications Department to develop a bid proposal to purchase a new campus-wide telephone system that includes a quick-dial feature. The university's current telephone system was installed fifteen years ago by Regional Telephone. Over the last few years, Regional and one other vendor have sold add-on equipment to five of the university's fifteen departments. This add-on equipment is expensive and represents a major investment to the five departments, one of which is the Communications Department. Departments that have the quick-dial equipment are pleased with the results; departments that do not have quick dial cannot afford it and are unhappy with Regional.

FIGURE 7.4

City of Tempe: Water Utilities Department

Department Purpose:
To provide the residents, businesses and visitors of Tempe with a reliable and economical supply of drinking water that meets or exceeds all federal, state and local standards of quality, and to protect the health, safety and overall environment of our community through wastewater and storm water management and the collection and disposal of household hazardous materials.

Department Description:
The Water Utilities Department is responsible for Operations, Water Resources, Administration, and SROG. The Operations Division is comprised of Plant Operations, Field Operations, Environmental Services, Environmental Health & Safety, and Security. Water Resources is responsible for the water conservation program, Tempe Town Lake, and hydrology services. The Administration Division includes Capital Improvement Program (CIP) management, Finance, and Aviation. The Sub-Regional Operating Groups (SROG) division is responsible for administration of the SROG program.

FY 2006-07 Budget Highlights:
Funding was approved for laboratory supplies and testing, compound meter replacement, sewer cleaning, and a rate study for water, sewer and irrigation. In addition, funding for two temporary intern positions was approved to address an increased workload at the Household Products Collection Center (HPCC).

Expenditure by Type	2004-05 Actual	2005-06 Budget	2005-06 Revised	2006-07 Budget
Personal Services	$ 9,878,309	$10,846,863	$10,805,993	$11,510,134
Supplies and Services	12,055,360	12,825,110	13,348,528	14,036,150
Capital Outlay	229,835	222,100	384,933	283,200
Internal Services	3,684,064	3,375,861	3,372,724	3,309,785
Contributions	1,000			
Expenditure Total	**$25,848,568**	**$27,269,934**	**$27,912,178**	**$29,139,269**
Per Capita	**$158.65**	**$165.91**	**$169.82**	**$175.75**

Expenditures by Division	2004-05 Actual	2005-06 Budget	2005-06 Revised	2006-07 Budget
Operations	$16,327,978	$17,574,531	$18,175,519	$19,079,336
Water Resources	607,459	1,073,629	892,387	1,052,672
Administration/CIP Management/Finance/Aviation	4,516,225	4,216,435	4,444,003	4,604,428
SROG	4,396,906	4,405,339	4,400,269	4,402,833
Total	**$25,848,568**	**$27,269,934**	**$27,912,178**	**$29,139,269**

(Continued)

FIGURE 7.4

City of Tempe: Water Utilities Department (*continued*)

Authorized Personnel	2004-05 Actual			2005-06 Revised			2006-07 Budget		
	Full Time	Perm FTE	Temp FTE	Full Time	Perm FTE	Temp FTE	Full Time	Perm FTE	Temp FTE
Operations	113	0.50		117	1.00		116	1.00	
Water Resources	4			4			4		
Admin./CIP Mgt./Finance/Aviation	12		0.49	11	0.50	0.49	12	0.50	0.49
SROG	1			1			1		
Total	130	0.50	0.49	133	1.50	0.49	133	1.50	0.49

Related Strategic issue: Neighborhood Quality of Life and Public Safety

Goal: To provide a safe and adequate domestic water supply to all citizens in Tempe, while at the same time minimizing cost

Objective: 1) To monitor increases in water treatment costs for the Johnny G.Martinez and South Tempe Water Treatment plants; and 2) maintain an Operating and Maintenance Cost per 1,000 gallons treated under eighty cents

Measures (*Comparative Benchmark*)	2004-05 Actual	2005-06 Budget	2005-06 Revised	2006-07 Budget
Total Water Treatment Operating and Maintenance Cost	$9,186,874	$10,995,858	$10,995,858	$10,849,927
Number of Customer Accounts	41,532	41,532	41,532	42,000
Total Gallons Treated (Million Gallons)	15,152	18,800	17,563	17,900
Operating and Maintenance Cost per 1,000 gallons treated	*$0.61*	*$0.59*	*$0.63*	*$0.61*
Operating and Maintenance Cost per customer account	$221.20	$264.76	$264.76	$258.33

Related Strategic issue: Neighborhood Quality of Life and Public Safety

Goal: To reduce operating and maintenance costs of the wastewater collection system

Objective: To achieve wastewater collection costs that are less than $10,000 per mile

Measures	2004-05 Actual	2005-06 Budget	2005-06 Revised	2006-07 Budget
Total Wastewater Collection Operating and Maintenance Cost	$3,153,522	&3,445,996	$3,445,996	$3,453,689
Miles of Mains in Collection System	500.0	502.2	502.2	502.2
Operating and Maintenance Cost per mile	$6,307	$6,862	$6,862	$6,877

Related Strategic issue: Neighborhood Quality of Life and Public Safety

Goal: To minimize the number of resident complaints related to water quality and respond to those complaints within twenty-four hours

Objective: To maintain low resident complaints and to respond within twenty-four hours

Measures	2004-05 Actual	2005-06 Budget	2005-06 Revised	2006-07 Budget
Taste and Odor Complaints	6	N/A	17	<17
Hardness Complaints	2	N/A	1	<1
Other Complaints	9	N/A	5	<5
Response within twenty-four hours of the complaint	100%	N/A	100%	100%

SOURCE: City of Tempe Annual Budget, July 1, 2006 through June 30, 2007, Performance Budget (pp.194–195). Retrieved April 7, 2007 from www.tempe.gov/budget/FY%2006–07%20docs/ 5%20Performance%20Budget.pdf.

Tom has updated you on the status of the proposal. The communications office has insisted throughout the proposal process that the new phone system must be capable of using the existing quick-dial equipment. Tom tells you that if that is the case, only Regional and two or three other vendors would be able to bid on the system. Six other vendors with their own quick-dial equipment would not be able to respond to the bid. Tom explains that in some cases, a whole new system was less expensive than hooking up one of Regional's systems to existing quick-dial equipment. Tom also tells you he has heard that several staff members from the Communications Department have threatened to quit if the bid goes to a company other than Regional. After 15 years, they feel Regional is the best and only qualified vendor. Tom wants to know how he should proceed to satisfy both the university's needs and the vendors' rights to a fair bidding process.

SOURCE: The Preceding case was provided by Bill Carney.

    a. How should Tom proceed to ensure that all bidders have an equal chance to participate in the bid process?

    b. How can the procurement office avoid the practice of vendors helping buyers to write a bid proposal?

    c. What about Tom's responsibility to taxpayers? (Thousands of dollars would be wasted if the quick-dial equipment that has already been purchased was scrapped.)

3. The following simulation reenacts a series of budget discussions held at the University of Southern Anonymous (USA) during a time of significant budget reductions. To conduct the simulation, divide the class into five groups, each of which will represent one character in the simulation. All students in the class should read the following general description of the situation facing USA. Then members of each group should read only the character description assigned to their group. (It is important that you read only the description assigned to you.) The role descriptions of the following characters can be found after the general description of the situation in the following pages.

Vice President Cooper
Dean Berryderry, College of Liberal Arts
Dean Stevens, dean of Science
Dean Dudley, dean of Education Dean Dollar, dean of Business

After everyone has had a chance to read the general description of the situation and the specific information pertaining to their character, each character group should meet separately for fifteen to twenty minutes. During this period, the group should: (1) select a representative to play the character at a meeting to be held in Vice President Cooper's office, and (2) develop detailed strategies and information for that person to use in representing your group's interests in the meeting.

Following the individual group meetings, the five individuals selected to play the five characters should meet around a table near the middle of the room. Vice President Cooper will call the meeting to order, present any opening remarks he or she wishes to make, then preside over the remainder of the discussion. All other students should remain quiet during this part of the simulation. During the course of the meeting, any member may request a recess to consult with his or her group (for no longer than five minutes). When the meeting in Vice President Cooper's office reconvenes, the person who called the recess will have the floor. The meeting should continue until a consensus is reached concerning the reductions or until Vice President Cooper feels the meeting is stalled and he or she will have to make a decision independently. Enjoy the discussion!

General Description of the Situation

The University of Southern Anonymous (USA) has been informed by the state adminis-tration that its budget for the current year will be reduced by several million dollars. The president of the university, I. M. Fearless, has informed Vice President for Academic Affairs Cooper that the various colleges in the university will be required to reduce their budgets by an average of eight percent. In turn, Vice President Cooper has chosen not to implement across-the-board cuts of eight percent for all colleges, but has discussed different target percentage reductions with each of the deans of the four colleges—Liberal Arts, Science, Education, and Business. In response to a request from several of the deans, Vice President Cooper has called a meeting of the four deans to get their reactions to his targeted amounts for each college and to find out how each college plans to implement the required reduction.

USA is a medium-sized Midwestern university whose mission is providing students with a broad-based liberal arts education as well as a limited graduate program, primarily in business and education. The school serves a regional constituency in the southern part of the state, though it draws students from around the country, many of whom first heard of USA because of its reputation as a leader in intercollegiate billiards. (In fact, some cyn-ics refer to USA as "Cue U.")

Though the university has traditionally enjoyed a good relationship with the governor and members of the legislature, President Fearless has antagonized many in the state capital with his rough and abrasive manner. Many on campus see the president as bring-ing the university the same administrative style he employed as a colonel in the Marine Corps. Despite these difficulties, most academic programs at the university are considered sound, with some exceptions. Similarly, many feel some programs are not suited to the mission of a regional Midwestern university, notably the school's long-standing program in oceanography, which some feel is out of place because the university is seven hundred miles from the nearest ocean.

Character Descriptions

Vice President Cooper In your five years as vice president at USA, you have never faced such a difficult situation. You recognize that the university's president is in some political trouble and may be asked to resign soon. As a ploy to reduce the heat on his office, he has passed on the largest part of the budgetary reductions to you. If you can come through this situation in good shape, you will receive considerable notoriety and be likely candi-date for the presidency should the president be forced to resign. You will, however, need to be sure that you maintain the support of all the deans of the colleges, because their support is essential for your promotion. On the other hand, a major disruption at the university, in which you might lose support of the deans, would end any chances of your attaining your ambition. In fact, you might be fired along with the president!

Given the instructions from the president, there seems to be little you can do other than assign reductions to the colleges. After reviewing the various programs within the colleges, however, you have decided that across-the-board cuts would be inappropri-ate and that some colleges could indeed stand to be cut more than others. You have, therefore, assigned differential reductions to each college, with Education receiving the greatest reduction (20 percent), Liberal Arts receiving the second greatest reduction (10 percent), Science next (7 percent), and Business last (2 percent). You have chosen these figures based on your assessment of the quality of programs, the quantity of students (faculty/student ratios), the nature of the programs, and their suitability to the mission of your university.

The total reductions you have assigned to the deans exceed the total the president has required you to complete. Your reasons for this strategy are twofold: (1) If any of the deans complain too loudly, you can fall back to the figure you actually need as a compromise; and (2) If you persuade all the deans to accept the assigned reduction, then you will have some money available for internal reallocations, which you would like to achieve anyway.

For the most part, you are willing to let the various deans assign reductions within their colleges as they see fit, as long as each seems to be doing a thorough job in the assignment. Later, if there is money available, you can make other needed reallocations to add needed new programs or strengthen others.

However, you are personally interested in a couple of particular areas. First, your favorite uncle chairs the oceanography program. Second, your own degree is in higher education administration, and you have enjoyed periodic classroom visits to that department. Third, the governor has expressed a strong interest in the integrity of the public administration program.

Dean Berryderry College of Liberal Arts (target reduction—10 percent). You approach the meeting with the vice president with some trepidation, because you realize that your college is likely to be high on the list of cuts. You would prefer across-the-board cuts that would not place a special burden on your college. Several of your programs, however, are of minimal quality and simply have not been attracting students over the years. For example, your program in German has graduated an average of two majors per year over the past several years, with a faculty of only three. Several other programs, such as anthropology and geography, are showing similar results. These programs, however, are important to a broad-based liberal arts education. You feel that students should at least have the opportunity to enroll in such programs if they see fit.

On the other hand, there are some programs currently housed in your college you would just as soon see ended. For example, the graduate program in public administration is a professional program that you feel is inconsistent with the liberal arts perspective of the college. The total faculty salaries in this department would just about equal the total by which you need to reduce your budget. This is an obvious area to eliminate.

Next, it has occurred to you that your staff of professional advisors could be eliminated and all academic advising performed by members of your faculty. This could be accomplished with no faculty or program reductions.

You feel a natural alliance with the College of Science and would prefer to see reductions occur in either Education or Business rather than in Liberal Arts or Science. However, Dean Stevens of the College of Science has always been somewhat antagonistic toward you, perhaps because of your critical remarks about the oceanography program, which you think should be eliminated.

Finally, several personal considerations enter into your thinking. First, if the vice president were to become president, you would probably be the leading candidate for the vice presidency. You find that very attractive. Second, although you don't want to appear to favor any department, your home department, the Department of Political Science, is putting strong pressure on you to support expansion of the program. Across-the-board cuts *within* your college would make that impossible. Third, a member of your faculty was recently offended by sexual advances from the dean of the School of Business, Dean Dollar.

Dean Stevens Dean of the College of Science (target reduction—7 percent). You have conducted a thorough analysis of the possibilities for reduction within your college. You feel that by eliminating one visiting professorship, four graduate teaching assistantship positions, and two staff positions, you'll be able to accommodate the reductions. You are quite aware, however, that others see your Department of Oceanography as a primary target for elimination. This is, however, one of your oldest and strongest programs, certainly one of the leading oceanography programs in the Midwest. You want to protect the program as it is; however, even if you are required to reduce that program, you wish to do so only by eliminating several faculty positions rather than the entire department. You also feel this program will be protected because the chair of that department is the vice president's uncle.

Several other personal considerations affect your thinking. First, you feel that the entire College of Education could be eliminated with no real loss to the university. Other programs within the state clearly produce enough graduates in that field. Eliminating the entire college would mean no reductions would be needed in any other college. Second, you think Dean Berryderry is an idiot. You were especially incensed by Berryderry's comments about oceanography. If Berryderry can't run his own college, why should he try to run yours? Third, one of your faculty members recently was offended by sexual advances from the dean of the School of Business, Dean Dollar.

Dean Dudley Dean of the College of Education (target reduction—20 percent). You know you are in trouble! Over the past several years, enrollments have been dropping in Education to the point that you are considerably overstaffed. At the same time, other programs in the state have developed and now have better reputations. This is especially true for your Department of Higher Education Administration. Another campus in the state boasts one of the country's leading programs in this area. Your best hope is to argue for across-the-board cuts that would affect all colleges equally. Your suspicion is that the College of Business will receive the lowest reduction, and the College of Liberal Arts and the College of Science will be somewhere above. One of them would probably benefit from across-the-board cuts as opposed to targeted reductions; the other would probably lose—but you don't know which one.

In addition, several personal considerations guide your thinking. First, nearly all the athletes who are part of the school's winning billiards program are students in your college. You doubt if they could pass their coursework elsewhere. Second, the chair of the Department of Higher Education Administration has been one of your strongest critics over the years, and eliminating that department would eliminate one of your biggest problems. Third, a member of your faculty was recently offended by sexual advances from the dean of the School of Business, Dean Dollar.

Dean Dollar Dean of the School of Business (target reduction—2 percent). Though you realize that your college will have to take a token reduction, you are certain that your reduction is far less than that required from other schools. Consequently, you are highly supportive of the vice president's selective reduction and opposed to across-the-board cuts. Your college has grown by leaps and bounds in the past several years, and you are in desperate need of more faculty, not fewer. At the same time, salaries have increased dramatically in your field, and retention of capable faculty is a problem. You can probably accommodate the reductions assigned to you through minimal staff changes and will not have to fire faculty.

You see all this as a possibility for considerable reorganization of programs. One program that you would particularly be interested in bringing into the college is that in public administration. This program is viewed with great favor by the governor and, consequently, by those higher in the university's administration. Moreover, the program would seem to be consistent with the interest of your college in management. You wonder if perhaps somewhere in all of this redistribution of money you might be able to acquire a new program. If you can discredit Dean Berryderry's interest in public administration and champion that field, you should stand a good chance of receiving support from the higher administration. All in all, you see this process as opening the possibility of adding to your college rather than reducing it. This result, however, depends on selective reductions rather than across-the-board cuts and upon reallocations *beyond* the amount required for the president's stated budget reduction.

You also have several personal concerns. First, you think both the College of Education and the Department of Oceanography (in the College of Science) could be eliminated outright and you could use the money. Second, you have heard that the chair of the Department of Oceanography is the vice president's cousin. Third, you have just met a very attractive person who is an advisor in the College of Liberal Arts. You think you are falling in love—again!

Do not read this paragraph until after the simulation.

Following the simulation, the entire class should discuss each group's strategies and tactics. Sometimes it is helpful to ask first what others thought each dean was trying to do and then ask that group to describe its strategy. Pay particular attention to strategies of cooperation and competition, as well as to strategies that have little to do with actual budget reductions. (For example, shifting a program from one location to another doesn't save the university any money.) Note also the inevitable lack of information, as well as the roles of rumor and false impressions in the budget process. (Both these features are more typical of budget decisions than you might think!) Finally, just for fun, have Dean Berryderry read the last line of his or her description, then have Dean Stevens do the same, then Dean Dudley, and then Dean Dollar.

FOR ADDITIONAL READING

Briffault, Richard. *Balancing Acts*. Washington, DC: Brookings Institution, 1996.

Clynch, Edward J., and Thomas P. Lauth, eds. *Governors, Legislatures, and Budgets: Diversity Across the American States*. Westport, CT: Greenwood Press, 1991.

Frank, Howard A. *Forecasting in Local Government: Near Tools and Techniques*. New York: Quorum Books, 1993.

Garner, C. William. *Accounting and Budgeting in Public and Non-Profit Organizations: A Manager's Guide*. San Francisco: Jossey-Bass, 1991.

Gosling, James J. *Budgeting Politics in American Governments*. White Plains, NY: Longman Publishing Group, 1992.

Gross, Malvern, and Richard Larkin, eds. *Financial and Accounting Guide for Non-Profit Organizations*. New York: John Wiley & Sons, 1999.

Jones, Vernon Dale. *Downsizing the Federal Government*. Armonk, NY: M. E. Sharpe, 1997.

Kettl, Donald F., and John Dilulio, Jr. *Cutting Government*. Washington, DC: Brookings Institution, 1995.

Light, Paul. *Thickening Government*. Washington, DC: Brookings Institution, 1995.

Maddox, David. *Budgeting for Not-for-Profit Organizations*. New York: John Wiley & Sons, 1999.

Mikesell, John L. *Fiscal Administration*. 2nd ed. Pacific Grove, CA: Brooks/Cole, 1986.

Miller, Gerald J. *Government Financial Management Theory*. New York: Marcel Dekker 1991.

Reed, B. J., and John Swain. *Public Finance Administration*. Englewood Cliffs, NJ: Prentice Hall, 1990.

Reischauer, Robert D. *Setting National Priorities*. Washington, DC: Brookings Institution, 1997.

Rubin, Irene S. *The Politics of Public Budgeting*. Chatham, NJ: Chatham House, 1990.

Scott, David, John D. Martin, and Arthur J. Keown. *Basic Financial Management*. Upper Saddle River, NJ: Prentice-Hall, 1999.

Shick, Allen. *The Federal Budget*. Washington, DC: Brookings Institution, 1995.

Wildavsky, Aaron, and Naomi Caiden. *The New Politics of the Budgetary Process*. 3rd ed. New York: Longman, 1997.

CHAPTER 8

THE MANAGEMENT OF HUMAN RESOURCES *(through time)*

Nothing is more critical for an administrator than to effectively manage the people who work in his or her organization. Yet, the hiring and treatment of public employees often seem so bound up in rules, regulations, and "red tape" that effective management is extremely difficult. Many managers feel that civil service systems (and central personnel offices), originally designed to attract and retain competent personnel, exist merely to complicate the manager's life and make it more difficult to manage. Instead of simply hiring someone for a job, the manager must advise an applicant to take a competitive examination and join many other candidates on a register for the position (some of whom may be given special preferences in the hiring process) and then to wait until all the paperwork clears. After someone has been hired, the manager finds there are limits to the "rewards and punishments" that can be offered to encourage improved job performance. And, should the person fail to perform adequately, the paperwork and justifications required to terminate his or her employment seem endless. You may wonder how anything else gets done!

But there are good reasons for the way human resources or personnel management in government has developed. Even though it is true that some civil service systems have become overly rigid, even "fossilized," most of the requirements relating to government employment are deeply rooted in important political and ethical principles. An understanding of how government personnel systems operate includes a knowledge of personnel techniques and a sensitivity to the values that underlie human resources management in public organizations.

Nowhere is the contest between the competing values of efficiency and responsiveness played out more clearly than in the area of human resources or personnel. On the one hand, staffing government agencies with the most competent people available is essential to effective management. On the other hand, those who staff the offices of government should be responsive to the citizenry. In any case, the human resources or personnel system for any public organization ultimately reflects the political priorities of the particular public involved. In certain cases or at certain times, managerial concern for efficiency may receive preference; in others, the democratic concern for responsiveness may be paramount.

NETWORKING

For general information on personnel issues, see the International Personnel Management Association at www.ipma-hr.org. For jobs and recruiting, see www.aspanet.org, www.fedworld.gov, www.careersingovernment.com, and www.govtjob.net.

■ Merit Systems in Public Employment

Because the Constitution made little mention of either administrative structures or how they would be staffed, early leaders at all levels of government experimented with many different approaches to hiring, working with, and firing personnel. In the late 1800s, however, growing concern about the composition of the civil service led to a new focus on competence and professionalism and, in turn, to legislation establishing the merit principle in public employment. The *merit principle*, though widely varied in its application, generally means that selection and treatment of government employees should be based on merit or competence rather than on personal or political favoritism. Despite the apparent simplicity and appeal of this notion, the development of public personnel systems has been infused with controversy.

Spoils versus Merit

Most of the early American presidents followed George Washington's lead in seeking people of high competence and integrity—what he called "fitness of character"—to hold governmental positions. This approach resulted in a stable and fairly skilled government workforce, but not without several problems. Because there were few well-educated people in society and because those with education tended to be from the wealthier classes, the newly formed civil service soon took on a somewhat elitist character. Moreover, partisan considerations began to enter into the process as well. Presidents and members of Congress began to recognize not only that government employees needed to be loyal to the new government (and presumably the party in power), but also that public offices (and salaries) could be rewards to the party faithful. Finally, there was the question of tenure: Should civil servants hold office for life, thus providing experience and continuity, or should they change with each administration, providing loyalty (and jobs) to the incoming party?

All these concerns were dramatically illustrated in the administration of Andrew Jackson. Jackson was swept into office on a strong wave of democratic sentiment and was especially concerned with making government more accessible to those previously excluded: the "common people." Though Jackson was not the first to employ the *spoils system* (the notion that "to the victor belong the spoils"—in this case, the ability to give government jobs to the party faithful), his administration was notable for its expansion of the system and for its elaborate justification of it. Jackson argued that the common people had as much right to government jobs as the wealthy and that most government jobs could be done without special training.

Jackson is sometimes portrayed as something of a villain for his defense of the spoils system, though far greater abuses occurred later at all levels of government. At the same time, however, Jackson made several positive contributions to democratic government; for example, there is no question that he democratized the civil service of his era and set a tone for greater representativeness within government agencies for decades to come.

Even Jackson could not have foreseen the corruption and abuse that would soon become associated with the spoils system (see Box 8.1). Succeeding presidents went far beyond Jackson in applying the system, as did political bosses at the state and local levels.

BOX 8.1

THE EARLY SPOILS SYSTEM

By the late 1800s, the spoils system was firmly a part of political life in most jurisdictions. One aspect of the system was collecting funds from appointees to help sustain the party in power. Although such practices persisted in some jurisdictions well into the 1950s and even the 1960s, they were hardly as blatant as the tribute requested in the letter from a state party committee in 1870.

Dear Sir:

(We) have great and imperative need of funds at once, to carry the campaign to successful issue. An assessment of one percent on the annual gross receipts of your office is therefore called for, and you will please enclose that amount, without delay, to the treasurer, E. S. Rowse, in the envelope enclosed. This assessment is made after conference with our friends at Washington, where it is confidently expected that those who receive the benefits of Federal appointments will support the machinery that sustains the party which gives them pecuniary benefit and honor. The exigencies are great, and delay or neglect will rightly be construed into unfriendliness to the Administration. We do not look for such a record from you, and you will at once see the propriety and wisdom of the earliest attention to the matter.

Isaac Sheppard

Chairman of Committee

The quality of the civil service rapidly declined, and even those who found jobs in government became disenchanted with the financial contributions exacted from them each election year. The system also became a problem for each new president, as thousands of office-seekers came to press their claims for patronage positions, and presidents soon grew weary of the long lines of people seeking jobs.

These factors set the stage for reform, but even more important in eventually bringing about change was the increasing corruption in government. There were kickbacks from contractors, private sales of surplus public property, skimming of tax receipts, and many other abuses. Corruption was becoming a normal way of doing government business.

The various ills that grew from the spoils system eventually led to a strong and active reform movement, spearheaded by such groups as the National Civil Service Reform League. The reformers made vigorous and eloquent appeals, but their eventual success was assured more by a historical accident—the assassination of President Garfield—than by eloquence. Though Garfield had hardly been a proponent of civil service reform and had drawn criticism from reform groups for his failure to support a reform bill, the fact that he was killed by a disappointed office-seeker made him a martyr for the reform cause.

A man named Charles Guiteau had hoped to be consul to Paris. After weeks of making his case and after repeatedly being turned away from Garfield's office, he followed Garfield into a train station and shot him twice in the back. As he did so, he shouted that now Chester Arthur, a noted spoilsman, would be president. The reformers capitalized on this comment, portraying the situation as the obvious result of the evil spoils system. In a sudden change of heart (and reality), they described Garfield as a proponent of reform. After two more years of pressure, the Republican Congress finally acknowledged the rising sentiment for reform and passed the Pendleton Act, which was signed into law in January 1883.

The Pendleton Act is one of two landmark pieces of legislation in federal personnel administration (the other being the Civil Service Reform Act of 1978). The Pendleton Act was primarily an effort to eliminate political influence from administrative agencies and, secondarily, an effort to ensure more competent government employees. It pursued these aims through the following major provisions.

1. A bipartisan commission, the U.S. Civil Service Commission, was created within the executive branch to establish and implement personnel rules and procedures for the federal government.

2. Open and competitive examinations to test job-related skills were developed wherever practical within the agencies covered by the law and were to become the primary basis upon which to make hiring decisions.

3. Employees were given protection against political pressures, such as assessments (mandatory contributions) or "required" participation in campaign activities.

4. *Lateral entry* into government positions (that is, entry at any level as opposed to only the beginning level) was encouraged, thus maintaining an important element of Jacksonian openness.

5. Positions in Washington offices were to be apportioned among the various states, in an effort to provide geographical representation in the civil service.

6. The president was given authority to extend coverage to other groups of government employees beyond the approximately 10 percent of federal employees covered by the act.

These provisions, especially the last, provided the basis for the gradual extension of the idea of a merit system throughout most of the federal government as well as state and local governments. A respected writer on public personnel provides the following definition of the civil service system that emerged: "Throughout its history, the civil service idea has rested on three basic principles: (1) that the selection of subordinate government officials should be based on merit—the ability to perform the work rather than any form of personal or political favoritism; (2) that since jobs are to be filled by weighing the merits of applicants, those hired should have tenure regardless of political changes at the top of organizations; and (3) that the price of job security should be a willing responsiveness to the legitimate political leaders of the day" (Heclo, 1977, p. 20). The concept of "merit" is so central to the American approach to public personnel administration that "merit system" and "civil service system" have become almost synonymous.

The Pendleton Act, although important in establishing the notion of a merit system of public employment, merely provided a framework within which a more full-blown system might develop. Unfortunately, development of the system was not well coordinated. Although the merit system was gradually extended to more and more government

[Handwritten margin notes:]
Pendleton Act 1883
- eliminate pol. influence
- ensure more competent govt
① Civil Service Com.
- est. + imp. rules + procedures for Fed. Govt.
② Exams wherever practical
③ Protection from political pressure
④ Lateral entry (other than entry level)
⑤ Washington offices apportioned among states for representation
⑥ Pres. can extend coverage

employees, its values were not always the primary motivation for extension. For example, one unlikely set of agents for the extension of personnel reforms turned out to be out-going presidents. Many of them sought to "blanket in" those they had appointed to patronage positions by making the positions subject to the merit system. In this way, merit coverage was extended from its original 10 percent of all federal employees in 1883 to approximately 70 percent by the end of World War I and some 90 percent today.

Other changes in the system also occurred slowly. The Pendleton Act contained provisions for examinations, but other devices for improving the quality of the workforce, such as position classification, standard pay schedules, and objective performance appraisals, had not yet been developed. Over the next decades, these ideas too became a part of the federal system of civil service. The Classification Act of 1923, for example, established a system for classifying jobs according to qualifications needed to carry them out and tying them to various pay grades, thus providing uniformity throughout the system.

Changes were also required to respond to a newly professionalized workforce and a larger and more activist government. In the early days, the main jobs in government were essentially clerkships, but as government grew and entered new fields, there was a need for more professional and more highly specialized people. Similarly, especially through the Roosevelt years, a multitude of new agencies were created, each placing different demands on the personnel system. Prior to this time, the Civil Service Commission had assumed the role of the government's central personnel agency; now it was necessary to decentralize personnel responsibilities to the various agencies, with the commission setting regulations and monitoring implementation.

The merit system has now become firmly established at the federal level. Nine out of ten federal employees are covered by either the general merit system or by one of several special systems created by law to pursue merit principles within specific agencies: the Postal Service, the Federal Bureau of Investigation, the Foreign Service, and so on. The remaining positions are exempt because they are not amenable to competitive selection or to regular personnel procedures; they include seasonal workers, those in intelligence, and a limited number of policy-making/confidential positions. Any incoming president now has over 2,000 positions to fill on a purely political basis—a number that has actually risen substantially in the George W. Bush administration, after being reduced in the Clinton years. Questions about the background and preparation of political appointees were raised with the resignation of Michael Brown, a former commissioner of the Arabian Horse Association, as director of the Federal Emergency Management Agency (FEMA) after Hurricane Katrina. In addition, both the head of the recovery division and the FEMA chief-of-staff were political appointees, whose counterparts in the Clinton administration were career officials with decades of experience.

Many questions have been raised in recent years about whether there are too many political appointees in the federal government or, in other words, whether the federal bureaucracy has become too highly politicized. This concern has been intensified as the growth in numbers of political appointees has been accompanied by increasing centralization of the appointment process in the White House. At present, nearly all the political appointments that occur at the federal level—executives, members of boards and commissions, ambassadorships, and judgeships—are cleared through the White House personnel office.

The Civil Service Reform Act and Its Aftermath

For nearly 100 years, the Pendleton Act provided the primary statutory basis for federal civil service. That changed with the passage and implementation of the Civil Service Reform Act of 1978. During the 1960s and 1970s, it became increasingly clear that there were serious problems in the federal personnel management system. The problems were in large part a result of the fairly haphazard pattern through which the system had been established. Responsibilities for personnel management were spread among the president, Congress, the courts, the Civil Service Commission, and various agencies; but there was often not agreement on the basic principles that should guide the development of the system.

Even within the Civil Service Commission itself, there was confusion about the direction of personnel policy. On the one hand, the commission existed to execute the president's personnel directives; on the other hand, it was also responsible for protecting employees from political abuse. At times, the two objectives came into conflict. As a result, the numbers of rules and regulations were not only excessive, they often directly conflicted with one another.

President Carter made reform of the personnel system one of the central themes of his administration and targeted at least five problem areas.

1. *Technical overkill.* Critics charged that those in charge of the personnel function had, in their drive to achieve political neutrality, created overly detailed regulations for recruiting, testing, selecting, classifying, and releasing employees. In many cases, these technical rules became a maze that prevented rather than aided action, and sorting through the procedures to replace a key manager could take as long as two years. Firing one Commerce Department employee who consistently failed to show up for work without valid reasons took twenty-one months!

2. *Excessive protection of employees.* Similarly, many felt that the drive to achieve political neutrality created excessive protections for employees. Although these protections were initiated for the best of reasons—so that employees would not be unduly or arbitrarily punished or dismissed—they sometimes resulted in incredible outcomes, such as an award of almost $5,000 in back pay to a postal employee who had been fired for shooting a coworker in the stomach! On the other hand, protections were needed in other areas. For example, employees who pointed out cases of waste, fraud, and abuse in public agencies—"whistle blowers"—were often subjected to harassment or even dismissal.

3. *Lack of management flexibility.* Managers, especially political appointees, claimed that civil service regulations were so inflexible that they could not manage effectively. In an effort to counter this tendency, one official in the Nixon administration prepared a document, known as the Malek Manual, suggesting 130 ways that managers could subvert the intent of the merit system and do what they wanted to do. One entry described how to get rid of someone who doesn't enjoy traveling: "[He] is given extensive travel orders crisscrossing the country to towns (hopefully with the worst accommodations possible) of a population of 20,000 or under. Until his wife threatens him with divorce, unless he quits, you have him out of town and out of the way. When he finally asks for relief you tearfully reiterate the importance of the project and state that he must continue to obey travel orders or resign."

4. *Inadequate incentives to eliminate inefficiencies.* It was also charged that a system that seemed to grant raises according to longevity rather than performance and that made raises

and promotion appear almost automatic encouraged inefficiency. Over 99 percent of the nearly 3 million federal employees regularly received satisfactory performance ratings that entitled them to raises. Alan Campbell, a leading advocate of reform, wrote: "The current system provides few incentives for managers to manage or for employees to perform."

5. *Discrimination.* Many—notably women and minorities—felt the federal personnel system was not adequately promoting their representation within the bureaucratic ranks. They wanted to make sure that any new system would be more attentive to their interests and better able to cope with the increasing number of complaints in this area.

The Civil Service Reform Act was proposed to "restore the merit principle to a system which has grown into a bureaucratic maze" (Carter, 1978). The act sought to deal with the often contradictory roles of the Civil Service Commission by creating a new office of Personnel Management responsible for policy leadership and a Merit Systems Protection Board to handle investigations and appeals. OPM is "the President's principal agent for managing the federal workforce"; it has responsibility for human resource management and enforcement of personnel regulations (Campbell, 1978, p. 100). The Merit System Protection Board, on the other hand, is the "watchdog" of the personnel system, hearing and resolving complaints, as well as protecting whistle blowers from reprisals. The previously conflicting responsibilities of the Civil Service Commission were split between the two new agencies.

Beyond establishing the two new agencies, perhaps the most striking feature of the Civil Service Reform Act was the creation of the Senior Executive Service (SES). Following ideas that had been discussed for nearly forty years and specifically proposed but not adopted in the Nixon years, the SES created a separate personnel system for the highest-ranking civil service officials, permitting greater flexibility in assignments and establishing a new system of incentives for top-level managers. Basically, eligible managers would apply for positions in the SES and, if accepted, would hold SES rank as individuals, rather than being limited to the rank of a particular position. This meant that, within certain limitations, SES managers could be moved from agency to agency depending on their talents and the needs of the agencies. A new system of performance evaluations and pay increases closely tied to performance was also developed, along with an elaborate system of bonuses for exceptional executives. A 1991 "deal" involving pay plans and performance measures required SES members to be "recertified" every three years.

In addition to these major features, the Civil Service Reform Act made several other changes: giving agencies greater flexibility to administer their own personnel systems, establishing a new and more sophisticated performance appraisal system, creating a merit pay system for managers just below the SES range, providing protection for whistle blowers, assigning the federal Equal Employment Opportunity program (previously with the Civil Service Commission) to the Equal Employment Opportunity Commission, and creating a more independent Federal Labor Relations Authority.

After more than two decades, the Civil Service Reform Act is still receiving mixed reviews. The most favorable opinion is that there is little wrong with the act itself, but that implementation has been flawed by lack of funding and administration pressures to increase the number of political appointees. Others suggest the act was based on questionable assumptions about the nature of the federal workforce and was doomed from the beginning. In any case, the Civil Service Reform Act represented the first major change in personnel policy at the federal level since the Pendleton Act. Its confirmation of the principle of merit, its effort to sort out the multiple responsibilities of the personnel system, and its attempt to produce greater managerial flexibility have been significant.

NETWORKING

The Office of Personnel Management is located at www.opm.gov.

Reinvention and the National Performance Review

During the 1990s, Vice President Gore's National Performance Review (NPR), and the reinventing government movement generally, had a dramatic impact on personnel systems within the federal government. The goal of NPR was to enhance government productivity by streamlining processes, increasing accountability, and decentralizing authority to encourage entrepreneurial behavior. Federal administrators searched for innovative ways to conduct the business of government while cutting costs. An immediate consequence of NPR was an overall shift in the culture of federal organizations. Decentralization and the focus on results have instituted a fundamental change in the way government agencies, and thus personnel systems, work. Public employees are now held accountable for customer service and productivity. And they are rewarded based on their agency's efficiency and performance. The NPR improved the performance of federal government by, "among other things, granting public managers and line staff increased flexibility in exchange for increased accountability," especially through decentralized and competitive customer services and incentives for performance (Page, 2006, p. 167). While the NPR has given way to other reforms, and other administrations, its impact on the culture of the federal government has been substantial.

The Bush administration has had its own approach to administrative reform in the federal government. In August 2001, President George W. Bush introduced the President's Management Agenda (PMA). Management and performance measurements are the main focus of PMA. Among the five areas of improvement, human capital development was the first to be emphasized. As an MBA business-oriented administrator, President Bush saw the need for competent and competitive personnel as a key to effectively delivering government services to the citizens (Breul, 2007). Agencies were given the flexibility to "use their performance management and awards programs to develop results-based elements and standards, to align employee performance plans with organizational goals and objectives, and to design recognition and incentive programs that reward employees for accomplishing those goals and objectives to develop a strong performance culture within their organizations" (Office of Personnel Management [OPM], n.d., p. 35). While Bush continued the practice of giving chief operating officers the responsibility for day-to-day operations, he strengthened the requirements for performance-oriented management, focusing primarily on the results achieved by each individual department and agency (Breul, 2007, p. 22).

In 2002, the OPM established the Human Capital Assessment and Accountability Framework (HCAAF). According to the HCAAF, each agency has to "maintain a current human capital plan and submit to OPM an annual human capital accountability report" (OPM, HCAAF, n.d.). Human capital management in every organization is followed by the level of achieving certain merit standards in five key human capital areas: (1) strategic alignment (planning and goal setting), (2) leadership and knowledge management (implementation), (3) results-oriented performance culture (implementation), (4) talent management (implementation), and (5) accountability (evaluating results). For the relationship among these elements, see Box 8.2.

BOX 8.2

HUMAN CAPITAL ASSESSMENT AND ACCOUNTABILITY FRAMEWORK

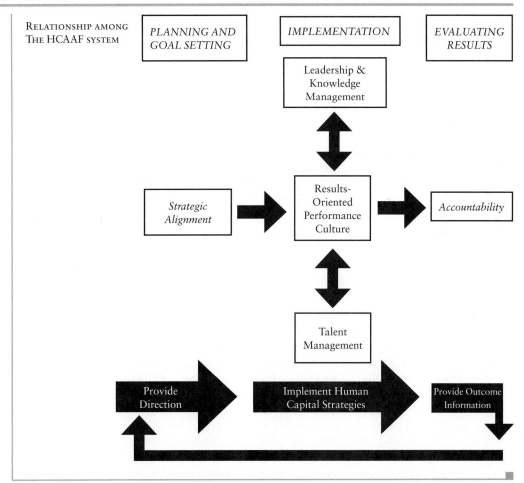

SOURCE: Office of Personnel Management (November, 2005). Relationships among the HCAAF Systems, Retrieved May 12, 2007, from www.opm.gov/hcaaf_resource_center/assets/introhcaaf_rlshps.pdf.

State and Local Personnel Systems

Many of the same problems that led to institution of the federal civil service system in the late 1800s also existed at the state and local levels—indeed, the problems were often more severe. Although the federal government was certainly influenced by politicians interested in maintaining power through patronage, it was never so completely dominated by political bosses and machines as were the states and, especially, the cities.

Even after the federal government created its civil service system, states and localities were slow to follow. New York adopted the first state civil service law in 1883, followed by Massachusetts in 1884. It was twenty years, however, before another state joined these two. By 1935, only twenty states had adopted merit systems. Today nearly all states have relatively sophisticated civil service merit systems, although those systems don't cover everyone. Even now, only about 60 percent of state government employees are covered by merit systems.

The story is much the same at the local level: Albany, New York, was the first city to adopt a civil service system (1884), and a few other cities and counties followed prior to the turn of the century, but reform came slowly at the local level. Moreover, even where formal systems were adopted, patronage practices and political manipulation of the government workforce continued. Chicago and Cook County were among the first to adopt civil service systems. Yet, even today, mayoral candidates often run on a platform of reducing machine control in Chicago. Today almost 90 percent of local jurisdictions with populations of over 50,000 have some type of merit system on the books.

What Would You Do?

A department director that reports to you has had six sexual harassment claims filed against him over the last four years. All six have been investigated but dismissed. What would you do?

Over the years, a primary motivator for adopting merit systems at state and local levels has been the number of federal laws requiring such systems in order for states and localities to receive federal funds. By 1980, every state and thousands of local governments had federal grants that required personnel systems that met a set of federal standards. The result has been that most state agencies receiving large amounts of federal funding are now covered by merit systems; those that receive limited or no federal funds are much less likely to have a merit system. In addition to these requirements, the courts have extended due process protections to many public employees and have supported affirmative action and other personnel-related actions that place greater burdens on state and local governments for detailed testing, classification, and reporting. Many states have thus found it advisable to establish or to extend merit concepts for their own protection.

Though these regulations have been somewhat relaxed in recent years, it seems unlikely that state and local governments will return to massive use of the spoils system. Indeed, there is some evidence that governments are pursuing many of the same reforms pursued at the federal level in the late 1970s, which some charge have led to greater politicization of the public workforce. For example, states and localities are experimenting with decentralization of personnel functions, greater responsiveness of managerial and political authority, and closer ties between performance appraisals and merit pay. It remains to be seen whether elected officials at state and local levels will be subject to the same temptation as were those at the federal level to employ the new devices in a more politicized approach to public personnel.

Hiring, Firing, and Things In Between

Most provisions of public personnel systems exist to protect public employees from excessive political interference; however, in some cases, they appear to make public personnel actions unduly complicated. Knowing the "rules of the game" will be a considerable help in your administrative work, and if you are looking for a job in a government agency.

Classification Systems

The key to most public personnel systems is the notion of *position classification:* the arrangement of jobs on the basis of duties and responsibilities and the skills required to perform them. A position classification system usually begins with a set of job descriptions, each based on a thorough analysis of the work and the required capabilities. A *job description* typically contains the following elements: job title, duties required, responsibilities associated with the position, and qualifications needed to carry out the job. A clerk-typist position, for example, might be described as including duties such as typing reports, maintaining correspondence records, answering telephone and walk-in inquiries, arranging for meetings and conferences on behalf of the supervisor, and other duties "as assigned." Qualifications might include a high school diploma or the equivalent, typing speed of forty words per minute, and two years secretarial experience.

Typically, sets of jobs that are closely related are then grouped together in classes that indicate increasing levels of difficulty—Clerk-Typist I, Clerk-Typist II, Clerk-Typist III, and so on. In larger jurisdictions, such as the federal government, classes may also be grouped into grade schedules that group jobs of varying levels of difficulty. For example, the federal General Schedule, which covers clerical and professional positions, lists a variety of different occupations under the grade GS-11.

Organizations use personnel classification systems for several reasons: to maintain an objective inventory of positions, to provide equity across similar jobs, to connect tasks and the skills required to perform them, and to provide standards for judging the work of specific employees. Historically, such systems developed out of a concern for objectivity and equity consistent with the idea of protecting employees from political abuse. The Position Classification Act of 1923, for example, required grouping jobs into classes on the basis of duties and responsibilities and, in language sounding much more contemporary, committed the federal government to providing "equal compensation for equal work, irrespective of sex." With this early impetus, most public organizations have developed rather sophisticated classification systems that are usually more advanced than their private-sector counterparts.

Although most people agree that the objective of current classification systems—equal pay for substantially equal work—is basically sound, many have argued that classification systems have become burdensome, inflexible, and unfair. Specifically, many argue that the complexity of the system creates excessive requirements that interfere with agency performance. The National Academy of Public Administration (NAPA) developed an alternative classification scheme that groups hundreds of federal job categories into occupational "families" based on similarities in career progression, basic skills, recruitment training, and performance measurement. Families might include such areas as general support, office services, technical, engineering, health, or law enforcement. NAPA has also recommended the adoption of broadbanding for pay classification. (In broadbanding, the upper and lower limits are defined, but the number of different levels in between is reduced.)

The Recruitment Process

Having objective statements of duties, responsibilities, and qualifications makes it possible to recruit personnel based not on who one knows, but on what one knows and what one can do. Recruitment efforts in the public sector must also be concerned with assuring fairness, openness, and representativeness. Typically, the recruitment process involves the following steps:

1. Advertising or giving notice of a vacancy to be filled
2. Testing or otherwise screening applicants
3. Preparing a list of qualified candidates
4. Selecting someone to fill the position

In most jurisdictions, a personnel officer within a particular agency or someone from a central personnel department is significantly involved in the first three steps. Testing or screening processes have been subject to special scrutiny in recent years. Screening can occur through a review of written applications and recommendations, aptitude or ability testing, performance examinations, interviews, or assessment centers. Of the aptitude or ability tests that public organizations use, some measure general knowledge, others measure personality characteristics, and still others measure specific job-related knowledge or abilities. Performance examinations, such as typing tests, measure specific job capabilities.

The method of testing should relate to the job to be filled. Though individual interviews are a common part of the hiring process, for example, they tend to be poor predictors of eventual job performance. Generally speaking, *structured interviews,* in which a previously developed set of questions is used with each applicant, and *panel interviews* which involve more than one interviewer, are preferable. Similarly, carefully constructed assessment centers using several independent raters may be used. (An *assessment center* puts several job applicants through a series of job-related simulations to observe their performance under "real-life" conditions.)

After testing or screening, a small number of eligible applicants are certified and forwarded to the hiring agency, often with rankings based on the candidates' qualifications. Most merit systems require that at least the top three names be forwarded to the agency so the manager will have some flexibility to consider personal or subjective characteristics in the final selection. This "*rule of three*" provision has proven controversial, however; many claim that it has been used as a device to discriminate against women and minorities. (Under this provision, for instance, a sexist employer could hire a male even if a woman candidate were objectively more capable.) An equally controversial provision of many merit systems requires that veterans (or sometimes even relatives of veterans) receive extra points in the ranking system. Obviously, such a provision works against the interests of nonveterans, most of whom are women; however, it is strongly supported by veterans' groups and has been upheld by the courts.

What Would You Do?

One of your employees, whose work is otherwise quite good, has annoyed many of her fellow employees with her arrogant attitude. You don't want to lose her, but her behavior is clearly bothering others and, they claim, affecting the quality of their work. What would you do?

The centralized process of recruitment traditionally underlying public personnel systems itself has come under fire in recent years. Many suggest that it places decision-making authority in the hands of human resources staff as opposed to public managers. For example, NPR recommended that federal agencies be given the power to establish their own recruitment and examining programs. The report concluded that managers in each policy area can be more effective in recognizing the skills and abilities needed to make the agency more productive and that they are in the best position to determine when to increase hiring levels.

As a result, the trend toward decentralized recruitment has gained in popularity even in larger, more diverse agencies within the federal government. Decentralized processes may rely on similar selection criteria as a centralized system, but the primary difference is that agency heads, rather than personnel managers, select the viable candidates. Those with the greatest knowledge of the policy field, therefore, choose the individuals they believe will enhance the organization. Moreover, by not having to engage in the selection process, personnel staff members are free to concentrate on broader concerns, such as diversity, affirmative action, and other factors affecting the organization.

NETWORKING

For employment opportunities in the federal government, go to the Office of Personnel Management at www.opm.gov, or USAJOBS at www.usajobs.opm.gov/infocenter/howjobsgetfilled.asp, or www.careersingovernment.com, or visit any of the federal agencies online. Those interested in employment at other levels of government can go to www.aspanet.org, the new www.PublicServiceCareers.org, or www.govtjobs.com. For nonprofit-sector jobs, go to www.philanthropy.com or www.opportunitynocs.org.

For those interested in applying for positions in the federal government, or in other levels of government, and the nonprofit sector, the Internet has become a vital resource. Applicants can complete the necessary forms and submit their materials online, and in some cases the entire recruitment process can occur without the candidate ever visiting the hiring organization. Whether it's done in person or online, be sure to submit the appropriate application materials. In some cases this may be as simple as sending in a current resume with the vacancy number and level. Usually, however, resumes should be accompanied by the proper application forms. Many recruiters will not consider application materials unless they are submitted in a style and format consistent with those called for in the vacancy announcement. (In the federal government, candidates may submit their information using forms that can be downloaded from the OPM Website.)

Pay Systems

Naturally, both the recruiting process and the individual's job performance are affected by compensation patterns, including wages and benefits. Generally speaking, pay is determined by the nature of the work and the quality of job performance. But pay plans in the public sector are difficult to construct, for they must embody two often contradictory principles. To be fair and equitable, they must be highly structured; to be competitive, they must be responsive to changing political and economic conditions.

Most large government personnel systems (including states and big cities) base their pay plans on classification systems, which usually define a series of grades, each containing a set of jobs that are comparable in terms of difficulty, and a number of steps within each grade. These steps represent approximately equal increments of pay, with the highest about 20 to 30 percent above the lowest. In most cases, the grades are slightly overlapping so the first step in one grade is equal to one of the higher steps in the grade below. Individuals are assigned to a particular grade and step depending on the position description and individual qualifications for the position.

Employees in this type of system may receive pay increases in several ways. One way is to change grades; however, for an employee to change grades, either the position would have to be reclassified or all equivalent positions would have to be moved to a higher range. For an employee to receive increases within grade, either the entire pay plan must be adjusted upward—for example, through a legislative action to improve overall pay (such as through cost of living increases)—or the individual may receive a raise. Raises can be based on several factors, ranging from seniority to merit pay (pay for performance).

The idea of *merit pay* is simply that increases in salaries and wages should be tied to the actual quality of the work being done, so that those who perform better or more productively receive greater rewards. Although governments have used various merit pay systems, such systems have not always worked well. In many cases, the money available for merit raises for a few is spread so thinly that meritorious employees aren't differentiated from others. Part of the reason for this is the difficulty of objectively measuring an individual's performance and the fact that many managers find it awkward to evaluate their employees' work.

Recall that the Civil Service Reform Act of 1978 sought to remedy this situation by requiring merit pay based on formal performance appraisal systems. Although agencies have been given considerable flexibility as to what systems they adopt, efforts have been made to base evaluations on critical elements of the individual's job or to develop results-oriented systems that tie evaluation to specific job outcomes. Any system of performance appraisal must be both accurate and fair.

> Performance-appraisal systems must be based on the real requirements of the task. They must reflect realistic levels of performance, and be couched in terms that the workers understand, while at the same time providing workers with some insights on where and how performance improvements need to be made. (Siegel & Myrtle, 1985, p. 337)

One aspect of compensation policy that has received substantial attention over the years is the comparability of wages and salaries in the public and private sectors. Efforts to make such comparisons are similar to comparing apples and oranges, thus early studies tended to show public-sector salaries considerably below those in the private sector—today ranging between 22 and 38 percent, depending on grade level. (Incidentally, the greatest differences are at top-level positions.)

Under these conditions, the federal Pay Comparability Act of 1990 required the federal government to close the gap between the public and private sectors, beginning by closing the gap 20 percent in 1993 and then 10 percent in subsequent years. Both Presidents Reagan and Bush in the 1990s cited the country's economic problems as reason to impose lower wages than those suggested by comparability studies. President Clinton, although proposing some increases, rejected the comparability targets, arguing that the law's formulas were based on flawed methodology. More recently, President George W. Bush argued that full statutory pay raises would interfere with the nation's ability to fight terrorism.

Reagan, Bush (Jr + Sr), + Clinton rejected PCA 1990 for various reasons.

Conditions of Employment and Related Matters

There are several contemporary issues in personnel management that relate either to conditions under which employees are hired or under which they must work. For example, increasing numbers of employers in both the public and private sectors are recognizing that substance abuse is responsible for greater absenteeism, higher accident rates, and generally lower productivity. Consequently, programs have been established to identify and aid or dismiss employees who have problems with drugs or alcohol.

Testing for drugs, primarily through urinalysis, has become quite common. Despite the fact that such programs violate personal dignity and have a variety of technical problems, a substantial number of private companies now use drug testing. Whereas in 1983 only about 3 percent of private firms used drug testing, today over 75 percent do so. Employees in private firms have little protection from testing and, in the absence of collective bargaining agreements to the contrary, may be tested at management discretion. Because public employees (at least civilian employees) are more clearly protected against illegal search

NETWORKING

The following sites track contemporary issues in personnel management. Many others are available—conduct your own search.

www.ipma-hr.org (International Public Management Association for Human Resources; benefits)

www.shrm.org (Society for Human Resource Management; benefits)

www.cdc.gov/hiv/pubs/facts.htm (AIDS links from CDC)

www.hr.com (general information relating to human resource management)

www.hr-guide.com (index of subjects relating to personnel management) www.lawinfo.com/index.cfm/fuseaction/Client.main (overview of sex discrimination) www.faa.gov/acr/ocr/ACR-MWE-Comm-attch.htm (diversity, affirmative action, discrimination-free)

www.careermag.com (*Career* magazine)

www.unions.org (unions listed by state and country) www.shrm.org/hrmagazine (*Human Resources* magazine)

and seizure and are guaranteed equal protection and due process, programs to test public employees have frequently been challenged in the courts. For the most part, the courts have held that random mandatory testing is a violation of employee rights, but that testing may be required where there is reasonable suspicion of abuse or where testing is made a part of the hiring process. But questions continue to be debated. For example, what type of testing is appropriate for those in "sensitive positions," such as air traffic controllers or those in contact with nuclear or chemical weapons?

Sexual Harassment

Another contemporary concern is establishing a work environment that is supportive of and sensitive to the needs of all people, regardless of gender. One aspect of this concern is sexual harassment, a topic that has received considerable national attention in the wake of several highly publicized cases. *Sexual harassment* may be defined as any unwanted and nonreciprocal verbal or physical sexual advances or derogatory remarks that the recipient finds offensive or that interfere with job performance. Sexual harassment especially includes (though is not limited to) situations in which one person in a position of power or influence uses his or her position to encourage or coerce a subordinate or coworker into undesired sexual activity, even to the point of withholding or taking away promotions or raises. The courts consider sexual harassment a type of inequality that employers must deal with, both in terms of eliminating offensive behaviors and creating a less hostile or intimidating work environment for both men and women.

Although there appear to be many instances of sexual harassment, many remain unreported. (The number of reported incidents rose dramatically during the 1990s with the increase in public awareness.) One reason for unreported cases may be the complex and often ambiguous procedures many organizations have for dealing with complaints. Most tend to be lengthy, expensive, and psychologically draining. For this reason, public organizations are currently reviewing their policies on sexual harassment, establishing more clearly the seriousness of the offense, and developing strong enforcement and disciplinary measures, including dismissal. The goal is to eliminate specific instances of harassment and create a work environment that is fully supportive of the potential of all employees. In fiscal year 2006, the federal Equal Employment Opportunities Commission received about 12,000 charges of sexual harassment, with 85 percent of those charges filed by women. EEOC resolved nearly all of these sexual harassment charges and recovered $48.8 million in monetary benefits for the charging parties (www.eeoc.gov/types/sexual_harassment.html).

NETWORKING

Two sites dealing with sexual harassment are www.de.psu.edu/harassment and www.eeoc.gov/facts/fs-sex.html.

AIDS Policy = AIDS victims Qualify under ADA: no medical basis for refusal to work w (AIDs victim)

Other issues relating to a positive work environment arise as public organizations, like others, work to protect the rights of individuals with HIV/AIDS. The Office of Personnel Management provided one of the first directives for federal agencies, setting a policy that prohibits the discrimination against employees with AIDS and that allows managers to take disciplinary action against anyone who refuses to work with an employee who has AIDS. The guidelines said that employees with AIDS "should be allowed to continue working as long as they are able to maintain acceptable performance and do not pose a safety or health threat to themselves or others in the workplace." Moreover, because there is no medical basis for refusing to work with employees with AIDS, where managers feel the refusal is "impeding or disrupting the organization's work, [the manager] should consider appropriate corrective or disciplinary action against the threatening or disruptive employees" (Havemann, 1988a, p. 34).

These considerations have become even more important with the passage of the 1990 Americans with Disabilities Act (ADA), which considers those infected with HIV/AIDS as disabled individuals. (The ADA will be discussed in more detail later in this chapter.) Consequently, many agencies are developing HIV/AIDS plans for the workplace. Despite this attention, much work remains to be done to create a positive work environment for this protected group.

Workplace Violence

In recent years, incidents of violence in the public workplace have had a dramatic effect on work environments. Although multiple murders and acts of terrorism, such as the 1995 Oklahoma City bombing, tend to capture the public's attention, other forms of violence pose an equally significant threat to workplace safety and quality. Violent crime affects organizations in all sectors; however, the government remains a primary target. In 2005 alone, the U.S. Department of Labor reported that 32 percent of all state employees reported some type of workplace violence as compared to 15 percent of local government employees and 5 percent of the employees in private industries (www.bls.gov/iif/oshwc/osnr0026.pdf).

The increase in violence over the past decade has prompted administrators to implement strategies for reducing the risk of workplace crime. While the Department of Labor reported in 2006 that 70 percent of public workplaces do not have any formal plan to address workplace violence, preventive measures include improving the physical environment, adding security and related staff, and reducing hours of operation during high-risk periods (www.bls.gov/opub/ted/2006/oct/wk5/art02.htm). However, as we noted, many public administrators have yet to realize the actual threat of violence that affects their organization. Some continue to view occupational violence as someone else's problem. Recent research on violent crime, though, suggests otherwise. The political nature of government, the deterioration in public perception of government workers, and the increase in stress loads among public employees combine to make public organizations likely targets for workplace violence.

Removing Employees

Occasionally things don't work out on the job. An employee may not live up to expectations or may become unproductive. In cases such as these, your first step as a manager is to try to improve the individual's work (a strategy that is far easier than recruiting and training a replacement). You may encourage or counsel the employee, either personally or, better, through an employee assistance program. In a surprising number of cases, you may be able to restructure the job to better motivate the employee. Concerns about an employee's work can often be addressed in positive and productive ways that are helpful to both the individual and the organization.

But if your efforts to help the employee fail, you may have to resort to disciplinary action: formal reprimands, reduction of pay, suspension without pay, or outright dismissal. In all cases, it is important to be able to demonstrate that there is adequate cause for disciplinary action. Simply firing someone for personal reasons unrelated to the job opens both you and the organization to possible lawsuits; and firing someone for political reasons is contrary to the whole concept of merit employment in the public sector.

There is a strong presumption that public-sector employees are entitled to notice and an opportunity to be heard before disciplinary action or before dismissal. This does not mean that a person cannot be demoted, suspended, or terminated but rather that the employer cannot take such action in an arbitrary way.

At the federal level, the Civil Service Reform Act encourages development of performance appraisal systems that make it easier for managers to document employee incompetence and remove them from the organization. At the state and local levels, various court cases have indicated that employees being terminated have certain due process rights, such as advance notice and the opportunity for a hearing. In any case, if you decide to pursue disciplinary action, you should build a clear case to demonstrate the underlying reasons for your action.

Personnel Reform Efforts

There have been a number of efforts to reform the federal personnel management system. Two recent experiments have underscored the importance of agency flexibility in personnel matters. In November 2002, when the Department of Homeland Security (DHS) was created, it was given authority to work with the Office of Personnel Management to create a personnel system unique to its needs. DHS responded by creating a system with more open pay ranges, performance pay pools, and specific market-based pay adjustments. Similarly, in November 2003, the Department of Defense (DOD) was asked to create a National Security Personnel System, again one unique to its needs. The flexibilities that DOD incorporated included a broadband pay system, performance-based pay, and a simplification of the employee appeals process.

Similar recommendations have come from other sources. In 2001, a National Commission on the Public Service, chaired by former Federal Reserve Chairman Paul A. Volcker, was convened to analyze and report on the state of the public service at the federal level. The Commission released its report, titled Urgent Business for America, in January 2003, commenting that "the organization of the federal government and the operation of public programs are not good enough: Not good enough for the American people, not good enough to meet the extraordinary challenges of the century just beginning, and not good enough for the hundreds of thousands of talented federal workers who hate the constraints that keep them from serving their country with the full measure of their talents and energy." In contrast the Commission made a series of recommendations to improve the quality of management of the federal government (see Box 8.3).

The Changing Character of Labor-Management Relations

An interesting issue that cuts across the field of public personnel management is the rise and decline of public-sector unions. At the federal level, many rather narrow issues, having to do primarily with working conditions, are resolved through collective bargaining, though more controversial issues, such as compensation and hiring practices, are rarely considered. At state and local levels, there is a patchwork of labor relations practices, ranging from highly restrictive to extremely permissive labor legislation.

The early development of public-sector unions was tied to the reform of the patronage system. With the establishment of merit principles in public employment, employees had greater protection from political intrusions, but they also had fewer direct ways to get the attention of political leaders. To combat the possibility that they might simply be ignored, public employees began organizing in the late 1800s and early 1900s. At first, political leaders strenuously opposed these efforts; at least two presidents issued *gag orders* to prevent federal workers from pursuing wage demands except through departmental channels. In response, the newly organized employees, led by the postal workers, pressed Congress for recognition, which they finally received in the Lloyd-LaFollette Act of 1912. The only statutory basis for public-sector unionization for more than half a century, this act permitted federal employees to join unions (that did not advocate the right to strike) and to appeal directly to Congress.

BOX 8.2

URGENT BUSINESS FOR AMERICA
THE ORGANIZATION OF GOVERNMENT:

Fundamental reorganization of the federal government is urgently needed to improve the capacity for coherent design and efficient implementation of public policy.

The federal government should be reorganized into a limited number of mission-related executive departments.

The operating agencies in these new departments should be run by managers chosen for their operational skills and given the authority to develop management and personnel systems appropriate to their missions.

The President should be given expedited authority to recommend structural reorganization of federal agencies and departments.

The House and Senate should realign their committee oversight to match the mission-driven reorganization of the executive branch.

LEADERSHIP FOR GOVERNMENT:

Effective government leadership requires immediate changes in the entry process for top leaders and the long-term development of a highly skilled federal management corps.

The President and Congress should develop a cooperative approach to speeding and streamlining the presidential appointments process.

Congress and the President should work together to significantly reduce the number of executive branch political positions.

The Senior Executive Service should be divided into an Executive Management Corps and a Professional and Technical Corps.

Congress should undertake a critical examination of "ethics" regulations imposed on federal employees, modifying those with little demonstrated public benefit.

Congress should grant an immediate and significant increase in judicial, executive, and legislative salaries to ensure a reasonable relationship to other professional opportunities.

Congress should break the statutory link between the salaries of members of Congress and those of judges and senior political appointees.

OPERATIONAL EFFECTIVENESS IN GOVERNMENT:

The federal workforce must be reshaped, and the systems that support it must be rooted in new personnel management principles that ensure much higher levels of government performance.

More flexible personnel management systems should be developed by operating agencies to meet their special needs.

Congress and the Office of Personnel Management should continue their efforts to simplify and accelerate the recruitment of federal employees.

Congress should establish policies that permit agencies to set compensation related to current market comparisons.

Competitive outsourcing should follow clear preset standards and goals that advance the public interest and do not undermine core competencies of the government.

SOURCE: The National Commission on Public Service, *Urgent Business for America.* (www.brookings.edu/gs/cps/volcker/reportfinal.pdf).

With the early emergence of unions at the federal level, a few agencies, such as the Tennessee Valley Authority, developed advanced patterns of labor-management relations; elsewhere, however, public unions emerged slowly, especially in comparison to their counterparts in the private sector. The slow development of public unions can be explained in part by several difficult questions.

First, there was the issue of sovereignty, the notion that the ultimate power to decide issues of public policy in a democracy lies with the people or their elected representatives and cannot properly be delegated, even partially, to some nongovernmental group such as a union. Illustrating this position, President Franklin Roosevelt wrote, "The process of collective bargaining, as usually understood, cannot be transplanted into the public service. . . . The very nature and purpose of Government makes it impossible for administrative officials to represent fully or bind the employer in mutual discussions. The employer is the whole people who speak by means of laws enacted by their representatives in Congress" (Klingner & Nalbandian, 1985, p. 292).

A second set of factors restricting the growth of public unions concerns the nature of governmental services, which are considered either essential to the community (police, fire, national defense) or unprofitable (systems of mass transportation). In the case of essential services, the ultimate union weapon—the strike—may be seen as holding the public interest hostage and can backfire. In the case of low-profit undertakings, the balancing factor of the market—the fact that a company may go out of business if pressed too far—does not appear to operate. In either case, the private-sector model of collective bargaining seems to apply only loosely.

A third factor limiting the growth of public-sector unions through much of this century is the varied nature of government employment and the difficulties this presents for unionizing. Traditionally, unions have organized around occupational groups, such as truck drivers or garment workers. But government employs people in thousands of occupational groups; to have a union for each group would lead to endless and unsuccessful bargaining for both sides. The federal government is also characterized by geographic dispersion (only about 10 percent of the federal workforce is located in the Washington area) and the fact that there are so many white-collar workers in government, who have been historically reluctant to organize. Thus, the question of finding an appropriate focus for union activity has been especially difficult at the federal level.

NETWORKING

For information on labor-management issues, see www.labornet.org and www.dol.gov. On specific unions, see www.afge.org and www.afscme.org.

Yet, unions have been able to organize. Sparked at least partly by the success of unions in the private sector, where the right to bargain collectively was never seriously questioned after passage of the Wagner Act in 1935, public employees continued to press for recognition of their right to negotiate labor-management disputes. Soon even the sovereignty argument was eroded; Secretary of Labor Willard Wirtz commented, "This doctrine is wrong in theory; what's more, it doesn't work" (Levitan, 1983, p. 6). Bills providing recognition for unions in the public sector were introduced (although unsuccessfully) in every session of Congress from 1949 to 1961.

Just as another such bill seemed stalled in Congress, President Kennedy took the initiative in reforming public labor-management relations by issuing Executive Order 10988 in 1962. Kennedy's order affirmed the right of federal employees to form and join unions, set up conditions under which unions would be recognized for purposes of "meeting and conferring" (*discussing*, not necessarily *negotiating*) with management on certain issues, and established limits on the kinds of issues that could be discussed. Though the order placed a great deal of administrative authority in the hands of the various agencies, it did seek some uniformity in application through the Civil Service Commission.

The Kennedy order was expanded somewhat by several executive orders during the Nixon and Ford administrations. Principally, Executive Order 11491, issued in 1969, sought a more coherent labor policy at the federal level through establishment of the Federal Labor Relations Council (FLRC) and slightly expanded the scope of bargaining. The essential items of wages and benefits, however, remained outside the bargaining process.

The next landmark in federal employee unions was the Civil Service Reform Act of 1978. Though the CSRA did little to expand areas of bargaining or to alter administration of federal labor practices (other than replacing the FLRC with a Federal Labor Relations Authority separate from the Office of Personnel Management), the act was important in that it based federal labor relations on a single, comprehensive statute rather than a series of executive orders.

Currently, some three out of every five federal workers are represented by unions, the largest of which is the American Federation of Government Employees (AFGE), a part of the AFL-CIO, which has 600,000 federal employees as members. But because Congress has refused to permit a "union shop" among federal workers, though it exists in the private sector, the actual membership of federal unions is significantly less than it might otherwise be. (*A union shop* is an arrangement under which all members of an agency are required to join the union that represents them.) The AFGE, for instance, negotiates agreements that apply to three times its actual membership. Despite that fact, however, the percentage of federal workers who pay dues to unions compares quite favorably to that among workers in the private sector; public unions have done quite well in terms of membership. Indeed, overall, public-sector union membership is higher than that in the private sector. In 2003, for example, the membership rate among public employees was almost four times that of private sector employees. While government union membership has remained fairly stable over the last thirty years, that in the private sector has declined significantly. The largest number of public employees in unions are at the local level, many in highly unionized occupations of teachers, firefighters, and police officers. (ftp://ftp.bls.gov/pub/news.release/Hirstory/union2.01212004)

At state and local levels, there is incredible variety in the kinds of labor-management relations permitted by law. Though there has been occasional talk of uniform federal statutes to govern state and local practices, the case of *National League of Cities v. Usery* (1976) seemed to indicate that states have considerable sovereignty over public employees. More recently, however, the case of *Garcia v. San Antonio Metropolitan Transit Authority* (1985) again opened the possibility of further federal intervention. But until federal legislation is passed, states will continue to exercise control over labor relations in widely varying ways. At present, some states follow the "meet and confer" model of the Kennedy program, while others establish a "negotiations" process similar to the private-sector model. Some states differentiate between state and local employees, while others differentiate among various occupational groups as well. Some states require enforced arbitration of one kind or another, and eight states permit strikes by public employees.

In all, forty-three states have comprehensive labor-relations laws, most of which are more favorable to unions than the existing federal legislation. Over the last thirty years, in fact, the two most rapidly growing unions in this country were the American Federation of State, County, and Municipal Employees and the American Federation of Teachers, both of which operate exclusively at the state and local levels.

Steps in the Bargaining Process

The first and major steps in the bargaining process are recognizing the union's right to exist, determining the type of bargaining permitted, and determining the scope of bargaining. Scope of bargaining is a source of continuing debate in many jurisdictions. Legislation may prescribe areas where negotiation is permitted, where it is prohibited, and where it is required. But the applicable legislation may range from a prohibition on negotiating wages and salaries (as exists at the federal level) to situations in which wages and salaries are at the heart of the process (as in many states and localities). Even beyond these questions, many other issues are less clear. For example, does inclusion of "work methods and procedures" in a bargaining arrangement for public schools mean that teachers can negotiate class sizes?

The typical procedure requires that organizers who wish to represent employees petition the administrative authority to establish a *bargaining unit* that will represent the employees in conferring or negotiating various issues. (The decision to include or exclude certain groups in the bargaining unit is called *unit determination*.) Whereas the traditional standard for setting unit boundaries has been to establish a "community of interests," governments have loosely applied this concept, in some cases recognizing agency-based units (the Department of Social Services or the Department of Mental Health) and in others recognizing units based on occupational classes (nurses, custodians, or security officers). After deciding on the bargaining unit, some mechanism must be established to ensure coordination among the various groups and to prevent *whipsaw tactics* (arguing that pay or benefits negotiated by one group should apply to others as well).

A similar concern is where to draw the line between managers and workers; for example, are first-line supervisors part of the bargaining unit or part of management? The importance of this issue was illustrated in the case of *NLRB v. Yeshiva University* (1980), in which it was determined that faculty at Yeshiva University, a private university, are management personnel, participating in decisions such as curricula and scheduling, and therefore outside the coverage of federal labor laws. Similar questions are raised in almost any unit determination; inclusion or exclusion of supervisors in the bargaining process varies greatly from place to place.

After appropriate bargaining units have been established, the administrative authority may either voluntarily recognize a particular union, essentially by petition, as representing a group of employees, or it may conduct an election to determine which, if any, union will represent the employees. Once a union has been recognized, it is usually granted exclusive representation of employees in the unit, including the ability to bargain on all issues required or permitted by law. (The reverse of this process, *decertification*, is rare, though it can occur.) Bargaining may then begin, typically with both sides bargaining in *good faith*—attempting to resolve the issues at hand even while following the strategy they feel will be most advantageous to them. In most cases, the bargaining process results in an agreement; occasionally it does not. Where an *impasse* occurs, there are several possibilities for resolving the issue: mediation, fact-finding, and arbitration.

1. *Mediation* involves the use of a neutral third party to attempt to work out a settlement. The work of the mediator is to assist the parties in communicating and clarifying their positions, but not to impose solutions. Though the mediator's recommendations are not binding, professional mediators are remarkably successful in helping parties reach agreements.

2. *Fact finding* employs the third party in a somewhat more investigatory and judicial role: to examine evidence on both sides of the issue, present the evidence, and, in most cases, make specific recommendations for a settlement. Some jurisdictions require making the recommendations public on the assumption that public pressure will then lead toward an agreement.

3. *Arbitration* is a form of impasse resolution involving fact-finding followed by specific recommendations that are usually binding on the parties. One form of arbitration that has received attention recently is *final-offer arbitration,* a technique in which both parties must present their best offer with the understanding that the arbitrator will choose one or the other without modification. Presumably, since both parties know that unreasonable proposals will lead to the arbitrator choosing the opposing proposal, it is in the interest of both parties to submit their most reasonable position.

To Strike or Not to Strike

If impasse resolution fails, the employee organization may consider a strike. Although most governmental jurisdictions prohibit strikes by public employees, they do occur. There are usually several hundred work stoppages in public agencies each year. These strikes raise difficult questions for public-sector, labor-management relations. Certainly public employees have the right to form associations, and one might argue that they should have the right to withhold services just as employees in the private sector do. On the other hand, the importance of public services, especially those such as fire or police protection, may justify different standards in the public sector.

Experts make the following arguments against public employee strikes:

1. Strikes violate sovereignty (conceding authority to any special-interest group contravenes the public interest).

2. Public services are essential and cannot be interrupted. In effect, all government services are vital.

3. Traditional channels of influence on public policy exist for unions: lobbying and voting.

4. Whereas strikes in the private sector are usually of an economic nature, those in the public service are political. They are strategies that use the leverage of public inconvenience to cause a redirection of budgetary priorities (Siegel & Myrtle, 1985, pp. 377–378).

On the other hand, advocates of public employees' right to strike make these points:

1. Public employee strikes occur whether or not they are illegal and regardless of heavy penalties prescribed by law.
2. In strike situations, labor-management conflict becomes channeled and socially constructive: Both labor and management gain greater understanding of each other and of the consequences of work stoppages.
3. The right to strike enhances a union's strength as a bargaining agent. Lack of the ultimate ability to withdraw services weakens labor's position at the bargaining table.
4. Many private workers doing the same work that public employees do (for example, in transit, health care, garbage collection, and communications) have the right to strike, and for many other public employees (clerks, for instance), the public consequences of striking would be little different from what they are when private-sector clerks strike.

Though strikes at the state and especially at the local level are more frequent, two landmark strikes at the federal level were especially dramatic. The postal workers' strike of 1970 occurred when members of the Manhattan-Bronx Branch of the National Association of Letter Carriers voted to strike against the U.S. Postal Service. The immediate issue was the low wage scale for carriers—a scale that left a substantial number of postal workers on welfare. Beyond this concern, the postal workers desired the right to negotiate wages and benefits, especially if the Nixon administration followed its plans to make the post office a government corporation. The strike began with about 25,000 postal workers in New York City, but soon spread up and down the East Coast and to several major cities around the country, ultimately involving some 200,000 union members. As the situation became more intolerable, President Nixon sent 27,500 National Guardsmen into New York to sort and deliver the mail. He also broke a long-standing precedent, however, and agreed to permit postal workers to bargain for wages. Following this agreement, the postal workers returned to work, most claiming victory in the strike. Eventually, the Postal Reorganization Act was passed, setting up the government corporation Nixon sought, and also providing for a bargaining pattern similar to that in the private sector.

A quite different result occurred when members of the Professional Air Traffic Controllers Organization (PATCO) went on strike in August 1981. PATCO had earlier established itself as one of the most powerful and most militant of the public unions, boasting 90 percent of the FAA's air traffic controllers as members (probably the highest percentage among federal-level unions at the time). Early in the year, the Federal Aviation Authority (FAA) was pressured into negotiating with the union concerning issues of wages and working conditions, even though it had no statutory power to do so and could only recommend wage increases to Congress. The union, arguing that the controllers were underpaid and subject to severe job stress, presented several demands, including a $10,000 across-the-board annual salary increase for the controllers and a four-day, 32-hour work week. Although the FAA did not meet these demands, Secretary of Transportation Drew Lewis agreed to support a $40 million package of improvements, including a $4,000 wage increase. However, 95 percent of the union membership rejected this proposal.

After a final round of negotiations was unsuccessful, the union decided to strike; union leader Robert Poli declared, "The only illegal strike is one that fails" (Steele, 1982, p. 38). As it turned out, this strike was to fail. What had begun as a confrontation between the union and the FAA now became a confrontation between the union and the White House.

President Reagan acted decisively, fining the union and firing nearly 11,500 striking controllers for participating in an illegal strike. Although there was severe disruption in the air transportation system for several days, new controllers were hired, airline schedules were altered, and training programs were accelerated. The situation soon gave at least the appearance of a return to normalcy. Beaten in the strike and decertified by the Federal Labor Relations Authority (FLRA), less than a year later PATCO filed for bankruptcy.

Unions Redefined

While the PATCO example has made strikes by public employees extremely difficult, unions still exert significant influence, especially at the state and local levels. But, in many ways, the character and role of organized labor has undergone a fundamental change during the last three decades, as efforts to reinvent government and reform personnel processes have redefined the ties between labor and management. In some respects, the influence of unions has been diminished by the more businesslike approach taken by government agencies. Contracting out and privatization, too, have contributed to labor's troubles, due to more and more services being delivered by private or nongovernmental organizations. The net result has been a drop not only in the power of unions, but also in some cases in the level of union membership. While some 1.1 million federal employees belong to unions, many unions have seen decreases in membership recently. For instance, although AFGE still represents more than 600,000 employees, its roster of members was cut nearly in half during the last three decades. But since a few public employee unions grew during this period, the overall trend has been fairly stable membership numbers.

What remains the same, however, is the often confrontational nature of the labor-management relationship, with many identifying collective bargaining as a key contributor to bitter contests between management and staff personnel. As a result, an adversarial climate has often prevailed. Public organizations often spend months, or sometimes years, trying to reach agreements or attempting to effectively manage existing contracts. Meanwhile, the relationship between managers and union employees becomes bogged down over what amounts to minuscule matters.

During the past decade, however, both labor and management have sought more peaceful, less adversarial alternatives to bargaining and dispute resolution. A major step toward this goal came in 1993, when President Clinton issued Executive Order 12871, which encouraged the two sides to form partnerships and take a cooperative approach to labor issues. To carry out these objectives, the order created the National Partnership Council, with representatives from public unions, management, and the Public Employee Department of the AFL-CIO. However, in 2002, President George W. Bush used Executive Order 13203 to eliminate the requirement for partnerships in federal agencies, preferring a less structured form of labor-management cooperation.

A significant recent development in labor–management relations in the federal government has been the increasing use of alternative dispute resolution (ADR). As we noted earlier, ADR was encouraged in federal legislation passed in the early 1990s and reaffirmed in the Administrative Dispute Resolution Act of 1996. ADR typically involves the use of

ADR—works + sometimes better than without

a neutral third party, often a mediator, who can help the disputing parties arrive at some agreement, short of imposing legal remedies. In addition, ADR may involve conciliation, problem solving, dispute panels, fact finding, and facilitation. While ADR is not intended to replace more traditional approaches, it often can lead to solutions that are not only quicker and less costly, but have significant buy-in from the parties involved. The Bureau of the Treasury's Engraving and Printing Bureau began using ADR in 1997 and, in its first five years, processed over 165 cases with an estimated cost avoidance of 3 to 4 million dollars (www.opm.gove/er/adrguide_2002).

Change in labor-management relations also has been targeted in the culture and leadership styles that characterize public organizations. Many public agencies have opted for a more participatory form of management, thus precluding the legalistic, not to mention lengthy, process of collective bargaining. Administrators work to dismantle bureaucratic hierarchies and distribute power throughout the organization. Public employees enjoy a more meaningful form of empowerment than could ever have been facilitated through traditional channels. The result is a more effective and productive organization.

Of course, such an alternative does not completely resolve the issue. The structural factors that pit the two sides against each other, for the most part, remain in place. Public unions still hold a level of power in government personnel administration, and the gains made on behalf of workers through lobbying and court decisions continue to influence the administrative process. However, the relationship is changing. Though the direction of this change remains to be seen, reform of the system and the search for alternative forms of communication between labor and management appear necessary.

■ Correcting Patterns of Discrimination in Public Employment

Whereas civil service systems have traditionally emphasized the concept of "merit" in public employment, other values have become increasingly important. Most prominent is a concern for correcting patterns of discrimination in hiring and treatment of workers in public agencies. The two terms that have been central to that debate are "*equal employment opportunity*" and "*affirmative action*." Equal employment opportunity refers to efforts to eliminate employment discrimination on the basis of race, ethnic background, sex, age, or physical handicap. It simply seeks to ensure that all people have an equal chance to compete for and hold positions of employment based on their job qualifications. Affirmative action, on the other hand, involves the use of "positive, results-oriented practices to ensure that women, minorities, handicapped persons, and other protected classes of people will be equitably represented in the organization" (Hall & Albrecht, 1979, p. 26).

The concept of equal opportunity has a firm basis in constitutional and legal history, but the primary piece of federal legislation guiding current practices is the Civil Rights Act of 1964. (Many states had passed equal employment legislation in advance of the federal act.) Title VII of the Civil Rights Act banned employment discrimination in areas such as selection, promotion, and training based on race, national origin, sex, or religion and created the Equal Employment Opportunity Commission to investigate complaints of discrimination in the private sector. In 1972 the act was amended through the Equal Employment Opportunity

Act to extend coverage to all public-sector employees (at the federal, state, and local levels) and to provide for stronger actions, including filing suits, against those who did not comply with the act.

The original Civil Rights Act did not require affirmative action to correct past patterns of discrimination; this requirement was included in an executive order issued by President Johnson. Executive Order 11246 sought to secure compliance with the Civil Rights Act by requiring that federal contractors not discriminate on the basis of race, creed, or national origin and that they develop affirmative action programs leading to equal employment practices. President Johnson's Executive Order 11375 later added women to the list of protected groups and specified requirements for affirmative action plans.

These requirements were first applied to federal contractors, but were soon adopted elsewhere in government and the private sector. The Civil Rights Act of 1964 had declared "that it shall be the policy of the United States to ensure equal employment opportunities for federal employees," but it was an executive order issued by President Nixon in 1969 that required agency heads to create "affirmative programs" in eliminating patterns of discrimination (Shafritz, Hyde, & Rosenbloom, 1981, pp. 185–186). Similarly, state and local governments were brought under the provisions of the Civil Rights Act in 1972 and were threatened with loss of federal funds in the event of noncompliance. Title IX of the Higher Education Act of 1972 was interpreted to require universities to provide equal athletic opportunities for both sexes in intercollegiate sports; the penalty was withdrawal of federal funds from universities found not in compliance.

During the past two decades, however, there has been a waning of support for equal employment opportunity programs. Beginning in 1984, with the Supreme Court's ruling in *Grove City v. Bell* (1984), limits on the applicability of civil rights legislation have been the source of considerable controversy. In *Grove*, the Court narrowly interpreted the law as it regarded sex discrimination to mean that federal funds were to be restricted from the particular program receiving funds rather than from an educational institution as a whole. This meant that if an English department was found guilty of discrimination, its federal funds would be cut off, but funds to other parts of the institution would not be.

Obviously, the effect of the *Grove* case was to severely limit enforcement power of the federal legislation dealing with sex discrimination, and, by implication, similar legislation dealing with discrimination based on race, age, or handicap. Barely a week after the *Grove* ruling, for example, the Department of Education dropped charges against the University of Maryland's athletic programs because they did not receive federal aid—though the institution as a whole received substantial federal funding in scholarships, research money, and so on. Not surprisingly, legislation was soon introduced in Congress to put teeth back into the various civil rights laws. The Civil Rights Restoration Act, passed by an over-whelming bipartisan majority, applies not only to educational institutions, but also to a wide range of other public and private organizations receiving federal funds.

The Civil Rights Restoration Act, in many respects, proved to be the last of Congress's progressive stances on civil rights. Since then, equal opportunity legislation has come under fire from a conservative judiciary (for example, *Kimel v. Florida Board of Regents* [2000] and *University of Alabama v. Garrett* [2001], which will be discussed in more detail), as well as from a conservative trend in legislatures at all levels of government. The result has been a shift in the balance of power toward employers and away from those petitioning on the grounds of discrimination (see Box 8.4).

ADA

In 1990, the Americans with Disabilities Act was passed. The purpose of the ADA is to prohibit discrimination against 43 million Americans who live with some type of disability. Beginning in 1992, the ADA prohibited employers of twenty-five or more people from discriminating against those with disabilities who can satisfactorily meet the expectations of the job they hold or seek, with or without reasonable accommodation. A disabled person must be qualified, meet educational and skill requirements, and be able to perform the essential functions of the position. However, the employer is required to make reasonable accommodations to the work environment so the disabled person can perform to the best of his or her ability (Bishop & Jones, 1993, p. 122).

With respect to public services, the ADA prohibits excluding a person from participating in programs or activities of a public entity or denying an individual benefits of its services. A public entity is defined to include not only the federal government but any part of state or local government. Other sections of the act deal with transportation, public accommodations, and telecommunications.

Although the ADA has substantially changed both employment patterns and the design of public facilities, a recent Supreme Court decision dealt a major blow to the enforceability of

BOX 8.4
THE COURTS AND EMPLOYMENT DISCRIMINATION

Employees of state governments cannot file suit against their employers on the grounds of discrimination, in this case under the ADA, since suits of this nature abrogate state governments' immunity under the Eleventh Amendment.

Age discrimination in employment is not a suspect classification under the Equal Protection Clause, so states may discriminate on the basis of age without violating the Fourteenth Amendment, as long as the age classification is related to state interests.

Broad-scale programs aimed at promoting affirmative action rejected by federal courts; instead affirmative action programs must be limited to specific conditions and circumstances.

University of Alabama v. Garrett (2001)
Kimel v. Florida Board of Regents (2000)
Hopwood v. University of Texas Law School (1996)
Bakke v. The Regents of the University of California (1978)
United States v. Paradise (1987)
Johnson v. Transportation Agency (1987)

the law. In *University of Alabama v. Garrett* (2001), the Court reviewed a petition brought by employees of the state who claimed to have been discriminated against under the ADA. The Court ruled against the plaintiffs, stating that suits of this nature abrogate states' immunity under the Eleventh Amendment. In doing so, the Court effectively blocked the rights of state employees to file suit for monetary damages in federal court for discrimination under the ADA.

Questions of Compliance

Early efforts to prove discrimination against an employer required proof of "evil intention": evidence that the employer was knowingly discriminating. The difficulty of proving intent led to a new focus on "unequal treatment": proof that an employer used different selection procedures for different groups or used the same procedure in different ways. Still, under this definition, minorities made little progress entering the workforce.

In 1971, however, the Supreme Court, in *Griggs v. Duke Power Company,* settled on a new definition: *adverse or disparate impact.* The *Griggs* decision held that it was no longer necessary to prove discriminatory motive or differential treatment; it was simply necessary to show that employment practices affect one group more harshly than another. The Court stated, "Practices, procedures, or tests neutral on their face, and even neutral in terms of intent cannot be maintained if they operate to 'freeze' the status quo of prior discriminatory practices" (Hays & Reeves, 1984, p. 354).

The notion of adverse impact has been articulated more fully in a set of *Uniform Guidelines* agreed upon by federal agencies. Under the Uniform Guidelines, employers are required to keep records indicating the relationship between those hired and minorities, including women, and the comparative success of various groups in selection for a position. If, for example, women constitute 50 percent of the labor market, yet only 20 percent of the workforce are women, there is evidence of adverse impact. (Actual figures show that about 41 percent of employees in local government are women, 41 percent in state government are women, and 43 percent in federal government are women. Women are disproportionately represented in lower-paying positions, such as secretarial or clerical jobs.)

The guidelines also follow another aspect of the *Griggs* case. Employers whose practices are found to have adverse impact are required to demonstrate the *job relatedness* of tests or procedures used in hiring or promotion decisions. That is, if a screening test cannot be shown to relate specifically to job performance, then it cannot be used as a criterion in making employment decisions. Elimination of the Professional and Administrative Career Examination (PACE) is a classic case of the job-relatedness issue. In a court challenge, it was ruled that the PACE exam, at that time the primary test given to applicants for federal managerial positions, was not related to the eventual jobs these people would hold and had an adverse impact on African Americans and Hispanics. For this reason, the exam was shelved.

A conservative shift in the Supreme Court, however, led to an end in these protective standards. In *Wards Cove v. San Antonio* (1989), the court reversed the *Griggs* interpretation of Title VII and ruled that plaintiffs, not employers, must substantiate their position in discrimination cases. In particular, the court deemed unconstitutional the earlier ruling that allowed the establishment of a prima facie case based on the "four-fifths rule"—that is, when minority hires constitute less than 80 percent of the nonminority hires. Although the Wards Cove packing plant paid minority employees less and segregated their living and dining quarters, justices said that the workers would have to prove that such practices created a gap between the percentage of minorities actually employed and the percentage in the workforce.

Federal lawmakers tried repeatedly to counter the Wards Cove ruling and restore the more progressive provisions of *Griggs*, finally adopting the Civil Rights Act of 1991. In many respects, though, the act only confused the issue of Title VII protection. Progressive critics argued that too much had to be sacrificed to gain the act's approval. Although it contained several important provisions, such as extending the definition of discrimination to personnel decisions other than hiring and promotion, the act still placed in the court's hands the final decision on what can be considered discrimination in the workplace.

Consequently, the courts have continued to narrow the bounds on what constitutes discrimination. The Supreme Court's decision in *University of Alabama v. Garrett* (2001) was discussed previously, but another example of this trend can be seen in *Kimel v. Florida Board of Regents* (2000). In *Kimel*, the Court considered a challenge to the Age Discrimination in Employment Act (ADEA) that allows suits to be filed against state governments for monetary damages on the grounds of discrimination in employment decisions. The case was filed by three sets of petitioners in Florida, who claimed to have experienced discrimination on the basis of age during the employment process. However, the Court not only ruled against the plaintiffs, but also criticized Congress for passing the ADEA in the first place. The Court held that (1) "age is not a suspect classification under the Equal Protection Clause, and so states may discriminate on the basis of age without offending the Fourteenth Amendment, if the age classification in question is rationally related to a legitimate state interest," and (2) Congress had "failed to identify a widespread pattern of age discrimination by states, and it concluded this failure confirms that Congress had no reason to believe that broad prophylactic legislation was necessary in this field" (Wise, 2001, p. 348).

The long-term impact of the *University of Alabama v. Garrett* and *Kimel* decisions remains to be seen, but the immediate effect is that the burden of proof now lies with the plaintiff on matters of discrimination. Moreover, given the underlying message in the Court's rulings, it appears that even the statutory foundation of equal opportunity employment has come under scrutiny, leaving us to wonder if our days of formal protection against discrimination may be numbered.

Burden of Proof w/ plaintiff in discrimination.

Affirmative Action and Reverse Discrimination

Another area of intense controversy involves attempts to correct past patterns of discrimination against minorities and women through the use of *affirmative action programs*. Such plans typically include (1) a statement of policy indicating a commitment to correct discrimination in employment practices, (2) an analysis of existing practices and their results, and (3) a statement of goals to improve those practices.

Unfortunately, a great deal of popular and legal confusion has developed around the notion of goals and quotas, often resulting in charges of *reverse discrimination* against white males. Although quotas require hiring specific numbers of people from specific groups (and

Quotas in Action →

are rarely used in actual practice), goals or timetables are intended to be flexible and are to be established internally by the employer. Both goals and quotas may involve numbers (and this causes some of the confusion), but the goals are merely intended to show a direction in which an employer wishes to move. Generally, a good faith effort in that direction will be viewed as satisfactory in terms of providing opportunities for equal employment.

Even the Supreme Court has found it difficult to clarify exactly what is acceptable and what constitutes reverse discrimination. In *Bakke v. The Regents of the University of California* (1978), the Supreme Court ruled that it was illegal for a university to reserve a specific number of slots in its medical school for minority applicants who were less quali-fied than other students who were rejected. The Court agreed that race could be consid-ered one factor in an admissions decision, but only one among several.

On a slightly different issue, the Court held in *United Steel Workers of America v. Weber* (1979) that a training program that admitted black workers before white workers with more seniority was acceptable. The key here seemed to be that the company initiated the program voluntarily to eliminate obvious patterns of discrimination and that it did not necessitate the discharge of white workers (Stewart, 1983). On the other hand, in *Firefight-ers Local Union #1784 v. Stotts* (1984), the Court held that a lower court could not order an employer to lay off more senior employees in favor of less senior employees on the basis of race to preserve a specific percentage of minority employees. The emerging consensus, reflected in such recent cases as *United States v. Paradise* (1987) and *Johnson v. Trans-portation Agency* (1987), seems to be that affirmative action programs will be limited to specific needs and circumstances. Broad-scale programs are not likely to be accepted.

More recently, federal courts have begun to hear challenges to affirmative action programs used by universities to increase student diversity. The Supreme Court sought to clarify the use of race in admissions in two University of Michigan decisions. In *Grutter v. Bollinger* (2003) the court upheld the law school's policy of narrowly tailoring the use of race in admissions policy, but the same Court upheld *Bakke* in *Gratz v. Bollinger* (2003) that the use of a point system awarding minorities extra points in undergraduate admis-sions was illegal given that it, in effect, was a quota system.

Given this trend, as well as the increasingly conservative view in Washington and in many states, as evident in California's Proposition 209 (1996) that ended affirmative action programs, the future of affirmative action seems questionable. Some suggest that although preferences and so-called set asides leveled the playing field, they no longer offer what the nation needs to ensure a diverse workforce. Unfortunately, the discourse on the issue often degenerates into political rhetoric with both sides losing sight of an impor-tant principle: that is, not only must all people have an equal opportunity to serve but also that the distinct contribution made by each person must be appreciated. By pursuing an agenda to enhance diversity, organizations may gain important contributions from a broader range of viewpoints.

A few alternatives have been offered for promoting and sustaining diversity, including several strategies that target the underlying culture of organizations. The process begins with creating a shared sense of purpose toward diversity, then empowering those at all levels to contribute action steps for achieving this goal. Periodic assessments can be used to determine how successful the organizational change has been and to identify any future barriers the group may need to overcome.

The Glass Ceiling

Unfortunately, extending diversity throughout the organization, especially at the highest levels of management, has proven difficult. Although the representation of women and minorities in the federal workforce has generally improved along with their representation in the middle- and upper-management levels, certain groups remain underrepresented in the overall workforce, and white women and all minorities remain underrepresented in the key jobs that lead to middle- and upper-management positions. Similarly, at the state and local level, about 41 percent of government employees are women, but they still fill only 27 percent of the management positions.

The "glass ceiling" encountered by many women and minorities has been recognized in several recent studies. Data from OPM revealed that "women were promoted less than men who had comparable amounts of formal education and experience and who entered government at the same grade levels as the women; and women face obstacles to advancement at lower levels in the pipeline. For those women who have advanced, it usually meant staying late, relocating, or working longer hours" (Desky, 1992, p. 1). Recognizing these concerns, the Civil Rights Act of 1991 set up a "glass ceiling" commission to study the barriers to the advancement of women and minorities in the private sector.

However, efforts to remove the "glass ceiling" have been thwarted by similar trends affecting affirmative action, and only rarely does the issue of equitable treatment for women in the workplace receive its share of the national spotlight. Congress in 2000 addressed the issue by passing the Equity Contracting for Women Act, which encourages contractors to do business with women-owned businesses in industries where women are underrepresented. The downside of the legislation is that it relies mainly on market forces to achieve parity, meaning that firms are not obligated to contract with women contractors.

The result of these trends is that despite some gains made by women to achieve equal treatment, they still experience a significant gap in pay, job status, and overall employment opportunity. Recent figures show that more women are becoming entrepreneurs now; in the period between 1997–2002, the number of women-owned companies increased by 14 percent nationwide (Kephart and Schumacher, 2005, p. 11). About 18.5 million employees work for women, meaning that every fourth employee works for a woman. The pay gap in 2006 has closed to about 78 cents to each dollar earned by men. However, the largest gap is for women age 55–65 as compared to men of the same age group (73 cents for each men's dollar earned). The smallest gap is for women age 65 and over (81 cents for each men's dollar earned) (www.bls.gov/cps/cpswktabs.htm). But supporters of women's rights argue that these figures, rather than marking a significant improvement for women, tend to be used more as ammunition for lawmakers who want to end affirmative action and other civil rights programs.

The political debate in Washington, and in communities across the country, has shifted so far away from any type of "set asides" or "preferential treatment" that even advocates for women find themselves sidestepping the labels outright in their efforts to lobby for new legislation. In fact, even some advocates for protection on the basis of race, sexual preference, and other factors have turned away from protection of women, arguing that women have achieved equal opportunity and that continuation of affirmative action would not only provide an undue advantage but would soon negatively affect women's self-perception.

Political Appointee–Career Executive Relations

The tension between political responsiveness and managerial effectiveness that characterizes public management is especially well illustrated in the relationship between political appointees and career executives. Each newly elected administration, whether at the federal, state, or local level, has a certain number of top-level managerial positions to fill with people of its choosing. These appointees become the "bosses" of career civil servants who staff the various agencies of government. As you might imagine, there is occasionally some tension between the two groups. Incoming presidents are usually elected on a platform of change and view career employees as representing opposition to change. The political executive wants to move in new policy directions, but often has little experience in government operations; the career executive, on the other hand, has both knowledge and expertise, but, aware of potential problems, may appear reluctant to change.

At the same time, the legality of using political appointments, or patronage, for certain kinds of positions has been challenged in the courts. Political patronage practices were declared unconstitutional by the U.S. Supreme Court in three cases between 1976 and 1990. In *Elrod v. Burns* (1976), the Court held that the Sheriff's Office of Cook County, Illinois, could not fire employees because of their political affiliation. It would be a violation of their First Amendment rights to freedom of belief and association. Similarly, in *Branti v. Finkel* (1980), the Court found that assistant public defenders in Rockland County, New York, could not be terminated because of their party affiliation. These protections were extended to include politically motivated transfers, promotions, recalls from layoffs, and hires in *Rutan v. Republican Party* in 1990. The only exception to this prohibition against patronage is when a position can be shown to have partisan affiliation as a necessary requirement for effective performance. As a practical matter, this still allows appointment of political executives, but curtails the use of noncivil-service appointments for other types of employees.

What Would You Do?

You are the top civil service official in a large federal agency. The new administration has just appointed the cabinet secretary and her top political appointees. You want the agency to work well but are afraid that the new appointees, all drawn from large corporations, may not understand how government works and may make some mistakes that could be damaging to some of your most important programs. What would you do?

In any case, sorting out the relationship between politically appointed executives and career executives brings us back to the old question of politics and administration. One interpretation suggests that the role of the career executive is solely to execute orders given by superior authorities—elected officials and their app\ointees. In the most extreme formulation of this view, the career executive should be isolated from any involvement in policy development and should concentrate on implementing policies handed down from above.

In contrast to this extreme position, career executives and many others find another interpretation of the politics-administration issue more appealing. This view holds that there are important reasons for career executives' involvement in policy development. Certainly, career executives have the background and expertise to contribute substantially to developing practical and effective public policies. In addition, these executives are likely to be more effective in implementing policy if they have been involved in developing it, if they understand the need for policy changes, and if they feel some sense of "ownership" of the new policies.

Political appointees, on the other hand, generally come to government with relatively little knowledge about their subject matter (at least compared to career bureaucrats) and certainly with little understanding of how policies are developed in a governmental setting. While the average tenure of career civil servants is over thirteen years, political executives last an average of only eighteen to twenty-two months. If the stereotype of the bureaucrat is one of hostility to any change, the stereotype of the political appointee is someone brash, inexperienced, and intent on bringing about change.

There appear to be at least three areas in which further improvements might be made in the relationship between political appointees and career executives. First, political appointees must receive the training and orientation they need to effectively manage public organizations and to work with career executives both in developing and implementing policies. Second, an exchange of views between political leaders and careerists, including team-building sessions, may help to develop greater understanding between the groups and forge more effective working relationships. Third, Congress should reassess the structure of executive management in government and make whatever structural changes are needed to establish a more balanced political-career interface. But the basic dilemma continues: The political appointee must make sure that the bureaucracy is responsive to the policy directives of the current president; the career executive must maintain high standards of professionalism so that the work of the organization is carried out in the best way possible.

■ Summary and Action Implications

Personnel systems in the public sector have evolved in response to a variety of competing demands. Much of the earliest personnel legislation at the federal level was directed toward ensuring a neutral and competent bureaucracy protected from the potentially corrupting influences of politics. More recent efforts have sought greater responsiveness on the part of the bureaucracy to political leadership. Personnel systems in the public sector—like systems of budgeting and financial management—reflect important, though sometimes changing, values.

The development of merit systems of public employment reflects such concerns. At the root, policies governing recruitment and classification in the public sector reflect the fact that public organizations must, by definition, operate in the public interest. Similar concerns significantly affect the way contemporary issues such as conditions of employment (drug testing, etc.), labor-management relations, and pay equity are played out in the public sector.

As a manager, you must be concerned with recruitment, training, and retention of the best possible people to work in your organization. You may often feel that public personnel systems and the people who monitor them are simply roadblocks to effective management. Fortunately, in many jurisdictions, the relationship between manager and personnel officer is shifting in a more positive direction.

Personnel managers have been given the responsibility of protecting the merit system from abuse by maintaining detailed records of personnel transactions and enforcing personnel rules and procedures. Personnel officers have thus often been placed in the position of exercising control over the activities of program managers. But public personnel officers, like their private-sector counterparts, have always had another role as well—helping managers employ and utilize personnel effectively.

Although this service aspect of the personnel officer's role has often been treated as a secondary function, there is every reason to believe that the more progressive personnel systems will increasingly emphasize this aspect. Increasingly, personnel officers are shifting from the traditional emphasis on compliance to a new emphasis on consultation. In this role, those in personnel will be available to help with human resource management questions of all kinds. For example, a personnel specialist might be called in to help develop a productivity improvement program or to advise on legal questions. As this new orientation becomes established, line managers will tend to view the personnel officer more as an ally than as a protagonist.

Consequently, you are likely to be more effective as a public manager if you are able to develop a good understanding of the technical details of personnel transactions and an effective working relationship with the personnel professionals in your agency. The support of trained experts in the field of personnel management can help improve your organization's performance and, in turn, its service to the public.

TERMS AND DEFINITIONS

Adverse or disparate impact: Criterion for showing that employment practices affect one group more harshly than another.

Affirmative action: Use of positive, results-oriented practices to ensure that women, minorities, handicapped people, and other protected classes of people will be equitably represented in an organization.

Bargaining unit: The organization that will represent employees in conferring and negotiating various issues.

Equal employment opportunity: Refers to efforts to eliminate employment discrimination on the basis of race, ethnic background, sex, age, or physical handicap; ensures that all people have an equal chance to compete for employment and promotions based on job qualifications.

Final-offer arbitration: Technique in which both parties must present their best offer with the understanding that an arbitrator will choose one or the other without modification.

Job description: A thorough analysis of the work to be done and the capabilities for a job; typically contains these elements: job title, duties required, responsibilities, and job qualifications.

Lateral entry: Entry into government positions at any level.

Merit pay: Increases in salary and wages that are tied to actual quality of work performed.

Merit principle: Concept that selection and treatment of government employees should be based on merit or competence rather than personal or political favoritism.

Position classification: Analyzing and organizing jobs on the basis of duties, responsibilities, and knowledge and skills required to perform them.

Rule of three: Provision of most merit systems that requires at least the top three applicants' names to be forwarded to the hiring official to allow some flexibility in selection.

Sexual harassment: Any unwarranted and nonreciprocal verbal or physical sexual advances or derogatory remarks that the recipient finds offensive or that interfere with his or her job performance.

Spoils system: The ability to give government jobs to the party faithful; "to the victor belong the spoils."

Structured interviews: Those in which a previously developed set of questions is used with each applicant.

Unit determination: Decision to include or exclude certain groups in a bargaining unit.

Whipsaw tactics: Argument that pay or benefits negotiated by one group should be applied to others.

STUDY QUESTIONS

1. "To the victor belong the spoils" was a phrase used to define the spoils system for filling vacancies of government jobs. Discuss the historical use of this system and its contemporary manifestations.

2. What was the Pendleton Act, and how did it help to reform federal personnel procedures?

3. Explain the basic principles of the civil service system.

4. Discuss some of the basic problems President Carter faced regarding personnel/civil service reform.

5. The Civil Service Reform Act provided for various changes in personnel procedures. Explain the importance of this legislation and discuss the impact of major provisions on the civil service system.

6. What are some of the criticisms of the Civil Service Reform Act?

7. List the steps in recruiting for a government position.

8. Identify various methods of testing and screening applicants.

9. Discuss government methods to combat discrimination in employment activities.

10. What are some of the tools governments use to ensure compliance with equal employment opportunity regulations?

11. With changing labor-management relations, public unionization has become an issue. Explain the factors public managers must recognize to unionize the public sector.

12. Discuss the major components of the bargaining process.

13. Identify arguments against strikes by public employees and give a few examples of strikes that have occurred.

14. Discuss the relationship between political appointees and career executives and how it might be improved.

CASES AND EXERCISES

1. Consider the following case: You are Steve Style, a programming director in a large city's data-processing department. You manage five sections of computer programmers, each made up of a senior programmer and three to four trainees. The department generates computer systems for the other city departments, thus requiring you and your staff to spend a lot of time with the users of the systems. Your staff has a reputation throughout the city for being highly professional. For some time, your boss, Isabel Info, has been talking about the need to expand the programming staff by adding a database administrator.

   A few months ago, a new police chief was hired, brought in from another city. In the past, when a new department head came in, if he or she were married, the spouse also found a job somewhere in city government. You had heard that the police chief's wife has a degree in computer science. On Monday, Isabel calls to tell you she has just hired Theresa Topcop as the database administrator in your area. Isabel is happy to get someone with Theresa's education and background, which includes working for several software companies. Isabel also tells you that Theresa is the police chief's wife and that she will be making more money than any of your current senior programmers.

Excited about the addition of a database administrator, you go to tell the staff about the program expansion. Rather than the positive reaction you had expected, theirs is quite negative. David Denman, the most experienced programmer, is upset for two reasons: First, isn't she the police chief's wife? It sounds to him like a deal was made. And second, why didn't any of the current staff have a chance to interview for the new position? Another staff member leaves the meeting grumbling about how much money Theresa will be making in comparison to the other senior programmers.

You go back to your office trying to figure out how to deal with this problem. You're looking forward to having a database administrator, and from what Isabel tells you, Theresa is well qualified. You are concerned about the staff's reaction. You know you will face an uphill battle to convince the users that Theresa is qualified for the position.

- As a practical matter, how does an administration deal with the problem of a "qualified spouse"?
- How do you justify to your staff the fact that Theresa is making a higher salary than any of them and that they didn't have the chance to interview for the position?
- How does the personnel office handle this problem in light of the city's civil service system?

SOURCE: The preceding case was provided by Perri Lampe.

2. Through contacts with the U.S. Office of Personnel Management, the state's personnel office, and the city's personnel office, learn as much as you can about finding employment in a government agency in your area. Ask the following questions.
   - What kinds of positions are typically available?
   - What should you expect in terms of the salary range for entry at the bachelor's or master's level?
   - What benefits and salary increments are associated with these positions?
   - What is the hiring process (how do you apply; what types of tests or interviews are required; who makes the final decision)?

   In addition, contact a variety of nonprofit organizations in your community or a representative of the American Society of Association Executives to discuss career possibilities in the nonprofit sector. Make your report available to students on campus through your academic department and through your school's placement center.

3. Obtain a copy of your school's policy (or policies) on sexual harassment regarding administrators, faculty, staff, and students. Based on conversations with knowledgeable faculty and other school officials, as well as your own reading and research, analyze the policy in terms of the following questions.
   - Does the policy define sexual harassment in terms that are generally understandable?
   - Does the policy specify particular types of actions that will be considered harassment?
   - Are there clearly defined procedures through which charges of harassment can be brought and heard?

- Are there specific penalties, including dismissal from the school, for prohibited actions?
- Has the policy been employed in actual cases with success?
- Does the policy act as a deterrent to sexual harassment?
- Are there training programs or other educational materials available to help administrators, faculty, and students understand the issue of sexual harassment specifically and gender sensitivity more generally?
- What would you suggest to strengthen, clarify, or more easily enforce the policy?

SOURCE: The preceding exercise was adapted from material provided by Charles Sampson of the University of Missouri-Columbia.

4. Form small groups to complete the following exercise.

You have just accepted membership on the Energy Resources Commission Recruitment Task Force. This task force was recently created by the newly elected governor. The purpose of the task force is to develop recruitment strategies to staff the ERC, which has just been established to fulfill the following functions.
- Determine the future energy needs for the state
- Develop strategies to meet these needs
- Provide technical assistance to the public utilities and agencies involved in meeting these needs

Special recruitment problems are anticipated because this is a completely new agency that will require a significant number of professional and technical personnel. The task force has been charged with the responsibility for developing specific action plans to recruit the required personnel over the next three years. The ERC will require approximately 250 employees by the end of this three-year period, in the following categories.

1. Management and management staff (50 employees)

2. Clerical support staff (65 employees)

3. Professional/technical personnel (100 employees)

4. Blue-collar/maintenance-type personnel (35 employees)

Factors that may or may not complicate the recruitment effort include the following.

1. The primary sources of employment in the state are in agriculture, mining, and transportation.

2. The population of the state totals 10 million, but almost 40 percent of the population resides in a single upstate metropolitan district.

3. The political environment has traditionally been characterized by conflict between upstate Democrats and downstate Republicans.

4. This political competition has produced extensive reliance on patronage as the means for staffing most public agencies.

5. Control of state government has just shifted to the Republicans after twelve years of Democratic control, but one of the new governor's major campaign promises was to professionalize the personnel system and expand civil service coverage to most state employees.

6. During the campaign, the governor also committed himself to hiring within the state whenever possible.

7. The state is currently involved in two employment discrimination lawsuits: one brought by the National Organization for Women and the other by the NAACP.

8. Racial minorities compose 15 percent of the population, but most of these individuals reside in the upstate metropolitan area.

9. Of the total state workforce, 22 percent are women and 4 percent are classified minority.

10. The unemployment rate for the state is 12 percent, but most of the unemployed reside in the upstate area.

11. The unemployment rate by occupational class is as follows: 18 percent blue-collar, 7 percent white-collar, and 3 percent professional/technical.

12. The unemployment rate for minorities is 21 percent, and the rate for women is 16 percent.

13. Public-sector unionization is in its early stages of development in the state. Unions are competing for membership and becoming more and more militant. A key demand, which is currently before the legislature, is to establish an "agency shop" for public utility employees.

14. Citizens' groups and professional associations actively lobbied for the creation of the ERC.

15. The ERC is being partially funded by a federal grant-in-aid program that, in addition to requiring 50 percent matching funds from the state, also requires establishment of a merit system to ensure nondiscrimination in employment.

The task force is to design a specific recruitment strategy to meet all the staffing needs of the new Energy Resources Commission. Besides paying particular interest to the preceding characteristics, you might also consider the following in your deliberations.

1. Need and approach for determining the commission's specific staffing requirements.

2. Characteristics of the labor market geographically and by occupational field.

3. Level and availability of the state's labor resources.

4. Extent of search process for candidates geographically and occupationally; type of institutions/organizations/agencies to be covered in recruitment process.

5. Qualification standards (education, training, work experience, residency, physical characteristics, and so on) that should be required for each occupational category in the commission.

6. Implications of these standards for the recruitment effort.

7. Selection devices (practical or aptitude tests, credentials examination, interviews, and so on) and their effect on recruitment.

8. Whether recruitment should be for specific jobs or for a career (and the implication of this decision for qualification standards, selection devices, and so on).

9. Recruitment approaches for each occupational category—for example, job announcements, written brochures and materials, recruitment visits (and institutions that will be covered, if any), use of professional/collegial contacts (whose?), and so on.

10. Consideration of the factors to emphasize to prospective candidates (that is, what would be the attractive aspects of a job/career in this agency in this locale?).

FOR ADDITIONAL READING

Beaumont, P. B. *Human Resource Management: Key Concepts and Skills*. Newbury Park, CA: Sage Publications, 1993.

Capozzoli, Thomas, and R. Steven McVey. *Managing Violence in the Workplace*. Delray Beach, FL: St. Lucie Press, 1996.

Cayer, N. Joseph. *Public Personnel Administration in the United States*. 2nd ed. New York: St. Martin's Press, 1986.

Coleman, Charles J. *Managing Labor Relations in the Public Sector*. San Francisco: Jossey-Bass, 1990.

Cooper, Phillip J., Linda P. Brady, Olivia Hidalgo-Lardeman, Albert Hyde, Katherine C. Naff, Steven Ott, and Harvey White. *Public Administration for the Twenty-First Century*. Fort Worth, TX: Harcourt Brace College Publishers, 1998.

Dresang, Dennis L. *Public Personnel Management and Public Policy*. Dallas: Pearson Publications, 1999.

Farnham, David. *Managing People in the Public Service*. Basingstoke, U.K.: Macmillan Business, 1996.

Goldstein, Irwin L. *Training in Organizations: Seeds Assessment, Development, and Evaluation*. 3rd ed. Pacific Grove, CA: Brooks/Cole, 1993.

Guy, Mary E., ed. *Women and Men of the States*. Armonk, NY: M. E. Sharpe, 1992.

Huddleston, Mark, and William Boyer. *The Higher Civil Service in the United States*. Pittsburgh: University of Pittsburgh Press, 1996.

Ingraham, Patricia, and Carolyn Ban, eds. *Legislating Bureaucratic Change: The Civil Service Reform Act of 1978*. Albany: State University of New York Press, 1984.

Jackson, Susan E., ed. *Diversity in the Workplace: Human Resource Initiatives*. New York: Guilford Press, 1992.

Kearney, Richard C. *Public Sector Performance Management, Motivation and Measurement*. Boulder, CO: Westview Press, 2000.

Klingner, Donald E., and John Nalbandian. *Public Personnel Management*. 5th ed. Englewood Cliffs, NJ: Prentice-Hall, 2002.

Lane, Larry M., and James F. Wolf. *The Human Resource Crisis in the Public Sector: Rebuilding the Capacity to Govern*. New York: Quorum Books, 1990.

Maranto, Robert, and David Shultz. *A Short History of the United States Civil Service*. Lanham, MD: University Press of America, 1991.

National Academy of Public Administration. *Modernizing Federal Classification: An Opportunity for Excellence*. Washington, DC: National Academy, 1991.

Nigro, Lloyd G., and Felix A. Nigro. *The New Public Personnel Administration*. 4th ed. Itasca, IL: F. E. Peacock Publishers, 1993.

Pynes, Joan E. *Human Resources Management for Public and Nonprofit Organizations*. 2nd ed. San Francisco: Jossey-Bass, 2004.

Risher, Howard, Charles H. Fay, et al. *New Strategies for Public Pay*. San Francisco: Jossey-Bass, 1997.

Robinson, Dana Gaines, and James C. Robinson. *Performance Consulting*. San Francisco: Berrett Koehler Publishers, 1995.

Selden, Sally Coleman. *The Promise of Representative Bureaucracy*. Armonk, NY: M. E. Sharpe, 1997.

Shafritz, Jay M., Albert C. Hyde, and David H. Rosenbloom. *Personnel Management in Government: Politics and Process*. 4th ed. New York: Marcel Dekker, 1991.

Sloane, Arthur A., and Fred Witney. *Labor Relations*. 8th ed. Englewood Cliffs, NJ: Prentice-Hall, 1994.

Sylvia, Ronald D. *Critical Issues in Public Personnel Policy*. Pacific Grove, CA: Brooks/Cole, 1989.

CHAPTER 9

LEADERSHIP AND MANAGEMENT SKILLS IN PUBLIC ORGANIZATIONS

All the ideas and approaches we have examined are helpful in understanding what is going on in public and nonprofit management. But putting those ideas into practice requires the ability to lead and work effectively with other people. Ideas about what leadership is, who can be a leader, and the roles that leaders serve have changed over time. While early perspectives on leadership focuses on those holding top-level positions, more modern views recognize that leadership can and should be exercised at all levels of organizations. By carefully considering and constantly practicing good leadership, you can become more effective in whatever position you occupy in an organization.

Effective leadership and management involve decision making, communication, self-awareness, the ability to motivate others and manage group dynamics. It should be recognized, however, that leadership and management in practice is often complex and fluid, demanding both a strong skill set and enormous flexibility. For instance, you may be called upon to up a situation and take appropriate action, often within a matter of seconds. As a leader, you will necessarily and appropriately analyze and understand the situation in terms of your own approach or theory. But you will also have to act and engage with others in decision making. In doing so, you need to have the ability to influence others and to exercise power constructively and responsibly.

Putting ideas into action not only requires that you have the ability to make decisions and delegate tasks, but to do so in a manner that energizes and engages others. Doing so requires both confidence and self-awareness. Employees look to leaders not only for direction, but also for cues about how to feel about their work and their part in achieving organizational goals. Interestingly, however, successfully exercising these leadership skills depends on several essential "personal" skills that are a part of one's social and psychological makeup. Some of these personal skills reflect your approach to the world, others have to do with your capacity for creativity or effective decision making, and still others have to do with how you deal with ambiguity or lack of clarity. For example, the manager suddenly promoted to the directorship of the mental health department will certainly have important (and immediate) decisions to make perhaps involving creative solutions to organizational problems left by the departing director. The new manager will also have to be able to operate, perhaps for months, in a highly ambiguous situation.

■ Leadership and Power

Many commentators have argued that improved leadership is essential for us to successfully meet the challenges of the coming century. Public opinion data reveal widespread loss of faith in the leadership of business, government, labor, and other private and public institutions. But many argue that the problem relates not merely to formal positions of power; rather the failure of leadership is pervasive throughout society. Effective leadership sometimes involves the use of power. The capacity to understand power, especially the capacity to recognize and use the resources one has available to influence others, is essential in modern organizations of all types. But power is a far narrower term than leadership. We will consider power as one aspect of the larger question of how one might develop greater skills in public leadership.

Early leadership studies attempted to identify and understand the attributes of "great men." Such approaches focused on the personal characteristics of existing or historical leaders, assuming that leaders were "born, not made." These so-called "trait studies" were reviewed by Ralph Stogdill in the 1940s, who found that although leaders do appear to possess traits that make them different from other people, there was a lack of agreement about exactly what were those traits (1948). For example, some of the studies that Stogdill reviewed had found that leaders were more intelligent and active, others found that leaders were taller and more dependable. Overall, Stogdill concluded that leaders encouraged cooperative behavior, were sensitive to others, exercised initiative, and had self-confidence (1974). But, having those traits did not necessarily mean that you would be an effective leader.

Although the trait approach to leadership offered some insights, it became evident over time that it left a number of important questions unanswered. For example, beyond personal characteristics, what did leaders actually do? Why was it that the same leaders might be effective in one situation but not another? These questions led researchers to focus on the behavior of leaders and the exercise of leadership in particular contexts. One of the more important studies of leadership behavior was initiated at The Ohio State University in the 1940s. Leadership was conceptualized as based on two types of behaviors. The first type was called "consideration" which was behavior focused on relationships and concern for others. The second type was called "initiation of structure" which was behavior aimed at task definition and completion (Bass 1990). A similar study at the University of Michigan referred to these same sets of behaviors as "employee orientation" and "job or production orientation." Based on these dimensions, Blake and Mouton (1964) came up with a Managerial Grid which plotted behaviors associated with production and people on a scale of 1 to 9. The ideal in their model was to be a "9.9" manager—that is, to have a high concern for both people and production.

Other researchers began to focus on the context of leadership, trying to match different types of organizational situations with the appropriate mix of leadership behaviors. One such "situational" leadership model was developed by Hersey and Blanchard (1988). In this model, the key to assessing a situation was the readiness and ability of the follower to accomplish a particular task. For example, a person lacking in ability needs the leader to use high task behavior to provide instruction and guidance. Then, once that person begins to show a willingness to try, the leader should be encouraging using high relationship behavior. On the other hand, a person who is ready and willing to accomplish a task, needs neither high task or high relationship behavior—in this case, the leader should just get out of the way!

NETWORKING

For different perspectives on leadership, visit the James MacGregor Burns Academy of Leadership at www.academy.umd.edu, the National Initiative for Leadership and Institutional Effectiveness at www.ced.ncsu.edu/ahe/nilie, or the Centre for Advanced Studies in Leadership at www.casl.se.

More contemporary perspectives on leadership embrace the idea that leadership is not just the responsibility of those in the executive suite, but can and should be exercised throughout an organization. John Gardner, the former cabinet secretary and founder of Common Cause, stated, "In this country leadership is dispersed among all the segments of society and down through all levels, and the system simply won't work as it should unless large numbers of people throughout society are prepared to take leaderlike action to make things work at their level" (Gardner, 1987). In this view, leadership is a pervasive phenomenon occurring in families, work groups, businesses, and at all levels of government, society, and culture. Leadership, then, should be seen not merely as a position someone holds, but rather as something that happens in a group or organization, something that comes and goes, something that ebbs and flows as the group or organization does its work.

As we have seen, modern society can be described as (1) highly turbulent, subject to sudden and dramatic shifts; (2) highly interdependent, requiring cooperation across many sectors; and (3) greatly in need of creative and integrative solutions to problems. Under such circumstances, ambiguity is increasingly a hallmark of decision making, and the involvement (rather than the control) of many individuals in group decisions will be necessary. "Leadership . . . will become an increasingly intricate process of multilateral brokerage, including constituencies both within and without the organization. More and more decisions will be public decisions; that is, the people they affect will insist on being heard" (Bennis, 1983, p. 16). Leadership for the future cannot be equated merely with the exercise of control by those in formal positions of power.

So what do we know about leadership, especially shared or public leadership? What do we know about leadership in the increasingly common situations where no one is really "in charge"—student organizations, churches, political groups, and so on? Often, much of their work is done through committees or other even less formal groups. And those committees seem to waste a lot of time and energy, partly because of lack of leadership. Even though one person may be designated the "leader," rarely does he or she exercise much control. Usually, things drift for a while—maybe a long while—until someone finally puts forth a suggestion that people pick up on and get excited about. At that point, we can say that someone has exercised leadership.

Somewhat more formally, then, we can define leadership as "the character of the relationship between the individual and a group or organization that stimulates or

Leaders energize the group (handwritten margin note)

releases some latent energy within the group so that those involved more clearly understand their own needs, desires, interests, and potentialities and begin to work toward their fulfillment" (Denhardt & Prelgovisk, 1992, pp. 33–44). Where leadership is present, something occurs in the dynamics of the group or organization that leads to change. What is central to leadership is the capacity of the leader—whether or not called a leader—to "energize" the group.

What Would You Do?

The state government division that you head is going through several significant changes in a very short period of time. You are moving to a new location and at the same time embarking on some major new programs. All of this is occurring in a year in which your staff has been substantially reduced by retirements and transfers and you are in the midst of hiring replacement personnel. It promises to be a really difficult year, filled with change and uncertainty. You want to make things go as smoothly as possible for your staff. What would you do?

Leadership involves helping the group become aware of a new direction in which to move.

The leader merely taps and reshapes the "consciousness" of the group. Acts of leadership express a new direction, but one that is determined by the emerging interests of all members of a group. We can say that one exercises public leadership who (1) helps the group or organization understand its needs and potential; (2) integrates and articulates the group's vision; and (3) acts as a "trigger" or stimulus for group action. The essence of leadership, therefore, is its "energizing" effect. But often the people we formally refer to as leaders don't really lead; at best, they "manage" things successfully by keeping the group running more or less smoothly.

To energize the group, for example, the leader must know how to "sense" its underlying desires, sometimes even before those desires are clear even to the group members themselves. The leader must also be able to act in ambiguous situations and to take risks; leadership involves change, and change is often difficult for both group and leader. Developing the personal strength to face change is important. Leadership has often been viewed in terms of the exercise of power by one person or group over another—getting people to do what one wants them to do by manipulating power and influence. Leadership in the future will be more and more independent of power, and the most critical leadership skills will be the personal (rather than interpersonal) skills associated with correctly empathizing with and "reading" a group, acting with a sense of direction in the presence of ambiguity, and having the courage to take risks when change is warranted.

Sally Helgesen calls this new approach "grass-roots leadership." She argues that today's organizations differ dramatically from those created in past generations. Power becomes shared throughout the group and, in turn, leaders "are to be found not only among those at the top, the 'lead horses,' but also among those who constitute what in the industrial era we called the rank and file" (Helgesen, 1996, p. 21). Accordingly, each individual plays a key role in shaping the organization; each helps the group deal with issues of organizational change.

In fact, although power may be an important resource to the leader, one need not exercise traditional power to bring about change (see Box 9.1). Efforts to control a group are often ultimately destructive of leadership. On the other hand, when the direction of the group or organization is selected through a developmental process that gives priority to group members' needs and desires, leadership is much more likely to be enduring. Leadership, in this context, relates more to sharing power among the group rather than using power for the purpose of control. So for the new knowledge-based organizations

---

BOX 9.1

BASES OF SOCIAL POWER

Power is really much more complex than we often think. For example, the power we exercise is based on a number of different factors that operate in social situations. A classic research article describes the following "bases of social power":

1. *Reward power.* The ability to meet the needs of another, or control the other by rewarding the desired behavior. Pay, promotions, or bonuses may be ways that organizations exert reward power over employees.
2. *Punishment power.* Coercive power, or the ability to deliver a painful or punishing outcome to others, and hence control them by their desire to escape the punishment. Firing, ridiculing, or disciplining an individual are common techniques of punishment.
3. *Expert power.* Power based on the ability to understand, use, and deliver information that others need. Engineers or scientists may exert great influence in an organization based on their knowledge of scientific techniques for manufacturing a product, and so forth.
4. *Legitimate power.* Control or influence exerted by virtue of one's holding a particular position in the organizational structure. The "power" is vested in the rights and responsibilities of the position, not the person. Thus, a company president or chairman of the board has power by virtue of the rights and responsibility given to whoever holds the office. Compliance with legitimate power occurs because other individuals in the organization respect the organizational structure and the rights and responsibility that accompany particular positions.
5. *Referent power.* Liking, charisma, or the desire to comply with someone's wishes because you are attracted to him or her are examples of referent power. Control based on referent power depends on the power-holder's ability to have others like and be attracted to him or her, and to follow his or her leadership because of this attraction.

SOURCE: Adapted from John R. P. French, Jr., and Bertram Raven, "The Bases of Social Power," in Dorwin Cartwright and Alvin F. Zander, eds., *Group Dynamics*, 2nd ed., New York: HarperCollins Publishers, 1962. © 1962 by Dorwin Cartwright and Alvin F. Zander. Reprinted by permission.

[handwritten marginalia: Leadership = doing the right things, right]

of today to be successful, greater autonomy and decision-making capacity should be distributed to the front line, with those closest to the situation serving as the leaders of change.

Perhaps most importantly, leadership is not just about doing things right, but about doing the right things (Bennis & Nanus, 1985). In the public sector particularly, the goals sought by leaders inevitably involve important public values. Public leaders, at all levels, must play a "transformational" role in helping people to articulate and act on shared ideals and values within the context of democratic governance. Transformational leaders understand and support the needs of followers, work with them to define and seek higher-level needs, and engage followers as whole people. "The result of transformational leadership is a relationship of mutual stimulation and elevation that converts followers into leaders and may convert leaders into moral agents" (Burns, 1978, p. 4). In fact, leadership in the public sector involves not only attention to the needs and values of those within the organization, but also the values and preferences of citizens.

Communication

All the good ideas in the world are worth very little if they cannot be shared with others. Communication is the basis for setting goals, engaging others, and ensuring cooperation. Hales (1986) found that between two-thirds and four-fifths of a manager's day is spent giving or receiving information, and that most of this giving and receiving takes place in face-to-face interactions. In fact, the ability to communicate well is necessary for any adult to function successfully in virtually any role in American society. Indeed, research has shown that, on the average, adult Americans spend 70 percent of the waking day in some form of communication activity (Rankin 1929). He classified how people spent their communication time and found that 9 percent of the time was spent writing, 16 percent reading, 30 percent speaking, and 45 percent listening. We will discuss the communication modes of listening, speaking, and writing. (We will not address reading, except to note that the special skill known as "speed reading" is probably one a manager might find useful.)

Listening

We spend time listening more than any other form of communication. Recent research focusing exclusively on managers reveals that managers spend a greater than average portion of their time listening—about 63 percent of a typical day. But doing a lot of listening does not mean that managers listen well. Listening is not the same as hearing, and although hearing cannot be altered without medical or technical intervention, one can substantially improve the quality of one's listening with proper motivation and training. Let us first review some basics of effective listening (see Box 9.2).

BOX 9.2

PRINCIPLES OF EFFECTIVE LISTENING

1. Have a reason or purpose.
2. Suspend judgment initially.
3. Resist distractions.
4. Wait before responding.
5. Rephrase what you listen to in your own words.
6. Seek the important themes.
7. Use the thinking-speaking differential to reflect and find meaning.

Have a Reason or Purpose This is the most important principle of those we will discuss. Having a purpose or a reason to listen provides the motivation to listen, and, generally speaking, you will do things you are motivated to do better than if you are not motivated. Listening is no exception. One must be motivated to listen well; it does not just happen. Without motivation, you will not use the other six principles, or you will not use them as well as you could.

But, you ask, what if I don't have a reason to listen? In such cases, it is a good idea to actively search for a reason to listen to what is being said. Ask yourself, "How can this information help me do my job better?" or "How can I use this information in some way, on the job or elsewhere?" Finding a reason to listen will provide the motivation to use all the other principles and techniques.

Suspend Judgment Initially The key word in this phrase is "initially." You will obviously need to evaluate the material you listen to, but you should wait until you hear the entire message before you begin the evaluation. This can be difficult. In an election year, for example, if we know a particular candidate's party, we are likely to evaluate what the candidate is going to say before he or she even begins speaking. It is not coincidental that television and radio advertising for many candidates does not prominently identify the candidate's party. The advertisers want to increase the chances of having the message heard rather than losing half the audience immediately by identifying the speaker as a Democrat or a Republican. To make a judgment before listening carefully to what someone is saying is the opposite of the "suspension" principle.

Resist Distractions Many things can distract us when we are trying to listen. The "distraction" principle tells us to fight back, to actively resist whatever may be distracting us. Among the many things that distract us, various sounds are usually the most powerful. The sound may be a nonverbal noise, such as the siren from a passing fire engine or ambulance; the voices of several people speaking at once; or something about the way the speaker talks. Regardless of what type of sound is creating the distraction, the remedy is to resist, to try harder. In this case, "trying harder" means that you should increase your concentration. If you are in a face-to-face situation with a speaker, make sure you maintain constant eye contact. You can also lean a little bit in the direction of the speaker. By increasing your level of concentration, you can resist distractions you would have thought impossible to overcome. And that is the problem with distractions—they become an excuse for not even trying to listen because "It's impossible to hear what she's saying."

A common classroom demonstration in listening skills illustrates the "distraction" principle (as well as others). Two volunteers are positioned in front of the class, about fifteen feet away from each other. Each reads aloud a brief paragraph (that only takes thirty to forty seconds to read). Each student in the class is assigned to listen to one or the other of the volunteers, but not to both. The students are instructed not to take notes while the paragraphs are being read, but at the end of the reading they are to write down something about each of the major points in the paragraph they listened to. The trick is that each volunteer not only reads a different paragraph, but they read them simultaneously! After the first round of the exercise usually only a small number, and sometimes none, of the students in the class are able to write down something about every major point their speaker read. The instructor then reviews the eye-contact and leaning points, picks two new volunteers, gives them two new paragraphs, and repeats the exercise. The second time around it is not unusual to find that 20 percent to 25 percent of the class has written down something about each major point. This exercise demonstrates that there is variability in the quality of listening, both between and within individuals. It also shows that it is possible to resist even a major distraction, that our ability to resist distractions is much higher than we realize, and that we can overcome a great deal to improve the quality of our listening.

Some distractions are less obvious and are perceived only semiconsciously. One such distraction for many Americans is listening to English spoken with a foreign accent or with a different regional accent. Professor Allen Bluedorn recalls learning this in a listening course that he took while he was in the U.S. Army. Bluedorn wondered if he had been using people's accents as an excuse not to listen to them. (He was stationed at Fort Bliss in El Paso, Texas, and frequently heard English spoken with a Spanish accent.) He tested his theory by concentrating harder the next time he conversed with someone with a Spanish accent. To his surprise, he found that he clearly understood everything the person said. He concluded that he had indeed been succumbing to the distraction of the accent, and it had become an excuse not to listen well. This lesson is important in today's increasingly multicultural organizations, where English is often spoken with a wide variety of accents. But the larger and more important lesson is that even substantial distractions can be overcome.

Wait Before Responding   The "response" principle suggests that one relax and wait for natural opportunities to speak instead of jumping into the conversation immediately. When we are burning to contribute to a discussion, we may get so excited about what we want to say (as soon as we get the chance) that we don't listen to the person who is speaking. The "response" principle suggests that one wait for a natural opportunity to contribute; try to flow with the conversation as an event rather than interrupting.

Rephrase What You Listen To in Your Own Words   The "rephrasing" principle suggests an incredibly simple, yet powerful, way to check one's understanding. The idea is merely to take something you hear (an opinion, instructions, and so on) and put it into your own words. You then repeat it to the person who gave you the information and ask if that is what was meant. As easy as it seems, this is an excellent way to check understanding and avoid mistakes. When you give instructions, you can ask the person who is receiving them to do the same thing. You can say, for example, "I'm not sure I explained that very well. Please tell me what you got out of that."

Seek the Important Themes The "thematic" principle indicates that the main ideas are more important than facts—so important that they are the general keys to understanding and retaining what is said. Understanding the main ideas provides a framework for organizing the facts, which makes the facts themselves easier to remember.

The man usually credited with starting the listening movement over thirty years ago, Ralph Nichols, demonstrated this point in his research. He discovered that A and B students reported different listening habits than C and D students. In surveys of hundreds of students, he discovered that the A and B students gave a much different response to the question "What do you listen for first when you attend a lecture?" than did the C and D students. The A and B students predominantly gave a response like "I listen for the main ideas first," whereas C and D students said, "I listen for the facts." (This finding probably does not entirely explain the differences in these students' GPAs, but it is undoubtedly part of it.)

Use the Thinking-Speaking Differential to Reflect and Find Meaning The "meaning" principle reflects the fact that people think faster than they speak. Although it varies by region, people in the United States speak at a rate of about 150 words per minute, but in terms of language, they think at a rate of about 500 words per minute. Thus, we normally think more than three times faster than we speak. This differential creates an opportunity to listen more effectively, but the opportunity can also be a temptation to do things that interfere with our listening. The extra time can also be used for things that distract from the listening process—concentration lapses, daydreaming, thinking about something other than what the speaker is saying, and so forth. All of these can interfere with good listening, so extra time can be a two-edged sword—both opportunity and temptation.

Listening is both the most widely used and most widely misused communication skill. It is also the skill least often taught in the American education system at all levels (Steil, Barker, & Watson, 1983).

Speaking

Most of the speaking that managers do is informal, one-on-one or small group communications in their offices, on the phone, and in meetings. To demonstrate how we can improve our speaking, we will focus on giving instructions, because a significant amount of manager-initiated communication consists of giving instructions to others. The managerial activity of delegation, in fact, would be virtually impossible without being able to properly give instructions. The key to doing so successfully is the ability to put yourself in the position of the person who is getting the instructions. Ideally, you want to give exactly the right amount of information–neither too much nor too little. (If one must depart from the ideal, however, it is usually better to give too much rather than too little.)

[handwritten marginalia: Not too much, not too little information.]

These two questions can help you put yourself in the position of the individual to whom you are giving the instructions.

1. What does the person *need* to know to carry out the instructions? *[handwritten: Get it done]*
2. What does the person *want* to know to carry out the instructions? *[handwritten: Don't insult.]*

The ability to decide what information is necessary is, incidentally, a justification for promoting from within—making managers out of those who have done the jobs they will be managing. People who have done the job should be able to determine more accurately what their subordinates need to know when they receive instructions. Unfortunately, not everyone who is promoted to the management level takes full advantage of this knowledge.

[handwritten marginalia: – Doing a job helps one manage others doing that job → what they need to know]

To demonstrate how difficult it is to identify what information to transmit, we'll look at another classroom exercise on how you can put yourself in the position of the person who will be receiving the instructions. Students form pairs, and one member of each pair is given a diagram. The students are seated back to back, and the one with the diagram gives the other one instructions for drawing the diagram on a piece of paper. Only the instruction giver is allowed to speak and may not look at the partner's drawing. After the drawing is completed, it is evaluated with a set of scoring rules. The partners then switch roles, a new diagram is used, and verbal instructions are again given to a draw the diagram.

It has been found that the scores in the second round are usually higher than those in the first, even if the second diagram is more complex. Why? The answer seems to be that the instruction giver in the second round has been in the position of receiving instructions already and thus has a better idea of what information is really helpful. Furthermore, the instruction givers during the second round know the scoring rules and can focus on what elements of the diagrams will be scored when the copies are evaluated. Most important, however, the instruction giver who understands what information someone needs is better able to provide that information.

Writing

Writing is a less common form of managerial communication than speaking and listening, but it is important nevertheless. Most managerial writing is brief, often one or two pages. The memo is the most common type of written communication for many managers. Sussman and Deep (1984) offer six rules for effective managerial writing that they call the "Six Cs."

1. *Clarity.* To be clear, one must put oneself in the reader's position—much as the instruction giver must put himself or herself in the receiver's position. Write in the active voice (such as, Dave painted the house) rather than the passive (such as, The house was painted by Dave); avoid jargon; and try to use the simple format of introduction, body, and conclusion.
2. *Courtesy.* Courtesy involves knowing your readers, adapting to their moods, and writing at their level, providing neither too much nor too little information. Again, there are clear parallels with instruction giving.
3. *Conciseness.* This is the rule of brevity: Be short and to the point. Sometimes you may want to repeat something for emphasis, but the general rule is the shorter the

better. Think of it this way: Which are you more likely to read—a fifty-word memo or a ten-page report? You are likely to read the fifty-word memo on the spot; the ten-page report goes into the "when I get a chance" pile.

4. *Confidence.* Always write with confidence. Confidence is really a matter of the writer's judgment, based on one's knowledge of one's readers. Judgment is especially important in avoiding two extremes: overbearing (too confident) and wishy-washy (not confident enough).

5. *Correctness.* You must be correct in grammar and composition, the technical rules of writing that include spelling and punctuation. Inaccurate spelling is especially conspicuous.

6. *Conversational tone.* To achieve a conversational tone, write the way you talk, and try to imagine one specific person to whom you are writing. Thinking of a specific individual rather than an abstract category makes it much easier to write. (It is much easier to write to John Jones than to "all economics professors.") Occasionally, conversational writing calls for violating some formal rules of grammar, but this breach can make things smoother, more understandable, and easier to follow.

Communication will affect nearly every aspect of your work as a public manager. Your ability to persuade others of your position, your clarity in sharing ideas, and your ability to deal effectively with difficult people will shape your image as an administrator (see Box 9.3). Fortunately, you can improve your ability to listen, to speak, and to write. So, practicing your communication skills whenever possible will pay dividends whatever your career.

■ Delegation and Motivation

Management can be defined as "the process of getting things done through others." To get things done through others, it is necessary to communicate with others and, often, to motivate them as well. Much of the time, those "others" are the people you supervise. After all, if you can do all the work yourself, you should just go ahead and do it. As a manager, however, you are not there to do the actual work but to do the managerial work.

BOX 9.3

SECRET WEAPONS FOR ORGANIZATIONAL COMMUNICATION

Here are several methods for dealing with difficult situations in the work setting.

1. Remember that people do things for their own reasons, not yours. Someone's anger may mean he or she actually sees the situation from a completely different perspective, so try to understand that view.

2. When under attack, use a calm, even tone of voice and low-key body language. The content of what you say can be the same—just modify your delivery; in face-to-face communication, words carry 7 percent of your message, tone of voice 38 percent, and body language 55 percent.

3. Use conversational fantasy to anticipate a really sticky situation by saying exactly what you want to say. Then tone it down to what you know you should say.

(Continued)

(Continued)

4. Remember to rehearse so that you are prepared to cope with the situation when it arises. Practice receiving and returning "verbal hardballs."
5. If necessary, use emotional jujitsu. The principle of jujitsu is to flow with your opponent's strength, to turn his own force against him by redirecting it rather than resisting it. Rather than defending yourself, agree. Your critic will be instantly disarmed, and then you can begin to deal with the causes of the emotion rather than the emotion itself.

SOURCE: Excerpted from "Personal Productivity: Organizational Communication," *Government Productivity News* 3 (September 1989): p. 4.

Delegation

Delegation is the process of assigning tasks to others. Like so many other managerial tasks, it may be done poorly or it may be done well. As Fraser Parks discovered, poor delegation can be nearly fatal. To delegate well, you need to try to delegate an equal amount of authority and responsibility for a job. Authority is the legitimate power to do the job, and responsibility is the accountability the individual has to you for getting the job done. The idea that an individual should have equal amounts of both is the *parity principle.* Managers often complain that they will be held responsible for something, but have not been given enough authority to get the job done. Less frequent, but equally troublesome, is an individual who has authority but is not held responsible for its use.

Generally speaking, you should delegate jobs with complete and clear instructions, and you should delegate tasks to the appropriate level. Holding everything else equal, the appropriate level is the lowest level in the hierarchy where the task can be accomplished competently. You should also provide support for the delegated tasks. This support can take many forms, including delegation of authority in a public statement (such as saying at a meeting, "Betty is in charge of inspections in the northern district now").

It is often helpful to involve subordinates in the process of delegation, encouraging them to make suggestions about the kind of work they can or should be doing. Delegation should be a two-way process. On the other hand, do not fall victim to the upward delegation phenomenon. Upward delegation occurs when subordinates bring problems to their managers that the subordinates should be solving themselves. This is the opposite of effective delegation, and you should refuse to take on such problems. An effective technique is to insist that any subordinate who wants advice about an issue (the way the upward delegation attempt is often presented) should first think of at least one potential solution before coming to you to discuss it. To allow for creativity and motivation in the delegation process, it is best to hold subordinates accountable for results and leave the "how" up to them. This principle assumes, of course, that the "how" will be within the constraints of legal and ethical behavior as well as the constraints of public or organizational policies. Finally, tasks should be delegated consistently when the workload is light as well as heavy and when the jobs are fun as well as unpleasant.

Besides getting things done through others, delegation helps to develop employees, thereby making them more valuable to you and to the organization. Some managers are threatened by the idea that they may be developing possible replacements (that is, competitors). But there is another way to look at this situation. Unless you are at the very top of the organization, you probably want to be promoted. But you cannot be promoted if you cannot be replaced. Developing your subordinates through delegation is a way of providing, to your advantage, your own potential replacements!

Motivation

Whether members of an organization perform well depends partly on ability and partly on motivation. A person must already possess or be able to learn the right mix of skills and abilities to do a job and must be motivated to do the job well. When you can help develop your employees' skills through instruction, training programs, and so forth, you are likely to have a significantly greater impact on their motivation.

Pay and Job Satisfaction When one thinks of motivation in a managerial context, monetary compensation is a subject that naturally comes to mind. Frederick Taylor (1923) based the entire incentive system of his scientific management program on economic factors. Contemporary thinking about motivation is more sophisticated than Taylor's, however, as pay is seen to interact with other motivators in complex ways.

Even as early as the 1950s, Frederick Herzberg developed a model of motivation known as the *two-factor theory*. Herzberg (1959) argued that two sets of variables were relevant to the question of motivation: "hygiene factors," which impact job dissatisfaction, and "motivators," which impact job satisfaction.

Hygiene factors included variables such as pay and working conditions; motivators were factors such as chances for achievement, recognition, and advancement. Herzberg argued that improvements in hygiene factors such as pay would not increase job satisfaction; instead, any improvements would simply reduce dissatisfaction. If an individual's pay got worse or did not increase fast enough, dissatisfaction would increase. Conversely, motivators such as achievement or advancement would not affect dissatisfaction, but would increase or decrease job satisfaction. The lesson for managers was that motivating employees is a far more complex task than simply changing salary levels.

Other approaches to motivation were based on psychologist Abraham Maslow's theory of human development, the assumption that everyone has a need to grow and develop and to establish a sense of meaning in his or her life. Maslow (1954) suggested a *hierarchy of needs* that all human beings must fulfill. At the first level, we must meet our physiological needs for food, clothing, and shelter. Next we have a need for safety and security. Beyond these basic needs, we have social needs, which we meet by being a part of a group. Then we have a need for ego satisfaction and self-esteem. Finally, at the highest level, we have a need for development or self-actualization. This final level, which can only be reached after the other four levels have been achieved, describes that state of psychological development through which we reach our greatest human potential.

Controversy about the effect of job satisfaction goes back at least as far as the Hawthorne studies conducted during the mid-1920s and early 1930s. Recall from Chapter 5 that these studies began as a research project to investigate the effects of physical working conditions, such as lighting, on workers' productivity. Given some unexpected findings early in the studies, the investigators changed the focus of the research to investigate the impacts of social and supervisory variables on performance. Some authors interpreted the results of the later studies as indicating that higher levels of job satisfaction led to higher levels of worker performance, a conclusion that some argue was never present in the original research reports and is thus a misinterpretation (Organ, 1986). But misinterpretation or not, the Hawthorne studies are usually credited for the "discovery" that a "happy worker is a productive worker." Other studies of the job satisfaction–performance relationship produced mixed results. Some theorists argued that the job-satisfaction-leads-to-better-performance thesis was wrong in terms of the causal ordering—that it was actually the other way around, with higher levels of performance causing higher levels of job satisfaction.

Although there is still not complete agreement on this issue, support is accumulating for a third interpretation of the job satisfaction–performance relationship: that there will only be a relationship between job satisfaction and performance if the rewards one receives are based on one's performance. If rewards are based on performance, there should be a positive correlation between job satisfaction and performance (the higher the performance, the higher the job satisfaction) because higher performance will lead to higher rewards, which will produce higher job satisfaction. If this is true, one part of the manager's job will be to make sure that performance is directly linked to rewards—monetary as well as others. One method to achieve this linkage is reinforcement theory.

Reinforcement Theory   Reinforcement theory and related approaches have been given various labels, including behaviorism, operant conditioning, stimulus-response psychology, and Skinnerian psychology. All of the labels refer to more or less the same thing: an approach to explaining behavior based on Thorndike's law of effect, which states, "Of several responses made to the same situation, those which are accompanied or closely followed by satisfaction (reinforcement) . . . will be more likely to occur; those which are accompanied or closely followed by discomfort (punishment) . . . will be less likely to occur" (Daft & Steers, 1986, p. 51).

The law of effect as it relates to learning in both animals and human beings has been studied for more than a century. Results of this research have produced a number of generalizations about the specifics of reinforcement. There are four basic scenarios or results that may follow a specific behavior. If a reward follows the behavior, the individual is more likely to repeat the behavior; this is called positive reinforcement. Reinforcement will also occur when behavior is followed by the removal of something unpleasant, called negative reinforcement.

On the other hand, if an unpleasant event or punishment follows the behavior, the individual is less likely to repeat it. Note that negative reinforcement is not the same as punishment, even though the terms have become synonymous in ordinary usage. From the standpoint of the recipient, punishment would be considered a bad outcome, whereas negative reinforcement would be considered a good outcome. The final possibility is that nothing will happen following a behavior, or at least no reinforcement will occur in connection with it. When this is the case, the individual is less likely to repeat the behavior and will eventually stop doing it altogether. This cessation of behavior is called extinction.

Regardless of which of the four possibilities one is considering, a common theme, and one of the key principles of the reinforcement approach, is that whatever response is given to the behavior, the response should follow the behavior as soon as possible. If there is too long a delay following the behavior, the response (reward, removal of an unpleasant situation, and so on) may be misinterpreted and associated with other behaviors that have occurred in the interval.

Other important considerations of the reinforcement approach are the patterns, frequency, and basis for providing the response. In terms of frequency, responses can be given every time the behavior occurs (continuous reinforcement schedule) or for only a certain proportion of occurrences (partial reinforcement schedule). The basis for making the responses can be either the number of times an event occurs (ratio schedules) or the passage of time (interval schedules). The pattern of responses can be either consistent (fixed schedules) or random (variable schedules). Research indicates that fixed schedules lead to faster learning, but lead to quicker unlearning or forgetting when the schedule is abandoned. Conversely, variable schedules lead to slower learning, but once the behavior is learned, the unlearning or forgetting is much slower when the schedule is abandoned.

This description of reinforcement approaches probably conjures up images of laboratory animals running through a maze to earn food or to avoid electric shocks, and these are indeed how reinforcement has been studied in the laboratory. An obvious and natural parallel applying reinforcement theory in a managerial context is to link pay in some way to an individual's performance. This can be done, but pay (wages or salaries) tends to be set only once a year, and because organizational policies often dictate pay scales, many managers have only a partial impact on establishing their subordinates' salaries. This limits the extent to which the manager can use pay as a motivational tool.

An article in the *PA Times* identified several assumptions underlying pay-for-performance forms of motivation.

1. An individual's performance could be accurately or reasonably measured according to some criteria.
2. This system could affect an employee's decision to leave or remain with his or her organization and influence an employee's willingness to work harder for his or her organization than those who are not under the system.
3. An employee will place high value on monetary rewards in the workplace (Lee, 2001, p. 3).

Beginning with the first assumption, though, we can see the challenges faced by public and nonprofit managers in employing such a system in practice. As the author found, "It [a performance-based system] may work in private companies, since they have a clear goal (maximization of profit) that can be measured in quantitative ways. However, this doesn't seem to be working in most public agencies" (Lee, 2001, p. 3). Unclear goals, combined with the need to balance between competing interest groups, tend to make establishing such clear-cut objectives impossible in the delivery of public services.

Moreover, the author found in his study of public employees in New Jersey that people who work in public and nonprofit organizations tend to seek more than financial incentives: "[I]f a public-sector employee is committed to his or her supervisor, he or she is more likely to remain with the agency and make an extra effort on behalf of the organization. In other words, a major motivating factor is not monetary reward, but an effective personal relationship among employees" (Lee, 2001, p. 3). Pay-for-performance may boost some forms of productivity, but it shouldn't be viewed as a building block for a truly high impact organization.

Goal Setting   Goal setting is another method of motivating that can be used by itself or in conjunction with reinforcement techniques. In fact, you can use it to motivate yourself as well as other people. A goal is a desired state of affairs one attempts to achieve, and, as research has shown, just the act of setting goals seems to increase the probability of success. But some ways of setting goals are better than others in terms of motivational impact. Research indicates there are at least eight necessary characteristics for a goal to have maximum motivational impact.

1. Write down a goal rather than just keep it in mind. In a technical sense, one does not "do" a goal, but *achieves* a goal. Therefore, the proper way to write a goal statement is with the word *to* followed by an action verb—for example, "To finish reading this chapter by 5 o'clock." Something about writing down a goal creates greater commitment on the part of the writer. It is harder to ignore, and seeing it on your desk or in your notebook constantly makes the goal harder to forget. Writing down a goal can also facilitate planning because you are consciously identifying the actions you must take to achieve the goal.

2. Because specific goals are much better motivators than general goals, a properly stated goal should be very clear. For example, a field experiment on goal setting at the Weyerhauser Lumber Company in Oklahoma several years ago tested the relative impacts of general and specific goals. The objects of the experiment were truck drivers who hauled logs from one location to another. The federal government established safety standards for how much weight the truckers could carry, and this amount was taken to be the maximum capacity of the trucks, or 100 percent. The researchers and managers at Weyerhauser noted that the truckers normally only hauled about 62 percent of capacity. The first part of the experiment consisted of management informing the truckers that they wanted more weight to be carried on each load and that the truckers were to do their best to achieve this goal.

   The truckers' performance was tracked for the next three months, and there was little or no improvement (1 or 2 percent at most). The truckers were then informed that a goal had been set for them: to haul 94 percent of capacity on each load—a much more specific goal than "Do your best." After three months, the truckers were averaging over 90 percent of capacity per load, very close to the 94 percent goal the managers had set for them.

   No pay increases were given for the increase in weight hauled, although the truckers were told they would not be asked to make any more runs than they normally did as a result of hauling more weight. This remarkable change in behavior saved Weyerhauser over $250,000 annually, and subsequent checks on the truckers have found they have maintained this level of performance for several years. So a specific goal indeed makes a difference.

3. The means for verifying whether a goal has been achieved should be specified. In the study at Weyerhauser, the truckers weighed in at the delivery location for the logs, which provided a precise way to measure the amount of weight they were hauling

and, in turn, how close they were to the goal. (Incidentally, the weigh-in procedure was not added by the experiment; the truckers had been following it for many years as part of their job.)

4. A date or time by which the goal is to be accomplished should be specified. The presence or absence of a deadline is a critical attribute of any goal-setting exercise. Deadlines stimulate action, and the closer the deadline, the more motivation to act. The absence of a deadline makes the urgency of the goal indefinite and hence less motivating. For example, there are a disproportionately large number of plays during the last few minutes of a football game because the team that is behind faces a deadline for scoring more points or losing the game. Similar increases in activity occur toward the end of the trading period each day on the New York Stock Exchange. Think of your own behavior when a test date is rapidly approaching, and you begin to increase your preparation activities.

5. A goal should be perceived as attainable. Impossible goals often are demotivating because there is no reason to try if they cannot, by definition, be attained. (Problems may also occur, however, if the goal is too attainable.)

6. Although a goal should be attainable, it should also be challenging. There is little or no satisfaction in achieving a goal that presents little challenge. The best goal in terms of motivation is one that is perceived as attainable yet challenging, that can be achieved, but only with significant effort.

Psychologist David McClelland (1985) demonstrated this phenomenon many years ago. Children were asked to throw beanbags into a box from various distances, including a position located right next to the box. After they had thrown from various distances, they were asked from which position they preferred to throw. Very few picked the location next to the box; most picked a position farther away—a decision consistent with the properties of attainability and challenge. In effect, the children were setting their own goals, and the goals they set were challenging but attainable.

7. When setting a goal for someone else, the goal must be understandable to the people for whom you are setting them. If they cannot understand the goals, how can you expect them to achieve them? As in so many areas, clarity is extremely important.

8. It was originally believed that if the participants were not involved in setting the goals, they would reject them. Subsequent research, such as in the Weyerhauser study, in which the truck drivers did not take part in establishing the goals, has shown that people are quite willing to accept goals that others set for them. This does not mean, however, that involving people in establishing goals is a waste of time. Among other things, if the people who will actually be trying to accomplish the goals take part in formulating them, there is a greater chance that they will more completely and accurately understand the goals. And although people may be willing to accept goals established by others, there may be greater motivation if they participate.

Managers often worry about involving subordinates in decision making, including decisions about goals and goal levels. A study comparing goals that managers set for their subordinates to goals for the same activities set by the subordinates themselves revealed that the subordinates set more difficult goals (Hitt, Middlemist, & Mathis, 1983, p. 289). Although this may not happen all the time, it is an intriguing finding that supports the notion of including subordinates in the goal-setting process.

Individual Decision Making

One could argue that decision making is the most universal managerial activity because it is involved in all the other functions of management. It is impossible to plan, control, staff, direct, organize, or perform any of the miscellaneous management functions without making decisions. All management involves either explicit or implicit decisions. We will examine decision making at the individual level and explore several models of how decisions should be made and how decisions are actually made.

A great deal of research has been conducted concerning rational processes for decision making, some of which we discussed in terms of rational policy analysis. In its purest form, the rational model of decision making suggests the following steps.

1. Find an occasion for decision making ("decide to decide") and then formulate the problem in the best way possible.
2. Develop as many alternative solutions as possible.
3. Choose the alternative that maximizes the possibility that we will attain our goals or standards.

In essence, analyze the problem, generate alternative solutions, and choose from among the solutions. For our purposes, the most important lesson of the rational decision model lies at the beginning—becoming aware that a problem exists and correctly defining the problem. If you are not aware of a problem, you will not go through the rest of the process to solve it. Your chances of solving the problem are obviously low. (The probabilities are not zero, however, because problems are sometimes solved by accident.) Even if you are aware that a problem exists, if you do not identify the problem correctly, your chances of solving it do not increase very much. How you define the situation is the result of your own perception of reality. Human beings need to make sense of things. We do not tolerate chaos well, and thus are continually defining and redefining situations in which we find ourselves. Aside from our need to make sense of things, defining the situation is important because that will be the basis for our actions and decisions. All mentally healthy individuals behave in a way consistent with their definitions of situations.

When it comes to problem solving, incorrect diagnosis of the problem (that is, an incorrect definition of the situation) can be disastrous. A good example of this can be seen in the Cold War days of the early 1960s. During this period, the United States and its allies had installed long-range radar systems to monitor the Soviet Union and to give warning of any Soviet attack by either missile or bomber. Soon after the radar systems were installed, the commander of an installation in England was made aware of a set of images on the station's screens that looked as if the Soviet Union were launching a massive missile assault against the United States It was the commander's job to evaluate the information, report it to Washington, and include a recommendation and an evaluation of the accuracy of the information.

Obviously, since missiles travel pretty fast, the commander did not have a great deal of time to contemplate the situation. But, being a calm and collected individual, the commander thought things over for a few minutes before he made his report. He remembered that Nikita Khrushchev, then premier of the Soviet Union, was in New York City addressing the United Nations that day. He thought it would be an unlikely time for the Soviets to attack. He also took into consideration the fact that the radar system was new and that new systems sometimes have "bugs" in them. Putting all this together, he made his report, including in it his relatively low confidence in the information on his screens. He stated that he believed there was a malfunction somewhere in the system and recommended that the radar images not be interpreted as an attack on the United States. Obviously he was correct; there was no attack by the Soviet Union. But what was actually happening?

It turned out that the radars were so powerful that some of the radiation they broadcast traveled far out into space. The system operated smoothly for about a week, but then the moon orbited into position and was hit by some of the radiation, which it reflected back to the radar antennas, creating images on the screens that looked very much like a group of missiles heading toward the United States. The computers in the radar system had not been programmed to disregard radiation bouncing back from the moon.

The commander was presented with a problem: the decision of interpreting the images and making his report. He had two interpretations. One was that the Soviet Union had started World War III, and the other that he had a malfunctioning system. One definition of the situation might have actually started World War III, but the other would prevent that catastrophe. So you can see why correctly identifying the problem is critical in a problem-solving situation.

The rational decision model is often presented as the way people actually go about making decisions (or at least the way they should), and this is probably true to a certain extent. It is also clear that, in many cases, solutions to problems are arrived at in a far different way. The basis of the rational problem-solving process is the economic assumption that people attempt to maximize their outcomes when they make choices (that is, decisions). Theoretically, people select a criterion, such as income or profit, then evaluate all decision alternatives in terms of that criterion, and finally select the alternative that will produce the best results.

As we discussed in Chapter 5, Herbert Simon, in his studies of organizational decision making, found that the rational model rarely describes human problem-solving or decision-making behavior in real life. He argued that maximizing outcomes is simply not possible in most situations and identified several reasons that it is usually impossible (Simon, 1957, p. xxvi). All the reasons Simon offers add up to constraints on human beings' abilities to acquire and process information. There are time limits for making most decisions, and there are only so many resources available to gather information. Moreover, because we care more about some problems than others, our motivation to solve problems varies. We are willing to spend more mental and physical energy on some problems than on others.

Even if we had access to unlimited information about any problem, there are cognitive limits to how much information we can process at any given time. Furthermore, particularly in managerial situations, we seldom have the luxury of being able to deal with just one problem at a time. Other problems compete for our attention, time, and energy, which further taxes our cognitive limits.

Putting all these constraints together, Simon argues that human beings attempt to be rational, but they can be rational only within certain limits or bounds. What Simon calls "bounded rationality" (see Chapter 5) suggests that choices will be evaluated, but only within the bounds of these constraints. This results in a "satisficing" criterion for evaluating alternatives, rather than in a maximizing one.

Limits of Rational Decision Making [handwritten marginal note]

A *satisficing decision* is one that is just "good enough" in terms of some criterion. Bounded rationality leads to satisficing decisions, and the process, in its pure form, operates as follows: When an individual faces a choice situation in which a decision must be made, rather than attempting to gather all possible information, generate all possible alternatives, and choose the alternative likely to produce the best results, the decision maker decides what level of outcome (in terms of some criterion) will be satisfactory or "good enough." The individual then examines choice alternatives one at a time and selects the first one that equals or exceeds the minimal ("good enough") criterion level. The process stops at this point, and the choice becomes the decision. No attempt will be made to examine other, potentially better, options.

That human beings vary in attempts to maximize suggests something of a continuum between satisficing and maximizing. But Simon's work suggests that most decisions, most of the time, fall much closer to the satisficing end of the continuum than the maximizing end, even where we are making important (and potentially costly) decisions. Marketing research shows, for example, that people tend to seek out most of the information they acquire about new cars after they purchase a new car rather than before.

Thus, the rational decision-making process can be considered a prescriptive model that tells us what we should do to make better decisions, but it does not give us an accurate picture of how human beings actually make decisions. Because we tend to satisfice rather than maximize, a modified and more limited version of this process, the satisficing model, provides the more accurate description. Hence, we can call it a descriptive model, which attempts to describe how things actually happen without regard to how they should happen. Given the nature of managerial work, satisficing may be the only way a manager can deal with the constant stream of problems and choice situations that arise daily.

Interestingly, one alternative model of decision making in the public sector claims to be both prescriptive and descriptive. Charles Lindblom's incremental model of decision making assumes that most governmental decisions (and others) usually begin by analyzing the existing situation and then move marginally or incrementally away from that position. In making a case for new programs, for example, managers often talk about how a new idea "builds on" existing strengths. This descriptive aspect of the model has a familiar ring. But, in a curious twist, Lindblom also suggests that the incremental model may even make sense normatively: Because incremental proposals focus on well-known experiences, they reduce the number of alternatives to be considered and thus reduce the complexity of the problem at hand (Lindblom, 1968, p. 27).

■ Group Dynamics

Individuals acting alone make a majority of organizational decisions, but sometimes two or more people combine efforts to solve a problem or make a decision. Research has shown that sometimes a group should make a decision and that certain advantages come from group decision making, but there are also disadvantages. Similarly, studies of group dynamics have established fairly predictable patterns of interactions.

Advantages of Group Decision Making

An old cliché has it that two heads are better than one—probably because two heads hold more information than one. Put any two people together, and it is very likely that each knows something the other does not. Create a group of five or six, and there is even more information available. We have already seen that generating alternatives is one of the fundamental steps in the rational decision-making process, even under satisficing conditions. Because there is more information in a group, there is greater potential for generating more alternative solutions to a problem than could be generated by a single decision maker. But these advantages will surface only if the group is managed properly.

Groups may also benefit from synergy: the notion that the whole is greater than the sum of the parts. Synergy can occur in a group, but it is a precious commodity that is not easy to create. Consider the following case.

Three people get together to solve a problem. Bob proposes a solution, and Allen proposes a different solution. Betty has been listening to the proposals, which gives her an idea about how to solve the problem in a completely new way. The idea represents something new that was not present before in the group. If it were possible to quantify the information in the group at the beginning of the discussion, the total information would equal the sum of the information held by the individual members. With Betty's new idea—an idea stimulated by the group discussion—the sum is now greater than the sum of the individual parts.

We want to do more than just make a good decision. The final step in the decision-making process is always implementation. If the people who make the decision are the ones who will be implementing it, commitment to the decision should help with implementation. Research also reveals that satisfaction with the group and its processes increases as the networks become more decentralized. Satisfaction is not exactly the same thing as commitment, but the two are closely related. In most cases, then, as participation in making the decision increases, so should commitment to the final decision.

What Would You Do?

You are the leader of a task force composed of a dozen members, each selected for his or her significant expertise in the field. Drawn from several different professional areas, these are "the best and the brightest" your organization has available. As your meetings progress, however, you recognize that, although these are very smart people, many of them take a rather narrow view of the world and are almost contemptuous of anyone who sees things differently. You recognize that unless something changes, the task force will fail to achieve its goal. What would you do?

An interesting property of group decision making, the *risk shift,* can be either an advantage or a disadvantage. The risk shift refers to how daring the decisions would be if made as a group compared to the average risk of the same decision if each member made it alone. It was originally thought that groups would always make riskier decisions than

[handwritten margin note: Groups are more or less risky than average – but not average]

would individual members. As more research was conducted, however, it was discovered that sometimes the shift works in the opposite direction: that groups sometimes make decisions that are less risky than those made by members working alone.

Sometimes a daring decision produces better results, but sometimes it makes things worse. Because the same can be said about more conservative decisions, the dilemma is that it is often impossible to predict whether a more conservative or more daring decision will yield better results. The most we can say is that a group decision will normally be either more daring or more conservative than the average riskiness of a decision made by each member acting individually.

Disadvantages of Group Decision Making

[handwritten margin note: ① Time ② Cost ③ Groupthink]

Along with the advantages of group decision making, there are potential problems. One of the obvious constraints on human beings that results in our "bounded rationality" is the constraint of time. Time not only limits the efforts of individual decision makers to acquire and process information, but it also limits the possibilities for groups to make decisions. Normally, it takes a group much longer to make a decision than it takes an individual to make a decision about the same problem. Time thus becomes an important constraint on a manager's ability to use group decision making.

Another constraint may be cost. Even if group decision making and individual decision making were equally fast, the group is still more expensive. Compare a single decision maker whose pay is $100 per hour who takes one hour to reach a decision with a committee of five managers who are paid $100 each and also reach a decision in one hour. The cost to the organization for the single decision maker is $100, whereas the cost of the committee is $500.

Another property of groups is groupthink, which is the opposite of synergy. If synergy is the concept that the whole is greater than the sum of the parts, groupthink makes the whole (the group) less than the sum of the parts. Groupthink was first defined and analyzed by Irving Janis as "a mode of thinking that people engage in when they are deeply involved in a cohesive in-group, when the members' strivings for unanimity override their motivation to realistically appraise alternative courses of action" (Janis, 1983). Because the group is so cohesive, greater emphasis is given to conformity than to making good decisions.

[handwritten margin note: Groupthink: Morality/negative stereotyping, invulnerability, rationalization, conformity]

Janis identified characteristics of groups victimized by groupthink and cautioned managers to interpret the presence of these characteristics in a group carefully. For example, groups experiencing groupthink have an illusion of morality, a belief that the group's position, whatever it may be, is inherently ethical and moral in comparison to positions held by other individuals and groups. Such groups also engage in negative stereotyping of other people and groups, often viewing outsiders as the "enemy" and as being too different to negotiate with. Groupthink tends to produce an illusion of invulnerability, which makes decisions seem less risky than they really are. Rationalization is commonly employed as a way to discredit information critical of the group or its decisions, and there is frequent self-censorship of dissenting views, which minimizes the amount of critical or contrary information to which the group is exposed. A strong conformity pressure permeates the group and puts further pressure on group members to agree with the dominant position.

Finally, an illusion of unanimity results in the belief that everyone in the group has confidence in the group's decisions and judgment. Obviously, groups that are victimized by groupthink are limited in their constructive abilities.

Groupthink has been used to explain flawed decision-making processes in situations such as the Bay of Pigs, Watergate, and the *Challenger* space shuttle disaster. In the case of the *Challenger* disaster, a Presidential Commission investigated the accident and identified faulty decision making as a primary cause. Moorehead, Ference, and Neck (1991) analyzed the testimony of those involved and found the situation had many characteristics associated with groupthink. For example, the Commission found that those testifying displayed a strong sense of overconfidence because of the extraordinarily successful history of NASA (National Aeronautics and Space Administration). Even though engineers predicted during the final launch approval process that critical joints would fail, flight center officials discounted the analysis and rationalized that the conclusions were faulty or questionable. Two of the three top NASA officials stereotyped and criticized the views of others, particularly the engineers who warned them about the dangers of proceeding with the launch. Dissenters were pressured to either change their minds or remain silent. As a result of these and other problems, the launch was authorized and the shuttle exploded, killing all seven astronauts.

Interpersonal Dynamics in Groups

Interpersonal relationships affect the work of groups or teams. To illustrate the problems that can arise, imagine that two people who despise each other are assigned to the same committee. Obviously, these two individuals will not work as well together as two people who are neutral toward each other or who like and respect each other. Even if the conflict is not manifested, personal animosity may contribute to building a *hidden agenda,* where privately held goals and priorities motivate actions more directly than the overt and publicly stated reasons. Obviously, the operation of hidden agendas disrupts the group and diminishes its effectiveness.

But the interpersonal dynamics of groups in action are much more subtle and complex than these examples suggest (Gardner, 1974, pp. 8–11). For example, groups often follow a fairly predictable pattern of development. Typically, at the outset of the group's work, its members are highly dependent on the leader of the group. They ask for direction and become quite frustrated if they don't get it. If the leader allows the group to become overly dependent, however, its productivity will suffer in the long term. The leader can resist dependency by referring questions back to the group's members for input.

Often, however, a period of counterdependence will often follow, in which members may show hostility toward the leader. Although still wanting some direction, the group's members are now also experiencing a need for independence, just as an adolescent may simultaneously love and hate his or her parents. Counterdependency seems especially likely to occur in authoritarian work environments, where members' actions are too closely regulated.

On the other hand, in a group where members feel they can openly express themselves and their ideas without fear of retaliation, feelings of interdependence may develop. At this stage, group members recognize the purposes they hold in common and come to have greater trust and respect for one another. The group will probably be most effective when it reaches this stage.

As the group moves through these stages of development, certain patterns of behavior are likely to occur. Early in the group's development, some members may seek flight, actually withdrawing from the work of the group or through silence, irrelevant comments, or self-serving remarks. Most flight behavior is an implicit attempt to say that nothing significant will happen unless the leader gives in to the group's desire for explicit direction. In the counterdependent stage, members may engage in fight behavior or in pairing. Fighting the group's leader in some symbolic fashion is, of course, a fairly straightforward act of rebellion; pairing or breaking off into small groups or alliances is somewhat more subtle, but it expresses the same emotion.

Finally, as the group reaches the stage of interdependence, the actual work of the group can be accomplished in reasonable and satisfying ways. At this stage, a variety of leadership functions must occur for the group to maintain its effectiveness (see Box 9.4). These functions can all be performed by a single person, typically the group's formal leader, but they can also be performed by a variety of different people active at different times in the group's development. In either case, if you wish to help the group meet its objectives, you should be attentive both to the stages of group development and to the extent to which the various leadership functions are being fulfilled.

BOX 9.4

LEADERSHIP ROLES IN GROUP DYNAMICS

1. *The coordinator role.* Communicate to all members about meetings, schedules, tasks, procedures, and similar matters; act as an information clearinghouse for all group members and as a contact person with other groups or outsiders.
2. *The facilitator role.* Set up procedures and a structure for group work; assist members in identifying problems, defining issues, summarizing progress, and working together. (This role involves minimal direct influence on the group task. It concentrates on establishing an interpersonal network that helps members work together to solve problems.)
3. *The trainer role.* Teach group members ways of approaching problems; provide the group with methods of learning from their own experiences; arrange for outside consultants to train the group.
4. *The observer role.* Be alert to how the group is functioning and particularly to which functions are not being met; describe to members what is happening in terms of the group process; show the group areas in which change might facilitate their work.
5. *The gap filler role.* Fulfill those functions that are not being handled by anyone else, particularly the functions of summarizing, clarifying, synthesizing, or facilitating compromise.
6. *The monitor role.* Once the group has determined a procedure to follow or a solution to a problem, see to it that the group is reminded of responsibilities, functions, and assignments necessary for implementation of the decision; provide copies of budgets, schedules, assignment sheets, and agendas to members so they can complete their work on schedule.

SOURCE: Excerpted from Ernest Stech and Sharon Ratliffe, *Working in Groups* (Lincolnwood, IL: National Textbook Company, 1976), pp. 220–221. Reprinted by permission of The McGraw-Hill Companies.

Specialized Techniques for Group Decision Making

Brainstorming is a technique that was developed to enhance the alternative-generation portion of the decision-making process. The goal is to generate as many ideas about some problem as possible, although suspending judgment about each idea. The task before the group is to develop ideas about a problem, or even solutions to the problem, and the more of them generated, the better.

Once the assignment is announced, group members begin to propose ideas. The ideas are described orally, and someone records each idea on a chalkboard or flipchart for everyone to see. No evaluations of ideas are permitted during brainstorming. The session continues until everyone is out of ideas or the leader feels the session has lasted long enough. The purpose is to bring out the information held by different group members and to encourage synergy by stimulating new ideas.

Although brainstorming helps enrich the alternative-generation portion of the decision-making process, the nominal group technique generates both alternatives and solutions. A major purpose of the design is to avoid groupthink. A *nominal group* is a face-to-face meeting that allows only very limited interaction among participants. A problem is presented, but unlike brainstorming, the group is expected to make a decision about how to solve the problem. After the problem has been presented, each member, working alone, writes down as many solutions to the problem as he or she can formulate. When everyone is finished writing, the leader calls for the solutions. Each person in the room presents one solution until all the possible solutions have been heard.

The solutions are recorded publicly as they are presented, again usually on a chalkboard or a flipchart. Other members may ask questions for clarification if they do not understand a solution, but only clarifying questions are allowed. Members may not debate the merits of particular solutions. After every solution has been presented and all questions answered, the group makes a decision by means of a written poll, taken as a secret ballot. Each member rank-orders the different solutions from best to worst. The rankings are submitted to the meeting leader without any identifying material on the ballot. The leader or someone assisting the leader tabulates the ballots, and the solution that receives the highest average preference becomes the group's decision.

Quality circles are the most comprehensive specialized technique for group decision making in that they are explicitly concerned with every step in the decision-making process, from recognition that a problem exists through implementation of solutions. Quality circles also incorporate other specialized techniques such as brainstorming.

Now that we have examined the advantages and disadvantages of group decision making, how do we know when to use group decision making rather than an individual decision maker?

Participation in Group Decision Making

The Vroom-Yetton model of participation in decision making focuses on the manager's decision concerning the extent to which subordinates should participate in making a specific decision (Vroom & Jago, 1988; Vroom & Yetton, 1973). The most impressive study supporting the model was an investigation of 200 actual managerial decisions. Managers made these decisions as part of their jobs without the aid of the model; the model was then applied, after the fact, to determine the effectiveness of various patterns of involvement in decision making.

Vroom and his associates identified the 200 decisions and gathered data about how much subordinate participation was involved in making each decision. The researchers also gathered information about the consequences of each decision specifically, whether or not each decision produced successful results. When decisions were made using a level of subordinate participation consistent with levels recommended by the Vroom-Yetton model, 68 percent of the results or outcomes were judged successful (remember, none of the managers knew anything about the model at the time they made the decisions). When the amount of participation by subordinates was not at a level consistent with the model's recommendations, only 22 percent of the outcomes were judged successful.

This is a remarkable difference. In both relative and absolute terms, the managers who involved subordinates to a degree consistent with the model's recommendations had extremely good results. In relative terms, the outcomes were more than three times better. In absolute terms, 68 percent success is excellent, because factors other than how a decision is made determine whether it produces good results. We would not expect any decision-making method to produce successful outcomes 100 percent of the time, so the results in the study were quite impressive.

The Vroom-Yetton model involves the choice of various levels of involvement in decision making; the choice is not merely between a single individual and an entire group. These two alternatives frame a continuum with several other levels of participation in between. As Vroom and Yetton conceptualized them, there are five levels of participation along this continuum (see Box 9.5). The Vroom-Yetton model indicates which level of participation is appropriate in a particular situation. (Note that for some situations, two or more levels are equally likely to produce decisions that will generate successful results.)

To use the model, you must understand (1) how to identify the different situations and (2) how to match the situation with the appropriate levels of participation. Both issues are resolved by combining the use of two tools: the set of alternative courses of action listed in Box 9.5 and the decision tree shown in Figure 9.1.

BOX 9.5

ALTERNATIVE COURSES OF ACTION

Symbol	Definition
AI	You solve the problem or make the decision yourself using the information available to you at the present time.
AII	You obtain any necessary information from subordinates, then decide on a solution to the problem yourself. You may or may not tell subordinates the purpose of your questions or give information about the problem or decision on which you are working. The input provided by them is clearly in response

(Continued)

(*Continued*)

	to your request for specific information. They do not play a role in the definition of the problem or in generating or evaluating alternative solutions.
CI	You share the problem with the relevant subordinates individually, getting their ideas and suggestions without bringing them together as a group. Then you make the decision. This decision may or may not reflect your subordinates' influence.
CII	You share the problem with your subordinates in a group meeting. In this meeting you obtain their ideas and suggestions. Then you make the decision, which may or may not reflect your subordinates' influence.
GII	You share the problem with your subordinates as a group. Together you generate and evaluate alternatives and attempt to reach agreement (consensus) on a solution. Your role is much like that of chairperson, coordinating the discussion, keeping it focused on the problem, and making sure that the critical issues are discussed. You can provide the group with information or ideas that you have, but you do not try to "press" them to adopt "your" solutions and you are willing to accept and implement any solution that has the support of the entire group.

SOURCE: Reprinted from *Leadership and Decision-Making* by Victor H. Vroom and Phillip W. Yetton, by permission of the University of Pittsburgh Press. © 1973 by the University of Pittsburgh Press.

FIGURE 9.1
Decision Tree Governing Group Problems

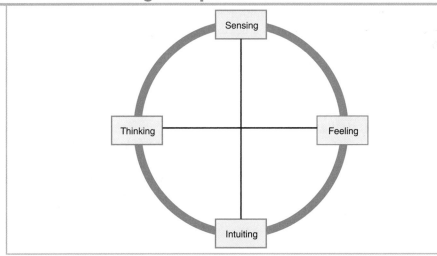

SOURCE: Reprinted from Leadership and Decision-Making, by Victor H. Vroom and Philip W. Yetton, by permission of the University of Pittsburgh Press. © 1973 by University of Pittsburgh Press.

The decision tree may look complex, but it is actually quite simple to use. One begins under point A by answering question A (all questions must be answered either "yes" or "no"; "maybe" or "sometimes" is not allowed). Depending on the answer, you proceed to either question D (for a "no" response to A) or to question B (for a "yes" response to A). One continues answering the questions as indicated by the decision tree until you reach an end point.

Each end point is numbered, with a set of participation levels listed after each end point. These are feasible sets; all the participation levels listed in a feasible set are equally likely to result in a successful outcome. This does not mean, however, that there is no reason to pick one style over another within the feasible set. The decision styles are arranged in the order of the amount of time it will take to reach a decision using the styles. The style listed first is the fastest, followed by the second fastest, and so on. In most situations, one should choose the fastest style in the feasible set.

Again, the answers to the questions along the path reaching the particular end point define the situation, and the participation levels indicated in the feasible sets provide guidance concerning the appropriate level of involvement. Although the model, even as presented here in simplified form, may initially seem cumbersome and complex, managers who practice it for several days seem to be able to utilize it without notes thereafter.

Conflict, Bargaining, and Negotiation

Differences and conflicts inevitably arise in public and nonprofit organizations. But as Richard Box explains, finding a way to equitably resolve differences is a key interpersonal skill, opening the door to more citizen-oriented governance. "For elected leaders and public service practitioners, this means a flexible attitude toward change, shedding of protective feelings about personal turf, and a willingness to engage in open dialogue on issues facing the community" (Box, 1998, p. 12).

What Would You Do?

Your division of purchasing is composed of two sections, one that acquires goods and another that acquires services. Over time, the two section heads have developed an intense rivalry that has increasingly turned ugly. The two are basically at war, with insults flying back and forth at every occasion. They are forcing you into the position of having to choose sides—which you don't want to do. What would you do?

Roger Fisher and William Ury (1981) of the Harvard Negotiation Project have suggested that negotiation is a natural process that occurs where two parties share certain interests but are opposed with respect to others. Negotiations often move quickly to positions that are held by one party or another. For example, a union representative requests a 10 percent raise, but the city negotiator takes the position that only a 2 percent raise is possible. Moving quickly to a position and allowing it to become hard and fast not only produces undesirable results, but damages the continuing relationship between the parties. Positional bargaining seems to move participants to one of two postures: a soft posture that emphasizes the ongoing relationship and seeks agreement among participants, or a hard posture that assumes an adversarial relationship and in which each party seeks victory over the other.

Fischer and Ury suggest an alternative method called "principled negotiation." Principled negotiation is based on four elements of negotiation: people, interests, options, and the criteria for solution. Four guidelines emerge from these elements (see Box 9.6).

According to Fischer and Ury, following these guidelines leads to negotiated settlements that are more equitable and more likely to lead to continued effective working relationships than are more traditional modes of bargaining. Remember that negotiations occur in all kinds of situations, from deciding which movie to see to resolving matters of war and peace. However, the same general guidelines may be employed in all negotiations to generate more effective and responsible solutions (Fischer & Ury, 1983).

More recently, managers of public and nonprofit organizations have adopted systems for Alternative Dispute Resolution (ADR). ADR can be thought of as any conflict management strategy outside of formal adjudication. Approaches range from preventative measures, including consensus-building and setting clear parameters on interpersonal (and interorganizational) relationships, to more formal approaches, such as court-based mediation and arbitration (Constantino & Sickles-Merchant 1996).

NETWORKING

For information on conflict resolution, visit the Conflict Resolution Center at www.crnetwork.ca, the National Association for Community Mediation at www.nafcm.org, or Illinois's Center for Analysis of Alternative Dispute Resolution Systems at www.caadrs.org, which offers insight into specific examples of ADR at the state level.

BOX 9.6

GUIDELINES FOR SUCCESSFUL NEGOTIATIONS

1. Separate the people from the problem.
2. Focus on interests, not positions.
3. Generate a variety of possibilities before deciding what to do.
4. Insist that the result will be based on some objective standard.

SOURCE: From *Getting to Yes.* 2nd ed. by Roger Fisher, William Ury, and Bruce Patton. © 1981, 1991 by Roger Fisher and William Ury. Reprinted by permission of Houghton Mifflin Company. All rights reserved.

■ Summary and Action Implications

Leadership involves more than power and control. To lead others, you must first know yourself. Thus, understanding yourself is an essential prerequisite to acting effectively and responsibly in public organizations. Moreover, to the extent that you are able to learn about yourself, your strengths and weaknesses, your desires and frustrations, you will be much more effective in your work with others. Whereas power may be a resource, leadership capabilities are more likely to arise from the ability to understand the emerging desires of a group, to articulate the vision or direction the group wishes to follow, and to stimulate the group to action. Leadership unquestionably requires social or interpersonal skills, but it is based in empathetic understanding, the ability to express the aspirations of the group, and the confidence to undertake the risks associated with change.

All the knowledge, values, and skills you possess are expressed in the moment of action. Whether you are a manager or a policy analyst, or hold some other position in a public organization, your ability to act effectively and responsibly "in the real world" will determine your success. Your actions will usually occur in social settings and require working with others. Especially in a managerial position, you will engage in almost constant interaction with other people, so no matter how much you know or how proper your values, your effectiveness will be limited if you cannot work well with others.

Today we recognize that interpersonal skills, like other skills, can be developed and improved over time. Just as artists or athletes can improve proficiency, so can you improve your skills in areas of communications, delegation, negotiation, and group dynamics. The key to improving your skills in public management, as in other areas, is practice and repetition, accompanied by self-reflection and self-critique.

If you want to be a better communicator, for example, you should seek opportunities to practice communicating with others. Find opportunities to make presentations; practice listening with special concentration and sensitivity; try to develop your writing skills. As you practice, be conscious of your own and others' reactions. Reflect upon your successes and failures and try to learn from both. Over time, you'll improve your skills and find yourself far more effective.

Throughout this book, we have described public management as involving cognitive, conceptual, technical, and human skills. In the moment of action, however, the areas cannot be separated. Indeed, your capacity to bring together knowledge, technique, and interactive skills at the moment of action will determine success or failure in most situations. Public management can be studied in the abstract, but it must be lived in the real world—a world of stress, complexity, and uncertainty. In few other fields do so many aspects of the human personality have to come together. But it is this very difficulty that makes public service so challenging and rewarding.

TERMS AND DEFINITIONS

Brainstorming: Technique for enhancing the alternative-generation portion of the decision-making process.

Delegation: Assigning tasks to others.

Hidden agenda: Privately held goals and priorities.

Nominal group: Face-to-face meeting that allows only limited interaction among participants.

Parity principle: Idea that an individual should have equal amounts of authority and responsibility.

Risk shift: Difference in the daringness of decisions made by group members compared to the average risk of the same decision if each member made it alone.

Role ambiguity: Occurs when the rights and responsibilities of the job are not clearly understood.

Role conflict: Occurs when one faces two different and incompatible sets of demands.

Satisficing decision: One that is just "good enough" in terms of some criterion.

Support system: Network of people with whom one can talk about problems.

Two-factor theory: Model of motivation involving two variables: job satisfaction and job dissatisfaction.

STUDY QUESTIONS

1. What are the seven basics of effective listening?

2. Why is speaking an important interpersonal skill?

3. Discuss the "Six Cs" for effective written communication.

4. Management can be defined as "the process of getting things done through others." Discuss how delegation and motivation enable the work of management to occur.

5. Explain reinforcement theory and its four basic scenarios or results.

6. Goal setting is another motivation technique. Discuss what characteristics a goal should have for maximum motivational impact.

7. What features are present in rational decision making?

8. What are the elements of "principled negotiation"?

9. Discuss advantages and disadvantages associated with group decision making.

10. Explain the fundamentals of managing group dynamics.

11. Identify and discuss various techniques for group decision making.

CASES AND EXERCISES

1. Although power should not be equated with leadership, it can certainly be an important resource to public managers. To illustrate some types of power, think back over the past week or two as you attended class and worked in various groups and organizations, and answer the following questions:

   a. Who were the two or three people during this period who exercised the greatest power over you?
   b. Who were the people during this period over whom you exercised the most power? Now return to the "Bases of Social Power" in Box 9.1. What was the basis for the power that others exercised over you? What was the basis for the power that you exercised over others? How might you most effectively build up your power base in groups and organizations to which you belong?

2. Chapter 1 listed management skills developed by the U.S. Office of Personnel Management. Part of that list is reproduced here. Go through the list and assess your level of development in each of the skills. You might want to verify your evaluations by talking with others who know you well and have seen you operate in groups and organizations. After you have a sense of your own level of skill development, try to identify the activities (classes, workshops, readings, and so on) that would help you improve your skills in areas that need some work.

The "How" of Management Effectiveness Characteristics

Broad perspectives: Broad, long-term view; balancing short- and long-term considerations.
Strategic view: Collecting, assessing, analyzing information; diagnosis; anticipation; judgment.
Environmental sensitivity: "Tuned into" agency and its environment; awareness of importance of nontechnical factors.
Leadership: Individual; group; willingness to lead, manage, and accept responsibility.
Flexibility: Openness to new information; behavioral flexibility; tolerance for stress, ambiguity, change; innovativeness.
Action orientation: Independence, proactivity; calculated risk taking; problem solving; decisiveness.
Results focus: Concern with goal achievement; follow-through, tenacity.
Communication: Speaking; writing; listening.
Interpersonal sensitivity: Self-knowledge and awareness of impact on others; sensitivity to needs, strengths, and weaknesses of others; negotiation; conflict resolution; persuasion.

Technical competence: Specialized expertise (such as, engineering, physical science, law, accounting, social science).

3. Divide your class into groups of three. Taking turns, have one person choose a topic from the following list and begin a conversation with the group. Follow the rules of effective communication.

    a. You are short of cash and want to take a winter vacation to an island off the coast of Mexico. You need to borrow at least $300 for the trip. You are pretty sure you can pay it back in three months.

    b. The two classmates you are talking with have been working with you on a class project. Actually, the problem is that they haven't been working! You have to do something to get them busy, or your grade will suffer. You need at least a "B" in the course to graduate.

    c. You have been working in behalf of the homeless in your community for the past two years. A march on Washington has been scheduled for next week, and a bus has been chartered to take people from your community to Washington at a cost of $83 each. The problem is that unless you can find two more people to make the trip, the bus won't go. You want to convince your two friends to go with you.

4. Imagine that you are an administrative assistant to the director of the Department of Social Services in your state government. The director is interested in starting a new strategic planning process and wants to send a letter to all the managers and employees in the department describing the new process and enlisting their support. You have been asked to draft the letter. Using the information about strategic planning in Chapter 6, draft an appropriate letter.

    After everyone in the class has drafted a letter, each draft should be shared with and analyzed by at least one other student. Your analysis should take into account the specifics of the situation (what should be said, how much should be said, how it should be said) as well as the more general Six Cs of effective communications listed in this chapter.

5. Divide the class into groups of three. Have one person in each group play the role of Chris, the supervisor, and another play the role of Brett, the employee. (Each person should read only his or her own role description and not that of the other person.) The third person in each group should observe the discussion between Chris and Brett, then comment on the motivation strategies employed. The scene begins as Brett walks into Chris's office and says, "Someone said you wanted to see me."

Chris: You are 28 years old and recently received your MPA from a fairly prestigious school in the East. You have worked for the federal government for four years, moving rapidly from a presidential management internship to your current position supervising a small unit that produces health and safety brochures for industry. Brett has worked with the agency for 23 years as a design specialist. Throughout this period, from what you understand, Brett has done an excellent job. In the few months you have been with the agency, however, you have noticed a decided drop in both the amount and quality of

Brett's work. With a heavy workload anticipated over the next several months, you decide that you have to do something to improve Brett's performance. You have asked Brett to come and speak with you.

Brett: You have worked for 23 years as a design specialist for a small federal government unit that produces health and safety brochures for industry. Throughout your career, you have taken great pride in your work and have done an excellent job. Over the last few months, however, you have been increasingly troubled by painful back spasms, the source of which you have not been able to identify. The problem with your back has triggered a lot of concerns about your health, your age, your work. Although you haven't shared these concerns with anyone, you find that you spend long periods daydreaming about them. Even drinking a few martinis each evening hasn't calmed your fears. You still enjoy your design work, but somehow the projects you have had recently just don't seem all that exciting. What's worse, your supervisor, a kid probably half your age, has been hinting that your work may not be up to par.

6. Consider the following case. You have recently been appointed head of a new agency established to monitor pollution emissions from coal-fired power plants throughout the Midwest. The data you collect will have a direct impact on an anticipated presidential decision concerning "acid rain" in the Northeast and Canada. You must try to develop the most comprehensive and precise measures possible, and then monitor as many plants as you reasonably can during the relatively short period prior to the presidential decision. Most of your staff have been in the pollution control field much longer than you and are highly committed to the goals of your agency. They have been arguing that a new piece of equipment, an Emission Systems Monitoring Instrument (ESMI), is the only device that is capable of precise measurements of the particular pollutants with which you are concerned. The problem is that the ESMI is both extremely expensive and would require nearly half the time you have available just to be delivered. You are skeptical about whether the ESMI is worth the cost, but even more concerned that its limited availability will mean that you will fail to meet your deadline. You also think, though you are not sure, that the rough estimates generated by the existing equipment are sufficient for the purposes of your report to the president. Do you go ahead with the existing equipment, or do you buy the ESMI? Using the Vroom-Yetton model for decisions about delegation, work through the various aspects of this problem to determine the appropriate level and pattern of delegation.

7. Divide the class into task groups of five people each, with three observers assigned to each group.

The task groups should complete the following task: List what you consider the five most important guidelines for effectively managing a large organization. After the task group completes its work, the observers should lead a discussion of the group dynamics they observed in the work of the task group.

For observers only: During the discussion, you should silently watch the discussion and take notes about the operation of the group. Try to identify patterns of group development such as those presented in the chapter. Pay special attention to shifting patterns of leadership and communications. If this same group were to perform a similar task, what would you suggest to improve its effectiveness?

8. The following "classic" exercise in group problem solving will illustrate several important aspects of the decision-making process.

Your spaceship has just crash-landed on the moon. You were scheduled to rendezvous with the mothership 200 miles away on the lighted surface of the moon, but the rough landing has ruined your ship and destroyed all the equipment on board, except for the following fifteen items.

You and four to seven other people should take this test individually, without knowing one another's answers, then take the test as a group. Share your individual solutions and reach a consensus—one ranking for each item that best satisfies all group members.

Your crew's survival depends on reaching the mothership, so you must choose the most critical items available for the 200-mile trip. Your task is to rank the fifteen items in terms of their importance for survival. Place 1 by the most important item, 2 by the second most important, and so on through 15, the least important.

- box of matches
- food concentrate
- fifty feet of nylon rope
- parachute silk
- solar-powered portable heating unit
- two .45-caliber pistols
- one case of dehydrated evaporated milk
- two 100-pound tanks of oxygen
- stellar map (of the moon's constellation)
- self-inflating life raft
- magnetic compass
- five gallons of water
- signal flares
- first-aid kit containing injection needles
- solar-powered FM receiver-transmitter

SOURCE: Jay Hall, "Decisions, Decisions, Decisions," *Psychology Today* 5 (November 1971): pp. 51–88. Reprinted with permission from *Psychology Today Magazine*. © 1971 by Sussex Publishers, Inc.

Note: NASA experts have determined the best solution to this task. Their answers appear in Appendix A.

FOR ADDITIONAL READING

Allison, Graham, and Philip Zelikow. *Essence of Decision: Explaining the Cuban Missile Crisis.* 2nd ed. New York: Longman, 1999.

Bass, Bernard M., and Bruce J. Avolio, eds. *Improving Organizational Effectiveness through Transformational Leadership.* Thousand Oaks, CA: Sage Publications, 1993.

Bechard, Richard. *Changing the Essence: The Art of Creating and Leading Fundamental Change in Organizations*. San Francisco: Jossey-Bass, 1992.

Bingham, Richard D. et al. *Managing Local Government: Public Administration in Practice*. Newbury Park, CA: Sage Publications, 1991.

Bozeman, Barry, and Jeffrey D. Straussman. *Public Management Strategies: Guidelines for Managerial Effectiveness*. San Francisco: Jossey-Bass, 1990.

Burns, James MacGregor. *Leadership*. New York: Harper & Row, 1978.

Cohen, Stephen R. *Principle-Centered Leadership*. New York: Simon and Schuster, 1991.

Conger, Jay A. *Learning to Lead: The Art of Transforming Managers into Leaders*. San Francisco: Jossey-Bass, 1992.

Covey, Stephen R. *The Seven Habits of Highly Effective People: Restoring the Character Ethic*. New York: Simon and Schuster, 1990.

Denhardt, Robert B. *The Pursuit of Significance: Strategies for Managerial Success in Public Organizations*. Belmont, CA: Wadsworth, 1993.

Denhardt, Robert B., Janet Vinzant Denhardt, and Maria Pilar Aristigueta. *Managing Human Behavior in Public and Nonprofit Organizations*. Thousand Oaks, CA: Sage Publications, 2001.

Fischer, Roger, and William Ury. *Getting to Yes*. 2nd ed. New York: Penguin Books, 1991.

Frederickson, H. George. *The Spirit of Public Administration*. San Francisco: Jossey-Bass, 1996.

Garnett, James L. *Communicating for Results in Government: A Strategic Approach for Public Managers*. San Francisco: Jossey-Bass, 1992.

Gortner, Harold F., Julianne Mahler, and Jeanne Bell Nicholson. *Organization Theory: A Public Perspective*. Pacific Grove, CA: Brooks/Cole, 1987.

Holzer, Mark, ed. *Public Service: Callings, Commitments, and Contributions*. Boulder, CO: Westview Press, 2000.

King, Cheryl Simrell, and Camilla Stivers, eds. *Government Is Us: Public Administration in an Anti-Government Era*. Thousand Oaks, CA: Sage Publications, 1998.

National Academy of Public Administration. *Leading People in Change: Empowerment, Commitment, Accountability*. Washington, DC: National Academy, 1993.

Murray, Nancy. *An Inner Voice for Public Administration*. Westport, CT: Praeger Publishers, 1997.

Vroom, Victor H., and Arthur G. Jago. *The New Leadership*. Englewood Cliffs, NJ: Prentice Hall, 1988.

Whetten, David A., and Kim S. Cameron. *Developing Management Skills*. 2nd ed. New York: HarperCollins, 1991.

APPENDIX A

"Lost on the Moon" Exercise: Answers from NASA Experts

1. Two 100-pound tanks of oxygen: most pressing survival need

2. Five gallons of water: replacement for tremendous liquid loss on lighted side

3. Stellar map of the moon's constellation: primary means of navigation

4. Food concentrate: efficient means of supplying energy requirements

5. Solar-powered FM receiver-transmitter: for communication with mothership; but FM requires line-of-sight transmission and short ranges

6. Fifty feet of nylon rope: useful in scaling cliffs, tying injured together

7. First-aid kit containing injection needles: needles for vitamins, medicines, and so forth; will fit special aperture in NASA spacesuits

8. Parachute silk: protection from sun's rays

9. Self-inflating life raft: Carbon monoxide bottle in military raft may be used for propulsion

10. Signal flares: distress signal when mothership is sighted

11. Two .45-caliber pistols: possible means of self-propulsion

12. One case of dehydrated evaporated milk: bulkier duplication of food concentrate

13. Solar-powered portable heating unit: not needed unless on dark side

14. Magnetic compass: magnetic field on moon is not polarized; worthless for navigation

15. Box of matches: no oxygen on moon to sustain flame; virtually worthless

CHAPTER 10

ADMINISTRATIVE REFORM AND TECHNOLOGY

Over the past fifteen years, you may have heard the expression the "New Public Management," or "reinventing government." This idea is based on a belief that public organizations, or, more accurately, the systems underlying public organizations, lack the capacity to meet the challenges and opportunities of the twenty-first century, and need to be thoroughly reformed. Thus, the concept of reinvention, and the broader effort known as the New Public Management (NPM), in many ways can be considered approaches to a rather old question: How can we improve government performance and accountability?

However, the reform movement in the public and nonprofit sectors should not be equated simply with a call for increased productivity. Proponents of reform recognize that public and nonprofit agencies, particularly in America, constitute some of the most productive institutions in the world, even more so than private institutions. (For example, over the past generation, government productivity has increased at double the national average.) Instead, NPM and other reformist themes suggest that government should not account merely for its own activities but should be assessed on its capacity to achieve substantial public outcomes.

NPM and reinvention are, however, closely related to issues of quality and productivity in government. The two stem from similar sources. Concern about government productivity centers around issues of efficiency and accountability. These issues have, of course, been debated throughout the country's history; modern expression is typically dated back to the passage of Proposition 13, a tax limitation initiative passed by California voters in the late 1970s. Following the California example, other states and localities also began efforts to limit what voters perceived as the excessive cost of government services.

At the federal level, the desire to avoid new taxes meant reduction or elimination of numerous domestic programs, especially during the Reagan years. Many of these programs provided aid to state and local governments. When the reductions were combined with the desire to limit state and local taxation, many governments were severely constrained in trying to provide sufficient revenues to support important, even basic, services. But despite these limitations, these governments were often asked to "do more with less," to provide increased services, with the same or even with reduced funding.

We examined some of the implications of this situation in Chapter 7 with respect to budgeting and financial management, as many governments were forced to search for alternate funding methods, including privatization and so forth. But the same governments also sought new ways to improve both the quality and quantity of work without extra cost. Many governments and agencies at all levels initiated, or at least intensified efforts to find new solutions, to break from the traditional assumptions, and to find more effective means of meeting their objectives.

Public organizations started to lose their traditional bureaucratic structure, becoming instead more lateral systems of shared power and teamwork. Systems of management, too, were transformed into more equitable, less controlling forms of leadership. And government agencies began to form meaningful partnerships with other institutions and citizens in response to public problems.

Nongovernmental organizations (NGOs) also underwent a transformation of sorts. During the 1990s, NGOs became drivers of policy issues in a variety of areas, such as human rights, economic development, urban revitalization, and even governmental reform.

Advances in information technology (IT) played an integral role in transforming public and nonprofit organizations worldwide. The impact was twofold. First, increased capacity for communication and information sharing redefined the distribution of authority within institutions. Every member of the organization had access to the latest news and information, and so shared one of the more important sources of power. Second, IT-enabled public and nonprofit organizations to engage more effectively with their counterparts in other sectors and around the world, as well as with citizens. Such change restructured the ways in which governments and other public service agencies responded to opportunities and challenges.

So whether we call it an effect of NPM, reinvention, or efforts to improve quality and productivity, public and nonprofit administration at the beginning of the twenty-first century is quite different from that of merely a generation ago. The ways in which we organize ourselves, engage with others, and respond to public concerns have undergone a huge change or, to use Don Kettl's phrase, "a transformation in governance" (Kettl, 2000, p. 488). Yet, as we explore the various aspects of reform, keep asking these questions: Have we improved service to the public? Is the work we are doing today consistent with our expectations for a system of democratic governance? Are we truly acting in the interest of citizens?

■ NPM, Reinvention, the Management Agenda, and Nonprofit Reform

The current reform agenda in public administration can be traced to several worldwide trends. First, and perhaps most significant, the social, political, and economic dialogue in industrialized countries underwent a rightward shift during the late 1970s and early 1980s, as political leaders recognized the unsustainable nature of comprehensive, centralized systems of public service delivery. Leaders in Europe, Asia, and North America started to examine more cost-efficient, effective ways of providing public services, including public welfare, transportation, health care, and others. Second, fiscal challenges brought on by the changing nature of the global economy prompted scholars and practitioners to explore new ways of thinking about public administration. By the early 1990s, many public managers around the world, using slogans like NPM and reinvention, had embarked on a journey to restructure bureaucratic agencies, streamline agency processes, and decentralize policy decision making.

The New Public Management

The New Public Management, or NPM, is a term used to describe a set of principles and practices in the public service, which has emerged during the past several decades in a variety of countries around the world (Barzelay, 2001, p. xi). Although the application of NPM has varied country by country, the reform agenda has remained consistent in its drive to create organizations that are mission-driven, decentralized, and incentive-based. Reformers strive for more flexible public organizations and more responsive interorganizational networks, guided by the key principles of accountability, responsiveness, and a commitment to outcome-based governance (Boston, 1996; Peters, 1994).

Perhaps the best example of the NPM principles at work can be seen in New Zealand's administrative reforms. Beginning in 1985, New Zealand's national government took several bold steps aimed at transforming its system of public administration. Among the most significant reforms, the government redeveloped its personnel system as an attempt to make top executives more performance-oriented; instituted a comprehensive performance measurement system based on a new process of measuring the productivity and effectiveness of government agencies; and reengineered its departmental systems to reflect the Labour administration's commitment to governmental accountability (Boston, 1996).

The effectiveness of New Zealand's reform agenda, as well as parallel activities in Canada, Great Britain, and the United States, prompted public administration reformers around the world to adopt many of the principles from NPM, as well as use these principles as a new framework for public policy and governance (Barzelay, 2001, pp. xi–xv; see also Kettl, 1997). For example, reports from the United Nations' Commission on Global Governance and other international bodies reinforced this international movement, advocating decentralized decision making, civil society, empowerment, and a reliance on third-sector organizations for achieving public outcomes (Commission on Global Governance, 1995).

Reinventing Government

In the early 1990s, Osborne and Gaebler's (1992) landmark work, *Reinventing Government,* brought many of the NPM principles to American shores. For Osborne and Gaebler, the reform agenda represented a response to what they call "the bankruptcy of bureaucracy"—that is, the ineffectiveness of government organizations. The authors believed that public agencies had failed to keep pace with changing conditions in the postindustrial society, with government still attempting to respond to public issues with a "one-size-fits-all" approach. As a result, the systems in which public administrators function had become the problem, not the solution, and consequently citizens had begun to lose faith in the capacity of government to serve their needs.

A central theme in reinvention is that only more entrepreneurial forms of government will enable public administrators to effectively deal with problems and capitalize on opportunities in contemporary society. Yet, in contrast to most interpretations, Osborne and Gaebler actually avoided the more traditional view that government should be run like a business: "Government and business are fundamentally different institutions.

What Would You Do?

You are a top-level manager in a state transportation department. You have been planning to widen and realign an existing highway that runs through some of the most picturesque countryside in the state, part of which is in a national forest and the remainder of which is in two different resort communities and the county. There are several businesses along the route, all of which could be hurt if the new highway pulls traffic away. Some of your staff have suggested a lengthy process of public involvement in the design of the highway. You are concerned, however, that such a process could raise major controversies and take at least an extra year. You think the highway is needed now. What would you do?

Business leaders are driven by the profit motive; government leaders are driven by the desire to get reelected. . . . Differences such as these create fundamentally different incentives in the public sector" (p. 20). Although encouraging public administrators to derive insights from successful experiences in all sectors, Osborne and Gaebler maintain that public and private sector organizations face a distinct array of challenges.

Entrepreneurial government, then, refers to more streamlined, flexible, and responsive systems of public policy and administration. Osborne and Gaebler cite example after example of public organizations that had chosen innovative strategies for doing more with fewer strategies for increasing the value of public services without raising costs for public consumers. These ranged from privatization efforts in Phoenix, Arizona, that enhanced competition among service providers, thus raising significantly performance standards, to public school initiatives in East Harlem, New York, that empowered residents with greater choice for students' learning opportunities. The authors suggest that these common themes—competition and empowerment—combined with more attention to public outcomes and action based on customer priorities rather than bureaucratic imperatives represent the future of successful government.

To carry out the reform agenda, Osborne and Gaebler provide ten principles underlying reinvention and public entrepreneurship:

1. Catalytic government: steering rather than rowing
2. Community-owned government: empowering rather than serving
3. Competitive government: injecting competition into service delivery
4. Mission-driven government: transforming rule-driven organizations
5. Results-oriented government: funding outcomes, not inputs
6. Customer-driven government: meeting the needs of the customer, not the bureaucracy
7. Enterprising government: earning rather than spending
8. Anticipatory government: prevention rather than cure
9. Decentralized government: from hierarchy to participation and teamwork
10. Market-oriented government: leveraging change through the market

Osborne and Gaebler intended these ten principles to serve as a new conceptual framework for public administration—an analytical checklist to transform the actions of government. "What we are describing is nothing less than a shift in the basic model of governance used in America. This shift is under way all around us, but because we are not looking for it—because we assume that all governments have to be big, centralized, and bureaucratic—we seldom see it. We are blind to the new realities, because they do not fit our preconceptions" (p. 321). By applying the ten reinvention principles in the context of any given policy area, a new universe of opportunity, an altogether different system of governance, would evolve.

NETWORKING

Global perspectives on the NPM are available from The Canada School of Public Service at www.myschoolmonecole.gc.ca/main_e.html and the OECD Public Management and Governance Service at www.oecd.org.

The Management Agenda

The "reinvention" movement was the centerpiece of the Clinton administration's effort to bring about administrative reform. But, as we have already mentioned in previous chapters, George W. Bush has also initiated several managerial reforms in the executive branch of the federal government—though these efforts continue to build on the basic ideas of the New Public Management. The President's Management Agenda (PMA), emphasized five core initiatives:

- Strategic management of human capital
- Competitive sourcing
- Improving financial performance
- Expanded e-government
- Budget performance integration

For each of these reforms, the President appointed four political appointees in the Office of Management and Budget (OMB), and one in the Office of Personnel Management (OPM), as "owners", who should be held accountable for the success of the initiatives (Breul, 2007). In addition, the Bush administration developed an "Executive Branch Management Scorecard to track the implementation of the PMA" known as the Program Assessment Rating Tool (PART). PART is essentially a questionnaire designed to follow the implementation of the executive programs in terms of meeting the requirements imposed by the PMA. While, the PMA and PART are well-known reforms, we should note two other Bush initiatives that died in Congress. The first, the Freedom to Manage Act of 2001, would have given "expedited congressional consideration" to the management reform measures. The second, the Managerial Flexibility Act of 2001, would have given flexibility to the executive managers in the fields of "personnel, budgeting, and property management and disposal" (Bruel, 2007, p. 23).

Nonprofit Management Reform

Since the 1990s, the reform agenda in government has had a substantial impact on the nonprofit sector. We have discussed the interconnected nature of public-nonprofit relations, but as governments use contracts, grants, and other strategies to devolve public services to nonprofits, they also have begun to hold their not-for-profit counterparts accountable to many of the same performance and outcome objectives. Consequently, nonprofit organizations in today's world find themselves buoyed by the "tides of reform" affecting the public sector (Light, 2000).

The factors precipitating reform in the nonprofit sector, of course, go beyond the government-imposed. In fact, Paul Light (2000, pp. 17–43) has identified several important trends influencing the nonprofit reform movement, including "nationalizing trends" relating to productivity, recruitment, resource development, and technology, combined with "local realities" of ensuring consistency, building patterns of shared responsibility, and enhancing nonprofit capacity for public service delivery.

Unfortunately, nonprofit organizations have experienced less of the tides of reform and more of a tidal wave! "The nonprofit sector has never been under greater pressure to improve. Despite two decades of phenomenal growth, the sector suffers from a general impression that it is less efficient and more wasteful than its government and private competitors. Even if the sector could prove that it has achieved "ordinary excellence," spending money wisely and producing measurable results as a natural by-product of organizational design, it faces a serious public relations problem among clients and funders alike" (Light, 2000, p. 1). As a result, nonprofits have been flooded with demands to reform systems of administration, service delivery, and accountability, with each set of demands often reflecting divergent philosophies.

As Light explains, the movement to enhance productivity and accountability in nonprofit organizations can be categorized into these four reformist principles.

- Scientific Management—Management should be based on the "one best way," with individual organizations seeking to implement codes of internal conduct and basic best practices of administration.
- War on Waste—Management should be based on a drive for external efficiency, with organizations and alliances reengineering to achieve efficient, streamlined systems for administration and service delivery.
- Watchful Eye—Management should be based on creating more transparent patterns of administration, with organizational stakeholders holding agencies accountable for openness and compliance.
- Liberation Management—Management should be based on achieving positive outcomes, with agencies working together in the public interest (pp. 46–71).

While on a theoretical level these philosophies may not seem incompatible, the struggle to apply such principles in management practice has taken a toll on nonprofits. Indeed, when faced with competing demands by funders and donors, a single nonprofit may find itself swept away in attempts to implement multiple reform strategies at the same time. Foundations, government grant-makers, and other institutions that provide financial support to nonprofit organizations, even at the local level, have a poor track record for engaging in a substantive dialogue concerning policies and procedures, much less for coordinating funding programs and reporting standards. As a result, nonprofits must be prepared to structure their administrative practices and reporting systems to correspond with each funder's demands.

The problem here, though, is that few can agree on what constitutes a "good" nonprofit, this despite an emerging trend for foundations and government grant-makers to fund "capacity-building" activities (for discussion, see Greene, 2001, pp. 1–12). Although scholars, management consultants and program officers have attempted to bring order out of chaos, the results have amounted to little more than platitudes. The *Chronicle for Philanthropy*, for example, offered the following "expert tips."

- Management challenges are normal for nonprofit organizations . . . There are no quick fixes . . .
- Ideas are nothing, thinking is everything . . . Proffer the pole, not the fish . . .
- In times of great change, our support can reap great dividends . . . Don't redesign the kitchen while the house is on fire . . .
- Speak the truth . . .
- Change demands a champion . . .
- Building a nonprofit organization is a long, hard haul . . . We don't know enough yet . . . (Kibbe, 2001, p. 10)

Even the application of a particular reformist agenda may be carried out in different ways, depending on those implementing the strategy and on what level the implementation occurs. For example, a United Way–based "outcome measurement" system in one community may vary significantly from another just miles away; or the definition of "impact" as interpreted at the state level may be off the mark with agencies at the grassroots.

The challenge for nonprofit management in the future will be to balance the drive to adopt sound management practices from the private sector with a dedication to public service. Such a balance will be difficult, though, as demands for reform seem to be increasing, and the tides appear to be toward the former rather than the latter. Perhaps even more important, greater attention needs to be placed on those activities that fall outside of the individual nonprofit. Foundations, government agencies, and other funders, in conjunction with the nonprofits they support, must begin a more substantive dialogue around ways to coordinate grant-making and reporting requirements, as a way of bringing a level of consistency and coordination to an increasingly fragmented public policy process, and of easing the administrative burden on nonprofit organizations. Indeed, reforming the nonprofit sector will be as much about improving the dialogue among leaders in philanthropy, business, and government as it is building the capacity of nonprofit organizations.

The Results of Reform

It will be some time before we can fully assess the impact of NPM, reinvention, and the drive to improve nonprofit organizations. However, many have begun to question the lessons learned from the reform movements. Proponents point out that some of the key reform-oriented initiatives, such as the Government Performance and Results Act (GPRA), have helped improve the public service. Kathryn Newcomer and Aaron Otto (2000) recently summarized some of GPRA's benefits at the federal level.

- Amplifying conflicting/polarizing expectations—GPRA has raised consciousness over some of the terms and concepts underlying management reform (p. 1).
- Strengthening programmatic communities—Federal agencies have started working more collaboratively on achieving shared objectives (p. 2).

- Asking the right questions about program performance—GPRA has helped to enhance the quality of the discourse around performance measurement (p. 2).
- Effectively reporting performance—Federal officials have improved their agencies' capacity for accurately and appropriately measuring program impacts (pp. 2, 6).

On the other hand, critics of NPM and reinvention suggest that even though certain aspects of the reform agenda have contributed to meaningful improvements in public service, the application of these principles has produced a variety of negative externalities not envisioned by early reformers. In practice, the adoption of business practices and the reliance on market forces by public organizations degenerated into a sense of *managerialism*—a belief that government could and should be run like a business based on strictly economic principles. As public managers began to apply their reform agendas, many focused on the pursuit of administrative efficiency more than maintaining the democratic principles of effective governance.

Another point of concern is that the reform movement has concentrated on customer-centered instead of citizen-centered public administration. Critics argue that "citizens are not the customers of government; they are its owners who elect leaders to represent their interests. A customer-centered model puts citizens in a reactive role limited to liking or disliking services and hoping that administrators will change delivery if enough customers object" (Schachter, 1995, p. 530, citing Frederickson, 1994). In contrast, citizen-centered public administration restores the public to an ownership position—a proactive relationship in which citizens engage with the institutions of governance to achieve public outcomes.

Despite this criticism, however, the NPM and reinvention movements have had a pervasive impact on public administration in this country and around the world. As we will see later in the chapter, the principles underlying these reform efforts have contributed to major initiatives to enhance government performance and accountability. Public organizations at all levels have employed a variety of strategies to streamline work processes and enhance the public service.

■ Information Technology, the Internet, and Management Reform

Advances in information technology (IT) have played a key role in the move toward a more entrepreneurial public and nonprofit organizations. Beginning with the PC revolution in the early 1980s, when personal computers started to appear in every office (not to mention every home), IT has been a central part in the drive to increase public and non-profit performance. Yet, in the age of reform, IT was transformed from being a tool for enhancing productivity to a metaphor for the very way in which we organize. We began to view ourselves as actors in "wired organizations," members of "virtual communities," and citizens in a growing web of "e-public administration."

By the beginning of the twenty-first century, the transformation of the Internet, which began as an electronic network of researchers and scholars into a global, online community, supported our change in perspective. We could, in real-time, have a virtual chat with colleagues around the world on matters of public policy (or anything else, for that matter), exchange insights on common challenges, or swap information relating to management innovations. Governments and nonprofit agencies soon turned to online resources for many of their core functions, including economic development, human and social service delivery, health care, and engagement with citizens. So we can say that in less than a generation, the Internet and improvements in IT generally have helped to reshape our notions of governance and public space.

Electronic Organizations

From a management perspective, the most immediate impact of IT has been to redefine our concept of organization. Intranets, e-mail, and other networking resources have allowed, or in some cases forced, agencies to transform work processes and integrate strategies for meeting public objectives. In fact, some even consider IT and integrated forms of organizing, such as team-based approaches, to be at the heart of management in today's society. Mankin, Cohen, and Bikson (1996), for example, suggested that "information technology can make teams more effective, and teams can help fulfill the promise of information technology. Together, teams and new information technology can catalyze dramatic improvements in organizational performance" (p. ix). The connection between teamwork and IT provides a gateway for organizational performance.

Accordingly, IT became a key theme in Vice President Al Gore's National Performance Review (NPR) of the 1990s. The NPR plan, as well as the Information Technology Management Reform Act of 1996, focused on the use of IT in the reengineering process of federal agencies. Specific NPR recommendations included the creation of an information infrastructure that would allow for a more effective use of government resources, as well as facilitate the modernization of processing and customer service centers; the development of an efficient electronic mail service, improving federal agencies with messaging and communications capabilities; and the implementation of an incentive system to reward innovation, a system that would enable agencies to reinvest dollars saved into information technology (Gore, 1993).

The NPR recommendations have translated into important innovations relating to the use of IT in the reinvention process (see Box 10.1). At a recent conference organized by the International Quality and Productivity Center, administrators from a variety of federal agencies shared their experiences and insights on one of the crucial advancements: the use of government intranets or internal websites for public organizations. Noted one participant, "An intranet is much more than a glorified e-mail or groupware solution . . . [It] can be customized and tailored to a specific work environment, enabling employees to not just communicate internally, but collaborate, interact, and become part of a team connected through their desktop computers" (Kerwood, 1997, p. 1).

Of course, the application of IT has not been limited to the federal government. State and local authorities around the country have forged relationships with private service providers to expanded their IT infrastructure and take the "business of government" online. State governments in Pennsylvania, Virginia, Washington, and elsewhere are capitalizing on IT innovations to create seamless systems of service delivery in the areas of health care, education, public safety, and corrections. Many states are also viewing high-tech companies as key drivers of economic development, and some have adopted incentive programs to support IT-related industries (Stoneman, 2000, pp. 34–50).

NETWORKING

Check out Neighborhoods Online at www.neighborhoodsonline.net, Harvard's National Center for Digital Governance at www.ksg.harvard.edu/digitalcenter, the Center for Technology in Government at www.ctg.albany.edu, and the National Science Foundation Digital Government Research Program at www.digitalgovernment.org

At the local level, public agencies are using IT and online networks to manage the regulatory process, interact with citizens, and increase the efficiency of public services. We mentioned the city of Baltimore's use of Citistat in Chapter 7 in our discussion of financial management systems. But another role of Baltimore's Citistat has been to track the effectiveness of interagency partnerships in addressing important health and human service concerns (see also Box 10.1). For example, as part of its "Leadstat" initiative, city officials use GIS technology to pinpoint actual cases of lead poisoning, using a red "dot" on a GIS map, and then assess the effectiveness of their abatement strategies by monitoring the number of dots to change from red to green, with a green dot marking a successful abatement (Swope, 2001, p. 23).

BOX 10.1
SERVICE TO THE CITIZEN, BY THE CITIZEN

New technologies are alleviating the headaches of doing business with the government by enabling citizens to do much of the work themselves.

It's lunchtime—peak business hours at the Department of Motor Vehicles. A line of frustrated customers waits to step up to the service counter. Clerks register automobiles, administer driver examinations, and try to reduce the waiting lines. But the same thought crosses the mind of almost everyone in the room: "Isn't there a better way?"

Until recently, the answer was no. Whether a citizen needed to register an automobile or obtain a Social Security card, it meant a harrowing day of hustling between agencies and waiting for a number to be called. For government employees, a day at work meant subduing dissatisfied customers and spending time on repetitious paperwork.

But in today's wired age, citizens are beginning to help themselves. Self-service kiosks, informational or interactive websites, and toll-free telephone lines are helping public agencies revolutionize the way they serve the public. And, for the most part, people love it. Experts say electronic government is unique because both parties can reap benefits. Consumers profit from increased government accessibility and faster response time, while governments can cut costs and improve reliability. Janet Caldow, director of IBM Corp.'s Institute for Electronic Government, said government is undergoing a dramatic technological transformation. "Electronic government has the potential to change the relationship between elected leaders and constituents," she said. "These vital technologies will change and empower both governors and the governed."

Government one day may resemble a neighborhood convenience store: one location that offers everything the citizen needs from public agencies, anytime he or she needs it. The U.S. Postal Service's Web Interactive Network of Government Services (WINGS) is a step in that direction. WINGS is one of the first intergovernmental efforts to reduce the complexity and confusion people experience when dealing with the government.

The website, www.wings.gov, offers local, state, and federal government services and information by way of the Internet.

"The WINGS infrastructure provides the complete functionality to enable electronic commerce between the public and their government," said WINGS Program Manager Susan Smoter. "Basically, the Postal Service relieves other agencies of the burden of secured delivery, freeing them up to concentrate on the services that fall into their individual missions."

Caldow said saving time and trouble is one of the prime benefits of systems like WINGS. "There is not a citizen in the world who wants to take a vacation day and stand in line to get a driver's license," she said. "That's why one of the trends we're seeing is the next generation of websites for government, where it's not just information on government, but actually service that can be performed from a computer or kiosk." Experts predict that government provided interactive kiosks, IVR (interactive voice recognition) systems, and web services soon will be commonplace. "Everyone is pursuing it quite aggressively," Caldow said. "Kiosks are going to be as common as bank ATMs in the not-too-distant future."

"The stuff you only find on the Internet now, it's going to be pervasive enough that anyone will feel it is common," Mechling agreed. Progress in voice systems means that in about a decade, "a lot of machines we'll be talking to, instead of using keyboards for," he predicted.

The days of waiting in line at government offices may be numbered. And that's good news for customer and agency staff alike.

SOURCE: Maxwell, Alison. "Service to the Citizen, By the Citizen." *Government Technology* 29 (special insert with *Government Executive*, Oct. 1997) 6–16.

Technology and the rise of the IT sector also have made a significant impact in the philanthropic sector, opening new doors for resource development and performance measurement. But the process has come with its share of challenges. During the late 1990s, the boom in high-tech firms created what seemed to be a new generation of philanthropists. The Bill and Melinda Gates Foundation of Seattle, for example, which was started by the family of Microsoft's multibillion-dollar chairman, became the nation's largest foundation, with assets in 2000 exceeding $21 billion (an increase of more than 25 percent over 1999). However, the halcyon days of the dotcoms quickly vanished, and by mid-2001 the *Chronicle of Philanthropy* was reporting a "sober view of the Internet's future" on charitable giving (Marchetti, 2001, p. 1).

Rather than give up on technology, many nonprofits began using the new landscape as a way of expanding their strategies for IT-based fundraising. Some charities are now using their websites to receive direct contributions, and many more are turning to e-mail and other forms of electronic engagement to solicit gifts from the more e-savvy philanthropists. Goodwill Industries has taken this to new ends, using an eBay-type online auction house to raise more than $2 million since 1999. There has even been a growth in the number of online fundraising collaboratives, such as Helping.org, which raises money on behalf of several philanthropic organizations (Hruby, 2001, p. 10).

E-Governance

The pervasiveness of IT in public and nonprofit management has many talking about a new era of electronic governance (e-government). E-government can be defined as the use of IT to provide information, deliver services, support organizational management systems, and/or to offer opportunities for dialogue and citizen input. Dean and Stage outlined some examples of e-government, including "government websites, pages, e-mails, and service delivery over the Internet. It can also mean digital access to government information or electronic licensing or payments." But the most significant aspect of the public service in this information age involves what they call a "revolution" in governance, a "dramatic shift in the methods by which political and social power are organized and used today" (Dean & Stage, 2000, p. 3).

This revolution began well before the "dotcom" craze of the late 1990s. Its origins can be traced to the utopian forms of governance conceived during the early part of the twentieth century. But the actual emergence of what's called "cyber-democracy" dates from the early 1990s and the growth in community networks (for discussion, see Browning, 1996; Bryan et al., 1998). Alexander and Grubbs define community networks as "a low cost, easy-to-use computer network that provides citizens with access to electronic mail, public bulletin boards, and electronic information relevant to their locality" (1998, unnumbered, online journal). These networks are usually used to enhance local community organizations, facilitate neighborhood capacity-building programs, and foster citizen participation in public decision making. In recent years, these networks have gained in complexity and strength, with some even branching into providing Internet access, GIS technology, and computer-based civic and educational courses.

Community networks serve as models for what Grossman (1995) calls a "key-pad" democracy—an electronic republic in which public participation occurs in virtual settings.

- Greater communication with public officials and administrators is possible through e-mail, faxing, and audio-video conferencing.
- Information necessary for rational decision making can be disseminated to the public via the Web and advanced multimedia presentations.
- Elections and public referenda may be conducted more accurately through electronic voting mechanisms (Alexander and Grubbs, 1998, unnumbered, online journal). Thousands of local authorities across the United States, and an increasing number in Europe and elsewhere, have begun to use community networks to connect with citizens; and, there are even more grassroots efforts being initiated by private citizens to reach out to governmental and nongovernmental leaders (Bryan et al., 1998, pp. 1–2). When online services are available, indications are that Americans are increasingly willing to use such technology. According to a 2004 study conducted by the PEW Internet and American Life Project, 29 percent of respondents said that they had visited a government website, and 18 percent had used e-mail to contact a government official or agency. Of those who use the Internet, 77 percent of, or approximately 97 million, Americans have

used the Internet to access information from or contact a governmental organization, a 50 percent increase over the previous year (Horrigan, 2004).

Although they vary in quality and ease of use, at present virtually all federal agencies and states and most local governments have established websites. The White House launched FirstGov in 2000, a website that currently provides a portal for citizens, businesses and organizations, and federal employees to access a wide variety of information and governmental services ranging from applying for a passport or for a student loan, obtain information on government contracts and rules, and access information and directories for federal agencies. As of the summer of 2004, it was receiving 6 million visitors per month. States are using e-government approaches as well. For example, the state of Texas, in conjunction with the advocacy group America's Promise, allows parents to search for multiple kinds of assistance for their children in one place, regardless of which of the twenty to thirty agencies of government might be involved. In Kansas, the Department of Health has established a Web-based Public Health Information Exchange to share confidential information among public health professionals across the state. A study on digital governance in municipalities ranked New York City's website number one in the world in content and fourth overall after Seoul, Hong Kong, and Singapore (*PA Times*, December 2003). For an up-to-date list of state and local government websites, visit www.statelocalgov.net/index.cfm.

What Would You Do?

Review any public sector website—federal, state, local, or nonprofit. Assume that you work for that agency in responding to this situation: A highly placed federal official addressing a meeting you are attending comments that, while most government websites aren't as good as Amazon.com, they are generally better than most private sector websites. In a discussion with others at the conference, people start making suggestions about how their own websites could be improved. What would you do?

While e-government offers many opportunities for better information sharing, efficiency, and better service to citizens, it also creates significant challenges. In a recent study on e-government, David Lazar and Maria Binz-Scharf identified two key challenges: (1) novelty—the fact that electronic medium offers a very wide range of fundamentally new possibilities for governmental processes and operations; and (2) cooperation—it often requires new and unprecedented levels of cooperation between agencies and organizations (IBM Institute for the Business of Government). Novelty can make it difficult to choose among the vast array of choices, some of which involve profound changes in organizational processes, relationships, and culture. Interagency cooperation is also critical because the best websites are designed around citizen needs, not agency structures. As Laura Larimer, chief information officer for Indiana, comments, "Citizens really shouldn't have to—and don't want to—understand the organizational structures of how government is delivering services to them. . . They shouldn't have to care whether they get a license they need at the city, state, federal, or township level. In the long run, we ought to have doors into government that allow them to traverse those lines without having to understand our system" (Perlman, 2002).

There are other challenges as well. IT almost always involves significant resource commitments. Budget restrictions make it difficult for many jurisdictions to develop and maintain Web-based sites. Ensuring broad-based access can be problematic as well. About one-third of Americans do not have access to the Internet (Horrigan, 2004). Access can also be limited for non-English-speaking or disabled individuals, although government agencies are making some progress in this regard. Finally, security issues must also be considered. Not only must systems be protected from viruses and hacking, but sensitive information and transactions must be safeguarded so they are not revealed or used inappropriately.

Despite these challenges and barriers, the benefits of e-government are potentially great. In addition to access to information and services, the Internet also offers opportunities for new kinds of two-way communication between citizens and government. For example, one way that government can obtain citizen input is through the use of simulation games. For example, Governor Baldacci of Maine used a budget-balancing game for citizens that provided a list of programs on one side of the screen and revenues on the other. Players were asked to balance the budget, and then they could send the results to the governor's office. Virginia is using a "regulatory town hall" to facilitate public comment on regulatory changes. As comments are made, they are publicly posted so participants can read what others are saying and submit responses (Swope, 2004). The federal government also uses Internet technology to invite participation in its rule-making process. The website at www.regulations.gov provides interested parties with a one-stop site to review and comment on proposed revisions to regulations in any federal agency. So although we may have to wait a few years until we can vote online (although it may be sooner than we think!), our capacity for interacting with public officials and building a virtual civil society has never been greater.

■ The Human Side of Technological Innovation

Whether designing new vehicles for collecting garbage, developing new techniques for space exploration, or creating broad-based management information systems, the technical questions are always accompanied by a related set of "human" concerns, most having to do with how human beings work together to solve technical problems. For example, what is the proper relationship between government and industry in supporting research and development activities? How can technological innovations be transferred from one jurisdiction or organization to another? What are the human consequences for a particular organization in adopting particular approaches? How can people in the organization be helped in adapting to the new technology?

One group that has been deeply involved in responding to questions such as these is Public Technology, Inc. (PTI) which began in 1969. A group of local government managers joined together to establish PTI as a way to apply technologies developed by NASA to problems encountered by local governments. Throughout most of its history, NASA has had a special mandate to support civilian applications of space technology. For example, local officials were concerned about inadequate or bulky air supplies for firefighters. From conversations with NASA employees who designed life support systems, the local officials gained access to high-pressure, lightweight air tanks; devices that can help people see through smoke; and other tools (Toregas, 1988, p. 3).

In addition to specific technical contributions, PTI focused on the human element of technology transfer. Public Technology Inc. felt that what came to be called "orgware"— the combination of human and interpersonal skills needed to cope with the frustration and fear associated with new technologies—was more important than the technical hardware or software itself (Toregas, 1988, p. 3). Emotional issues can often get in the way of applying improved technology; for example, firefighters considered a new, automated, radio-controlled nozzle for fire trucks such a threat to their jobs and their normal way of fighting fires that it was abandoned almost immediately.

Experiences such as this led PTI to adopt a formula for technology management: For every $5 spent on hardware, $15 must be spent on software, and $80 must be spent on orgware training, organization development, and so on. Organizational members' concerns about introduction of new technologies can be dealt with effectively, but implementing a change to new technologies is time-consuming and costly. In any application of new technology, you must keep the human element very much in mind. For this reason, many agencies establish joint technology design committees to analyze how employees will respond to the changes brought about by new technology (*Government Productivity News*, September 1992, p. 4).

Other dimensions of the human side of advanced technology, especially advanced IT, are also important. The first has to do with the impact of IT on day-to-day work patterns. As already noted, managers' work is not only information-based, but highly interpersonal as well. There is no question that computer networking, for example, will increase the information available to managers and decrease the time spent waiting for it. Moreover, extensive networking should improve managers' capacity to more effectively integrate the work of various groups within the organization. On the other hand, managers with access to computer networks may spend much less time in face-to-face conversations or in visits to various locations where the work is done, and these interpersonal tasks are essential.

Second, we should expect greater dependence on advanced IT to raise several very personal concerns for those who work in or deal with public organizations. The depersonalized nature of computerized control and evaluation systems may prove highly stressful for either employees or clients. In the private sector, for instance, there have already been experiments with automated systems of accountability measuring the number of keystrokes a typist generates or the number of calls a salesperson makes. Similar applications in the public sector could well lead to the same negative reactions that have often occurred in the private sector applications.

Third, the use of advanced IT raises questions about how organizations of the future are likely to be structured. Networking can simultaneously allow for greater centralized control and greater decentralization. Some argue that "knowledge is power," and that making more information available to top officials on a timely basis will permit them to accumulate even greater power (perhaps to the detriment of others). Some argue instead that new technology will spread information throughout the organization, and, consequently, power will be decentralized. The latest studies take a different position: that information technology in and of itself does not necessarily lead an organization toward either more or less central control. Rather, the organization's initial structure, history, and culture, as well as the behavior of its managers are the determinants. Information systems, it seems, can be designed to either centralize or decentralize. (To examine a system designed for collaboration, see Box 10.2.)

BOX 10.2

COLLABORATIVE PUBLIC MANAGEMENT IN SAN FRANCISCO

In the case of the city and county of San Francisco, Mayor Gavin Newsom has illustrated the concept of collaborative public management through two successful programs known as SFStat and the HOME Team project. Both large and complex, San Francisco departments tend to operate in isolation from one another within an environment characterized by intense competition over limited budgetary allocations decided by the Board of Supervisors.

Seeking to emulate a data and technology-driven management model employed by other large cities, such as Baltimore (CitiStat) and New York City (CompStat), Mayor Newsom launched SFStat with the intention to create an efficient, effective, citizen-based government. SFStat is a forum in which essential city departments present data on budgets, human resources, and service delivery to a panel comprising the mayor, his chief of staff and budget director, the controller, the city attorney, and the human resources director on a routine basis.

SFStat is a successful management instrument that is marked by several characteristics:

- It provides a forum in which the city's primary decision makers can be located within one room. This allows decision makers to receive the same information at the same time in the same manner. Departments, in turn, receive the collective expertise and guidance of these individuals in a timely manner.
- By emphasizing the reporting and tracking of data, SFStat creates a safe, accountable operating environment for department directors. Through the routine provision of data, operational issues surface and departments discuss strategies for improving operations. The effect of these strategies is monitored through data tracking. Departments are held accountable for providing accurate data and implementing strategies

Yet in an operating environment devoid of collaborative public management, the ability to realize these shared cultural norms would have been diminished by the divergent paths created by large and complex government. In essence, Mayor Newsom created a process that enabled multiple organizations to collaborate in order to bring coherence to the service delivery model, think creatively about improving services, and successfully manage entrenched social problems.

SOURCE: Sharon Friedrichsen. "Collaborative Public Management in San Francisco," *Public Administration Review*. Vol. 66, pp. 150–151, 2006.

■ Human Resources, Innovation, and Performance

Whereas advanced technology can improve productivity and performance, other (and sometimes far greater) improvements are possible through more effective use of human and organizational resources. Many approaches for improving the commitment, motivation, and creativity of employees (including managers) have been developed over the years. Most today are considered merely good management practice, but many specific techniques are more often used in formal productivity improvement programs than as ongoing managerial processes. We will provide a historical review of four techniques:

1. management by objectives (MBO)
2. quality of work-life programs (especially job enrichment)

3. quality circles (or similar group approaches)
4. incentive programs, as well as more recent efforts to encourage innovation

Management by Objectives

One of the oldest productivity improvement techniques to be used systematically in business and government is *management by objectives (MBO)*. Management by objectives became especially popular in the late 1960s and through the 1970s. President Nixon extended MBO concepts throughout many federal agencies, a pattern many state and local organizations soon followed. Although MBO has fallen into some disfavor in government agencies, many of its key elements, such as objective setting and performance appraisal, remain in place today in many agencies.

Essentially, MBO is a highly participatory approach to establishing clear and measurable objectives throughout an organization. First, MBO assumes that the organization as a whole will benefit by clarifying its broad-range goals and by targeting the work of all organizational units and all individuals in pursuit of those goals. Second, MBO assumes that all elements of the organization, from top to bottom, will benefit from establishing realistic objectives each year and measuring progress toward the objectives as the year goes by. Third, MBO assumes that the process of establishing goals and objectives should involve a broad spectrum of organizational members, both to solicit the fullest range of ideas and to build patterns of effective communication and commitment.

MBO is based on an image of the organization as a hierarchy of linked goals and objectives. The organization's broad goals are developed at the top of the hierarchy and become the basis for negotiating more specific objectives at the next level down. These objectives in turn become the basis for negotiating objectives at the next level and so on down through the organization, even to the level of setting objectives for each individual employee. In a fully developed MBO system, the broad agency goals theoretically provide a framework within which everyone in the organization, including both managers and other employees, has before him or her a set of performance objectives to guide his or her work during the course of the year (Jun, 1976, pp. 15–16).

Note that the objective-setting process is not one in which objectives decided "from above" are merely handed down to each successive level. Rather, MBO involves a highly decentralized objective-setting process in which each supervisor works with each subordinate manager or employee to arrive at a reasonable set of objectives. Ideally, this process of negotiation involves face-to-face conversations in which objectives at various levels are worked out; however, in many applications of MBO, the objective-setting process occurs through an exchange of memos and written forms.

For objectives to most effectively guide the work of all those in the organization, special attention must be paid to the *type* of objectives being developed (Morley, 1986, p. 186). These are considered the most useful.

Clear and specific. The objectives should state exactly what is to be done (that is, to reduce response time to three minutes), rather than vague and subjective (that is, to respond in the shortest possible time).

Realistic. The objectives should be challenging to the unit or the individual, but not beyond reach. It also should be clear that the resources and support necessary to meet the objectives will be available.

Measurable (or otherwise verifiable). There must be some way for both the supervisor and subordinate to know when the objective has been met.

Prioritized. Both the superior and subordinate should agree on which objective is most important, which is next most important, and so on.

The resulting objectives may be stated in several ways: in terms of amount of work (cases processed per week), effectiveness of work (applicants placed each month), quality of work (a minimum error rate), completion dates and target costs, or some combination of these (Morley, 1986, p. 186). The objective-setting process should be followed by a more detailed examination of what must be done to meet the objective. Usually an action plan is developed, indicating how, when, and by whom the actual work will be done to meet the objectives. (At this point, of course, it is important to agree on the resources and support necessary to attain the objective.) Finally, managers must assign specific responsibility to those in their units for completing the necessary task.

As mentioned, MBO has been tried in many different government and nonprofit organizations here and abroad. Recently, MBO has been widely criticized, largely because of the extremely detailed paperwork that many organizations required as part of their MBO system, but many organizations still use important features of MBO. For example, setting goals and objectives and developing accompanying action plans are central to more contemporary strategic management efforts. Similarly, one of the most important features of MBO systems, which has been retained in many organizations long after the demise of a full-blown MBO system, is the frequent review and revision of objectives, accompanied by detailed *performance appraisal*—that is, a specific evaluation with respect to an individual's progress in completing specified tasks. By setting a standard against which to measure performance (which is often especially difficult at the professional or managerial level), MBO-based performance appraisal systems provide a base against which results can be measured. Finally, the emphasis in MBO on frequent communications up and down the organizational ladder has clearly been maintained in other approaches to productivity improvement, as well as in management practice more generally.

Quality of Work-Life/Job Enrichment

For a period, MBO took on the aura of a "movement," complete with classic texts, disciples and other advocates, and strong commitment to "the cause." Much the same is true of the recent concern for quality of work-life (QWL). The QWL "movement" traces its ancestry back to the development of child labor laws, passage of workers' compensation legislation, and more general concerns for human relations arising in the 1930s. Its more recent impetus, however, has come primarily from a group of European scholars and practitioners associated with the Tavistock Institute for Human Relations in London.

The Tavistock group was initially concerned with how organizations might become more adaptive to a society engaged in a shift from a production base to a service base, one expected to exhibit a high degree of social change and "turbulence." According to the Tavistock researchers, most organizations reflect their technological bases; that is, their organizational structure models their technology. Unfortunately, such a structure limits adaptability. The Tavistock group urged attention to the interaction of social and technical systems.

For at least some QWL advocates, creating a work environment of high quality was even more important than improving productivity. The most important question to ask, they argued, is whether a particular organization is doing all it can to contribute to a more humane and progressive work environment. Others, however, felt that one didn't have to trade productivity for quality. Rather, by improving the quality of work-life, productivity would rise as well. Indeed, studies seemed to show that improving the quality of work-life led to decreased absenteeism and turnover, greater job satisfaction, and greater commitment to the organization and its goals—all features that should improve an organization's productivity as a whole.

Obviously, any movement directed toward concerns as broad as these may lack some focus, and that has been a problem with efforts to improve the quality of work-life; the term has become so embracing as to be unclear. Some scholars, however, have focused on three paramount concerns: the autonomy, the responsibility, and the authority granted to individual workers. "The general objective is to arrange organizations, management procedures, and jobs for the maximum utilization of individual talents and skills, in order to create more challenging and satisfying work and to improve organizational effectiveness" (Jenkins, 1983, p. 2). Another writer inserts the objective of QWL efforts into this question: "How can jobs be designed so that effective performance is linked with meaningful, interesting, and challenging work?" (Suttle, 1977, p. 1).

This question leads to a specific productivity improvement effort—job enrichment—that is concerned with designing or redesigning particular jobs so that workers experience greater meaning and satisfaction from the work and, consequently, can be more productive. Job enrichment efforts usually assume that people will perform better (1) where they perform a diverse array of tasks; (2) where they have a high degree of autonomy in their work; and (3) where they get clear feedback on the quality of their work.

Diversity, autonomy, and feedback in a particular job can be enhanced through a variety of mechanisms. For example, you might combine tasks so that instead of a series of individuals, each involved in only one part of an assembly process, each individual would be responsible for the entire product. Jobs might also be enriched through vertical loading—that is, giving individual workers responsibilities and controls previously reserved for management, such as responsibility for deciding on work methods or for training new workers (Hackman, 1983, p. 249). Presumably, workers in enriched jobs not only find the quality of work-life improved, but also become more productive.

Quality Circles and Related Ideas

The "quality circles" concept has been widely used over the past several decades. Hundreds of reports of documented savings and solutions to work-process problems—some involving public-sector organizations—have appeared in the popular and business press.

More important, although the term *quality circles* seems to be fading from use, some of the principles underlying quality circles have reemerged under the concept of "self-managed teams" and through the application of the techniques of quality management.

A quality circle is a small group of people who do similar or connected work and meet regularly (usually an hour a week) to identify, analyze, and solve work-process problems. Quality circles involve six to twelve employees, who are led by their first-line supervisor (often called a team leader) and assisted by a trained facilitator, usually from outside the work unit. The circle chooses its own problems to work on and approaches them through a structured, problem-solving process. Resulting recommendations are usually presented to the team leader's immediate supervisor, who in turn may carry the recommendations further up the hierarchy.

Because quality circles offer frontline employees the opportunity to get involved in decisions affecting their work, circles have proven popular among employees (as well as employers) in many organizations. In some places, employees have never been asked how they think work processes might be improved, yet they are the experts in providing patient care, processing tax returns, or developing procedures to remove hazardous wastes. The benefits for these employees are thus twofold: First, they are given time to solve problems that cause frustrations and that keep them from completing their jobs, and second, by taking greater responsibility for work-process problems, they gain a greater awareness of solutions and may have greater interest in the success of those solutions.

The team leaders, facilitators, and circle members receive training in quality circle operations and in group dynamics and problem solving. An open atmosphere concerning circle activities helps managers to feel comfortable with the circle concept, a natural step toward acceptance and institutionalization of the entire program.

A key ingredient in the success of a quality circle program is the support of top management. This factor needs careful attention at the beginning stages of a quality circle program. Without active support from the top, quality circle members may feel their recommendations will not be taken seriously, and managers elsewhere in the organization may see no incentive to start quality circles in their work areas. Although quality circles are a bottom-up approach to problem solving, the implementation process is very much topdown; information about the concept must be presented to those at all levels of the organization.

Although managerial support is necessary for long-term success, the real core of any circle program is the participants themselves; without a large proportion of highly motivated and properly trained circle leaders and members, the circle program cannot succeed. Members of the organization must be introduced to the notion of quality circles, and team leaders, facilitators, and group members must be trained.

Although quality circles and related ideas are usually employed to solve specific work-process problems, and are more frequently used in units where such problems are found, the basic quality circle principles of widespread participation and group problem solving are applicable elsewhere. For example, *task forces* (groups brought together to work on specific organizational problems) may consist of members from different parts of the organization. They may address work-process problems or issues of organizational policies or broader public policies; however, the approach to problem solving may be much like that modeled by quality circles.

Incentive Programs

Many, if not most, personnel systems in public agencies emphasize merit considerations in deciding which employees receive larger and smaller raises. This is an effort to build into the system a reward or incentive for high-level performance. In addition to pay increases, there are several other types of incentive plans that reward extraordinary performance. The rewards are usually money, but they may sometimes be nonmonetary incentives such as merchandise or time off. The incentives seek to reward increased output (measured quantitatively), improved performance (measured qualitatively), or improved behavior (such as reduced absenteeism or fewer accidents) (Morley, 1986, p. 118).

A variety of incentive plans are currently used in public agencies (Greiner et al., 1981, pp. 28–29). Among the most common are: performance bonuses, piecework bonuses, gainsharing plans, suggestion awards, behavioral awards, and employee recognition.

Performance bonuses are one-time monetary awards based on superior performance on the job generally or in a particular task. Often used to reward professional or managerial employees, bonuses may be presented annually or upon completion of a specific task. There are, however, several difficulties with bonus systems in the public sector. Many people, including many legislators, seem to feel that performance evaluation is so difficult to manage that there is no fair basis for deciding which employees receive bonuses and which do not. Consequently, bonus systems may become mechanisms for rewarding friends and favorites in the organization. Although these concerns can be addressed in several ways, in many jurisdictions they have led to legislation prohibiting bonus systems.

Piecework bonuses are performance incentives that tie the worker's productivity in a given task to monetary rewards. These systems may either tie the monetary reward directly to the number of units produced or use some formula to determine which workers are exceeding a standard level of performance. For example, keypunch operators in many jurisdictions are paid according to number of entries. Similarly, painters and electricians in some areas are paid according to what degree they meet or exceed a standard of performance set in advance. The effectiveness of piecework bonuses depends on arriving at specific measures of performance that will be clear to all concerned.

Gainsharing plans provide a monetary award for a group of employees based on savings the group generates. Based simply on the idea of rewarding those who produce more, this kind of plan is easy for both employees and citizens to understand. Washington, for example, has operated such a program for nearly a decade. Through the state's Teamwork Incentive Program, employees in groups that develop significant savings can receive up to 25 percent of the documented savings. State employees have received as much as $6,273 per employee (*Government Productivity News,* April 1989, p. 1).

Gainsharing can also be combined with a quality circle program. If, for example, a quality circle designed a new computer program that saved a state government $6,000 a year, it might split as much as $600 among the circle members. Again, this system depends on careful documentation of the savings generated by the work of the group.

Suggestion award programs provide incentives for employees who make specific suggestions that result in savings for the organization. Such systems are widely used in American industry; firms such as General Motors have major suggestion "contests" that result in thousands of dollars, even hundreds of thousands, in awards to individuals and, of course, even greater savings for the companies. Suggestion programs have only recently become widespread in public agencies and are still less well established than in the private sector.

Behavioral awards reward specific behaviors that management wishes to encourage. If absenteeism is a problem, a system might be designed to reward good attendance; if workplace accidents are a problem, a system might be designed to reward excellent safety records. Again, it is important to establish clear standards for performance and relate them to specific benefits.

Employee recognition programs, although they do not provide monetary incentives, are often an effective way to acknowledge special contributions of certain employees or groups. An employee-of-the-month program, for example, allows top management (the governor, a department head, or a city manager) to recognize individuals who have done work "above and beyond the call of duty." Similarly, special recognition of groups of employees involved in quality circles or interdepartmental task forces is a good way to highlight work of exceptional quality. At little or no real cost, such programs provide a surprisingly good incentive for employees and emphasize the high-quality work that most employees of public organizations do. As one productivity leader pointed out, "You always hear about the bad things that happen in government. An employee-of-the-month program gives us an opportunity to talk about the good things that happen!"

What Would You Do?

As head of a state agency, you are concerned that your employees have fallen into the old trap of assuming that "the way things have always been done" is the way they should be done in the future. You would like your agency to be one known for its innovation practices, for being on the cutting edge of what's happening in your field. What would you do?

All in all, incentive programs are effective mechanisms for encouraging employees to make more significant or more appropriate contributions to the organization. You must be careful, however, to identify specific behaviors that will lead to improved productivity, devise specific measures so you know when the objective has been met, and provide an appropriate and meaningful incentive. As the success of employee recognition programs testifies, incentive programs do not work merely because employees need more money. Employees also respond because they take pride in their work and in their contributions to the organization's success.

Innovation

A more recent strategy for improving productivity in public and nonprofit organizations involves encouraging innovation by public servants (see Box 10.3). Unfortunately, although many managers and consultants search for ways to innovate, the concept of innovation tends to be one of the least understood in management. Some view it simply as implementing some new system or process within an organization or as improving the business of government. Others appreciate innovation as a way of adding public value or serving more effectively in the public interest. Most will agree, however, that at its core, innovation involves challenging the "prevailing wisdom" in management theory and practice (Light, 1998, p. xvi).

BOX 10.3
AWARDING INNOVATION IN PUBLIC AND NONPROFIT ORGANIZATIONS

In 1985, the Ford Foundation launched an award program in conjunction with Harvard University's Kennedy School of Government to celebrate innovations by public-sector organizations. Since then the Innovations in American Government Program has recognized 280 programs with more than $17.2 million in Ford Foundation grants. The Ford Foundation also became the principal sponsor of the Kennedy School's Institute for Government Innovation, which provides support to scholars and practitioners in the form of research forums, conferences, case studies, and other resources.

Similarly, the Alliance for Innovation (a partnership of the International City Management Association, the former Innovation Groups, and the Arizona State University School of Public Affairs) presents several awards for innovation in local government. Criteria for the awards include: how it successfully addressed an important dilemma of public service delivery concerns, how it has had a positive impact and tremendous benefit to the community or jurisdiction, a quantum leap of creativity, and tangible effectiveness and results.

The Peter F. Drucker Foundation offers a similar award program for innovations by non-profits. Each year the foundation recognizes a nonprofit organization that finds new ways of touching the lives of those it serves, based on Peter Drucker's definition of innovation: *Change that creates a new dimension of performance.* To be eligible, the nonprofit must show how the innovation (1) advances the organization's mission; (2) helps the organization achieve clear, meaningful outcomes; (3) features a "new dimension" of performance; (4) makes a difference in the lives of clients; and (5) serves as a model that may be replicated by other nonprofits. The award includes a $25,000 prize and a short documentary video.

SOURCE: The Innovations in American Government Home Page (www.harvard.edu/innovat/home.html) and the Peter F. Drucker Foundation Innovation Award Information Page (www.pfdf.org/award/about.html) (August, 2001).

H. George Frederickson (2000, p. 8) recently attempted to sort out some of the different ways of thinking about innovation, contrasting between "managed innovation" and "sustaining innovation." First, in managed innovation the primary driver of change tends to be the visionary, with the main objectives being productivity, efficiency, and the improving government's "bottom-line." This type of innovation becomes communicated through best-practices research for other organizations to diffuse into their administrative practices.

The managing innovation approach begins with the core mission of the organization, often as articulated by the visionary leader. Staff roles involve setting objectives for accomplishing the mission and implementing the innovative practices set out by management. It is a linear process, at the end of which the organization is able to achieve a new level of productivity. But, as critics point out, it also results in a much shallower form of innovation, one that fails to take into account the underlying values of the organization or provide for managing through rapidly changing conditions.

Sustaining innovation, on the other hand, builds from Paul Light's (1998) work by the same name and depends less on the visionary hero and more on leaders inside and outside of the organization. Unlike its more linear counterpart, the sustaining innovation approach involves as much of a process of searching for questions as it does searching for answers. Frederickson wrote, "Under conditions of sustained innovation it is far better to approximate an answer to the right question, which is often vague, than to search for the exact answer to the wrong question. Such answers can always be made more precise; they are still answers to the wrong question" (Frederickson, 2000, p. 8). The underlying belief is that each organization faces competing goals, based on each group of stakeholders, and often must work harder to identify the problems, not just the solutions.

According to Light (1998), sustaining innovation begins with removing barriers to excellence and what he calls "debunking the myths"—for example, innovation being limited to just a few, perfect organizations—that tend to block natural forms of creativity in public and nonprofit agencies. Light challenges managers to give up the quest for absolute efficiency and search instead for "preferred states of being"—that is, "an ecosystem in which an organization's innovativeness depends upon four factors that ignite and sustain new ideas: (1) the external environment in which a given organization exists, (2) its internal structure, (3) its leadership, and (4) its internal management systems" (Light, 1998, pp. 12–13).

The sustaining innovation approach provides greater flexibility and places the opportunity for innovation into the hands of those at all levels. As a result, this approach allows organizations to deal more effectively with ambiguity—both in goal-setting and in relations in the external environment. Given its open engagement with external stakeholders, the sustaining innovation approach also enables organizations to anticipate change and maintain effective, meaningful relationships for the long term.

Recent Examples of Performance Management

Public and nonprofit organizations at all levels have experimented with formal efforts to improve quality, productivity, and overall performance. Generally speaking, public productivity is concerned with how organizations can achieve their objectives as efficiently and effectively as possible—how they can improve their performance. Some emphasize technological innovation, while others emphasize human resources management; some operate through centralized productivity improvement staffs, while others are more decentralized. But most have successfully demonstrated the value of managing for results.

NETWORKING

Now that the NPR site has closed, information on examples of reinventing government have been archived at http://govinfo.library.unt.edu/npr. Additional sites about NPR, reinvention, and reengineering include www.gsa.gov/Portal/gsa/ep/home.do?tabId=0 and www. reengineering.com.

GAO Cites Best Practices for Performance Management   The Government Accountability Office (GAO) recently completed a comprehensive survey of twenty-five federal and state regulatory agencies to determine best practices for performance-based management and measurement. Agencies selected for participation had been identified either by the GAO or other sources as leaders in designing and implementing performance management systems. The GAO study provided twelve recommendations based on best practices shared across the various sites.

1. Focus on building effective performance management strategies by making managing-for-results a top priority and dedicated resources to enhance core organizational competencies.
2. Ensure ownership of performance management and measurement activities throughout the agency.
3. Redesign work processes, internal structures, and lines of responsibility to be consistent with the new performance measurement systems.
4. Forge solid alliances—in this particular case, with regulated agencies, as well as with partners in service delivery.
5. Develop ties with counterparts, which in the case of regulatory agencies were other organizations in programs with crosscutting jurisdictions.
6. Adopt a systems-thinking approach to understand the influences and impacts of individual programs.
7. Establish clear, measurable performance goals and objectives that are in line with the new performance measurement rationale.
8. Identify appropriate performance targets for each of the goals and objectives in the system.
9. Select appropriate, reliable data sources to support the performance goals and objectives.
10. Focus analysis on specific functions—in this case, regulatory interventions—with an emphasis on maximizing results and targeting action at all phases of action.
11. Integrate into their performance analysis consideration of internal and external factors affecting the agency and its interventions.
12. Engage in processes of continuous improvement to ensure ongoing appropriateness in performance measurement systems (Government Accounting Office, 1999).

Although the study focused on regulatory agencies, the GAO anticipates that its findings can be used by nonregulatory organizations at all levels to enhance productivity and performance (for discussion, see the CAP Corner, *PA Times*, December 1999, p. 10).

Measuring Performance in Arizona   The state of Arizona has been working to transform its productivity and accountability system to concentrate on "what matters" in public service. Arizona initiated the transformation in 1993, when the state legislature passed a bill requiring state agencies to engage in strategic planning and to tie their strategic goals and objectives to measurable performance targets (similar to GPRA). Agencies currently submit performance information at the program level through program operating plans that include goals, performance measures, and budgetary information.

Although all facets of Arizona's performance management system have not yet been fully implemented, some of the early signs suggest a definite cost savings as a result of the state's dedication to performance management. The general consensus among state officials is that the new system has contributed to a slower growth in the amount of state government expenditures and a corresponding decline in the level of taxation, but without a negative impact on government productivity.

Most importantly, the performance management system has enabled state agencies to become more effective in achieving public outcomes and in more effectively modeling its service delivery to accommodate performance objectives. The Department of Economic Security, for example, in the past was able to report only on isolated cases of support to children and their families. Under the new performance measurement system, the department has been successful in identifying systemswide service targets and now can track its delivery to make sure it remains focused toward accomplishing the agency's strategic objectives. State officials thus have removed the guesswork from decision making, relying instead on "knowledge-driven" management.

A key contributor to the success of Arizona's performance management system has been its integration throughout the state hierarchy. Department heads take a leading role in designing the system's framework, but the ownership and sustainability of the system has been with staff. Many state employees have come to recognize the usefulness of the performance measures for improving internal operations. The state's report on the system stated, "This has helped institutionalize the use of performance measures and contributed to the continued evolution of using measures of performance within the executive branch. . . [It should also] aid in their use by the legislative branch" (Governmental Accounting Standards Board, 2000a, p. 2). As with the sustaining innovation approach discussed previously, the sense of shared ownership should enable the state to maintain a flexible, effective management system well into the future. (For discussion, see Governmental Accounting Standards Board, 2000a.)

Benchmarking and Performance Improvement in the City of Portland   In the City of Portland, Oregon, public officials have implemented several performance measurement tracking systems aimed at enhancing productivity and effectiveness of government programs. Underlying Portland's system is the use of benchmarks, which provide performance standards and points of comparison for the city's leadership and staff. The city also has integrated productivity and outcome targets in its strategic planning and budget decision-making processes.

City officials at all levels have a key role to play in Portland's performance management system. Due to the decentralized nature of the city government, this means that department heads, middle managers, and staff share responsibility for setting strategic objectives, tracking effectiveness, and reporting to key stakeholders on the performance results. Moreover, the city uses its community outreach to bring citizens into the performance management process. Portland relies on both formal mechanisms of public participation, with citizens serving on the Portland-Multnomah Progress Board, and informal approaches to citizen engagement.

Besides the benefits for productivity, Portland's performance measurement system has given the city government exciting new forums for sharing progress and facilitating organizational learning. The city's report stated, "Communicating results is seen as a driving force behind the intent and expectations of Portland's performance measurement efforts, involving both communication within the government as well as communication to stakeholders and the public" (Governmental Accounting Standards Board, 2000b, pp. 2–3). City officials use a variety of messaging strategies to inform their colleagues internally on performance issues and to connect with the public on citizen priorities.

However, the Portland experience has not come without its share of obstacles. Among the most significant roadblocks have been (1) setting solid, measurable performance targets; (2) ensuring the quality and reliability of performance data; and (3) covering the time and cost required to maintain the reporting and tracking under the new system. The result has been concerns relating to the consistency of the system agency-by-agency and the capacity of city departments to continue tracking performance over time.

Like Arizona, the principal strength of the Portland initiative is the high degree of ownership for the system throughout the city government. If this was seen by staff as something imposed by department heads or elected officials, there might be a higher level of resistance. Under such conditions it would be questionable if the performance management approach would be sustainable in the future. But in Portland the city government as a whole appears to have embraced this new system as a way of serving more effectively in the public interest, and as a result, performance management seems to be a key part of the city's policy and administrative decision making.

Implementation Issues in Quality and Productivity

Whatever approach to improving quality, productivity, and performance you undertake, the design of your intervention will be important to its success.

Productivity in public organizations, as in others, can often be improved through technological innovations. Many areas of federal, state, and local governmental activity rest on a strong technical base. In areas such as the design and construction of waste-to-energy plants, development of pollution control devices (including hazardous-waste treatment centers), or building of public housing, new technologies may help governments to be not only more effective in meeting their objectives, but also to be more cost efficient.

NETWORKING

Several organizations offer resources, case studies, and links to other sites on the issue of productivity, including the NPR archives at http://govinfo.library.unt.edu/npr, the National Center for Public Productivity at www.ncpp.us, and the American Productivity and Quality Center at www.apqc.org. The Benchmarking Exchange at www.benchnet.com also features information on benchmarking and performance measurement.

Think for a moment about the changes that are likely to occur in the country's transportation system over the next twenty years. In the not-too-distant future, high-speed intercity rail systems or vehicles that move on cushions of air may well displace planes, cars, and trains as the primary means of transportation between major urban areas. Designing the systems, regulating them, coordinating among various systems, providing communications and control—all these and many more functions will fall at least in part to government, and all will benefit from advanced technology.

Other efforts, such as those associated with the reinventing government movement, are more concerned with changing the culture and practices of the organizations, but these can vary in scope. Some programs simply require you to undertake new efforts to motivate your employees. Others are more programmatic; for example, you might emphasize greater responsibility on the part of lower-level personnel through a job enrichment strategy, or you might develop a recognition program within the unit.

You might also work with a broader program, such as undertaking a reinvention effort throughout a local government or establishing a governmentwide employee suggestion award system.

Steps to Productivity Improvement

Whatever the level or organization of the quality and productivity effort, there are certain basic issues to consider.

1. *Identify ripe areas.* Identify areas that are "ripe" for productivity improvement. Any program, however great its ambitions, must start small. It makes sense to start where you are most likely to achieve immediate gains, because you will identify savings most quickly here, and because a few early successes will encourage productivity improvement efforts elsewhere. To identify areas, managers should be particularly attentive to:
   - functions continually faced with large backlogs of work or slipping deadlines.
   - operations where visible problems have already been hinted at (citizen complaints, high employee turnover).
   - operations that appear to be using an unusually large percentage of resources.
   - operations where large numbers of employees perform essentially repetitive tasks (payoffs will be especially evident here because of the effect of multiplying any increase by the number of employees).
   - availability of new techniques or technology already proven workable elsewhere (that is, computer installation to improve police response time).
   - receptivity of managers and supervisors to new ideas coupled with an ability to follow through (Holzer, Rosen, & Zalk, 1986, pp. 9–15).

2. *Locate models in other jurisdictions.* Whatever your organization, it is likely that there are others like it and that others have experienced similar problems. Having some idea of how others approached the issues you are now confronting is especially helpful. Fortunately, such information is readily available, either through publications such as the Governmental Productivity News or through professional organizations such as the American Society for Public Administration or the International City Management Association. From these sources, you may discover new approaches to productivity improvement, or you may find that approaches you are considering have either been successful or have failed elsewhere.

3. *Define roles.* Define the roles of those who will be involved in planning and implementing the program. Some programs are oriented to a particular department, while others cut across several departments within a jurisdiction; in either case, some staffing for the

productivity effort will be necessary. Staffing at the department level will provide a specific focus to the productivity program and will allow you to build technical expertise (such as, in fire or police work). A centralized productivity staff will enable you to give broad impetus to the program and to build general expertise in productivity techniques. Presumably, this general knowledge can then be applied in various departments.

4. *Set realistic goals and objectives.* As noted, productivity programs in public organizations have been stimulated by public demand for "doing more with less." You may thus be tempted to set high expectations for a new productivity improvement effort; resist the temptation. Setting realistic goals and objectives and actually meeting them is more helpful in the long run than setting too-high expectations and falling short.

5. *Choose among alternative programs.* Different approaches range from changes in management style to technological innovations to specific productivity efforts, such as quality circles or incentive programs. In implementing a productivity program, it is advisable to fit the solution to the problem rather than the other way around. Though this advice seems obvious, you may find yourself tempted to pursue an immediate opportunity rather than engage in more careful planning. For example, a vendor might herald a new telecommunications system as the solution to all your problems. Even though you may not view communications issues as your highest priorities in terms of productivity improvement, you may be tempted to adopt the new technology "just because it's there." A more reasonable approach, of course, is to establish a prioritized list of problems, then seek to develop solutions that match your most important concerns.

6. *Anticipate problems.* Many problems can arise in implementing a productivity improvement program, especially one of high visibility. Many of the problems are based on misconceptions about what productivity improvement is all about and can be anticipated and dealt with early in the program. Employees might feel that a quality circles program will lead to elimination of jobs, or they may feel that safety standards will be lowered; in fact, neither outcome is likely. But these are serious concerns that should be thoroughly discussed as the program is begun. To the extent possible, all participants and all people likely to be affected by the program should have a chance to learn about and comment on the proposed program. Dealing with questions up front minimizes confusion and disruption later.

7. *Implement the program.* After carefully analyzing the need for a productivity improvement program and deciding on a course of action that will address the identified needs, you will face the difficult task of implementation. Implementation may, in fact, be the most difficult phase. Expectations may be too high; needed legislation may be difficult to pass; organization "turf" issues may interfere; there may not be enough money to invest in the program.

You can avoid some of the difficulties by starting the program on a modest basis, then expanding to other areas. Limiting objectives at the outset can help keep expectations from rising too high and will make it easier to demonstrate the viability of the effort. Beginning the program in an area where you might reasonably expect quick and identifiable gains will enable you to claim early success and in turn make the program more likely to be adopted elsewhere. Similarly, keeping a low profile for the program in its early days will make it less threatening to labor and management. Whatever publicity is accorded to the program (and many political leaders will want high-profile efforts), you should monitor the program carefully in its early days to avoid misconceptions.

The most serious limitations, however, are the difficulties in institutionalizing the program. Implementation is not merely a short-term concern; you should be concerned from the beginning about how durable the program is likely to be. Several factors work against institutionalization of productivity improvement programs. Programs may be dependent on a particular individual, such as a governor or mayor or a particular department head, and may be discontinued when that person leaves office. Many programs lack an organizational home and thus find it difficult to sustain support over a period of years.

8. *Evaluate the program.* Most productivity improvement programs require an initial investment of money and time; you have to spend money to save money, and many people may be skeptical of the program's value. Skeptics are likely to be unconvinced by general statements of program advocates; they will want to see specific, objective data. Types of information you should collect from the beginning are documented cost savings, increased output that has been achieved at a similar or reduced cost, or increased citizen satisfaction with the agency's services. This information can be made public through periodic reports to legislators or other decision makers or through press conferences or news releases.

An aspect of evaluation that needs special attention is the development of an appropriate measurement system to ensure that the proper information is being acquired at an appropriate time. You must be sure that information is gathered on a timely basis and that it is accurate. The information must also be fully relevant to measuring the improvement effort. It is difficult to develop a measurement system, but it may be critical to sustaining your program over time.

We have already discussed ways to measure objectives. For example, a social service agency might measure the number of clients served, a police department might measure response time, or a public works department might measure numbers of miles of streets and highways paved. Matters are complicated, of course, by the fact that most organizations seek several objectives simultaneously. The social services agency is not concerned only with screening clients, but may also make referrals to other agencies or distribute money to certain clients. Each of these multiple objectives, and each of the activities that contribute to the objectives, may require its own separate measure.

Even more important, those who measure the effects of productivity improvement programs need to be attentive to what properly reflects the quality of work performed. Obtaining an increase in cost savings at the expense of courtesy or promptness is questionable at best. Responding to requests for information or help "when it is convenient" to the agency may be less costly, but will probably not be acceptable in terms of quality. You may wish to consider either a separate measure of quality or implementation of a quality control system. You might also be able to develop composite measures that combine considerations for output and quality. For example, the streets department might measure repairs made within a certain number of working days, or the revenue department might measure the number of tax returns processed without error.

Three conditions appear to be required for productivity improvements to occur: "(a) the performance of individuals or groups must be assessed in a valid, objective manner, emphasizing the public purposes of the services provided by those employees; (b) such assessment should be closely linked to some type of reward or penalty, whether monetary or nonmonetary; and (c) there should be both early meaningful involvement by employee organizations as well as adequate advance participation and training for those affected, including supervisory as well as nonsupervisory employees" (Greiner et al., 1981, p. 411). Developing programs with these considerations in mind will help ensure not only early successes in productivity improvement, but will also help sustain the program through the years.

■ Summary and Action Implications

Technical innovations are often dramatic in their impact, sometimes saving thousands, even millions, of dollars. But technological innovations do not occur independently of the skills and attitudes of those who work in an organization. Innovations seem to flourish in a climate where human creativity is encouraged and usually require human changes—what one group calls "orgware"—to be successfully implemented.

Improved productivity appears to depend at least in part on a shift from the traditional authoritarian approach to management to a more open and participatory approach. This shift has been especially apparent in implementing productivity improvement programs at all levels of government. In many cases, we find a shifting orientation toward management that places greater emphasis on the involvement of all employees. (The resulting orientation was perhaps best expressed by the head of a state productivity council, who described his philosophy this way: "Those who do the work know the work best and know best how to improve the work.") The result is an approach to management that seems not only more human in scale and perspective, but that many authorities are coming to believe is far more productive as well.

A study by the Canadian government of "well-performing" governmental organizations in that country twenty years ago outlines some of the basics of this approach in terms that are still relevant today. That study identified five factors leading to organizational success, which we may take as recommended patterns of action for managers to seek in trying to improve productivity.

Emphasis on people. People are challenged, encouraged, and developed. They are given power to act and to use their judgment. There is a belief that high performance is a product of people who care rather than systems that constrain. People do not preoccupy themselves with the risk of failure, but are confident they can tackle virtually any challenge.

Participative leadership. Leadership is not authoritarian or coercive, but participative whenever possible. The leaders envision an ideal organization, define purpose and goals, then articulate these and foster commitment. Staff communicate easily. They feel comfortable consulting peers as well as those above and below them. Although formal levels exist for administrative purposes, there are no boundaries that inhibit collaboration in achieving goals.

Innovative work styles. Staff reflect on their performance. They learn from the effects of their actions. They seek to solve problems creatively. They maintain strong monitoring, feedback, and control systems as useful tools. They are self-reliant, rather than dependent on control from an outside authority.

Strong client orientation. These organizations focus strongly on their clients, deriving satisfaction from serving the client rather than the bureaucracy. There is an alignment of values and purpose between the well-performing agency and their political and central agency masters.

A mindset that seeks optimum performance. People hold values that drive them to always seek improvement in their organization's performance. When conditions change, they adjust their methods, not their values. Because of this orientation toward performance and adaptability, the organization performs well even in a changing environment. This mindset may be the most important feature of all *Government Productivity News*, December 1989, p. 4).

SOURCE: Extract originally from the *Report of the Auditor General of Canada to the House of Commons for Fiscal Year Ending 31 March 1988,* Chapter 4: "Attributes of Well-Performing Organizations." Minister of Supply and Services, Canada, 1990.

As a manager, one of the primary technical concerns you will face is improving your organization's productivity. Whereas you may be able to accomplish great gains through technological innovations, the most significant long-term gains will come from a proper emphasis on the human factors in organizational effectiveness. To be judged successful, you will always have to balance your concern for the technical side of your agency's work and your attention to the human side of the organization.

TERMS AND DEFINITIONS

Behavioral award: Used to reward specific behaviors that management wishes to encourage.

Employee recognition program: Effective way to acknowledge special contributions of certain employees or groups to the organization.

Expert systems: Computer programs that mimic the decision-making processes of human experts within a particular field.

Gainsharing plan: Monetary award for a group of employees based on savings generated by the group.

Management by objectives: Participatory approach to establishing clear and measurable objectives throughout the entire organization.

Performance appraisal: Specific evaluation with respect to an individual's progress in completing specified tasks.

Performance bonus: One-time monetary award based on superior performance on the job or in a particular task.

Piecework bonus: Incentive that ties the worker's productivity in a given task to the monetary rewards he or she receives.

Quality circle: Small group of people who do similar or connected work and meet regularly to identify, analyze, and solve work-process problems.

Suggestion award program: Incentive for employees who make specific suggestions that result in savings for the organization.

Task forces: Groups brought together to work on specific organizational problems.

STUDY QUESTIONS

1. Discuss the relationship between the growing use of computer-based systems and the human element involved in technology transfer.

2. What is management by objectives, and how can this approach benefit an organization?

3. Identify the eight categories for judging the quality of work-life.

4. Discuss the variety of incentive plans currently used in public agencies. Explain the usefulness of each approach.

5. Productivity improvement has become a major concern of public managers. What basic issues should one consider when undertaking a quality of productivity program?

CASES AND EXERCISES

1. Using the material in this chapter, develop a set of criteria for evaluating the quality of work-life. Working in groups of five to seven, choose two or three jobs that members of the group have previously held and analyze the quality of work-life in those jobs. In each case, members of the group should interview the person who held the job, asking questions about each category in the chart. When everyone has a complete understanding of the nature of the job, the group as a whole should draw conclusions with respect to the quality of work-life for someone holding that job.

   Following this activity, choose two or three jobs to which members of the group might reasonably aspire in ten to fifteen years. Have one individual imagine in detail what the job would be like from day to day, and then follow the same procedure to interview the "job holder" and draw conclusions about the quality of work-life. In what ways do you expect that future jobs will be of higher "quality" than those in the past? Why should there be any differences?

Finally, choose one job from the "jobs already held" and one from those "to which you aspire." Then consider these jobs from the standpoint of the person to whom the individual job holder would report. How could the manager improve or "enrich" the particular job? Specifically, could adjustments in authority or responsibility improve the quality of work-life for the job holder? How would those changes affect the individual's productivity? Report your conclusions to the class.

2. Divide the class into groups ranging from seven to ten members each. Have each group select a reasonably small public agency—federal, state, local, or nonprofit. Based on interviews with several top managers and a sampling of employees throughout the organization, analyze the organization's existing system of incentives. Design a new incentive program you think would result in improved quality and productivity. (If you have difficulty locating or gaining access to a particular organization, simply develop a research design through which you might test an incentive system. Assume an organization of 200 people engaged in manual processing of tax receipts for a state government. What kinds of questions would you ask of which individuals in the organization?)

3. Academic departments, like other organizations, can benefit from information and advice from employees and clients (faculty, staff, students, alumni, potential employers, and so on). Consider the department of your major. How would you design a comprehensive program of employee and client involvement that would help the department improve the quality of its offerings? (After designing a program, you might interview the department chair to find out what mechanisms are already in place.)

FOR ADDITIONAL READING

Altshuler, Alan A., and Robert D. Behn, eds. *Innovation in American Government: Challenge, Opportunities and Dilemmas.* Washington, DC: Brookings Institute, 1997.

Barzelay, Michael. *The New Public Management: Improving Research and Policy Dialogue.* Berkeley: University of California Press/Russell Sage Foundation, 2001.

Cohen, Steven, and Ronald Brand. *Total Quality Management in Government: A Practical Guide for the Real World.* San Francisco: Jossey-Bass, 1993.

Dilulio, John, Jr., Gerald Garvey, and Donald Kettl. *Improving Government Performance.* Washington, DC: Brookings Institute, 1993.

Garson, David G., ed. *Handbook of Public Information Systems.* 2nd ed. Boca Raton, FL: Taylor & Francis, 2005.

Gore, Albert. *Common Sense Government.* New York: Random House, 1995.

Gore, Albert. *Businesslike Government.* Washington, DC: Government Printing Office, 1997.

Gore, Albert. *Serving the American Public.* Washington, DC: Government Printing Office, 1997.

Kamensky, John M., and Albert Morales, eds. *Competition, Choice, and Incentives in Government Programs.* Lanham, MD : Rowman & Littlefield, 2006.

Kelman, Steven. *Unleashing Change: A Study of Organizational Renewal in Government.* Washington, DC: Brookings Institute, 2005.

Lane, Jan-Erik. *New Public Management.* London: Routledge, 2000.

Light, Paul C. *The Tides of Reform.* New Haven, CT: Yale University Press, 1997.

Matzer, John, Jr., ed. *Productivity Improvement Techniques.* Washington, DC: International City Management Association, 1986.

National Performance Review. *From Red Tape to Results: Creating a Government That Works Better and Costs Less.* Washington, DC: Government Printing Office, 1993.

Osborne, David, and Ted Gaebler. *Reinventing Government.* Reading, MA: Addison-Wesley, 1992.

Osborne, David, and Peter Plastrik. *Banishing Bureaucracy.* Reading, MA: Addison-Wesley, 1997.

Pollitt, Christopher, and Geert Bouckaert. *Public Management Reform: A Comparative Analysis.* 2nd ed. New York: Oxford University Press, 2004.

Pollitt, Christopher, and Colin Talbot, eds. *Unbundled Government: A Critical Analysis of the Global Trend to Agencies, Quangos and Contractualisation.* London: Routledge, 2004.

Rocheleau, Bruce. *Public Management Information Systems.* Hershey, PA : Idea Group Pub., 2006.

Schachter, Hindy L. *Reinventing Government or Reinventing Ourselves.* Albany: State University of New York Press, 1997.

Stanton, Thomas H., ed. *Meeting the Challenge of 9/11: Blueprints for more Effective Government.* Armonk, NY: M. E. Sharpe, 2006.

Swiss, James. *Public Management Systems: Monitoring and Managing Government Performance.* Englewood Cliffs, NJ: Prentice-Hall, 1990.

Wholey, Joseph S., and Kathryn E. Newcomer. *Improving Government Performance: Evaluation Strategies for Strengthening Public Agencies and Programs.* San Francisco: Jossey-Bass, 1989.

CHAPTER 11

THE FUTURE OF THE PUBLIC SERVICE

For those considering work in the public service, whether for a relatively short period or for an entire career, several considerations may shape your thinking. As we have noted, the rewards of public service are not likely to be primarily financial. Salaries in most public organizations lag somewhat behind comparable salaries in business or industry. At the same time, however, those in public organizations are likely to be given a broader range of responsibilities earlier in their careers than their counterparts in business or industry. Moreover, the challenges and complexities of public service provide a special excitement that comes from being a part of unfolding major events—local, state, national, or even international.

If you want to be a part of what's happening in a changing society, then the public service is the place for you. Think about the incredible variety of work in the public sector. Public managers are key actors in foreign affairs, the human services, environmental policy, educational reform, the space program, and an endless variety of other important areas. Indeed, it is fair to say that every major local, state, national, or international issue now being discussed will provide challenges and opportunities for public managers in the future. If you are interested in meaningful work—work that makes a difference in people's lives—then you should find involvement in public service quite appealing.

■ The Importance of Public Service

Throughout most of our country's history, public service has been recognized as an important undertaking that contributes to the betterment of society, supported by citizens and politicians alike. Unfortunately, for the past twenty-five years or so, support has wavered. From the late 1960s through the middle 1980s, the public service seemed to be under fairly constant attack. Through the candidacies of both Jimmy Carter and Ronald Reagan, national politicians of both parties organized their campaigns at least in part around attacks on Washington and the bureaucracy. Public administrators were criticized as both unresponsive and overly responsive—unresponsive to the common citizen and overly responsive to special interests. Public organizations were accused of being highly ineffective and inefficient, failing to achieve their objectives and wasting enormous sums of public funds.

Fortunately, the environment of the public service has changed considerably over the past several years, leading us to be somewhat more optimistic about its future image. The first President Bush and President Clinton were more supportive of the federal public service, and President George W. Bush appears to be continuing this trend.

In policy areas, over the past decade, Americans have seen tax reductions and tax reform at the federal level, as well as tax limitations at the state and local levels. These actions have helped to mitigate the view that the government tax machine is running wild. Similarly, throughout the last five presidential administrations, there has been a move to deregulate certain activities. Some areas (such as transportation) were significantly deregulated, while others were put under special scrutiny by the Office of Management and Budget. In general, an impression developed that excessive government intervention was being brought under control.

Finally, the political climate has been changing, even to the point that we might suggest the reemergence of a positive view of government. Such a view has been most evident at the state and local levels. In several important areas—notably education, economic development, and environmental concerns—the states are taking positive actions. And at the same time, public confidence in state and local governments is growing.

Moreover, with growing national concern about such problems as AIDS, hazardous waste, ocean dumping, the greenhouse effect, drugs, foreign competition, the homeless, and child care for working families, we might even speculate that a new era of national action is on the horizon. Certainly the success of the Clinton administration in reducing the size of government and contributing to a projected federal surplus, at the same time encouraging substantial economic growth, suggested the possibility of a more activist era, as well as one in which the men and women who constitute the public service will be treated with greater dignity and respect. On the other hand, several widely publicized problems in the Bush years, problems ranging from the slow response to Katrina and possible mishandling of intelligence prior to the Iraq war, may have undercut that possibility. In any case, the current concerns seem to be directed more at the policy level than the level of administration.

Efforts in support of the public service return our country to a long-standing tradition. At other periods—and even today in other countries—the public service has been considered a proud and honorable profession. John F. Kennedy's inaugural statement continues to have relevance today. Recall that Kennedy said, "Ask not what your country can do for you; ask what you can do for your country." In another speech, Kennedy amplified the point: "Let the public service be a proud and lively career. And let every man and woman who works in any area of our national government, in any branch at any level, be able to say with pride and honor in future years: I served the United States Government in that hour of our nation's need." Those who work in the field of public administration at all levels of government carry forward that long and proud tradition (see Box 11.1).

■ Trends in the Public Service

The challenges that will face those in the public service over the coming years are substantial, for they not only require resolving important public-policy problems, but resolving them in a way that restores and then maintains public confidence. The efforts to restore meaning and integrity to the public service are much needed in our society and in societies around the world, but they should be accompanied by a clear understanding of several important trends in our field that are reshaping the values and commitments of public service itself. What are the major trends worldwide that those entering the public service in the next decades are likely to experience?

BOX 11.1
MAIN CONCLUSIONS OF THE VOLCKER COMMISSION

The central message of this report of the Commission on the Public Service is both simple and profound, both urgent and timeless. In essence, we call for a renewed sense of commitment by all Americans to the highest traditions of the public service—to a public service responsive to the political will of the people and also protective of our constitutional values; to a public service able to cope with complexity and conflict and also able to maintain the highest ethical standards; to a public service attractive to the young and talented from all parts of our society and also capable of earning the respect of all our citizens.

A great nation must demand no less. The multiple challenges thrust upon the Government of the United States as we approach the twenty-first century can only reinforce the point. Yet, there is evidence on all sides of an erosion of performance and morale across government in America. Too many of our most talented public servants—those with the skills and dedication that are the hallmarks of an effective career service—are ready to leave. Too few of our brightest young people—those with the imagination and energy that are essential for the future—are willing to join.

Meanwhile, the need for a strong public service is growing, not lessening. Americans have always expected their national government to guarantee their basic freedoms and provide for the common defense. We continue to expect our government to keep the peace with other nations, resolve differences among our people, pay the bills for needed services, and honor the people's trust by providing the highest levels of integrity and performance.

At the same time, Americans now live in a stronger, more populous nation, a nation with unprecedented opportunity. But they also live in a world of enormous complexity and awesome risks. Our economy is infinitely more open to international competition, our currency floats in a worldwide market, and we live with complex technologies beyond the understanding of any single human mind. Our diplomacy is much more complicated, and the wise use of our unparalleled military power more difficult. And for all our scientific achievements, we are assaulted daily by new social, environmental, and health issues almost incomprehensible in scope and impact issues like drugs, AIDS, and global warming.

Faced with these challenges, the simple idea that Americans must draw upon talented and dedicated individuals to serve us in government is uncontestable. America must have a public service that can both value the lessons of experience and appreciate the requirements for change; a public service that both responds to political leadership and respects the law; a public service with the professional skills and the ethical sensitivity America deserves.

SOURCE: Excerpted from The National Commission on the Public Service, *Leadership for America: Rebuilding the Public Service*. Washington, DC, 1989, pp. 1–2.

Economic Changes and Redefining Government

First, remember that a significant redefinition of the public service is now taking place. Note specifically that changing economic conditions are affecting both the mission and structure of the public enterprise. Our economy has been transformed in several ways from a production base to a service base, from a national base to a global base, and from a growing public commitment to a limited commitment. In each case, there are direct implications for those in the public service.

- Challenges face public managers in areas where traditional industries, such as steel or timber, have suddenly declined, as "high tech and high touch" has become a banner for economic growth.
- Challenges face those at the state and local levels who must play new and important roles in economic development, including international economic development, which may require them to know as much about business decisions in Japan as in their own state capital.
- Challenges face those operating public programs, especially in the human services, who have found government spending severely restricted at a time when the need for the services seems ever increasing.

Our economy is presenting important challenges to government, but in responding to these challenges, government is not alone. The challenges have led to new ways of thinking about public-private relationships in the provision of public services. As a result, public-service work is no longer the work only of government, but an effort in which governmental agencies, nonprofit and third-sector organizations, and corporate and business interests participate. Consider these examples.

- In many states, the number of people employed by private security forces exceeds the number employed by local police departments.
- In some cities, the chamber of commerce is so involved in public programs that it receives more funding from government than it receives from private business.
- In major urban areas, fewer than half of human services are delivered by government; the majority are delivered by nonprofit and private agencies.

Some of these trends, such as privatization and contracting for specific goods and services, are becoming familiar; others are quite distinctive, because they involve third parties' discretion in the use of public authority and in spending of public funds. This development suggests a significant reshaping of the public service and raises serious questions about equity and accountability in the management of public programs.

Trends associated with the reform agendas in the public and nonprofit sectors reflect more recent responses to our changing social and economic condition. We have noted that the reform agenda stems from the belief that government has failed to keep pace with the dynamic environment in the postindustrial world. Consequently, the reform movement already has had a dramatic impact on the character and processes of government organizations at all levels. And given the attention this reform movement has received, such trends promise to continue into the future.

An important consideration with respect to the reform movements relates to the application of entrepreneurial practices and business values in public service. Although transforming the relationship between a government and its citizens economic terms— that is, viewing the citizen as a customer—may generate cost savings and lead to more streamlined public organizations, the question remains as to what the long-term impact will be for issues of citizenship and public participation. Although creating a government that "does more with less" may produce a stronger bottom line, it could also have harmful effects for issues of citizen engagement with the institutions of governance.

On the other hand, one international group cautions would-be reformers to avoid what it calls "reform fatigue," or "the condition in which public servants become cynical and tired of reform" (OECD, 2001, p. 5). In its study of thirty countries that have implemented some type of reform agenda, the OECD found that the most successful reforms were not imposed from the executive leadership level but were embraced (and in most cases initiated) by those at all levels. Most importantly, successful reforms resulted not from change simply for change's sake, but rather from attempts to build more adaptive, responsive organizational systems. (See Box 11.2.)

Globalization

Second, changing economic conditions have combined with technological developments to make the international dimensions of public administration more important than ever. Understanding the activities of political and administrative officials in other countries is important not only for those who will spend part of their careers outside the United States, but also for those who will work at home. Increasingly, city managers, for example, find that to be effective in local economic development activities, they must be experts in international business. But global interdependencies will affect us in other ways as well; for example, the deforestation in Brazil,

BOX 11.2

CHALLENGES FOR THE FUTURE

The OECD's Public Management and Governance Service (or PUMA) recently released its prediction of "government of the future," citing the following questions facing public officials in the twenty-first century.

- How can governments best prepare themselves for reform challenges?
- How can the public sector develop a culture responsive to change?
- What types of leaders are needed?
- How can governments better communicate with citizens?
- How can governments avoid "reform fatigue"?

Although the OECD recognized the need for reform in some cases, it also cautioned reformers to take stock of the scope of change and make sure the reform agendas remained in line with citizen-oriented outcomes. Moreover, the OECD challenged reformers to make this a shared process. "Public management reform has important stakes for all members of society, but too often people are forced into opposite sides in discussions on reform: by dividing people into winners and losers, the stage is set for conflict rather than success" (OECD, 2001, p. 1). The key challenge will be to use the opportunity created by the improving image of government to build a consensus around the goals, as well as the underlying values, of the reforms.

SOURCE: OECD, *Government of the Future*. PUMA Policy Brief No. 9, Paris: OECD, June 2001.

NETWORKING

For information concerning international perspectives on governance and public administration, visit the OECD at www.oecd.org or the United Nations at www.un.org/esa. Local issues on a global scale, including decentralization and sustainable development, can be researched online at the ICMA at www.icma.org/resources/index.htm or at the International City Government Resource Centre at www.geocities.com/Paris/9925.

Africa, and the Philippines will directly affect the quality of our own environment. And, of course, we cannot overlook our obligation to help reduce poverty and hunger throughout the world.

Several diverse—indeed, competing—views have emerged relating to this globalization trend. They range from a critical perspective, in which the trend is seen as an attempt by developed nations to introduce Western values into other regions, to what supporters believe to be a chance to extend employment opportunities and wealth creation into impoverished nations. This latter view suggests that, over time, all of us in the global village will benefit from the forces of globalization and the internationalization of economic markets.

The impact of globalization on public administration should not be underestimated. However, relating to the internationalization process is a pattern that carries perhaps even greater implications: decentralization. Central governments increasingly are handing over new powers and responsibilities to local and regional authorities. Whether triggered by declining revenues at the national level, or the nation-state's diminished powerbase, the result has been growing demand for services and decision making by subnational administrations. And in many cases, these administrations lack the capacity and resources to deal effectively with their newfound authority.

To better understand these trends, and what they mean for public administration, the development of more globalized, comparative forms of analysis will be critical. Such analysis serves both as a source of understanding international issues, as well as enhancing the way we deal with issues in our own communities. So as we continue to live in our "global village," we will be challenged to deal with opportunities and threats that defy national boundaries. Our systems of governance, consequently, will need to reflect our concern for the public interest—both at home and abroad.

Technology and the Work Environment

A third area of concern is the changing environment in which public servants work. New people and new values are entering the public workplace. Greater diversity in public agencies has had important and positive impacts on the values of those agencies. Public organizations have taken on entirely new shapes, a feat that would have been impossible with the established, more traditional views of organizing that characterized public bureaucracies in the past. In turn, this diversity has contributed to important changes in the way we under-stand leadership, as diverse cultural and organizational views become translated into more equitable, power-sharing systems of authority. One hopes that present trends toward equity and involvement will continue.

Similarly, we have experienced a transformation in the public workplace brought on by new forms of technology. The influence of information technology—in particular, on how we conduct the public's business—has been remarkable, and there is no reason to expect that the technological revolution is over. Pressure to integrate work processes and create more flexible, networked organizations will continue to fuel the drive for more effective forms of communicating and sharing information. We will, more and more, work in vir-tual groups, with much of our interaction being transferred into cyberspace.

As just one example, the Norwegian government has begun to use information and communications technology for more than enhancing internal systems; its Electronic Government Action Plan lays out guidelines on ways public officials can use technology to engage with citizens. As part of the plan, the government has implemented a strat-egy to achieve high levels of public access to the Internet in schools, libraries, homes, and places of employment. A primary purpose is to expand Norway's tradition of civic engagement into the electronic age, something that is being pursued by many localities in the United States.

Of course, the most prevalent argument for technology remains grounded in the more instrumental purpose—that is, the use of technology to enhance government performance. The changing character of government organizations reflects this purpose, as virtually all systems and work processes feature some form of automation. However, we should not lose sight of the fact that technology may also help us achieve more value-oriented goals of public service. Technology in the form of civic networks and other resources may help us shift the orientation of our public organizations to be more external in nature. We may, through our emerging technology, be able to enjoy more meaningful forms of engagement with citizens.

Still, as this trend develops, it raises important concerns for the human consequences of advanced technology. How technology affects the relationship between government workers and their clients, how to cope with the seemingly inevitable impersonality of the information age, and how to resolve the difficult ethical questions relating to privacy and abuse—these and many other issues will continue to confound us over the coming decades as the technological society pursues its present course.

The Role of Citizens in the Governance Process

The fourth issue involves the participation of citizens in the governance process and the notion of civil society. More and more, public decisions are being made through meaning-ful interaction with citizens. This means that citizens are playing an important role not as recipients of government services but as contributors to the policies and programs that affect their lives. In many ways, this emerging form of citizen participation represents a return to important principles that underlie our system of democracy. It appears that we are becoming more concerned with equity and justice, as opposed to merely efficiency and performance. Yet, the change from the more traditional representative democracy to a direct form poses unique challenges for elected and administrative officials.

As it stands, many public administrators view citizen participation as a source of tension. That is, they associate civic engagement with public hearings, legal and administrative arbitration, and other formal mechanisms that tend to be time-consuming and highly confrontational. Public involvement, accordingly, comes to represent a hindrance to efficient management. In turn, public involvement is limited to being a source of legitimacy, through hearings and similar forums, of decisions that have already been made through more rational approaches. However, such limited forms of civic engagement not only result in policies which are detached from the actual needs of affected populations, but over time create barriers between the local institutions of governance and citizens.

Many public officials have started to open governance processes to more substantive forms of engagement. In the Netherlands, for example, public officials at the national and local level have initiated more interactive forms of decision making, where government decisions result not just from consultation with citizens but with direct involvement of the public in the decision-making process. The government also has opened doors for "legal resistance" to governmental actions, giving citizens the opportunity to challenge the government on policies believed to run counter to the public interest.

The move to more direct forms of civic participation opens the door for effective and responsible citizenship. But the theme also cuts in another way, suggesting that those in government must be willing to listen and act in a responsive manner. Only by pursuing this "two-way street" between citizens and government will the most healthy relationship between government and citizens be brought about. For those in public administration, the challenge will be to sustain these meaningful forms of engagement and civil society.

To guide public administrators in this capacity, Janet and Robert Denhardt (2003) offer seven principles of what they call "the New Public Service."

1. The primary role of the public servant is to help citizens articulate and meet their mutual interests rather than to attempt to control or steer society in new directions.
2. Public administrators must make the creation of a collective, shared notion of the public interest paramount.
3. Policies and programs to meet public needs can be most effectively and responsibly achieved through collective efforts and collaborative processes.
4. The public interest is the result of a dialogue about shared values rather than the aggregation of individual self-interests.
5. Public servants must be attentive to more than the market; they must also attend to statutory and constitutional law, community values, political norms, professional standards, and citizen interests.
6. Public organizations and the networks in which they participate are more likely to be successful in the long run if they are operated through processes of collaboration and shared leadership based on a respect for all people.
7. The public interest is better advanced by public servants and citizens committed to making meaningful contributions to society rather than by entrepreneurial managers acting as if public money were their own.

■ The Ethical Challenges Facing the Public Service

Establishing a proper ethical basis for public action is itself one of the most important challenges facing the public service. If your generation has one significant contribution to make to the development of the public service, it may be to identify and elaborate the moral and ethical dimensions of public administration and to assert moral leadership.

As we have seen, early writers in the field portrayed public administration primarily as a managerial concern with the technical processes of implementing public policy. Over the years, public administrators have developed considerable skill in managing public programs—probably more than they are usually given credit for.

Others soon came to recognize that public administration is also a political concern—that administrators at all levels are deeply involved in shaping public policy. Despite recent rhetoric in Washington, there is every reason to expect that those in public organizations will increasingly be called upon to do more than simply respond to legislative mandate; they will be asked to identify and to articulate important public interests.

Beyond a view of public administration as a managerial or a political concern, public administration today is increasingly an ethical concern. Indeed, all the "spontaneous" little actions you will take as an administrator will carry important value implications. At the root of every act of every public servant, whether in developing or executing public policy, lies a moral or ethical question.

What does it mean, then, to recognize public service as not only a managerial and political concern but also as a moral and ethical concern? For one thing, it means that public administrators must demonstrate in their own actions the highest standards of behavior. Beyond that, to see the public service as a moral and ethical concern requires recognition that every action an administrator takes involves an effort to discover or to clarify the public interest.

The future public servant will likely be both active in policy development and responsive to the public interest. Our constitutional structure not only permits but encourages an active executive and administrative role. Even more important is the implicit philosophical directive of the Constitution that public service is a special calling in a democracy and that those who participate in the public service, regardless of background or occupation, are guardians of a public trust.

This point is most critical at a time when our definition of public service is shifting. As we have noted, the public service is no longer merely that group of political and administrative officials employed by government agencies. Public service today involves a wide range of private and nonprofit organizations in the delivery of public goods and services. This development raises managerial concerns, political concerns, and most of all, moral and ethical concerns. Under these conditions, public administrators must assume leadership in establishing a high moral tone for the public service generally. In contrast to the often-heard advice that public administrators should follow the model of business, we might propose just the opposite: that public organizations and the values and commitments they represent should become models for all organizations, at least those involved in the management of public programs.

Ethical considerations have become a central theme in public administration around the world. In Japan, for example, lawmakers at the national level recently passed comprehensive legislation to ensure ethical practices by governmental officials. Among other provisions, the National Public Service Ethics Act, which took effect in April 2000, established a national ethics board to continuously monitor compliance of government officials and to oversee investigations and punishment for violations of ethical standards.

For the public service to regain its proper role in our society, we will have to establish and maintain throughout government and the public service a true commitment to the values of democracy. Trust in the public service and the public willingness to participate in the work of government will occur only if the public is convinced that those in office, whether political or administrative, seek the public interest (not merely their own) and do so with skill and responsibility. Only when our commitment to democratic practices and ideals is clear to all will we once again be able to establish public service as the highest calling in our society.

Commitment to democratic ideals involves concerns such as responsiveness and involvement, but also commitment to equity and justice. Consider for a moment the reasons that bring people to public service. No doubt high on the list would be "concern for the well-being of others." At one point in our history, we seemed to feel that the primary measure of success of the public service was the elimination of human suffering. Public officials are still at the forefront of dealing with the complex and difficult issues of homelessness, poverty, and drug addiction. Perhaps more than any other group, public administrators are uniquely situated to see and understand these concerns. They certainly should be able to pinpoint the failures of past policies, to suggest alternatives, and to work actively toward implementation with elected leaders. Indeed, they have a moral responsibility to do so.

■ A Final Note

The challenges to the public service are substantial and pose managerial, political, and ethical questions for all who participate in public programs. They will require careful analysis and effective action on the part of academics and practitioners in the field of public administration and beyond. Most of all, they are challenges that will require responsibility both in the sense of acting responsibly and in the sense of accepting responsibility for our ideas and actions. The frontiers of public service will present quite difficult personal and professional choices. But responsible public servants will find their solution very rewarding. Albert Schweitzer once said, "I don't know where you will go or what you will do, but the ones among you that will be most happy will be those who serve." We would only add that especially happy will be those who serve the public, well and faithfully.

STUDY QUESTIONS

1. Discuss some of the changes in the image of public service over the last thirty years.

2. What would you recommend to attract and retain "the best and the brightest" in the public service?

3. Discuss future trends in the field of public administration.

CASES AND EXERCISES

1. By most objective measures, public agencies are, on the average, highly productive—at least in comparison to their private-sector counterparts. (Obviously, there are wide variations in both sectors, but the general conclusion seems valid.) The general public, however, seems to have exactly the opposite impression: that government agencies are hopelessly inefficient and unproductive. Part of the problem seems to be that people are more critical of government in the abstract than where it directly touches their lives. In fact, one study found most people highly critical of the coldness and inefficiency of government in general, but highly complimentary of specific government employees with whom they had dealt most recently.

   In any case, there seems to be some disparity between image and reality—a disparity that is often quite damaging to the morale of the public workforce. Write an essay explaining why you think governments are considered less productive and less efficient than they really are. Consider the issue from several viewpoints. How would the issue appear from the perspective of a legislator? A public manager? A citizen? On the basis of your analysis, what should be done to improve the image of the public service?

2. In this chapter, we have considered a number of trends that are likely to affect the public service over the next decade or more. What do these trends mean in terms of the skills that individual public managers will require? Review once more the set of public management skills in Chapter 1 and then in small groups discuss the following questions: What specific skills will public managers likely utilize more frequently in the future than in the past? What, if any, will be de-emphasized? To what extent will the demands of the future public service change the mix of conceptual, technical, and human skills needed for effective public management? Finally, how will the values that underlie the work of public managers shift as we move through the coming years?

FOR ADDITIONAL READING

Denhardt, Janet V., and Robert B. Denhardt, *The New Public Service*. Armonk, NY: M. E. Sharpe, 2003.

Donahue, John D., and Joseph S. Nye, eds. *For the People: Can We Fix Public Service?* Cambridge, MA: Visions of Governance in the 21st Century, 2003.

Frederickson, George. *The Spirit of Public Administration*. San Francisco: Jossey-Bass, 1997.

Hesse, Joachim Jens, Christopher Hood, and B. Guy Peters, eds. *Paradoxes in Public Sector Reform: An International Comparison*. Berlin: Duncker & Humblot, 2003.

Ingraham, Patricia W., and Donald F. Kettl. *Agenda for Excellence: Public Service in America*. Chatham, NJ: Chatham House, 1992.

Ingraham, Patricia W., and Laurence E. Lynn, Jr., eds. *The Art of Governance: Analyzing Management and Administration*. Washington, DC: Georgetown University Press, 2004.

Ingraham, Patricia W., and Barbara Romzek. *Governance and the Public Service: Rethinking the Research Agenda for Public Sector Change*. San Francisco: Jossey-Bass, 1994.

Kettl, Donald F. *The Global Public Management Revolution.* 2nd ed. Washington, DC: Brookings Institute, 2005.

King, Cheryl Simrell, and Camilla Stivers. *Government Is Us.* Thousand Oaks, CA: Sage, 1998.

Lane, Jan-Erik. *Public Administration and Public Management: The Principal-Agent Perspective.* London: Routledge, 2005.

National Commission on the Public Service. *Leadership for America.* Washington, DC: National Commission, 1989.

Nye, Joseph S., Jr., Philip D. Zelikow, and David C. King, eds. *Why People Don't Trust Government.* Cambridge, MA: Harvard University Press, 1997.

OECD. *Government of the Future.* PUMA Policy Brief No. 9. Paris: OECD, June 2001.

Thomas, John C. *Public Participation in Public Decisions.* San Francisco: Jossey-Bass, 1995.

Tummala, Krishna K., ed. *Comparative Bureaucratic Systems.* Lanham, MD: Lexington Books, 2003.

References

Chapter One

Appleby, Paul. *Policy and Administration.* University, AL: University of Alabama Press, 1949.

Blumenthal, W. Michael. "Candid Reflections of a Businessman in Washington." In *Public Management,* edited by James L. Perry and Kenneth L. Kraemer. Palo Alto, CA: Mayfield Publishing, 1983.

Flanders, Loretta R., and Dennis Utterback. "The Management Excellence Inventory." *Public Administration Review* 45 (May/June 1985): 403–410.

Katz, Robert L. "Skills of an Effective Administrator." *Harvard Business Review* 52 (September/October 1974): 90–102.

Office of Personnel Management, "Guide to Senior Executive Service Qualifications," October 2006. www.opm.gov/ses/pdf/SES_Quals_Guide_2006.pdf.

Redford, Emmette S. *Democracy in the Administrative State.* New York: Oxford University Press, 1969.

Rosenbloom, David. *Public Administration.* New York: McGraw-Hill, 1993.

Herbert A. Simon, Donald W. Smithburg, and Victor A. Thompson. *Public Administration.* New York: Knopf, 1950.

White, Leonard D. *The Study of Public Administration.* New York: Macmillan, 1948.

Willoughby, W. F. *Principles of Public Administration.* Baltimore, MD: Johns Hopkins Press, 1927

Wilson, Woodrow. "The Study of Public Administration." *Political Science Quarterly* 2 (June 1887): 197–222.

Chapter Two

American City & County "Council-Manager System." (September 2006):121 (10): 16.

Archibald, Samuel J. "The Freedom of Information Act Revisited." *Public Administration Review* 39, no. 4 (July/August 1979): 311–317.

Boris, Elizabeth T. "Nonprofit Organizations in a Democracy: Varied Roles and Responsibilities." In *Nonprofits and Government: Collaboration and Conflict,* edited by Elizabeth T. Boris and C. Eugene Steuerle, pp. 3–29. Washington, DC: Urban Institute Press, 1999.

Bowman, Ann, and Richard C. Kearney. *The Resurgence of the States.* Englewood Cliffs, NJ: Prentice-Hall, 1986.

Caldwell, Lynton. *Administrative Theories of Hamilton and Jefferson.* New York: Russell & Russell, 1964.

Cooper, Phillip J. *Public Law and Public Administration.* Palo Alto, CA: Mayfield Publishing, 1983.

Cooper, Phillip J. "Conflict or Constructive Tension: The Changing Relationship of Judges and Administrators." *Public Administration Review* 45, special issue (November 1985): 643–652.

Cooper, Phillip J. *Public Law and Public Administration.* 3rd ed. Itasca, IL: F. E. Peacock Publishers, 2000.

Crenson, Matthew A. *The Federal Machine*. Baltimore, MD: Johns Hopkins University Press, 1975.

Dodge, William R. "The Emergence of Intercommunity Partnerships in the 1980s." *Public Management* (July 1988): 2–7.

Dudley, E. Susan. "The Bush Administration Regulatory Record." *Regulation 27 (4)*: (Winter 2004–2005): 4–9.

Federal Administrative Procedures Source Book. 2nd ed. Washington, DC: Administrative Conference of the United States, 1992.

Gilmour, Robert S. "Agency Administration by Judiciary." *Southern Review of Public Administration* 6, no. I (Spring 1982): 26–42.

Henry, Nicholas. *Governing at the Grassroots*. Englewood Cliffs, NJ: Prentice-Hall, 1980.

Hill, Larry B. "The Citizen Participation-Representation Roles of American Ombudsmen." *Administration and Society* 13, no. 4 (February 1982).

Johannes, John R. *To Serve the People*. Lincoln: University of Nebraska Press, 1984.

Johnson, Stephen F. "The Legislative Veto in the States." *State Government* 56, no. 3 (1983): 99–102.

Jones, Charles O. *An Introduction to the Study of Public Policy*. 3rd ed. Monterey, Calif.: Brooks/Cole, 1984.

Karl, Barry D. *Executive Reorganization and Reform in the New Deal*. Cambridge, MA: Harvard University Press, 1963.

Katz, Michael B. *The Price of Citizenship: Redefining the American Welfare State*. New York: Henry Holt, 2001.

Kessler, David. *A Question of Intent: A Great American Battle with a Deadly Industry*. New York: Public Affairs, 2001.

Kettl, Donald F. "The Transformation of Governance: Globalization, Devolution, and the Role of Government." *Public Administration Review* 60, no. 6 (2000): 488–497.

Kingdon, John W. *Agendas, Alternatives, and Public Policies*. 2nd ed. New York: Harper Collins, 1995.

Kraft, Michael E., and Scott R. Furlong. *Public Policy: Politics, Analysis, and Alternatives*. 2nd ed. Washington, DC: CQ Press, 2007.

Light, Paul C. *The Tides of Reform: Making Government Work, 1945–1995*. New Haven, CT: Yale University Press, 1995.

Light, Paul C. *Making Nonprofits Work: A Report on the Tides of Nonprofit Management Reform*. Washington, DC: Brookings Institution/Aspen Institute, 2000.

Lowi, Theodore. "Four Systems of Policy, Politics, and Choice." *Public Administration Review* 32 (July/August 1972): 298–310.

McLaughlin, Curtis. *The Management of Nonprofit Organizations*. New York: Wiley, 1986.

Moe, Ronald C. "The Emerging Federal Quasi Government: Issues of Management and Accountability." *Public Administration Review* 61, no. 3 (2001): 290–312.

Municipal Year Book. Washington, DC: International City Management Association, 1992.

Nelson, Michael. "A Short, Ironic History of American National Bureaucracy." *Journal of Politics* 44, no. 3 (August 1982): 747–778.

Pfiffner, James P. "The First MBA President: George W. Bush as Public Administrator." *Public Administration Review*. 67 (2007), 6–20.

Piotrowski, Suzanne J. and David Rosenbloom. "Nonmission-Based Values in Results-Oriented Public Management: The Case of Freedom of Information." Public Administration Review 62, no. 6 (2002): 643–657.

Reich, Robert B. "Public Administration and Public Deliberation: An Interpretive Essay." *Yale Law Review* 94 (1985): 1617–1641.

Ripley, Randall B., and Grace A. Franklin. *Congress, the Bureaucracy, and Public Policy.* 4th ed. Pacific Grove, CA: Brooks/Cole, 1987.

Rosenbaum, David E. "Subject to Review." *New York Times* (June 8, 2001), A1–A22.

Rourke, John T. "The GAO: An Evolving Role." *Public Administration Review* 38 (July/August 1978): 453–457.

Salamon, Lester M. *America's Nonprofit Sector: A Primer.* 2d ed. New York: Foundation Center, 1999.

Sanger, David E. "Trying to Run a Country Like a Corporation." *New York Times* (July 8, 2001): 1–3.

Walsh, Annmarie Hauck. *The Public's Business.* Cambridge, MA: MIT Press, 1978. White, Leonard D. *The Federalists.* New York: Macmillan, 1948.

U.S. Census Bureau. *Statistical Abstract of the United States.* Washington, DC: Government Printing Office, 2002, 2003, 2005.

Chapter Three

Beam, David R. "New Federalism, Old Realities." In *The Reagan Presidency and the Governing of America,* by Lester M. Salamon and Michael S. Lund. Washington, DC: The Urban Institute, 1984.

Berman, David. "State/Local Relations." In *Municipal Yearbook.* Washington, DC: International City Management Association, 1992.

Berrios, Ruben. "Government Contracts and Contractor Behavior." *Journal of Business Ethics,* 63 (2006): 119–130.

Blackstone, Edwin, and Simon Hakim. "Private Ayes: A Tale of Four Cities." *American City & County* 112 (February 1997): 4–8.

Bowman, Ann O'M., and Michael A. Pagano. "The State of Federalism, 1989–1990." *Publius* 20 (Summer 1990): 1–25.

Bowman, Ann O'M., and Michael A. Pagano. "The State of American Federalism, 1991–1992." *Publius* 22 (Summer 1992): 1–20.

Bryson, John. *Strategic Planning for Private and Nonprofit Organizations.* San Fransisco, CA: Jossey-Bass. 1995.

Carver, John, and Miriam Mayhew Carver. *Basic Principles of Policy Governance. CarverGuide Series on Effective Board Governance, Volume 1.* San Francisco: Jossey-Bass, 1996.

Center on Philanthropy, Indiana University. *Giving USA 2001: The Annual Report on Philanthropy.* Indianapolis, IN: AAFRC Trust, 2001.

Cooper, Phillip J. *Governing by Contract.* Washington, DC: CQ Press, 2003.

Cooper, Phillip J., Linda P. Brady, Olivia Hidalgo-Lardeman, Albert Hyde, Katherine C. Naff, Steven J. Ott, and Harvey White. *Public Administration for the Twenty-First Century.* Fort Worth, TX: Harcourt Brace College Publishers, 1998.

Council of State Governments. *Private Practices: A Review of Privatization in State Government.* Lexington, KY: Council of State Governments, 1997.

Eggers, William D. "There's No Place Like Home." *Policy Review* 83 (May/June 1997): 43–47.

FEMA, *Florida Disaster Aid Tops $2 Billion,* news release October 27, 2004.

Forester, John. "The Effects of the Elimination of General Revenue Sharing on U.S. Cities." Unpublished manuscript, 1988.

Fredericksen, Patricia, and Rosanne London. "Disconnect in the Hollow State: The Pivotal Role of Organizational Capacity in Community-Based Development Organizations." *Public Administration Review* 60, no. 3 (May/June 2000): 230–239.

Gore, Al. *From Red Tape to Results: Creating a Government That Works Better and Costs Less. Report of the National Performance Review.* New York: Times Books, 1993.

Greene, Stephen G. "Ranks of Volunteers Swell to a Record but Donations Dip, Survey Finds." *Chronicle of Philanthropy* 11, no. 20 (October 21, 1999): 16.

Greene, Stephen G. "Getting the Basics Right." *Chronicle of Philanthropy* 13, no. 14 (May 3, ajsdl2001): 1, 9–12.

Gullo. Theresa. "History and Evaluation of the Unfunded Mandate Reform Act." *National Tax Journal* 57, no.3 (September 2004): 559–570.

Gurwitt, Rob. "The Lonely Leap." *Governing* 13, no. 10 (July 2000): 38–44. Hernandez, Shawn. "Power of Partnerships." *Governing* 14, no. 9 (June 2001): 10.

Hult, Karen M., and Charles Walcott. *Governing Public Organizations.* Pacific Grove, CA: Brooks/Cole, 1990.

Kettl, Donald F. "Transformation of Governance: Globalization, Devolution and the Role of Government." *Public Administration Review* 60, no. 6 (November/December 2000): 488–497.

Kettl, Donald F. "Wisconsin Considers Sweeping Changes." *PA Times* 24, no. 5 (May 2001): 1, 8.

Kincaid, John. "From Cooperative to Coercive Federalism." *Annals of the AAPSS* 509 (May 1990): 139–159.

Kostro, Charles. "The Road to Cheaper Services." *American City & County* 109 (August 1994): 16. Lenkowsky, Leslie. "Court Ruling Upholding Political Advocacy Should Be Seen as a Warning to Charities." *Chronicle of Philanthropy* 13, no. 12 (March 22, 2001): 40.

Light, Paul. *Making Non-Profits Work.* Washington, DC: Brookings Institution Press, 2000. MacManus, Susan. "Enough Is Enough." *State and Local Government Review* (Fall 1992): 103–111.

Mariani, Michele. "e-Permitting 101." *Governing* 14, no. 7 (April 2001): 86–88.

Nathan, Richard P., Fred C. Doolittle, and associates. *Reagan and the States.* Princeton, NJ: Princeton University Press, 1987.

Nice, David C. *Federalism: The Politics of Intergovernmental Relations.* New York: St. Martin's Press, 1987.

Osborne, David, and Ted Gaebler. *Reinventing Government: How the Entrepreneurial Spirit is Transforming the Public Sector.* Reading, MA: Addison-Wesley, 1992.

PA Times, 27, no.8 (August 2004):1.

Pear, Robert. "Bush and Health Care Companies Promise Medicare Drug Discounts." *New York Times* (July 14, 2001): A1.

Reagan, Ronald. "Inaugural Address." Washington, DC, January 20, 1981.

Rosenau, Pauline Vaillancourt, ed. *Public-Private Policy Partnerships.* Cambridge, MA: MIT Press, 2000.

Sagawa, Shirley, and Eli Segal. *Common Interest, Common Good: Creating Value through Business and Social Sector Partnerships.* Boston: Harvard Business School Press, 2000.

Smith, Bucklin & Associates. *The Complete Guide to Nonprofit Management.* 2nd ed. New York: John Wiley & Sons, 2000.

Smucker, Bob. *The Nonprofit Lobbying Guide.* 2nd ed. Washington, DC: Independent Sector, 1999.

Stone, Charles F., and Isabel V. Sawhill. *Economic Policy in the Reagan Years.* Washington, DC: The Urban Institute, 1984.

U.S. Census Bureau. *Statistical Abstract of the United States.* Washington, DC: Government Printing Office, 2003, 2005.

Walker, David B. "The Advent of an Ambiguous Federalism and the Emergence of New Federalism III." *Public Administration Review* 56 (May/June 1996): 271–280.

Walters, Jonathan. "The Welfare Bonanza." *Governing* 13, no. 4 (January 2000): 34–36.

Wise, Charles R. "Judicial Federalism: The Resurgence of the Supreme Court's Role in the Protection of State Sovereignty." *Public Administration Review* 58, no. 2 (March/April 1998): 95–98.

Wise, Charles R. "The Supreme Court's New Constitutional Federalism: Implications for Public Administration." *Public Administration Review* 61, no. 3 (May/June 2001): 343–358. Wright, Deil S. "A Century of the Intergovernmental Administrative State." In *A Centennial History of the American Administrative State*, by Ralph Clark Chandler, pp. 219–260. New York: The Free Press, 1987.

Wright, Deil S. *Understanding Intergovernmental Relations.* 3rd ed. Pacific Grove, CA: Brooks/ Cole, 1988.

Chapter Four

American Society for Public Administration. *Ethical Dilemmas.* Washington, DC: ASPA, n.d.

Arendt, Hannah. *Eichmann in Jerusalem.* New York: Viking Press, 1963.

Blum, Lawrence A. "Gilligan and Kohlberg: Implications for Moral Theory." *Ethics* (April 1988): 472–491.

Bowman, James S. "Ethical Issues for the Public Manager." In *Handbook of Organization Management*, edited by William B. Eddy, pp. 69–102. New York: Marcel Dekker, 1983a.

Congressional Quarterly Weekly. Washington, DC: Congressional Quarterly Press (March 6, 1993): 511.

Cooper, Terry L. *An Ethic of Citizenship for Public Administration.* Englewood Cliffs, NJ: Prentice Hall, 1991.

Cooper, Terry L., and N. Dale Wright, eds. *Exemplary Public Administrators.* San Francisco: Jossey-Bass, 1992.

Council of State Governments. *Book of the States, 1992–1993.* Lexington, KY: Council of State Governments, 1992.

DeGeorge, Richard T. *Business Ethics.* New York: Macmillan, 1982.

Finer, Herman. "Administrative Responsibility in Democratic Government" In *Bureaucratic Power in National Politics*, edited by Frances Rourke, pp. 165–175. Boston: Little, Brown, 1972.

Fleishman, Joel L., and Bruce L. Payne. *Ethical Dilemmas and the Education of Policy Makers.* Hastings-On-Hudson, NY. The Hastings Center, 1980.

Friedrich, Carl J. "Public Policy and the Nature of Democratic Responsibility." In *Bureaucratic Power in National Politics,* edited by Frances J. Rourke, pp. 176–186. Boston: Little, Brown, 1972.

Hilberg, Raul. *The Destruction of the European Jews.* Chicago: Quadrangle Books, 1961.

Kohlberg, Lawrence. "From Is to Ought." In *Cognitive Development and Epistemology,* edited by T. Mishel, pp. 151–235. New York: Academic Press, 1971.

Lewis, Carol. *The Ethics Challenge in Public Service.* San Francisco: Jossey-Bass, 1991.

Masters, Marick F., and Leonard Bierman. "The Hatch Act and the Political Activities of Federal Employee Unions." *Public Administration Review* (July/August 1985): 518–526. McKeon, Richard. *Basic Works of Aristotle.* New York: Random House, 1941. Milgram, Stanley. *Obedience to Authority.* New York: Harper & Row, 1974.

Pastin, Mark. "The Thinking Manager's Toolbox." In *Ethical Insight, Ethical Action,* Washington, DC: International City Managers Association, 1988: 91–104.

President's Commission on Federal Ethics Law Reform. *To Serve With Honor: Report and Recommendations to the President.* Washington, DC: U.S. Department of Justice, 1989.

Rawls, John. *A Theory of Justice.* Cambridge, MA: Belnap Press of Harvard University Press, 1971.

Reich, Robert B. "Public Administration and Public Deliberation: An Interpretive Essay." *Yale Law Review* 94 (1985): 1617–1641.

Rubin, Hank. "Dimensions of Institutional Ethics." In *The Nonprofit Organization,* edited by David Gies, J. Steven Ott, and Jay Shafritz. Pacific Grove, CA: Brooks/Cole, 1990.

Svara, James. *The Ethics Primer for Public Administrators in Government and Nonprofit Organizations.* Sudbury, Massachusetts: Jones and Bartlett Publishers, 2007.

Truelson, Judith A. "Protecting David from Goliath: On Blowing the Whistle on Systematic Corruption." *Dialogue* (Spring 1986): 1–23.

Chapter Five

Argyris, Chris. *Interpersonal Competence and Organizational Effectiveness.* Pacific Grove, CA: Brooks/Cole, 1962.

Argyris, Chris. *Knowledge for Action: A Guide to Overcoming Barriers to Organizational Change.* San Francisco: Jossey-Bass, 1993.

Barbour, George, P., Jr., Thomas W. Fletcher, and George A. Sipel. *Handbook: Excellence in Local Government Management.* Washington, DC: International City Management Association, 1984.

Bryson, John M., and Barbara C. Crosby. *Leadership for the Common Good: Tackling Public Problems in a Shared-Power World.* San Francisco: Jossey-Bass, 1992.

Chrislip, David D., and Carl E. Larson. *Collaborative Leadership.* San Francisco: Jossey-Bass, 1994.

Cohen, Michael D., James G. March, and Johan P. Olsen. "A Garbage Can Model of Organizational Choice." *Administrative Science Quarterly* 17 (1972): 1–25.

Collins, Jim. *Good to Great and the Social Sector, A Monograph to Accompany Good to Great.* Boulder, Colorado, 2005.

Cyert, Richard M., and James G. March. *A Behavioral Theory of the Firm.* Englewood Cliffs, NJ: Prentice-Hall, 1963.

Denhardt, Robert B. *The Pursuit of Significance: Strategies for Managerial Success in Public Organizations.* Belmont, CA: Wadsworth, 1993.

Dimock, Marshall E. "The Criteria and Objectives of Public Administration." In *The Frontiers of Public Administration,* edited by John M. Gaus, Leonard D. White, and Marshall E. Dimock. Chicago: University of Chicago Press, 1936.

Fayol, Henri. *General and Industrial Management.* Translated by C. Storrs. London: Isaac Pitman and Sons, 1949.

Gerth, H. H., and C. Wright Mills. *From Max Weber: Essays in Sociology*. New York: Oxford University Press, 1946.

Golembiewski, Robert T. *Renewing Organizations*. Itasca, IL: Peacock, 1972.

Gulick, Luther. "Notes on the Theory of Organization." In *Papers on the Science of Administration*, edited by Luther Gulick and L. Urwick, pp. 1–46. New York: Institute of Public Administration, 1937a.

Gulick, Luther. "Science, Values, and Public Administration." In *Papers on the Science of Administration*, edited by Luther Gulick and L. Urwick, pp. 189–195. New York: Institute of Public Administration, 1937b.

Guy, Mary Ellen, and Meredith A. Newman. "Women's Jobs, Men's Jobs: Sex Segregation and Emotional Labor," *Public Administration Review* 64 (3), (2004) 289–298.

Hatch, Mary Jo. *Organization Theory: Modern, Symbolic and Postmodern Perspectives*. Oxford: Oxford University Press, 1997.

Kaufman, Herbert. *The Forest Ranger*. Baltimore, MD: Johns Hopkins University Press, 1960.

MacGregor, Douglas. *The Human Side of the Enterprise*. New York: McGraw-Hill, 1960.

March, James G., and Herbert Simon. *Organizations*. New York: John Wiley, 1958.

Mintzberg, Henry, Duru Raisinghani, and Andre Theoret. "The Structure of Unstructured Decision Processes." *Administrative Science Quarterly* 21 (1976): 246–275.

Mooney, James, and Alan C. Reiley. *The Principles of Organization*. New York: Harper & Row, 1939.

Ostrom, Vincent, and Elinor Ostrom. "Public Choice: A Different Approach to the Study of Public Administration." *Public Administration Review* 31 (March/April 1971): 203–216.

Peters, J. Thomas, and Robert H. Waterman. *In Search of Excellence*. New York: Harper & Row, 1982.

Redford, Emmette. *Democracy in the Administrative State*. New York: Oxford University Press, 1969.

Schein, Edgar H. *Organizational Culture and Leadership*, 2d ed. San Francisco: Jossey-Bass, 1997.

Selznick, Philip. *TVA and the Grass Roots*. Berkeley: University of California Press, 1949.

Senge, Peter M. *The Fifth Discipline: The Art and Practice of the Learning Organization*. New York: Currency Doubleday, 1990.

Simon, Herbert A. *Models of Man*. New York: Wiley, 1957.

Taylor, Frederick W. *Scientific Management*. New York: Harper & Row, 1923.

Thomas, John Clayton. *Public Participation in Public Decisions*. San Francisco: Jossey-Bass, 1995. *Washington Post* (September 8, 1993): A17.

White, Leonard. *Introduction to the Study of Public Administration*. New York: Macmillan, 1926.

Willoughby, W. F. *Principles of Public Organization*. Baltimore, MD: Johns Hopkins Press, 1927.

Chapter Six

Bardach, Eugene. *The Implementation Game*. Cambridge, MA: M.I.T. Press, 1977.

Carter, Karen. "Performance Budgets: Here by Popular Demand." *State Legislatures* 20 (December 1994): 22–25.

Chelimsky, Eleanor. *Program Evaluation: Patterns and Directions*. Washington, DC: American Society for Public Administration, 1985.

Gulick, Luther. "Notes on the Theory of Organization." In *Papers on the Science of Administration*, edited by L. Gulick and L. Urwick. New York: Institute of Public Administration, 1937, 1–46.

Hakes, Jay E. "Performance Measurement and Organization Change." *PA Times* 20 (July 1997): 10, 17.

Hammer, Michael, and James Champy. *Reengineering the Corporation: A Manifesto for Business Revolution.* New York: Harper, 1993.

Hatry, Harry, Therese van Houten, Margaret C. Plantz, and Martha Taylor Greenway. *Measuring Program Outcomes: A Practical Approach.* Alexandria, VA: United Way of America, 1996.

Joyce, G. Philip. "Linking Performance and Budgeting: Opportunities in the Federal Budget Process" (2003) In *Integrating Performance and Budgets: The Budget Office of Tomorrow (2007)* by Jonathan Breul, and Carl Moravitz (eds). IBM Center for The Business of Government. New York: Rowman & Littlefield Publishers, Inc.

Jennings, Edward T. Jr., Dale Krane, Alex N. Pattakos, and B. J. Reed, eds. *From Nation to States .* Albany: State University of New York Press, 1986.

Kaplan, Robert and David Norton. *The Balanced Scorecard: Translating Strategy into Action.* Boston, MA: Harvard Business School Press, 1996.

Latane, Henry A. "The Rationality Model in Organizational Decision Making." In *The Social Science of Organizations,* edited by Harold J. Leavitt. Englewood Cliffs, NJ: Prentice Hall, 1963.

Linden, Russell M. *Seamless Government: A Practical Guide to Reengineering in the Public Sector.* San Francisco: Jossey-Bass, 1994.

Mayne, John. "Public Sector Reforms: International Perspectives on Performance Monitoring." *PA Times* (July 20, 1997): 1, 16.

Melkers, Julia and Katherine Willoughby. "Staying the Course: The Use of Performance Measurement in State Governments" (2004) In *Integrating Performance and Budgets: The Budget Office of Tomorrow (2007)* by Jonathan Breul and Carl Moravitz (eds). IBM Center for the Business of Government. New York: Rowman & Littlefield Publishers, Inc.

Newcomer, Kathryn E. "Reaction to the Government Performance and Results Act." *PA Times* 22, no. 9 (September 1999): 10.

Pressman, Jeffrey, and Aaron Wildavsky. *Implementation.* Berkeley: University of California Press, 1973.

Quade, E. S. *Analysis for Public Decisions.* 2nd ed. New York: North-Holland, 1989.

Shirley, Robert C. "Limiting the Scope of Strategy." *Academy of Management Review* 7 (April 1982): 262–268.

Stokey, Edith, and Richard Zechauser. *A Primer for Policy Analysis.* New York: Norton, 1978.

Thompson, James D. *Organizations in Action.* New York: McGraw-Hill, 1967.

Wholey, J. S., H. P. Hatry, and K. E. Newcomer, eds. *Handbook for Practical Program Evaluation.* San Francisco: Jossey-Bass, 1994.

Chapter Seven

Congressional Quarterly Weekly. Washington, DC: Congressional Quarterly Press (March 20, 1993).

Council of State Governments. *Book of States, 1992–1993.* Lexington, KY: Council of State Governments, 1993.

Joyce, Philip G. "The Federal Line Item Veto Experiment: After the Supreme Court Ruling, What's Next?" *Public Budgeting & Finance*, Vol. 18, (December 1998) 3–21.

Lynch, Thomas D. *Public Budgeting in America.* 2nd ed. Englewood Cliffs, NJ: Prentice Hall, 1985. McGowan, Robert P., and Gary A. Lombardo. "Decision Support Systems in State Government."

Public Administration Review 46, special issue (November 1986): 579–583.

PA Times, (September 2004):1.

Pechman, Joseph A. *Federal Tax Policy.* 4th ed. Washington, DC: The Brookings Institution, 1983.

Schick, Allen. "The Road to PPB: The Stages of Budget Reform." In *Perspectives on Budgeting,* 2nd ed., edited by Allen Schick. Washington, DC: American Society for Public Administration, 1987.

Stevenson, Richard W. "Congress Passes Tax Cut, With Rebates This Summer." *New York Times* (May 27, 2001): A1–A26.

Swope, Christopher. "Restless for Results." *Governing* 14, no. 7 (April 2000): 20–23.

Thomassen, Henry. "Capitol Budgeting for a State." *Public Budgeting and Finance* 10 (Winter 1990): 72–86.

Uchitelle, Louis. "Taxes, The Market, and Luck Underlie The Budget Surplus." *New York Times* (October 20, 2000): A1.

United Press International, "Bush Cuts Would Affect over 100 Programs," February 4, 2004.

U.S. Census Bureau. *Statistical Abstract of the United States.* Washington, DC: Government Printing Office, 2000.

Washington Post, p. A01, Friday, October 8, 2004.

Wildavsky, Aaron. *The New Politics of the Budgetary Process.* Glenview, IL: Scott, Foresman, 1988.

Williams, Grant. "Lobbyists' Labours Lost?" *Chronicle of Philanthropy* 13, no. 17 (June 14, 2001): 26–30.

Chapter Eight

Bishop, Peter C., and Augustus Jones, Jr. "Implementing the Americans with Disabilities Act of 1990." *Public Administration Review* 53, (March/April 1993): 121–128.

Breul, Jonathan D. "Three Bush Administration Management Reform Initiatives: The President's Management Agenda, Freedom to Manage Legislative Proposals, and the Program Assessment Rating Tool." *Public Administration Review* 67, no. 1 (2007): 21–26.

Campbell, Alan K. "Civil Service Reform: A New Commitment." *Public Administration Review* 38 (March/April 1978).

Carter, Jimmy. "State of the Union Address." January 19, 1978.

Desky, Joanne. "Glass Ceiling Slows Down Women in Government." *PA Times* (December 1992): 1.

Gore, Al. *From Red Tape to Results: Creating a Government That Works Better and Costs Less. Report of the National Performance Review.* New York: Times Books, 1993.

Hall, Francine, and Maryann H. Albrecht. *The Management of Affirmative Action.* Santa Monica, CA: Goodyear, 1979.

Havemann, Judith. "The Government Takes a Stand on AIDS in its Office." *Washington Post National Weekly Edition* (March 28–April 3, 1988a): 34.

Havemann, Judith. "Sexual Harassment." *Washington Post National Weekly Edition* (July 11–17, 1988b): 30–31.

Hays, Steven W., and Zane T. Reeves. *Personnel Management in the Public Sector.* Boston: Allyn & Bacon, 1984.

Heclo, Hugh. *A Government of Strangers.* Washington, DC: Brookings Institution, 1977.

Kephart, Pamela and Lillian Schumacher. "Has the 'Glass Ceiling' Cracked? An Exploration of Women Entrepreneurship." *Journal of Leadership and Organizational Studies* 12, no.1 (2005): 2–15.

Klingner, Donald E., and John Nalbandian. *Public Personnel Management*. 2nd ed. Englewood Cliffs, NJ: Prentice Hall, 1985.

Levitan, Sar. *Working for the Sovereign*. Baltimore, MD: Johns Hopkins Press, 1983. Lorentzen, Paul. "A Time for Action." *The Bureaucrat* 13 (Fall 1984): 5–11.

Lorentzen, Paul. "Stress in Political-Career Executive Relations." *Public Administration Review* 45 (May/June 1985): 411–414.

Office of Personnel Management [OPM]. (n.d.). Post Reform: Gains, Losses, and Constant Change. Retrieved May 10, 2007, from www.opm.gov/BiographyofAnIdeal/docs/Bio1979-Present.pdf.

Page, Stephen. "The WEB of Managerial Accountability: The Impact of Reinventing the Government." *Administration and Society* 38, no. 2 (2006): 166–197.

Risher, Howard, Charles H. Fay, and associates. *New Strategies for Public Pay: Rethinking Government Compensation Programs*. San Francisco: Jossey-Bass, 1997.

Shafritz, Jay M., Albert C. Hyde, and David H. Rosenbloom. *Personnel Management in Government*. 2nd ed. New York: Marcel Dekker, 1981.

Siegel, Gilbert B., and Robert C. Myrtle. *Public Personnel Administration: Concepts and Realities*. Boston: Houghton Mifflin, 1985.

Steele, Randy. "Strike Zone." *Flying* (March 1982): 34–41.

Stewart, Debra W. "Assuring Equal Employment Opportunity in the Organization." In *Handbook of Public Personnel and Labor Relations*, edited by Jack Rabin, Thomas Vocino, W. Bartley

Hildreth, and Gerald J. Miller. New York: Marcel Dekker, 1983.

Wise, Charles R. "The Supreme Court's New Constitutional Federalism: Implications for Public Administration." *Public Administration Review* 61, no. 3 (May/June 2001): 343–358.

Zuck, Alfred M. "Education of Political Appointees." *The Bureaucrat* 13 (Fall 1984): 15–18.

Chapter Nine

Argyris, Chris. *Intervention Theory and Method*. Reading, MA: Addison-Wesley, 1970.

Argyris, Chris. *Knowledge for Action*. San Francisco: Jossey-Bass, 1993.

Bass, Bernard M. *Handbook of Leadership*. New York: The Free Press, 1990.

Bennis, Warren. "The Artform of Leadership." In *The Executive Mind*, edited by Suresh Srivastya. San Francisco: Jossey-Bass, 1983.

Bennis, Warren, and Burt Nanus. *Leaders: The Strategies for Taking Charge*. New York: Harper & Row, 1985.

Benson, Herbert. *The Relaxation Response*. New York: Morrow, 1975.

Box, Richard C. *Citizen Governance: Leading American Communities into the 21st Century*. Thousand Oaks, CA: Sage Publications, 1998.

Burns, James MacGregor. *Leadership*. New York: Harper & Row, 1978.

Constantino, Cathy A., and Christina Sickles-Merchant. *Designing Conflict Management Systems*. San Francisco: Jossey-Bass, 1996.

Cooper, Kenneth H. *The Aerobics Way*. Toronto: Bantam Books, 1978.

Daft, Richard L., and Richard M. Steers. *Organizations: A Micro/Macro Approach*. Glenview IL: Scott, Foresman, 1986.

Denhardt, Robert B., and Kevin Prelgovisk. "Public Leadership: A Developmental Perspective." In *Executive Leadership in the Public Service*, edited by Robert B. Denhardt and William H. Stewart. Tuscaloosa: The University of Alabama Press, 1992.

Fisher, Roger, and William Ury. *Getting to Yes: Negotiating Agreement Without Giving In*. New York: Penguin Books, 1983.

Gardner, John. Remarks to the National Conference of the National Association of Schools of Public Affairs and Administration, Seattle, October 23, 1987.

Gardner, Neely. *Group Leadership*. Washington, DC: National Training and Development Service, 1974.

Hales, Colin P. "What Do Managers Do? A Critical Review of the Evidence." *Journal of Management* 23 (1986): 88–115.

Helgesen, Sally. "Leading from the Grassroots." In *The Leader of the Future: New Visions, Strategies, and Practices for the Next Era*, edited by Frances Hesselbein, Marshall Goldsmith, and Richard Beckhard. San Francisco: Jossey-Bass, 1996.

Hersey, Paul and Kenneth H. Blanchard. *Management of Organizational Behavior, 5th ed.* Englewood Cliffs, NJ: Prentice Hall.

Herzberg, Frederick. *The Motivation to Work*. New York: Wiley, 1959.

Hitt, Michael A., Dennis R. Middlemist, and Robert L. Mathis. *Management Concepts and Effective Practice*. St. Paul, MN: West, 1983.

Hopper, Linda. "Unstressing Work." *Public Management* 17 (November 1988): 1–4.

Janis, Irving. *Groupthink*. 2nd ed. Boston: Houghton Mifflin, 1983.

Kanter, Rosabeth Moss. *Men and Women of the Corporation*. New York: Basic Books, 1977.

Kotter, John P. *The General Manager*. New York: The Free Press, 1982.

Lakein, Alan. *How to Get Control of Your Time and Your Life*. New York: Signet Books, 1973.

LeBoeuf, Michael. *Working Smart*. New York: McGraw-Hill, 1979.

Lee, Seok-Hwan. "Does Performance-Base Pay Motivate? Maybe, Or Maybe Not . . ." *PA Times* 24, no. 4 (April 2001): 3.

Lindblom, Charles E. *The Policy-Making Process*. Englewood Cliffs, NJ: Prentice Hall, 1968.

Lippitt, Gordon L., Peter Langseth, and Jack Mossop. *Implementing Organizational Change*. San Francisco: Jossey-Bass, 1985.

Maslow, Abraham. *Motivation and Personality*. New York: Harper & Brothers, 1954.

McClelland, David. *Human Motivation*. Glenview, IL: Scott, Foresman, 1985.

Moorhead, Gregory, Richard Ference, and Chris P. Neck. "Group Decision Fiascoes Continue: Space Shuttle Challenger and a Revised Groupthink Framework." *Human Relations* 44, no. 6 (1991): 539–550.

Nichols, Ralph. *Are You Listening?* New York: McGraw-Hill, 1967.

Organ, Dennis H. "A Review of Management and the Worker." *Academy of Management Review*, 11, no. 2 (April 1986): 459–464.

Price, Virginia Ann. *Type A Behavior Pattern*. New York: Academic Press, 1982.

Rankin, Paul. "Listening Ability." Proceedings of the Ohio State Educational Conference, Ninth Annual Session, 1929.

Selye, Hans. *Stress without Distress*. Philadelphia: Lippincott, 1974.

Simon, Herbert A. *Models of Man*. New York: Wiley, 1957.

Steil, Lyman K., Larry L. Barker, and Kittie W. Watson. *Effective Listening*. Reading, MA: Addison-Wesley, 1983.

Stogdill, Ralph M. *Handbook of Leadership*. New York: Free Press, 1974.

Sussman, Lyle, and Samuel Deep. *Comex*. Cincinnati, OH: Southwestern, 1984.

Taylor, Frederick W. *Scientific Management*. New York: Harper & Row, 1923.

Vroom, Victor H., and Arthur G. Jago. *The New Leadership*. Englewood Cliffs, NJ: Prentice-Hall, 1988.

Vroom, Victor H., and Philip W. Yetton. *Leadership and Decision Making*. Pittsburgh, PA: University of Pittsburgh Press, 1973.

Whetten, David A., and Kim S. Cameron. *Developing Management Skills*. Glenview, IL: Scott, Foresman, 1984.

Ziller, R. C. "Toward a Theory of Open and Closed Groups." *Psychological Bulletin* 64 (1965): 164–182.

Chapter Ten

Alexander, Jason Hansen, and Joseph W. Grubbs. "Wired Government: Information Technology, External Public Organizations, and Cyberdemocracy." *Journal of Public Administration and Management* 3 (January 1998): unnumbered, on-line journal.

Barzelay, Michael. *The New Public Management: Improving Research and Policy Dialogue*. Berkeley, CA: University of California Press/Russell Sage Foundation, 2001.

Boston, Jonathan, ed. *Public Management: The New Zealand Model*. Auckland, New Zealand: Oxford University Press, 1996.

Breul, Jonathon D. "Three Bush Administration Management Reform Initiatives: The President's Management Agenda, Freedom to Manage Legislative Proposals, and the Program Assessment Rating Tool." *Public Administration Review* 67, no. 1 (2007): 21–26.

Browning, Graeme. *Electronic Democracy: Using the Internet to Influence American Politics*, edited by Daniel J. Weitzner. Wilton, CT: CyberAge, 1996.

Bryan, Cathy, Roza Tsagarousianou, and Damian Tambini. "Electronic Democracy and the Civic Networking Movement in Context." In *Cyberdemocracy: Technology, Cities, and Civic Networks*, edited by Roza Tsagarousianou, Damian Tambini, Cathy Bryan. London: Routledge, 1998.

CAP Corner, *PA Times*, 10 (December 1999).

Commission on Global Governance. *Our Global Neighborhood*. Report issued to the United Nations. Oxford, United Kingdom: Oxford University Press, 1995.

Dean, Mahnaz A., and Betty Roberts Stage. "In the World of 'E'—Where is E-Public Administration?" *PA Times* 23, no. 5 (May 2000): 3.

Frederickson, H. George. "The Seven Principles of Total Quality Politics." *PA Times* (January 17, 1994): 9.

Gore, Al. *From Red Tape to Results: Creating a Government That Works Better and Costs Less. Report of the National Performance Review*. New York: Times Books, 1993.

Government Accounting Office. *Managing for Results: Strengthening Regulatory Agencies' Performance Management Practices*. Washington, DC: Government Printing Office, 1999.

Governmental Accounting Standards Board. *State of Arizona: Focus on Performance*. SEA Research Case Study. Norwalk, CT: GASB, 2000a.

Greene, Stephen G. "Getting the Basics Right." *Chronicle of Philanthropy* 13, no. 14 (May 3, 2001): 1–12.

Greiner, John M., Harry P. Hatry, Margo P. Koss, Annie P. Miller, and Jane P. Woodward. *Productivity and Motivation.* Washington, DC: The Urban Institute Press, 1981.

Grossman, Lawrence K. *The Electronic Republic: Reshaping Democracy in the Information Age.* New York: Penguin, 1995.

Hackman, J. Richard. "Designing Work for Individuals and for Groups." In J. Richard Hackman, Edward J. Lawler, and Lyman W. Porter, *Perspectives on Behavior in Organizations.* 2nd ed. New York: McGraw-Hill, 1983, pp. 242–257.

Holzer, Marc, Ellen Doree Rosen, and Constance Zalk. "Steps in Productivity Improvement." In *Productivity Improvement Techniques,* edited by John Matzer, Jr. Washington, DC: International City Management Association, 1986.

Horrigan, John B. *How Americans Get in Touch With Government.* Washington, DC: PEW Internet and American Life Project, May 24, 2004.

Hruby, Laura. "All Aboard." *Chronicle of Philanthropy* 13, no. 17 (June 14, 2001): 8–13.

Jenkins, David. "Quality of Work Life." In *The Quality of Work Life and the 1980s,* edited by Harvey Kolodny and Hans van Beinum, pp. 1–32. New York: Praeger, 1983.

Jun, Jong S. *Management by Objectives in Government.* Beverly Hills, CA: Sage Publications, 1976.

Kerwood, David. "Government Intranets." (Article submitted to the Federal Communicators Network, National Performance Review, December 15, 1997). Washington, DC: National Performance Review, 1997.

Kettl, Donald F. "The Global Revolution in Public Management: Driving Themes, Missing Links." *Journal of Policy Analysis and Management* 16 (Summer 1997): 446–462.

Kettl, Donald F. "The Transformation of Governance: Globalization, Devolution, and the Role of Government." *Public Administration Review* 60, no. 6 (November/December 2000): 488–497. Kibbe, Barbara. "Improving Non-Profit Operations," *The Chronicle of Philanthropy,* May 3, 2001. Available at www.philanthropy.com/free/articles/v13/i14/14001001.htm.

Lazar, David and Maria Binz-Scharf, *Information Sharing in E-Government Projects: Managing Novelty and Cross-Agency Cooperation,* IBM Institute for the Business of Government, 2004. Light, Paul C. *Sustaining Innovation: Creating Nonprofit and Government Organizations that Innovate Naturally.* San Francisco: Jossey-Bass, 1998.

Light, Paul C. *Making Nonprofits Work: A Report on the Tides of Nonprofit Management Reform.* Washington, DC: Brookings Institution, 2000.

Mankin, Don, Susan G. Cohen, and Tora K. Bikson. *Teams and Technology: Fulfilling the Promise of the New Organization.* Boston: Harvard Business School Press, 1996.

Marchetti, Domenica. "High-Tech Hopes Meet Reality." *Chronicle of Philanthropy* 13, no. 17 (June 14, 2001): 1, 20–22.

Morley, Elaine. *A Practitioner's Guide to Public Sector Productivity Improvement.* New York: Van Nostrand Reinhold, 1986.

Newcomer, Kathryn, and Aaron A. Otto. "Is GPRA Improving Federal Government?" *PA Times* 23, no. 1 (January 2000): 1–6.

Osborne, David, and Ted Gaebler. *Reinventing Government.* Reading, MA: Addison-Wesley, 1992. Perlman, Ellen. "The People Connection," *Governing Magazine,* (www.governing.com/archive/2002/sep/eg2c.txt) 2002.

Peters, B. Guy. "New Visions of Government and the Public Service." In *New Paradigms for Government: Issues for the Changing Public Service,* edited by Patricia W. Ingraham and Barbara S. Romzek. San Francisco: Jossey-Bass, 1994.

Schachter, Hindy Lauer. "Reinventing Government or Reinventing Ourselves: Two Models for Improving Government Service." *Public Administration Review* 55 (November/December 1995): 530–537.

Stoneman, Bill. "Old-Line to Online." *Governing* 13, no. 12 (September 2000): 34–50.

Suttle, J. Lloyd. "Improving Life at Work." In *Improving Life at Work*, by J. Richard Hackman and J. Lloyd Suttle. Santa Monica, CA: Goodyear, 1977, 1–29.

Swope, Christopher. "E-Government's New Gear," *Governing Magazine,* March 2004, p. 52.

Swope, Christopher. "Restless for Results." *Governing Magazine,* April 2001, 20–23.

Toregas, Costis. "Technology and Our Urban Communities: Who Shall Lead?" *Public Management* 17 (May 1988): 2–5.

Chapter Eleven

Denhardt, Janet V., and Robert B Denhardt. *The New Public Service: Serving, Not Steering.* Armonk, NY: M.E. Sharpe, 2003.

Organization for Economic Co-operation and Development (OECD). *Government of the Future.* PUMA Policy Brief No. 9 (June). Paris: OECD, 2001.

Appendix

Journals

Academy of Management Perspectives
www.journals.aomonline.org/amp/

Academy of Management Review
www.aom.pace.edu/amr/

Administration & Society
www.sagepub.com/journal.aspx?pid=12

Administrative Science Quarterly
www.johnson.cornell.edu/publications/asq/

American Review of Public Administration
www.sagepub.com/journal.aspx?pid=10

Australian Journal of Public Administration
*www.ingentaconnect.com/content/bpl/ajpa;jsessionid
=15e55k489s4rk.victoria?*

California Management Review
www.haas.berkeley.edu/news/cmr/

Canadian Public Administration
www.ipac.ca/pubs/cpa_journal/

Criminal Justice Policy Review
www.cjp.sagepub.com/

G.A.O. Journal
www.gao.gov/

Governance
www.sog-rc27.org/Governance/journal.htm

Governing
www.governing.com/

Government Executive
www.govexec.com/

Harvard Business Review
www.harvardbusinessonline.hbsp.harvard.edu

*International Journal of Public Administration www.
informaworld.com/smpp/title~content=t713597261*

International Public Management Journal
www.inpuma.net/editors.htm

Journal of Management
www.jom.sagepub.com/

*Journal of Organizational Behavior www.inter-
science.wiley.com/cgi- bin/jhome/4691*

Journal of Policy Analysis and Management
www.interscience.wiley.com/cgi-bin/jhome/34787

*Journal of Public Administration Research and
Theory www.jpart.oupjournals.org/*

Journal of Public Affairs Education
www.naspaa.org/initiatives/jpae/jpae.asp

Journal of Public Management and Social Policy
www.andromeda.rutgers.edu/~ncpp/jpmsp/

National Civic Review
www.ncl.org/publications/ncr/

National Tax Journal
www.ntj.tax.org/

Organization Studies
www.degruyter.de/rs/270_1791_DEU_h.htm

Policy Studies Journal
*www.blackwellpublishing.com/journal.asp?ref=0190
-292X*

Public Administration and Development
www.interscience.wiley.com/cgi-bin/jhome/2821

Public Administration Review
*www.blackwellpublishing.com/journal.asp?ref=0033
-3352&site=1*

*Public Budgeting and Finance (NOTE NAME
CHANGE)*
www.abfm.org/public_budgeting_finance_journal.htm

Public Finance Review
www.pfr.sagepub.com/

Public Integrity
www.mesharpe.com/mall/results1.asp?ACR=pin

Public Management
www.icma.org/pm/8605/index.htm

The Public Manager
www.thepublicmanager.org/

Public Performance & Management Review
www.jstor.org/journals/15309576.html

Public Personnel Management
*www.ipma-hr.org/index.cfm?navid=
74&id=263&tcode=nws2*

Public Voices
www.andromeda.rutgers.edu/~ncpp/pv.html

Review of Public Personnel Administration
www.rop.sagepub.com/

Spectrum: Journal of State Government
*www.csg.org/CSG/Products/spectrum/
default.htm*

State and Local Government Review
www.cviog.uga.edu/publications/slgr/index.php

Organizations

American Planning Association
www.planning.org/

American Public Human Services Association
www.aphsa.org/Home/home_news.asp

American Public Health Organization
www.apha.org/

American Public Power Association
www.appanet.org/

American Public Works Association
www.apwa.net/

American Society for Public Administration
www.aspanet.org/

*Association of Public Policy Analysis and
Management*
www.appam.org/

Council of State Governments
www.csg.org/csg/default

Education Commission of the States
www.ecs.org/

Government Finance Officers Association
www.gfoa.org/

IBM Center for The Business of Government
www.businessofgovernment.org/

International City Managers Association
www.icma.org/main/sc.asp

*International Public Personnel Management
Association for Human Resources*
www.ipma-hr.org/

National Academy of Public Administration
www.napawash.org/

National Association of Counties
www.naco.org/

National Association of Schools of Public Affairs
and Administration www.naspaa.org/

National Association of State Budget Officers
www.nasbo.org/

National Civic League
www.nationalcivicleague.org/

National Forum for Black Public Administrators
www.nfbpa.org/

National Institute of Governmental Purchasing
www.nigp.com/

National League of Cities
www.nlc.org/

Public Technology, Inc.
www.pti.org/

APPENDIX OF FEATURED CASES*

THE DEATH AND LIFE OF AN AGENCY

It was an unmitigated disaster! The hearing had gone so badly that Caleb Kasper didn't even want to go home. What he really wanted to do was slink away to some isolated mountain retreat and spend the rest of his life fishing. When the state legislature passed the agency review statute, he had been a supporter. As part of the effort to improve government, a reform-minded governor and state legislature had passed a "sunset" law, which required all non–cabinet-level agencies and departments to be reauthorized every ten years. The initial list of agencies to be reviewed had included the Industrial Development Agency that Caleb had headed for the past six years.

The opportunity to be among the first agencies to be reauthorized under the new law had stimulated Caleb and his staff to a frenzy of activity. Months of preparation had gone into the careful crafting of an impressive set of internal review reports. The original mission of the Industrial Development Agency (IDA) was to stimulate the industrial development of the state. The original director had been recruited from one of the largest corporations in the state. His idea had been to have the IDA serve as a clearinghouse for starting industrial parks throughout the state. The agency quickly hired and trained staff to prepare grant applications for federal grants to do the site preparation in urban areas. The IDA had provided technical assistance to local governments in rural areas, where there was a possibility of starting an industrial park on entirely new land.

This part of the agency's past was well documented, and even the most hostile legislators at the hearing had praised the former director's efforts. When Caleb was appointed to head the agency, change had been inevitable. The federal programs that had allowed IDA to receive grants for industrial redevelopment in urban areas were being scaled back and in some cases eliminated. Most of the choice sites in the rural areas had been identified and industrial parks had been started. Caleb had called a week-long planning retreat for top administrators, during which they took stock of where the agency should be headed in the future.

At the retreat, two issues had been identified as the most pressing problems for the IDA. Under many of the grants from the federal government, the IDA was obligated to ensure

*These cases are adapted from Robert B. Denhardt and Barry R. Hammond, *Public Administration in Action* (Pacific Grove, CA: Brooks-Cole, 1992).

that all applicable federal regulations were being observed in the redevelopment projects. The IDA had included the stipulation in the contracts it had signed with the developers, but very little checking had been done on whether the regulations were actually being followed. Caleb and his administrative group had decided to form an enforcement and investigations group, which they called the Compliance Review Bureau.

The second issue to emerge from the discussion of the agency's future was the growing number of bankruptcies among the developers. During the initial spurt of development, only a very small percentage of the projects were in financial difficulty. The original director had managed to get the legislature to authorize a modest bond issue, which provided funds to keep these projects going. Over the past two years, the rate of insolvency among the developers had grown. Caleb, whose background had been in banking, suggested that the IDA set up a refinance group to help those developers secure additional funding from private sources. They decided to call this division the Bureau of Refinance.

The two new bureaus experienced the usual problems. The contractors were not very happy about the Compliance Review Bureau's investigations of their projects. Two of the industrial parks were required to completely redo their waste-water management facilities because they didn't meet federal standards. One developer was discovered to have denied an occupancy application to a minority-owned business without justification. Rather than comply with the nondiscrimination requirements, the developer had sold his interest to another company. The Bureau of Refinance was quite successful. In fact, it was so good at finding private funding for distressed developers that some of the residential building companies began to complain that the IDA was making it hard for them to get money to build large residential developments.

With these new directions going so well, Caleb had anticipated no problem with the Government Operations Committee during the review. He could not have been more wrong. The first hint Caleb had came in the list of parties wishing to give testimony before the committee. Along with the usual groups were several that he had not anticipated. The Home Builders Association was on the list. The Industrial Resources Council was on the list. The Save Our Forests group was on the list. The Citizens for Taxpayer Justice was on the list. Because the list had been released only two weeks before the hearing, Caleb had only sketchy information about what these groups were going to say.

The hearing had started with an opening statement by the committee chairperson, who reviewed the reasons for the hearing and reminded the committee members that the vote on reauthorization would be taken immediately after the hearing. As one group after another testified that it thought the Industrial Development Agency had served its purpose in the past but ought to be abolished, Caleb got a sinking feeling in his stomach. Even the Industrial Resources Council offered only lukewarm support. By the time the Economy League testified that industrial parks were no longer an appropriate development technique because of environmental hazards associated with concentrations of industry, Caleb was beginning to panic.

Caleb's prepared testimony carefully reviewed the history of the agency and pointed to the success of the two new bureaus as indication that the work of the agency was not yet done. As he concluded his remarks, he asked permission to comment on the previous testimony. The chairperson consulted with the other committee members and agreed—with an admonishment to be brief.

Caleb looked around the room at the unsmiling faces and began in a low voice: "What you have heard today reflects on the changing role of the agency in state government. When the agency began its work, there was agreement between the developers and the agency officials. We all wanted to establish new industrial parks—and we did. The agency served to channel funds from the federal government to developers. Over the years, however, our role has changed. We are now required to regulate the development in order to ensure compliance with federal rules. That means that the agency officials and developers are often in conflict over the interpretation of the regulations." Caleb took a deep breath and went on. "In addition, we are now serving as a transfer agent to facilitate the flow of capital from the private sector to public sponsored projects. This has not made everyone happy. The agency recognizes that it must be responsive to the people it interacts with, but the agency also recognizes that it must serve the public at large, as well as its individual clients. We believe that we are doing a good job and deserve to be reauthorized for another ten years. Thank you very much for this opportunity to testify."

DISCUSSION QUESTIONS

1. Explain how you would vote on the question of reauthorization if you were a member of the Government Operations Committee.
2. What other arguments would you have used, if you were Caleb, to justify the reauthorization?
3. Did the administrators in the Industrial Development Agency do anything inappropriate when they redefined their mission at the planning conference?

This case is especially associated with material in Chapter One.

THE DANGEROUS REPTILES CASE

Adventurous Pets, Inc., an animal importer incorporated in the state of Delaware and doing business in forty-six other states, had imported approximately two-hundred horned lizards from South America. Selling these lizards as "pets" through a chain of pet stores, the company advertised these animals as "safe as household pets." During the past six months, thirteen children have been hospitalized after playing with the lizards. All of the children exhibit a fever and a rash that resists antibiotics. No deaths have been reported. Investigators for local health authorities have been unable to establish the exact process by which the animals might have caused the condition.

Adventurous Pets maintains that the lizards were not involved and that the connection is purely coincidental. They are, however, willing to meet and discuss the situation. So far, Adventurous Pets has not agreed that the lizards fall under government regulation, and they have not submitted any data concerning the lizards. Approximately 130 lizards have been sold to date.

Under the authority of the lead investigator for the Bureau of Noxious Fauna and pursuant to the Dangerous Reptile Act of 1988, Shawn Archer was charged with determining what action if any would be taken in the case. The director called a meeting to draw up a plan of action that would cover all eventualities. The director was willing to go to the full extent of authorized agency action, if required. The following excerpts from the act were applicable:

> The Bureau of Noxious Fauna [herein after BNF] is authorized to investigate all cases of suspected animal-caused injury to humans and, after consideration of the information so gathered, to issue seizure orders, restraining orders, requirements of licensing for vendors and/or owners, impositions of special conditions of sale, requirements for chemical or surgical modifications of animals prior to sale or captivity, issuance of findings and publicity of same, and other actions as may be authorized by law.
>
> The BNF shall, upon receipt of three or more complaints of a serious nature concerning a single species, respond to such complaints within 10 days. Actions undertaken to investigate such complaints may encompass subpoena power and seizure of records, property, or other evidences. BNF shall be permitted, but not required, to use evidence, information, or other data collected by state and local authorities, but shall not rely solely upon such in final action.

All sectors of the Administrative Procedures Act as amended shall apply to BNF unless otherwise superseded in the statute. Final agency action shall be reviewable as to substantial evidence on the record. Procedures for the making of the record shall be promulgated by the agency. Emergency action by the agency shall be permitted to prevent serious and imminent danger to the health and/or safety of the public. Such action shall not be subject to injunctive relief by a court of law.

Definitions: "reptile" shall be any animal which reproduces by egg laying AND is cold blooded; "dangerous" shall mean likely to cause harm or suffering. . . .

Two other pieces of information were considered by Shawn before he began his investigation. First, one of the children in the hospital is the daughter of a powerful congressman whose staff has brought this situation to Shawn's attention. Second, the agency has been involved in two judicial reviews of former action. In one, the court upheld the destruction of a family of "pit vipers" brought back from India by a university and kept by a professor. In the other case, the court overturned an order requiring that "poisonous fish" be surgically altered before sale.

Shawn's recommendations were such that contingencies based on the possible actions of Adventurous Pets were explored and a time line was established for action. The results of Shawn Archer's recommendations led to the following court case.

ADVENTUROUS PETS, INC. V. THE BUREAU OF NOXIOUS FAUNA

Pursuant to its authority under the Dangerous Reptile Act of 1988, the Bureau of Noxious Fauna ordered Adventurous Pets, Inc., (an animal importer incorporated in the state of Delaware and doing business in forty-six other states) to destroy all remaining unsold South American lizards in its possession. Further, the bureau ordered Adventurous Pets to repurchase all of the lizards sold at the original purchase price from as many customers as could reasonably be found. Finally, the bureau subpoenaed the import records of Adventurous Pets, Inc. in order to determine whether any violations of import regulations had taken place.

Adventurous Pets, Inc. filed a motion in the District Court of Washington, D.C., seeking to quash the order to destroy the remaining lizards. The district court ruled that the Dangerous Reptiles Act of 1988 prevented injunctive relief and refused to grant the order. The reptiles were destroyed under the supervision of federal marshals. Adventurous Pets has filed a new motion to set aside the order to repurchase the previously sold lizards. Claiming that the agency had no substantial evidence on which to base the order, Adventurous Pets has refused to release its customer records. The district court determined (1) that the order exceeded the authority granted to the Bureau of Noxious Fauna and (2) that insufficient evidence existed on the record to warrant the seizure of records.

The Bureau of Noxious Fauna appealed to the Supreme Court on a writ of certiorari contending (1) that the emergency powers granted under the act were sufficient to justify the order and (2) that a public danger continues to exist unless the lizards are located and destroyed. Further, the bureau contends that no formal record is required under the emergency powers granted in the act and that therefore the district court erred in granting the stay of the order.

FACTS

The Bureau of Noxious Fauna convened a special meeting on June 22, 1990, at which no representative of Adventurous Pets was present. Adventurous Pets had submitted an affidavit of "harmlessness" drawn by its staff veterinarian, certifying that the lizards were completely safe. The bureau's reptile expert (Ph.D. in herpetology) argued that too little was known about this species of reptile for anyone to be able to guarantee that no harm could be caused. She argued that further research was needed before the lizard should be allowed to be sold to the general public. The chief investigator, Shawn Archer, indicated that seven complaints had been filed and that eight days had passed since the receipt of the fourth complaint. The bureau lawyer suggested that the agency take action in order to prevent a lawsuit from an injured party claiming that the agency had violated the law by not acting. A member of the staff of a congressman was present at the meeting.

On June 23, 1990, the director of the bureau signed an order seizing the remaining lizards, ordering their destruction, and ordering Adventurous Pets to repurchase the original lizards and to surrender records indicating from whom the lizards had been purchased. Adventurous Pets refused to cooperate and tried to have the order quashed. Failing in its attempts, Adventurous Pets refused to cooperate with the bureau, failed to return phone calls, and denied the bureau's investigators access to its files. Federal marshals entered Adventurous Pets' stores and destroyed the lizards on June 28, 1990.

DISCUSSION QUESTIONS

1. Did the Bureau of Noxious Fauna exceed its authority under the Dangerous Reptiles Act when it: (a) ordered the destruction of the lizards? (b) ordered the seizure of business records? (c) ordered the repurchase of the lizards by Adventurous Pets?
2. Were the procedures used by the bureau adequate due process under the Fourteenth Amendment in terms of protection of property?
3. Was adequate notice given of the action to be taken by the bureau?
4. Was there sufficient evidence on the record to justify the action taken by the bureau?
5. Was the presence of a nonagency person at the meeting inappropriate as an ex parte contact?

This case is especially associated with material in Chapter Two.

LOW-LEVEL NUCLEAR WASTE DISPOSAL

Ever since the near disaster at Three Mile Island, Jim Bates had a particular sensitivity to the public reaction to radiation hazards. When he was appointed chief of staff of the governor's Commission on Low-Level Nuclear Waste Disposal, he was determined to keep a low profile. The previous year, Pennsylvania, New York, New Jersey, and West Virginia had signed an agreement to cooperate in building a low-level nuclear waste disposal site. The agreement had been reached only after intense pressure from the Nuclear Regulatory Commission in Washington, D.C, Now that the agreement was signed, it was Pennsylvania's responsibility to implement it. Jim's first six months on the job were mostly devoted to identifying the people who needed to be brought together to make the commission successful. The list was a long one, with some obviously difficult matchups.

At the top of the list were the federal officials from the Nuclear Regulatory Commission staff. The federal government was understandably very sensitive about the issue of nuclear waste. The debacle at Hanaford, Washington, was still a sore point with the staff. Jim met Yavette Collins at a conference and casually mentioned that he was planning to draft the multistate disposal plan required by the Hazardous Waste Disposal Act of 1985. Yavette, a twenty-year veteran of the NRC staff, offered to act as a liaison with the NRC but cautioned Jim that he must go slowly if he wanted to avoid the usual premature opposition from local officials. She suggested that he begin with a site survey before drafting the plan.

While Jim was pondering how to select a site, he was called to the governor's policy planning meeting. At the meeting, he was told to make arrangements to attend the governor's annual conference, where he would meet his counterparts in the three other states that would be sending low-level nuclear waste to Pennsylvania. "By the way," said Bill Olson, the governor's chief legislative assistant, "be sure that you brief Senator O'Connell when you get back. He was really angry that we agreed to build the site in our state. Even though we generate 60 percent of the waste in the three-state area, he felt that we could have agreed to pay 60 percent of the cost and shipped the waste to one of them."

At the governor's conference, the four key people had a brief meeting. The three other state representatives pressed Jim to move quickly to identify the site. They each would have to arrange for the transportation of the waste and needed to know exactly where it would be going. Marty Vieto from New York was particularly insistent that the site be selected within the next six months. "Look," he said, "we all know that there is going to be lots of local resistance, no matter where it is. The sooner we start the process, the sooner we can get over all of the road blocks and protests and court challenges." Paul Sands from New Jersey agreed that the preliminary geologic reports indicated that there were only four general areas in Pennsylvania that were suitable according to the NRC regulations, so those people wouldn't be surprised when the decision was announced.

Sandy Montwell wasn't so sure that speed was all that desirable. Her state, West Virginia, didn't plan to ship a large volume of waste, but she knew from experience that without extensive and gradual preparation, local officials and citizens could quickly mobilize significant political pressure against a project. Sandy suggested that Jim start discussions with the local officials in all four areas and try to discover which group was most amenable. Her final comment to Jim as the meeting broke up was based on hard won experience. "Jim," she said quietly, "look at the unemployment figures in each area and start with the argument that construction of the site will take several years and provide lots of jobs."

Soon after Jim returned to his office he called Senator O'Connell. They agreed to meet the following week to go over the planning process for the site. Senator O'Connell ended the conversation with a warning: "This project had better have some advantages for us or the whole thing will become a political time bomb. The governor sold us out last time and now he had better have some good things to announce." Jim wondered, as he replaced the phone, how to keep Senator O'Connell from turning the site selection into a major controversy. The conflicting advice he was getting about how much citizen involvement to solicit didn't help him decide what to do next.

Senator O'Connell arrived at the meeting with Jim in a sour mood. He had just come from a budget hearing and wasn't pleased that two of the projects he had suggested had been turned down. Jim began by discussing the geologists' reports and indicating that the low-level site would have to be in one of the four areas designated as geologically safe. The senator looked at the map and growled, "One of those areas is in my district!" "I know that," Jim replied, "and 1 have a proposal to make." Jim outlined his proposal to locate the site in Senator O'Connell's district. Part of the proposal was a massive local public-works project to build new roads, bridges, and dams to ensure the safe transportation of the waste. Jim pointed out that after the facility was completed, the area would have the best chance to attract new industry because of the excellent access provided by the improvements. Jim finished his proposal and looked directly at Senator O'Connell. "The problem, as you well know, is going to be getting the local communities to accept all this."

A shrewd look passed across Senator O'Connell's face. "So you want me to be the one to organize the local groups to support the project?" "That's right," said Jim. "You'll be able to help us to identify the right people to contact and the people who might cause trouble." "I'll think about it for a few days and get back to you," Senator O'Connell said slowly. "If we do this right, I might even get a big boost for my next campaign. On the other hand, it could all blow up in my face." "Isn't that the way it always is when you do something really important?" said Jim softly.

DISCUSSION QUESTIONS

1. If you were Senator O'Connell, would you help Jim organize the community groups?
2. What would you do next if you were Jim, and Senator O'Connell agreed to help?
3. If you lived in one of the communities where the waste disposal site was going to be located, what role would you see for yourself and others in the process?

This case is especially associated with material in Chapter Three.

To Tell the Truth—but the Whole Truth?

Senator McClain left the committee room and headed for the elevator that would take him to the underground train back to his office suite. As he stared idly at the closed doors of the elevator, he reminded himself that humility in victory was a virtue. The meeting of the Subcommittee on Investigations for the Committee on Overseas Trade had gone quite nicely. He had managed to obtain the appointment as chairman of the selection committee for foreign trade ambassador. Senator McClain knew that with all the other work the committee had to do before recess, this post put him in position to literally name the new trade ambassador. Yes, he would have to work with the people from the White House and, yes, he would have to listen to the majority leader's staff people, but in the final analysis he would be the one to present a name to the committee. He had a very good idea what that name would be.

While Senator McClain was riding the train back to his office, Jason Masters was winding up the morning staff meeting. Jason had served as Senator McClain's administrative assistant for the past two terms. Prior to that, he had been a legislative assistant in another senator's office, Jason Masters was an insider on Capitol Hill. "The last item for today is the probable appointment of the senator to head up the selection of the new trade ambassador. Sandy and Wendy, I want you to be on this project. The senator will probably be calling a meeting with the White House people for next week. Make sure that you leave your mornings flexible. That's all for now; let's remember that all calls from the media about this will be referred to me."

Wendy Sanko quickly went back to her desk and phoned her roommate. "Bad news," she began when her roommate answered. "I've got to work next week, so have fun at Atlantic City." Just as she put the phone down, Sandy Carpenter dropped into the chair next to her desk. His short, blond, curly hair, which explained his nickname, was already rumpled from his constant habit of running his hands through it. "So, what do you think old Mastermind Masters wants us to do with this one?" Sandy was the newest member of Senator McClain's staff and had not yet learned the innate caution practiced by the more experienced members. "Ask him yourself," Wendy solemnly murmured, "he's standing right behind you." "In my office—right now," growled Jason.

When a sheepish Sandy and a resigned Wendy had settled into the plush chairs around the small conference table in Jason's office, he let the silence stretch out for just a few moments longer than necessary. Finally, he leaned back and folded his hands over his stomach. "I picked you two for a reason. Sandy, despite your uncontrolled mouth, you're the best researcher in the office—at the moment. Wendy, I think you have talent and you're about ready to move up. If you handle this right, I may start mentioning you for one of the assistant positions coming vacant." Sandy and Wendy knew better than to make any comment at this point. Jason would ask them if they had questions at the end, and both knew he hated to be interrupted.

"Here is a list of names that I want you to start working on. Sandy, you'll be responsible for digging up all the financial data on them so that we won't be surprised in the hearings. Wendy, you start mentioning these names to the staff people of the other senators on the committee. Be sure to leave them with the impression that we don't need any more names. The current biographic descriptions are in these packets." Jason slid a bulky manila folder across the table to each of them. "Any questions?" Wendy paused, then said firmly, "Are these clear with the leadership?" "Good question," replied Jason, "You let me worry about the leadership. I'm having lunch with the majority leader's chief of staff today. By this afternoon, we'll have the clearance."

That's one smart lady, Jason thought as Wendy and Sandy left the office. I hope that she is smart enough to get the message I sent her. Jason turned to the pile of papers on his desk and began to skim them for content and possible controversy. The door opened and Senator McClain strode in with a jubilant look on his face. "It's in the bag, Jason," he beamed. "Call Toliver and tell him to get ready to go under the microscope." "He's already been warned, Senator," Jason replied. "I talked to his lawyer yesterday about the problem and was told they were fixing it." "Good," Senator McClain grinned, "I'm going over to the Trade Department this afternoon to lay the ground work with the secretary. I don't want him to feel like he isn't on the inside track on this one."

Two weeks later, Wendy and Sandy sat together in the senate cafeteria over coffee. Sandy was clearly upset. "I tell you that it doesn't make any sense. Why would Masters have me doing this research? It's so easy the summer intern could do it. Every time I call somebody, it's as if they expected the call and had the information on their desk. Not one person has said they'll get back to me." Wendy shrugged her shoulders. "So what? Most of these people have been trying to get an appointment for years. They probably have their background information updated monthly." Sandy frowned. "Perhaps that's true of their own people, but when was the last time a major bank didn't tell you that it would have to check with its client before it released financial data?" Wendy thought a moment then offered, "Maybe the FBI has already done the background security check so the figures were recently compiled." "Doubtful, but possible," said Sandy as he finished his coffee.

Wendy stopped Jason in the corridor later that day. "Jason, we've finished the background stuff on that list of names for trade ambassador. What do you want us to do with it?" "Put it on my conference table—including any notes you or Sandy made," Jason paused. "And by the way, nice job." Wendy was puzzled. Jason never complemented people for routine work. In fact, Jason rarely complimented people for extraordinary work. As Jason walked away, Wendy got the feeling she was missing something. Wendy didn't like that feeling, so she decided to do a little digging on her own.

By the end of the week, Wendy had put it all together. She asked for a meeting with Jason and was scheduled for early Monday morning. Wendy was strangely calm as she began the meeting. "I found out something very interesting about Wolford Toliver. Did you know that he declared bankruptcy in 1952? Moreover, did you know that he was subsequently involved in an insider trading scheme that the Security and Exchange Commission investigated?" Jason was perfectly still. "The thing that I'm sure you do know is that none of this is indicated on his financial disclosure forms," Wendy finished.

Jason steepled his fingers in front of his face and tapped them gently together. "I was wrong; you're the best researcher in this office, not Sandy." Jason got up from the table and walked over to look out the window. "Wendy, you may as well get used to this if you plan to go any further in your career. Wolford Toliver is far and away the best person for this appointment. Senator McClain has been trying to entice him into government service for a long time. Toliver has always objected by saying he couldn't stand the light of day. Six months ago, he finally told the senator about his early financial problems and the brush with the Security and Exchange Commission. We did some legal research and discovered that the bankruptcy court sealed the records and the SEC investigation resulted in no charges. His disclosure forms are technically correct."

When Jason swung around to face Wendy there was a look of determination on his face. "Most of the people who could do this job have a few skeletons in their closet. I'm asking—no, I'm telling you that what you have discovered isn't relevant to his appointment, and that you are going to forget you ever knew anything about this matter." "What about Sandy?" inquired Wendy. "If he suspects anything, he has sense enough to keep quiet about it," replied Jason. Wendy gathered her papers and started for the door. "I'll let you know what I have decided this afternoon."

DISCUSSION QUESTIONS

1. If you were Wendy, what would you do?
2. Do you think that the requirement for full and complete financial disclosure prevents many people from serving in government?
3. How helpful would the ASPA Code of Ethics be in resolving Wendy's problem?
4. Why is it important to understand the difference between something that is technically legal and something that is ethical or moral?

This case is especially associated with material in Chapter Four.

THE HOSPITAL EXPANSION PROJECT

Greenvault Memorial Hospital has served as the only hospital in Folkstown for the past eighty years. As the town grew, the hospital expanded and modernized. Three years ago, a new board chairperson started a capital campaign to raise money for a major addition. As the plans were drawn up, it became apparent that the only available space for expansion lay across the city line in the adjoining township. Although this was recognized as a problem, the decision was made to go ahead with the plan, as everyone assumed that the expansion would be in the interest of the residents of the township as well as of those in the city.

The entire hospital board spent three days at a local resort going over the architect's plans and suggesting revisions. The final plans were approved with only one dissenting vote. The newest member of the board voted against the project because he felt that the cost estimates were too high and that the design was unnecessarily fancy. With a great deal of publicity, the board announced that it was ready to approve construction project bids. When the bids were opened, only one bid was within 5 percent of the projected cost; all of the others were much higher. The board awarded the bid even though the contractor insisted that any delay in beginning the project would invoke a penalty clause that required the hospital to bear the additional costs.

One week after the bid was awarded the first problem became apparent. The application for a construction permit was routinely approved by the city, and a preliminary estimate of the tax on the new addition was provided by the city assessor. The assessor had included the entire cost of the addition. At the same time, the township commissioners had also granted a permit, and they had also included the full cost of the addition in their tax estimate. Wallace Becker, business manager for Greenvault Hospital, contacted the township and the city to request a meeting to work out the problem. During the conversation, Frank Pliance, the township regulations officer, casually remarked that this would be a good time to work out the parking problem. "What parking problem?" Wallace inquired. Frank replied, "Didn't you get my addendum to the building permit? Well, never mind, I'll bring it to the meeting."

At the meeting, Frank explained that the township had, indeed, made an error in the computation of the tax estimate. He commented that because the tax status of the hospital had only recently gone from nonprofit to for-profit, the township staff was unfamiliar with the process. Wallace was relieved and relaxed in his seat. Judy Rankin, assistant to the city manager, began to collect her papers in preparation for the conclusion of the meeting.

"So the only problem remaining is the provision for an additional 430 parking spaces," said Frank. "Wait a minute," Wallace sputtered. "Four hundred and thirty—that's preposterous! Where did you get that figure?"

Frank slid a short document toward Wallace with a resigned look on his face. "This should have been attached to the building permit, but it's all in the township records." Wallace briefly scanned the document:

Greenvault Hospital has recently changed from an all-residential treatment facility to a combination outpatient, clinic, and residential facility. As a result, the hospital is now considered a mixed occupancy facility under the township zoning ordinance Section 6.01 E. The requirements for medical and dental clinics are one space for each fifty square feet of gross floor space. The computed square footage for "clinic" use (excluding administrative, record keeping, and waiting areas) is 41,943. This requires 838 parking spaces. The submitted plan provides only 400. In order for this permit to be valid, a revised plan must be submitted to accommodate the additional spaces.

Wallace looked up at Frank. "What's going on here?" "Actually," said Frank, "you ought to ask Judy." Wallace turned to Judy who was fidgeting in her seat. Slowly she turned to Wallace. "The problem has been getting worse over the past several years. The hospital sits on the edge of a residential neighborhood. As you have more and more outpatients, they park on the street and walk into the clinics. The residents have been complaining to the mayor to do something. We know that you don't have room to expand your parking lots in the portion of the hospital located in the city, so we asked the township to help us with the problem." Wallace was angry now. "So that's it. The city wants us to accommodate all of the traffic without any use of the city parking capacity. I thought when we were forced to start paying taxes we could expect some cooperation."

Judy flushed. "That's not fair." She rose from her seat and began to pace around the room. "We could have raised this question years ago, but we were sensitive to your limited options. Now that you are expanding, we thought it was reasonable to request the township to change the zoning category and ask for the additional spaces." Wallace leaned over the table and looked directly at Frank. "It's too late to change the plans. We have already awarded the construction bid and there isn't enough room to add the spaces. Besides, I don't think that you can require us to solve the city's problem using the township's zoning ordinance." Frank looked startled. "I wouldn't count on that," he replied. "The permit isn't valid unless you revise the plans. If you start construction we'll get a court order to make you stop."

Two weeks passed as the attorneys from the hospital and the township solicitor tried to work out some solution. Wallace became more and more concerned that the construction would be delayed by the dispute. Finally, he decided to offer his own compromise. Quickly he jotted down some figures and made a few phone calls. He called Judy and Frank and asked them to meet him at the township building the next day. He then invited the mayor and the chairperson of the township board of commissioners to join the meeting. When they were all assembled, Wallace explained what he had in mind. "I've arranged to lease a two-acre plot in the township about a mile from the hospital. We'll operate a shuttle bus from the site to the hospital and require nonmedical regular shift employees to park there.

That should increase the available on-site parking by the required 400 spaces without necessitating a revision in the plans."

Judy and Frank looked pleased. The mayor had a few questions about how the hospital would prevent the employees from parking on city streets anyway, but was generally in favor. The chairperson of the township board of commissioners was delighted. He had become increasingly uneasy about whether the change in zoning could be sustained in court. "I think that we ought to have a long-term development plan for the hospital submitted to a joint planning meeting between the city and the township," he offered. "It's time we started cooperating rather than competing."

DISCUSSION QUESTIONS

1. Explain whether you think the township was correct in changing the zoning designation of the hospital.
2. Discuss the kind of intergovernmental agreement the city and the township could have made that would have solved this problem.
3. Was the city correct in waiting until the expansion plans were proposed to formally raise the parking problem?

This case is especially associated with material in Chapter Five.

The Fifty-Five Mile Speed Limit

Foster Atwood had been asked by the newly elected governor of a large Middle Atlantic state to join the governor's policy planning staff. His specific assignment was to develop a plan that would revise the method of patrolling the state's highways. The problem stemmed from a report by the federal Department of Transportation that an independent sampling of traffic in the state indicated that far too many motorists were exceeding the federally mandated speed limit. The report went on to threaten a cutoff of all federal highways funds to the state if something were not done. Foster wasn't surprised; when he drove on the interstate at the legal speed limit, most of the cars and many of the trucks passed him quite easily. Perhaps of greater urgency, however, was Foster's awareness that the number of accidents per 1,000 miles driven was rising dramatically.

Foster was not the first person to study this problem. His predecessor, Sheila Williams, had already looked at the problem and gathered some of the information necessary. Her report provided him with a set of alternative strategies for patrolling the highways and with the associated costs and probable reductions in both accidents and speeders. Also included in the materials was a study of the revenue generated by the issuance of citations. Foster found a table that summarized the information.

Attached to the table were the following explanatory notes:

The cost of servicing each accident that occurs during a patrol is 250 dollars. The likelihood of accidents, however, differs depending on the type of patrol being used. The stationary patrol results in a .50 probability of two (2) accidents per shift; the cruising patrol results in a .30 probability of two (2) accidents per shift; and the airplane patrol results in a .25 probability of two (2) accidents per shift. Finally, the number of citations issued per shift varies by type of patrol: stationary patrols issue 8 citations on average; cruising patrols issue 5 citations on average; and airplane patrols issue 3 citations on average.

	Stationary	Cruising Car	Airplane/Chase
Car cost per shift	$600	$800	$1,500
Revenue per shift	$600	$375	$225
Cost of each accident to state	$250	$250	$250
Likelihood of two (2) or more accidents per shift	.50	.30	.25

Foster decided that he needed to meet with the Federal Department of Transportation people. A previous study indicated that accident rates of *less* than an average of one (1) per patrol were typical of states in which the Department of Transportation found acceptable levels of speeding. But the crucial question was whether an increase in the numbers of patrols would actually satisfy the requirement. From the information supplied by Ms. Williams, it appeared that changing the type of patrols would be more effective.

Serge Amisis had worked for the Department of Transportation for nine years. He had started as a policy analyst and still considered himself a pretty good researcher. Since his last promotion, however, he had spent less and less of his time with the data and more time negotiating agreements with state officials. His first appointment of the day was typical. He hoped that Foster Atwood would be reasonable. Serge poked the intercom button and told his secretary to send in Mr. Atwood.

Foster and Serge exchanged the usual greetings and settled down to the business at hand. "The dilemma as I see it," Foster started out, "is that we could spend a lot of money trying to reduce the average speed motorists travel on our highways and still not necessarily affect the number of accidents." Serge raised one eyebrow. "I assume that those two things are connected—don't you?" Foster nodded. "They are, but not directly. For example, if the weather is particularly bad in a given month and we have changed to airplane patrols, the planes won't be able to patrol and the bad weather may contribute to an increase in the number of accidents. What I really need to know is whether you people are more interested in reducing the number of accidents or in reducing the average speed at which people travel."

Serge regarded Foster with an appraising glance. "Your question is really about our methodology, isn't it? I'll tell you how we measure and you can decide what to do. We have a list of states in which the accident rate per thousand miles driven is one standard deviation above the mean or higher. Those states are examined to determine whether any peculiar physical explanation—lots of winding mountain roads, for example—can account for the rate of accidents. If no peculiar circumstances exist, we send out teams of DOT monitors to check the average rate at which people drive on the highways. When that data is analyzed, we inform the state that their federal highway funds are in jeopardy."

Foster thought about what Serge had said. "So, if our accident rate is around normal, it doesn't matter how fast our drivers are going, because you wouldn't be monitoring, right?" Serge frowned. "Not necessarily. We do some spot checking in the states with normal accident rates, but essentially we believe the single most important explanation for the accident rate is the speed of travel." Foster leaned forward. "But other factors do enter into it, don't they?" "Well, yes they do," Serge admitted. "We have adjustments, for example, for states that have no inspection of motor vehicles. We also adjust for the proportion of miles of limited access as opposed to regular access roads."

Foster jumped in quickly, "Let me guess—limited access roads have fewer accidents than regular access, right?" "On average that's correct," Serge replied. "So if my state would concentrate on building more limited access roads, we might reduce our average accident rate to the point where you only did not checks," Foster offered. "Perhaps," said Serge, "but we have also found that the average speed is higher on the limited access roads. So it might not help you escape the penalty imposed for excessive speeding." "So," Foster mused out loud, "its really a question of whether we want to avoid your monitoring or try to get the motorists to slow down on the interstates."

Serge stood up to indicate that the meeting was over. "My advice to you is to concentrate on better enforcement of the speed limits. While it may cost you more money in the short run, it may enable you to build better highways in the long run. When we started this program, we were trying to save gasoline by getting people to travel at the most efficient speed. We've discovered that the reduction in accidents was pretty dramatic. With better crash protection technology in the newer cars, we expect even better results in the future." Foster left the meeting still worried about whether more or different enforcement would enable his state to escape the penalties. It might take quite a while for people to change their driving habits, and the political pressure from irate motorists would be fierce.

On the plane going home, Foster began to rough out a plan. First, he would recommend that the fines for speeding be increased dramatically. That would help with the cost of more airplane patrol enforcement. Then, he would recommend that the state begin a long-term plan for changing from regular to limited access on some major highways. Finally, he would suggest that the state department begin its own monitoring program to predict when the federal limits were being exceeded. As Foster put away his calculator and leaned back in his seat, his mind drifted back to something his first supervisor had told him: "Trying to affect the behavior of a large number of people is like trying to predict the weather. There are so many variables that it's more an art than a science."

DISCUSSION QUESTIONS

1. Do you think that Foster's recommendations will reduce the speed at which motorists travel in his state?
2. Do you think the methods used by Serge to decide how to monitor are reasonable and fair?
3. What other actions would you recommend that Foster suggest?

This case is especially associated with material in Chapter Six.

Tomorrow's Bill Comes Due Today

Carlos Monteriva left the bank with a frown on his face. His meeting with two of the bank officers had not turned out the way he had hoped it would. They had been polite—even concerned—but not very helpful. Carlos had hoped that they would give him some ideas for resolving the latest financial crisis in Desert Rock. Ten years ago, when Carlos had become the chief financial officer of Desert Rock, he had looked forward to a relatively easy finish to his twenty-eight-year career in public service. Desert Rock's population had been growing at a steady rate of about 17 percent a year. The dry climate and spectacular scenery of the Southwest high desert was attracting a steady stream of retired couples to the area. The tax base was expanding, as new retirement communities with moderately expensive homes were built within the city limits.

Planning the expansion of city services to meet the growth curve had been exciting. New sewers, streets, parks, and a civic center had all been financed with very modest tax increases every other year. Carlos chuckled as he remembered how carefully those increases had been scheduled in the off-election year to spare the councilman the embarrassment of running for reelection right after increasing taxes. The bond issue to build the civic center had been more difficult to pass, but an aggressive publicity campaign stressing the future benefits had convinced the voters that the construction was an investment in the future of the community.

The first sign of any problem came just two years ago. The Economy League at the state level decided to do a study of employer pension plans in the state. The league was interested in the topic because so much of the net income of residents in the state depended on pension payments. The debate at the national level over Social Security had alerted them to a potential problem. Carlos had been eager to see the results because Desert Rock was one of those communities in which pension payments were a primary source of income. When the study was released, Carlos and his counter-parts in other cities in the state were shocked.

The study pointed out that the private employers in the state were doing a good job of ensuring that money was being put aside to support the projected pensions of their employees. The public sector, however, was in serious trouble—at least from the point of view of the league. Unlike the private employers, most of the local governments were paying pensions out of current revenues. With a very small number of employees currently on retirement, this was not a significant percentage of the annual budget. The study raised a concern, however, about the future. As the size of the local government work force rose to meet the demands for more and better services from a growing population, the number of people scheduled to retire over the next twenty years would grow exponentially. By the year 2010, the study predicted, more than 30 percent of local budgets would be devoted to pension payments.

Last year, the state legislature had responded to the study and to the pressure of the Economy League and the Public Employees Advocacy lobby. The Public Pension Act of 1989 mandated that local governments were required to reduce their unfunded pension liability to zero over the next thirty years. As Carlos walked back to his office overlooking the piazza, he mentally reviewed the provisions of the act:

1. All municipalities were required to set up a trust fund into which payments were to be made to cover pensions.
2. All municipalities were required to submit biannual actuarial studies indicating the "normal cost" of fully funding pension liabilities.
3. During the first ten years, the municipalities were required to phase in their payments, beginning with 10 percent in the first year and rising by an additional 10 percent each year to 100 percent in the tenth year.
4. Failure to make the proper payments would result in the subtraction of state money of the same amount in the Local Government Assistance account.

Carlos had gone to the bank earlier to discuss setting up a pension trust fund. The First National Bank of Desert City had regretfully indicated that it did not engage in that kind of business. Moreover, it knew of only one bank in the state that did. When Carlos pointed out that the bank might wish to consider starting such a fund, the president of the bank, John Rodgers, looked over his reading glasses and commented: "We've tried to stay out of local politics because someone always gets angry. We don't intend to lose any of our customers over this issue."

Later in the week, Carlos received a reply to his letter of inquiry from the Setting Sun Bank in the state capital. They would be happy to set up the trust fund under their normal arrangements, which they had included. Skimming over the agreement, Carlos discovered that Setting Sun Bank was going to make a tidy little profit by investing Desert Rock's pension money. Worse yet, the penalty clauses for failure to deposit the required amounts were very severe. The final insult was a requirement that Desert Rock transfer its payroll deposits to Setting Sun as part of the agreement.

Carlos pulled the phone toward him and dialed the number for Naomi Winterwind. Naomi had joined his staff four years ago after working for her tribal investment company. She was an expert in budgetary systems with an emphasis on computertized systems. Naomi arrived with a stack of printouts and a puzzled look on her face. "We've already done the initial run on next year's budget for the council. Any changes now would have to be hand written in the margins." As Carlos explained the problem, Naomi began to smile. "I don't see anything to smile about in all of this," snorted Carlos. "Oh but 1 do," beamed Naomi. "I've been after you and the council to install a two-year budget process ever since I started here. This is the perfect opportunity."

The council room was practically deserted when the meeting began. Carlos gave his standard report and then asked for permission to address the council on the pension fund issue. Richard Cowper, mayor of Desert Rock, nodded for Carlos to proceed. Quickly

Carlos outlined what he had discovered and the various steps that he thought should be taken. When he finished, he asked if there were any questions. "I'll start," said Percy Whitworth, one of the council members. "Does this mean that we can't hire more people in the future? It seems the more people you hire, the larger the required payments." "Maybe we should start hiring more part-time people," said Mayor Cowper. "They don't have the same pension liability, do they?"

"My solution," piped up Alonzo Chiesa, the city attorney, "is to renegotiate the contracts with the employees. We could change to a private pension plan, where all we do is pay the premium and the private company worries about funding." "But how do we control the cost of that?" shot back Mayor Cowper. "You know what is happening to insurance premiums." City Manager Jim Carson held up both hands, leaned forward in his chair and spoke softly: "Before we rearrange everything over just one issue, let's look at the whole picture. I suggest that we ask Carlos to bring us a proposed revision of next year's budget to the next meeting." Jim looked down the table with a twinkle in his eye. "I'll bet someone on your staff could even come up with some figures for the year after next."

DISCUSSION QUESTIONS

1. Do you think that the state legislature was wise in requiring the local governments to fully fund their pension plans?
2. What advantages *and disadvantages* would a two-year budget process have for the city?
3. What other effects would you expect this state requirement to have on personnel policies, aside from the ones mentioned in the council meeting?

This case is especially associated with material in Chapter Seven.

A Working Manager: Classification as if People Mattered

Morning found the usual smells and sounds in Rockwall State Penitentiary. Just as in the previous endless mornings, the smell of too many bodies mingled with the sounds of too many loud voices. Joel Haskins looked up from his empty coffee cup and squinted through the bars that confined his observation room. Just beyond his line of sight, he could sense the day shift assembling in the ready room. They were laughing and exchanging crude jokes as they lined up for inspection. Joel checked the status board and grimaced. Four red lights winked on and off among the forty or so steady green ones. "Another below strength watch," he thought. "That's the third one this week, and the tenth this month."

Pulling the duty rooster down from the rack, Joel began to make notes in the margin. As he reassigned people from one group to the other to balance the work crews, he wondered for the hundredth time why he had agreed to take the experimental position of lead guard. As the most experienced member of the forty-five member guard unit, he had felt that maybe his experience could help straighten out an increasingly chaotic situation. Over the past five years, Joel had watched as the inmate population doubled and the guard strength increased by only six men. To make matters worse, the new warden had decided that all new officers had to have a college degree in some relevant subject. The final blow had come with the opening of new positions in the federal prison system for experienced corrections officers. Three of the officers at Rockwall had immediately applied for and been accepted into the federal system, leaving only two regular officers to supervise the entire force at Rockwall.

As Joel was briefing the new watch in the duty room, Alicia Eggers was driving through the front gates. Two months ago, Alicia had transferred from the central office in the state capital to Rockwall. She still felt funny as she stopped at the gates for identification and a search of her car. "Big day for you today?" inquired the guard, as he handed back her ID. "Does it show that much?" Alicia gulped. "Naw, just a little. You're all dressed up and the look on your face reminds me of my daughter on her wedding day—excited and nervous." Alicia smiled and relaxed. "Well, its not quite that important, but I have to make a presentation to the prison Board of Visitors this afternoon about my special project." "Good luck to you," the guard mumbled as he turned away to the next car in line.

Alicia parked her car in the area marked "staff and walked slowly up the steps to the main administration building. She knew that she had to make a decision that morning and then sell it to the Board of Visitors that afternoon. Three years ago, when she had graduated from the Master of Public Administration Program at the state university, she hadn't anticipated feeling this nervous. Then she had been sure that hard work and careful preparation would allow her to make the right decisions and prepare her to justify them to anybody. Now she knew better. As she walked to her office, she mentally reviewed her special project.

Immediately after graduation, she had taken a position with the State Department of Corrections as a classification specialist. She had done very well in her personnel courses and had quickly caught on to the elaborate job descriptions, union contracts, and legal definitions in the state personnel system. Her first project, the reclassification of positions in the central records office, had been a success. She had managed to reduce the work force and still make progress on the backlog of records waiting to be processed. That success had brought her to the attention of the executive director of the State Prison Board.

He had called her to his office and explained that the commissioner wanted someone to investigate the possibility of creating a middle ground between the rank-and-file guards and the officers in the prison system. The problem, he explained to her, was that a recent manpower study indicated that the system needed to hire some 180 new guards over the next several years to keep up with the growth of the inmate population. Normally, that would have meant promoting about eighteen people to officer level. Unfortunately, the system was experiencing a decline in the number of officers, as some retired and others left for better jobs in the federal government. Because, by law, officers had to have five years of experience or a degree in criminal justice, the system couldn't simply promote more guards to the rank of officer. What he wanted Alicia to do was to define a new level between the rank and file and the officers so that expansion could take place without overtaxing the remaining officers.

Summoning her courage, Alicia had agreed on one condition. She didn't want this to be a long-distance, on-paper project. She wanted to be able to run a pilot project at one of the prisons to see how the new position would work before she proposed it as a permanent classification. The executive director had agreed, and Alicia had chosen Rockwall as the best trial situation. From the central office, it had seemed like a straightforward exercise. She had carefully reviewed the various responsibilities, authorities, and training requirements of the guard positions and of the officer positions. On paper, it appeared to be a matter of shifting a few duties from the officers to a guard. After two months at Rockwall, she knew it wasn't that simple.

When Alicia reached her desk, she make a quick decision. Picking up her phone, she called the main guard station and asked the duty officer to send Joel Haskins down to her office at his earliest convenience. Replacing the phone, she pulled out her latest file on the project and began to reread her report. Originally, she had divided the responsibilities into three categories: managerial, supervisory, and technical. Her list now looked like this:

Managerial Responsible for preparation of monthly budget requests, including routine equipment replacement

Responsible for scheduling vacations, personal days, sick leave and other leave days as specified in the contract

Responsible for recommending policy changes concerning the movement and confinement of inmates

Supervisory Responsible for biweekly fitness reports on each member of the guard force on the shift

Responsible for twice daily head counts of inmates within the assigned unit

Responsible for changes in the daily duty roster according to required duties and prevailing policies.

Technical Visit each observation station at least twice each day to ensure that proper procedures were being followed

Check all "pass through" areas for proper mechanical functioning at least once each shift

Brief the shift as it reported for duty and debrief as it reported off duty, and transfer information to the new watch officer before signing out

Alicia frowned as she studied all of the comments she had written on the sheet over the past weeks. She and Joel had met weekly to discuss the way things were working. Joel had convinced her to drop several of the original technical assignments because there wasn't enough time in the eight-hour shift. She wasn't sure that he was very happy about all the paperwork that remained, but this would be the last chance to revise the list before she made her presentation.

DISCUSSION QUESTIONS

1. If you were Alicia, what questions would you ask Joel when he came to your office?
2. If you were Joel, what aspects of the new position would you try to change?
3. If you were a member of the Board of Visitors, what questions would you have for Alicia after she finished her presentation?

This case is especially associated with material in Chapter Eight.

SOLVING ONE PROBLEM CREATES ANOTHER

Thomas Winker had been hired by the mayor to work on a project for New York City. Thomas, formerly a free-lance consultant, liked the idea of working when he wanted to work, but he had mixed feelings about coming in "at the top" as a political executive. Nevertheless, his last project had been overseas, and he was glad to be back in New York, his original home town. The mayor had hired Thomas to analyze the advisability of either "contracting out" garbage collection, expanding city garbage collection capacity, or going to a twenty-four-hour collection system. Thomas saw evidence of the problem that morning as he drove over the bridge to Manhattan. At that very moment, he could look out the window of his car and see the garbage barges being towed down the East River; they weren't a pretty sight.

As Thomas watched the traffic inch forward over the bridge, he thought over the initial briefing he had received by fax two weeks ago in Paris. The city currently operates a sanitation department of 2,538 people using 781 garbage trucks. The cost of one day for each truck is $720 in wages for three people (eight-hour shift) and $200 for maintenance. The collective bargaining contract calls for a "shift differential" of 15 percent above the standard $30 per hour for the truck crews if the crews work other than 6:00 A.M. to 3:00 P.M. or any other nonstandard eight-hour shift. The contract has three years to go before it expires.

A recent study indicated that there is a 60 percent chance that the amount of garbage to be collected in the city will increase by 14 percent the next year and by 18 percent the following year. The briefing also indicated that many of the larger firms in the city are contemplating using a private garbage service (WE-HAUL, Inc.), which had recently begun competing with the city. The briefing concluded that whereas the amount of garbage to be collected would rise, there was a 40 percent chance that the amount the city would be required to collect might either fall slightly or remain steady.

As the traffic sped up after the bridge, Thomas reviewed the list of the information he still needed that he had made the night before. First, he needed to know what it would cost to maintain the current fleet of trucks if the city collected garbage twenty-four hours a day. Second, he needed some information about what new trucks would cost. If he recommended that the city expand its garbage pickup, he was sure that the mayor's office would want cost estimates. When he reached his office, Thomas went right to work. A quick check of the maintenance records for the large trucks indicated that he could expect a 20 percent increase in maintenance costs if he recommended that the city operate the trucks twenty-four hours a day. Thomas called the TIDY-TRUCK manufacturer and got a quote of $82,000 for a new truck if the city ordered that year. They also told him that they expect a 6 percent price increase next year.

Just after Thomas put down the phone, his liaison with the city, Rachael Swiniki, called to tell him that the private contractor (WE-HAUL) had offered to collect the additional garbage at a "special rate" for the city of $18 per ton for the first year and $20 per ton for the second year. Rachael ended the conversation by casually adding, "Just so that you know, since you're relatively new in town, WE-HAUL is a nonunion company." Thomas thoughtfully replaced the phone in its holder. He swiveled his chair around to his computer and called up his appointments for the next few days. The day after next, he was scheduled to meet with the president of the local sanitation workers' union. When the union heard about the offer from WE-HAUL, they were going to be quite concerned about the possibility of the city contracting to a nonunion operator.

Antonio Piace was not what Thomas had expected as the president of the sanitation workers' union. When Antonio entered the office, his most prominent feature was the very expensive suit he wore—or perhaps it was the Harvard Law School tie. Thomas had the feeling that Antonio knew more about him than he did about Antonio when Antonio began the conversation by asking Thomas how it felt to be back in New York after all these years. "It's nice to see a home-town boy get some of the work from the city," Antonio purred. Thomas leaned back in his chair and regarded Antonio through half-shuttered eyes. "Why don't we save the 'good old boy' routine for later?" Thomas said softly. "By the way, your Bronx accent certainly doesn't show at all."

Antonio relaxed and grinned. "So you've done your homework, too. Good, that will save me the trouble of establishing my tough-guy side." Thomas returned the smile and suggested that they get right to the point. Antonio arranged some papers in his lap and began what was obviously a carefully prepared statement. "The union signed an agreement four years ago that included a clause prohibiting the contracting of bargaining union work to outside organizations. In addition, the contract contains a clause that requires union approval of any change in hours or working conditions beyond those necessitated by emergency situations. Finally, the contract provides for an expedited grievance process for policy grievances." Antonio looked directly at Thomas. "We intend to make sure that the contract is either enforced or renegotiated entirely."

Thomas allowed the silence to stretch out to a full minute. Then he slowly leaned over the desk toward Antonio. "First of all, the city legal department's interpretation of the no-contracting clause is that it applies only to 'current bargaining unit work.' They are quite confident that new garbage collection can be contracted out by calling it a 'special service.' Second, emergency conditions may include a public health hazard, which persists when garbage is not collected promptly. Such a condition might last for several years. Finally, the grievance process you refer to requires the city to appoint a neutral arbitrator who is mutually acceptable. I'm sure you can appreciate just how long that might take if one side or the other were very hard to please." The two men looked at each other with measured stares.

Antonio rose to leave. As he put his papers back into his briefcase he paused, shrugged his shoulders, and slipped one across the desk to Thomas. "Before you make your final recommendation to the city, I suggest that you look into this issue." On the paper Thomas saw three names and a rather large figure with a dollar sign in front of it. "Should I recognize these names?" said Thomas in a puzzled tone. "You would if you knew who owned WE-HAUL," said Antonio. At the door he turned and said, "The money represents the total campaign contributions made to the mayor by those people. Have a nice day."

Thomas picked up the piece of paper and looked at it with distaste. He had wondered why the city had created a new position to make the recommendation when the Sanitation Department had people who were almost as well qualified. He had wondered even more why the mayor had called him back from Europe to do the report. Some of the reasons were becoming clear. The numbers made contracting out the most prudent financial option, but it was sure to cause labor trouble. Now the suggestion that the outside contractor had exercised some political pull to get the inside track made it even more obvious why Thomas had been asked to do the study. If a newly appointed "expert" recommended that the city contract out, it would look better than if the city simply decided to award the contract to a well-connected firm. Thomas closed his eyes and rubbed his forehead. He had left Paris for this?

DISCUSSION QUESTIONS

1. Do you think that the union is right when it insists that garbage collection has to be done by members of the union?
2. Should it have any effect at all on Thomas's recommendation that the owners of WE-HAUL were heavy contributors to the mayor's campaign?
3. In making his recommendation, what compromise could Thomas advise the city to offer the union?

This case is especially associated with material in Chapter Nine.

Contracting for Mandatory Recycling Services

"That tears it," said Loretta, as she slammed down the phone. Turning to her assistant borough manager, Carson Smith, she ran her fingers through her hair and propped her head up with her hands. "The legislature just passed the Recycling Act, and our lobbyist says that the governor will sign it as soon as he gets it." "Is that all that bad?" responded Carson. "The good part is that we do need to recycle; the bad part is that the legislature wants the law to go into effect in six months," moaned Loretta. "We'd better get cracking on that recycling plan we started several weeks ago," Carson said. "More importantly," replied Loretta, "we need to call the mayor and tell him that the option to do it ourselves isn't available anymore."

Loretta Mihn had been aware of the problem since her last meeting of the Borough Manager's Association. She had listened carefully to the explanations by the experts from the Department of Environmental Services about the decisions facing the boroughs. The easy ones were what to recycle. The boroughs had to choose five of seven possible substances: glass, newsprint, plastic, aluminum, tin, cardboard, and organic yard waste. The hard decision was whether to use the borough garbage equipment to collect and recycle the items to industry, or whether to contract with a private firm.

Soon after she had returned to her office from the meeting, Loretta had asked Carson to start collecting information about the desirability of each of the seven products. At the next borough council meeting, she had presented the options and the likely profit from each item. Council had quickly picked aluminum, tin, newsprint, cardboard, and glass. The question of whether to contract out or do it with borough equipment and workers, however, split the council into three groups. One group wanted to use the borough equipment because it believed that it was possible to make some income from the service. A second group wanted to contract out because it believed that the profits would disappear because, as the new law made tons of materials available, the purchasers of those items would quickly be oversupplied. The third group indicated that it wanted more information about the choice and could see arguments in favor of both options.

The day after the meeting, the mayor stopped by to see Loretta. Mayor Althouse was up for reelection in the fall and was particularly conscious of the reaction of the voters to any new programs. He had agreed with the third group and was determined that he would be able to explain his vote during the campaign. Loretta called in Carson, and the three of them spent the afternoon going over the options in some detail. At the end of the session, the mayor indicated that he thought using the borough equipment was the cheapest route because the only additional expense at first would he the additional hours of labors and the fuel and maintenance on the trucks. "Besides," he said, "we can always contract out later if we don't come out ahead."

When the mayor left, Loretta asked Carson what he thought. "Well," said Carson thoughtfully, "it might be hard to contract out after the law goes into effect. If we can't sell at a ptofit, it will be pretty obvious to the bidders. Since all this will be public information, I don't see how we will convince anyone to take over our program at a loss." "Maybe we should go ahead and look at both options for the time being," sighed Loretta. "You look into doing it with our trucks, and I'll see about having the borough lawyer draw up a request for bids."

Two weeks later, Loretta and Carson went to lunch to compare notes on the two options. Carson seemed uneasy as he started to outline his findings. "To begin with, we don't have enough trucks, and we haven't really got a place to hold the stuff until we can collect enough to make it feasible to transport to the buyer. Second, the union isn't too happy about the overtime needed to collect it. They say that one extra shift per week is all they think we can ask for under the current contract. The only way I can see it working is if we buy two additional trucks and hire four more people."

"What about the buyers?" asked Loretta. "Will they come and pick up the stuff for us, and what kind of price are they offering?" "Well, three of the buyers said that they don't own any trucks to pick it up, and the other two said that if they come to get it, the price they are willing to pay goes way down," replied Carson. "One company said that they would come and get it all—meaning all five types—at a fixed price, but only if we can guarantee a certain volume. If we don't have the volume, then they get the stuff free."

"My option is even worse," said Loretta. "The solicitor drew up the request for bids and I called several of the major companies likely to bid. All of them said that they were willing to bid only if we allowed them to charge the customers directly. More importantly, they said that they would only agree to a charge rate for six months at a time." Loretta looked down at the figures on a sheet of paper and frowned. "According to some of the numbers suggested, it will cost about five dollars a month for a pickup once a week."

"What happens after six months?" asked Carson. "They would be able to raise the rate up to 50 percent for the second six months. And if the contract is for more than one year, they would have that option in each six-month period." "Would the council be able to do anything about it if they raised the rate to the maximum each time?" Carson asked. "Not without voiding the contract and having to pay severe penalties," Loretta responded. "But that wouldn't solve the problem, since the state still requires us to maintain the program."

The day after the phone call from the state capital indicating that the legislature had passed the Recycling Act, the mayor showed up in Loretta's office. "Are we ready to go with our recycling plan?" he asked. Loretta indicated that he should pull up a chair and prepare for some bad news. "To put our program into effect within ninety days with our own equipment is just not possible. We don't have the money in the budget to buy two new trucks or to hire four new workers. The collective bargaining agreement with the borough workers still has two more years to run, so we can't even start with the trucks and people we have." "So where does that leave us?" asked the mayor.

"Our only option now is to publish the request for bids and hope that we get something reasonable," sighed Loretta. "I want to look more closely at how to protect our residents from being exploited," grumbled the mayor. "I'm not going to let some outfit come in here and rip everybody off just because the governor wants to take credit for getting this program in place immediately."

DISCUSSION QUESTIONS

1. What provisions would you put into the contract to protect the residents?
2. What other courses of action might the borough take?
3. Explain how "privatization" might provide an advantage for the borough after the initial period of adjustment.

This case is especially associated with material in Chapter Ten.

A Room With a View—at a Price

The national Fair Accommodations Act had only been in force for a few months when the first serious problems began to arise. The Congress had debated the issue of discrimination in hotel, motel, and resort reservations for more than five years. The statute that emerged was hailed as a victory for the consumer. All businesses providing overnight accommodations for more than fifty people were required to participate in the World Reservations System. Each business was required to input their reservations into a computer network based in Denver. Included in that information was the name, address, race, religion, and national origin of each customer. The Bureau of Fair Accommodations ran an analysis of the composition of each business on a quarterly basis to determine whether discriminatory patterns were present.

The technology to run the system was superb. None of the predicted snags and glitches had occurred. The expense to most businesses was very modest. Many of the large hotel and motel chains were already connected to computerized reservations, and only the smaller businesses had to buy new equipment. At first the customers had balked at providing the information, but a combination of discounts on room rates and refusal to confirm guaranteed reservations by the large chains had overcome the resistance.

The first problem surfaced in the electronic mailbox of Sharif Untermeyer. Sharif was the information and analysis officer for the Bureau of Fair Accommodations. On his screen one morning was a request from Collections International for a listing of reservations at Mountain Hideout Resorts over the next two months. Sharif keyed in a set of instructions, and the screen indicated that there were two thousand or so reservations in the system. Several more instructions made the request make sense. In three of the categories used by the bureau, there was only one reservation listed. Sharif blanked his screen and typed a quick query to his supervisor.

Months before, the bureau had promulgated rules concerning the release of information from the system. Essentially, the rules stated that specific names, addresses, or other unique information identifying individuals could not be released. The rules did allow for release of analytic reports on individual businesses. There had been some grumbling about "competitive trade secrets" being jeopardized, but generally the accommodations industry had gone along with the system. What Sharif now suspected was that certain debt-collection agencies were using the system to try to locate people who had peculiar backgrounds. For example, in the reservation system for the coming month, Mountain Hideout Resorts listed only one Caucasian, Buddhist of Irish descent.

Under the much strengthened Freedom of Information Act, the electronic mail message that requested the data had automatically triggered a similar message in the Department of Justice information system. If, within ten days, Sharif did not release the information or file a statement identifying the rule that precluded its release, the Department of Justice system would alert Collections International and automatically file a petition with the federal district court for a court order requiring the release of the information.

Ben Carrado, Sharif's supervisor, muttered a mild oath in Spanish when he read the query. He had only forty-eight hours to respond to Sharif. The new Public Productivity Monitoring Program had logged the query and would deduct points from his base monthly rating if he took longer to respond. Last month, he had lost points because his monthly review of employee morale had been twelve hours late. "These damn machines have no mercy," he sighed. Quickly he phoned the legal department.

When Jeb Disque's face appeared on the visaphone, Carrado knew he had called at a bad moment. Jeb's normally composed features were twisted into a scowl. "I'll bet you called about the Collections International request," jeb growled. Startled, Ben stammered, "Well, yes, um, I was." Jeb rubbed his face with his hands, "Those turkeys have been driving me nuts all day. I've called a teleconference with the Justice Department for tomorrow morning. Collections International's legal department faxed me a copy of the suit they intend to file if we don't comply. To top it all off, my friend from Barney, Biddle, and Brown tipped me off that they intend to file daily requests as soon as we start releasing the information."

Ben Carrado turned away from his desk and looked out the window. If we give the information to one collection agency, all the others will want it too, he thought. On the other hand, someone is sure to sue us for invasion of privacy if they get served with legal papers while on vacation. Worse yet, the only people whom the collection agencies will be able to find will be minority group members who will stick out in our reports. Information is always a two-edged sword, Ben concluded; it allows us to monitor conditions to prevent one wrong while it makes it possible for other wrongs to take place.

DISCUSSION QUESTIONS

1. What should Ben recommend that Sharif do—release the information or deny the request, and why?
2. What new rules should the agency establish to protect the identity of the people staying at the travel lodges and resorts?
3. Does the "right to privacy" mean that a person should be able to travel without anyone knowing where he or she is staying?
4. Should the government help private businesses locate people who haven't paid their debts?
5. Does the increasing amount of information collected by the government and the increasingly sophisticated technology for retrieving this information threaten basic rights of citizens?

This case is especially associated with material in Chapter Eleven.

Glossary

Accounting: The process of identifying, measuring, and communicating economic information to permit informed judgment and decision making.

Adverse or disparate impact: Criterion for showing that employment practices affect one group more harshly than another.

Affirmative action: Use of positive, results-oriented practices to ensure that women, minorities, individuals with disabilities, and other protected classes of people will be equitably represented in an organization.

Agenda setting: Phase in public policy process when certain problems come to be viewed as needing attention.

Allotments: Amounts that agencies are authorized to spend within a given period.

Apportionment: Process by which funds are allocated to agencies for specific portions of the year.

Appropriation: Legislative action to set aside funds and create budget authority for their expenditures.

Area of acceptance: Area within which the subordinate is willing to accept the decisions made by the supervisor.

Authorizing legislation: Legislative action that permits establishment or continuation of a particular program or agency.

Autocracy: Government by one.

Bargaining unit: The organization that will represent employees in conferring and negotiating various issues.

Behavioral awards: Used to reward specific behaviors that management wishes to encourage.

Block grants: Grants in which the money can be used for nearly any purpose within a specific functional field.

Bond: Promise to repay a certain amount (principal) at a certain time (maturity date) at a particular rate of interest.

Boundary spanning: Representing an organization to outside groups and organizations.

Bounded rationality: Seeking the best possible solution, but not necessarily the most rational, from a purely economic standpoint.

Brainstorming: Technique for enhancing the alternative-generation portion of the decision-making process.

Budget padding: Proposing a higher budget than is actually needed.

Business cycle: Periods of economic growth featuring inflation and high employment followed by periods of recession or depression and unemployment.

Capital expenditures: Spending for items that will be used over a period of several years.

Capital grants: Grants for use in construction or renovation.

Categorical or project grants: Grants requiring that the money may be spent for only a limited purpose; typically available on a competitive basis.

Charter: Local government's equivalent of a constitution.

Cohesion: Degree to which members of a group are uniformly committed to the group and its goals.

Comparable worth: Notion that men and women in jobs that are not identical but require similar levels of skill and training should be paid equally.

Constituent policy: Policy designed to benefit the public generally or to serve the government.

Continuing resolution: Resolution permitting the government to continue operating until an appropriations measure is passed.

Cooperative federalism: Greater sharing of responsibilities between federal and state governments.

Cooptation: Situations in which citizens are made to feel involved, but allowed to exercise little real power.

Coproduction: Using volunteer activity to supplement or supplant the work of government officials.

Cost-benefit: Identifying and quantifying both negative impacts (costs) and positive impacts (benefits) of a proposal, then subtracting one from the other to arrive at a net benefit.

Councils of government: Oversight bodies representing various localities to help coordinate local affairs.

Cross-cutting requirements: Rules that apply to most grant programs.

Debt capacity: Value of a city's resources combined with the ability of the government to draw on them to provide payment.

Decision analysis: Technique wherein decisions are likely to be made sequentially and under some degree of uncertainty.

Decision tree: Technique that identifies various possible outcomes, given the risk associated with each.

Deferral: Decision by the president to withhold expenditure of funds for a brief period.

Delegation: Assigning tasks to others.

Democracy: A political system in which decision-making power is widely shared among members of the society.

Deontology: Belief that broad principles of rightness and wrongness can be established and are not dependent on particular circumstances.

Dillon's Rule: Municipalities have only those powers granted in their charters; cities are creatures of the state.

Direct orders: Requirements or restrictions that are enforced by one government over another.

Discretionary spending: That portion of the budget still open to changes by the president and Congress.

Distributive policy: Policy involving use of general tax funds to provide assistance and benefits to individuals or groups.

Dual federalism: Pattern in which federal and state governments are struggling for power and influence with little intergovernmental cooperation.

Effectiveness: Extent to which a program is achieving or failing to achieve its stated objectives.

Efficiency: Relationship between inputs and outputs.

Employee recognition program: Effective way to acknowledge special contributions of certain employees or groups to the organization.

Entitlement grants: Grants that provide assistance to persons who meet certain criteria.

Entitlement programs: Programs that provide a specified set of benefits to those who meet certain eligibility requirements.

Equal employment opportunity: Refers to efforts to eliminate employment discrimination on the basis of race, ethnic background, sex, age, or physical handicap; ensures that all persons have an equal chance to compete for employment and promotions based on job qualifications.

Equality: The idea that all persons have an equal claim to life, liberty, and the pursuit of happiness.

Ethical or moral relativism: Belief that moral judgment can be made only by taking into account the context in which action occurs.

Ethics: Process by which we clarify right and wrong and act on what we take to be right.

Ethics audit: Evaluation of the value premises that guide an organization's action.

Excise tax: Tax applied to the sale of specific commodities.

Executive order: A presidential mandate directed to and governing, with the effect of law, the actions of government officials and agencies.

Expert systems: Computer programs that mimic the decision-making processes of human experts within a particular field.

Exploratory evaluation: Investigating a variety of hunches or intuitions about program operations.

Fiduciary funds: Funds used when government must hold assets for individuals or when government holds resources to be transmitted to another organization.

Final-offer arbitration: Technique in which both parties must present their best offer with the understanding that an arbitrator will choose one or the other without modification.

Fiscal policy: Public policy concerned with the impact of government taxation and spending on the economy.

Fiscal year (FY): Government's basic accounting period.

Formula grants: Grants that employ a specific division rule to indicate how much money any given jurisdiction will receive.

Franchise: Exclusive award to one firm (or a limited number) to operate a certain business within a jurisdiction.

Functional principle: Horizontal division of labor.

Gainsharing plan: Monetary award for a group of employees based on savings generated by the group.

General fund: Fund that handles "unrestricted" funds of government.

Grants: Transfers of money (and/or property) from one government to another.

Grantsmanship: Skills needed to compete successfully in the grant process.

Gross National Product (GNP): Measure of total spending in the economy; includes total personal consumption, private investment, and government purchases.

Hidden agenda: Privately held goals and priorities.

Home rule: Provision allowing cities greater autonomy over local activities.

Impoundment: Withholding of funds authorized and appropriated by law.

Independent agencies: Agencies intentionally created outside the normal cabinet organization.

Individualism: The idea that the dignity and integrity of the individual are of supreme importance.

Institutional subsystem: Responsible for adapting the organization to its environment and for anticipating and planning for the future.

Intergovernmental relations: A term encompassing all the complex and interdependent relations among those at various levels of government.

Interorganizational networks: Pattern of relationships within and among various groups and organizations working in a single policy area.

Interventionist: External consultant brought in to reveal dysfunctional patterns of behavior and to try to develop more effective working relationships.

Iron triangle: Term given to a coalition of interest groups, agency personnel, and members of Congress created to exert influence on a particular policy issue.

Item veto: Allows a governor to veto specific items in an appropriations bill.

Job description: A thorough analysis of the work to be done and the capabilities for a job; typically contains these elements: job title, duties required, responsibilities, and job qualifications.

Lateral entry: Entry into government positions at any level.

Legislative veto: Statutory provision that gives Congress the authority to approve or disapprove certain executive actions.

Liberty: The idea that individual citizens of a democracy should have a high degree of self-determination.

Line-item budget: Budget format for listing categories of expenditures along with amounts allocated to each.

Management by objectives: Participatory approach to establishing clear and measurable objectives throughout the entire organization.

Managerial subsystem: Concerned with providing necessary resources for accomplishing a technical task and mediating between the technical and institutional subsystems.

Mandate: Order requiring a government to do something.

Merit pay: Increases in salary and wages that are tied to actual quality of work performed.

Merit principle: Concept that selection and treatment of government employees should be based on merit or competence rather than personal or political favoritism.

Morality: Practices and activities considered right or wrong and the values those practices reflect.

Negotiated investment strategy: Bringing together representatives of all affected groups to set priorities for funding.

Neutral competence: The belief that a neutral public bureaucracy following the mandates of a legislative body will meet the requirements of democracy.

Nominal group: Face-to-face meeting that allows only limited interaction among participants.

Nonprofit organizations: Organizations prohibited by law from distributing surplus revenues to individuals.

Objective responsibility: Assurance of responsiveness through external controls.

Oligarchy: Government by the few.

Ombudsman: Permanent office that receives complaints and acts on behalf of citizens to secure information, request services, or pursue grievances.

Operating grants: Grants for use in development and operation of specific programs. **Organization development:** Process-oriented approach to planned change. **Organizational culture:** Basic patterns of attitudes, beliefs, and values that underlie an organization's operation.

Parity principle: Idea that an individual should have equal amounts of authority and responsibility.

Participant-observer: Someone in either the target population or the agency who makes observations and draws conclusions based on firsthand experience.

Performance appraisal: Specific evaluation with respect to an individual's progress in completing specified tasks.

Performance auditing: Analysis and evaluation of the effective performance of agencies in carrying out their objectives.

Performance bonus: One-time monetary award based on superior performance on the job or in a particular task.

Performance budget: Budget format organized around programs or activities; includes various performance measurements that indicate the relationship between work actually done and its cost.

PERT: A way to monitor the time or costs of various activities required to complete a project, showing the sequence in which the activities must be completed.

Picket-fence federalism: Pattern of intergovernmental relations in which the horizontal bars represent levels of government and the vertical slats represent various substantive fields.

Piecework bonus: Incentive that ties the worker's productivity in a given task to the monetary rewards he or she receives.

Planning-programming-budgeting system (PPBS): Effort to connect planning, systems analysis, and budgeting in a single exercise.

Policy: Statement of goals and intentions with respect to a particular problem or set of problems.

Policy analysis: Process of researching or analyzing public problems to provide policy makers with specific information about the range of available policy options and advantages and disadvantages of different approaches.

Policy analysts: Persons who provide important information about public programs through research into the operations and impacts of the programs.

Policy entrepreneur: A person willing to invest personal time, energy, and money in pursuit of particular policy changes.

Political economy approach: Focusing on politics and economies as categories for analyzing organizational behavior.

Position classification: Analyzing and organizing jobs on the basis of duties, responsibilities, and knowledge and skills required to perform them.

Preaudit: Review in advance of an actual expenditure.

Preemption: Federal government efforts to preempt an area traditionally associated with state government.

Privatization: Use of nongovernmental agencies to provide goods and services previously provided by government.

Process charting/flowcharting: Graphically demonstrating the various steps in an operation, the people who perform each step, and relationships among those elements.

Program managers: Persons ranging from the executive level to the supervisory level who are in charge of particular governmental programs.

Progressive tax: One that taxes those with higher incomes at a higher rate.

Proportional tax: One that taxes everyone at the same rate.

Proprietary funds: Used to account for government activities that more closely resemble private business.

Public administration: The management of public programs.

Public corporation: An essentially commercial agency in which work requires greater latitude and acquires at least a portion of its funding in the marketplace (e.g., Tennessee Valley Authority).

Public policy: Authoritative statements made by legitimate governmental actors about public problems.

Quality circle: Small group of people who do similar or connected work and meet regularly to identify, analyze, and solve work-process problems.

Reconciliation bill: Legislative action that attempts to reconcile individual actions in taxes, authorizations, or appropriations with the totals.

Redistributive policy: Policy designed to take taxes from certain groups and give them to another group.

Regressive tax: One that taxes those with lower incomes at a proportionally higher rate than those with higher incomes.

Regulatory commission: Group formed to regulate a particular area of the economy; usually headed by a group of individuals appointed by the president and confirmed by the Senate.

Regulatory policy: Policy designed to limit actions of persons or groups to protect all or parts of the general public.

Rescission: Presidential decision to permanently withhold funds.

Revenue sharing: Grant pattern in which the money can be used any way the recipient government chooses.

Risk management: Ways that public organizations anticipate and cope with risks.

Risky shift: Difference in the daringness of decisions group members make as a group, compared to the average risk of the same decision if each member made it alone.

Role ambiguity: Occurs when the rights and responsibilities of the job are not clearly understood.

Role conflict: Occurs when one faces two different and incompatible sets of demands.

Rule making: Administrative establishment of general guidelines for application to a class of people or a class of actions at some future time.

Rule of three: Provision of most merit systems that requires at least the top three applicants' names to be forwarded to the hiring official to allow some flexibility in selection.

Satisficing decision: One that is just "good enough" in terms of some criterion. **Scalar principle:** Vertical division of labor among various organizational levels.

Scientific management: Approach to management based on carefully defined laws, rules, and principles.

Sexual harassment: Any unwarranted and nonreciprocal verbal or physical sexual advances or derogatory remarks that the recipient finds offensive or that interfere with his or her job performance.

Special districts: Local governments created for a specific purpose within a specific area.

Spoils system: The ability to give government jobs to the party faithful; "to the victor belong the spoils."

Staff managers: Persons who support the work of program managers through budgeting and financial management, personnel and labor relations, and purchasing and procurement.

Stakeholders: The many different persons who are involved in a policy decision and are affected by the results.

Strategic planning: Matching organizational objectives and capabilities to the anticipated demands of the environment to produce a plan of action that will ensure achievement of objectives.

Structured interviews: Those in which a previously developed set of questions is used with each applicant.

Subjective responsibility: Assurance of responsiveness based on an individual's character.

Suggestion award programs: Incentives for employees who make specific suggestions that result in savings for the organization.

Sunset law: Provision that sets a specific termination date for a program.

Sunshine law: Provision that requires agencies to conduct business in public view.

Supplemental appropriation: Bill passed during the fiscal year, adding new money to an agency's budget for the same fiscal year.

Supply-side economies: Argument that decreased taxes and government spending will stimulate capital investment and economic growth.

Support system: Network of people with whom one can talk about problems.

System: Set of regularized interactions configured or "bounded" in a way that differentiates and separates them from other actions that constitute the system's environment.

Systems approach: Suggestion that public (or other) organizations can be viewed in the same general way as biological or physical systems.

Systems theory: Effort to identify the interactions of various internal and external elements that impinge on an organization's operations.

Task forces: Groups brought together to work on specific organizational problems.

Technical subsystem: Concerned with effective performance of an organization's actual work.

Time series analysis: Making a number of observations about the target population both before and after program intervention.

Two-factor theory: Model of motivation involving two variables: job satisfaction and job dissatisfaction.

Unit determination: Decision to include or exclude certain groups in a bargaining unit.

Urban renewal: Government program designed to provide cities with money for public housing and urban redevelopment.

Utilitarianism: Philosophy of the greatest good for the greatest number of people.

Whipsaw tactics: Argument that pay or benefits negotiated by one group should be applied to others.

Zero-base budgeting: Budget format that presents information about the efficiency and effectiveness of existing programs and highlights possibilities for eliminating or reducing programs.

Index

NOTE: Italic *b* following page number indicates box; italic *f* following page number indicates figure; italic *n* following page number indicates networking information; and italic *t* following page number indicates table.